D0918895

AMERICAN JURIES

FURTHER PRAISE

"Written by two of America's leading experts on juries, this book is a model of the intelligent use of social science to inform public debate. Vidmar and Hans are masters of their craft and their mastery is vividly on display. Comprehensive and lucid, *American Juries* takes up a wide range of criticisms of, and questions about, juries in civil and criminal cases. It judiciously marshals evidence and concludes with a persuasive defense of the jury system. It was a pleasure to read."

Austin Sarat
William Nelson Cromwell Professor of Jurisprudence and Political Science
and Five College Fortieth Anniversary Professor
Departments of Law, Jurisprudence & Social Thought, and Political Science
Amherst College

"Since its publication in 1986, *Judging the Jury* has been recognized as the definitive discussion of the jury and its place in the American legal system. It is tricky business to fiddle with a classic, but the authors of *American Juries* have done so, and have produced a book that is equally comprehensive, but even more engaging than the original. By weaving references to history and scholarly studies with verbatim jury transcripts gleaned from their recent studies, the authors have enlivened their discussion of the jury system and made their presentation of the findings of empirical research on the jury vivid and easier to understand. This book is both a good read and a solid and comprehensive survey of the large social science literature on the American jury."

Tom Tyler
Professor of psychology, New York University

"The American jury has a powerhouse pair of expert witnesses on its defense team. Neil Vidmar and Valerie Hans draw upon a now sizable body of empirical research to illuminate every facet of the jury system. This new book goes well beyond their classic *Judging the Jury*, portraying the jury system in its full historical and political context as a microcosm of the American democratic experience."

Robert MacCoun
Professor of public policy and law, University of California at Berkeley

"Neil Vidmar and Valerie Hans, two experts on the American jury system, have joined forces to write an exhaustive study of the origins of the modern jury, its historic role in American society, and how it functions at the present time. They rely heavily on empirical data to describe jury selection, the jury's decision-making process, jury nullification, juries' evaluation of expert testimony, and a range of other issues and topics about the workings and responsibilities of the American jury. It is a must read for anyone interested in jury behavior."

Rita J. Simon
University Professor in the School of Public Affairs and the
Washington College of Law at American University,
and author of *The Jury and the Defense of Insanity*

Neil Vidmar &
Valerie P. Hans

AMERICAN JURIES

THE VERDICT

59 John Glenn Drive
Amherst, New York 14228-2119

Published 2007 by Prometheus Books

American Juries: The Verdict. Copyright © 2007 by Neil Vidmar and Valerie P. Hans. All rights reserved. No part of this publication may be reproduced, stored in a retrieval system, or transmitted in any form or by any means, digital, electronic, mechanical, photocopying, recording, or otherwise, or conveyed via the Internet or a Web site without prior written permission of the publisher, except in the case of brief quotations embodied in critical articles and reviews.

Inquiries should be addressed to
Prometheus Books
59 John Glenn Drive
Amherst, New York 14228–2119
VOICE: 716–691–0133, ext. 210
FAX: 716–691–0137
WWW.PROMETHEUSBOOKS.COM

11 10 09 08 07   5 4 3 2 1

Library of Congress Cataloging-in-Publication Data

Vidmar, Neil.
American juries : the verdict / Neil Vidmar and Valerie P. Hans—1st American hardcover ed.
p. cm.
Includes bibliographical references and index.
ISBN 978–1–59102–588–7 (hardcover : alk. paper)
1. Jury—United States. 2. Verdicts—United States. 3. Damages—United States. I. Hans, Valerie P. II. Title.

KF8972.V53 2007
347.73'752—dc22   2007027089

Printed in the United States of America on acid-free paper

For JE and our respective offspring—and, with much joy, theirs
—NV

For Michael and Zachary
—VPH

CONTENTS

Foreword		9
Acknowledgments		11
Introduction		15
Chapter 1.	The English Origins of the Modern Jury: From Trial by Ordeal to the Decline of the "Little Parliament"	21
Chapter 2.	Criminal and Civil Juries in America from Colonial Times to the Present Day: Evolution, a Heroic Role, and Controversy	41
Chapter 3.	A Jury of Peers: Democratic Goals	65
Chapter 4.	Jury Selection: Juror Bias, Juror Challenges, and Trial Consultants	83
Chapter 5.	Problem Cases: Pretrial Publicity	107

Chapter 6. The Tasks of the Jury: Evidence Evaluation and Jury Decision-Making Processes 125

Chapter 7. Judging the Jury: Evaluating Jurors' Comprehension of Evidence and Law 147

Chapter 8. Trials in a Scientific Age: Juries Judging Experts 169

Chapter 9. Judging Criminal Responsibility: Erroneous Convictions, the *CSI* Effect, and the Victim's Role 191

Chapter 10. Deciding Insanity: Mad or Bad? 207

Chapter 11. Jury Nullification: The War with the Law 221

Chapter 12. Death Is Different: Juries and Capital Punishment 241

Chapter 13. Civil Liability: Plaintiff vs. Defendant in the Eyes of the Jury 267

Chapter 14. Deciding Compensatory Damages: Million-Dollar Questions 281

Chapter 15. Punitive Damages: Coffee Spills and Marlboro Cigarettes 303

Chapter 16. Juries and Medical Malpractice: Antidoctor, Incompetent, and Irresponsible? 321

Chapter 17. Concluding: The Verdict on Juries 339

Notes 347

Index 399

FOREWORD

American Juries breathes life and understanding into one of the most important duties we as Americans have in our justice system: serving on a jury of our peers.

The United States Constitution provides every citizen with the right to a trial by jury in both criminal and civil cases. That's how fundamental and essential the founders of this country and the framers of the Constitution believed the guarantee to trial by jury was to protect the rights of every citizen, from unfair prosecution or unfair claims on one's property or civil liberties, by the government or other individuals or institutions. Indeed, it has been said that the jury is the hand brake on the arrogance of power.

Like society, the makeup of the jury has evolved from all male, all white, all property owners to arguably the most diverse in American culture today.

Juries not only represent a unique blend of culture, race, religion, and ethnicity; they embody the moral values, community standards, and the belief that every American can be given, and should receive, a fair trial.

Indeed, as the authors of *American Juries* observe as they trace the history of the jury system, when juries are given the opportunity to learn the facts and clearly understand the law, they get it right in the majority of cases.

If you learn anything from *American Juries*, it should be that, given the right environment, the proper tools, and the appropriate instructions, juries are reliable, fair, and accurate.

Juries ensure that the future of our nation's democracy will not be determined by the powerful or wealthy alone but by all people, each with a vote equal to the other. Juries represent democracy of the people and for the people, as envisioned by the founders of this country.

Some believe that jury trials are on the decline, that alternative methods to dispute resolution are being used more widely, that the expense and the uncertainty of monetary awards have contributed to this phenomenon. While we may debate the reason for decline in jury trials, make no mistake that without a viable justice system that supports and encourages the use of jury trials, these dispute alternatives would not be as effective or as widely used.

Reading *American Juries* is a great way for citizens to appreciate and to take pride in their right to a jury trial and their right to serve on a jury. This book is appropriate for use in university and law courses and for legal professionals, but it is written to address broader audiences as well. It should be required reading in high school civics classes and would make for great conversation and education at monthly meetings of civic organizations and classes on leadership and citizenship, not to mention among everyday citizens.

Robert J. Grey Jr.
Past President, American Bar Association

ACKNOWLEDGMENTS

Like all authors, we have debts to many people, institutions, and funding sources.

We owe a huge debt to Professor Richard Lempert, a tremendously busy man who nonetheless took up with zest our request to make remarks on our draft manuscript. He offered extensive comments and criticisms that dramatically improved the book. Professor Brian Bornstein also gave invaluable advice, reviewing our draft manuscript and providing excellent suggestions about the relevance of current psychological research. Michael Bend, Zachary Bend, Paul Carrington, Joanne Ernteman, Paula Hannaford-Agor, Mike Levi, Elizabeth Hans McCrone, Jonathan McCrone, Bernie Meyler, Mary Rose, Amanda Stevens, and John Tryneski made important comments on individual chapters. Jennifer McGinnis, a Duke Law School student, conducted essential background research for the book and critiqued many of the chapters during later stages of the book's development. And we are also grateful to our editor, Linda Regan, who taught us a lot about writing more than twenty years ago when she was the editor of our coauthored book *Judging the Jury* (1986). She performed the same teaching role for this book.

Each of us benefited from our own networks of colleagues and research funding; in turn, these sources of support contributed to the development and completion of *American Juries*.

From Neil Vidmar: Particular thanks are due to Kara MacKillop, who served as my dedicated research assistant and colleague for over two years as she was earning her JD and MA at Duke. Faculty and administrators at Duke Law School, under the guidance of Dean Katherine Bartlett, were, as always, highly supportive of my scholarly efforts. Deep gratitude is owed to Russell M. Robinson II, who funded my chaired professorship. Thanks are also due to the Duke Law Library, especially librarians Melanie Dunshee, Jennifer Behrens, Laura Scott, and Kathryn Topolus. Linda Grace, Tracey Madrid, and Karen Britt provided crucial technical support. Over the past years, a large number of Duke Law students, too many to mention them all, have also assisted on various projects that form part of this book, but special note should be made of Brian Brook, Kieran McCarthy, David Landau, Jeffrey Rice, Matthew Wolfe, Jason Rimes, Nicholas Holland, and Mike Perry.

From Valerie Hans: During the development of *American Juries*, I moved from the University of Delaware to Cornell Law School. Both institutions provided critically important intellectual and practical support. Many wonderful colleagues and students at Delaware helped out along the way. Maggie Andersen's friendship and sociological insights once again offered support and inspiration. My department chair, Joel Best, deserves special mention for providing me with the necessary resources to keep this long-term project going. Many Delaware students made helpful comments on draft chapters or collaborated with me on work reported here. A well-timed sabbatical at the University of Pennsylvania Law School was invaluable.

At Cornell Law School, Dean Stewart Schwab made me an offer I couldn't refuse; his prediction that Cornell would be a felicitous environment for my scholarship has proven to be true. Law school faculty research funds and summer research grants in 2006 and 2007 allowed me to make good progress on the manuscript. Our book has also benefited from the generosity of my Cornell colleagues who shared their knowledge about the American jury system. In addition to insights from the empirical legal studies quartet of Ted Eisenberg, Michael Heise, Jeff Rachlinski, and Marty Wells, Kevin Clermont served as our civil procedure guru, and Steve Schiffrin helped out with background about the St. Patrick's Four. The fabulous Cornell Law School librarians Julie Jones, Nancy Moore, and Claire Germain know about their substantial contributions to this book and how indebted we are to them. Bonnie Jo Coughlin and Susan Tosto provided superb administrative support.

From both of us: Our book summarizes findings from many research studies we have conducted over the years, and it is appropriate to acknowledge the key sources of financial support that have been so significant in sponsoring our projects in the field of jury studies. Important examples in the book regarding civil juries are taken from original data collected as part of the Arizona Jury Project. Judge Michael Brown, then Presiding Judge of Pima County Superior Court, initiated the project; Vidmar's co-investigators on the project were Shari Seidman Diamond, Mary Rose, Leslie Ellis, and Beth Murphy. The team was funded by grants from the State Justice Institute (Grant SJI-97-N-247), the National Science Foundation (Grant SBR9818806), and the American Bar Foundation, as well as from Duke Law School and Northwestern Law School. Vidmar received valuable support for other research projects through the Eugene T. Bost Jr. Professorship funded by the Charles A. Cannon Charitable Trust No. 3; the State Justice Institute; the Robert Wood Johnson Foundation; the Project on Scientific Knowledge and Public Policy (SKAPP); and the Provost's Common Fund of Duke University. In writing about jury studies, we were also able to draw on research findings from Hans's projects funded by the National Science Foundation (Grants SES-8822598 and GER-9350498) and collaborative work she conducted with researchers from the National Center for State Courts, funded by the National Institute of Justice (Grants 98-IJ-CX-0048 and 2002-IJ-CX-0026). Her collaborators on these projects include Stephanie Albertson, Mike Dann, Erin Farley, Paula Hannaford-Agor, Sanja Ivković, David Kaye, Tom Munsterman, and Nicole Waters.

The book draws on the jury scholarship of many colleagues; we especially want to acknowledge Tom Green, Bill Haltom, Michael McCann, Neal Feigenson, and Scott Sundby, who all graciously gave us permission to quote from their work.

INTRODUCTION

American juries are an integral part of our nation's history and a major feature of our democratic society. Yet, over the past several decades American criminal and civil juries have been criticized for incompetence and irresponsibility. One alleged failure was the criminal jury that acquitted O. J. Simpson of stabbing to death his wife and her friend in Brentwood, California, creating a racial divide in opinions about the trial. Or take the civil jury that awarded nearly $3 million in punitive damages to an elderly woman after she spilled a cup of McDonald's coffee on her lap. John Hinckley Jr.'s "Not Guilty by Reason of Insanity" verdict, following his assassination attempt on President Reagan, still rankles many among the public. A recent *U.S. News & World Report* story told of a trial involving a woman who threw a soft drink at her boyfriend in a restaurant, slipped on the wet floor, and then won $100,000 in a lawsuit against the restaurant. The US Chamber of Commerce, the American Medical Association, and the American Tort Reform Association claim there are "judicial hellholes," or areas of the country where juries routinely render outrageous awards.

Dramatic and provocative jury trials rivet public attention. In these pages, we will examine what juries do and what research tells us about their performance. Are juries competent to evaluate DNA evidence or testimony about negligence in complicated medical malpractice cases? How does racial bias factor into jury decisions? Do juries sometimes nullify the law—essentially overruling the directions of the judge? Do juries give away money as if they were Robin Hood when the defendant is a rich business corporation? What causes juries to decide a defendant is not guilty by reason of insanity? What are the effects of jury consultants on the fairness of trials? These are important questions that need to be answered by evidence rather than anecdote. We present the evidence and offer a verdict.

JURIES DEFENDED AND JURIES ON TRIAL

Thomas Jefferson wrote in 1788 that "I consider trial by jury as the only anchor ever yet imagined by man, by which a government can be held to the principles of its constitution."[1] The right to a jury trial is enshrined in the US Constitution, the Bill of Rights, and the constitution of every state. Vigorous supporters of the jury promote it as an essential feature of democracy and a valuable protection against special interests. Trial judges, who preside over jury trials on a daily basis, overwhelmingly endorse the jury system, evaluating juries as conscientious, competent, and fair.[2]

Nevertheless, today, the American jury is under concerted attack.[3] Critics charge that high-priced criminal lawyers, their experts, and their jury consultants ostensibly cause miscarriages of justice, allowing obviously guilty criminals to go free. According to this viewpoint, juries make these mistakes because jurors are gullible, overly influenced by the media, and susceptible to "abuse excuses."[4] Over the last decade, cases in which DNA evidence has exonerated defendants who had been convicted by juries—including some prisoners on death row—have raised questions about how well juries evaluate trial evidence and reach their verdicts.[5] More recently, news media stories have claimed a "*CSI* effect"—named for the television program that showcases crime scene investigators—as a possible reason for handing out unwarranted jury acquittals. According to the stories, jurors who have learned about the marvels of modern investigation refuse to convict if the prosecution does not have definitive forensic evidence to prove the defendant's guilt.

Civil juries, like the one that decided the McDonald's coffee spill case, are equally condemned, accused of irrationality, unreliability, and prejudice against business corporations. The coffee spill case has become a poster child for those who oppose the jury system. *Newsweek* tells us that we have become a nation in which "Americans sue each other at the slightest provocation," hoping "they will get lucky and win a jackpot from a system that allows sympathetic juries to award plaintiffs not just real damages . . . but millions more for impossible-to-measure 'pain and suffering' and highly arbitrary 'punitive damages.'"[6] Some argue that as a result of juries' far-too-generous awards against doctors and manufacturers, healthcare costs have skyrocketed and the competitiveness of American businesses has been severely harmed. In the face of these attacks, will the venerable institution of trial by jury be replaced by other forms of dispute resolution?

JURIES ON TRIAL: BEYOND ANECDOTAL EVIDENCE

One of the unfortunate features of contemporary debates over the jury is the heavy prevalence of anecdotes or stories about a single jury. In some ways this is understandable because juries decide cases one at a time and individual jury trials and jury verdicts are highly visible. But the easy anecdotes in popular stories about the jury can be misleading about the broader picture of the institution.

Some anecdotes based on individual criminal juries do not hold up to empirical scrutiny. The so-called *CSI* effect claim, for example, is not the first time an assertion about acquittal-prone juries has been made. Following the O. J. Simpson acquittal, the hung jury in the Menendez Brothers case (the brothers who justified the planned shotgun killings of their parents with an abuse excuse), and the acquittal of the Los Angeles police officers who were videotaped beating African American Rodney King, some observers concluded that juries were becoming acquittal prone. Yet systematic studies of federal and state criminal jury trials going back at least a decade before that showed a steady increase in conviction rates, not a decline.[7]

What is more, many charges against the jury have been supported by anecdotes that are unsubstantiated or are partly or totally fictitious. The story of the woman who received a $100,000 award after throwing a drink at her boyfriend has been exposed as pure fiction. Another story in circulation involved a man who purportedly injured himself while using his lawn mower as a hedge clipper, and then won $500,000 in a lawsuit against the lawn mower company. It, too, was shown to be totally fictitious.[8]

We will go beyond anecdotes here to develop an empirically based portrait of the American jury. Over the last decades, a vibrant field of jury studies has emerged, devoted to understanding the historical, legal, and empirical dimensions of the jury as an institution. In writing this book, we are able to draw on substantial scientific investigations—our own as well as that of others—into the functioning and competency of American juries.

The two of us, trained as social scientists and holding doctorates in social psychology, have studied the jury system, often in collaborative projects, for the past thirty years. We have reviewed and assessed the work of other researchers, lectured to judges and lawyers, testified before legislative committees, and written briefs pertaining to juries in US Supreme Court cases.

Neil Vidmar's interest in juries began in 1971 when, as a young psychology professor, he was asked to testify about potential juror prejudice in a capital murder trial of a young African American man accused of killing a white policeman in Lucas County (Toledo), Ohio.[9] The panel from which the jury was to be selected was not representative of the population of Lucas County: it contained too few young and single persons, too few professional persons, and, especially, it contained far too few African Americans in proportion to their numbers in the Lucas

County population. Social psychologist Milton Rokeach testified about why the existing panel would not represent the full spectrum of life experiences that a jury needed to fairly evaluate the evidence. Vidmar testified about the likely effects that the absence of diverse viewpoints would have on the jury deliberations. The research forming the basis of their testimony was not specifically designed to address jury problems, but the judge understood the implications of their testimony for fairness of the trial and ordered a new jury panel that was more representative of Toledo's population. (The charges against the defendant were eventually dropped after two trials resulted in juries that could not reach consensus.)

The Toledo experience led to an invitation to participate in a conference on the death penalty held at Columbia Law School in the wake of *Furman v. Georgia*, the 1972 Supreme Court decision that temporarily abolished the death penalty. The interesting sociological and psychological issues that these experiences raised about creating impartial juries persuaded Vidmar to spend a year at Yale Law School to acquire a legal background in criminal and civil law. He then embarked on what has become decades of research and writing on juries. Complaints from doctors about their treatment by juries led him to focus on medical malpractice litigation and the jury's role within it. In addition to other projects, in 1998, along with co-investigators Shari Diamond, Mary Rose, Leslie Ellis, and Beth Murphy, he began an unprecedented study that videotaped the actual jury room deliberations of fifty civil juries in Tucson, Arizona. The project was carried out under the oversight of the Arizona Supreme Court and had consent from the jurors.[10] Many new insights garnered from the Arizona Jury Project are reported throughout this book.

Valerie Hans first became intrigued about jury research when she was an undergraduate student at the University of California at San Diego. A friend gave her a prepublication copy of an early mock juror experiment by University of Toronto social psychologist Anthony Doob.[11] The study examined whether people who read the facts of a robbery prosecution were biased when they learned of a defendant's criminal record (they were) and whether a judicial instruction to disregard the criminal record in deciding on guilt was effective (it wasn't). In a eureka moment, she realized that this kind of research could satisfy both her passion for conducting social science research and her desire to address questions of social justice. Accepted into the graduate program at the University of Toronto to work with Doob, she embarked on her own experiments about juries.[12]

Early on, she saw how jury research could be helpful to policymakers. Canada's Law Reform Commission was considering adopting a reform that England had taken a few years before, to allow nonunanimous jury verdicts, that is, verdicts in which a minority of jurors did not agree with the majority. Recommending that Canada stick with the requirement that all jurors agree on the verdict, the Law Reform Commission cited Hans's dissertation research that used mock juries to test the impact of allowing majority verdicts.[13]

As a university professor, Valerie Hans continues to research and write about the jury system, interviewing and surveying jurors, analyzing jury verdicts, and conducting experiments to test hypotheses about jury decision processes. In one study, she conducted face-to-face interviews with several hundred civil jurors who decided cases involving businesses or corporations.[14] Another major project, carried out with researchers from the National Center for State Courts, examined felony juries, and included distributing posttrial questionnaires to judges, jurors, and attorneys, asking for their views of the case and the jury decision. The research compared how juries and judges saw the same cases.[15]

In this book we draw on our collected work over three decades, and our experience in advising judges, lawyers, and policymakers. Insights about the operation of the American jury, however, also come from many other sources and texts, including statistical analyses of jury verdicts, experiments with mock jurors, juror interviews, recordings of jury deliberations, and surveys of jurors, judges, attorneys, and the public. Juries have a role in deciding real disputes, sometimes for life and death matters or claims for billions of dollars. An understanding of juries is incomplete without these true life stories, so we include cases such as the historical trial of William Penn; a long-ago murder at Harvard; and recent high-profile cases such as that of Andrea Yates (the Texas mother who drowned her five children in a bathtub), Scott Peterson (whose pregnant wife's body was discovered in a California bay), the Vioxx drug litigation, and the fraud trials following the collapse of energy giant Enron. And we discuss the iconic cases of O. J. Simpson and the coffee spill verdict that figure so heavily in public impressions of the American jury. We have also tried to write about the issues in such a way as to make the book accessible to a broad readership. At the same time, we offer details of legal matters and research studies which bear on juries and their performance, and which lawyers, social scientists, and students want to hear.

Our goal is to provide evidence, so that each of our readers—whether the reader is a layperson, a student, or a lawyer—can reach a verdict about the American jury.

Chapter 1

THE ENGLISH ORIGINS OF THE MODERN JURY

From Trial by Ordeal to the Decline of the "Little Parliament"

In his landmark treatise, *Commentaries on the Laws of England*, published around 1769, William Blackstone called the jury the "glory of the English Law."[1] Two hundred years later Sir Patrick Devlin continued to extol the virtues of the jury system, describing it as a "little parliament" and a symbol of democracy, "the lamp that shows that freedom lives."[2] An understanding of the modern American jury requires knowledge of its English origins and history. But describing the jury's evolution over almost a thousand years is a daunting task. We can only touch on the milestones.[3]

BEFORE JURIES: PUTTING AN ACCUSED "ON THE WATER" AND OTHER METHODS OF PROOF

All societies must deal with crime and other disputes among their members. In preliterate human organizations, the affected parties handled problems directly by sanctioned acts of revenge or payments to the injured parties or their families. In England during the Middle Ages colorful methods of proof were often used to settle disputes. Trial by wager of battle, trial by ordeal, compurgation, and trial by witnesses all preceded trial by jury.[4] These medieval methods of proof depended on shared religious beliefs about the directing hand of God.

In wager of battle the two disputing parties engaged in a formal duel under the assumption that God would determine which party was in the right and should prevail. The parties could fight each other or choose a surrogate, called a "champion," to fight for them. The duel followed certain prescribed rules and each party was forced to acknowledge that death was a possible result. Regardless, even if the losing party survived the battle, no appeal of the outcome was allowed.[5]

The *Judicium Dei*, commonly known today as the "ordeal," is the most intriguing form of trial. The hand of God in the affairs of men and women was assumed to be direct and underlay the rationale for ordeals. There were four basic forms of the ordeal: by cold water, by hot water, by hot iron, and by "corsnaed." The first two were usually reserved for the lowest classes, serfs and other persons not classified as free men. Trial by hot water or hot iron was reserved for freemen, and the last was for members of the clergy.

In a trial in which an accused person was judged by "putting himself upon the water," a solemn religious ceremony led up to the physical ordeal. The accused fasted for three days before being brought into church for a mass and communion. The accused was warned to refrain from communion if he or she was guilty. Following communion, the priest conducted a ritual asking God to cast the person forth if he or she was guilty and to receive the person into the depths if innocent. The person was stripped (perhaps a precaution against carrying stones in one's pockets, but more likely to prevent trapped air in clothes from floating the body), kissed the Bible and crucifix, was sprinkled with holy water, and was bound and tossed into a pond or a lake. If the accused floated to the top, execution, branding, or some other form of punishment awaited, whereas persons who sunk were pulled up and pronounced innocent.

Similar religious ceremonies took place if the accused chose trial by boiling water. The water was heated to boiling or near boiling in a vessel. If the alleged crime was relatively minor, the accused was required to plunge a hand up to the wrist and bring forth a stone suspended on a cord. If the alleged crime was grave, the stone was placed at a deeper level so that the arm had to be plunged to the elbow. The hand or arm was then bandaged. At the end of three days the bandage was removed. If it appeared that the burn was healing cleanly, the person was declared innocent; a festered arm was a sign of guilt. Ordeal by hot iron was similar except that a piece of iron weighing one or three pounds, depending on the seriousness of the charges, was heated to a certain temperature. Following a religious ceremony, the iron was raised from the embers and placed in the naked hand of the accused person, who had to carry it a distance of nine feet. As in the hot water test, festering after three days was interpreted as a sign of guilt.

Ordeal by "corsnead" (or "ordeal of the morsel") also involved religious rituals and was usually reserved for religious leaders. The clergyman was provided a small piece of barley bread or cheese and required to swallow it whole. If swallowing was accomplished without serious difficulty, the accused was found innocent, but if he choked or grew black in the face, he was judged guilty. Ordeal by morsel may have acted like a lie detector test. A cleric who believed in divine judgment and was truly guilty may have had a dry throat and been more prone to choke on the morsel.

Proof by ordeal lasted to some extent for more than a century after the Norman invasion of England in 1066.[6] Both the *Assize of Clarendon* (1166) and the *Assize of Northampton* (1176), gatherings of clergy and barons called by King Henry II to formally establish English laws, provided for trial by ordeal. However, even at that time its inadequacies as a method of proof were apparent to many members of the Church. Finally, in 1215 the Fourth Lateran Council forbade Catholic priests from participating in the religious rituals surrounding the ordeal and trial by battle, effectively terminating them as trial procedures.

Another early form of proof was compurgation, also called a wager of law. It was essentially a test of good character. A man needing proof that he should prevail in a dispute was required to bring forth a number of persons to swear under oath that he was a credible person of good reputation. Depending on the circumstances, the number of compurgators might range from one to as many as forty-eight persons, but by tradition it was twelve. If a litigant had a poor reputation, it was difficult to find the required number of compurgators. Formally, the compurgators testified only to the person's good character, but undoubtedly the degree to which they knew some facts about the dispute helped the person's case. In business disputes, oral oaths attesting to a person's good character were considered more trustworthy than written accounts, because the latter could be falsely altered.

Trial by witnesses was also common in both civil and criminal matters. These early witnesses gave testimony about facts in a dispute, unlike the compurgators who testified about character. Although these witnesses swore that their testimony was truthful, they were not like modern witnesses. They had to be men of the neighborhood with sufficient wealth and legal standing, and they were not examined to determine the accuracy of their testimony. The status of the witnesses in the community and the wrath of God if they violated their oaths were deemed to be sufficient to ensure honesty.

THE DOMESDAY BOOK AND EARLY FORMS OF THE JURY

The seeds of the jury system may have been in existence in the form of proof by witnesses before William the Conqueror defeated King Harald's army in 1066, but the Norman conquest of England set the stage for a more formal use of sworn testimony. Pollock and Maitland, two nineteenth-century legal scholars, described the early form of the jury as "a body of neighbors summoned by some public officer to give upon oath a true answer to some question."[7] In order to assess taxes on the countryside, the Norman kings required sworn testimony about who owned land, oxen, and other forms of property. The information obtained from the testimony was recorded in the great Domesday Book. Officially this book was "the description of England," but because it served as the basis of taxation it became known as the "doomsday" (or in ancient spelling, the "domesday") book. The procedure for collecting the information through sworn testimony, some scholars say, was one that had been used in France, although other scholars dispute the claim.[8] There is some evidence that Danelaw, in existence in England at least seventy years before the Norman Conquest, provided for "presentment" juries, the forerunner of grand juries. Eighteen or more citizens were summoned to hear preliminary evidence about alleged crimes, serving as a measure of protection from zealous government prosecutors.[9] By contrast, the Domesday inquiry was an exercise in power by the king. The sworn testimony provided by jurors was subject to penalties for perjury. Taxes were extracted on the basis of the testimony.

When the Church forbade trial by ordeal, the jury seemed a logical successor for both criminal and civil disputes. The idea developed slowly and unevenly throughout England. The early jurors were functionally witnesses who testified about events that they knew about or had heard about, perhaps even second- or thirdhand. The king's judges questioned the jurors to determine who provided the most credible accounts. We can obtain a sense of these cases from a 1221 jury trial reported by the nineteenth-century English legal historian William Frederick Maitland:

> Henry had been found dead and a knife was nearby. John Miller was arrested because he was the last person seen with Henry, but John denied even knowing the deceased. John asked to defend himself by battle and was not willing to let the matter be settled by jurors. Nevertheless, twelve jurors were asked for their verdict but they concluded under oath that "because John denied any association with Henry or any knowledge of him, and the jurors know this to be false, and further because Henry went out in John's company but did not return and because John was unwilling to place himself on the jury, they understand that he is guilty." Three other groups of jurors subsequently gave the same verdict, but the judges were not forced to decide the case because the master of the dead man gave the king 40 shillings to buy John the privilege of abjuring [leaving] the kingdom.[10]

John Miller's case illustrates a problem during this transitional period of development, namely, that trial by jury had uncertain legal standing. John was not required to submit to jury trial. Indeed, this uncertain status persisted for some time.[11] As a partial remedy, the first *Statute of Westminster* in 1275, an attempt to compile and codify English law, provided that "notorious felons, who would not put them selves upon the country [submit to jury trial] shall be put in strong and hard imprisonment." This remedy was later increased to "*peine forte et dure*" (strong and continuing pain). An accused person was tied or chained to the floor of the prison and covered with a platform. Then heavy rocks were placed upon the platform one at a time, until the accused agreed to be tried by a jury or died.

That some accused persons actually underwent this torture but still refused jury trial can be explained in two ways. First, if a man was found guilty of a heinous crime, he might be subjected to an even worse death. He would be hanged, cut down while still alive, and drawn and quartered. Second, all lands and possessions of a convicted person were forfeited to the Crown. By submitting to *peine forte et dure*, the man preserved his inheritance for his offspring. *Peine forte et dure* remained legally in force in England for centuries. There is a record of men being pressed to death as late as 1720.[12] After *peine forte et dure* was abolished in 1772, an accused person who refused jury trial was considered guilty. In 1872 the rule was changed so that a prisoner refusing jury trial was counted as entering a plea of not guilty.[13]

One of the quirks of the early jury system was that the *petit* jury ("small" jury consisting of twelve men) was often chosen from persons who served on the "presenting" jury that indicted the accused person. Thus, some of the same men who had knowledge about the crime and who served on the body that decided that there was enough evidence to put the accused on trial then sat on the jury that decided guilt. This mixing of the roles of jurors may have lasted as long as through the fifteenth century. Judge Bracton's treatise *On the Laws and Customs of England*, written about 1235, explained the reasoning:

> If the jurors are altogether ignorant about the fact and know nothing concerning the truth, let there be associated with them others who do know the truth. But even thus the truth cannot be known, but then it will be requisite to speak from belief and conscience at least.[14]

Over the course of time the presenting jury and the petit jury became distinct entities. The petit, or trial, jury evolved closer to an independent fact-finding body. Nevertheless, jurors in civil cases were still subject to harsh penalties for rendering a decision that the court considered improper. Under a *writ of attaint* they could be fined, imprisoned, or their lands could be seized if the court determined that they had rendered a false verdict. On occasion, sanctions were applied against criminal jurors as well.[15] Rendering a verdict unpopular with the authorities could be hazardous to a juror's freedom and finances.

Trials in the fourteenth and fifteenth centuries were short affairs, and juries typically decided many disputes in a single session.[16] It is likely that the accused person stood at the bar before the judge and jury, alone without a lawyer. In contrast to modern trials, the accused was not put under oath. In the legal thinking of the day, the accused had clear conflicts of interest in telling the truth and was therefore perceived as an unreliable witness. It is likely that the judge briefly questioned the accused. The jury listened to other witnesses and rendered a verdict. The verdict was usually guilty or not guilty. In some instances the jury might conclude that the accused had committed homicide but that the killing was in self-defense or by accident. However, along with its verdict the jury also recited the facts it had found. These recitations provide interesting details about how the jury served to mitigate harsh laws.

HARSH LAWS, CORONER'S FACTS, AND JURORS' DISCOVERY OF WALLS, HEDGES, AND DIKES

By about 1215 all felony convictions required a death sentence.[17] In many cases the jurors followed the law and convicted, and the accused was sent to the gallows. However, Thomas Green's leading scholarship on the early jury system shows that juries played a vital role in mitigating the harsh effects of the laws. Substantive law in the thirteenth through fifteenth centuries was rigid and formal. Generally speaking, there was no distinction made between murder and manslaughter. In cases of self-defense the law was very clear. To legally apply deadly force against an assailant, a man literally had to have his back against a wall and be threatened with death:

> . . . if a man assaults you in order to beat you it is not lawful for you to say you will kill him and to menace his life and limb; but if the case is such that he has you at such advantage that it may be understood that he is going to kill you as if you seek to flee and he is swifter than you and pursues you so that you are unable to escape . . . or if he chases you to a wall or a hedge or dike, so that you cannot escape, then it is lawful for you to say that if he won't desist, you want to slay him to save your own life, and thus you may menace him for such special cause.[18]

Green compared coroners' statements of facts at the scenes of the incidents with those subsequently found by the juries. His research shows juries engaged in some remarkable factual inventions.[19]

In Buckinghamshire, for instance, a coroner recorded that John Coles Sr. and his son, John Jr., stood talking to William Shepherde when an argument occurred.[20] Shepherde struck the senior Coles with a staff, whereupon John Coles Jr. "drew his knife and struck Shepherde in the right part of the neck wounding him mortally." The coroner finished his report with the phrase "and thus slew him feloniously." It appears pretty clear that John Jr. had not been attacked. However, at trial the jury found that Shepherde had begun the argument and struck the senior Coles and that the latter's son had tried to separate the men. Shepherde then turned on John Jr., who fled as far as a wall between two houses where, the jury concluded, he was forced to kill Shepherde in self-defense.

Another case indicates the jury's response to the slaying of an adulterer. While a man might chase his wife's lover away, he was not permitted to kill him.[21]

In 1341 an inquest jury found that Robert Bousserman came home at midday and discovered his wife having sexual intercourse with John Dougherty. Robert killed John with a blow of his hatchet. The petit jury, however, found the facts different, concluding that the events occurred at night and that John had trespassed. Deadly force could be used in the event of trespass.

> John Doughty came at night to the house of Robert in the village of Laughscale as Robert and his wife lay asleep in bed in the peace of the King, and he entered Robert's house; seeing this, Robert's wife secretly arose from her husband and went to John and John went to bed with Robert's wife; in the meantime Robert awakened and hearing noise in his house and seeing that his wife had left his bed and sought her in his house and found her with John; immediately John attacked Robert with a knife . . . and wounded him and stood between him and the door of Robert's house continually stabbing and wounding him and Robert seeing that his life was in danger and that he could no way flee further, in order to save his life he took up a hatchet and gave John one blow to the head.[22]

Professor Green's research shows that, notwithstanding facts found by coroners' inquests, petit juries had the power to find the facts to be quite different—and they did. Presumably the facts were reconstructed in accordance with the community's sense of justice in those ancient times.

PREACHING QUAKERS AND BUSHEL'S CASE

Between the fourteenth century and the seventeenth century, the jury system continued to evolve.[23] The petit jurors were less likely to be chosen from the presenting jury, or at least some of them would be independent of the body that rendered the indictment. The jury was slowly turning into an independent fact-finding body rather than a group of persons who had direct or indirect knowledge of the events at issue. But it was not quite independent. As we noted earlier, civil trial jurors were subject to the punishment of *attaint*.[24] Much like a witness who commits perjury, if a court concluded that jurors had rendered an improper verdict, the jurors could be subject to heavy fines, imprisonment, or even the loss of their property and possessions.

Jurors were also punished in some early criminal cases. In 1554, for example, Sir Nicholas Throckmorton was tried for high treason and for conspiring and plotting the death of Queen Mary.[25] The jury found Throckmorton not guilty. The Crown was not happy with the verdict. Eight of the twelve jurors were brought before the Star Chamber court. Three were fined two thousand pounds each; the others received fines of two hundred pounds. These were enormous fines by the standards of the day.

What became known as "Bushel's Case" in 1670 effectively put an end to sanctions on jurors. Foreman Bushel and several of his fellow jurors evoked the wrath of the trial court with their verdict in the trial of William Penn.[26] Penn was the son of wealthy Admiral Sir William Penn, who was highly respected and in good favor with the king and other powerful aristocrats.[27] However, the younger Penn became a convert to the Quaker religion, joining a group of zealous believers who were constantly in conflict with the Church of England. Consistent with their nonconformist beliefs and doctrines, Quakers wore unusual modes of dress and affected demeanors that accentuated their distinctiveness. They were viewed as rabble-rousers, radicals, and the most dangerous kind of extremists. William was nearly disinherited by his displeased father as a result of his religious conversion, but he courted much worse troubles. The authorities closed Quaker meetinghouses and forbade them from assembling and preaching in the streets. William and his fellow Quaker, William Mead, defied the ban. They were arrested, not for the first time, and put on trial.

The indictment read that Penn and Mead, along with "divers other persons . . . unlawfully and tumultuously assembled and congregated themselves together in Gracechurch Street in London." The indictment further charged that Penn, aided and abetted by Mead, preached and spoke to the people assembled in the street "by reason whereof a great concourse and tumult of people a long time did remain and continue, in contempt of the king and his law, and to the great terror and disturbance of many of his liege people and subjects."

Trials in London's Old Bailey and other urban courts in the 1600s, and even much later, appear to have been free from the dignity that we associate with courts today.[28] Spectators would noisily move in and out of the courtroom. They would talk, argue, and even shout at witnesses during the proceedings. Some scholarship suggests that the trial jurors sat in the public section of the courtroom rather than a jury box and mingled freely with spectators. In some instances the jurors did not retire to deliberate but simply looked at one another or had a huddled discussion. If there appeared to be agreement, one of them simply announced the verdict.

The Penn trial was no exception to the general lack of decorum. It took place before the Lord Mayor and the aldermen. The prosecution called several witnesses to testify that Penn had indeed preached in the streets and that Mead was present. After the recorder summarized the case for the jurors, they were sent to an upstairs room to consider their verdict. After ninety minutes, eight of the twelve jurors came down and indicated that they were ready to render a verdict, but four dissenting jurors remained upstairs. The dissenters were ordered to appear in the courtroom and one juror, Bushel, was singled out by the Court's recorder: "Sir, you are the cause of this disturbance, and manifestly show yourself an abettor of [this] faction; I shall set a mark upon you sir!" When Bushel protested, several of the aldermen yelled at him, characterizing him as an "impudent fellow" and a troublemaker.

The jurors were sent upstairs again. Eventually they returned to the courtroom and the court was called to silence. The clerk of the court turned to the foreman: "Look at the prisoners at the bar. How say you? Is William Penn guilty?" The foreman replied that Penn was guilty of speaking in Gracechurch Street. However, he said nothing about the charge of unlawful assembly.

Questions and threats were thrown at the jurors: "Is that all?" "You had as good say nothing." "Was it not an unlawful assembly?" While some of the jurors appeared cowed by this intimidation, Bushel and his allies stood their ground. The jury was instructed that the law of England would not dismiss them until they had rendered a proper verdict. The jurors were directed back upstairs for more deliberations. In short order they returned with a written verdict stating that Mead was not guilty and that Penn was guilty only of preaching in Gracechurch Street. The verdict contained not a word about unlawful assembly.

Accounts suggest that the court officials were nearly apoplectic. After some conferring among the various officials, the Lord Mayor said, "Gentlemen, you shall not be dismissed until we have a verdict that the court will accept; and thus you shall be locked up without meat, drink, fire and tobacco; you shall not think thus to abuse the court; we will have a verdict, by the help of God, or you shall starve for it." (Locking the jury up in this manner was standard practice when jurors could not reach a verdict.) The jury was led out and the court adjourned.

The next day the jury was summoned back to court and again returned its unpopular verdict: Penn was guilty only of speaking in Gracechurch Street. Once again the jurors were denounced by the court officials, with the Lord Mayor even threatening to cut Bushel's nose. And again they were ordered to reconsider. The next day the jurors returned with another written verdict, except this time it was signed by all the jurors: Not guilty!

The court polled each juror, but no one wavered. In response, the court recorder made the following pronouncement: "I am sorry, gentlemen, you have followed your own judgments and opinions, rather than the good and wholesome advice which was given you; God keep my life out of your hands; but for this the court fines you forty marks a man, and imprisonment until paid."

Even though the court finally had to accept the verdict, Penn was sent to Newgate prison for contempt of court. The jurors were also imprisoned but were eventually released. However, juror Bushel filed a lawsuit over his imprisonment. Chief Justice Vaughn heard the appeal and ruled in Bushel's favor. Vaughn argued that the jury had an age-old right to find facts and that a judge was never in a position to say with certainty that the jury had found against either law or fact.[29]

Bushel's case helped set a precedent for the freedom of the jury to find the facts as they saw them. It was not the final step in the evolution of the jury's power, because in routine felony cases the courts continued to pressure juries for the prosecution's preferred outcome. Nevertheless, Bushel's Case is still deservedly seen as a landmark in the development of the modern jury. It laid the groundwork for later legal developments allowing juries to nullify harsh laws or thwart unfair prosecutions

William Penn eventually reconciled with his father and later inherited his father's estate, a sizable fortune, including a large debt owed his father by King Charles II. To settle the debt, King Charles granted Penn certain lands on the North American continent under the condition that the new colony be called Pennsylvania in honor of William Penn Sr.[30]

SEVEN BISHOPS, SEDITIOUS LIBEL, AND THE JURY

A second major milestone in the development of the jury occurred less than two decades after Bushel's case, in the Trial of the Seven Bishops.[31] The importance of the controversy that led to the trial needs to be viewed by the standards of the seventeenth century rather than by today's standards. After ascending to the British throne in 1685, James II converted to Catholicism despite the fact that the official church of England was the Anglican church. Following his conversion, the king attempted to install Catholics in many important positions, including the administration of Cambridge University. Many anti-Catholic statutes had been passed by Parliament, which James attempted unsuccessfully to persuade Parliament to repeal. Asserting the divine right of kings, James took executive action. In 1687 he published a "Declaration of Indulgence" that effectively nullified the anti-Catholic laws. Today, we would probably view this as a significant protection for a persecuted religious minority. But at the time, the declaration was viewed as a serious threat to parliamentary government and its law-making powers.

English common law long recognized the crime of seditious libel. Any intentional publication of a writing that brought the government's reputation and integrity into question could be prosecuted.[32] Most indictments for seditious libel alleged that the accused had acted "falsely, seditiously, maliciously, and factiously [undermining authority]." The truth of the published words was not recognized as a defense. In seditious libel trials, the jury was required to find the defendant guilty if it found that the accused intentionally published the writing and that the writing bore the meaning alleged by the prosecution. The judge alone determined whether the publication was committed with criminal intent and whether the writing was seditious or defamatory.

At first James did not try to enforce the Declaration of Indulgence. However, in 1688 he reissued the declaration and suspended the anti-Catholic laws by royal prerogative. These actions evoked outrage in Parliament. Trouble truly began when James issued an Order in Council directing the Anglican bishops to have the declaration read in all parish churches. Recognizing the threat to their established religion, the Anglican bishops drafted a petition, phrased in very humble wording, requesting that they should not be compelled to comply with the order because doing so would constitute an illegal act. The bishops offered the petition on their knees before James in Whitehall Palace, but James was incensed, viewing the petition as an act of rebellion against his authority.

Within a few weeks, seven bishops were summoned before the Privy Council and ordered to withdraw their petition. The bishops argued that the best legal counsel advised them that their actions were correct under the law. Refusing bail, the bishops were committed to the Tower of London. The bishops had overwhelming public support because James's actions were seen as a direct threat to the English constitutional system and the religious establishment.

The subsequent trial of the bishops on charges of seditious libel lasted for ten hours. Four presiding judges each commented on the evidence and each provided his own version of the law. The jurors were charged with applying whatever version of the law they believed was correct. At seven in the evening the jury was locked up without food or water. The debate among the jurors was heated: listeners heard loud voices coming from the jury room. At four in the morning the jurors were given water for washing, which they promptly used to quench their thirst. Two hours later they announced that they had reached a verdict.

At ten in the morning the court convened and the Crown clerk asked the jurors: "Do you find the defendants guilty as charged?" The foreman replied, "Not guilty." The spectators became so riotous that the chief justice could not restore order. A number of the celebrants were taken into custody. The jurors became heroes along with the acquitted bishops and celebrations took place throughout London.

The *Seven Bishops Trial* is viewed as another milestone in English constitutional law, and a key incident in the Glorious Revolution that drove James II into exile. William of Orange, a Protestant, was brought from the Netherlands to replace him with the provision that William would be a constitutional monarch subject to the laws set forth by the English Parliament.

The trial also had major consequences for the jury as an institution. The verdict was taken as a vindication of the right of the jury to determine both intent and libelousness, affirming the jury's right to nullify the legal doctrine of seditious libel. However, this case eventually had even greater consequences. Prior to this time, criminal juries were asked to answer specific questions relating to the criminal charge. In contrast, the Seven Bishops jury returned a single statement of not guilty. In today's terminology the jury was permitted to return a "general" verdict instead of a "special" verdict requiring the jury to report specific findings so that the judge can apply the law in the light of those findings.

Hot debate over the role of the jury in the Seven Bishops case and subsequent cases eventually led to the legal doctrine that in ordinary felony crimes, the judge would provide the law to the jury, but the jury was to be the sole decider of facts and need only render a general verdict. Despite the Seven Bishops' precedent, seditious libel trials continued to be a source of controversy.[33] Finally, in 1792,

Fox's Libel Act specifically restored to the jury the right to determine not only whether a libelous article had been published but also what constituted libel in any given case and to determine whether the accused was guilty of it. The exclusive right of the jury to decide seditious libel is seen as a great landmark in English constitutional law.

THE THEATER OF TRIAL

In the eighteenth century, judges traveled from community to community and held an assize, or "sessions" court. The arrival of the court was an occasion of theater.[34] The judge and his retinue paraded through the towns, met by crowds of people and occasionally by celebratory cannon fire. They were received by the sheriff and other local dignitaries, dressed in their best finery. Often the judges in their scarlet vestments would attend the parish church for a sermon on the wisdom of the law and the righteousness of punishments before getting down to the court business before them. When court adjourned for the day, the judges and higher officials retired to the tavern for feasting and drink with the wealthier citizens of the community.

Up until the nineteenth century, juries decided nearly all criminal charges from property theft through felonies and murder. Almost invariably the sentence following a felony conviction was death. Legal historian John Beattie writes that "few sessions of the court . . . ended without the judge putting the black cloth on his full-bottomed wig and pronouncing the terrible words of the death sentence. In rare instances in which no one was condemned to death, the conclusion of a 'maiden session' was marked by another piece of theater, a gift of a pair of white gloves to the judge."[35] These ceremonies served the purpose of emphasizing the authority of law and the authority of the Crown.

GUILTY UNTIL PROVEN INNOCENT

In the eighteenth century, the crime victim was responsible for bringing charges against the alleged wrongdoer, except when the Crown's interests were at stake.[36] Virtually every jury trial began with the victim telling his or her story to the jury. In contrast to today, eighteenth-century judges actively questioned the witnesses. Sometimes the jurors themselves raised questions or made comments about the testimony during the course of the trial. In most cases neither the prosecuting party nor the defendant had lawyers. The prisoner might cross-examine witnesses, but without a lawyer to assist, most prisoners were at a serious disadvantage. The prisoner's main defense, if any, was expected to come after the prosecution had presented its case.

The foundational idea that an accused person is innocent until proven guilty is so central to contemporary English and American law that one might suppose that it has always been the case. Yet Beattie has convincingly demonstrated from historical records that this inference is wrong. Functionally, the law presumed accused persons were guilty and left them to prove otherwise. The idea of the burden of proof being on the accuser rather than the accused was not established before the beginning of the nineteenth century.[37] William Penn's trial, of course, clearly reflected a presumption of guilt. The defendant had the burden of providing an alternative explanation to the accusations. As an example, in one case a man merely responded that he was "not a thief" and the judge replied, "You must prove that."[38] Some prisoners may have had witnesses, but at least in the early part of the century the witnesses, like the accused, were not put under oath.

LAWYERS AND THE RULES OF EVIDENCE

Toward the latter part of the seventeenth century, lawyers began to assist in the prosecution's case, especially in important libel, sedition, and felony trials.[39] Accused persons were much slower in getting this privilege, but it appears that starting about 1730 in London's Old Bailey defense lawyers were cross-examining witnesses.[40] Yet even in 1800 approximately seven of ten prisoners on trial for their lives did not have legal counsel.[41] In 1836 the Prisoner's Counsel Act gave the accused the right to have legal counsel, but for the vast majority of prisoners the Act had no effect since most were too poor to retain a lawyer.[42]

The advent of lawyers slowly brought challenges to testimony.[43] Although some judges had raised issues about the reliability and fairness of confessions made before trial, defense lawyers put forth logical arguments as to why some confessions should not be placed before the jury. Similar arguments were made about the potential unreliability of accomplices who testified for the prosecution in order to avoid or mitigate their own punishment and of uncorroborated witness testimony. Other evidence rules that are recognized today gradually grew out of this foundation. Scholars have convincingly argued that the rise of the role of lawyers in the development of evidence and the questioning of witnesses gradually reduced the role of the judge in deciding procedural matters, "summing up" (reviewing the evidence at the end of the trial), and giving instructions on the law. Simultaneously, the rise of lawyers eroded the common practice of jurors asking witnesses questions and taking an active role in the trial. Instead, increasingly jurors were instructed to listen to the evidence and arguments, and to refrain from discussing the evidence, even with one another, until they had been instructed on the law and begun to deliberate.

THE JURY OF "PEERS"

The difficulty of assembling an unbiased jury of peers was apparent from the very beginning of the English jury system. Jury service could be tedious and costly since jurors might have to travel some distance to the court, arrange their own lodging, and perhaps stay for weeks on jury duty.[44] Many potential jurors, especially wealthy ones, found ways of avoiding it. During the reign of King William III, a 1692 statute set out qualifications that broadened jury service so that freeholders of ten pounds or more per year were eligible to serve on juries. This shifted jury duty more to farmers, craftsmen, and other established housekeepers, and away from the gentry and the laboring poor. Summoned jurors were regularly fined for nonattendance if they did not have a valid excuse.

One approach to eliminating biased jurors was the use of a "struck" jury. Each litigant could strike twelve jurymen from a panel of forty-eight names. The purpose of asking for a struck jury was to avoid incompetent or biased jurors called by the sheriff. Sheriffs often had difficulty in recruiting qualified jurors. Moreover, some sheriffs were corrupt. The jurors they called were frequently drunks or reprobates or had strong political opinions about one party or the other.

The problem of juror bias was formally recognized in the latter part of the eighteenth century. In his famous 1769 treatise on the laws of England, William Blackstone distinguished between "manifest prejudice," in which a juror had an obvious conflict of interest in the outcome of the case, such as family or financial ties to one of the parties, and "bias on the favor," by which he meant what today we would call prejudiced attitudes or beliefs. The prosecution or defendant in criminal cases, or either litigant in a civil lawsuit, could make a challenge. Challenges to manifest prejudice were decided by the judge, but bias on the favor was decided by two triors.[45] The triors were selected from the jury pool and sat as a sort of mini-jury as the challenged juror was questioned by the challenging party. The triors would then decide whether the accusation of lack of impartiality was true or not true. The trior procedure was also used in America, both before and after the Revolution.[46] Canada still retains this quaint procedure and uses it when the trial judge rules that there is concern about juror impartiality in a criminal trial.[47]

Blackstone additionally described "peremptory challenges" and "stand bys."[48] Each side would have a limited number of peremptory challenges through which a juror could be rejected without giving a reason. Peremptory challenges provided an additional measure of fairness to the trial by allowing the parties to act on a hunch that the juror was biased. In addition, the Crown prosecutor was provided an unlimited number of stand bys. Any juror called to the jury box whom the Crown did not like could be dropped to the back of the list and replaced by another juror. The theory was that the Crown had a royal interest in seeking jurors partial to its case. Stand bys may be seen as another reflection of bias in favor of the prosecution. In practice, stand bys gave the Crown a virtually unlimited ability to shape the jury. Canada abolished stand bys in 1992 but they are still available under certain conditions in English jury trials.[49]

THE EARLY JURY AT WORK

Notorious trials like that of William Penn and the Seven Bishops were exceptions.[50] Ordinary trials in the seventeenth and early eighteenth centuries were brief, sometimes lasting only a few minutes. Charges of murder and some robberies and burglaries might take longer, perhaps a few hours. John Beattie's description of the proceedings of a court session in Surrey in the summer of 1751 fleshes out a typical assize court session.[51] On Thursday and Friday the court dealt with grand jury and other business. On Saturday the court commenced at about seven in the morning. Beattie reports that the first case was an infanticide case that had ten witnesses. Next came a series of property crime trials, most of which were potentially capital offenses. By dinner adjournment, probably 2:00 in the afternoon, ten cases had been tried and the jury had returned verdicts. Not guilty verdicts were returned in the infanticide case and a shoplifting case. The jury found five felons guilty of reduced charges, convicting three others of the original charges, two of whom were later sentenced to death. The court commenced again at about 5:00 with four more felony trials and two of misdemeanors. No court sessions were held on Sunday. On the following Monday, Tuesday, and Wednesday, the court dealt with an additional thirty-seven men and women charged with felonies and six others charged with misdemeanors. Sentencing as well as other business took place on Thursday.

A jury was usually assigned to deal with a number of accused persons. The cases in the grouping, anywhere from two to twelve or more, were heard in serial order, with hardly a pause in between. In many instances, the jurors retired to render their verdicts only after testimony in all of the cases had been presented. Most juries had a number of jurors with previous trial experience. The rapid proceedings made it difficult to keep both the accused persons and the evidence clear in the jurors' minds. As a consequence, the court clerk provided the jury with a list of the accused and the charges against each. We noted earlier that jurors often stayed in the courtroom rather than retire for private deliberations. They might render a verdict without deliberating, merely taking a hurried survey or assenting to a lead juror who proposed a verdict.

This swift justice may have been in part due to the strong possibility that the evidence against most accused prisoners was overwhelming or that the accused offered little or nothing in the way of defense. Plea bargaining was not recognized, so all charged crimes tended to be adjudicated. However, the alacrity of the jury trials probably also reflects the legal and societal presumption that accused persons were presumed guilty until proven innocent.

EVOLVING LAW AND TRIAL BY MAGISTRATE IN THE NINETEENTH CENTURY

During the nineteenth century, both substantive and procedural law continued to evolve into the form that we recognize today.[52] Courts and Parliament had begun to make distinctions in degrees of criminal culpability and punishments. The rules of evidence became more elaborate and the novel presumption that an accused should be considered innocent until proven guilty was gaining favor by about 1820.[53] Prisoners being tried in the Old Bailey were assigned counsel at the time of trial, and although the legal help was perfunctory at best, it was an improvement over no legal representation at all. Jury verdicts were given greater scrutiny by appellate courts.

Nevertheless, justice was less than ideal by today's standards.[54] Before Irish independence, for example, the Crown continually exercised its authority by excluding Catholics from juries. The selection of the jury panel was left entirely to the discretion of the local sheriff, who often ensured a pool of jurors favoring a certain outcome. There were many complaints about class bias. Although defendants retained the rights of challenges for cause and peremptory challenges, judges did not allow detailed questioning of prospective jurors. Unless the jurors were already known to the defendant, this rendered the defense challenge privileges functionally useless. Despite the presumption of innocence having become an accepted principle of the law, juries were often not given instructions on that presumption.[55]

One of the most significant changes that began taking place in nineteenth-century England was the transfer of lesser crimes to magistrate courts.[56] This had a major impact on the frequency of jury trials because magistrates sitting without a jury tried these charges of lesser crimes. Parliament developed a criminal code that officially distinguished between indictable (more serious) offenses that were eligible for jury trial and summary (less serious) offenses that were not. This process of trying offenses before magistrates had actually begun before Blackstone's time, and he worried that the right to jury trial was being eroded. His concerns were justified. By 1900 more than 98 percent of criminal trials were decided by magistrates.[57]

THE SPREAD OF THE JURY SYSTEM THROUGHOUT THE WORLD

The English jury was transplanted onto American soil in all the colonies. Jury systems developed in other parts of the British Empire as well. These included Australia, Canada, and New Zealand, but also many other smaller colonies strung across the globe. Many of the colonies retained juries when they became independent countries. Today, fifty-two nations and territories retain jury systems derived from England. These include Malawi, Sri Lanka, Tonga, Guyana, and Caribbean nations such as Jamaica, Bermuda, and Trinidad.[58] On the continent of Europe even Napoleon, an enemy of England, admired the concept of the jury and included a version of it in his legal code that was imposed on the countries that he conquered. Nations such as Russia, Spain, and Portugal also created jury systems as a symbol of popular government, but later abandoned them. Recently, Spain and Russia have reintroduced jury systems that they had forsaken and Korea is developing a jury system modeled after United States juries. The rise, decline, and renewal of jury systems provide telling lessons about the jury's significance as a political and legal institution.

CHANGES IN TWENTIETH-CENTURY ENGLAND: THE DECLINE OF THE "LITTLE PARLIAMENT"

Strikingly, despite the fact that England gave birth to modern jury systems, there is no constitutional right to a jury trial in that country.[59] Unlike the United States, England does not have a written constitution with a bill of rights that provides for trial by jury. There is only a common law obligation to use juries for the cases that Parliament decides are indictable offenses. In theory, Parliament could abolish juries tomorrow with the passing of a simple statute. It is unlikely to do so any time soon, but the trend toward fewer jury trials that began during Blackstone's time continued into the twentieth century and shows signs of accelerating in the twenty-first century.

In the middle of the nineteenth century, English judges were granted the power to deny trial by jury in civil cases.[60] During the First World War, the military mobilization of so many of England's men left a severe shortage of persons eligible for jury service, and women could only serve as jurors in special cases involving female issues such as pregnancy. Civil jury trials were suspended. After the war the civil jury system was briefly revived but then fell into disuse.[61] Today, England's Supreme Court Act of 1981 provides a right to jury trial only for civil cases involving libel and slander, fraud, malicious prosecution, and false imprisonment. But even that right is qualified: a judge may decide the case is too lengthy or too complicated for a jury. In theory, a judge could grant a jury trial for a personal injury case under special circumstances, but it doesn't happen.

By 2001 juries decided only about 1 percent of criminal cases in England and Wales.[62] The English Parliament has progressively reclassified crimes to be summary judgment crimes or "triable either way" offenses, that is, offenses in which the defendant can elect to be tried by magistrates or elect to be tried in a higher court, where jury trial is available if the accused pleads not guilty.[63] The end result is that most cases are tried in magistrates' courts.

The vast majority of England's approximately 30,400 magistrates are persons without formal legal training who preside over hearings, usually in three-person panels.[64] Except for approximately one hundred stipendiary magistrates, these magistrates receive no compensation for their services. In this sense most English defendants have their guilt determined by laypersons, even if they are not jurors. If a defendant is found guilty, the magistrates can render a sentence of up to six months in custody and a fine of five thousand pounds. Magistrate courts today handle approximately 91 percent of all prosecuted crime in England.

The jury itself underwent major changes in England during the latter half of the twentieth century.[65] In 1972 jury eligibility was extended to anyone on the electoral register who is not ineligible for some reason, such as having a prior criminal record. This change was intended to make the jury more democratic in composition. But four years later the Criminal Justice Act of 1976 changed the ancient rule that lawful verdicts require all twelve jurors to be unanimous.[66] The Act allows majority verdicts from ten of the twelve jurors. In practice, the jury is told to deliberate and reach a unanimous verdict, but if after several hours of deliberation it has failed to reach unanimity, the judge will call the jurors to the court and instruct them that ten of twelve will suffice. In 1998, 20 percent of convictions were by majority verdicts.[67]

The other major jury change occurred in 1988.[68] The defendant's right to peremptory challenges was abolished. On the other hand, the Crown has retained the right to stand by jurors, retaining its advantage in forming the jury's composition.[69] In theory the stand by is to be used only under special circumstances, but there are no statistics on how often the procedure is actually employed.

As the twentieth century drew to a close, a significant change in the Criminal Justice and Public Order Act of 1974 affected the defendant's right to remain silent.[70] Beginning in 1996 judges were given the ability to instruct the jury that the defendant's unwillingness to talk to the police at the time of arrest or to testify in his or her own behalf at trial could be used in making inferences of guilt. This change has upset many English lawyers and others concerned with civil liberties.

In the mid-1980s concerns were raised that juries were not up to the task of deciding complex fraud cases. In 2001, Lord Justice Auld published a detailed analysis of the British court system, *Review of the Criminal Courts of England and Wales*.[71] The Auld report discussed the complexity of modern financial fraud cases, the lengthy trials required, the alleged inability of laypersons to comprehend these matters, and the hardships lengthy trials impose on jurors. Administrative costs of lengthy jury trials were also mentioned. The Auld report recommended trial by judge alone or trial by judge sitting with laypersons skilled in a field necessary to understand the financial transactions. In 2003 Parliament passed a bill permitting fraud trials by judge alone, and in 2005 the Attorney General of England and Wales attempted to get rid of fraud juries.[72]

The efforts brought an outcry from scholars and civil libertarians, and the House of Lords subsequently rejected the measure. Nonetheless, the Attorney General has promised to continue the effort to replace fraud juries with judges.

CONCLUDING OBSERVATION

We have explored how the English jury developed and evolved over the centuries. The jury that the American colonists inherited was copied almost verbatim from the eighteenth-century English jury. Yet, as we will see, the evolution continued: local circumstances, local culture, and physical distance almost immediately resulted in changes to the jury system the colonists had inherited.

Chapter 2

CRIMINAL AND CIVIL JURIES IN AMERICA FROM COLONIAL TIMES TO THE PRESENT DAY

Evolution, a Heroic Role, and Controversy

THE MORNING STAR OF AMERICAN LIBERTY: JOHN PETER ZENGER'S TRIAL[1]

Gouverneur Morris, a major drafter of the United States Constitution, asserted that John Peter Zenger's jury trial in 1735 was the "germ of American freedom, the morning star of that liberty which subsequently revolutionized America."[2] It is arguably the most important trial in American history—and one of the most dramatic. It had a significant influence on English law, both before and after the Revolution, and served as a symbolic event that helped generate the First, Fifth, and Sixth Amendments in the Bill of Rights.

The Dutch surrendered New Amsterdam to the English in 1664. The renamed New York colony, however, was always a bit more problematic to govern than the other American colonies, partly because its leading inhabitants were resentful merchants of Dutch rather than English ancestry. The colony was ruled by the Duke of York and his successors as a governorship and exploited for as much financial return as possible. At times all of the American colonies chafed under English rule, but when William Cosby was appointed governor of New York and New Jersey in 1731, public discontent at corruption and exploitation came to a head. Cosby did not arrive in New York for thirteen months. In the interim, Rip Van Dam, a prosperous merchant, served as a popular acting governor.

Cosby had a history of greed and corruption in his previous stint as governor of Minorca. Upon arriving in New York, he immediately began a dispute with Van Dam over his back salary, which Cosby claimed was his due even though he had been absent. Cosby created more controversy when he appointed his son as Secretary of New Jersey. Cosby made two unsuccessful attempts to sue Van Dam over the salary issue in established courts, but Supreme Court Chief Justice Lewis Morris took the side of Van Dam in a powerful opinion condemning Cosby. Still pursuing his alleged debt, Cosby then attempted to create a new special court of equity composed exclusively of judges. The New York Assembly had previously passed resolutions opposing special courts and Cosby's action brought many colonists to the side of Van Dam and his two lawyers, James Alexander and William Smith.

Zenger's *Journal*

Early on, newspapers played a vital role in American politics. After an apprenticeship and work experience in Maryland and New York, German-born John Peter Zenger opened his own print shop in New York in 1726. In 1733 he began publishing a newspaper, the *New York Weekly Journal*. In contrast to previous and contemporary newspapers, the *Journal* was openly partisan on politics and candid in its opposition to the governing New York establishment. Zenger was not especially literate, but in the bitter dispute between Cosby and Van Dam, the *Journal* carried leading articles ghostwritten by lawyers Alexander and Smith, as well as by Chief Justice Morris, Morris's son, and another prominent participant in the dispute, Cadwaller Colden. The writings addressed freedom of the press, corruption in government, and the legal process. Many were clearly intended to heap scorn on Cosby and his supporters.[3]

One satirical advertisement in the *Journal*, making an obvious reference to an ally of Governor Cosby, involved "A Large Spaneil, of about Five Foot Five Inches High" that "has lately stray'd from his Kennel with his Mouth full of fulsom Panegyricks . . . to abuse Mankind, by imposing a great many Falsehoods upon them."[4] Another article alluded to Cosby's successful maneuver in depriving Van Dam of a jury trial for a countersuit: "Deservedly therefore is this Tryal by Juries, ranked among the choicest of our fundamental Laws, which whosoever shall go about openly to suppress, or craftily to undermine, does ipso facto, ATTACK THE GOVERNMENT, AND BRING IN AN ARBITRARY POWER, AND IS AN ENEMY AND TRAYTOR TO HIS COUNTRY."[5]

All of this was too much for Cosby and his allies. While everyone knew that others had written the articles, Zenger was the only legally eligible target. Twice Cosby failed to persuade grand juries to indict Zenger for "seditious libel." Finally, he resorted to an "information" by his attorney general, which effectively served the same purpose as an indictment. Zenger was arrested and thrown into

New York's Old Jail. Chief Justice DeLancey, an ally of Cosby, set Zenger's bail at four hundred pounds.

Although Zenger did not have the resources to manage the huge bail, his political allies could have provided the money. But Zenger, probably in discussions with his allies, made a decision that it was politically advantageous to remain in jail. Zenger's wife, Anna Catherina, continued to publish the *Journal*, taking instructions from Peter in conversations through the keyhole of his dark cell. Through her, Zenger continued the political fight during the nine long months between his arrest and his trial. The circulation of the *Journal* increased dramatically during this time.

The Stacked Deck

In the meantime, lawyers Smith and Alexander saw that Cosby and his judicial allies were attempting to stack the deck by choosing a biased jury. Although the ploy was thwarted, Zenger's two lawyers began to search for assistance. They needed it. Governor Cosby appointed Chief Justice James DeLancey and Justice Frederick Philipse to preside over the trial, but their commissions as judges were made without the consent of the governor's council and were termed "at pleasure" rather than the standard appointment specifying "during good behavior," which meant they could be dismissed by Cosby at any moment. The terminology of the appointment thus compromised their judicial independence. Moreover, each man had been a party to the initial lawsuit against Zenger.[6]

Alexander and Smith made a careful technical challenge to the appointments that questioned the competence of DeLancey and Philipse to preside over the trial. In response, Chief Justice DeLancey disbarred them. Despite appeals by the lawyers, DeLancey ruled that the disbarment stood and it applied to their total practice as attorneys and as counsel. One writer on the Zenger case suggests, not unreasonably, that this action probably terrorized the rest of the established lawyers in New York.[7]

Zenger now asked that the court appoint new counsel. DeLancey assigned John Chambers, a new lawyer with absolutely no courtroom experience and who had recently publicly praised Governor Cosby. Chambers did enter a plea of not guilty for his client and moved for a struck jury and a trial date. Under the struck jury procedure, the sheriff selected forty-eight names and each side could strike up to twelve names. The remaining jurors were then subjected to questioning about their impartiality. DeLancey reluctantly approved the struck jury only on the first day of the trial, but spectators immediately noticed that there were aberrations in the selection process. These problems were eventually resolved. Yet, immediately afterward, the clerk of the court attempted to introduce new irregularities. Honorably, John Chambers argued against the deviations to a fair jury selection process and prevailed. As a result, the final jury contained a number of freeholders who were of Dutch rather than English ancestry.

The trial began with the reading of the information accusing Zenger, in part, of:

> being a seditious person; and a frequent printer and publisher of false news and seditious libels, both wickedly and maliciously devising the administration of His Excellency William Cosby, Captain General and Governor in Chief, to traduce, scandalize, and vilify both His Excellency the Governor and the ministers and officers of the king . . . [and] did falsely, seditiously and scandalously print and publish and cause to be printed and published, a certain false, malicious, seditious, scandalous libel entitled *The New York Weekly Journal*.[8]

Chambers replied to the information by arguing that great allowances ought to be given for what men speak or write and that after examination of the prosecution's witnesses it would be clear that the prosecution had failed to prove its case.

Andrew Hamilton

At this point, from the back of the courtroom, an elderly man rose to announce that he was attending the proceedings to represent Mr. Zenger. The court and all those in attendance, most likely including even Chambers, were stunned when the man introduced himself as Andrew Hamilton, a lawyer whose outstanding legal reputation was known throughout the colonies. Disbarred or not, Smith and Alexander had worked behind the scenes to find an experienced lawyer to lead Zenger's defense.

Andrew Hamilton's origins and much of his life are obscure.[9] He was born in Scotland. Some accounts suggest that he left for America after fighting a duel, while others hint he left for political reasons. When he arrived in America, Hamilton first went by the surname of Trent rather than Hamilton. He married a wealthy widow and then traveled to England to study law as a member of Gray's Inn. Upon returning, he settled in Pennsylvania and entered into colonial politics, eventually being appointed to the Pennsylvania Council and then elected to the Assembly of Pennsylvania. He became prominent in Pennsylvania business and handled legal cases for the descendants of William Penn and others. Hamilton had a reputation for opposing arbitrary acts by the Pennsylvania governor, especially with respect to the courts. He had a commanding personality and an astute mind, both of which were critical in his defense of Zenger.

Hamilton knew that, following English legal precedent in cases of seditious libel, Justice DeLancey would instruct the jurors that they were to find only that Zenger had published the articles and that the court would deliver the judgment on whether the articles were libelous. He also knew that, under English law, any truth contained in the articles was not a defense. In contrast to Chambers's legal strategy of disproving the allegations of the prosecution's witnesses, Hamilton immediately took an offensive strategy. He asserted that there was no need to examine the allegations. He conceded that Zenger printed and published the articles, but asserted that in doing so Zenger had committed no crime: "I hope it is not our bare printing and publishing a paper that make it a libel. You will have something more to do before you make my client a libeler. For the words themselves must be libelous—that is false, scandalous, and seditious—or else we are not guilty."[10]

Proscribed from directly confronting the law of seditious libel by Chief Justice DeLancey, Hamilton remained deferential to the court throughout his arguments, even defending the right and responsibility of government to defend against false accusations. Nevertheless, he simultaneously affirmed the right of citizens to protest publicly about injustice. Hamilton sparred with the prosecutor on the issue of truth, and Chief Justice DeLancey stepped in: "You cannot be admitted Mr. Hamilton, to give the truth of a libel in evidence. A libel is not to be justified; for it is nevertheless a libel that it is true."[11]

The Philadelphia lawyer politely but courageously disagreed with the chief justice, pointing out that the definition of a libel, contained in the indictment, was "false, seditious, and scandalous." Hamilton accepted the English law principle that questions of law were left to the judges while the jury determined only questions of fact, but he asserted that charges of libel involved an intertwining of law and fact: What makes a statement a libel is the factual question of whether it is a falsehood. To require the jury to return a special rather than a general verdict would, therefore, usurp the rights of the jury, since it was supposed to decide factual questions.

Furthermore, Hamilton suggested that although the laws of England might be good laws for England, they were not necessarily good laws for America, where there was greater equality between the people and those who governed them. Finally, Hamilton propounded to the jury a theory about the relationship between law and politics. It was not part of their English heritage, but it was one with which many New Yorkers would be sympathetic. Calling attention to the fact that Zenger was not dissimilar to the jurors themselves, he asserted that citizens had the right to criticize their rulers and that Zenger was on trial because he asserted that right. Central to Hamilton's theory was the notion that the state existed to protect the liberties of its citizens. When the state fails in this regard and the King's authorities use their power to destroy individual citizens, the citizens do not need to obey these authorities: "When the representatives of a free people are by just representations or remonstrances made sensible of the sufferings of their fellow subjects, by the abuse of power in the hands of the governor, they have declared . . . that they were not obliged by the law to support a governor who goes about to destroy a province or colony."

Hamilton began his summation to the jury with the following argument:

> You are citizens of New York. You are really what the law supposes you to be, honest and lawful men; and according to my brief the facts [printed by Zenger] were not committed in a corner. They are notoriously known to be true. Therefore in your justice lies our safety. And [as] we are denied [by the court] the liberty of giving evidence to prove the truth of what we have published, I will beg leave to lay it down as a standing rule in such cases that the suppression of evidence ought always to be taken for the strongest evidence; and I hope it will have weight with you.[12]

Hamilton extended this argument with erudite references to the injustices wrought by the discredited English Star Chamber courts, to the Seven Bishops case, the Bible, Roman history, and other esoteric law. He concluded with this appeal: "The question before the Court and you, Gentlemen of the Jury, is not of small or private concern. It is not the cause of one poor printer, nor of New York alone, which you are now trying. No! It may in its consequence affect every free man that lives under a British government in America. It is the best cause. It is the cause of liberty. "[13]

Chief Justice DeLancey had the final word, and he instructed the jurors that it was their duty to decide the case as stated in the indictment, namely, whether Zenger had published the articles. The jury withdrew, returned within a short time, and the foreman announced "Not guilty."[14] The courtroom broke into cheers that the chief justice could not suppress. Zenger was released the next day, although only after paying for the costs of his upkeep while in jail.

The Aftermath

The Common Council of New York feted Andrew Hamilton with honors. Zenger's *Journal* published a detailed account of the trial the next week. Two years after the trial, Zenger was appointed to the post of official printer to the New York Assembly and a year later as the printer for New Jersey.[15] Some have suggested that Zenger probably did not appreciate the full extent of the risks he was taking when he first printed the *Journal* articles but decided to stand on principle after he was arrested. In any event, he displayed admirable fortitude. Governor Cosby's effectiveness in office suffered severely and he died within the year. Both James Alexander and William Smith were reinstated to the bar in 1737, a year after the trial.

The arguments espoused by Andrew Hamilton were widely read in London, and applauded in some quarters. Nevertheless, even after the American Revolution, the Zenger precedent was not followed in other trials involving charges of seditious libel.[16] For example, in 1803 Harry Croswell was put on trial for seditious libel for criticizing President Thomas Jefferson. And the affirmation of his conviction by a divided court was legally more significant for the rights of a free press in America.[17] Yet Zenger's trial indisputably had an eventual influence on both English and American thinking. Zenger's account of his trial had fourteen printings prior to the Declaration of Independence. The trial was discussed in relation to Fox's Libel Act in 1792, which permitted English juries to return a verdict on both fact and law in libel cases. It appears to have encouraged greater boldness on the part of newspapers, and was a backdrop in deliberations about the jury in the construction of the American Constitution.

There is one final observation to be made about the Zenger case. In his arguments before Chief Justice DeLancey, Andrew Hamilton raised questions about whether it was always appropriate to apply English law and precedent in America because social, legal, and economic conditions were so different, asserting that "what is good law at one time and place is not so at another time and another place."[18] Although Hamilton was addressing the particular case of his client, Zenger, the logic of his argument was a prescient insight about future American divergence from English law and jury practices.

GENESIS: EARLY COLONIAL JURIES

We need to take a step back in time before the Zenger case to consider the initial transplantation of the English jury to American soil.[19] The 1606 charter to the Virginia Company provided for jury trial, and by 1624 juries were available for all civil and criminal cases. In 1623 the right to jury trial was recognized in New Plymouth.[20] The Massachusetts Bay Colony introduced jury trials in 1628. The Colony of West New Jersey formally recognized them in 1677, as did Pennsylvania in 1682.[21] In fact, juries were probably in use before their formal recognition. Rhode Island had jury trials even before the establishment of the colony's government and set of laws in 1647.[22]

Governor William Bradford of Plymouth Plantation reported in his diary the details of an interesting trial in 1642, giving us a glimpse of long-ago jury trial procedure.[23] Bradford's diary states that Thomas Granger, an adolescent servant, "was this year detected of buggery, and indicted for the same, with a mare, a cow, two goats, five sheep, two calves, and a turkey." Although Granger at first denied the charges, he eventually confessed to ministers and then to the court and the jury. The court required Granger to identify the specific animals in the herds and flock. Each of these animals, starting with the mare and then the cow, was killed in front of him, followed by the rest of the beasts, "according to the law, Leviticus xx.15; and then he himself was executed. The cattle were all cast into a great and large pit that was digged for that purpose for them, and no use was made of any part."[24]

The trial was bizarre and the punishment harsh from today's perspective.

However, legal historian David Bodenhamer points out that the magistrates did follow some important procedural rules. There was a formal indictment and a speedy and public trial by judges and jury. Granger's trial was not ordinary, but its religious underpinnings were typical. Other research suggests that among the English Puritans instructions to the jury began with the admonition to "Feare God and Keepe his Comandments." Before jury deliberations began, the charges against accused persons were made with reference to the Ten Commandments.[25]

AMERICANIZATION OF THE COMMON LAW

Although the charters of the colonies provided that the laws they established should not be contrary to the laws of England, this left much wiggle room for the individual colonies to modify both substantive and procedural law.[26] The isolation from England and the need to respond to local conditions almost immediately resulted in practices different from those of the mother country.[27] The colonies had different cultural, social, and religious foundations that led to divergences among them, a tradition that is still reflected in differing practices between states today.

Many of the colonists had left England at least partly because of bad experiences with English justice. As a consequence, rules and practices against double jeopardy in criminal trials developed early in the colonies. There was also a related mistrust of lawyers.[28] The Puritan colonies at first barred representation by lawyers in civil and criminal cases because it was assumed that lawyers would subvert the goal of justice by finding loopholes in the laws. By 1624 jury trials were available for all civil and criminal cases in Virginia, but in 1645 Virginia excluded lawyers from the courts. Lawyers were also banned in Connecticut, and frowned upon in the Carolinas, West New Jersey, and Pennsylvania. Only a handful of the colonists, in fact, had formal legal training and the few books on law were often outdated.[29] The practical realities of life in America did not allow for the luxury of legal cases to be based on technicalities.

Placing the jury between authorities and litigants was one way of assuring that justice was kept in the hands of the people. Moreover, the jury system allowed the injection of local norms and values into legal disputes. In his important treatise *Americanization of the Common Law*, William Nelson concluded that in the early years of colonial development in New England, juries were the central instrument of governance.[30] They enforced morality with respect to criminal violations, but also applied local norms in regard to civil matters such as debt and the proper laying out of highways. Massachusetts litigants had a right to a jury trial in all cases before superior and common pleas courts. Few legal disputes were decided without a jury.[31] Nevertheless, following English practice, some types of courts did not provide for jury trial. These included equity courts, which handled remedies other than money damages, and admiralty courts, which specialized in maritime cases. Minor civil disputes and minor criminal offenses were ordinarily not subject to jury trial.[32]

It almost goes without saying that colonial juries were composed exclusively of men, and ordinarily there were property qualifications. In procedures set out in 1648, Massachusetts juries were selected in town meetings of freemen (e.g., excluding indentured servants and slaves). As we shall see shortly, this process had crucial implications for later resistance to English governance. In Virginia juries were selected by the local sheriff, but there was a strong tendency to ensure that the jurors were persons with local knowledge and values.[33]

Jury service in all colonies was often an onerous and expensive obligation. The juror might have to travel many miles and be in residence at his own expense (often for days or weeks) because jurors, as noted earlier, were assigned to serve on many trials at a single sitting of the court. Some jurors simply did not show up and were fined for failure to appear. At other times, a juror might sit for some trials and then depart, leaving the court without the required twelve persons. Following English precedent, the court could simply conscript anyone in the courtroom or on the street to fill out the roster. These ad hoc jurors were called *talesmen*.[34] The common use of talesmen led to complaints that many juries were composed of "vagabonds" who were alleged to be incompetent or easily corrupted.[35]

Jury challenges were accepted as part of the trial process. Similar to the English procedures described earlier, challenges to "bias on the favour" were decided by two "triors," rather than the judge.[36] One consequence of using triors to decide who was or was not an impartial juror is that it provided a check on the power of the judge to control who sat on the petit jury. Peremptory challenges varied; some states allowed none or permitted them only in criminal trials.[37]

JUDICIAL CONTROL OF THE COLONIAL JURY

Analyzing historical debates about the right to jury trial in the colonial period is essential to understanding the controversies surrounding the jury's role that extended well into the nineteenth century (and are echoed in the twenty-first-century debate over jury nullification, that is, the jury's right to return a verdict that is contrary to the law).

A basic assumption of American thinking was that the common law was based on natural justice. In his legal papers, John Adams, later America's second president, remarked that the common law was known by everyone and "imbibed with the Nurses Milk and first Air."[38] In many cases judges gave the jury no instructions at all on the law. In still other cases, the three or more presiding magistrates might offer contradictory instructions on the law, allowing the jury latitude in interpreting the law.

The wide discretion of the colonial jury to decide law as well as facts did not mean that judges had no control over the jury. There were formal rules of pleading that could be used to limit the jury's decision to a simple factual finding, although in practice these rules were not used often. The presiding judges actively participated in the proceedings, questioned witnesses, and commented on the evidence in order to make the case clear and understandable to the jury.[39] There were rules of evidence, still rudimentary by today's standards, that precluded some evidence from the trial, especially that which might be considered prejudicial, such as hearsay.[40] There were provisions for special verdicts that required a jury to answer particular factual findings in addition to its general verdict.

Criminal trials typically were brought by the accuser, not a public prosecutor. This meant that neither accuser nor defendant in trials could testify under oath because it was assumed that they both had a personal interest in the case. (Note that in the Zenger trial, no consideration was given to having the defendant testify on his own behalf.) Sometimes even witnesses who were not a party to the dispute were excluded from giving evidence under oath. In 1763 a Baptist sued to recover money damages for unlawful collection of a religious tax. The court ruled that no Baptists could testify as witnesses because of their implied interest in the outcome.[41]

VARIATION BETWEEN COLONIES

In the early days of colonization, there was much variation between the colonies in their proclivities toward the use of juries. Rhode Island, West Jersey, and North Carolina strongly embraced them while New Haven, Massachusetts, Connecticut, and Virginia used them sparingly.[42]As the eighteenth century began, New England made greater use of civil juries.[43] Moreover, the role of jurors began to depart from English practice.[44] Unlike in England, grand jurors were not required to inform the court of any private crime or offense that did not imperil the colony. Both grand juries and petit juries were allowed to bring in special verdicts at their own discretion, including a partial verdict. The jury could not easily be intimidated by the judges, who did not hold the same authority as judges in England. Moreover, if the members of the petit jury were "not clear in their judgments or consciences, concerning any Case wherein they are to give their verdict," they all had the privilege "in open Court to advise with any man they shall think fit to resolve or direct them before they give their verdict."[45] This change from English practice probably resulted from the Puritans' reluctance to force anyone to act against their conscience.[46] In any event, it added to the power of the jury over judges and magistrates.

The courthouse and the jury trial played a central role in colonial Virginia.[47] Trials were often short, some perhaps lasting less than an hour. In contrast to the

English practice of having a jury hear testimony about a series of defendants before being sent back to deliberate, evidence suggests that verdicts were rendered at the end of each case. Virginia judges lacked the authority to comment on the evidence or to instruct the jury on the law, privileges they enjoyed in New England courts. On the other hand, the social and economic hierarchy of Virginian culture was reflected in both the process and the verdicts of juries. Historical records indicate that judges sometimes appeared as litigants in their own courts. Even in the 1790s, well after the Revolution, judges might temporarily step off the bench and into the witness box to testify about some fact at issue. Much of the trial evidence was focused on character and reputation. In cases involving disputes about debts, juries not infrequently returned damages verdicts of one penny that carried both symbolic and legal significance: the plaintiff received a moral victory of sorts but could not recover the amount of the alleged debt.[48]

Historian William Nelson has observed that the jury was a profoundly powerful institution spurring the Americanization of English law.[49] He writes: "The vital fact about the jury system, however, was not that juries tried nearly every case but that they had vast power to find both the law and facts in those cases."[50] These developments led to the jury system playing a critical role in resisting English imperial rule as many colonists sought freedom from taxation without representation.

WHIGS AND CIVIL TRAVERSE JURIES: DEFYING ENGLISH LAW

George Cradock was a temporary Collector for the Port of Boston.[51] In 1761 he seized a ship belonging to John Erving and confiscated contraband cargo. A case against Erving was filed in the Court of Admiralty. Erving appeared in court personally and agreed to settle for duties of 500 pounds sterling. Erving paid the sum and, according to the laws and custom of the day, it was meted out equally among the King, the governor of Massachusetts, and Collector Cradock. Erving then sued Cradock in the common law court for damages on the grounds of illegal seizure and trespass. Erving asserted that the payment he had made was involuntary and extorted by violence and duress. Unlike in admiralty courts, litigation in common law courts was eligible for jury trial.

Governor Bernard, who had already received his share of the settlement, immediately concluded that Erving's action was part of a general conspiracy to destroy admiralty jurisdiction and the customs service. If Erving was successful, other merchants would pursue this strategy. At trial two of the judges, apparently antipathetic to the Crown, directed the jury to find for the plaintiff. The jury did and returned a verdict against Cradock in the amount of nearly 600 pounds sterling, 100 pounds more than Erving had paid in his settlement. Cradock appealed to a superior court, which tried the case again. Chief Justice Thomas Hutchinson, presiding over the new trial, emphatically stated that "the decree of the Court of Admiralty, where it had jurisdiction, could not be traversed and annulled in a court of common law."[52] In other words, there were no exceptions: The jury had to return a verdict for Cradock. Regardless, the jury returned a verdict for Erving in the amount of 555 pounds sterling.

The basic strategy of the plaintiff in *Erving v. Cradock* was repeated in many cases in Rhode Island,[53] Massachusetts, New York, and South Carolina over the next fifteen years as the Whigs resisted English imperial laws controlling and taxing the colonists.[54] Among the successful plaintiffs was John Hancock, whose later signature on the Declaration of Independence was allegedly written boldly so that King George III would not need his spectacles to read it.[55]

Governor Bernard had correctly anticipated the problem. Lawyers for Whig plaintiffs argued to the jury that American interpretation of the law should take precedence over English interpretation of the law. Juries were encouraged to use civil tort (i.e., injury) damages as a sanction to punish revenue agents for enforcing unpopular English laws. And the jurisdiction of admiralty courts was challenged.[56] The strategy was successful because Whigs controlled the forums from which the jury panel was selected, thereby favoring jurors with Whig leanings or sympathies, and because civil juries were acknowledged to have the authority to decide both the law and the facts.

Both grand juries and criminal juries played similar roles prior to the Revolution.[57] Recall that Governor Cosby could not get grand juries to indict John Peter Zenger. American juries found criminal liability against authorities following the Boston Massacre.[58] But the greatest threat to imperial authority appears to have been the civil jury because it was used to defy the broad institutions of English governance in the colonies. Through the Sugar Act and the Stamp Act, Parliament attempted to institute new courts that would avoid juries. These actions were some of the most important parliamentary actions that precipitated the Revolution. The First and Second Continental Congresses, held in 1774 and 1775, respectively, decried the attempts by the Crown to avoid jury trial,[59] and a year later the Declaration of Independence echoed these grievances when the signers declared that, among many other abuses and usurpations, King George III was guilty of "depriving us, in many cases, of the benefits of Trial by Jury."

JURIES IN THE CONSTITUTIONAL DEBATES

Views about the right to a jury in criminal and civil contexts began to diverge. Immediately after independence, the new states passed constitutions that guaranteed rights to civil as well as criminal jury trials. Article III of the US Constitution, which limits the power of federal government, also provides that "[t]he Trial of all Crimes, except in Cases of Impeachment, shall be by Jury." This right to a jury trial in criminal cases is repeated in the Sixth Amendment. But despite the importance of civil juries to resisting English oppression before the Revolution, the right to a jury trial for civil disputes, eventually enshrined as the Seventh Amendment in the Bill of Rights, became a subject of hot controversy in the new republic.

Debates about the Constitution pitted the Federalists, who wanted a strong central government, against the Anti-Federalists, who were deeply concerned about infringements on the autonomy of state governments.[60] The Federalists emphasized the desperate need to finance the new nation through credit to be granted by both foreign merchants and American merchants. To survive, the country needed to borrow, but a major part of the difficulty in achieving this end, they believed, lay with civil juries.

The Federalists had reason to be concerned because of recent experiences. Civil juries—composed of men embittered against the English government and the destruction caused by English and Hessian troops during the Revolutionary War—often refused to recognize prerevolution debts incurred to English merchants and Americans with Tory leanings. Even when debts were recognized, juries drastically discounted the amounts allegedly owed. Furthermore, in disputes about debts incurred *after* independence, juries tended to disfavor both foreign and domestic creditors. The problem of credit imperiled relations with other foreign countries, most notably France.

A major part of the difficulty lay with the fact that, as noted above, civil juries had the right to decide law as well as facts. A second problem was that while all states recognized civil juries, their laws differed considerably in what was and was not eligible for jury trial, making a unified approach to federal civil juries difficult to achieve.

The Anti-Federalists, by contrast, retained deep reservations about the power of the federal government, in particular the whole federal judicial system. Historians have suggested that there were probably various and complex motives behind the Anti-Federalist objections to omitting the guarantee of civil juries from the federal constitution, but the matter struck a responsive chord in the general public and threatened to derail ratification of the Constitution.

The arguments of the Anti-Federalists on the issue of civil juries reflected suspicions of central government.[61] Civil juries provided protection against government officials. Recalling the actions of colonial officials, they argued that civil juries were essential in disputes between a citizen and the national government and in suits between the government and citizens under the revenue laws. Also, the civil jury was a protection against unjust legislation that might be rendered by Congress as well as protection against biased or corrupt judges. This view reflected a consciousness of class differences. One of the arguments was that judges were usually from the upper, educated classes and would hold a "bias towards those of their rank and dignity," whereas the jury "preserves in the hands of the people, that share which they ought to have in the administration of justice, and prevents the encroachments of the more powerful and wealthy citizens."[62] Finally, without a civil jury chosen from the local community, a debtor might be forced to fight a claim in a distant court. Because of the travel costs, debtors might have to submit to the demand without a chance of defending themselves.[63]

In the end, the contentious issue of civil juries was left to the first Congress to decide. James Madison drafted the Seventh Amendment and it was passed without much legislative debate. However, it was a compromise.[64] The Anti-Federalists got their civil juries, but the Federalists prevailed in having federal circuit courts retain jurisdiction over "diversity" cases involving citizens from different states or countries. They also prevailed in establishing provisions for nonjury equity courts that would have jurisdiction over many revenue cases. Consequently, the compromise wording of the Seventh Amendment limited jury trial to common law actions: "In Suits at common law, where the value in controversy shall exceed twenty dollars, the right of jury trial shall be preserved."

THE LOSS OF LAW-DECIDING POWER

Civil Juries

Between 1804 and 1810 the Massachusetts civil jury lost its legal right to decide law.[65] This provides an example of the forces that shaped changes in jury power in the rest of the country. Merchants and industrial developers were stymied in their desire for a coherent doctrine of commercial laws because juries in different locations applied local norms. Furthermore, business leaders were concerned that their commercial agreements might be upset by the whim of a local jury. Departing from the tradition of multiple judges, newly revised court systems provided for a single judge, thus giving juries a single statement of the law, rather than multiple interpretations from different presiding judges. By 1810 it was generally acknowledged that juries still had the right to decide the law but were entitled to the assistance of the judge. Further developments allowed appeals courts to overturn jury verdicts that did not appear to comport with the law.

Virginia, in contrast, was much slower putting curbs on juries.[66] Virginia was more agrarian, conservative, and resistant to the loss of local control to state or federal power. Juries chosen from the community would help retain that control. Virginia courts decided that there could be no clear distinction between law and facts, and thus juries would have to decide many issues in which facts shaded into law. Nevertheless, over time the pressures for uniformity became too great to resist and juries lost some of their unfettered power.

Criminal Juries

In the early 1800s judges in some states had slowly begun to assert more control over criminal juries, but not without some resistance.[67] For example, an 1828 case, *Townsend v. State*, involved an Indiana tavern owner convicted of selling liquor without a license. The Supreme Court of Indiana ruled that the jury must yield to the law as it was given by the judge. This decision ran contrary to contemporary popular sentiment about democracy and the role of the jury in it. Reflecting skepticism against perceived elitism of judges, one jury foreman is reputed to have asked the judge whether "what you told us, when we first went out, was *raly* the law, or whether it was *only jist* your notion."[68] In 1851 voters gave the jury the right to settle law as well as fact as part of the Indiana Constitution,[69] where it remains intact today.[70] Yet the judge's role in Indiana remained significant. In the same year the Supreme Court of Indiana upheld a trial judge's instruction to the jury that "duty dictates that they should take the law from the courts."[71]

Similar control over the jury's law-deciding power was occurring in federal courts as well. As early as 1797, James Calendar was convicted under the Alien and Sedition laws for attacking President John Adams as, among other things, "a repulsive pedant" and a "hideous hermaphroditical character which has neither the force and firmness of a man, nor the gentleness and sensibility of a woman."[72] Supreme Court Justice Samuel Chase ruled in Calendar's trial that it was inappropriate to accept the jury's right to interpret the Constitution simply because it could decide the law. He acknowledged that the jury had to interpret the law to the degree that the facts fit under the law but that it had no right to interpret the law itself.[73]

Matters came to a head a century later in *Sparf et. al. v. United States*.[74] Herman Sparf and Hans Hanson were convicted of the murder of shipmates on the high seas. In 1895 the Supreme Court heard an appeal in the case, one of the issues being the ability of the jury to be instructed that they were judges of the law. Justice Harlan—writing the majority opinion over a vigorous seventy-three-page dissent by two members of the Court—extensively reviewed case law authority in the federal courts, including the *Calendar* case, the state courts, and English law. He concluded that the jury did not have the right to decide the law.

Sparf effectively put an end to the right of juries to decide the law in federal courts, although that did not completely end the matter in the states. As late as 1931 an Illinois court struggled with the matter before deciding that juries had a duty to follow the judge on the law.[75] Today, the state constitutions of Georgia, Indiana, and Maryland still provide that jurors shall decide questions of law, but judicial decisions, like the Indiana Supreme Court's decision following *Townsend*, have, in effect, canceled or muted those provisions.[76]

Jury Sentencing

Before independence from England, most felonies were automatically capital crimes and the judge pronounced the death sentence after conviction. Following independence a nationwide trend—influenced by the writings of Italian criminologist Cesare Beccaria—replaced capital punishment for most felonies with imprisonment or forced public work.[77] Someone had to decide on the appropriate sentence. In Pennsylvania, sentencing authority was placed in the hands of the trial judge. New York, New Jersey, Maryland, the Carolinas, and the New England states followed suit.

In contrast, Virginia enacted a penal code in 1796 that put the decision in the hands of the jury. Kentucky, Georgia, and Tennessee followed Virginia's lead and eventually Arkansas, Missouri, Indiana, Illinois, Texas, and Oklahoma also provided for jury sentencing to varying degrees.

Professor Nancy King has offered a theory that Federalists, wary of the many Republican judges who were serving at that time, may have championed jury sentencing simply as a way of eliminating some of these judges' power. Virginia lawyers who migrated to Kentucky and other states probably promoted the Virginia model and played into anti-authority sentiments in Kentucky and other states that then constituted the American frontier. Today, on occasion, juries continue to sentence criminal defendants in a handful of states.

THE NINETEENTH-CENTURY TRIAL: MURDER AT HARVARD MEDICAL SCHOOL[78]

A portrait of the emerging American jury trial can be drawn by examining a notorious murder trial in the middle of the nineteenth century. In November 1849, Dr. George Parkman, a wealthy scion of Boston families, was seen entering Harvard Medical College. He disappeared. All of Cambridge and Boston were consumed by the mystery.

A janitor at the Medical College became suspicious of Dr. George Webster, one of seven professors at the college, a Harvard classmate, and a friend and social companion of Dr. Parkman for over fifty years. On his own initiative, the janitor opened a hole in the brick wall of the vault of Dr. Webster's private laboratory privy and found parts of a pelvis and other human remains. He confided his findings to authorities. They searched Dr. Webster's lab and found parts of teeth and bone in the laboratory furnace and a human torso in a trunk.

Dr. Webster was arrested and charged with murder. He denied involvement. There was evidence that he owed Dr. Parkman money. Much of his adult life had been marked by financial difficulties, but Dr. Webster asserted that he had paid an installment to Dr. Parkman on the day of his disappearance, using money obtained from student lecture fees. He insisted that Dr. Parkman had left the building after being paid. Many persons in the community could not believe Dr. Webster was involved, insisting that the charges seemed preposterous.

Dr. Webster was visited by leading members of society as he remained in jail awaiting trial. The only glitch in support for Dr. Webster was that most leading lawyers declined to act as counsel. Eventually, Judge Pliny Merrick and Edward Sohier, both well-respected and prominent lawyers, agreed to take the case.

The trial began on March 19, 1850. Large crowds of the curious filled the square in front of the courthouse awaiting a carefully controlled ten-minute visit to view the proceedings. During the twelve-day trial, as many as sixty thousand people filed in and out of the courtroom. Chief Justice Shaw and three associate justices presided. Before jury selection began, Shaw announced that under the Revised Statutes of Massachusetts he would put the regular questions about bias or prejudice to the prospective jurors to ascertain if they had preformed opinions about the case. (This strongly indicates that the English trior procedure for jury selection was obsolete in Massachusetts in 1850.)

Shaw also said he would excuse any jurors who had conscientious scruples against the death penalty, a decision that was immediately criticized by some legal commentators and later led to claims that the trial was unfair. He also ruled that any peremptory challenges by the defendant had to be exercised *before* the juror was interrogated. The question he put to the jurors was, "Have you expressed or have you formed any opinion on the subject matter now to be tried; or are you sensible of any bias or prejudice therein?" Of the persons called, seven were set aside because they stated that they had formed an opinion, three were excused for opposition to capital punishment, and fourteen were peremptorily challenged by the defendant.

The prosecution opened with an address lasting over an hour. Then the calling of witnesses commenced. On the second day of trial Shaw permitted the jurors, accompanied by lawyers for both sides and two police officers, to visit the Medical College. In addition to civilian witnesses, the prosecution called medical experts to offer opinions on a number of issues. One explained the best way to burn human flesh. His opinion was based on his experiments with the body of a pirate. A number of other medical professionals used drawings to show the parts of the body that were recovered, and offered opinions that the body was Dr. Parkman's. In cross-examination the defense obtained an admission that if they had not known Dr. Parkman was missing, they could not have identified him. However, Dr. Parkman's dentist testified that the bridgework recovered from the furnace belonged to Dr. Parkman.

Next, the prosecution turned to the janitor who had uncovered the body parts in the privy. He had been held in jail as a material witness until he posted a $2,000 bond. The janitor was clear and concise regarding how he had become suspicious, and he withstood a fierce cross-examination by the defense. Other witnesses testified about Dr. Webster's finances. Evidence suggested that he did not have the money to have paid the debt to Dr. Parkman as he had claimed. The prosecution produced other witnesses bearing on Dr. Webster's behavior immediately before and after Dr. Parkman's disappearance. The prosecution concluded after the seventh day of trial.

The eighth day began with the defense's opening statement, stressing the difference between homicide and manslaughter, between malice implied and malice expressed, and the burden of proof. The lawyers stressed the circumstantial nature of the evidence, and, finally, the mild character of Dr. Webster, suggesting that he lacked the temperament to commit murder. The defense produced sixteen witnesses regarding Dr. Webster's reputation. Dr. Webster's two teenage daughters also testified on his behalf. Two medical experts were called to rebut the prosecution's evidence that identified the human remains as being Dr. Parkman's. Finally, seven witnesses testified about their recollections of seeing Dr. Parkman alive after he had entered the Medical College. With these witnesses, the defense rested.

The tenth day began with several rebuttal witnesses followed by a six-and-one-half-hour summation by the prosecution that was extended into the eleventh day from nine o'clock until five, except for a recess for dinner. Then Chief Justice Shaw did something extraordinary. At that time in the development of the American jury the defendant was not allowed to testify at trial because, it was assumed that he was an interested party and the testimony would be untrustworthy. Nevertheless, Justice Shaw asked Dr. Webster if he wanted to add anything to his defense before he instructed the jury. To the dismay of his lawyers, Dr. Webster offered an unsworn peroration taking issue with some of the positions his legal counsel had taken, offering explanations of his behavior in the laboratory, denying he had killed Dr. Parkman, and asserting that "perversions" had been brought against him in the prosecution's case.

Although it was after five o'clock, Shaw called a brief recess before he delivered his summing up and charge to the jury. At eight o'clock the jury, which had been sequestered from the beginning of the trial, began deliberations with a prayer and continued until 10:45 when it returned a verdict: Guilty of murder. Court was adjourned until Monday, at which time Dr. Webster was sentenced to be hanged.

In the following weeks a writ of error was filed on behalf of Dr. Webster. A petition for pardon was signed by substantial numbers of prominent persons. The petition called for sympathy, arguing that Dr. Webster was clearly insane. It also asserted that the trial was unfair because of the admission of "unreliable scientific evidence," judicial rulings, and incompetent legal representation or what we would call today "ineffective assistance of counsel." These efforts failed and Dr. Webster was escorted to the gallows on August 30, 1850.

Dr. Webster's trial, occurring more than a century and a half ago, bears many similarities to a modern American trial. He was represented by lawyers. Expert witnesses had clashing opinions. Witnesses were cross-examined. Massachusetts law allowed the court to interrogate prospective jurors and decide on their impartiality. Chief Justice Shaw excused death penalty opponents from the jury, similar to procedures in today's capital trials.

There are also striking differences. Four judges rather than one presided over the trial. Some legal experts argued that the jury was "packed." The defense had to exercise its peremptory challenges before jurors were interrogated.[79] Women were ineligible for jury service, and to think otherwise would have been considered absurd. The defense was not allowed to make an opening statement but rather had to wait until the prosecution's case was completed.

Chief Justice Shaw gave the defendant the opportunity to make a statement at the conclusion of closing arguments, but it was unsworn testimony, and as a consequence, Dr. Webster could not be cross-examined. Additionally, Chief Justice Shaw "summed up" and commented on the evidence during his charge to the jury. There was also no separate penalty phase in which the jury might decide aggravating and mitigating circumstances and make a recommendation for a lesser punishment. After the jury returned a guilty verdict, the automatic sentence was death by hanging.

Finally, there was no appeal of the verdict to a higher court. The writ of error, a motion or pleading derived from English law, involved claims about errors in law at the trial. A formal hearing was held on the writ but it was decided by the same four judges who had presided at trial and who had made the initial rulings on law.

TURN-OF-THE-CENTURY JURY TRIALS

During the latter half of the nineteenth century, criminal law continued to evolve, and trials with it.[80] Defendants were granted the right to testify and could be cross-examined if they did. Lawyers played a larger role in the trial process, and in states like California, defendants were provided free counsel if they were on trial for a felony. In New York the rudimentary beginnings of a public defender system emerged.[81]

Major changes in the structure of the court system occurred. Separate courts of appeals were developed. Instead of the writ of error for appeal mandated in Dr. Webster's trial, challenged verdicts were appealed to these higher courts, which contained different judges from the trial judges. Whereas the writ of error allowed a review of the evidence as well as the law, except for special circumstances the appeals courts confined themselves to deciding only questions of law.

Yet that is not the full story. In the vast majority of cases, trials were swift and not concerned with wrangling over legal procedure. Legal historians Lawrence Friedman and Robert Percival conducted a study of Alameda County, California, at the turn of the nineteenth and twentieth centuries that showed that the median felony trial lasted slightly longer than one day. In one 1907 burglary case the jury took a vote without leaving the courtroom and in another the jury deliberated three minutes, though both cases were probably unusual.[82]

Friedman and Percival's examination of the record books of Leon County (Tallahassee), Florida, from the 1890s indicated that trials in that venue took, on average, a half hour or less. Sometimes there were as many as six trials a day in the same courtroom. The same jury heard all six cases.[83] The process in most cases was routine. Those authors concluded: "A jury was hurriedly thrown together. Case after case paraded before them. The complaining witness told *his* story; sometimes another witness or two told his story; sometimes another witness or two appeared; the defendant told *his* story, with or without any witnesses; the lawyers (if any) spoke; the judge charged the jury. The jury retired, voted and returned. Then the court went immediately to the next case on the list."[84]

A number of reasons explain the abbreviated trials. Many police and prosecutors were not full-time professionals. Scientific evidence such as fingerprinting or blood typing did not exist and thus there was not much evidence to produce. Defense lawyers, even if assigned as counsel, were poorly paid or not paid at all and had little incentive to put on a good defense. Moreover, both professional and public attitudes showed little concern for the rights of defendants who were assumed to be guilty in any event. It was not until the second half of the twentieth century that the US Supreme Court ruled that an accused person has a right to legal counsel in serious cases.[85]

An additional explanation for these expeditious trials was a decline of the criminal jury trial. Around 1900 in Alameda County about 40 percent of defendants had jury trials. If records earlier in that century were searched, they would possibly reveal an even higher percentage of jury trials.[86] The figures document a decline of trial by jury that is hard to dispute. But the figures need to be put into context.

What happened in the other cases in which defendants entered guilty pleas? In Alameda County between 1880 and 1910 there was no such thing as a bench trial; trial meant trial by jury. The concept of "plea bargaining" was not prevalent in Alameda County at the time,[87] although in major urban areas, guilty pleas disposed of significant numbers of criminal cases.[88] Some of the pleas may have been made because of lack of adequate legal representation or because the evidence against the accused was overwhelming, but many of the guilty pleas may have involved an agreement between the prosecution and the accused. Of the cases that went to jury trial the jury found the defendant not guilty about one third of the time. More than half were convicted, but nearly a third of the convictions were for lesser charges. Another eleven percent involved hung juries, and in most cases the defendant was not retried.[89]

We cannot be sure, but given the brevity of many trials it is reasonable to speculate that substantial numbers of the trials involved either overwhelming evidence that the accused was guilty or the opposite, that the prosecution had a weak case. The trial was brief and the jury decided. Better police and prosecutorial investigation and evidence, as well as more and better legal representation, may have eliminated many clear cases from the pool of contested disputes. Today, high-profile cases, ambiguous cases, and cases involving community concerns may go to trial at the same rate as they did a century ago.

NINETEENTH- AND TWENTIETH-CENTURY ORIGINS OF THE CONTEMPORARY CIVIL JURY CONTROVERSY

Civil jury trials have also declined, and far more drastically, leading some scholars to argue that the civil jury is no longer an integral part of American law—at least in respect to the percentage of civil disputes that it resolves.[90] Early in the nineteenth century, doctors bitterly complained that civil juries were biased against them in medical malpractice cases, a complaint that is leveled against juries in these cases today.[91] Nevertheless, in most respects the civil jury was relatively uncontroversial through the nineteenth and first half of the twentieth century. But by the middle of the twentieth century, changes in legal doctrines about personal injury put civil jury verdicts in the eye of a storm.

THE EXPANSION OF TORT LAW AND BUSINESS DISPUTES[92]

During the industrial revolution in the nineteenth century, many laws were designed to protect business interests. "Guest" statutes made it more difficult for injured parties to recover from a negligent innkeeper, driver of a vehicle, or business. Landowners were protected from injuries occurring on their property. "Fellow-servant rules" prevented an employee from recovering damages from his or her employer if the direct cause of injury was another employee. Contributory-fault doctrines prevented recovery by a plaintiff if the plaintiff was even 1 percent responsible for the injury. Presumptions concerning a plaintiff's "assumption of risk" prevailed in statutes and case law. These doctrines allowed judges to keep claims from going to juries.

In the early part of the twentieth century, things began to change. Industrial accidents were rife, and the enormous costs associated with them shifted public and legislative interest in having employers pay the bills through workers' compensation plans or lawsuits through the tort system, which, of course, involves civil juries. The practice of lawyers taking cases on a contingency fee basis for a percentage of the damage award rather than for a set fee became widespread and allowed more plaintiffs an opportunity to have their day in court. Some of the legal doctrines that limited recovery, such as contributory fault and assumption of risk, eventually eroded.

Around 1960 this trend in favor of consumers underwent a rapid acceleration. In medical malpractice cases the "locality rule," in which a plaintiff had to show that the care she received deviated from local practice, was relaxed. Experts outside the immediate medical community could testify, thereby allowing an end run around the reluctance of local doctors to testify against one of their colleagues. The judicial trend toward holding businesses to greater standards of accountability was accelerated by legal scholars' economic theories about spreading the costs of injuries. For instance, the economic concept of "enterprise liability" asserted that the costs of accidents should be spread as broadly as possible. The actors best positioned to spread those costs are the manufacturers of the products on the logic that the costs can be incorporated into the price of the product at its source.[93] These trends in legal thinking had profound positive effects on plaintiffs' ability to succeed in their injury claims against manufacturers of faulty products. Also around this time, the concept of a mass tort took on momentum. Judges began to develop procedural mechanisms, such as class actions, that allowed the combination of individual claims into a single lawsuit, thereby exponentially increasing the magnitude of the damages against corporations that otherwise might have been litigated on an individual basis.

Paralleling the period of tort law expansion, large corporations began increasingly to engage in lawsuits against one another over breached contracts, antitrust violations, and intellectual property disputes.[94] Business lawsuits against other businesses often involve large sums of money and complex and arcane claims about scientific, economic, or accounting procedures with respect to both liability and damages. For example, in 1985 oil giant Pennzoil sued oil giant Texaco over what Pennzoil claimed was a broken contract.[95] After a seventeen-week trial that produced a transcript of twenty-three thousand pages, Pennzoil was awarded $7.5 billion in compensatory damages and $3 billion in punitive damages. The award caused Texaco to file for bankruptcy. Eventually Pennzoil agreed to settle the dispute for $3 billion.

"Mega verdicts," whether they involve individuals suing doctors or manufacturers for catastrophic injuries or businesses suing businesses, have placed civil juries in a spotlight and engendered much criticism, especially from business interests. Claims have been made that today's civil juries are incompetent to deal with complex technical disputes, that they are biased against businesses, and that they render excessive damage awards.

THE DECLINE OF TRIAL BY JURY

The proportion of cases decided by juries has continued to decline. Although as we noted earlier, the percentages have to be put in perspective, in the twenty-first century fewer than five percent of charged felonies go to jury trial.[96] Civil juries also decide a tiny fraction of all civil disputes.[97]

Consider these numbers. Between 1962 and 2002, the overall number of civil trials in federal district courts dropped 20 percent—from 5,802 to 4,569.[98] However, interestingly, the big decline in absolute numbers was in trials before judges rather than juries. There were 2,765 federal civil jury trials in 1962, and 3,006 such trials in 2002. Even so, because of increases in civil case filings, the proportion of federal civil cases that were resolved by juries has gone from 5.5 percent to 1.8 percent of all civil case dispositions.

The number of criminal trials in the federal district courts fell an even greater amount, 30 percent, in the same time period—from 5,097 in 1962 to 3,574 in 2002, and the proportion of criminal cases resolved by trial also fell. But again, the biggest decline was in the number of trials with judges, rather than juries. In 1962, there were 2,710 jury trials and 2,387 judge trials, with juries having a slight numerical advantage. By 2002 the number of jury trials declined slightly to 2,655; but the number of judge trials plummeted to 919.[99]

The trends in state courts are similar and important, since the majority of jury trials take place in state rather than federal courts.[100] An analysis of statistical patterns in approximately half the states found that in 1976, there were 26,018 civil jury trials (1.8 percent of all civil dispositions) in these jurisdictions; by 2002 the number of trials declined to 17,617 (0.6 percent of all civil dispositions). The same study examined criminal case filings, discovering that in 1976 there were 42,049 criminal jury trials in these state courts (3.4 percent of all case dispositions); that number dropped to 35,664 (1.3 percent of all case dispositions) by 2002.[101] In the state courts, both judge and jury trials declined.

What accounts for this shift away from jury trials? The increasing popularity of alternative dispute resolution (ADR) has taken numerous cases off the court dockets and placed many decisions into the hands of mediators and negotiators. Plea bargaining, substantial in many jurisdictions since the early part of the twentieth century, has continued to expand, reducing the number of criminal cases that go to trial. The growth of administrative agencies set up by local and national government has removed a number of subjects and fields of law away from juries.[102] We will return again to the issue of the decline of jury trials.

A PERSPECTIVE ON AMERICAN JURY HISTORY

There are significant insights to be gleaned from this brief history of the American jury. Without historical as well as contemporary context, a full understanding of the jury system is not possible. Jury trial today continues to play an important and often controversial role in society. Like the English jury, it is not a static system but one continually in the process of adaptation and change. The role of the jury and its functions within the legal system are shaped by political, social, economic, and judicial forces. These forces sometimes expand the role of the jury and at other times contract it. Civil and criminal juries are not independent of one another. Procedural and substantive changes in one system tend to migrate into one another, although the connections are not always immediate. Perhaps the greatest change of all, at least with respect to questions about the jury's competence and fairness, is that over the past fifty years an ever-increasing amount of empirical research has examined how the jury system operates and how jurors perform their task. We now turn to examining the contemporary American jury in the light of half a century of research and investigation by lawyers and social scientists.

Chapter 3

A JURY OF PEERS

Democratic Goals

The Arizona jury was in deliberations, evaluating the testimony of the Hispanic plaintiff who was injured in an accident. Although the emergency room physician had given her a prescription for pain pills, she did not fill it. After more than a week of persistent pain, she went not to her family physician but instead to a Hispanic chiropractor who treated her over a period of many weeks.

Some jurors were highly skeptical of the degree of her injury as well as her complaint of continuing pain. They focused on the fact that she had not obtained the pain medicine or consulted a medical doctor. As one juror observed: "I'm sorry folks, I, I can't agree that the lady had that kind of suffering. . . . I just find it hard that a person could be in that kind of excruciating pain, for that number of days, and never go anywhere. . . . And why she didn't see uh, a different doctor other than a chiropractor? I mean, why wouldn't she go see an orthopedic doctor?" Yet, two other jurors provided a different perspective, drawing particularly on their experiences in the local Mexican American community. For example, one Hispanic juror whose wife worked for a chiropractor drew on that experience, relating that some (Hispanic) people "will only go to chiropractors . . . [and] don't believe in taking drugs. You know, so, uhh, I think that's something that needs to be taken into consideration that she didn't want to go to an MD. You know, and I know a lot of people that don't."[1]

This small slice of conversation, in which jurors from different backgrounds exchanged experiences and assessments as they discussed and debated the evidence, illustrates the potential and power of the representative jury. Diverse life experiences help to shape jurors' perceptions of the evidence. As we see here, they lead to different inferences about the trial facts: one a suspicion of malingering and the other an assessment of normality, two views that are debated in the back-and-forth of jury deliberation.

Juries are supposed to serve a number of important functions. Formally, their task is to engage in sound fact finding from the evidence produced at trial. However, juries are also supposed to represent the various views of the community, serve as a political body, and, through rendering fair and just verdicts, provide legitimacy for the legal system. A jury that is not representative of the community is likely to fail in these functions. In our not very distant past, American juries were often far from a jury of peers and, sadly, failed to dispense legally just verdicts, especially in the segregated South. Tremendous changes have occurred in the way that jurors are selected from the community. Although not perfect, American juries are now much more apt to reflect a wide swath of the citizenry.

THE ELITE JURY

Over time, the legal understanding of a representative jury of peers has shifted from a privileged slice of society to a broader and more encompassing entity. The earliest reference to a "jury of peers" referred to elite members of society. In 1215 England, the Magna Carta, or Great Charter, set out the requirement that any charges against barons should be heard by other barons, their "peers," rather than the king. The notion that a person of high standing in society could be adequately judged by a motley assortment of commoners would have seemed absurd. The jurors selected to judge others were required to be "freemen" and major property owners, a minority of the population of thirteenth-century England. Over time, as the demand for jury trial grew (and many noblemen evaded jury duty), eligibility to serve on juries expanded. Property qualifications decreased but were not completely eliminated in England until the 1900s, and it was not until much later that women regularly served on juries.

In the American colonies, land was cheaper, so a substantial proportion of adult white men were able to vote and serve on juries. But there was no early commitment, even after independence, to the idea that juries should be fully representative of the community. Women were not permitted to serve in most jurisdictions until they gained the right to vote in the 1920s, and barriers to full service such as outright exclusion and automatic exemptions from jury duty were not eliminated until as late as 1975. African Americans, too, were not found on juries in substantial numbers, at first because slaves were not free men and were thus ineligible, and later because of a variety of obstacles that local communities placed in the way of African American voting and jury service. In the recent past, some otherwise desirable groups, including lawyers, police, physicians, soldiers, the elderly, and mothers of young children, have been excluded by being granted the privilege to refuse jury service. As we shall see, in many jurisdictions these exclusions have been narrowed or eliminated, but this is only a recent development.

In a number of states, the jury pool was constructed from voter registration or property tax lists, so it included only voters or property owners. Furthermore, many jury commissioners favored the idea that jurors should be upstanding citizens of high intelligence and integrity. Therefore, some commissioners employed a "key man" system in which important members of the community such as local leaders, aldermen, bankers, and clergy recommended names of potential jurors. Alternatively, commissioners might obtain names from club directories or church memberships. They reviewed the recommendations or membership directories and compiled a list. The approaches based on key man recommendations and selective lists drastically limited the range of potential jurors and gave the commissioners power to determine the makeup of juries.

Glasser v. United States, a 1942 case, vividly illustrated the detrimental consequences of the selective approach.[2] Glasser, a US Attorney in the Northern District of Illinois in the 1930s, was in charge of prosecuting liquor violations. He was convicted of fraud in connection with his professional duties. Unusual at the time, his jury included a mix of men and women. However, all six women on his jury were drawn from the membership list of the Illinois League of Women Voters who, he claimed, had attended jury classes where lecturers had presented the views of the prosecution. While observing that jury commissioners may need to be selective in their assembling of jury lists to ensure the competence of jurors, the Supreme Court noted with disapproval that

> The deliberate selection of jurors from the membership of particular private organizations definitely does not conform to the traditional requirements of jury trial. No matter how high principled and imbued with a desire to inculcate public virtue such organizations may be, the dangers inherent in such a method of selection are the more real when the members of those organizations from training or otherwise acquire a bias in favor of the prosecution. The jury selected from the membership of such an organization is then not only the organ of a special class, but, in addition, it is also openly partisan.[3]

Still, the idea that jurors should possess special competencies has long been attractive, giving rise to the special, or "blue ribbon," jury.

THE BLUE RIBBON JURY

A special jury consists of citizens with relevant specialized knowledge or expertise that might help them decide the facts of a case.[4] The earliest documented special jury was in 1351, when a jury of cooks and fishmongers decided the case of a defendant charged with selling bad food.[5] One notable form of the special jury was the jury of matrons, an all-woman jury used particularly in cases in which a convicted woman awaiting execution "pleaded her belly," that is, claimed that she was pregnant and requested a stay of execution until the child could be born. The jury of matrons assembled to determine the truth of the claim.[6] Special juries were fairly common in England in the 1700s, but use of them slowly declined, and they were finally abolished in 1949.[7]

In the United States, special juries were also familiar. At the beginning of the nineteenth century, they were authorized by sixteen states.[8] Some appellate courts justified the practice of selecting special juries in cases with important issues or complex and difficult evidence. For example, in 1806 a special jury decided a zoning and land use case in which the New Windsor Turnpike Company sued one Ellison for constructing a competing highway close to the turnpike gate. The New York court affirmed the use of a special jury because of the case's widespread significance for the public.[9] A special jury was also upheld in a business contract case because of the value of business-savvy and intelligent jurors: "the jury's equipment of intelligence and of practical business experience should be of the best which any established method of selection may secure in the interests of substantial justice. Indeed, to grasp the facts and make a fairly intelligent estimate of the values involved each juror should have much of the capacity for financial analysis."[10]

Not infrequently, jurisdictions had elaborate procedures for assembling special juries, selecting not just those with advanced education but also other attitudinal views that seemed to make them more reliable prosecution or business juries. Consider New York's approach, revealed in the 1947 case of *Fay v. New York*.[11] In New York, members assigned to the special jury pool, consisting of about three thousand names, were culled from the regular jury pool of sixty thousand. They were chosen on the basis of their written responses to juror questionnaires and personal interviews before the jury commissioner. Among other criteria, persons with conscientious objections to the death penalty were excluded from the special jury list. Either side in the legal case could apply to have the case tried by a special jury. The trial judge would make a determination based on, for example, the importance or complexity of the case or the extent of pretrial publicity. Fay and his codefendant, both union leaders, were convicted by a special jury of the crimes of extortion and conspiracy to extort. Fay challenged the fairness of the special jury.

Fay's blue ribbon jury pool was not representative of the population. It included just one woman and no laborers, craftsmen, or service employees. Moreover, it was likely biased against him. A 1938 study conducted by the New York State Judicial Council showed that special juries were more apt to convict. The Council analyzed New York jury trials from 1933 and 1934 and found that special juries convicted over 80 percent of the defendants, whereas ordinary juries had conviction rates of around 40 percent.[12] (Later on, we will describe research showing that support for the death penalty is associated with conviction-proneness, so the inclusion of the death penalty question might well have produced more prosecution-oriented blue ribbon juries.)

The US Supreme Court upheld New York's blue ribbon jury statute nonetheless, determining that Fay had not proven the intentional exclusion of people from the special jury and questioning the relevance of the differential conviction data.

Justice Murphy, writing a dissent in the *Fay* case, sounded themes that anticipated later legal decisions emphasizing the importance of a jury drawn from a cross section of the community. He maintained that the blue ribbon jury violated the equal protection clause of the Constitution by excluding certain classes of people who were normally qualified to serve on juries. The questionnaires answered by prospective jurors were supposed to be used to determine the jurors' intelligence, but Justice Murphy argued that the selection procedure posed a danger by allowing "jury officials to formulate whatever standards they desire, whether in terms of intelligence or some other factor, to eliminate persons from the blue ribbon panel, even though they admittedly are qualified for general jury service."[13]

Despite compelling arguments against blue ribbon juries, appellate courts continuously upheld the use of special juries in cases following the *Fay* decision.[14] But the tide has turned. Although at one time half of the states had some form of special jury statute, today only a handful of states allow for special juries in complex civil cases.[15] Delaware has a specific statute allowing the use of special juries in complex civil cases, but it has become exceedingly rare to call a special jury; a number of special jury requests have been rejected because of "insufficient complexity."[16]

THE MIXED JURY

The early English trial system provided for a *jury de medietate linguae*, literally, a "half-tongue" jury, in cases with Jews or alien merchants as parties.[17] The *jury de medietate linguae* was formed with half its members from the local community and the other half from an alternative community, such as aliens or Jews. The jurors would listen to the evidence and deliberate, drawing on their respective laws and norms, and arrive at a single collective verdict.

This right to a half-alien jury was not necessarily derived from open-mindedness and concern about unfair prejudice for minority litigants.[18] As far as Jewish settlers went, Jews were often taxed at a disproportionately higher rate than Christians, and upon their deaths their fortunes would belong to the King. Therefore, the King had a direct financial interest in their treatment in civil lawsuits. As an alternative to entirely Christian juries that might decide cases on their basis of anti-Jewish prejudices, the *jury de medietate linguae* provided some protection for Jewish assets and hence the King's. Deborah Ramirez has pointed out that alien merchants won the right to have merchant law applied by half-English and half-alien members: "After the expulsion of the Jews, foreign merchants who took over their commercial role could simply stop conducting business in England if they did not believe that the English courts would protect their commercial interests. The Crown had to provide alien merchants with the perception of fairness, a perception then created by the right to a mixed jury."[19]

There were practical difficulties in assembling the alien half of the mixed jury. Often there were not many aliens to choose from. The message was an unwelcome one too; it assumed that Englishmen would be inalterably prejudiced against outsiders, and if so, that reflected rather badly on the glory of the English law. Nonetheless the actual and perceived fairness of the mixed jury kept it alive in England until 1870. After Parliament gave aliens the right to serve on juries as a general matter, the Naturalization Act of 1870 removed an alien's prerogative of asking for a mixed jury.[20]

The mixed jury initially survived in the American colonies but encountered obstacles. One was definitional. In a country with a Native American Indian population and substantial European immigration, just who were the aliens? In one early mixed-jury trial, which took place in 1674 in Plymouth Colony, three Indians were charged with the death of another Indian. Six American Indians were added to a jury of twelve colonists, and all agreed that the accused men were guilty.[21] Here we see that the colonists had the insight that the mixed-jury verdict would be viewed as more legitimate by the Native American population. The addition of Native Americans helped in finding the facts as well, lessening the chance that the defendants would be convicted based on faulty assumptions about Native American behaviors and tendencies.

As the federal government and states worked to develop sound procedures for jury trial in the new United States, the right to a mixed jury, although invoked occasionally, became increasingly rare. In the decades after the Civil War, there were some trials with juries that included African Americans. And at the turn of the twentieth century, as women argued for the vote and for jury service, some trials of women defendants called for mixed juries of both men and women. However, the model of the mixed jury was replaced, first in rhetoric and increasingly in reality, by the notion of a jury drawn from a representative cross section of the community.

THE RISE OF JURY REPRESENTATIVENESS AS AN IDEAL

The change over time in jury representativeness can be seen in the shifts regarding the participation on juries of racial and ethnic minorities as well as of women. Excluded by law in the colonial period, women and minorities began serving in substantial numbers only in the latter half of the twentieth century. Legal cases arguing for their right to serve on juries reveal that outright barriers, intentional discrimination, and special provisions limited their full participation on juries.

RACIAL MINORITIES AS JURORS

Before the end of the Civil War, African Americans, with very few exceptions, were excluded from juries, even in northern states. After the Civil War and passage of the Fourteenth Amendment, the Supreme Court ruled in several cases that rights of citizenship extended to all races, making African Americans theoretically eligible to serve on juries.[22] The most important decision came in 1880 in *Strauder v. West Virginia*, when the Court ruled that a West Virginia statute limiting jury service to whites violated the US Constitution:[23]

> The very fact that colored people are singled out and expressly denied by a statute all right to participate in the administration of the law as jurors because of their color, though they are citizens and may be in other respects fully qualified, is practically a brand upon them affixed by the law, an assertion of their inferiority, and a stimulant to that race prejudice which is an impediment to securing to individuals of the race that equal justice which the law aims to secure to all others.[24]

Although the *Strauder* opinion was sweeping in its insistence on equal protection of the laws, it had little immediate effect in practice on expanding the tiny number of African Americans serving on juries. African Americans in the South faced barriers to voting, so they were often not on jury lists to begin with. They were rarely named as suitable jurors by "key men" in the communities that relied on that method to generate jury pools. And courts insisted on proof that jury commissioners engaged in intentional discrimination, demanding evidence that the absence of blacks on juries was due to systematic exclusion.

It was not until 1935, in the notorious Scottsboro case involving a host of racial issues, that the Supreme Court loosened the requirements for proving race discrimination in jury selection.[25] Nine young African American men, ranging in age from twelve to twenty, stood trial in Alabama in 1931 on capital charges that they raped two white women on a freight train while traveling from Chattanooga to Memphis. The trial took place a mere two weeks after the alleged events. The Scottsboro Boys, as they came to be called, were divided into four groups for trial.

Four different all-white juries heard their cases and swiftly delivered their brand of justice. The trials lasted just three days and the jury deliberations averaged thirty minutes. All of the defendants were convicted of rape, and eight of the nine were sentenced to death, the exception being the twelve-year-old. Although these initial verdicts were set aside by a US Supreme Court ruling that the defendants were not represented by defense counsel, the attorney who took their case, Sam Leibowitz, one of the nation's leading criminal defense attorneys, faced another all-white jury pool. Apparently no blacks had served in this Alabama jurisdiction. Leibowitz challenged the composition of the jury pool, calling jury commissioners, who said they did not purposefully discriminate, but, nevertheless, they could not recall a single African American ever serving as a juror. There were a number of discrepancies in the jury lists, including the fact that jury commissioners had made the notation "col" (colored) next to the names of the few African Americans who actually made the initial list. Leibowitz also called African American citizens who had college degrees. They testified that they had never been called for jury service.

Although his motion was denied and the trials proceeded, Leibowitz raised the issue successfully on appeal, making an equal protection claim, under the Fourteenth Amendment, that blacks had been systematically excluded from the jury panels. In *Norris v. Alabama*, decided in 1935, the Supreme Court ruled that the jury commissioners' testimony that they had no intent to discriminate was insufficient. Once a defendant had established sufficient evidence of jury discrimination, the burden of proof shifted to the prosecution to prove it had not discriminated against blacks.[26]

A substantial number of cases on racial discrimination followed *Norris*, but in practice there was much room for discrimination, intentional or unintentional, to slip in when the eligible jury pool was formed and the jury selected. This was against the backdrop of overt segregation and discrimination. In one Georgia jurisdiction in which no African Americans had served on a jury, jury panel names were selected from a box. White jurors' names were printed on white tickets, while black jurors' names appeared on yellow tickets, making it easy to determine the race of prospective jurors.[27] In another case, a handful of mostly elderly African Americans appeared on the jury list, but they had never been called.[28]

Once the cases moved from pointing out the total exclusion of African Americans to claims that the racial group was underrepresented, judges had to interpret statistical arguments about proportional representation, and this proved to be a challenge. In the 1965 case of *Swain v. Alabama* before the US Supreme Court, Robert Swain argued that although 26 percent of the population of Talladega County Alabama was black, in the preceding ten years before Swain's trial, African Americans had constituted only between 10 and 15 percent of grand and petit jury panels and no African American had served on a petit jury since 1950. Writing the opinion in *Swain v. Alabama*,[29] Justice White concluded that the 10 to

15 percent of blacks on panels was not essentially different from 26 percent of the population and affirmed Swain's death sentence. But Justice White's statistical reasoning was erroneous: focusing on the absolute disparity rather than the comparative disparity vastly understated the degree to which blacks were left off the jury panels. A number of critiques appeared in law reviews and elsewhere, pointing out that the statistical odds of so few blacks being on the jury panels by chance was 1 in 100 million. In later cases, both the Supreme Court and lower courts began to apply the correct statistical reasoning to cases challenging the jury array.[30]

WOMEN ON THE JURY

Women had an equally long road to the right to jury service.[31] Before the Nineteenth Amendment gave women the right to vote in 1920, women occasionally served on juries. Early on they were called as members of special juries in cases involving pregnancy or children's welfare. As far back as 1870, women in Wyoming Territory served on juries, and there is evidence from that period of their serving in Utah, Washington, Kansas, and New Jersey during this period.[32] By 1923 eighteen states and the territory of Alaska permitted women to serve on juries.[33] However, suffrage did not automatically mean eligibility for jury service. In 1925, for example, the Illinois Supreme Court concluded that when the Illinois General Assembly had used the words *legal voters* and *electors* in 1874, they referred only to men. It took fourteen more years before the Illinois General Assembly passed legislation saying that the words also included women.

In 1921 the Oregon legislature passed a statute requiring that "in all cases in which a minor under the age of eighteen years is involved, either as defendant or as a complaining witness, at least one-half the jury shall be women." But, simultaneously, that same statute permitted women to claim an automatic exemption from jury service.[34] Exemptions for women were, in fact, frequent in many statutes that described jury eligibility. As late as 1961, the liberal US Supreme Court under Chief Justice Earl Warren upheld the constitutionality of a Florida statute that drafted men for jury duty but allowed women to serve only if they volunteered.[35] There was no dissent from the nine men on the court when *Hoyt v. Florida* stated that "woman is still regarded as the center of home and family life. We cannot say that it is constitutionally impermissible for a state . . . to conclude that a woman should be relieved from the civic duty of jury service unless she herself determines that such service is consistent with her own special responsibilities."[36]

In 1975 the Supreme Court, a more conservative court, under Chief Justice Warren Burger, overruled the Hoyt decision in *Taylor v. Louisiana*,[37] ruling that a state law excluding women from jury service violated the fair cross-section requirement of the Sixth Amendment. In 1979 the Court ruled in *Duren v. Missouri*[38] that a statute allowing women to apply for exemption from jury service was unconstitutional, even though no barriers were put in the way of women who wanted to serve.[39]

VALUES OF THE REPRESENTATIVE JURY

Thus, in fits and starts, the Supreme Court moved eventually toward a cross-sectional ideal of the representative jury. In stirring words, the Court linked jury service and democratic principles in the 1946 case *Thiel v. Southern Pacific Co.*:

> The American tradition of trial by jury . . . necessarily contemplates an impartial jury drawn from a cross-section of the community. This does not mean, of course, that every jury must contain representatives of all the economic, social, religious, racial, political and geographical groups of the community; frequently such complete representation would be impossible. But it does mean that prospective jurors shall be selected by court officials without systematic and intentional exclusion of any of these groups. Recognition must be given to the fact that those eligible for jury service are to be found in every stratum of society. Jury competence is an individual rather than a group or class matter. That fact lies at the very heart of the jury system. To disregard it is to open the door to class distinctions and discriminations which are abhorrent to the democratic ideals of trial by jury.[40]

The idea of a representative jury is a compelling one. A jury of people with a wide range of backgrounds, life experiences, and world knowledge will promote accurate fact-finding for several reasons. As the Arizona jury example at the beginning of this chapter illustrates, a diverse group is likely to hold varying perspectives on the evidence, encouraging more thorough debate over what the evidence proves. As with the mixed jury, the inclusion of minorities and women in a representative jury adds their life experiences and insights to the collective pool of knowledge.[41] Research on heterogeneous decision-making groups supports the claim that diverse juries are better fact-finders.[42] Minority jurors contribute their unique knowledge to the general discussion. Furthermore, when whites anticipate participating in a diverse jury, they tend to give more careful assessment of the evidence.

One interesting experiment examined how racially homogeneous and diverse juries discussed the same case. Samuel Sommers compared six-person mock juries of either all-white members of a jury pool or diverse juries of four white and two black members of the jury pool.[43] The diverse juries engaged in longer deliberations, discussed a wider range of information, and were more accurate in their statements about the case. Interestingly, this was not simply the result of distinctive behavior on the part of black jurors in diverse juries. White jurors acted quite differently when they were members of all-white or diverse juries. Compared to whites in homogeneous juries, whites in diverse juries appeared to be more careful and systematic in their decision making, making fewer factual mistakes and raising more evidence and issues for discussion.

A diverse and representative jury should decrease the impact of prejudice. United States Supreme Court Justice Sandra Day O'Connor once observed: "Conscious and unconscious racism can affect the way white jurors perceive minority defendants and the facts presented at their trials, perhaps determining the verdict of guilt or innocence."[44] Minority presence on the jury is likely to reduce the outright expression of racial bias. University of Michigan psychology and law professor Phoebe Ellsworth reports that when juries contain no minority members, they tend to be harsher toward minority defendants. "White people worry about being racist when they're reminded of it, but when it's all white people, it just doesn't occur to them to remember their egalitarian values."[45] Even if jury members have strong biases, diversity ensures a range of biases that could cancel each other out.

A representative jury also offers more legitimacy for the resulting verdict. United States Supreme Court Justice Clarence Thomas wrote in one Supreme Court opinion that "an all-white jury" was a common part of news stories, reflecting the fact that people take the race of the jury into account as they evaluate the resulting verdicts.[46] Whether or not the presence of minority jurors influences the actual verdict in a case, the verdict's legitimacy can be affected. In short, fully representative juries are superior on informational, normative, and legitimacy grounds.

The legitimizing benefits of a jury's racial diversity are unfortunately most obvious when they are absent. Take the case of the Rodney King beating trial in the 1990s.[47] Rodney King, an African American man, was beaten by police. A citizen captured the beating on videotape. The police officers' trial was moved from downtown Los Angeles, which would have increased the chances of a diverse jury that included African Americans, to the predominantly white suburb of Simi Valley. It was no surprise that the jury pool of two hundred and sixty people included just a half-dozen African Americans. The eventual jury that was chosen did not include a single African American. After listening to the evidence, the jury acquitted the police defendants of the charges. Within hours of the acquittal, the city of Los Angeles exploded in riots. Fifty-four people died and millions of dollars' worth of property was destroyed.[48] We can only speculate about whether the same decision by a jury composed of whites and blacks would have produced a less violent response. The many denunciations of the verdict as an illegitimate decision by an unrepresentative jury all point to the key importance of the jury's composition.

Although a representative jury is advantageous for improving fact-finding, reducing prejudice, and promoting legitimacy, it might not be sufficient. Political scientist Jeffrey Abramson has suggested that there could be a danger in overemphasizing the cross-sectional ideal in composing a jury.[49] Members of the jury may come to think of themselves as standing in for people like themselves and decide their prime function is to represent their outside constituency. Jurors who focus on the fact they're in the Asian-American slot, the Christian fundamentalist slot, or the business leader's slot may concentrate more on their imagined constituents than on their responsibility to engage in robust and vigorous debate. Abramson argues that jurors should aspire to the deliberative ideal—that deliberation among diverse members of the community, who contribute perspectives based on their different cultural and life experiences, is a surer route to just results than representational positioning. Since we don't select juries today with an eye to quotas or slots, we don't know whether Abramson is right, but it's an intriguing idea.

JURY REPRESENTATIVENESS: FROM THEORY TO PRACTICE

The theory of the representative jury is solid. However, when we look closely at the process of assembling a jury pool, and the selection of those individuals who will serve on particular juries, we observe substantial deviations from the representative ideal. There are a number of reasons why American juries fall short, but fall short they do. System-level bureaucratic problems and the potential jurors themselves create difficulties that lead to less than fully representative jury pools.

JURY SOURCE LISTS

The first step in the process is to develop a list of citizens eligible to serve as jurors.[50] Today, voters' lists are the most commonly used source of potential juror names, supplemented with other lists. Voters' lists are more representative of the community than the key man systems of prior times, but they still tend to underrepresent identifiable segments of the population. In particular, young people, racial and ethnic minorities, and the poor are less likely to be registered to vote. To cope with this, many jurisdictions supplement their voters' list with other lists of names. Drivers' license lists tend to be more representative of the population than voters' lists. One 1996 report found that twenty-five states use both voters' lists and drivers' licenses, fifteen use voters' lists only, and six states use drivers' licenses.[51] In combining discrete lists into a master list, duplicates must be removed to ensure that all names have an equal chance of being summoned for jury duty. Sometimes there are problems combining the lists and removing duplicate names. Jurisdictions update their lists with varying frequencies—some like California update them every year, trying to keep track of their mobile population, while others do so infrequently.[52]

THE JURY SUMMONS

A second step—summoning those selected to participate—also often creates less representative pools of prospective jurors, as UC Santa Cruz Professor Hiroshi Fukurai has shown in California.[53] A set of names is chosen from the master list, and the jury commissioner sends out to each person on the list a juror eligibility questionnaire. States differ in their practices; some send the questionnaire along with a specific summons date for jury duty, while others send the questionnaire alone, with the summons later mailed to qualified jurors. Typically, items on the questionnaire assess whether the prospective juror is qualified to serve, and capable of serving, on a jury.

Prospective jurors are required by law to respond to the request. However, a substantial number are not returned. In some urban jurisdictions, fewer than 20 percent of the citizens who are summoned initially ever serve.[54] This poor response rate has been identified as the biggest cause of nonrepresentative juries. The low jury yield conjures up an image of apathetic or hostile citizens who believe they have much better ways to spend their time.

When asked about jury duty in the abstract, American citizens are quite positive. A total of 84 percent of Americans polled by the American Bar Association agreed that they should participate in jury service even if it is inconvenient, rejecting the statement that jury duty is a burden to be avoided.[55]

Yet judging by the excuses people generate to avoid jury duty, in practice it appears that many people do not want to serve. Late-night talk show host David Letterman compiled a list of Top Ten Ways to Get Out of Jury Duty.[56] The list includes inquiring whether there will be opportunities to examine bloody undershirts, asking whether you get to execute criminals personally, flying into a rage whenever Norwegians are mentioned, and asking the judge if he's wearing Aramis cologne. Tom Munsterman of the National Center for State Courts has put together a list of strange but true jury duty excuses proffered to the judge: "I cannot get to the courthouse. My driver's license is suspended on account of Mr. Meaner convictions," and "I do not meet the second qualification on the juror affidavit ('must be of ordinary intelligence'). My IQ was tested at 144, which rates me in the higher level of intelligence."[57]

Evasion of jury duty is not only a modern problem. In 1607 in England, King James's "A Proclamation for Jurors" exhorted the best citizens to heed the summons to serve as jurors in order to preserve the high quality of trial by jury.[58] A 1922 book, *Impressions of an Average Juryman*, written by Robert Sutcliffe, who served as a juror in New York civil and criminal courts over an eighteen-year period, devotes an entire chapter to "Evading Jury Duty":

> The large number of men of affairs who do not serve on juries is impressive. . . . The busy man argues that his prominence in the business world and the many calls upon his time constitute a good reason why he should be excused from jury duty. As a matter of fact, the very conditions that he cites are the best reasons why he should serve. Successful men, with broad experience, are badly needed. . . . They and their kind are the greatest obstacle to success of the system. . . . They will not give their own time, but when a case is on trial in which they have a personal interest, they demand that it be tried before men who are competent to digest evidence in complex cases.[59]

A modern remedy to this perennial problem includes cracking down on jury scofflaws. Many states, including New York, North Carolina, and Arizona, try to deal with citizens who don't respond to their jury summons by levying contempt of court citations or fines. Arizona periodically holds a "Scofflaw Court" for the citizens who do not respond to the jury summons.[60] Tracked down by deputies, the errant citizens face contempt of court charges and fines up to $500, but most are simply rescheduled for jury duty. Massachusetts instituted a Delinquent Juror Prosecution Program in which those who don't respond are first sent warnings and then prosecuted.[61]

Researchers have tried to discover why it is that many jurisdictions, especially urban areas, have a high rate of nonresponse to jury summons.[62] One survey asked state and federal courts to provide information about the summons process and response rate. A poll tapped the views of four hundred citizens in four jurisdictions who, according to court records, had been summoned for jury duty. The first contact with the citizens occurred after they had been summoned but before the date that they were scheduled to serve as jurors. A follow-up telephone call was made to a sample of these summoned jurors after their jury service date. This allowed the researchers to compare those who responded to the summons with those who did not.

The most common reason for nonresponse turns out to be prosaic. Many jury summonses are never received. In the study, a substantial percentage of the jury summonses were undeliverable because the citizens had moved to another address. Once that group was eliminated, the researchers attempted to develop a picture of the remaining citizens who had ignored their jury summons. Were they lower income? Less educated? More hostile to the courts? All of these might have been expected. However, surprisingly, those who did and did not respond were similar in many ways, including their socioeconomic status. Both groups were generally positive about the legal system, agreeing that courts usually come up with just verdicts and that jury duty would be exciting.

The nonresponders, though, were much less likely to say that they knew enough about how the legal system worked to be a fair and impartial juror (54 percent, compared to 86 percent of those who responded to their summons). They were not as knowledgeable about how to get a needed deferral or an excuse. Nonresponders who had less income and education also said that jury duty posed some troubling economic issues for them. They were not as likely to be reimbursed by their employer for jury duty, and they were more likely to have children or dependents requiring care. More highly educated and wealthier nonresponders believed that they would have a lengthy wait and would not be picked to serve. Nonrespondents were also less likely to believe they would be punished for ignoring the summons.

To improve jury summonses, the American Judicature Society outlines what can be done.[63] The first order of business is to make sure the source lists are frequently updated, helping to deal with the problem of mobile citizens. Next, courts should follow up when there is no response. There should be consequences when a citizen does not respond. A program like New York City's, where a small number of no-shows are penalized and the stories are broadly reported in the local media, is cost-effective. Other recommendations deal with juror concerns. The jury summons should clearly state that a response is required and should with equal clarity describe how to obtain a deferral or an excuse. Tell recipients what the typical juror experience is likely to be in terms of waiting and the likelihood of serving on a jury. To alleviate the concerns of those who feel they aren't equipped to be jurors, emphasize the universality of jury duty—anyone can serve well as a juror, and even people with substantial knowledge of law are not automatically excused from jury duty. Finally, if a jurisdiction is serious about broadening participation, it will deal with the economic issues that limit participation at the lower end of the income scale by raising juror pay and providing childcare.

DISQUALIFICATIONS, EXEMPTIONS, AND EXCUSES

Once juror eligibility questionnaires are returned to the court, the jury commissioner's office reviews the responses to determine whether the prospective juror is qualified to serve, or whether the individual merits an exemption, a deferral, or an excuse. Although in the past it was typical to have a broad range of disqualifications and exemptions, jury reforms have reduced the scope of those who are eliminated, to maximize the representativeness of the jury pool.

Each jurisdiction has its own criteria for disqualifications, but typically they include characteristics that in the eyes of the legislature would make a person unsuitable or undesirable as a juror. Lack of citizenship, inability to speak and read the English language, a serious criminal record, and serious physical impairment are among the most frequent characteristics that disqualify prospective jurors.

In many jurisdictions, felons—those who have been convicted of serious criminal offenses—are barred completely from jury duty, or barred for a certain number of years after the completion of their criminal sentences.[64] Inherited from England,[65] felony disenfranchisement laws prohibit felons from voting, holding public office, and serving on juries. In the United States, one scholar who has studied the matter reports that thirty-one states and the federal government ban felons permanently from jury service.[66] The disqualification of felons is based on the premise that felons as a group are dishonorable; furthermore, they are believed to be hostile to the government in criminal cases and thus unable to follow the legal requirement of impartiality in decision making.[67]

Interestingly, there is a movement, albeit modest, to reinstate civil rights for felons. The biggest focus has been on restoring the right to vote, but some of the same arguments that apply to permitting felons to vote also have relevance to the right to serve on a jury. First, some of the arguments against felons and jury duty have been analyzed and found wanting.[68] Whether felons are always hostile to the government's case is doubtful; even so, the jury selection process provides methods for removing biased jurors. And any presumed tendencies to disfavor the government shouldn't matter as much in civil cases, where the government is not a party to the litigation.

Second, and more significant, the permanent removal of felons' civil rights disproportionately affects minority communities. One estimate is that about thirty percent of African American men are permanently barred from serving as jurors because they have felony convictions.[69] This makes it more difficult to assemble a representative cross section of the community.

Another set of disqualifications stems from physical problems—such as blindness or severe hearing impairment—that would make it very difficult to follow evidence in a trial. Many people with these disabilities do not serve. However, some advocates have argued on behalf of blind or deaf citizens summoned for jury duty for their inclusion. Rather than wholesale exclusion, the advocates say, a court should accommodate such physical disabilities to enable blind and deaf citizens to serve as jurors.[70]

Other citizens might be desirable jurors, but they or others would experience hardship if they served. Various occupational groups—including physicians, firefighters, teachers, clergy, police officers, embalmers, and newspaper reporters—succeeded in getting exemptions for their members on the grounds that their time was much too valuable to spend on jury duty or that lawyers would always challenge them. In New York, before contemporary reforms that swept away most exemptions, the automatic exemptions from jury duty included a broad swath of the public.[71]

Today, many jurisdictions have eliminated these automatic exemptions, aiming to send the message that no one is too important for jury duty. (Except, perhaps, the president of the United States.)[72] Most notably, judges and lawyers, once routinely exempted from jury duty, are now eligible to serve in many places. In fact, there is a small but enthusiastic literature of opinion pieces written by judges and lawyers who have served on a jury and have come away reportedly impressed with their experience and their fellow jurors. Shirley Abramson, the Chief Justice of the Wisconsin Supreme Court, served on a criminal jury that was asked to decide a petty theft case. Although her jury couldn't reach a unanimous decision, she favorably concluded that "I am on the side of the jury. The system works. I have seen it."[73]

The one change in an exemption rule that we might debate is allowing judges to serve. In other countries, when judges and lay jurors decide cases together, the judges tend to dominate the jurors.[74] But in favor of American judges' participation on juries, judges who have served as jurors report that they worked assiduously to avoid dominating the jury. In any event, they may serve on relatively few cases, as lawyers might be apt to challenge them peremptorily. And, the overall message that no one is exempt from jury service may outweigh any disproportionate impact they might have. Indeed, a judge sitting in the jury pool is a highly visible illustration of an equally shared duty.

Thus, it continues to be challenging to put together jury pools that reflect a cross section of the community. The lack of representativeness of source lists, the failure of many jury summonses to reach their mark, the fact of nonresponse, and disqualifications, exemptions, and excuses all undermine efforts to draw from all segments of society. That said, a dynamic movement to promote jury representativeness has led to substantial improvements. The employment of multiple lists has increased, compensating for some of the deficiencies in the voters' lists; many jurisdictions have dramatically limited their exemptions and excuses, even narrowing the list of characteristics for disqualification. The strength of the jury system—for both criminal and civil cases—is dependent upon a true jury of "peers." While the ideal of juries truly representative of the population has not been entirely solved, today the American jury is more representative than ever before in its history.

Chapter 4

JURY SELECTION

Juror Bias, Juror Challenges, and Trial Consultants

Nineteen-year-old single mother Gracealynn Harris was pregnant again. A high school graduate working part-time at the local mall, Gracealynn already had a five-month-old son and hoped one day to become a nurse. That was not to be. On September 16, 1997, her mother and brother drove Gracealynn to the Delaware Women's Health Organization clinic to have a scheduled abortion.[1] Dr. Mohammad Imran, a clinic doctor, performed the procedure that day, then left for his private office in New Jersey shortly afterward while Gracealynn was in the recovery room.

Gracealynn was not doing well. Weak after the abortion procedure, she needed a wheelchair to leave the clinic. The family took her home, where she dozed on a couch for the rest of the day. Things took a turn for the worse that evening, and at 8:00 PM she suffered a seizure. Within two hours she was dead from massive internal bleeding caused by a perforated uterus. The Delaware Right to Life organization publicized Harris's death in a billboard campaign, showing her high school picture accompanied by the text "One abortion, two deaths."[2]

Gracealynn's family sued Dr. Imran and the clinic on behalf of Gracealynn's young son. From the start, the attorneys on both sides felt that jury selection was critical. The civil lawsuit involved the morally and politically controversial issue of abortion. Would jurors who strongly opposed abortion damn the doctor who performed them regularly? Or would they think a woman who had sought out an abortion deserved any negative consequences, even if she died in the process? What about the fact that the plaintiff was a single mother? She was African American. The doctor was an immigrant from Pakistan. Would race or ethnicity issues affect the jurors, and if so, how?

The case would be heard in the Superior Court of Delaware, which has a strong tradition of minimal judicial questioning of prospective jurors. Typically in Delaware, a group of potential jurors is randomly selected and taken to a courtroom. The judge or clerk reads a short list of questions to the group of potential jurors. Questions are phrased so that only a yes or no answer is required. Potential jurors are asked general questions such as whether they know the attorneys, judge, parties, and witnesses, or whether they have any reason to be biased in the case. Occasionally, potential jurors are asked several questions specifically related to the case. For example, in a medical malpractice case, jurors might be asked whether they have experienced similar medical problems or operations. Prospective jurors who answer yes to any of the items are asked to come forward and are questioned individually by the judge.

The judge in the Harris case, though, was concerned that such a limited approach might miss the latent and unspoken prejudices of many jurors. Views about the morality of abortion had the potential to negatively affect both sides—the plaintiffs, because Gracealynn Harris had chosen an abortion, and the defendants, because they provided abortion services. Both attorneys were worried about possible prejudice.

Therefore, in a rare departure from the usual practice, Judge Jurden ordered a modification of the jury selection procedure. She read an extended list of specific questions to members of the jury pool, asking whether they knew anything about the case; whether they knew any of the parties or witnesses; whether they believed abortion was legally or morally wrong; whether they had any bias or prejudice regarding abortion, women who sought abortions, or abortion clinics; and whether they knew anyone who had undergone an abortion. Questions about their views about the medical field and medical malpractice were also addressed. After hearing all of the questions, the prospective jurors who responded yes to any question were asked to stand. Each was taken to a conference room and questioned individually by the judge, then questioned by the attorneys.

As Judge Jurden and the lawyers feared, many things that surfaced in the questioning gave them pause. Eighty-one of the nearly one hundred jurors responded affirmatively to one or more of the initial questions. Individual questioning revealed very strong views about abortion that colored many jurors' views of the case. The judge excused fifty-four of the eighty-one "for cause" (for actual or likely bias) mostly because of their views about abortion. In one juror's words, abortion is "a violation of God's law, tantamount to murder. So as far as I'm concerned, the woman that had the abortion, the parents that allowed the children to have the abortion, and the doctor that performed the abortion are all wrong."[3]

Another juror stated: "I'm a strong disbeliever of abortions. In fact, I consider it murder. . . . I would have a problem finding compassion in this case."[4] One man revealed that he was very much against abortion and did not allow his daughter to have an abortion when she became pregnant as a high school senior.[5] A woman asserted her "strong views on abortion" when she added, "I am a Catholic and I think its [*sic*] murder, and I would have a hard time dealing with that."[6] A former attorney who worked to overturn *Roe v. Wade*, the Supreme Court case permitting abortion, frankly stated that he regarded the abortion industry as an unsavory one.[7] A juror who had been reading the book *The Power of God* while waiting to be questioned admitted, "[T]his case poses a series of dilemmas. On the one hand, I'm opposed to abortion but, on the other hand I . . . tend to be on the side of tort reform and against the idea of punitive damages, as well, and the joke is I might make an exception for an abortionist. I don't know. But this is clearly a tough and emotional one."[8]

There were some hints that antiabortion views might fall more heavily on the plaintiff. One juror stated: "I'm just 100 percent pro-life. That's part of my religion, the way I feel." He said his pro-life views might interfere with his ability to listen to the evidence and sit as a fair and impartial juror, but he added that his views would lead him to be more biased against the person choosing to have an abortion than the doctor.[9] One self-described pro-life advocate thought her antiabortion sentiment went both ways, but she also confessed she felt more negativity toward the individual seeking an abortion than the doctor performing the abortion.[10]

Many jurors knew friends or family members who had had abortions, and while a good number of them supported the women's choice to have the procedures, these experiences were sometimes a source of anguish. The aunt of one prospective juror had complications from an abortion and now was unable to have children. This juror admitted that he would tend to favor the plaintiff in the case.[11] The friend of another juror had an incomplete abortion that caused hemorrhaging. She, too, worried that she would tend to lean toward the plaintiff.[12] A man revealed that "my first wife had my son aborted" without his knowledge. When he subsequently joined the military, an illness left him sterile, and he had been unable to have any children.[13]

To add to the challenges, one of the prospective jurors showed up for the afternoon session of jury selection wearing a pin saying, "Helpers of God's Precious Infants,"[14] which reflected her antiabortion advocacy and raised concerns that she had discussed the abortion issue with other prospective jurors while they waited to be called for questioning.[15] This prospective juror told the court that she was an officer of the Helpers of God's Precious Infants for the Diocese of Delaware: "I counsel moms and dads that have had abortions. My husband and I had one back in the '70s. So, you know, I know how wrong it is. I'm—I know this case. I go to this clinic—well, it's not at the same location where this young lady lost her life. . . . But I go there and pray the rosary as often as I can." Excused by the judge, the juror promised that she would be "praying for you guys."[16]

Although the "Helper's" advocate was removed from the panel, the defendant's attorney was still troubled about the impact she may have had on the other potential jurors: "I thought it was somewhat suspicious that she had appeared with the button. . . . None of the jurors, presumably, would have known the nature of this case when they were asked to come here to the courthouse. . . . If someone was willing to engage in that type of display . . . we need to at least address to the jurors whether there was any contact with that juror."[17] Judge Jurden then asked the members of the jury pool whether anyone had attempted to discuss the case or influence them, but no one reported an attempt.

After this extended interviewing process involving jurors who responded affirmatively to the questions put to the whole panel, a group of jurors was randomly selected to serve as the trial jury and alternate jurors. That group included some jurors who had not been individually questioned. If the jurors survived the peremptory challenges, which the plaintiff and defense lawyers could exercise without providing reasons, this group of twelve would decide the case. The judge and the attorneys were uneasy with the extensiveness of the prejudice uncovered in the earlier questioning. Judge Jurden decided to interview each one individually, asking them why they had not responded affirmatively to her earlier set of questions. Of these eleven jurors, four were ultimately removed for cause because their answers revealed a degree of bias and prejudice.

The final jury consisted of nine men and three women. About half of them knew women who had had abortions; several had expressed antiabortion sentiments but thought they could be fair. Thus, the final jury consisted of people who said that they had no problems being fair in the case, a striking difference from the overall jury pool, where close to two-thirds had been excused for bias.

At trial the plaintiff goes first. Witnesses from the clinic were called to testify about the procedures used in Gracealynn's abortion. Then, a medical doctor testified, offering a conclusion that Dr. Imran's actions fell below the standard of care. In his expert opinion based on standards of care for abortion procedures, Dr. Imran should have performed the second trimester abortion in a hospital; should have employed osmotic dilators instead of metal dilators; should have used a sounding device to identify the position of the uterus; and should have used ultrasound to guide the instruments.[18] The clinic was also at fault, according to the expert, by failing to monitor the vital signs of the patient and by releasing her while she was weak and unstable.[19] In his defense against these claims, Dr. Imran testified that he had done the procedure properly, given that Gracealynn had nine months previously given birth to her son and did not require as much time for preparation. He noted that uterine perforation was a danger in abortion procedures and that she had signed a consent form that informed her of this danger.

The prospective juror who had sported the antiabortion button attended the trial along with other antiabortion advocates. She took a front-row seat in the courtroom, praying the rosary as the trial evidence was presented. Nonetheless, the jury, so different in composition from the jury pool, reportedly did not engage in a polarizing discussion of the merits of abortion during deliberations. In fact, whether abortion was right or wrong reportedly never came up in their discussions. Rather, they approached the case as a dispute over a medical procedure.[20] In the end, the jury found the clinic 60 percent responsible and Dr. Imran 40 percent responsible for Gracealynn's death and awarded $2.2 million in damages. Because the clinic settled prior to the trial, Gracealynn's son would receive $900,800 (40 percent of the jury's total award) from Dr. Imran.[21]

THE HISTORY OF VOIR DIRE AND CHALLENGES

Voir dire, a term with a French origin meaning roughly "to see them say," is used to denote the process whereby prospective jurors are questioned about their biases during the jury selection process (although the term is also used for special hearings once the trial is under way). The number of excused jurors in the Gracealynn Harris trial helps to illustrate that voir dire is not so much about juror selection as it is about juror *de-selection*. The de-selection can be done by two means. A "challenge for cause" is an assertion by one of the lawyers that a potential juror is not impartial. In modern times the judge rules on whether the challenged juror should be excused or stay on the panel. Lawyers for both sides also have a limited number of "peremptory" challenges they can use to reject a juror without giving a reason. Essentially, the lawyer vetoes the service of one prospective juror, hoping that the replacement will be more favorable to the client's case—but there are no guarantees.

Two interrelated rationales justify peremptory challenges. The first is that the questioning of the juror, or even the decision of the triors (or judge), might not satisfy the parties that the person truly is impartial. The second is that the mere fact of questioning the juror may provoke resentment by the juror that could result in prejudice.

Voir dire has a long and interesting history in American law. John Miles was put on trial for bigamy in Utah Territory in 1879.[22] The prosecutor challenged one of the prospective jurors, Oscar Dunn, for bias. Three triors were appointed by the court to decide whether the challenges were valid. Dunn testified that he "believed polygamy to be right, that it was ordained of God, and that the revelations concerning it were revelations from God . . . [and that] he who acted on them should not be convicted by the law of the land." The triors found the challenge to be true and Dunn was excused.

Triors were used to decide impartiality as a regular part of the trial process in America, both before and after independence. In the nineteenth century, federal courts[23] and various state statutes or practices provided for triors.[24] But by the beginning of the twentieth century, only a few jurisdictions retained triors.[25] In New York, an 1873 act made the judge the decider of all challenges.[26] Shifting of the decision on challenges for cause to the judge was part of the general trend toward greater judicial control over the trial process.[27]

Following English law, the "stand by privilege" for prosecutors survived in some American jurisdictions at least into the 1890s.[28] These included Florida, North Carolina, South Carolina, and Georgia. Pennsylvania did not abolish stand bys until 1903.[29] In the federal courts the stand by was abolished in 1877 when the prosecution was granted peremptory challenges.[30]

In the debates about the Constitution, many speakers expressed concern that there was no clear language specifying the right of the parties to challenge jurors. Patrick Henry of Virginia argued:

> If [the people] dare oppose the hands of tyrannical power, you will see what has happened elsewhere. They may be tried by the most partial powers, by their most implacable enemies, and be sentenced and put to death, with all the forms of a fair trial. I would rather be left with the judges. An abandoned juror would not dread the loss of character like a judge. From these and a thousand considerations I would rather trial by jury were struck out altogether. There is no right of challenging partial jurors. There is no common law of America, nor constitution, there can be no right to challenge partial jurors. Yet the right is as valuable as the trial by jury itself.[31]

Henry and others were won over when they were assured that the right to jury trial necessarily included those rights.

Up until the middle of the twentieth century, case law in most jurisdictions held that the parties themselves had the right to question prospective jurors—although the nature and extent of the questioning were to be supervised by the judge.[32] However, around 1973 Chief Justice Burger began to criticize lawyer control of voir dire as inefficient and consuming too much time, a view echoed by other courts.[33] The *Federal Rules of Criminal Procedure*, amended in 1966, eased the way for judge-conducted voir dire by stating that either the court or the parties could have responsibility for juror questioning about bias.[34] Gradually, judges in federal courts took over the questioning role and by 1977 about three out of four judges conducted the questioning by themselves.[35] The practice took hold in many state courts as well.[36] In recent years attorneys have been able to regain a foothold in some courts, but the earlier change reflects an additional example of judicial assertion of control over the jury trial.

VOIR DIRE PRACTICE IN THE CONTEMPORARY UNITED STATES

The practice of voir dire and jury selection varies tremendously among the states. At one end of the continuum is the most limited form of voir dire, the typical approach in Delaware where Gracealynn Harris's case was decided. In these states, judges tend to ask a small number of questions about the potential bias of prospective jurors. The questions tend to be narrowly focused upon bias specifically related to the case, and are presented to the jurors requiring only yes or no answers. Jurors are questioned in a group, and the court relies upon them to come forward if there is a potential for bias. At the other end of the continuum is the most expansive form of voir dire, in which the judge and the attorneys both participate in the questioning of prospective jurors. The questioning is wide-ranging and tends to be done individually, one juror at a time. Jurors answer yes or no questions as well as open-ended questions that allow them to give responses in their own words, often with a follow-up request to elaborate further. Thus, the judge and attorneys are able to make independent evaluations of the potential bias of the prospective jurors rather than relying exclusively on the juror's self-assessment of bias.

Today, in a majority of state courts, both the judge and the attorneys participate in the questioning.[37] In six states, including Delaware, only the judge usually asks questions, whereas in five states, attorneys conduct the voir dire themselves. Federal judges surveyed in the 1990s were more likely than judges in the 1970s to say that they ordinarily allowed attorneys to participate in the questioning of prospective jurors.[38] In the 1990s, six of every ten judges said attorneys played a role, up from about 30 percent in 1977.[39] Interestingly, whether judges or attorneys in the federal courts questioned the jurors did not change the amount of time it took to select a jury.

A large national survey of trial courts has found that the average time for jury selection in felony trials is 3.8 hours in state courts and 3.6 hours in federal courts. Jury selection in civil cases typically takes a bit less time: 3.1 hours in state courts and 2.3 hours in federal courts.[40]

The length of the jury selection, and the number of prospective jurors questioned, varies considerably. At the high end are capital trials, cases with substantial pretrial publicity, and trials that are expected to be lengthy. The largest jury panel in a California study, for example, involved 864 prospective jurors. It was for a capital murder trial with five defendants and was expected to last eighty-five days.[41] That dwarfs even the six hundred potential jurors from Eagle County, Colorado, who were summoned to court to fill out jury questionnaires in basketball star Kobe Bryant's rape case—which was dismissed before the trial began.[42]

HOW THE CONDUCTING OF VOIR DIRE AFFECTS THE SEARCH FOR BIAS

Short, limited voir dire presents serious problems for identifying biased jurors.[43] When Gregory Mize served as a Superior Court judge in Washington, DC, he felt uneasy about the jury selection process that he and other judges in the court conducted. He decided to investigate.[44] After posing an initial set of questions to a group of about sixty prospective jurors in the open courtroom, he and the attorneys would follow up individually with those jurors who had responded affirmatively to the initial questions. However, using a novel procedure for the DC court, he decided to interview every potential juror regardless of whether they responded affirmatively to the initial questions, just as Judge Jurden did in Delaware's Harris trial.

Judge Mize prompted each juror who had not indicated a "yes" response to any of the initial questions by asking, "I notice you did not respond to any of my questions. I just wondered why. Could you explain?" or "Is it because the questions did not apply to you?"[45] Mize reports that although many jurors indicated that the questions did not apply to them, a significant minority said that they did have something to say in response to the questions. Some of these jurors provided information that led to their removal. For example:

- "I do not understand your questions or remember the past very well" (suggesting a mental incapacity bearing on the juror's competence).
- "I was frightened to raise my hand. I have taken high blood pressure medications for twenty years. I am afraid I'll do what others tell me to do in the jury room."
- "I was on a hung jury before—I don't know if I can follow instructions of the court for gun possession—that was the problem in my other trial" (in a trial for a gun offense).
- "My grandson was killed with a gun so the topic of guns makes my blood pressure go up" (in a trial for a gun offense).
- I'm the defendant's fiancée.[46]

What Judge Mize uncovered in his courtroom led him to conclude that individual voir dire of all prospective jurors was indispensable to a fair trial.[47]

A number of other studies reinforce Judge Mize's conclusion that a limited form of voir dire is not very effective in detecting which prospective jurors may be biased.[48] Richard Seltzer and his colleagues observed jury selection in thirty-one criminal trials in Superior Court in the District of Columbia and recorded what jurors said about their views.[49] Then, the researchers conducted posttrial interviews with jurors who had decided cases. Voir dire answers and information from the posttrial interviews differed in important ways. Some prospective jurors did not reveal to the court that close friends and family worked in law enforcement.[50] Jurors who had been crime victims did not always admit it in court.[51] During the posttrial interviews, about half the jurors maintained that a defendant must prove his or her innocence (contrary to the legal rule of innocent until proven guilty), although that view wasn't asserted during voir dire.[52]

A study in California took a similar approach in observing four voir dires in felony cases and interviewing jurors after the trial.[53] The voir dires were more expansive than some of the other ones we've discussed. They lasted about five hours on average, with both the judge and two attorneys questioning prospective jurors. The researchers found that prosecutors and defense attorneys were able to identify and eliminate some potential jurors who would have been hostile to their respective sides. Still, some jurors who had served on a trial disagreed with the presumption of innocence.[54] Other jurors admitted they had not been able to set aside their personal feelings or biases during the trial.[55]

Another systematic set of studies compared the effects of different types of voir dire in capital cases.[56] Researchers Michael Nietzel and Ronald Dillehay concluded that limited voir dire in capital cases decreased the likelihood of successful defense challenges for cause. In their first study, the researchers compared four types of voir dire methods in thirteen Kentucky capital trials. Some voir dires were conducted one-on-one, out of the presence of the jury panel, while in others the questioning of prospective jurors took place in open court and in the presence of other potential jurors. The researchers found that the type of voir dire used affected the rate of successful challenges for cause. Defendants were more successful in securing challenges for cause when jurors were questioned individually than when they were questioned en masse. A second study replicated the basic finding with voir dire examinations from South Carolina, California, and Kentucky death penalty trials.[57] Challenges for cause were more likely to be granted with more extensive questioning because the judge and attorneys were better able to obtain more relevant information about prospective jurors.[58]

WHY IS LIMITED VOIR DIRE SO INEFFECTIVE?

Why can't we easily detect the biases and prejudices of prospective jurors? Some jurors, probably the minority, consciously and purposefully lie—whether to get on or off the jury. More often, the right questions aren't asked, or jurors fail to disclose pertinent information. Still others may not recognize their own biases. But it's not foreordained. The court's conduct of the questioning can minimize or exacerbate these problems.

Asking only a small number of questions may mean that critically important areas of potential bias are missed. With modest information about prospective jurors, judges and attorneys may be completely unaware of prospective jurors' relevant experiences and background and therefore may be oblivious to the importance of exploring such experiences in depth during voir dire. For example, post-trial interviews Hans conducted, with jurors chosen in trials with mostly limited voir dire, revealed that more than occasionally, jurors had experiences the parties would want to know about. For example, in a case in which the plaintiff claimed knee problems, one juror had a permanent limp caused by a childhood knee injury. Yet it had not surfaced during voir dire questioning.[59] Lacking information, judges and attorneys cannot review and assess pertinent data.

The form of the question is critical. Is it a leading question, where the legally and socially appropriate answer is obvious? Lawyers, of course, are well aware of the dynamics of asking leading questions during trial, posed not to obtain information but to suggest a particular stance on the part of the witness. Attorneys sometimes take advantage of this approach in questioning prospective jurors. Social psychologists have documented a phenomenon they label the "social desirability effect."[60] People are motivated to present themselves in a positive, socially desirable light. Yet questions posed to jurors in limited voir dire often suggest the right, socially desirable answer. For instance, a leading question might be: Do you have any biases against this defendant? whereas an open-ended question might be: What have you read or heard about this defendant? Can you please elaborate on that? Such alternative wording is almost always more effective in obtaining useful information.[61]

A major drawback of group questioning is that it requires prospective jurors to identify their own potential biases and come forward in front of other jurors. Jury duty is often stressful for jurors, and some may be too shy or nervous to come forward even if they have a pertinent experience to share. For example, civil litigation can involve accidents, personal injury, or medical procedures. A juror with similar experience may be too embarrassed to volunteer it or see its relevance to how it might prejudice her view of the case. Crime victims may feel the same way. Even if jurors are willing to reveal all, they may be unaware of their own biases.[62] When questioning is individual and private, hesitancies and other signs of unease may be followed up. Hidden prejudices and barely salient experiences may be uncovered. (Some attorneys have identified one potential advantage of the group setting, however. When one prospective juror admits to a particular bias, it may be easier for others to follow suit.)

The person conducting the questioning may also play a role. Judges may not be quite as effective as attorneys in uncovering biases. Attorneys, at this point, know much more about their case than the judge does and therefore are better able to identify potential areas for questioning. Research evidence suggests that jurors may be more willing to self-disclose personal information to lawyers than to judges.[63]

Another technique for improving the accuracy of the voir dire process is to provide jurors with a written questionnaire in advance of courtroom questioning.

Filling out such a questionnaire permits greater concentration on the part of the juror and allows greater self-disclosure than oral answers from a nervous juror in a crowded courtroom. The judge and lawyers can then sensitively explore biases that might prevent a juror from evaluating the evidence impartially as the law requires.[64]

A CAVEAT ON IMPLEMENTATION OF AN IDEAL VOIR DIRE

We need to offer a serious caveat. Courts have limited time for each trial. There are other cases waiting in the queue. There is also the fact that the official goal of voir dire is to determine juror bias, and attorneys may attempt to use the occasion to ingratiate themselves with the jury or to project their case themes. Detailed questioning can be time consuming and costly, and judges are rightfully very concerned about these matters. Our analysis suggests an ideal model that cannot be applied to every case. Yet, in some cases, the stakes are high: someone's liberty or life, or compensation for a disastrous injury to a person or business. In other cases, the likelihood of juror prejudice is great. In these circumstances, half measures seem inappropriate.

REMOVING JURORS FOR CAUSE

Judges have the exclusive ability to remove jurors for cause when they conclude that the juror is or might appear to be biased. Jurors who are linked in some way to the parties in the case—personal friends, close neighbors, coworkers, or investors—are usually removed for cause. People with highly relevant or similar experiences are often eliminated as well. In Gracealynn Harris's case, for instance, Judge Jurden removed a juror who had an abortion herself, as well as other prospective jurors with close friends who'd had medical complications stemming from abortions. The thinking in such circumstances is, no doubt, that these experiences would color a juror's perceptions so that the juror would not be able to listen openly to the evidence for both sides.

As for strong views about issues that will arise at the trial, there is more latitude. Judge Jurden usually asked prospective jurors whether, in light of their strong views about abortion, they could still be fair. If prospective jurors assert that they can be fair and impartial, despite having some strong feelings about the issues in a case, the judge may well determine they are suitable jurors. For instance, in Gracealynn Harris's case, some antiabortion jurors remained on the jury, in part, because they convinced the judge of their ability to decide the case fairly on the evidence presented at the trial. A Catholic woman, for example, asserted that "I do believe it is a human life" and that she did not agree with abortion, but she convinced the court that she was "not a judgmental person" and remained in the jury pool.[65]

Judges appear to rely mainly on jurors' own assessments of whether or not they can decide a case fairly. And one key factor is how confident prospective jurors appear in their ability to remain impartial in evaluating the evidence and reaching a verdict. In trying to determine whether someone is right or wrong about a particular fact, confidence can be a useful predictor. But we all know highly confident people who are absolutely sure—and absolutely wrong.

Social scientists Mary Rose and Shari Diamond decided to examine this question of the importance of juror confidence in judicial decisions about challenges for cause.[66] They developed a set of jury selection vignettes based on actual court cases. The vignettes described jurors' relevant personal experiences or relationships with witnesses. But they varied the juror's confidence in his or her ability to be fair. In some vignettes, prospective jurors were quoted as saying that they were very confident that they could be fair, while in others they were quoted as giving a more equivocal answer. Trial court judges reviewed the vignettes and reported whether they would be likely to remove the prospective jurors for cause. In line with expectations, judges differentiated between the certain jurors and the equivocating jurors, saying they would be more likely to remove the equivocating jurors.[67]

Prosecutors and public defenders also reviewed the vignettes and rated the jurors' level of bias and whether, in their view, a judge would be apt to remove the juror for cause. Attorneys sharply differentiated between prospective jurors who were confident versus those who were equivocal. Attorneys thought that jurors who would "try" to be fair were much more likely to be excused for cause. Public defenders were more likely than prosecutors to express concern about juror bias on the basis of personal experiences and key relationships.

In addition to expressed prejudice, close relationships, or biasing experiences, there is one other reason likely to give rise to a challenge for cause. This is when a prospective juror knows a lot about a case and, in particular, when the juror has through the press or other means learned information that will not emerge at trial, such as the defendant's criminal record, or knowledge of seized evidence that is inadmissible at the trial. Even here, however, judges may sometimes deny a challenge for cause if the juror asserts that he or she will disregard the factual information learned outside the courtroom.

How often people are removed for cause has not been extensively studied. The judge can, on his or her own initiative, decide to dismiss a juror for cause, or may rule on a motion for dismissal from the attorneys. In the California study, to the researchers' surprise, judges initiated most of the challenges for cause rather than responding to attorney requests.[68] The researchers observed jury selections in eighteen trials, including one hundred instances in which the judge, prosecutor, or defense attorney made a motion for a challenge for cause. The judge initiated a juror's removal eighty-nine times. Defense counsel made ten motions; six were granted. A prosecutor made just one motion, which was denied.[69] Overall, the California study found that 16 percent were excused for cause. So, the Gracealynn Harris case was unusual in that a very high proportion of prospective jurors were excused for cause.

Not surprisingly, how often jurors are dismissed for cause is linked to the extent of the jury questions. Of course, when there are great concerns about potential bias, judges are more open to expansive questioning. When the question period is longer, more thorough, and more individualized, more facts are uncovered to form the basis for challenges for cause.

PEREMPTORY CHALLENGES

The 1986 video training tape is grainy and jumpy. But the jovial tone of experienced homicide prosecutor Jack McMahon is clear.[70] McMahon, an assistant district attorney in Philadelphia, imparts his jury selection advice to new prosecutors, urging them to look for conviction-prone jurors who are predisposed to accept the government's claims at face value. The best jurors, he counsels, are not particularly bright; instead, they are conservative, well dressed, and from good neighborhoods. He asserts that "blacks from the low-income areas" are the worst jurors because they resent law enforcement and authority. He confides that he'd much prefer older blacks who have more respect for the law. Irreverently, he claims that "[y]ou do not want smart people. Now, I wish that you could ask everyone's IQ. If you could know their IQ, you could pick a great jury all the time."[71]

The training tape caused a sensation when it was released by McMahon's opponent during an election campaign for the office of Philadelphia's district attorney. It pulled back the curtain on what is usually a highly secretive process, namely, how attorneys go about exercising their peremptory challenges in jury trials. It confirmed many people's worst fears that even the most successful attorneys rely on stereotypes and biases in jury selection.

Mystique and controversy surround the lawyers' use of peremptory challenges. Depending on the type of case, attorneys have a limited number of challenges that they may exercise to remove prospective jurors without providing a specific reason. And many court observers complain that the removals are unreasonable.

Take the Jackson County paternity case that the state of Alabama brought—before the days in which DNA testing in such cases was routine—on behalf of Teresa Bible, the mother of a young child, against the child's putative father, James E. Bowman.[72] A panel of thirty-six potential jurors was selected to try the case, including twelve men and twenty-four women. The court removed three jurors for cause, two men and one woman, leaving just ten men out of the thirty-three remaining jurors. Then the adversarial game began, with the state using nine of its ten peremptory strikes to remove men, and Mr. Bowman's attorney employing all but one of his strikes to remove women. The final jury consisted entirely of women. Their verdict: Mr. Bowman was indeed the father. He was quickly ordered to pay child support. A fair jury? A legitimate approach to jury selection? Mr. Bowman didn't think so. He asked the US Supreme Court to review his case.

Until 1986, attorneys could base their peremptory challenges on any aspect of a prospective juror's appearance, demeanor, demographic characteristics, or answers on voir dire. And from what we can tell from the historical record, reliance on racial and gender stereotypes to dismiss prospective jurors was common. In fact, the US Supreme Court established an impossibly high standard that had to be met to fight improper peremptory challenges even if they were based on dubious factors, like a juror's race.

In the disturbing case of *Swain v. Alabama*, discussed earlier, the US Supreme Court in 1965 refused to overturn the conviction of an African American man on death row.[73] An all-white jury convicted African American Robert Swain of raping a white woman and sentenced him to death. His jury panel included eight African Americans, but two were excused, and the prosecutor used peremptory challenges to remove the remaining six. What is more, in Swain's county, no African American had served on a trial jury since 1950. The Court rejected Swain's claim of an unfair jury selection, though, saying he had not met the burden of proving the prosecutor had discriminated on the basis of race. If systematic evidence was uncovered of discrimination in case after case, that might meet the burden of proof, but Swain had not done that, the Court observed. (Swain's death sentence was eventually commuted to life in prison.)[74]

In 1986, the Supreme Court reversed course, partly because in the intervening years, it further developed its jurisprudence about the necessary proof for discrimination. In *Batson v. Kentucky*, the Court concluded that a prosecutor could no longer rely on a prospective juror's race as a basis for a peremptory challenge.[75] In subsequent cases, the Court expanded the race prohibition to defense attorneys in criminal trials and both sides in civil trials.[76]

In *J. E. B. v. Alabama*, the Supreme Court used Mr. Bowman's appeal of his paternity case conviction to conclude that using gender as the basis for peremptory challenges also violated the Equal Protection clause of the Fourteenth Amendment: "We hold that gender, like race, is an unconstitutional proxy for juror competence and impartiality."[77]

As the Supreme Court expanded the prohibited grounds for peremptories over this set of cases, an interesting shift in the rationale for representative juries took place. In *Batson*, the first case that it decided, the justices emphasized the rights of a criminal defendant to have a jury that was selected without a prosecutor's discriminatory actions. But in subsequent cases, the justifications expanded to embrace the rights of the excluded jurors. Prohibiting lawyers from challenging jurors because of race or gender is now centrally motivated by a desire that all citizens be able to participate in jury service.[78]

The Supreme Court outlined a procedure that was acceptable for examining the touchy subject of the grounds for a trial attorney's peremptory challenge, and the procedure is now labeled a *Batson* challenge. During jury selection, if the judge or an attorney believes that one side has based one or more peremptory challenges on prohibited grounds, the individual may raise a *Batson* challenge. If the judge believes there are sound reasons for such concern and concludes that a prima facie case of discrimination has been made, the burden then shifts to the attorney who made the peremptory to provide legitimate reasons for removing the juror.

Law professor Nancy Marder observes that *Batson* has had some benefits in that it has changed what is acceptable discussion about jurors' race and gender among lawyers and may reassure the parties to a legal proceeding as well as the jurors.[79] But, despite the fact that attorneys are now officially prohibited from relying on race and gender in deciding which jurors to challenge, recent studies of the voir dire process indicate that a juror's race continues to play a role in trial lawyers' thinking and use of peremptory challenges. And it's not hard to escape the consequences of the *Batson* regime; a survey of appeals shows that *Batson* challenges are rarely granted.[80] When Jack McMahon delivered his controversial remarks about whom to eliminate and whom to keep on the jury, he observed that as a defense to claims of racial discrimination in peremptory challenges, prosecutors should keep records of "legitimate" reasons for striking each black person from the jury.[81] Judges face a serious challenge trying to distinguish between the illegitimate factor of race and race-neutral reasons as the actual cause of strikes; one recent case, in fact, showed US Supreme Court justices at odds about whether or not the voir dire transcript in the case revealed racial motivations.[82]

Contemporary studies of peremptory challenges show clear patterns linked to race. For instance, law professor David Baldus and his colleagues studied the racial characteristics of prospective jurors challenged by the defense and the prosecution in Philadelphia death penalty cases during a seventeen-year period. They discovered strong and opposing patterns of strikes by prosecutors and defense attorneys. The Philadelphia prosecutors followed a pattern espoused by Jack McMahon, using their strikes against prospective black jurors. They also seemed to be somewhat more likely to exercise challenges against younger potential jurors.[83] Defense counsel, on the other hand, challenged whites much more often than blacks. They also showed a greater tendency to strike older jurors. Thus the strikes of the prosecutors and defense attorneys were almost reverse images of each other. Gender effects were not strong but again showed a reverse image quality, with defense attorneys striking more men than women and prosecutors doing the opposite. Further analysis showed that although prosecutors used fewer peremptories than defense attorneys overall, the prosecutors targeted a narrower population with their strikes and they were more effective than defense attorneys in removing their targets from the jury.

Mary Rose conducted a study of peremptory challenges in a southern court, finding very similar patterns to the Philadelphia study in the reverse images of prosecutorial and defense peremptory challenges.[84] Of the African Americans excused from service, seven out of every ten were challenged by the prosecution. In contrast, the defense challenged eight of every ten whites who were dismissed. Typically, defense attorneys made more strikes than prosecutors. Because defense attorneys were more likely to challenge whites than African Americans, some of the final juries wound up with greater proportions of African American jurors compared to their presence in the local population. Most juries, though, were similar in composition to the local population.

The racial patterns are troubling. But can we prove they are motivated by racial animus of the attorneys or driven by the attorneys' impermissible group stereotypes about good prosecution and defense jurors? It could be that African American jurors make more supportive remarks about the defense during jury selection, while whites are more apt to make comments favorable to the prosecution. In individual cases, one might be able to prove differential treatment based on race if both African American and Caucasian jurors make similar statements, yet one group is challenged and the other is not.

That was the approach taken recently in an experiment on race and peremptory challenges conducted by Tufts University professor Samuel Sommers and his Harvard Business School collaborator, Michael Norton.[85] Using college students, advanced law students, and practicing attorneys, Sommers and Norton presented them with a hypothetical robbery and assault case with a black defendant. They were also given two juror profiles and photographs. One profile described a journalist who wrote stories concerning police misconduct; the other, an executive who voiced skepticism about statistics and forensic analysis. The race of these hypothetical jurors was varied randomly; sometimes the first juror was identified (through the photograph) as black, and other times the second juror was identified as black. The study participants then were asked to assume the role of a prosecutor and select one of the jurors to strike peremptorily.

The results showed a clear effect for race. When the journalist was portrayed as black, he was challenged 79 percent of the time by the practicing attorneys, compared to only 43 percent of the time when he was white. Similarly, when practicing attorneys saw the executive as black, he was chosen for a challenge 57 percent of the time, compared to 21 percent when he was shown as white. College students and law students followed the same pattern. Not surprisingly, participants rarely said they exercised their challenges on the basis of race; instead, they justified their challenges with race-neutral factors such as the juror's knowledge of police misconduct or the negative views of statistics.

Analysis of actual peremptory challenges in Texas criminal trials converges with these experimental results.[86] Reviewing transcripts of Texas voir dires, journalists at the *Dallas Morning News* discovered that there appeared to be differential strikes based on race, even once the jurors' specific responses given during the questioning were taken into account. For instance, jurors' views on the desirability of rehabilitation were key to whether or not they were struck. Prosecutors eliminated through peremptories 79 percent of the black prospective jurors who endorsed rehabilitation over punishment but only 55 percent of the white prospective jurors who did so. If we combine the data from actual jury selections with the experimental results, it's hard not to conclude that race is a prime factor in exercise of peremptory challenges, and the race-neutral reasons provided for strikes are, in Professor Nancy Marder's words, a "charade."[87]

HOW EFFECTIVE ARE ATTORNEYS IN EXERCISING PEREMPTORY CHALLENGES?

All other things being equal, can a good attorney stack the jury? As Solomon Fulero and Steven Penrod have pointed out, when voir dire is limited and attorneys rely primarily on demographic characteristics to strike jurors for cause, they are not likely to do well.[88] That is because in most cases such characteristics are only weakly and inconsistently related to jury verdicts. If a lawyer obtains further information about jurors' attitudes and views about issues in the case, that could improve the lawyer's chance of success. But usually the importance of jury selection is an unanswerable question, because jurors who are challenged leave the courtroom and never decide the case. We can't normally compare how those jurors would have voted with the decision of the actual jury.

Enter Hans Zeisel and Shari Diamond, who did just that in a Chicago trial court some years ago.[89] After receiving the court's permission, they observed jury selection in a dozen trials and then asked the challenged jurors to participate in a research project. The excused jurors sat in the courtroom during the trial and at the trial's conclusion reached a verdict together with the other excused jurors. Zeisel and Diamond asked for their initial individual verdicts and then constructed a hypothetical jury profile that included the excused jurors and the actual jurors. They concluded on the basis of their profiles that two or three of the twelve cases might actually have resulted in different verdicts had the challenged jurors been included rather than dismissed. Some attorneys were remarkably better than others, apparently being able to spot unfavorable jurors. Other attorneys' challenges were essentially like a coin flip, having no noticeable impact on the resulting opinion of the jury.

David Baldus and his colleagues in the Philadelphia jury selection study concluded that the lawyers' jury selection strategies based on race likely made a difference in the jury's willingness to give a death sentence.[90] Drawing on their data, they concluded that prosecutors' removal of African American jury pool members raised the chance of a death sentence by about ten percentage points and increased the differential between black and nonblack defendants' sentences by an even greater amount.[91] Although strong efforts by the defense increased the proportion of African Americans on juries, and reduced the racial disparities, the defense efforts didn't appear to reduce the overall death-sentencing rate.

Cathy Johnson and Craig Haney studied four California felony trials and concluded that both the demographic and attitudinal compositions of the jury were affected by the jury selection process.[92] Comparing the demographic characteristics of the original group of prospective jurors with the selected jurors, they found that racial minorities and the elderly were less likely than other types of jurors to survive the voir dire questioning. The researchers also compared the criminal justice attitudes of the prospective and selected jurors. These attitudinal comparisons showed that prosecutors tended to challenge prospective jurors who were more pro-defense, and in return, the defense attorneys were apt to challenge more pro-prosecution jurors. So, in one sense, the attorneys were effective at identifying people who were likely to be hostile to their arguments and evidence. However, the effectiveness was limited: A number of strong pro-prosecution and pro-defense individuals remained unchallenged, even though each side had additional challenges it could have used to eliminate them from the jury. Furthermore, the retained jurors did not differ much from the jurors who would have been randomly selected without any challenges.

SHOULD PEREMPTORY CHALLENGES BE ABOLISHED?

Justice Thurgood Marshall presciently observed in the *Batson* case that "[t]he decision today will not end the racial discrimination that peremptories inject into the jury-selection process. That goal can be accomplished only by eliminating peremptory challenges entirely. . . . The inherent potential of peremptory challenges to distort the jury process by permitting the exclusion of jurors on racial grounds should ideally lead the Court to ban them entirely from the criminal justice system."[93]

The mixed record on the effectiveness of peremptory challenges, and new evidence of the continuing role of race in attorney peremptory challenges, have produced a heated debate over whether it is time to abolish the peremptory challenge in the United States. As we noted earlier, England went this route in 1988 when Parliament eliminated the defense's long-cherished right to peremptorily challenge prospective jurors.[94]

Jury reform commissions have studied whether the United States should follow England's example. The jury reform commission in the District of Columbia advocated eliminating or sharply reducing peremptories.[95] The commission report notes that trial judges in the District routinely observed attorneys in both civil and criminal cases exercising challenges in patterns that, at a minimum, gave the appearance of being based on race and gender. Judicial opinions in a number of cases found actual discrimination. In addition, it found that the elimination of peremptories would make for a more efficient jury selection process; fewer prospective jurors would need to be called. The right to peremptory challenges does not appear to be required by the US Constitution, and their use can flagrantly violate other constitutional rights. There is worry that jurors who are struck might be resentful and become more negative about the courts. In her research on the voir dire process, Mary Rose found that jurors are occasionally resentful when they are struck, particularly when they believe their personal characteristics, including race, are the cause of their removal. However, the majority of jurors who are removed recognize the adversarial nature of the trial and accept the decision.[96]

Because of these concerns, some DC commission members believed that peremptories should be drastically reduced, while others held that they should be eliminated entirely. The view on the DC jury reform commission was not unanimous, however. Other members staunchly maintained that the peremptory continues to play a significant role in promoting fairness and the appearance of justice in the legal system. Arguments cited in support include the fact that the peremptory was originally provided to the defense as a protection against state power. If the judge becomes the sole arbiter of who sits on the jury, with no input from the parties, then both actual and perceived fairness may suffer. The parties' opportunity to challenge peremptorily increases the likelihood that more of the biased jurors are removed from the case. They assert that it is an important supplement to the challenge for cause and should be retained.

Although we (Vidmar and Hans) are troubled by the biases inherent in peremptory challenges, on balance we agree with the arguments that ceding all of the control over the jury's composition to the trial judge is unwise. A primary reason is the way that challenges for cause are decided. As we've seen, jurors whose views and circumstances are strongly suggestive of bias commonly avoid elimination for cause by their simple assertion that they can be fair. Even when such responses are honest, and sometimes they are not, they are often mistaken. Human psychology is such that people cannot avoid their biases simply by vowing that they won't be affected by them. Absent changes in the treatment of challenges for cause, peremptory challenges are sometimes important to the seating of impartial juries.

The vigorous dissent among members of the legal community suggests that peremptory challenges will not be easily eliminated in the near future. But a number of jurisdictions are moving ahead to reduce the number of peremptory challenges, as the DC Commission recommended. The National Center for State Courts study of California voir dire found that on average, attorneys used just half of their allotment of peremptory challenges. The NCSC calculated the likely impact of proposed reductions, and concluded that the impact would be felt most in misdemeanor cases and civil trials and less so in serious criminal cases.[97] However, the study's authors report their observations that in a number of instances questionable jurors survived challenges for cause and had to be removed by the parties' peremptory challenges. Attorneys don't bother to debate the judge's ruling; rather, they use their peremptory challenges to remove the juror. All that will change if peremptories are reduced drastically or eliminated. If peremptory challenges are abolished, the administration of the challenge for cause must change radically as well. But radical changes would be hard to bring about, considering the wide latitude given to judges in conducting a trial.

TRIAL CONSULTANTS

Attorneys seeking advice on jury matters can now turn to a burgeoning number of trial consultants. For an often hefty fee, trial consultants conduct focus groups, mock juries, and community surveys. Analyzing the results and the local jury pool, consultants identify issues in the case that are likely to prove troublesome to a jury and make recommendations about favorable and unfavorable jurors. They may develop themes and graphics and help in witness preparation. Depending on their findings, they may advise the attorneys to settle if the case engenders strong opposition.

Jury consulting first became popular in the 1960s in controversial American trials dealing with antiwar demonstrations and racial and political protests.[98] Many of the methods that social scientists developed in these early cases are still in use, although they have been expanded and refined over the years. A community survey may be conducted, usually by telephone, to obtain responses to questions about the upcoming case. Results from scientifically conducted polls provide the lawyers with information about local knowledge and sentiments, which in turn are used to fashion questions for jury selection and approaches to the trial. Or, if bias is widespread, the survey results may be used to support a motion to move a trial to another location.

Trial consultants today frequently employ focus groups and mock trials, which vary widely in quality and scope. The consultant assembles a group of individuals, ideally a representative one from the local community. These individuals, paid for their participation, join focus groups with discussion organized around particular themes and issues, or serve in mock juries, in which they read or listen to an abbreviated version of the evidence and key witnesses and deliberate about the case to reach a verdict. The participants also complete extensive questionnaires tapping their attitudes and demographic factors that the consultant then uses to develop profiles of favorable jurors.

Trial consultants also play a key role in courtroom jury selection, analyzing the jury pool, formulating voir dire questions, systematically observing the prospective juror's body language and verbal responses, and weighing in on recommendations to accept or reject particular jurors.

In high-stakes civil trials, it's common for both sides to hire jury consultants. Prosecutors have also become more willing to hire them in high-stakes criminal cases, especially when the defense employs a consultant. The 2006 trial of Enron executives Jeffrey Skilling and Kenneth Lay on criminal conspiracy and securities fraud charges had three well-known consultants. *American Lawyer* interviewed all three of the consultants to obtain their perceptions of how they contributed to the case and what led to the ultimate conviction of the two defendants.[99] Working for the prosecution was Jo-Ellan Dimitrius, perhaps the best-known trial consultant nationwide. She skyrocketed to national prominence after her successful work with the O. J. Simpson defense team in his criminal trial. The defense also had highly regarded consultants: Houston consultant Robert Hirschhorn worked on Lay's defense, while Reiko Hasuike worked for Skilling. Their interviews provide an insider's glimpse at the work done by consultants in a high-stakes trial.

Dimitrius and her firm conducted multiple surveys of the Houston community and a companion survey in Phoenix. The surveys showed extensive prejudice against Lay and Skilling—surprisingly, in both communities! A total of 63 percent of Houston residents said that Lay and Skilling were definitely or probably guilty; 68 percent of Phoenix respondents felt similarly. Based in part on these findings, the trial judge decided to keep the trial in Enron's hometown of Houston, which some observers believe made obtaining an acquittal even more difficult for the defense.[100] Dimitrius also worked with other trial team members to come up with a clear and persuasive storyline for the prosecution in this complex accounting case. The prosecution team created graphics and themes that would convey the wrongful nature of the defendants' actions to jurors. To aid the prosecutors in their jury selection, Dimitrius used the community surveys and juror questionnaires to develop profiles of desirable jurors.

On the other side, Hirschhorn and Hasuike worked ferociously to try to counteract what many saw as the Enron prosecution's decided advantage. After the defense failed to get the trial moved out of Houston, the consultants ran mock-jury studies. As a harbinger of things to come, the mock juries mostly found the defendants guilty as charged. Hirschhorn told the *American Lawyer*: "The biggest problem we were constantly fighting was their belief that the CEO of a corporation is the captain of the ship, and captains know everything."[101] Still, the defense consultants drew on their research and hundreds of juror questionnaires to identify people who might question the government's case or agree that others at Enron were responsible for the company's fall. During the trial, Hasuike advised the attorneys on cross-examination and expressing their points more clearly. In the end, though, the jury convicted both men on multiple charges.

Two questions come to mind from the Enron case. Did the presence of these three consultants change the outcome of the trial? After all, high-profile cases in which consultants are employed are often litigated by extraordinarily successful attorneys. But, more generally, even if lawyers can't stack juries, could trial consultants do it for them? As far as the Enron trial goes, the consultants may have had little opportunity to affect the jury's verdict, considering the strong feelings in the community against the defendants prior to the trial, combined, of course, with the quality of the legal advocacy and the strength of the trial evidence. However, developing the statistical portrait of community sentiment that convinced the judge to keep the trial in Houston, and working on case themes that organized and clarified the problematic accounting issues, might have helped the prosecution. Likewise, the crafting of defense arguments that resonated with some of the jurors was worthwhile even if it did not affect the eventual verdict.

Jury and trial consulting may make a difference in some cases, although rigorous research proving it is lacking.[102] However, when it comes to assessing the effectiveness of trial consulting, the job of trial consultant should be divided into two separate categories. The first is trial preparation and presentation. Through focus groups and surveys the lawyers can learn about weaknesses in the presentation of their case and attempt to correct those weaknesses before trial. Relying on methods backed up by basic research in communication, consultants can assist attorneys in framing their opening statements and closing arguments, and develop graphics and other media that will more clearly illustrate evidence. This function of trial consultants is about communication.

The second function is jury selection, or as we have pointed out, jury deselection. Surveys can provide information on which jurors might favor one side or the other and suggest questions for the voir dire process. This assistance is more likely to have an impact when the evidence is ambiguous rather than strong for one side or another, because trial evidence is the most powerful predictor of jury verdicts. If the case polarizes the community, and views about the case are linked to obvious demographic factors or attitudes that can be detected and explored during the voir dire, jury consultants and lawyers may be better able to identify jurors who are biased against their side and make challenges for cause or exercise peremptory challenges.

Nevertheless, the influence of jury consultants on trials should not be overestimated, especially when it comes to voir dire. Some consultants have made extravagant claims about their ability to psychologically analyze jurors.[103] These claims fly in the face of research on psychological prediction. Even in highly controlled settings using standardized psychological tests, it is often very difficult to accurately estimate how any particular individual will behave. The voir dire process in a courtroom does not have the advantage of these standardized psychological tests. Furthermore, the process does not allow the deep analysis of people and their likely motives. Moreover, even when a jury consultant and the lawyer decide that a juror is highly favorable to their side, it is likely that the opposing lawyer will make a challenge for cause or exercise a peremptory challenge against that juror. Once again we are reminded that jury selection is really jury de-selection in which both sides have some vetoes over the other side's favorite juror. Furthermore, emphasis on the personalities and presumed predilections of jurors assumes that trial evidence, judicial instructions to be impartial, and the deliberations of twelve independent minds don't count very much. The Enron case suggests otherwise.

Chapter 5

PROBLEM CASES

Pretrial Publicity

Scott Peterson, a California man, was charged with killing his pregnant wife, Laci Peterson, on Christmas Eve 2003 and dumping her body in San Francisco Bay. The search for the missing woman; the discovery of her decomposed body and that of her unborn child in the bay; the reports by the police naming Scott Peterson as a suspect; and the stories about Scott Peterson's affairs, arrest, and police evidence against him dominated local and national news long before his trial. Throughout the trial, nationwide media coverage was intense. One of the jurors was dismissed during the trial because of improper contact with a media representative at the courthouse. Once the jury convicted Scott Peterson of first-degree murder, the Peterson jurors were released until the start of the penalty phase of the trial, when they were to consider evidence relating to the death penalty. However, they went from the courthouse into a public space saturated with congratulatory media coverage of the verdict, including much praise for the wisdom of their guilty verdict. One surely must worry about how that affirmation of their guilty verdict influenced the jurors when they returned to the courthouse to deliberate about Scott Peterson's death penalty.[1]

Scott Peterson's trial does not stand alone. Cases with public figures can get even more attention. O. J. Simpson's murder trial was televised live, providing a daily dose of real-time courtroom drama to many Americans, who were continually polled on whether they thought him guilty.[2] In fact, so many people tuned in to hear the announcement of the O. J. jury's verdict that it became a major social and political event. Other cases include the Michael Jackson trial (Jackson was accused of molesting young boys invited to his Neverland Ranch) and the Enron trial of Kenneth Lay and Jeffrey Skilling. However, the list also contains people like Scott Peterson who were unknowns and achieved nationwide notoriety only after being charged with a crime. Among these, we can consider Timothy McVeigh, charged with the Oklahoma City bombing; Susan Smith, charged with killing her two children by purposely guiding her car into a lake with the children inside; and Andrea Yates who pleaded not guilty by reason of insanity after drowning her five children in the family's bathtub. While the above examples attracted nationwide interest, many other cases are notorious only within a particular community. But, even there, public interest and reactions can be equally intense.

Pretrial publicity and reactions can occur in civil cases as well. Merck—the US drug company that manufactured the drug Vioxx—asked for a two-month postponement of the first wrongful death lawsuit over Vioxx, when, one week before the trial was slated to begin, the Texas attorney general filed another lawsuit against them. This time, he alleged that Merck had committed Medicare fraud by minimizing Vioxx's risks.[3] The judge, nonetheless, denied the motion, and the trial proceeded on schedule.[4] However, the challenges that businesses like Merck face in maintaining their profitability and good reputation in the face of highly publicized lawsuits has produced the new business specialty of "litigation communications."[5]

Cases with strong public interest and involvement have always presented special problems for a fair trial, even before the advent of today's mass media—such as when a local crime stirs passions in the community. As a result, the law pertaining to juries developed mechanisms to deal with the possibility that prospective jurors might be so tainted by publicity or gossip that they could not be fair and impartial in deciding guilt or innocence.[6] These mechanisms include probing voir dire, postponing the trial until passions have cooled, sequestering the jury during the trial, and changing the venue or trial location to a community less inflamed by passions.[7]

Modern mass media, including newspapers, radio, television, and the Internet, create additional problems. England, Canada, Australia, and New Zealand severely limit mass media coverage of criminal cases after charges have been laid. These countries also limit what can be published about the court proceedings while the trial is in progress, enforcing proscriptions through contempt of court laws.[8] In addition, these countries generally prohibit jurors from commenting about their verdict to the media or anyone else after the trial is over.

United States practice stands in sharp contrast. The First Amendment to the Constitution has been interpreted to allow broad public access to court proceedings.[9] American mass media have virtually unlimited ability to cover all phases related to a trial, including pretrial hearings and the trial itself. In some state courts proceedings may be televised live. It is common today to watch evening news broadcasts that feature video clips of the day's trial proceedings or to have gavel to gavel coverage on local television or CourtTV. It is also common for jurors to grant interviews and even occasionally sell their stories following the trial. In the midst of the O. J. Simpson trial, for example, a juror was dismissed in mid-trial after it was discovered he was taking notes with plans to sell the inside story of the jury deliberations.[10]

LEGAL RESPONSES TO EXCESS PUBLICITY

A series of criminal cases beginning in the 1960s caused the Supreme Court to consider the effects of pretrial and mid-trial media coverage of criminal cases. The Indiana case of *Irvin v. Dowd* generated extensive media coverage.[11] Implicated in ten murders in rural communities, the defendant was tried and convicted. The case had been moved from one county to an adjoining county, but the Supreme Court noted that even though the jurors asserted that they could be fair and impartial, a "'pattern of deep and bitter prejudice' shown to be present throughout the community . . . was clearly reflected in the sum total of the *voir dire* examination of the majority of the jurors finally placed in the jury box." The Court asserted that statements of impartiality in such cases "can be given little weight." In *Rideau v. Louisiana*, the Supreme Court overturned a murder conviction after a movie tape with accompanying sound track of the defendant making a jailhouse confession was televised three times in the parish from which the jury had been chosen.[12]

In one of the most highly publicized cases up to that time, Sam Sheppard was convicted of brutally murdering his wife in 1954, despite the fact that he claimed an unknown intruder had killed her. Eventually, the United States Supreme Court reversed his conviction based on the "deluge of publicity" and the "carnival atmosphere" in which the trial took place.[13] Speaking for the Court majority, Justice Clark admonished, "Given the pervasiveness of modern communications and the difficulty of effacing prejudicial publicity from the minds of the jurors, trial courts must take strong measures to ensure the balance is never weighed against the accused."[14] (Sheppard was released after serving ten years in prison, tried again two years later and found not guilty. More than fifty years later there is debate about whether the first or the second jury "got it right.")[15]

Notably, however, in the 1991 case of *Mu'Min v. Virginia*, the Supreme Court placed on defendants a higher burden of demonstrating juror prejudice than might have been inferred from the case of Sam Sheppard.[16] Dawaud Mu'Min, already serving a sentence for first-degree murder, was convicted of slipping away from an outside-prison work detail and committing the double murder of an elderly couple. The case received a great deal of publicity, but the trial judge refused to question prospective jurors about their reactions to specific details of news reports to which they had been exposed. Chief Justice Rehnquist wrote an opinion upholding the trial judge's decision, ruling that although such questions might have been helpful, they were not required by the Due Process clause of the Sixth Amendment. *Mu'Min* thus leaves a great deal of latitude to the judge over the conduct of juror questioning.

A few examples will illustrate the problems of extraordinary publicity in both criminal and civil trials.

THE TIMOTHY McVEIGH TRIAL

Timothy McVeigh stood trial in 1997 on multiple charges related to the 1995 bombing of the Alfred P. Murrah Federal Building in Oklahoma City, Oklahoma in which 168 people, including 19 children, died.[17] During the nine months after the bombing, 939 articles about it appeared in the major Oklahoma City newspaper, and 105 of them were front-page stories.[18] A third of the stories were accompanied by pictures. Content analysis of the stories showed that they included many statements about the emotional impact of the bombing on survivors and the families of victims. During a pretrial hearing on a defense request to move McVeigh's trial because of the extensive negative publicity, experts presented the presiding judge, Richard Matsch, with the results of a public opinion survey. It revealed that people who lived close to the bombing site knew more about it, were more emotionally affected by it, were more negative about McVeigh, and were more likely to already have judged him guilty of the bombing.[19] Roughly half the survey respondents in the Oklahoma towns of Tulsa and Lawton said they were absolutely confident that McVeigh was guilty. The more that people knew about the case, the stronger their beliefs were that McVeigh was guilty.

In weighing the opinion polls and other evidence, Judge Matsch concluded that "the entire state had become a unified community, sharing the emotional trauma of those who had become directly victimized."[20] He further decided that Oklahomans were "united as a family," that there was "extraordinary provocation of their emotions of anger and vengeance," that there was "a prevailing belief that some action must be taken to make things right again," and that the common reference in articulating these feelings was "'seeing that justice is done.'" As a result, the trial was moved to Denver, Colorado, where McVeigh was convicted by a jury and sentenced to die. He was executed by lethal injection on June 11, 2001.

CHICKEN MANURE AND GARBAGE TRUCKS

Tulsa v. Tyson was a 2003 civil case in which the city of Tulsa, Oklahoma, sued Tyson Foods and four other Arkansas companies on the grounds that the excessive use of manure from their chicken farms as fertilizer on Arkansas fields caused nitrates from the fertilizer to leach into rivers, which ultimately contaminated a lake in Oklahoma. The lake is a main source of Tulsa's drinking water and a major recreational area.[21] The high costs of purifying the water were being borne by Tulsa's citizens. Tulsa newspaper and television media ran many stories blaming Tyson for the problem and emphasizing the costs to Tulsa's taxpayers. The trial was scheduled to be held in a federal court in Tulsa. A survey of Tulsa residents indicated not only high levels of awareness of the case but also considerable anger about the financial costs. In contrast, a survey of citizens of Wichita, Kansas, who were part of the same federal judicial district but had been exposed to much less publicity and whose taxes would not be affected, indicated low levels of knowledge and much less emotion about the dispute. The case was eventually settled, making the evidence moot, but the trial could have encountered significant issues of fairness if it had proceeded in Tulsa.

A similar problem arose in a 1991 North Carolina case.[22] A garbage truck belonging to the city of Durham caught fire, and the ensuing flames destroyed ten other trucks, creating losses of almost $2 million. The city sued the manufacturer and a maintenance company for its losses and asked for punitive damages. Durham newspapers extensively covered the garbage truck story because the trucks were self-insured and taxpayers would bear the burden of the loss. Based on affidavits (including one by Vidmar) and other evidence, the trial judge granted a motion to move the trial to another county on the grounds that jurors chosen from Durham would have a conflict of interest.

THE SOURCES AND EFFECTS OF PRETRIAL PREJUDICE

Studies examining how pretrial publicity affects jury decision making have discovered multiple avenues of influence.[23] One effect is that, compared to jurors who have not been exposed to pretrial publicity, those who read or watch substantial amounts of pretrial publicity about a case in the mass media are more prone to believe the defendant is guilty.

Mass media are not the sole source of the problem, however. Sociologist Kai Erikson has offered a profound insight about community reactions to crime: "The deviant act . . . creates a sense of mutuality among people of a community by supplying a focus for group feeling. Like a war, a flood, or some other emergency, deviance makes people more alert to the interests they share in common and draws attention to those values which constitute the 'collective conscience' of the community."[24] The group solidarity response is true to a degree for most crimes, but it is especially true when the crime is viewed as a general threat to community safety or values. The Oklahoma response to the McVeigh bombing, as articulated by Judge Matsch, is a prime example of community responses, but there are many other cases.

The killing of a two-year-old child in rural Ontario, Canada, evoked gossip and rumor about the accused parents, who were generally known and perceived as unsavory.[25] Invoking Canadian law, which differs from American law, his lawyer asked a judge to prohibit the publication of stories bearing on the details of the case before trial, so there was no media coverage after charges were filed against the parents. Nevertheless, when the case came to trial nearly two years later, many people had gained extensive knowledge about the case through gossip. A community survey showed that many people had discussed the case with family and neighbors. Some of these people held factually erroneous and highly pejorative beliefs about the child's death that had been gained through the gossip. Additionally, a number of people remarked about the shame that the killing had visited on their community; such awful crimes were supposed to happen only in big cities and not in their community with its strong family values.

In a 1991 Florida case, *Lozano v. State*, a riot resulted when a Hispanic police officer killed an African American motorcycle driver, creating problems for a fair trial in that community.[26] In short, pretrial prejudice can arise solely out of community responses, but they interact with the available media coverage to multiply the effects. Crime information and misinformation learned outside the courtroom can slant the jurors' view of the trial evidence.

Once they are seated as jurors, those who have been exposed to extensive negative and accusatory pretrial publicity tend to see the prosecution's evidence as stronger and to make more negative character assessments of the defendant, compared to those who have not been exposed to such publicity. Jurors begin to develop a narrative account of the evidence that more strongly favors guilt because they are more apt to selectively attend to the evidence that points toward guilt and to discount the evidence that points toward innocence. Consistent with their preexisting views, they tend to weigh prosecution evidence against the defendant more heavily and are more persuaded by pro-prosecution arguments during the jury deliberation.[27]

Psychological research on trial prejudice has distinguished between potentially biasing factual knowledge (such as the defendant having a criminal record that is not admissible at trial, or rumors of a confession) and beliefs that have strongly negative emotional content (for example, the gore-filled crime scene).[28] An experiment by British researchers illustrates how the biasing works. They conducted a simulation of the highly publicized English fraud trial of Kevin Maxwell, the well-known son of a wealthy deceased publisher and public personality.[29] Maxwell, his brother, and two other people were accused of conspiring to defraud the beneficiaries of company retirement funds, leaving hundreds of retired people practically destitute. In the actual trial, the defendants were acquitted, but many English citizens were very dissatisfied with the verdict.

Many months after the trial, the British researchers carried out research to explore the effects of attitudes on juror reasoning. Jury-eligible participants were interviewed to determine their recall of the case and then asked to participate as jurors in a six-hour video simulation of the trial, which used actors working from verbatim transcripts. The jurors also had copies of crucial documents from the trial. They were interviewed at four time periods during the video presentation and asked to describe their impressions of the evidence.

Recall of factual details of the Maxwell case had minimal influence on jurors' judgments about the trial evidence. Negative attitudes about Maxwell and the loss of pensions did have an effect, but in a complicated way. In the first interview period, jurors with greater degrees of negative emotion about the Maxwell case were not significantly different than those with lesser negative affect. However, as the trial progressed, a "sleeper effect" started to emerge. Jurors with negative feelings began to express reasoning that favored a conviction. By the end of the prosecution's case, their reasoning about guilt began to solidify, and the effect persisted after the defense presentation. The researchers hypothesized that these jurors had withheld judgment at the early stages of evidence presentation because they were waiting for more evidence before reaching a decision. This suggests that the jurors were not preemptively deciding guilt but rather that their negative emotions encouraged them to evaluate the evidence in a way that ultimately favored the prosecution.

A phenomenon known as *generic prejudice* may also come into play in high-profile cases.[30] Public attention to the issues of child abuse, including child pornography, sexual violations, and physical harm, gained widespread attention in the 1980s that continues to this day. At a 1990 symposium, Judge Abner Mikva coined the term *generic prejudice* and explained: "I do not think that you can get a fair child abuse trial before a jury anywhere in the country. [I] do not care how sophisticated or law smart jurors are, when they hear that a child has been abused, a piece of their mind closes up and this goes for the judge, the juror and all of us."[31] Whether or not Judge Mikva truly believed this always was true, his statement started social psychologists thinking about the issue.

Generic prejudice exists when a juror transfers general biases and prejudices about categories of persons or other matters to the trial setting. Stereotypes of a defendant—because of his race, religion, occupation, other personal characteristics, or the type of crime for which he is charged—may affect the way jurors perceive the evidence in the case.

Judge Mikva's assertion that child abuse might affect jury verdicts was supported in a study of actual jury trials.[32] In twenty-five Canadian criminal trials involving charges of sexual abuse, 849 prospective jurors were asked under oath whether they could hear the evidence, follow the judge's instructions on the law, and decide the case with an impartial mind. Knowing only the nature of the charges, on average 36 percent of the jurors in these trials stated that they could not be impartial. A recent study conducted with US citizens is consistent with the Canadian study.[33]

A defendant's race may give rise to generic prejudice to the extent that a juror believes that African Americans in general are prone to certain behaviors, like selling drugs, for example. Similarly, racial, ethnic, and religious backgrounds can trigger prejudicial attitudes toward people accused of terrorism in the wake of the 2001 terrorist attacks on the United States.

Generic prejudice can operate in civil cases too, where the nature or reputation of the business may be negative. Some respondents to the Tulsa survey in the chicken manure case had very strong negative impressions of the Tyson company and other large poultry producers. Some members of the public view large oil companies and tobacco companies as immoral corporations.

Taken together, numerous studies on the pretrial publicity and the psychology of prejudice indicate that pretrial publicity may have improper influences at various stages of the trial. Such publicity can prejudice jurors' initial assumptions about a defendant's guilt; improperly influence the evaluation of evidence through selective attention and the weighing of evidence so as to be consistent with preexisting biases; affect predeliberation verdict preferences; influence the initial distribution of juror verdicts; promote jury deliberations that enhance the initial biases of the jurors; and instigate a "rotten apple" effect, whereby one or more tainted jurors infect other jurors with emotional appeals during deliberation.

REMEDIES FOR PRETRIAL PUBLICITY

In recent years judges have worked to counter the protection the First Amendment to the Constitution gives to media coverage of American trials by exerting more control over what trial participants say to the media. They increasingly issue gag orders that prohibit the trial lawyers and other participants from discussing inflammatory aspects of the case before and during the trial. They may also seal motions and evidence on grounds of national security or for other reasons so that no one can read or report what has transpired. Thus, some potentially informative, prejudicial, or exculpatory material is unavailable to the public.

As in the Merck lawsuit over the drug Vioxx, judges may consider a trial delay to allow passions to cool or memories to fade. However, in a high-profile case, whenever the trial eventually begins, an upsurge of renewed media coverage will likely take place, reproducing the original problem. Broad Internet access to older news stories also lessens the value of trial delays.

Another option, used in the McVeigh bombing trial, is a change of venue, moving the trial's location from a jurisdiction that has extensive media coverage and other evidence of community prejudice to a more neutral community whose members are less likely to have already formed opinions about the case. Especially in cases where the media coverage has been localized, this can be a good option.

But there are strong arguments for keeping a trial in the jurisdiction where the crime or injury occurred. Historically, trials have always been local matters, a fact enshrined in the Sixth Amendment right to trial by jury in criminal cases. Witnesses and other trial participants can attend with greater ease. And if justice must also be seen to be done, having a trial in the jurisdiction in which a crime or injury occurred makes sense. The local community usually has the greatest stake in the trial's outcome. Its members have suffered the injury or been victimized, and their desires to see retribution or compensation are often paramount. Jurors who come from the same community as the defendant and victim or plaintiff possess a richer understanding of the local norms and environmental context of the dispute. So, history, law, efficiency, legitimacy, and sound fact-finding all point toward the desirability of keeping a trial in the jurisdiction in which the dispute or crime occurred.

Not surprisingly, then, even in the face of substantial pretrial publicity and evidence of strong local community prejudice, judges are highly reluctant to move the trial to another community. The expense and inconvenience of a change of venue, and the community's possible loss of access to trial proceedings, must be weighed against the likelihood of jury bias. Often, the judge will therefore decide to stay put, expressing faith in a vigorous jury selection process to eliminate biased jurors and the efficacy of judicial instructions to be impartial. Changes of venue remain rare.

The judge can also sequester the jury, having the jurors live at a hotel at public expense during the entire trial or during the jury deliberations. In this way, the judge can more tightly control the media exposure and outside influence that a jury receives about the case. The O. J. Simpson jury was sequestered for that lengthy trial, and the many books written about the trial reflect the jurors' unhappiness with the forced separation from home, work, family, and friends.[34] And it may not have worked. The lead prosecutor in the O. J. case, Marcia Clark, wrote about her suspicions that much outside information was transmitted to the sequestered O. J. jurors during family weekends: "The proceedings were being broadcast, so their families could hear and see it all. I shuddered to think what information they were imparting to their sequestered loved ones during visiting hours…". Jury sequestration has fallen out of favor largely because of the extraordinary stress and disruption it causes for jurors. It also seriously compromises the representativeness of juries, since many people are unable to be completely away from their jobs and families for an extended time. Indeed, defendants who might reasonably push for sequestration sometimes refrain for fear that jurors will hold the sequestration against them.

The favored remedy is the voir dire. Judges tend to place great faith in the voir dire process. They argue that it is effective, especially when it is supplemented by instructions to avoid media coverage during the trial. This way the jurors will focus only on the trial evidence and disregard anything they have learned from outside sources. Additionally, they argue that jurors take an oath to be fair and impartial and that during deliberations the jurors will correct one another in evaluating the evidence and applying the law. The faith is probably justified in ordinary cases with adequate voir dire, but special problems arise in the exceptional cases.

Professor Edward Bronson studied the voir dire in a case that had extensive pretrial publicity.[35] In a small Florida town a brutal killing occurred in 1978. News reports indicated that a nineteen-year-old white woman had been abducted from the convenience store where she had been working. Residents of the community were frightened. The victim's body was found, and news reports quoted the sheriff as saying the woman had been raped. Johnny Copeland and two codefendants, all African Americans, were arrested and charged with armed robbery, kidnapping, and first-degree murder. The prosecutor sought the death penalty. Newspaper and television stories carried items that listed details of the defendants' prior criminal records, which included burglary, two robberies, an attempted robbery and a stolen van—all of which had been committed when the accused were under the age of eighteen. Other stories were similarly strongly suggestive of the defendants' guilt.

Research conducted by the defense revealed that the crime generated a great deal of informal gossip in the community. The findings indicated that hostility was widespread and that many people already assumed the defendants' guilt. Comments were often openly racist as in the following examples: "It's a shame all those niggers come down from Tallahassee and commit crimes," "They ought to lynch those niggers," "They ought to be hung in front of the courthouse," and "People are ready to take the jail apart . . . they better not get turned loose." The surveys estimated that 99 percent of the residents had heard of the case. Many residents knew the victim or her family, and nearly three-quarters of the study participants expressed anger, racist attitudes, presumptions of guilt, or other biases. As one respondent said, "Well, people here were very upset. They have very strong feelings about this death and the way the defendants have been handled. They have been handled too good." Despite inflamed community sentiment, the trial judge refused to grant Johnny Copeland a change of venue. (Copeland was convicted after a four-day trial, and the jury recommended death after one hour of deliberation. His sentence was eventually commuted to life in 1992; in 2006 he was still an inmate in the Florida prison system.)

Sometimes the questioning of jurors during jury selection is done individually and outside the presence of the whole jury pool, a method that is better suited to probing attitudes, as we described earlier. Often, however, the questioning takes place in the courtroom, as noted earlier, with the full panel present. This poses the problem of jurors learning what they are expected to say as they watch other jurors being questioned and challenged.[36] The Copeland trial voir dire was conducted with all the potential jury members present. Some jurors conceded their biases, but a striking number of jurors displayed what Professor Bronson labeled the "minimization effect," that is, the use of vocabulary to suggest that the person has little knowledge of the case. One juror said, for example, "*Only* thing I have read is what's in the newspaper," later adding, "I didn't read all of it; I *just* glanced at [the paper]." Another said, "I've heard it discussed and I read *some* but not a whole lot." Still another said about her exposure to the news, "*Not much*, just newspaper and television coverage" and "*only* what might have been in the *Democrat* [a local newspaper]." Thus, despite almost overwhelming evidence of widespread hostile community feeling about the defendants, Professor Bronson found continual use of words like "just," "only," "that's all," and "nothing but."

Minimization responses are not necessarily conscious lies. One problem that we have already alluded to is the strong possibility that some jurors may not recognize how their biases—arising from pretrial publicity and community gossip—affect their ability to be fair and impartial. Striking examples come from research on pretrial juror attitudes in two cases involving charges of terrorism.

THE "AMERICAN TALIBAN" CASE

Contemporary terrorism trials occur in an explosive social and political context, deeply influenced by the September 11, 2001, al Qaeda attacks on New York City's World Trade Center, the Pentagon Building in Washington, and the aborted attempt on the White House that resulted in a plane crash in western Pennsylvania.[37] The memory of the September 11 attacks is repeatedly refreshed by public leaders in the United States, who continue to warn about ongoing threats from terrorist organizations. As a result, it's fair to say that many Americans today consider themselves to be actual or potential victims of terrorist activity. This sense of victimization encompasses not only physical harm but also extends to a threat against deeply held personal and political values held by most Americans.

A young American, John Walker Lindh, was captured along with others fighting with the Taliban in Afghanistan during the US invasion of that country. CNN and other national media sources saw him being interrogated in Afghanistan by a CIA agent, Johnny "Mike" Spann. Shortly after his interrogation, an uprising of captured Taliban members occurred, and many of the prisoners temporarily escaped. Lindh hid with them but was recaptured. Agent Spann was killed during the uprising.

Lindh was sent back to the United States and indicted on multiple charges of conspiracy to murder US citizens, providing support to al Qaeda, and providing services to the Taliban.[38] He was scheduled for trial in Federal Court in the Northern District of Virginia, Alexandria Division—nine miles from the Pentagon—and in the home region where Agent Spann's family lived. Many US officials, including President Bush and then Attorney General John Ashcroft, had made widely publicized comments on the Lindh case. In preparation for jury selection, the defense attorneys commissioned a public opinion survey about Lindh in an attempt to get a change of venue.[39] Surveys were carried out in the Northern District of Virginia and four alternate venues.

The survey data from the Northern District of Virginia showed that many people knew someone injured or killed in the Pentagon attack, that many feared a future attack that would affect the members of their families, and that many had strong opinions that Mr. Lindh was guilty. Seventy-four percent of respondents said, however, that they could be fair and impartial jurors for his upcoming trial. These people were also asked to explain in their own words why they believed they could be impartial, and many gave explanations such as "[Guilt] must be proven with facts" or "I believe in the system and everyone should have a fair trial."

For many of the survey respondents, however, their statements of impartiality were belied by other responses to survey questions. Consider two examples:

> *Respondent #165* asserted she could be impartial in deciding Mr. Lindh's guilt or innocence and explained why by saying, "It must be proven with facts." Yet in response to an earlier question in the interview, this woman indicated that she had a "strongly unfavorable" impression of Mr. Lindh, she had asserted that "he is a traitor," that he was "definitely guilty," that "he killed Americans and should be shot." She further said that if a trial by judge and jury were to find Mr. Lindh not guilty, the verdict would be "very unacceptable." Finally, this woman also said that Lindh should experience "death by hanging" for the reason that "I want him to feel pain."

> *Respondent # 506* also said he could be an impartial juror by explaining, "I believe in the system and that everyone should have a fair trial." But similar to comments by Respondent #165, other interview responses raised questions about his openness of mind. He said Mr. Lindh was a "punk-a traitor" who was "definitely guilty" because "they captured him with a gun in his hand where [a] CIA agent was killed." This respondent further stated that if a trial by judge and jury found the accused not guilty, he would find the verdict "very unacceptable."

Thirty-five percent of those who professed impartiality as a potential juror gave responses similar to these two examples. This finding raises questions about whether people were giving socially desirable answers or whether they actually did not see the relationship between their beliefs and feelings and their ability to be impartial. And, the inconsistency in their answers raises questions similar to those in the Johnny Copeland trial in Florida. Despite the survey findings and other evidence, the judge denied a motion for a change of venue. Before jury selection got under way, Mr. Lindh pleaded guilty to a number of the charges and was sentenced to nineteen years in prison.

The Lindh research findings have additional implications. Responses from the surveys in four other areas of the country yielded responses roughly similar to those from Virginia, both in intensity and in underlying beliefs. People felt a strong sense of anger toward Mr. Lindh and his association with terrorism. Their responses also indicated that the events of September 11 had created a sense of cultural as well as physical threat. Just as Judge Matsch concluded that everyone in Oklahoma was affected by the McVeigh bombing, it is fair to suggest that, as noted above, the September 11 terrorist attacks have made many Americans feel a sense of victimization. This, of course, raises a question of whether anyone accused of acts of terrorism today can receive a fair trial. Let's consider a second case.

THE TRIAL OF SAMI AL-ARIAN

Beginning in the early 1990s, a Kuwaiti-born, US-educated, University of South Florida computer science professor, Sami Al-Arian, began to generate considerable controversy in his local Tampa Bay community because of his support for and involvement in Palestinian causes.[40] He formed several pro-Palestinian groups. One of these, officials in Israel and the United States asserted, was linked to the terrorist organization called the Palestinian Islamic Jihad, which claimed responsibility for suicide bombings in Israel.[41] In 1996, he was put on paid leave from the University of South Florida during a two-year investigation of his possible ties to terrorist front organizations, but he was never charged. He continued to publicly support Palestinian causes, created and raised money for Palestinian charities, and often used inflammatory rhetoric about Israel and about US policy in the Middle East. A spirited debate over the handling of his case erupted in a Florida senate race in which the former president of the University of South Florida, Betty Castor, was a candidate. Al-Arian had also appeared as a guest on the popular Fox Network news show *The O'Reilly Factor*. During the show, conservative host Bill O'Reilly openly called Dr. Al-Arian a terrorist.

In the wake of the 9/11 bombings and many public complaints about Al-Arian's continuing presence on campus, the university suspended Al-Arian with pay, on the grounds of campus safety. Ultimately, he was fired in 2003 after a federal indictment charged him with being an Islamic Jihad leader, running a criminal enterprise, and conspiring to injure and kill others overseas.[42] He faced trial with several codefendants, all charged with fronting for the Palestinian Islamic Jihad.

The defense hired jury experts to examine the extent of pretrial publicity and community opinions about Sami Al-Arian and his codefendants. The experts strongly urged that the trial's location be moved.[43] Professor Edward Bronson, who wrote about the Johnny Copeland case and who has been involved in many other high-profile trials, including that of Timothy McVeigh, analyzed public opinion surveys that had been commissioned by one of the other defendants. Those surveys found that 96 percent of the respondents from Tampa recognized the case against Mr. Al-Arian.[44] Of those who recognized the case, 55 percent believed that he was definitely or probably guilty of the crimes charged.[45] Many respondents also described him as a terrorist.[46] Open-ended comments showed hostility and vehemence toward Al-Arian and revealed a strong presumption that he was dangerous and guilty as charged.[47] Compared to the Tampa survey, polls conducted in three other Florida cities and in Atlanta, Georgia (also in the same federal district), showed much lower levels of case recognition and presumptions of guilt.[48]

Jury questionnaires, distributed by the judge as part of the initial screening process for jury selection, were analyzed by one of the present authors (Vidmar).[49] The questionnaire consisted of eighty-three questions and required the jurors to answer under oath. The answers of some jurors revealed extensive prejudice against the defendants in the case. Dr. Al-Arian's local notoriety, his ethnic background, his Muslim religion, and his publicized associations with Palestinian causes all created a strong presumption of guilt among many potential jurors. Here is an example taken from one of the juror questionnaires:

> Juror 316: "I feel they are both guilty of terrorism acts against the U.S.; I feel Al-Arian is a threat either directly or indirectly to the U.S. citizens, and that he is guilty of the crimes as charged. Yes, my opinions are formed and extremely unlikely to change; What I've read/heard points to Al-Arian's guilt when he's labeled a terrorist. Yes, it is very difficult to be impartial. I am biased; He is guilty. Reports on the defendant's connection to terrorist organizations, money laundering charges, monies paid to individuals to carry out suicide attacks; There are reasons why I could not be impartial; Terrorism charges are hard to swallow after 9/11; if you live in America you should not be involved in activities that are harmful to American citizens."[50]

Question 81 on the juror questionnaire asked: "Is there any reason you could not be fair to the defendants in this case?" and question 82 asked them to explain why. Of the 388 potential jurors who returned the questionnaire, 112 frankly stated that they could not be impartial in response to these two questions for reasons reflected in the examples given above. However, another seventeen jurors who asserted that they could be impartial in response to question 81 gave answers like the following to earlier items on the questionnaire:

> Juror 067: I saw newscasts, read it in the newspaper and heard it on the radio. I did not think it was right for Dr. Al-Arian to remain employed at USF with such

> serious allegations against him. . . . There were allegations that stated that Betty Castor knew Al-Arian was a terrorist supporter. I feel that it was wrong to fund terrorist groups. I don't think I would be impartial because I have heard too much about Dr. Sami Al-Arian. I already have an impression he funded terrorist groups.[51]

> Juror 204: I believe on what I have seen on TV, he should have been arrested a long time before he was. Yes, I think he is 99.9 percent likely to be guilty of what he is charged with based on what I have seen, heard, and read on TV and in the newspaper.[52]

> Juror 480: I have a daughter attending USF in Tampa and the jerk was a professor there. . . . I saw him all sweaty and screaming with laundry wrapped on his head on those film clips. Looked obvious to me. . . . What I've read and seen in the media you can take my vote now and save all that taxpayer money. . . . Remember 9/11?[53]

Juror 480's comment illustrates another finding from the juror questionnaire that was not uncommon among jurors who said they were unable to judge the case with an impartial mind, namely that they revealed stereotyped or negative beliefs and attitudes toward Muslims, Palestinians, and Arabs. About half of all the jurors who returned the questionnaire expressed the view that members of such groups were more violent than other ethnic groups.[54]

Other potential jurors expressed fears for their safety. Juror 280 said, "Due to the nature of the case, I would potentially fear for the safety of self and family." Juror 343 asked: "What if these defendants are found guilty? What about retaliation against the jurors? What's to stop their terrorist affiliates from coming after us? Or bombing the courthouse, etc.?" Similarly, Juror 367 wrote, "I think the biggest fear of people to serve on this jury will be reprisal. How do you know if you are in harm's way from these people? I feel intimidated." Juror 422 said: "If these men are guilty and associated with terrorists how safe will it be for myself and family?"

Despite these findings, Judge Moody, presiding over the Al-Arian trial, ultimately rejected the defense motion to move the trial outside of Tampa.[55] However, he deviated from common procedures in federal trials in which the judge alone conducts a brief voir dire on prospective jurors. After conducting some preliminary questioning himself, he allowed both defense and prosecution lawyers to conduct further questioning. A number of jurors were dismissed on hardship grounds because of the expected length of the trial, and other jurors were dismissed for cause or through peremptory challenges. The final jury consisted of twelve people plus four alternates.

The trial lasted six months. The government produced over one hundred witnesses, many flown in from Israel specifically for the trial. Other evidence consisted of hours of surreptitious Federal Bureau of Investigation wiretaps of conversations involving Mr. Al-Arian and other defendants. After the prosecution closed its case, Mr. Al-Arian's defense counsel, William Moffitt and Linda Moreno, concluded that the prosecution's case was so weak that there was no need to call defense evidence. After final arguments and judicial instructions, the case was placed in the hands of the jury. After thirteen days of deliberations, the jury rejected the charges that Mr. Al-Arian and the three codefendants operated a North American cell for Palestinian Islamic Jihad. The jury unanimously found Mr. Al-Arian not guilty of conspiring to commit murder abroad, money laundering, and obstruction of justice; it could not reach consensus on other counts against him. Two of the other defendants were acquitted of all charges; a third was found not guilty of the main charges. The jury could not reach consensus on the remaining charges.[56]

There is no way of determining for sure if the Al-Arian case would have turned out differently without the findings from the surveys and jury questionnaire as interpreted by the experts. It does seem unlikely that the judge would have been as flexible in the voir dire process. And without the voir dire it is quite likely that some of the jurors chosen for the trial would have harbored strong feelings against the defendants that might have tilted the jury toward guilt or resulted in a hung jury, even with what appeared to be a weak case for the prosecution.

THOUGHTS ON TRIAL PREJUDICE

Certain crimes raise special problems for jury trials. The problem is not just mass media coverage but the concomitant underlying sociological and social psychological reactions to those crimes. The Vioxx, Tulsa, and Durham cases we described indicate that problems arise as well in trials involving civil disputes. Issues of race have always posed problems, especially when the events evoke strong emotional reactions in the media and the community, as exemplified by the Johnny Copeland trial. An important review of forty-four empirical studies concluded that people exposed to negative publicity in criminal cases were more likely to judge defendants guilty than people with little or no exposure.[57]

Yet research on the subject of pretrial publicity has too often focused only on the direct effects of mass media exposure. A number of the examples in this chapter indicate that civil or criminal events that affect community values are likely to cause gossip and the formation of community solidarity against a trial participant that operates both independently of and in conjunction with the newspaper, television, and radio coverage. In short, such cases involve sociological as well as psychological elements. Increasingly the Internet may also contribute to pretrial prejudice problems through blogs, commentary, court documents, and case stories. The central questions for judges and lawyers for these exceptional cases are the degree to which the publicity has tainted the potential jury population, and then which judicial remedy or remedies will best ensure a fair trial.

We have drawn attention to the special problem of trials of people accused of being terrorists or supporting terrorists. In the wake of 9/11 there exists suspicion and hostility toward those of Arab, Pakistani, or other ethnic backgrounds combined with religious prejudice against Muslims. Both of these factors are inextricably associated in some people's minds with terrorism.

The Al-Arian case indicates that it is possible to have a positive outcome for the defendant in such cases. Indeed, some might argue that the outcome is strong evidence that even in a highly charged trial where community prejudice is widespread, an impartial jury can be seated. The real test, though, is whether all of the evidence is weighed impartially, uninfluenced by pretrial prejudice, and the verdict fairly decided. Perhaps, in a less hostile community, Al-Arian and his codefendants might have been acquitted on all counts. In some circumstances, the change of venue remedy used in the McVeigh case may have to be combined with extended voir dire procedures to achieve a just trial process in cases with extensive pretrial publicity.

Chapter 6

THE TASKS OF THE JURY

Evidence Evaluation and Jury Decision-Making Processes

What does the legal system ask juries to do? How is evidence presented to the jury, and what constraints are placed upon the presentation of the evidence? How does the jury evaluate and integrate the evidence to reach its verdict? These questions need to be addressed. Without an understanding of the legal context in which jury decisions are made, jury performance cannot be fairly evaluated.

DECIDING HISTORICAL FACTS

Juries are asked to decide an incredibly varied array of disputes concerning both criminal and civil matters. Consider the bare bones issues from typical cases that juries hear.

Case 1. A man broke into the apartment of a sleeping woman and sexually assaulted her at knifepoint. In a police lineup the victim identified the defendant as the assailant. The accused person claimed that it was a case of mistaken identity; he was not the assailant. There is no question that the crime was committed; the jury must decide if the accused was the assailant.

Case 2. The executive officers of a large corporation were charged with fraudulent accounting practices that resulted in inflated stock prices. Each of them was enriched by millions of dollars before the scheme was discovered and the company was forced into bankruptcy. The defendants assert that their actions were consistent with standard business practices and that the fall in the prices of the stock was a direct result of market pressures greatly exacerbated by the criminal charges. The jury must decide if the accounting practices were fraudulent and whether they were adopted to inflate the stock price.

Case 3. A college student purchased a rifle and ammunition and hid them in his room. Two weeks later he walked onto the campus and killed two students before being apprehended by the police. At trial he pleaded not guilty by reason of insanity, asserting that he believed that the police were listening to his thoughts through his television set. In conflicting expert testimony, the prosecution's expert witness concluded that the student likely knew right from wrong, while the defense psychiatrist asserted the opposite. The jury must decide if the student's account is believable, assess the expert testimony, and determine whether an insanity verdict is merited.

Case 4. A woman claims that during her nine years of marriage she was subject to numerous physical assaults by her husband. She was forbidden to leave the house without her husband's permission and had no access to money. One day while her husband was sleeping in a drunken stupor she took a kitchen knife and stabbed her husband to death. Charged with the killing, she pleaded self-defense. The jury must decide if the woman's claims are credible and, if so, the degree to which her beliefs mitigate or excuse her action.

Case 5. A young man was convicted of murder in the death of an elderly friend and faced the possibility of capital punishment. His defense at the death penalty hearing raised the facts that he was of borderline intelligence, that he had been brutally physically and sexually abused by his stepfather since he was a toddler, and that he was now remorseful for the act. The jury must weigh these mitigating factors against any aggravating factors associated with the killing and decide if his life should be spared.

This list could be expanded into hundreds, even thousands, of examples, but these illustrative cases vary in instructive ways. In some cases a crime occurs, but the defendant asserts that someone else did it. In some cases the issue is whether a crime occurred at all—the defendant says it was an accident, that the behavior was in self-defense, that the actions were within the bounds of acceptable business practices, or that the complainant consented to sex. In other trials, the defendant asserts that ordinarily it would have been a crime, but he or she lacked the mental capacity to distinguish right from wrong. Or the defendant admits to engaging in a crime but one involving a lesser degree of culpability such as second- rather than first-degree homicide. The defendant may plead diminished capacity. In the death penalty hearing, the issue is whether the defendant merits a death sentence.

Evidence in typical trials may include testimony about facts observed by civilian witnesses, expert opinions about such matters as entry wounds, blood spatter, fingerprints, and mental state, documents and other physical evidence and testimony by the defendant and the victim. The type and volume of evidence differ according to the issues in the case, legal strategies, and judicial rulings about admissibility of evidence.

The common thread running through all of the examples is that in each of them, the jury is charged with deciding about a historical event. Was the defendant at the scene and did he commit the rape? Did the stockbroker think the company's accounting followed accepted business standards? Did the college student believe that voices in his head told him to kill people? Did the woman judge at that time that her life and those of her children were in danger? The prosecutor in each case presents evidence and arguments supporting one conclusion, and the defense presents evidence and arguments supporting an opposite conclusion. During deliberations, the jury has to evaluate these conflicting stories, decide which is most likely correct, and render a verdict.

Civil juries also reconstruct history. One of their jobs is to decide liability, but they are given additional tasks. Consider these examples:

Case 6. The driver of a Honda Civic was severely injured as a result of a collision with a Ford Explorer. The Civic driver sued the Explorer driver, seeking $500,000 in damages. At trial the jury was asked to decide whether actual negligence occurred, to allocate the percent of responsibility each driver had for the accident and, if it found that the Explorer driver was to some degree negligent, to determine an amount of monetary damages to compensate the Civic driver for medical costs, lost wages, and pain and suffering.

Case 7. A truck negligently changed lanes, causing a collision that injured the driver of an automobile. The truck company and its driver admitted negligence but contested the plaintiff's claim of $170,000 in damages, arguing that the automobile driver's medical injuries were minimal and merited only $7,325. The defense argued that the plaintiff's alleged back pain and depression was the result of a preexisting condition due to a previous accident five years earlier. A doctor hired by the defense examined the plaintiff and gave testimony in court, followed by the plaintiff's doctor who testified on his behalf. The jury must assess the conflicting assessments of the cause and seriousness of the injury and arrive at a damage award.

Case 8. The plaintiff willingly dissolved his business relationship with his two partners with an understanding that he would receive a fair financial settlement from their various joint enterprises. He subsequently sued the partners for understating the fair market value of condominiums developed and held during their joint activities and for fraudulently excluding certain other equities. He asserted a claim for $45 million. The partners denied the claim and countersued, alleging fraud on the part of their former partner. Now the jury must sort out the competing claims.

Case 9. A woman sued her surgeon, her anesthesiologist, and a hospital, claiming that their actions breached standards of professional care, resulting in her severe and irreversible brain damage that paralyzed the left side of her body and required lifetime nursing home care. The hospital settled for $1.3 million prior to trial. The two physicians remained in the lawsuit and denied liability for the injury, leaving the jury to settle the question of whether their treatment violated professional standards.

Case 10. A thirty-two-year-old tradesman sprayed a polyurethane adhesive on a roof prior to setting roof tiles. The chemical vapors injured his eyes and lungs. The man sued the manufacturer for failing to warn of safety needs such as goggles, gloves, and a respirator. The manufacturer denied liability on the grounds that the workman was a trained professional and that the standard procedure for applying any such chemical is to wear protective devices. The jury must assess whether the injuries were caused by the chemicals and must determine the proper duties of the manufacturer and worker.

Civil juries also render verdicts in cases involving claims such as patent or trademark infringement; civil rights violations; slander and libel; the amount of money a state government must compensate a landowner for taking land; and mass injuries that claim the lives of hundreds or thousands from such causes as plane crashes, asbestos exposure, and cigarette smoking. Plaintiffs or defendants can include individuals, corporations, unions, nonprofit groups, governments, or the estates of deceased persons. There can be dozens of plaintiffs and multiple defendants as well as cross-claims and counterclaims.

The issues of liability can include determining the direct cause of an injury, identification of those responsible, deciding whether the defendant was careless or reckless or intended harm, and assessing whether the plaintiff was to some extent responsible for the injury. Claims for damages may include past and future medical expenses; past and future income losses; general damages including emotional distress, disfigurement, pain and suffering; and punitive damages. A single business dispute might include multiple claims involving, for instance, breach of contract, fraud, and punitive damages.

The civil jury's tasks often extend to deciding sanctions or remedies, and these decisions are often controversial. Punitive damages are allowed in some civil trials and in most states they take place in a separate hearing in front of the jury that held the defendant liable. In this phase of the trial, juries are presented with factual evidence about past behavior and likely future behavior by the defendant. They may also be told of the impact of the defendant's behavior on victims. In this sense the process in a punitive damages case is similar to the penalty hearing in a capital trial.

Before turning to the question of how the jury puts these historical facts together and attempts to make sense of them, we must briefly consider the process by which the facts are actually presented to the jury. The process is extraordinary and critical to any evaluation of the jury.

LEGAL FACTS AND ADVERSARY PROCEDURE

Legal scholars have long drawn attention to the fact that criminal and civil trials are not exclusively about finding truth. In fact, truth is often elusive. The jury considers the competing versions of the facts presented by the parties and arrives at a verdict in line with the burden of proof. In criminal trials, the well-known standard for convicting an accused person is "beyond a reasonable doubt." In civil trials, the plaintiff's burden is usually set at "the preponderance of evidence" (sometimes rephrased as "the balance of probabilities" or "more likely than not"), that is, a greater than fifty percent likelihood that the defendant is responsible for the injury. However, in some instances, such as when a jury is asked to decide whether punitive damages are warranted by a defendant's conduct, the burden may be set higher, at "clear and convincing evidence." None of the verbal formulas for these burdens of proof is clear, and juries report struggling with what is meant by such terms as "beyond a reasonable doubt."[1]

Trials have the additional goal of providing the parties and society as a whole with a sense that the procedure is fair and that justice has been done. This sense of procedural justice is important to the trial's legitimacy. Social psychologist Tom Tyler has shown the substantial value of a sense of procedural justice.[2] Litigants are more likely to accept the trial's outcome if they believe the procedure was fair. Likewise, a sense of procedural justice enhances the broader legitimacy of the justice system.

The American trial, whether by jury or by a judge deciding alone, is based on the assumption that the best way to achieve these multiple goals is to allow the disputing parties themselves to gather their own evidence and then present that evidence at trial in an adversarial format with judge and jury serving as passive, neutral arbiters.[3] The juror's formal role is as an observer of the proceedings.

In most settings outside of the common law courtroom, decision makers actively search for the evidence they think they need; obtain and evaluate it; gather additional information if they see important gaps; and then make a decision. In contrast, jurors depend on both sides to present the facts that they need. Furthermore, restrictions are placed on how they may consider those facts. After being seated in the jury box and sworn, jurors in most courts are told that they cannot discuss the case—even with their fellow jurors and even if the trial lasts many weeks or months—until all the evidence and arguments are presented by both sides and the judge has given them instructions on the law. In the classic jury movie from the 1950s, *Twelve Angry Men*, the juror played by actor Henry Fonda visits the neighborhood of the crime and buys a knife like the one used in the murder. But the American adversary system officially forbids this sort of unsupervised inquiry into a crime. To maintain their neutral, passive fact finder role, jurors are not supposed to gather evidence on their own. The law's ideal juror is a blank slate on which only attorneys can write.

An interesting departure from the overall rule of strict passivity is that in recent years, some courts now permit jurors, under carefully controlled circumstances, to ask questions of witnesses during the trial. When questions are allowed, jurors must usually write their questions out and submit them to the judge, who decides, after hearing any arguments that attorneys might offer, if the questions are legally permissible and whether they should be posed.[4] Even this active participation of the jury is conducted within the adversarial strictures of the trial.

The jury's predominantly passive role within adversary procedure stands in contrast to most European countries. Under what is called "inquisitorial" procedure typical of civil law countries, a judge or group of judges and their assistants may investigate the claims of the two parties, call witnesses, and conduct the examination of witnesses, all in the process of reaching a decision. John Jackson and Nikolay Kovalev's survey of European criminal procedure for serious criminal offenses describes an alternative that involves lay citizens: the mixed tribunal, in which judges and laypersons (called lay assessors or lay judges) decide together on the verdict and sentence.[5]

In addition to being adversarial, the American trial is primarily an oral proceeding. Even physical evidence, such as the alleged murder weapon or a document bearing on a contract, is typically introduced by a witness who interprets its meaning, unless the parties agree otherwise. For many years, jurors were discouraged or forbidden to take notes. This proscription was based on two main assumptions. The first was that if jurors took notes, they might pay less attention to the demeanor and credibility of the witnesses who gave oral testimony. The second assumption was that during deliberations, jurors who took notes might be more persuasive than those who did not. Note takers might even mislead the jury if their notes were incorrect. The opposition to note taking has been largely abandoned over the past two decades, in part because research has disputed the assumptions that attention to the witnesses is negatively affected and that note taking jurors are unduly persuasive.[6] Today, in many trials jurors are allowed, sometimes encouraged, to take notes on what they see and hear in the oral proceedings.

The trial typically begins with opening statements by both sides. In their openings, the opposing lawyers outline the evidence they will call at trial and how this evidence supports their client's claims. Often they'll attempt to fit the evidence into a story of the case, though evidence that questions the opponent's version of events may also be emphasized. Next, the prosecutor (in criminal cases) or the plaintiff (in civil trials) may call witnesses. The lawyers have almost total discretion in deciding the order in which their witnesses are called. Even if a certain witness might have relevant facts, lawyers usually have the discretion not to call that person if it might harm their client's case (although there is a risk that the other side might call that witness). After each witness testifies, the opposing lawyer is entitled (but not required) to cross-examine and challenge the details of the testimony or the witness's competence or integrity. Following cross-examination, the first lawyer may conduct a brief reexamination of the witness to clarify or rebut testimony. At the judge's discretion, further cross-examination or redirect may be allowed.

Laws of evidence exclude certain information that is potentially relevant to deciding the case but is deemed too prejudicial or violates other legal values. A rape complainant's prior sexual history may be excluded. Information improperly withheld in pretrial proceedings may be banned, as may documents that enjoy the protection of a privilege—state secrets, for example.

Unlike a prosecutor or a plaintiff, the defendant can win its case without presenting any evidence. The defendant simply needs to challenge, successfully, the case presented by the other side. For this reason, defendants sometimes present no case of their own. If the defendant has a criminal record, there is an additional reason to stay off the stand. If defendants testify, their criminal record can be used to impeach their credibility as witnesses. Judges instruct the jury that the criminal record should not be used as proof of guilt in the present crime, but it is a psychologically naive rule. Not surprisingly, research studies, like the one mentioned earlier by Hans and Doob, find that despite such instructions jurors who hear about a criminal record are more likely to assume the defendant is guilty.[7] But refraining from offering a defense case is a risky proposition. Jurors express a strong preference to hear the defendant's version of events.[8]

At the conclusion of the defense evidence, each side has the opportunity to offer closing arguments in which they try to explain what the evidence means for their client's case, in light of the law that the jury will be instructed to apply.

There are several important points to be made from this brief synopsis. First, the facts presented to the jurors are not necessarily presented in the order in which events happened. For tactical reasons, a lawyer may arrange the appearance of a particular witness for dramatic effect or necessity. A physician may describe the horrible condition of a brain-damaged child before jurors learn about the event that led to the injury; or an expert witness may be available only on a particular day. Second, the evidence is likely to be incomplete. The jury may find that an important part of the puzzle is missing and be forced to speculate about it.

Another challenge comes from the jury's task in reconstruction of historical events. When jurors—and judges too, for that matter—attempt to look back in time and gauge an actor's thoughts and motivations, the "hindsight bias" may affect them.[9] This psychological phenomenon refers to the fact that in hindsight, the likelihood of a particular outcome seems higher after it has occurred than before it has occurred. Like Monday morning quarterbacking, jurors may assume that the actor knew or should have anticipated that a particular outcome would occur when in truth the actor did not.

After this often fragmented, disjointed, and disputed presentation of evidence and arguments, the judge instructs the jury on the law. The jurors then retire to the jury room to decide what it all means and deliver a verdict. The individual jurors become a jury. How do they go about their task? Over the past twenty-five years or so, researchers have gained considerable insight into how the process operates.

JURORS' CONSTRUCTION OF STORIES FROM ADVERSARIAL PRESENTATIONS OF FACTS

In 1981 two political scientists, Lance Bennett and Martha Feldman,[10] drew attention to the fact that when lawyers describe how they will present their cases at trial, they frequently begin by saying, "Our story is . . ." In further research the two scientists examined how opposing lawyers attempt to focus the trial around forms of stories to persuade the jurors that their version of events is correct. The point is to develop consistent narratives that explain how and why the events at issue happened. Bennett and Feldman tested their hypotheses by observing trials and conducting a study that provided insights about the rules of story communication. Based on their research, they concluded that at the heart of trials were conflicting stories. Each side attempted to develop a story, or sometimes alternative stories, that were consistent with the position that favored them in the dispute. They also argued that jurors probably processed information in terms of the conflicting narratives, although they did not directly investigate juror decision making. Bennett and Feldman hypothesized that individual jurors would develop their narratives from the trial evidence based upon their own life experiences and biases. To reach a verdict, the jury would have to test different narratives and reconcile them within the framework of the most convincing trial evidence.

Bennett and Feldman illustrated their argument by reference to a famous trial from the 1970s.[11] Amid great political and social turmoil over the Vietnam War and the alleged role of capitalism in creating unjust conditions in society, Patricia Hearst, the daughter of a wealthy newspaper magnate, was kidnapped by a domestic terrorist group that called itself the Symbionese Liberation Army. The abduction instantly became nationwide news, and public attention remained focused on the case as the abductors continued to send messages to the press. Several months after her abduction, Hearst entered a bank with members of that group, carrying a gun. A videotape clearly identified her; she appeared to be standing guard while the others robbed the bank.

Hearst was eventually caught and put on trial. The prosecution and defense agreed that she had been kidnapped and they also agreed that she had been carrying a gun during the holdup. The issue was the meaning of her behavior during the robbery. Was she a willing participant? Had she, out of terror and abuse, come to identify with her captors? (This phenomenon is known as the "Stockholm Syndrome" after victims' reactions in a kidnapping case that occurred in Sweden.) The central issues at trial were whether her acts conformed to the definition of robbery and whether she had been forced to participate out of fear for her life.

Bennett and Feldman pointed out that the jury was faced with a number of normative questions. If the jurors decided Hearst had been afraid for her life, she could be found not guilty, or at least she could be held less responsible than if she acted under her own free will. Hearst took the witness stand and testified to numerous instances of physical abuse during her captivity. The defense tried to establish threat and coercion as the explanation of Hearst's behavior. The prosecutors argued, on the other hand, that by the time of the robbery, Hearst had become a loyal member of the group. She took regular guard watches at their hideouts, she went jogging by herself, she waited alone in a car with the keys in the ignition while her abductors robbed a store. Bennett and Feldman argued that the defense story was persuasive only as long as the jurors accepted a view that Hearst followed rules that members of society follow when they are in coercive settings. The prosecution, on the other hand, asserted that Hearst had not followed accepted rules of society.

Hearst was convicted. Bennett and Feldman suggest that the trial outcome might have been different if the defense had argued that Hearst was brainwashed rather than coerced, because it would have forced the jurors to consider a different set of societal norms. The lesson from the Hearst trial is that conflicting narratives about motives and behavior can be constructed out of the same evidence presented at trial. A slight shift in the defense arguments presented to the jury might have shaped the narratives in a different way, perhaps producing a different outcome. Bennett and Feldman's insights drew attention to the fact that societal norms and values—beyond the written laws—were implicated in how the jury viewed the trial evidence and interpreted it to reach their verdict.

Consistent with Bennett and Feldman's basic premises, a large body of research by social psychologists indicates that people intuitively use mental structures called "schemas" or "scripts" in order to explain how the world around them works.[12] The scripts are based on personal experience filtered by the culture in which the person lives. These mental structures contain assumptions about what typically happens when certain facts are present and what results from those facts. The scripts entail notions about physical and social causality and assumptions about what is typical and what is unusual or abnormal when humans engage in behavior. If facts are missing in a setting, people fill in the gaps, relying on what they know about the world. In a phrase, they develop narrative explanations of events. Many facts in a dispute are ambiguous. Different scripts could result in different narratives to explain a particular outcome, although some narratives are more plausible than others.

A few years after Bennett and Feldman's insightful book, social psychologists Nancy Pennington and Reid Hastie began a series of simulated juror studies involving a similar premise about the development of competing trial narratives.[13]

One of the case scenarios used in their research involved a defendant, Johnson, who was accused of first-degree murder in the death of Caldwell. Johnson pleaded not guilty on grounds of self-defense. Undisputed background facts included the following information. In the afternoon of the day of Caldwell's death, Johnson and Caldwell had had a quarrel in a bar. Caldwell was a much bigger man than Johnson. During the quarrel Caldwell threatened Johnson with a straight razor. Johnson left the bar. Later that evening both men appeared again at the same bar. They went outside together. They got into a fight. A policeman happened upon the scene but was some distance away, and before he could intervene, he saw Caldwell strike Johnson and Johnson retaliate by drawing a knife and stabbing Caldwell in the chest. Caldwell died at the scene. A straight razor was found in Caldwell's back pocket. The facts under dispute included: how the two men ended up outside together; the accuracy of eyewitness accounts; whether or not Caldwell pulled the razor during the fight; whether Johnson stabbed at Caldwell or just held his knife out to protect himself; whether or not Johnson intentionally went home to get his knife or usually carried it; and whether Johnson went back to the bar to find Caldwell or returned because that was one of his regular drinking places.

In analyzing mock juror responses to the hypothetical Johnson case, Pennington and Hastie found that their study participants made deductions from the facts that led them to draw certain conclusions relevant to reconstructing the killing. For example: (1) a person who is big and known as a troublemaker makes people afraid (a general premise based on life experience); (2) Caldwell was big and was known to be a troublemaker; (3) defendant Johnson was afraid of him. Using this logic, one juror might say, "If someone like Caldwell came up to me in a bar and threatened me, I would be afraid." The jurors' reactions also evoked competing narratives about certain events. One juror proposed: "I don't think Johnson was angry. If he had been angry, he would have gone right back to the bar. He didn't go right back." But this argument was rejected by another juror: "No, Johnson was afraid of Caldwell and he took his knife with him because he was afraid."[14]

Applying lessons from the body of research on schemas and scripts and their own experiments, Pennington and Hastie proposed that jurors impose a narrative story structure on the trial evidence by using three types of knowledge.[15] Jurors listen to the evidence at trial, and use their knowledge about analogous information and events, as well as generic expectations about what makes a complete story—that human actions are usually driven by goal-directed motives, for instance—to construct plausible, more or less coherent narratives explaining what occurred.

In a subsequent set of experiments, Pennington and Hastie found that, when factual gaps were purposefully left in the evidence presented to their subjects, jurors filled in the gaps by surmising the facts necessary to develop a complete narrative. In a third set of experiments, Pennington and Hastie examined the effects of variations in the order in which the facts were presented. When facts were presented in a coherent time sequence, what they called "story order," as opposed to witness order, their study participants were more likely to decide the case in line with the desired verdicts.

Combining their various findings, Pennington and Hastie named what they called the "story model" of juror decision making. Juror decision making consists of three stages: developing stories from the trial evidence, considering the verdict alternatives from the legal instructions provided by the judge (such as murder, manslaughter, or self-defense), and matching the various stories to these verdict categories. The verdict, according to the story model, is derived from the best fit between the narrative and the verdict category.

Many subsequent studies by these authors and other researchers have lent support to the basic assumptions of the story model and expanded on its implications.[16] In essence, jurors enter the jury box with beliefs and expectations about people and how the world works. Evidence is filtered through the individual jurors' beliefs. Evidence inconsistent with prior beliefs tends to be scrutinized more carefully than that which is consistent, and is more apt to be overlooked or rejected, a finding that has been demonstrated in many other domains of human behavior.[17] When jurors have prior beliefs about the law that conflict with a judicial instruction about the law, they may have difficulty following the instruction.[18] While the trial evidence and legal context set the parameters, the differing life experiences and beliefs frequently result in jurors drawing on different scripts and constructing divergent narratives.

INTEGRATING JUROR NARRATIVES IN JURY DELIBERATIONS

The research indicates that jurors construct narratives from the trial evidence and that differences between jurors may result in different shadings of what that evidence means and where it fits into available verdict options. Jurors may arrive at roughly similar narratives because they share similar life experiences, and a consensual interpretation may develop easily. But invariably, in some trials the jurors may strongly disagree about how to interpret the evidence. Deliberations are where jurors sort out the disagreements.

One important study by James Holstein looked at how jurors reconciled their differences during deliberations.[19] Holstein presented forty-eight groups composed of five or six former jurors with a twenty-minute videotaped simulation of a trial on charges of stealing bricks. The defendant, Harris, had removed approximately $200 worth of bricks from a site that had had little construction activity for several months. Harris was seen hauling the bricks from the property. After the owner of the bricks reported them missing, Harris admitted to the police that he had taken them. However, Harris asserted that he believed the site had been abandoned, and denied any intent to steal the bricks. The trial simulation was based on the testimony of three witnesses and the defendant. The judge then gave the jurors instructions on the law that emphasized the importance of establishing the defendant's intent to commit a crime. The deliberations of the juries were audiotaped and analyzed.

During their deliberations, Holstein's mock jurors focused on alternative interpretations of "what really happened" as they sought to develop a consensus. Some of the interpretations led to different conclusions. For example, in one instance a juror stated: "Harris knew what he was doing when he went on the property and drove away with those bricks. . . . He knew he was taking those bricks from someone. He knew they weren't his bricks, that he didn't own those bricks, so he intended to take them." In contrast another juror articulated an opposite interpretation: "Harris didn't, he didn't take things that were worth something . . . I, I got the very strong impression that he was a, a reasonably honest person and that he thought this really was property of no value. That it was old discarded burned down stuff. And he needed it for something, so he removed it." The statements of such views often resulted in a refinement of the defendant's motives. A few jurors suggested that the removal of the bricks was the act of a good Samaritan who was helping to clean up the neighborhood. In contrast, other jurors thought that Harris had attempted to plot a perfect crime by carrying the bricks out in broad daylight to make an act of theft appear innocent. Altogether the jurors proposed fifteen distinct interpretations of what might have happened as they attempted to develop coherent structural narratives that would justify a verdict.

Professor Neal Feigenson has similarly shown jurors constructing narratives in a simulation involving a medical malpractice case.[20] At issue was whether a doctor negligently failed to diagnose breast cancer in a woman. Part of the defense was based on the size of the lump in the woman's breast when she was examined and a claim that the doctor had no reason to suspect cancer. Here is a portion of the dialogue mock jurors engaged in, taken from Feigenson's book *Legal Blame*:

> Juror Mi: Size is an issue, though.
>
> Juror A: A lump that size—
>
> Juror S: Ten centimeters is about that much, two centimeters is almost an inch, about like that—
>
> Juror J: OK, so it was two this way and wide—
>
> Juror A: You would, you would feel that—
>
> Juror Mi: It's about the size of a kosher pickle, I don't know how you can miss a pickle, I mean—
>
> Juror A: Especially when you take a shower and you're washing you would feel it—
>
> . . .
>
> Juror J: Well, it depends on how big her breast is.
>
> Juror B: Well, that's another thing, we don't know what size of a woman she was.

Juror A: I mean, we don't miss something that large no matter how large your breast is.[21]

The Holstein and Feigenson results extend the story model of decision making by individual jurors articulated by Pennington and Hastie (and Bennett and Feldman's narrative theory) to the jury's group decision-making process as well. In deliberations it appears that juries try to reconcile their individual narratives and arrive at a consistent story they can all agree on. To do so they examine the narrative possibilities segment by segment to see if they can achieve consensus. But do these conclusions from laboratory experiments apply to real juries? Let us see if that is so.

INSIGHTS FROM A STUDY OF REAL JURIES

Although in most United States courts jurors are instructed that they should not discuss the evidence even among themselves until they begin formal deliberations, Arizona civil juries are allowed to engage in discussions of the evidence when they are in the jury room during recesses or lunch breaks or before the court opens in the morning. To study this innovation, the Arizona Supreme Court permitted researchers led by professors Shari Diamond and Neil Vidmar to videotape the discussions and final deliberations of fifty civil juries.[22] The exchanges of these juries provide additional evidence bearing on the development of juror thinking and add significant refinements to the story model. Consider some examples, as jurors attempt to make sense of the evidence:

Example 1. The jurors in this motor vehicle accident trial were attempting to determine the sequence of events that led to the accident.

Juror 1: He [plaintiff] said he [the defendant] sped up when he saw the yellow light and then it was red. I didn't get that straight—was it a yellow or a red light [the plaintiff] saw [the defendant] going through?

Juror 7: It was red and he had to go because he was stuck in the middle.

Juror 1: But another time he [the plaintiff] said he saw the other person see the light changing so he [the defendant] sped up, or maybe that is what the [other witness] told him. There was no left turn arrow.

Juror 7: Cause if you see someone speeding up, what do you do? I sit there.

Juror 1: Yeah.

Juror 6: That's why we have to wait for the judge to talk. What are the laws in this state?

Juror 1: Yeah, you are not supposed to be in the intersection . . .

Juror 6: Well, there was no turn signal, right? No arrow, what was he doing in the intersection?

Juror 7: We need witnesses to tell us if he ran the light . . .

In this example the jurors focused on conflicting testimony from witnesses and applied their own experience about whether the driver should have been in the intersection. In doing so they saw that, at this point in the trial, there was missing evidence they needed in order to make a complete narrative bearing on whether the defendant ran the light.

Example 2. In another motor vehicle accident trial, there was conflicting testimony from two experts about how the accident occurred:

> Juror 1 [explains an expert engineer's testimony]: If you're rear-ended, the first thing you do . . .
>
> Jurors 5 and 7 [interrupt]: You go backwards.
>
> Juror 1: You go backwards, but then you get the recoil going forward. And that's when the seatbelt catches you and stops you. What [the experts are] having arguments on . . .
>
> Juror 7 [interrupts]: Is whether he went forward first?
>
> Juror 1: Is, one . . . did [the plaintiff's car] go forward instantly? Did it accelerate? If it accelerated, you get the same thing . . . it's like you've been rear-ended: You're going to go back first and then go forward, recoil. If you all of a sudden decelerate, that means the car keeps going forward, I mean, the car also stops, but you're going to keep on going forward. And that's when you're going to hit. And the engineer was claiming that the time before they actually hit, when they crumpled each other and then when they started to turn, the time it took the crumple, the car was absorbing energy and . . .
>
> Juror 5 [interrupts]: That's when he went forward.
>
> Juror 1: He had enough time to go forward, before the car started turning. That's why when I asked those questions, he said "No, no, he'll have time to go forward and [injure himself] before he starts going forward and backwards," which I don't know is truly the case.
>
> Juror 5: But I think the question we were hearing from the other side is: if the hit was like this [hands are indicating diagonal impact at side of car], doesn't the [striking car] contribute some more energy to that sort of general forward movement in the car? Because it's not at right angles, and it's not head-on.
>
> Juror 1: My general impression is that that's true. If you have something going at an angle [makes same diagonal diagram with his hands], you have some motion going perpendicular to the car and you have some motion going along the car. And when you get hit, you get shoved [hands indicate motion to the side] and you also get shoved forward. And, at least for a short while, before friction, your car would actually go forward for a little while as it got hit, and you would go back. And that's why I was asking him and I was, like, "That seems a little strange." And he's saying there's something actually happening in between, while it's crumpling. And he didn't make that particularly clear. Hopefully we can read his report [Juror 5, murmurs agreement]. Because they keep referring to all the reports, and I say: Give me the dumb report and we'll read it.

Example 3. This plaintiff was injured in a work accident, but she had a preexisting medical condition. The jurors had to decide if that condition was the cause of the plaintiff's ills rather than the accident:

> Juror 5: That was a lot of force [that struck the plaintiff].
>
> Juror 8: Oh yeah, that's what I was thinking.
>
> Juror 4: And you know how hard her work is. I have no doubt this woman has pain.
>
> Juror 8: That whole issue of degenerative disc disease. She probably has it but it should not factor in . . . and if she was in the type of pain she was in yesterday . . . [referring to a "day in the life of the plaintiff" videotape]
>
> Juror 2: Yes, if that was really her level, geez . . .
>
> Juror 8: I have a friend who is going in for back surgery and his pain varies from day to day. I mean it will be interesting to watch the whole videotape. Are we going to watch the whole thing?
>
> Juror 3: A lot of people go to work with fused backs.
>
> Juror 1: Doesn't this degenerative back disease really hurt her chances? I mean they have not really proved to me that this was one instance that caused her back problem.
>
> Juror 8: Well, I think that at the end the judge will instruct us on what to consider and what not to, we haven't seen the whole thing yet.
>
> Juror 1: I thought the doctor's testimony was most useful. I mean, her daughter [who also testified] could never have seen what actually happened.

Here again we can see the beginning development of competing narratives. The plaintiff was struck with a lot of force that could have caused her condition, but, on the other hand, perhaps much of her pain and disability was due to her preexisting back condition or her job that required a lot of lifting. Juror 8 related his knowledge—that a friend with back problems had pain that varied from day to day—potentially explaining why the plaintiff might not be in severe pain all of the time.

Careful examination of the above examples shows the jurors engaging in two main types of information exchange. In Example 1, Juror 1 was uncertain about whether the testimony indicated that the light was red or yellow, and Juror 7 responded that it was red. The jurors were clarifying trial facts. However, other parts of the various exchanges involved inferences about what would likely follow if a fact were true. Consider some additional examples.

Example 4. Discussing conflicting testimony about when a letter was signed:

> Juror 8: I'm saying the letter wasn't signed until the 12th. How could they notify him or fax him until after they knew it?
>
> Juror 2: What would they have said to him on the phone? I would think . . .
>
> Juror 6 [interrupting]: They said working days, so I'm wondering so I'm wondering if it was a Tuesday or a Wednesday.

Juror 3: Well, I remember when [Witness X] was testifying they asked her if she remembered what day it was and she said it was a Thursday, so that means there must have been a weekend in there too.

Juror 3: Well, that must be why the letter didn't get signed; that seems so confusing.

Juror 6 [referring to her notes]: It was during the week, so there were five days . . .

Juror 8: Well the other calls were on a Friday, so that is more than five days they had to read it.

Juror 1: But they didn't use the mail; they faxed it.

Several jurors: The letter was faxed but the contract was returned on Monday.

Juror 5: They faxed the letter but the contract was returned on Monday. That was a reasonable amount of time.

Juror 9: The critical time is how long after the letter was received. That's the critical information.

Example 5. The details of an auto accident.

Juror 6: Let me ask a question. If the [other] car swerved to the right, then how could the damage have been only to the left bumper?

Juror 2: Yeah, right.

Juror 6: It seems to me that he could not have stayed in his own lane as he claims he did.

Juror 4: Well, he could have been in his own lane but turned the [steering] wheel at the last second to avoid the crash.

Example 6. This trial included testimony about a sequence of events in a claim about medical negligence and whether the health provider's notes contradicted her testimony.

Juror 1: . . . maybe she is telling the truth and just didn't write it down . . . if she had written everything down, they wouldn't have a case.

Juror 6: But you have to think in her eyes and mind, and what she's thinking at the time.

Juror 1: I agree, but she didn't document it.

Juror 3: A lot of time in medical stuff you think things but you don't write it down.

Juror 8: But you know, if it's not written down, it was never done, it was never thought, nothing, everything has to be documented, that's the biggest part.

Juror 7: You think something and you don't necessarily write it down . . . you don't write down what you think, you write down what you see.

Juror 8: I'm just saying that documentation counts, as [the opposing expert witness] said. She [the defendant] speculates a lot but doesn't have anything documented.

NORMS AND VALUES IN THE DECISION-MAKING PROCESS

The story model of juror decision making is a framework for understanding how the jury goes about its assigned tasks. However, with its focus on the facts introduced at trial, there is a tendency to see the jury's task as largely piecing together and matching the facts to reach a verdict. But a closer examination of what the law expects juries to do and what they actually do suggests more than just weighing and calculating the trial evidence. Bennett and Feldman's original work drew attention to other dynamics at play. In the Hearst case, for example, they argued that in order for the jurors to decide between the prosecution's argument that Patty Hearst was a willing participant in the bank robberies and the defense's case that she was forced into those acts, the jurors had to draw upon their knowledge of societal norms of behavior. The jurors had to decide which rules of behavior people should follow in circumstances similar to those in which Hearst found herself.

In Pennington and Hastie's Johnson case, the jurors constructed narratives around notions of whether Johnson might have been afraid. Holstein's case of alleged brick theft similarly demanded that jurors assess social norms to draw inferences about Johnson's intent.

Research by John Manzo has similarly drawn attention to the different considerations of proper conduct debated during jury deliberations.[23] Manzo taped deliberations of an actual civil jury trial of a dispute over a home-building contract. When there were long delays, the homeowners assumed that the builder had broken the contract and hired a second company to do the work. They then sued the construction company for expenses incurred as a result of the delays. The defendant countersued. In this excerpt from the deliberations, a juror who had experience with business contracts offered the opinion that the plaintiffs should have behaved differently if they wanted to void the contract, but at the same time the plaintiffs' expectations of the builder were reasonable.

> Juror 1: . . . when you got a contract . . .
>
> Juror 3: That's right.
>
> Juror 1: to this extent you know then if you wanna back outta this thing, you'd think, uh, I'd go to an attorney and say, hey, legally I wanna get out of this thing. How do I do it legally?
>
> Juror 4: Yeah, yeah, right.
>
> Juror 2: yeah, yeah, you can't say forget it. You're outta here.
>
> Juror 1: You can't say I assume.
>
> . . .
>
> Juror 1: Well, the thing too I can understand that they were disturbed when the construction didn't start, 'cause people not knowledgeable about construction say, "Hey, I signed this today, now tomorrow there's (Juror 4: Right, yeah) gonna be a hole."

Juror 4: Right.

Juror 1: That don't happen—they only brought out a very little portion, y'know, what goes on before you execute on the site . . .

In short, many inferences from facts are made in relation to social norms. While some narratives involve logical inferences about the relation between facts, in many instances the inferences require judgments about proper and improper behavior based on social norms. Similarly, in judging the intentions and motivations of the parties, jurors may need to refer to social norms.

We see that value judgments are an inherent part of the jury's task. Indeed, some are implicitly or explicitly contained in jury instructions. In judging the credibility of witnesses and many other matters, jurors are admonished that they should "apply common sense and life experience." To find second-degree murder, the jury is instructed to consider whether "a person of ordinary judgment would know [the act was] reasonably certain to kill or do serious bodily harm." Instructions on culpable negligence state: "Each of us has a duty to act reasonably toward others. . . . But culpable negligence is more than a failure to act reasonably. It must be gross and negligent behavior." In obscenity cases, jurors are called upon to apply community standards regarding what is "lewd" or "lascivious." In civil cases, the jurors are told that negligence is "failure to use reasonable care," and in instructions for deciding an amount for pain and suffering they are told that there is no exact standard for measuring pain and suffering; the amount should be fair and just.

In certain types of cases jurors are told to judge acts according to standards that may be outside of their ordinary life experience, such as whether a doctor's treatment fell within accepted medical practice, whether an accountant's behavior was consistent with the standards of her profession, or whether a drug company's warnings about its product were reasonable or consistent with trade practices. These cases reveal the complexity of the jury's task in evaluating and judging human action.

THE PROCESS OF GROUP DELIBERATION: FROM JUROR TO JURY

As we have seen, individual jurors construct narratives that are not always the same. But to reach a verdict, all (or in some jurisdictions and types of cases, a majority) of the jurors must agree on the legal implications of what they heard. This may, but need not, involve agreement on a common best story. Jurors may cling to different individual stories so long as they agree that their legal implications are the same. For example, in the Hearst trial all jurors could have agreed that Hearst had been coerced, but not to a degree that should have overcome her capacity to resist, and so arrived at a guilty verdict. Or some could have believed this while others might have believed she was simply a thrill seeker. Still others might have thought she agreed with her captors' goals from the outset. Yet for all these stories, the verdict would have been the same. Even so, much of the deliberation, no doubt, would have explored whether they could arrive at a common view of the evidence and a unified story.

Juries are rarely unanimous at first. How do they come to agree? The process by which individual jurors reconcile their perspectives and arrive at a group verdict has been studied for half a century, starting with mock jury deliberations in the famous Chicago Jury Project that began in the 1950s with a grant from the Ford Foundation.[24] Members of actual jury pools participated in these early studies. They listened to hypothetical cases and deliberated to group verdicts. These discussions were audiotaped and analyzed, revealing for the first time some of the social phenomena that characterize jury decision making. Since then, these early insights about jury deliberation have been replicated, extended, and modified in several hundred mock jury projects.[25]

The first order of business is typically the selection of a foreperson or jury leader, at least in those states in which the judge or court rules do not determine the jury leader. Although it usually takes just a few minutes, clear patterns have emerged about who is most likely to be picked to lead the jury and report its verdict. If the jurors themselves select the jury leader, it tends to be a person who is high in social status, has a college degree, and has experience in group settings, leadership positions, or prior jury service. Women are less likely to be chosen than would be expected from their representation on the jury.

Once the leader is chosen, the jury embarks on deliberating about the case. They begin in different ways; their choice of how to begin can relate to the jury's ability to reach a verdict. Some juries start by taking a formal vote, either through a show of hands or a secret ballot. In one approach, labeled the "verdict-driven" deliberation, jurors then align themselves with those who are on the same side and talk about the evidence that supports the verdict favored by their faction. In verdict-driven deliberations, polling tends to be frequent.

In contrast, in an "evidence-driven" deliberation, jurors tend to embark on a general discussion of the testimony, the facts, and their meaning. Rather than offer only the facts supportive of their preferred verdict, jurors tend to talk about all of the evidence as they collectively aim to develop a common story of the events. Several of the excerpts from Arizona jurors illustrated how jurors exchange their views and perspectives toward the goal of a shared understanding of the evidence. Balloting is infrequent and tends to occur later in the deliberation.

The verdict-driven style tends to be faster but also is more likely to lead to a situation in which the jurors cannot agree on a final decision. It's possible this is due to the fact that, in a verdict-driven deliberation, jurors announce and advocate for their individual preferences openly and often, and we know from other research that public commitments to a position make it more difficult to retreat or change one's mind.

A number of factors affect how much each juror contributes to the deliberation. Some factors relate to the juror's personal characteristics—men typically talk more, as do people with more education and higher-status occupations. The foreperson is usually one of the most active and most influential participants. Another factor is the size of the faction favoring a particular verdict. Large factions often include at least some jurors who say little.[26]

Studies of the group deliberation process have revealed that as the discussion proceeds, the sentiment tends to move in favor of the current majority view. There is a momentum effect: if one side gains a convert, another convert is more likely. Although the opinion change process is slow at first, things speed up the closer the jury gets to full agreement. As the size of the majority grows, the statements about evidence and arguments that support the majority position become more numerous than the comments that support the minority view, and there is increasing pressure on the shrinking minority to conform. These social transition phenomena, studied by social psychologists James Davis, Norbert Kerr, and their colleagues over many years, thus explain how groups use both informational and normative influence to arrive at a consensus verdict.[27]

JURY DECISION MAKING

Charged with deciding outcomes in legal disputes arising out of the seemingly infinite range of human behavior, juries hear evidence at trial under conditions that are quite different from the circumstances of their daily lives. The jury's task is to pull the threads together and reach verdicts.

The story model of jury decision making suggests ways in which the jurors integrate the evidence by developing alternative narratives, testing the narratives for completeness and consistency within their own minds, and arriving at collective understanding. Diversity of juror backgrounds, and long-held beliefs and attitudes among jurors, can produce different narratives, which underscores the value of a representative jury. But more than just a mechanical pulling together of facts is involved in juror judgments and jury verdicts. The subtleties and shadings of human motives and actions invite the jurors to apply normative values in making their individual and collective decisions about these facts. Judges and lawyers tend to stress to the jury that they are to decide only the facts, but implicitly they are aware that the jury's task requires application of value judgments to those facts. The deliberation provides an excellent opportunity for the jury members to influence one another on the meaning of facts and the value judgments implicit within them. As we will see, the ambiguity in the trial task allows for prejudice as well as mercy as the jurors evaluate evidence and collectively develop their own narratives, or stories, as they seek to understand contested facts and render verdicts. We now turn to consider how well juries perform. The story model and the role of value judgments provide an important framework for understanding many issues that the jury confronts.

Chapter 7

JUDGING THE JURY

Evaluating Jurors' Comprehension of Evidence and Law

"Trial by jury" is misleading. More correctly, trial by jury is actually "trial by judge and jury." The judge presides over the trial, deciding which evidence the jury may hear and which evidence it may not hear. The judge provides instructions to the jury at the outset of the trial and often before or after the presentation of certain evidence. At the end of both sides' presentation of evidence, the judge instructs the jury on the applicable law they must follow in arriving at a verdict. In criminal cases, the judge can set aside a verdict of guilty if she believes that the evidence does not support the verdict. In civil cases, the judge can override part or all of a verdict for either party by entering a "judgment not withstanding the verdict," can reduce or increase the damages awarded by the jury, or can order a completely new trial. Implicit in all of this power is the fact that the trial judge sees and hears the same evidence as the jury. Recognizing the judge's central role in the jury trial sets the stage for important studies bearing on jury performance.

AGREEMENT BETWEEN JUDGES AND JURIES

More than half a century ago, Harry Kalven and Hans Zeisel, two professors at the University of Chicago Law School, seized upon the simple insight that the trial judge sees the same trial as the jury. They conducted what has turned out to be the most famous and most important single study of juries. Kalven and Zeisel asked trial judges how they would have decided each case that they and the jury just heard. The participating judges were instructed to fill out a questionnaire while the jury was still deliberating. The questionnaire asked the judge to describe the nature of the case, the nature of the evidence, the difficulty of the evidence, and the degree to which the evidence favored one side over the other. Then the judge was asked to indicate how he would have decided the case. If the judge did as the researchers asked and recorded his own decision made before the jury's verdict was known, that decision could not be influenced by the judge's knowledge of the outcome. By comparing the judge's hypothetical verdict with the jury's verdict, Kalven and Zeisel were able to obtain rates of agreement between judges and juries. Over five hundred judges from around the United States participated in the research, eventually returning questionnaires on 3,576 criminal trials and over 4,000 civil trials. In 1966 Kalven and Zeisel published the results in their now classic book *The American Jury*.[1]

In criminal cases, judge and jury agreed that the defendant was guilty 64 percent of the time, and in 14 percent of cases, they agreed the defendant should be acquitted, for an agreement rate of 78 percent (64 percent +14 percent = 78 percent).[2] But what about the remaining 22 percent of cases in which they disagreed? If the cases had been tried by the judge alone, there would have been more convictions. In 19 percent of trials in which the jury said not guilty, the judge would have convicted. In only 3 percent of trials, the judge would have acquitted when the jury convicted. In short, judge and jury agreed in about four out of five cases; in the remaining cases the jury was more than six times more likely to be lenient (19 percent vs. 3 percent = 6.3:1). Was it because the jury misunderstood the evidence or the law?

The clever design of the research allowed Kalven and Zeisel to explore that possibility. Trials differ in the complexity of evidence. Recall that the judges were asked to comment on the trial evidence. The questionnaire asked for a rating of whether the evidence was very difficult, somewhat difficult, or easy to comprehend. If the judge-jury disagreement was because the jury did not understand the evidence, we should expect the cases of judge-jury disagreement to be ones in which the judge rated the evidence to be more difficult. This hypothesis was not supported. Judge and jury were just as likely to disagree on easy cases as difficult cases. Furthermore, if the judge disagreed with the jury, judges were asked to speculate about why they believed the jury's decision was different than their own. The judges almost never said it was because the jury failed to understand the evidence.

What accounted for the differences, if it wasn't the challenging nature of the evidence? The judges offered a number of reasons. If the trial contained no evidence of a prior criminal record, juries were more likely to give the defendant the benefit of the doubt. In some cases, the judge reported that he knew information that was withheld from the jury, such as a defendant's prior criminal record or that some charges had been dropped for lack of evidence. In other instances, the judges believed that the jury set the standard of proof of guilt at a higher level of probability than they themselves used. In a few instances, the judges believed that sympathy for the defendant influenced the jury. In a very few cases, the judges asserted that the jury just disagreed with the law. Juries in southern states, for example, tended not to convict in cases involving charges of poaching game. In other instances, juries acquitted defendants in drunken driving cases. Community attitudes about alcohol were different in the 1950s than they are today. While the law in both time periods proscribed driving while intoxicated, many people then saw the practice as harmless. Thus, while it appears that juries sometimes applied different standards and values than judges, their divergence from judges in criminal cases were not easily ascribed to their failure to understand difficult evidence. Kalven and Zeisel wryly noted that if jurors were sometimes "at war with the law," it was a small war.

The Kalven and Zeisel study yielded similar judge and jury concurrence in the four thousand civil trials, specifically a 78 percent agreement rate. In 47 percent of the cases, judge and jury both found in favor of the plaintiff, and in 31 percent they both found for the defendant. However, in contrast to criminal trials, the disagreement was more evenly balanced. Ten percent of the time, the judge favored the plaintiff when the jury favored the defendant, and 12 percent of the time, the judge favored the defendant while the jury decided for the plaintiff. The alleged bias of juries toward injured plaintiffs seems not to have existed.

The central findings from Kalven and Zeisel's research, then, are that agreement between judge and jury was substantial and that most instances of disagreement could not be ascribed to jury incompetence or unwillingness to follow the law. There will be other occasions to refer to findings from *The American Jury* later, but for now, consider an important question. Are their findings out-of-date? After all, the research was conducted more than a half century ago. In the intervening years, trials have become more technical and perhaps more complicated. Compared to then, civil and criminal trials today tend to demand more expert testimony. Some laws and procedures have changed; arguably, evidence has become more complicated. Fortunately, we have some recent research that allows us to consider this possibility.

One of the authors of this book (Hans) and her collaborators at the National Center for State Courts conducted a study of 382 felony jury trials that took place in four jurisdictions across the country in 2000 and 2001.[3] In addition to obtaining the jury's verdict as well as the judge's hypothetical "verdict," the study obtained the judge's rating of legal complexity as well as both the judge's and jurors' ratings of evidentiary strength and evidentiary complexity. Judge and jury agreement was similar to that found by Kalven and Zeisel almost fifty years before. And like Kalven and Zeisel, when judge and jury disagreed, the jury was much more lenient than the judge. The most important determinant of the jury's verdict was the strength of the evidence as rated by the judge and the jurors. The complexity of the law and the evidence did not help explain judge-jury disagreement, whether the judge's or jury's rating of complexity was used.

Further analyses of these felony jury trial questionnaires provided insights into why jurors and judges disagreed. First, their ratings of evidence sometimes differed; cases that looked strong to judges didn't seem that way to juries, and vice versa. Second, compared to judges, jurors appeared to have a higher threshold for "beyond a reasonable doubt." Jurors *required stronger prosecution cases to convict* than judges did.[4] A statistical analysis that controlled for a number of other factors showed that the impact of a judge trial compared to a jury trial was at least a 12 percent increase in the chance of a conviction for the defendant.[5]

Studies with smaller numbers of cases have found comparable, substantial rates of judicial agreement with jury verdicts. Another project Valerie Hans conducted with collaborators at the National Center for State Courts studied 153 civil jury trials that took place in Arizona in the middle of the 1990s.[6] Trial judges and jurors completed questionnaires to examine the impact of a jury reform. Each group then rated the evidence in terms of whether it favored the plaintiff, the defendant, or was evenly balanced. Jury verdicts tended to follow the judicial ratings of the evidence. Moreover, the rate of disagreement between the jury verdict and the judicial rating was unaffected by the complexity of the trial or the number of experts—another example of how case complexity does not appear to produce jury verdicts that diverge from those of legal experts. A study of California juries by the National Center for State Courts also found that judicial estimates of the strength and direction of the evidence were generally consistent with the jury verdicts.[7]

Larry Heuer and Steven Penrod conducted a study of ninety-three criminal and sixty-seven civil trials that took place in thirty-three states around 1990.[8] Participating trial judges filled out lengthy questionnaires about trials over which they had just presided. The questionnaires obtained information on the judges' perception of the complexity of the evidence, the law, and the arguments of the lawyers. The judges were also asked about the number of witnesses, the duration of the trial, the number of charges or claims, the number of pages of documents, and the number of parties in the suit. Finally, the judges were asked to indicate what their verdict would have been if they had decided the case. The rates of agreement between judge and jury were roughly similar to those in the Kalven and Zeisel study. As compared to the earlier research, juries in criminal trials were a little more inclined to acquit and in civil cases juries were a little more inclined to decide for the defendant. As with other projects, in this one too, the measures of trial complexity derived from the judges' assessments were not related to judge-jury disagreement. The judges also tended to express satisfaction with the juries' verdicts.

Thus, we have an answer to the question of whether Kalven and Zeisel's fascinating conclusions are dated. The answer is a solid no! The findings hold up remarkably well despite changes in trials, new types of evidence, and the demographic makeup of juries that contain far more women and minority group members than juries in the 1950s.

The agreement between the judges and juries in these studies is further mirrored in more general surveys of judges. A survey of state and federal judges in Georgia found high support for the jury system in civil negligence cases. Even when the judges said they might sometimes differ with the jury, they gave very positive evaluations of the jury for its competence and its fairness.[9] Two extensive surveys in 1987, one with 800 state and 200 federal judges, and the other with 348 state and 57 federal judges, also found strong support for juries. A Federal Judicial Center project examining complex trials questioned judges and lawyers about their perceptions of jury decisions. Even though the cases involved difficult issues, the judges generally reported that the juries had made the correct decision and had had no difficulties applying the appropriate standards to the case.

Legal professionals who preside over trials and observe the jury on a daily basis are in a good position to evaluate jury performance. It is striking that in most of the debates about jury competence, judges' opinions are seldom solicited. There are other ways of evaluating jury competence, but these reassuring data indicate that trial judges give them good marks.

JURY TRIAL OUTCOMES VERSUS JUDGE TRIAL OUTCOMES

In some cases, the disputing parties elect, within the boundaries that are set by law, to have their case tried by a jury.[10] In others they choose a judge to hear the dispute. This offers us another opportunity to compare how juries and judges overlap or differ. If we count, for example, how often judges convict criminal defendants in trials before them, and then compare that number with the number of convictions in jury trials, we can ask whether the conviction rates are similar or widely divergent. A number of researchers have taken this approach to analyzing jury verdicts.

There is a potential hazard of these direct comparisons of judge and jury trial verdicts. Are the cases before judges and juries similar, except for the fact that one was decided by a judge and the other by a jury? Common sense and careful analysis tell us that the answer is no. A host of factors go into the choice—if litigants have a choice—of whether to have one's case heard by a judge or a jury. A criminal defendant may believe that a jury will be more sympathetic to his plight—or more hostile to his insanity defense—and select a decision maker in line with these beliefs. A civil litigant may prefer the tutored evaluation of the judge in a complex case that turns on points of law, or a jury in a hometown community that benefits from jobs the litigant brings to the area. We have to be cautious in comparing jury-versus-judge verdicts because we might be comparing apples to oranges.[11] So long as we keep this caveat in mind, we can still gain some insights about trial by jury by comparing these decisions by juries and by judges.

Some scholars have compared judge and jury decisions in patent infringement cases, which can contain highly technical and complex testimony and legal rules. Kimberly Moore examined verdicts in all patent cases that reached trial between 1983 and 2000 and whose verdicts were appealed to a higher court. Although appeals courts primarily deal with issues of law, in some circumstances appeal court judges may review parts or all of the factual evidence and overrule the trial verdict. Moore's study drew on a total of 533 jury trials and 676 trials by judge alone.[12] She compared the respective sets of verdicts with the rates at which the appeals courts agreed with the verdicts or overturned them. In one part of her analysis, Moore observed that judge trial outcomes and jury trial outcomes differed somewhat, in that juries were more likely to find that patents were infringed. But, using the decision of an appeals court to uphold a verdict as a measure of correctness, she concluded that they seemed equally accurate.[13] In another analysis of some of these data, Moore was more negative about juries. She asserted that juries were more "xenophobic" or biased against foreigners than judges, because she discovered that foreign litigants in patent lawsuits prevailed just 36 percent of the time before juries, compared to 54 percent of the time before judges.[14]

Given the ubiquity of ethnic bias, it wouldn't be surprising if foreign parties suffered some prejudice in American courts. However, Cornell Law School professors Kevin Clermont and Theodore Eisenberg found a surprising pattern in their broader study of foreign litigants in a wide range of types of cases in US civil courts during the time period 1987–2005.[15] In contrast to Kimberly Moore, Clermont and Eisenberg found no significant differences in the treatment of foreigners by judges and juries over this larger time frame. But furthermore, they discovered that foreigners were actually *more* likely to win their cases over that time period before both judges and juries. Their explanation is that foreign litigants *thought* they would suffer prejudice in American courts and so brought only their strongest cases to trial in the United States. The lesson is that comparing decisions made in judge trials and jury trials can have more to do with who chooses trial by jury than with the supposedly distinctive decision-making approaches of juries.

CASE STUDIES OF JURY COMPETENCE

Case studies, including interviews of jurors, are another way to look at the competence of juries. Case studies raise questions of whether the findings can be generalized to juries as a whole, but they have the advantage of providing in-depth insights and the rich context of jury trials.

Richard Lempert systematically examined twelve complex jury trials.[16] The sample included corporate law violations, toxic torts allegedly causing injuries to many persons, conspiracies, stock manipulations, sexual harassment allegations, claims under antitrust laws, breaches of contract, and matters relating to the disclosure of trade secrets. In two cases, one with highly technical evidence pertaining to patents and trade secrets and the other with both epidemiological and hydrogeological testimony, the expert evidence was so complex and arcane, Lempert concluded, that it was likely that neither judges nor juries would have been able to properly understand it. Indeed, it is possible that only specialists in the fields could have made sense of it. These two cases present a dilemma, which suggests the possible need in a very few cases for extraordinary means of resolving disputes. Perhaps court-appointed experts could interpret the evidence for the judge and jury. However, in the remaining ten cases, Lempert argued that the evidence was not so esoteric that jurors would be confused by it and that there was no clear evidence that the jurors were befuddled in reaching their verdict.

One of the authors of this book (Vidmar) conducted case studies of five medical malpractice trials and a wrongful death case resulting from an automobile accident. Interviews were conducted with the people who served on the juries.[17] All of the cases had conflicting evidence. Analysis of jurors' reports in the trials indicated that the jurors sometimes had difficulty in resolving their views of the evidence and their application of the burden of proof, but in each trial they carefully scrutinized the testimony of expert and civilian witnesses. The accuracy of the final verdicts can be debated, since there was credible evidence on both sides, but the deliberation processes were carried out with competence.

Joseph Sanders conducted interviews with jurors who decided a case that concerned whether the drug Bendectin caused birth defects.[18] The trial featured conflicting testimony about human epidemiological evidence and animal studies, bearing on the potential effects of the drug. Sanders found a substantial range in the individual jurors' ability to summarize the scientific evidence after the trial, and he concluded that the jurors' deliberations fell short of generating a full understanding of the case. Yet, Sanders decided that some of the blame lay with how the defense lawyers presented the case and with the judge's instructions. He concluded that the jurors' performance was not due to their lack of effort or diligence. Their deliberations were not centered on the most important evidence, but they were pointed in that direction by both the legal instructions of the judge and the rules of evidence regarding research studies.

Researchers from the Rand Corporation interviewed jurors in a Texas trial involving the effects of exposure to asbestos.[19] Those authors concluded that the jurors failed to properly understand certain critical pieces of evidence. In posttrial interviews, the jurors had difficulty in remembering the judge's instructions and reported considering legally irrelevant factors in their determination of liability as well as damages. Austin observed two civil juries that heard an antitrust case and extensively interviewed some of the jurors afterward. He concluded that the jurors had a basic understanding of the facts but were somewhat confused about the economic evidence presented during the trials.

Case studies are problematic in drawing broad conclusions about juries, not only because the cases may not be representative, but also because reconstruction of the jury deliberations is dependent on the jurors' memories and perceptions of the deliberations. This is especially so when some time may have elapsed between the trial and the interviews. However, case studies do raise the possibility that juries do not always perform optimally. Yet sometimes, it appears the problems are rooted in the ways that lawyers present their cases and judicial rulings about how testimony can be presented.

SIMULATION STUDIES OF COMPLEX TRIALS

Mock jury studies, in which evidence is presented to research participants who assume the role of jurors and decide the case, are also used to explore the competence of juries. Mock jury research on the topic of jury competence is plentiful; we provide several illustrative examples.

The Maxwell Fraud Trial[20]

We earlier brought up England's Maxwell trial in discussing the challenges of emotional prejudice in jury trials. In 1991 Robert Maxwell—media baron and head of the worldwide Mirror Group empire, owner of the *New York Daily News*, controversial Labor member of Parliament (1964–1970), former professional soccer team owner, and always larger than life—disappeared from his yacht, the *Lady Ghislaine*, while sailing in the Canary Isles. His body washed up on the coast of Tenerife. Shortly afterward the British public learned that hundreds of millions of pounds were missing from the pension funds of companies that Maxwell had controlled, rendering thirty thousand pensioners destitute. Both the staid and the tabloid newspapers in Britain carried the news of the scandal day after day. In Parliament, speakers condemned Maxwell and his sons Kevin and Ian as rapacious thieves. In 1995, the Serious Frauds Office charged Kevin, Ian, and others as coconspirators in illegally raiding the Mirror Group pension fund of one hundred and twenty million pounds. After a seven-month trial in 1996, a jury found the Maxwell brothers not guilty. The acquittal raised an outcry in legal and public circles about the competence of juries and fostered calls for abolishing jury trials for complex fraud cases in England and Wales, calls that periodically have been made before and since.[21]

In a series of simulation experiments with jury-eligible people, Terry Honess, Michael Levi, and Elizabeth Charman assessed the ability of jurors to understand the evidence presented in the Maxwell trial.[22] Six hours of videotaped testimony incorporated the main issues from the actual trial. The simulation was carried out over several sessions and took place in a specially prepared room that allowed the participants access to two large video screens and copies of the documentary evidence. At four points during the trial presentation the participants were asked to summarize the evidence, offer a tentative verdict, rate their confidence in the verdict, and explain their reasons for choosing it. The jurors were then interviewed separately. Using the written responses and transcripts of the interviews, the researchers carefully assessed the quality of the reasoning used by the mock jurors and their comprehension of the evidence, and looked for improper reasoning that went beyond the trial evidence.

On an aggregate level the jurors reasoned competently with regard to both the prosecution and defense evidence. Nearly all participants showed a willingness to consider new arguments, one indication of higher-quality reasoning. In sum, most of the study's jurors passed the competence tests devised by the researchers, though this does not mean that they understood all the fine details of the case.

Severed and Joined Criminal Trials

Another way that criminal trials may be considered complex is when a defendant is accused of two or more offenses that are "joined" or combined into a single trial. The legal issue is whether joining the offenses may confuse the jury and lead to prejudice against the accused person.[23] Courts have recognized that prejudice might result because of confusion of evidence among the charges, accumulation of evidence across charges, or because jurors make inferences that by being involved in so many alleged acts the accused has a "criminal disposition."

A number of researchers have studied this problem through a variety of simulation experiments, some of which presented the evidence in videotaped trials lasting two or more hours.[24] The different experiments varied in the degree of similarity of the charges against the accused and the number of charges. Jurors in the experiments decided the cases in single trials or joined trials so that the researchers could compare differences between hearing charges individually or together. In addition the experiments varied the judicial instructions, including some intended to offset prejudice due to confusion.

These studies found that joining of offenses led to intrusions of facts from one offense to another, supporting the hypothesis that jurors can confuse evidence. The studies also revealed that joining led to unfavorable ratings of the defendant's character. Some of the studies also found that judicial instructions to the jurors were ineffective in reducing these biases. However, in follow-up research using more elaborate instructions that warned against such confusion, biases against the defendant were offset.

Joined charges and defendants are a special problem that applies only to certain criminal cases. One way to avoid the problem is to have separate trials on each of the charges. However, when trials are joined for reasons of efficiency, the research does suggest that special care with instructions can remedy potential deficiencies in jury performance.

Complex Civil Cases

Civil trials sometimes present problems that are roughly analogous to those in joined criminal trials. Many so-called mass tort trials involve multiple plaintiffs and multiple defendants. One example is the litigation by hundreds of workers suffering various asbestos-caused diseases brought against companies that used asbestos despite knowledge that asbestos posed severe dangers to workers' health. In the Northern District of Texas, Judge Robert Parker's court was faced with more than two thousand cases, so the judge certified a "class action" lawsuit in which all of the plaintiffs were joined.[25] Plaintiffs, however, had varying degrees of illnesses. Some suffered from mesothelioma, an aggressive and usually fatal form of cancer linked to asbestos exposure; some suffered from lung cancer; others from asbestosis; and still others from pleural disease. A central question is whether juries in such cases can differentiate between the various plaintiffs in deciding damages.

For nearly two decades, psychologist Irwin Horowitz and his colleagues have been investigating procedural complexity in a series of experiments and assessing the potential efficacy of ways to manage mass tort cases.[26] One experiment was based around a trial in which four plaintiffs were injured by a toxic chemical. Some of the jurors were told nothing about additional plaintiffs in the lawsuit, but others learned there were twenty-six other injured people, while still others learned that hundreds had been injured. In some versions of the trial presented to the participants, all of the plaintiffs suffered similar injuries, while in another version, one of the plaintiffs was an "outlier," who suffered a much more serious injury than the others. Some jurors heard each of the cases separately, but in others the plaintiffs were consolidated. The jurors were assigned to six-person juries, and the evidence was presented in a four-hour mock trial. The jurors were asked to decide causation, liability, compensatory damages, and punitive damages. To evaluate their reasoning abilities, the jurors also filled out questionnaires about their judgments regarding responsibility for the injuries, the credibility of witnesses, and the relative importance of trial witnesses.

When one of the plaintiffs was an outlier, or the size of the injured population was large, juries tended to give greater amounts for punitive damages. Compared to separate trials, consolidated trials resulted in the outlier receiving a larger award. Less severely injured plaintiffs also received larger awards than when they had individual trials. The findings showed that as the size of the population of other injured persons increased, so did the amount of responsibility assigned to the defendants.

In a second experiment, some juries heard all the evidence in a unitary trial, while other juries heard the evidence about causation and liability separately. Unitary trials resulted in more verdicts finding for the plaintiff than in trials separating the issues. There was no "right" verdict in these two experiments, but the research shows that different procedures produced different verdicts and different reasoning about verdicts.

Having demonstrated some problems in complex trials, in subsequent experiments, Horowitz and his colleagues examined what might promote juror understanding, including reforms such as instructing jurors at the start of the trial and allowing them to take notes.[27] One experiment concerned a large number of railroad workers who claimed their employer was responsible for the repetitive stress injury of carpal tunnel syndrome. Another was based on a medical malpractice case concerning a claim that a physician had not followed the then-current standard of medical care. Both cases involved complicated evidential issues that were presented by videotape and required a full day of participation by the jurors.

In typical American trials, judicial instructions in the law usually come at the end of the case presentation. However, in the Horowitz experiments, some of the jurors received pre-instructions on the complicated issues. The hypothesis was that pre-instructions would help them cognitively organize the evidence as it was presented. In other parts of the research the jurors were encouraged to take notes. The responses of the jurors in these conditions were compared to control conditions in which jurors did not have the advantage of such help. In addition to their verdicts, all of the jurors were asked to recall the evidence for the researchers; their oral statements were recorded for subsequent analysis by the research team.

Pre-instruction ameliorated many of the negative effects of trial complexity, particularly complexity created by the presence of multiple plaintiffs. When the individual jurors were allowed to deliberate with one another, the verdicts tended to be more legally correct than individual judgments. Note taking during the presentation of evidence also created greater comprehension by helping the jurors to better organize the evidence. The Horowitz experiments suggest that even when the evidence or the procedural complexity of the trial is difficult, juries can be assisted in making legally appropriate decisions by straightforward reforms.

UNDERSTANDING AND FOLLOWING INSTRUCTIONS

We've given the jury good marks for its comprehension of the evidence—and for jury verdicts that are consistent with the strength of the evidence and with the views of experts. Yet understanding the evidence is only one part of the jury's task. The jury must apply that evidence under the applicable law.[28] Here, the jury's report card is not always so glowing.

In 1975 Andre Sellars was charged with the murder of an acquaintance during a fight in a grocery store parking lot and pleaded self-defense.[29] The jury heard evidence that the deceased man and his brother had threatened Sellars throughout a weekend of arguing. At the end of the trial, the judge delivered a half hour of instructions replete with arcane legal jargon. The jury deliberated and announced its verdict that Sellars was guilty. Later in the jury lounge, several jurors discovered that they had misunderstood the instructions and had meant to find Sellars not guilty. They were under the impression that Sellars had acted in self-defense and that manslaughter rather than not guilty was the correct verdict because, after all, Sellars did fatally injure the other man. The misunderstanding was brought to the attention of the court, and a polling of the jurors resulted in a nine-to-three majority for acquittal, requiring a dropping of charges or a retrial. The Sellars trial is an unusual one. It occurred several decades ago when juries were seldom provided with written instructions to take into the jury room, but it raises the specter of the consequences of misunderstanding the law.

Legal scholars and social scientists have studied the issue in some detail. One problem is that judicial rules are filled with technical jargon that attempts to capture fine legal distinctions. Some jury instructions, as Professor Peter Tiersma has pointed out, use words that are unfamiliar to people without legal training, such as *quash*, *expunge*, or *res gestae*. In addition to specialized or esoteric language, many legal instructions are written in tortured and complex prose that is hard to follow. Many studies have been conducted on jurors' understanding of legal instructions, with mixed results, some showing adequate comprehension of the law and others revealing misunderstanding and confusion.

Over past years attempts have been made to remedy these problems, translating or explaining legal terms in pattern instructions so that they convey their legal meaning and still help jurors understand them. Consider a set of California instructions for "Murder with Malice Aforethought."[30] The older version was as follows:

> "Malice" may be express or implied.
>
> Malice is express when there is manifested an intention unlawfully to kill a human being.
>
> Malice is implied when:
>
> 1. The killing resulted from an intentional act,
> 2. The natural consequences of the act are dangerous to human life, and

3. The act was deliberately performed with knowledge of the danger to, and with conscious disregard for, human life.[31]

In a revised version of this rule, a judicial committee retained the archaic "malice aforethought" phrase, possibly on the grounds that jurors expect to hear it in a murder case or that it was reflected in the actual statutes. However, they dropped "express" and "implied" to produce the following version of the instruction:

> The defendant is charged . . . with (first degree/second degree) murder. You may find the defendant guilty of murder only if the prosecutor has proven beyond a reasonable doubt that:
>
> 1. The defendant caused the death of another person . . . AND
> 2. (He/She) caused the death by an act committed with malice aforethought AND
> 3. The killing was committed without excuse or justification.
>
> The defendant acted with malice aforethought if either:
>
> a. (He/She) intended to kill, that is, acted with express malice. or
> b. (He/She) intentionally did an act that (he/she) knew was highly dangerous to human life and acted with conscious disregard of that danger, that is, acted with implied malice.[32]

Undoubtedly, the revised version is better. Although "malice aforethought" is still retained, as are "express malice" and "implied malice," the A and B sections try to overcome the problem.

Researchers have conducted experiments to test whether revised instructions that improve vocabulary and syntax can enhance comprehension.[33] Some studies have provided jury-eligible people with variations of instructions and tested comprehension through multiple-choice tests or, in a few instances, by asking the jurors to paraphrase what the instruction means. In other research, jury-eligible people were exposed to a brief civil or criminal trial synopsis and asked to render a verdict under different versions of instructions. The percentages of "correct" verdicts were then compared across the various versions. Other studies varied procedures, such as providing preliminary instructions as well as final instructions or giving jurors written versus oral instructions. Remarkable improvements can be seen from such revisions and other procedural aids.

Another source of confusion—more difficult to remedy—is that certain legal terms are similar to familiar words, for example, *burglary*, *mayhem*, *complaint*, *aggravation*, or *insanity*, but they have specific legal meanings that differ from their commonly understood meanings.[34] The conflicts between everyday meaning and legal meaning may interfere with a proper application of the law. Social psychologist Vicki Smith conducted a series of experiments that demonstrated how jurors might be confused by these incompatibilities between lay and legal understandings of crimes.[35]

Consider a common instruction on burglary:

> A person commits the offense of burglary when he, without authority, knowingly enters a building with intent to commit a felony therein. To sustain the charge of burglary, the State must prove the following propositions: first, that the defendant knowingly entered a building; and second, that the defendant did so without authority; and third, that the defendant did so with the intent to commit a felony. If you find from your consideration of all of the evidence that each of these propositions has been proved beyond a reasonable doubt, you should find the defendant guilty. If you find from your consideration of all of the evidence that any one of these propositions has not been proved beyond a reasonable doubt, you should find the defendant not guilty.

Using this instruction, Smith presented groups of simulating jurors with trial scenarios that fit or did not fit laypersons' typical stereotypes of particular crimes. For example, in a study of burglary crimes, one scenario featured a defendant who picked a lock on a house while the owners were on vacation. He entered the home and took jewelry and stereo equipment. That fit the legal definition of burglary and matched people's stereotypes. Another scenario fit the legal definition of burglary because the defendant entered a building unlawfully with the intent to commit a felony: a deliveryman who was angry with his employer entered a closed warehouse through an unlocked window and unsuccessfully attempted to set the building on fire. Another scenario did not fit the legal definition: a defendant noticed a portable cassette recorder in a park and took it when the owner left it unattended.

The subjects in Smith's experiment tended to be confused by the atypical trial scenarios because they did not fit their preexisting beliefs about what constituted burglary. Although Smith experimented with different ways of trying to overcome the effects of prior stereotypes of law, such as avoiding the term *burglary* and providing preliminary or supplemental instructions to simulating jurors, these modifications were generally unsuccessful in improving performance.[36]

Smith's experiments raise questions about jurors' ability to follow the law and have been cited in that regard, but her studies as well as other mock jury investigations of juror comprehension of instructions have also been criticized on the grounds that the trial scenarios are frequently short, artificial, and miss the full adversarial context of the trial setting in which real jurors operate.[37] Attorneys often incorporate aspects of the legal instructions into the closing arguments to the jury, providing another way beyond judicial instructions to communicate the substance of the legal rules. In addition, most mock juror studies have focused on individual jurors' understanding, without giving them the benefits of group discussions about the case evidence and legal instructions that real jurors would have.

Instructions are given at the beginning and throughout a trial. Some instructions are procedural, such as admonitions not to talk about the evidence with other jurors until deliberations begin or how to choose a foreperson. Some are guidance instructions, such as how the testimony of expert witnesses is to be evaluated. Still others mix guidance and substantive law. Jurors may be told to disregard inadmissible evidence that a witness mentioned in testimony, such as the fact that the defendant holds an insurance policy. Limiting instructions tell the jurors how certain evidence should or should not be used and for what purposes. Thus, jurors may learn that an accused has prior convictions, but they are told that while this information can be used to judge the honesty of the accused person's testimony, it cannot be used as evidence that the accused committed the crime at issue in the trial that they are deciding. When both parties have presented their evidence and made their closing arguments, the trial judge instructs the jury on the applicable law. These instructions bear not only on the specific criminal or civil substantive laws at the heart of the trial, but also on such matters as the burden of proof, the weight of the evidence needed to find for the prosecution or plaintiff, and how damages are to be calculated.

Consider some illustrative examples of jury instructions that are particularly problematic.

The famous phrase *beyond a reasonable doubt* refers to the level of confidence needed to convict a defendant in a criminal trial. Geoffrey Kramer and Dorean Koening compared comprehension of the reasonable doubt standard of people who had recently served as jurors with people who had been called but did not serve on a jury.[38] Whether or not they had served as jurors, many of the participants tended to equate guilty beyond a reasonable doubt with absolute 100 percent certainty, which is not required by the standard. However, in contrast, another study found that jurors did have a sound understanding of reasonable doubt.[39]

"Presumption" instructions are important in civil and criminal trials. Presumptions are used when a fact is required but demonstrating it directly is difficult.[40] Thus, a letter shown to have been mailed is presumed to have arrived; a criminal defendant is presumed to be sane unless he claims he is not (and offers proof by an expert); a person who possesses stolen property may sometimes be presumed to have committed a crime even if there was no direct encounter between the victim and the defendant. Judicial instructions contain different types of presumption instructions, depending on the circumstances. A number of jury simulation experiments produced mixed results regarding laypeople's understanding of these instructions.

Jurors may also receive "limiting instructions" when evidence is introduced for one purpose but should not be used for another.[41] The most common example is when a defendant's criminal record is brought out at trial. As we discussed earlier, the criminal record may be used by the jury to assess whether the defendant's testimony is credible or, in some circumstances, as proof that the defendant had a motive, opportunity, or knowledge to commit a crime or in the past had engaged in a common pattern of criminal behavior. However, jurors are typically instructed that the information must not be used to infer that the defendant committed the present crime because of his general bad character or criminal tendencies. Numerous experiments have shown that this is a difficult instruction for jurors to follow. Valerie Hans's experiments with Anthony Doob, for example, found that deliberating groups of adults who learned of a defendant's prior criminal record were obedient to the judge's instructions, even admonishing each other that they were supposed to disregard the criminal record if one of them mentioned it. Yet, jurors who had the knowledge of a record were more likely to convict than those who did not hear about the prior convictions.[42] Later experiments by other researchers replicated that finding.[43]

Professor Sally Lloyd-Bostock devised a complex experiment to assess the effects of limiting instructions. Her experiment is a good example of how social scientists control variables in order to tease out potential factors that may influence jury decisions. She created video versions of three trials in which the defendants were charged with either handling stolen goods, indecent assault on a woman, or a deliberate stabbing.[44] For each trial scenario there were fact variations in the evidence. Some of the simulating jurors were not told anything about a prior criminal record, but others learned that the defendant had a single prior conviction. Sometimes the prior crime was similar to the current crime and in others it was dissimilar. In still another variation of the facts, the conviction was for an "indecent assault on a child." Some jurors learned that the prior conviction was in the distant past and others learned that it was recent.

The jurors who heard about a criminal record were provided limiting-use instructions. After viewing their video trial, the jurors were asked to indicate a verdict and to rate the likelihood that the defendant had committed the crime. Next, they met in groups to discuss the case for half an hour. Once again they gave their individual verdicts and likelihood ratings.

Lloyd-Bostock's experiments found that evidence of previous convictions had a prejudicial effect, particularly when the conviction was recent and for a similar offense. A conviction for an indecent assault on a child was particularly likely to increase convictions. But there was an unpredicted finding. When the defendant had a *dissimilar* prior conviction, the jurors rated the defendant as *less* likely to have committed the offense. Thus, jurors appeared to rely on beliefs about patterns of offending, which included both the assumption that offenders tend to commit similar crimes and the assumption that offenders who commit one type of crime are unlikely to commit other types.

An excerpt from an Arizona civil trial shows the jurors focusing on the limiting instruction to determine a witness's credibility in light of the legally sanctioned use of a witness's criminal record. In this case the jurors were troubled by contradictions between a witness's sworn testimony in a pretrial deposition and his trial testimony, a problem bearing on his credibility.

> Juror 2: Defense showed he changed his story and lied.
>
> Juror 4: That's my thing, I don't think we have enough actual facts to the . . .
>
> Juror 1: Is this burden here . . .
>
> Juror 7: I think we need to pay close attention to this stuff here, what the judge gave us, and let me read. I'll be the reader of these things if you want.
>
> Juror 4: Tell me which ones you read.
>
> Juror 7: Impeachment with felony conviction. Says here, "evidence that a witness has previously been convicted of a felony may not, may be considered only as it may affect the credibility of that person as a witness. You may not consider that evidence for any other purpose."
>
> Juror 1: Right, so that so everything is credibility.
>
> Juror 8: Credibility on that part because he didn't want to explain anything that happened.
>
> Juror 2: None of his facts are straight.

We see them bring up the issue of credibility and then draw upon the criminal record and the judge's limiting instruction. This portion of the transcript suggests that the jurors are appropriately employing the criminal record in assessing the defendant's credibility.

Even as we are heartened by this positive example of the Arizona civil jury, we would point out that the bulk of the research studies on following instructions leads to the conclusion that jurors do not always—and probably cannot always—faithfully follow instructions. They are imperfect decision makers. An important question, however, is whether judges could do better than jurors if they were the sole decision maker. Are they immune to such tendencies because of their legal training and experience?

Judges are more steeped in the substantive knowledge of the law, and their training should permit them to apply legal rules with a high degree of accuracy. Certain rules of evidence like limiting instructions, though, might be just as challenging for judges as for jurors. Stephen Landsman and Richard Rakos asked whether this was so in parallel experiments with judges and jurors.[45] Eighty-eight judges and 104 jurors from Ohio were presented with a synopsis of a product liability case. Some of the judges and jurors learned facts that could not legally be considered in deciding the case, while others, in a control condition, did not hear the objectionable facts. Half of the judges and jurors who heard the inadmissible evidence were given a limiting instruction directing that the evidence should be set aside, but the others did not receive this instruction. Compared to the control jurors, jurors who heard the inadmissible evidence were adversely affected by it. The verdicts of jurors who were instructed to disregard the information did not differ from those of uninstructed jurors, indicating that the jurors were unable or unwilling to follow the limiting instructions.

How did the judges do? Their performance was no better than that of the jurors! They, too, could not follow the instruction to disregard. Indeed, their decisions were almost identical to those of the jurors. The experiment suggests that legal training does not necessarily make judges less prone to make certain errors in following the law.

Law professors Chris Guthrie and Jeffrey Rachlinski joined forces with Judge Andrew Wistrich to conduct a series of research studies examining the extent to which judges are affected by the cognitive illusions that characterize the judgment processes of most people.[46] In making decisions, people often rely on mental shortcuts and heuristics, such as the hindsight bias phenomenon we described earlier. These techniques are often very helpful in ordinary decision making but can occasionally lead to errors. To study whether judges, too, made these common but systematic errors, the researchers administered questionnaires to federal magistrate judges. The questionnaires asked the judges to reach hypothetical decisions in different scenarios. Some judges were given information that tends to promote the use of mental shortcuts, while others did not receive the information. For instance, hearing an initial figure or an anchor number usually influences people's numerical estimates. The study revealed that judges—like the rest of us—are affected by anchors as well as other cognitive illusions. Compared to judges who did not hear any anchor figure, judges who heard an anchor value of $75,000 arrived at compensatory damage awards that were closer to that anchor. We come to the realization that judging guilt or liability is an imperfect process—whether it is done by juries or judges.

JURIES AT WORK: INTERACTIONS OF LEGAL INSTRUCTIONS AND FACTUAL DETERMINATIONS

Many judges today provide written copies of their oral instructions when the jurors are sent to deliberate. The Arizona Project showed that jurors frequently used those instructions as they worked to make sense of the conflicting evidence and to determine how the law was to be applied to that evidence. Brief excerpts from the deliberations in several of these real trials help to illustrate how jurors use instructions in the context of resolving conflicting claims.

One example comes from a malpractice trial with a chiropractor defendant. In order to determine whether negligence occurred, the jury was required to decide if the treatment was inconsistent with the prevailing standard of medical care. The standard of care was provided at trial in the form of expert testimony from medical providers. The jurors looked at exhibits from the trial as well as the written instructions. (As with all the examples from the Arizona Project reported in this book, the names given to the trial participants are fictitious.)

Juror 2: Is that okay or does everyone still need to look at it? Okay, I want to try to keep everything together here.

[Jurors return the exhibits to Juror 2.]

Juror 9 [reading from the instructions]: It asks whether the defendant, John Cerutti, was negligent, right? This information we are looking at is something that has been approved by both sides, both sides have . . .

Juror 5: What page are we on?

Juror 9: Page 10, and I think he was negligent because it says in here, it speaks of basing his processes and procedures according to what other chiropractors . . .

Juror 6: The standard of care!

Juror 9 [continues]: At the time as well, okay, I know I saw it . . .

Juror 8 [reading]: "Chiropractic negligence is the failure to comply with the applicable standard of care. To comply with the applicable standard of care, a chiropractor must exercise that degree of care, skill, and learning that would be expected under similar circumstances of a reasonably prudent chiropractic within this state."

Juror 9: Okay, we're looking at what they've given us, and I'm only talking here, I'm not saying he was negligent as far as causing, it says here, "the defendant negligence was a cause of injury to the plaintiff." I'm not agreeing with that, but I think he was negligent in the fact that he didn't take any notes [regarding the treatment he gave].

Juror 4: Ah, but wait a second, that's care, skill and learning, and we have to, we aren't looking at whether he took notes, or not, I don't think we are basing this thing on.

Juror 3: He was not required to take notes.

Juror 4: He was not required to and . . .

Juror 3: By law.

Juror 4: So there would be no standard at the time.

Juror 9 [reading from the instructions]: It says, ". . . and learning that would be expected under similar circumstances of a reasonably prudent chiropractor within this state." The only other chiropractic they brought as evidence from this state was Dr. Beale.

Juror 3: But, Dr. Beale was making records after the law was in effect.

Juror 9: Okay, so we don't . . .

[a few minutes later]

Juror 9: Do we agree, that we believe that the damage, whatever damage that happened, that he's, the alleged damage, if it was caused by Dr. Cerutti, primarily in March and not July 1?

Juror 4: Before we even ask that, does anybody here believe that Dr. Cerutti caused the damage that, uh, Mildred Stuart suffered?

Juror 8: If we agree on that we don't have to go any farther.

Juror 4: I mean, quite frankly, that's the main question, do we believe Dr. Cerutti caused the damage that Mildred Stuart is suffering?

We see the jurors moving back and forth in the discussion between the written instructions—which they read both individually and collectively—and attempt to apply the specific words and phrases to the details of the factual dispute. Clearly, multiple copies of the instructions are in the jury room, as more than one juror reads aloud and attempts to follow Juror 9, who takes the lead in reading relevant portions of the instructions to the group as a whole. They consider whether the chiropractor in question took notes and what the law said about his failure to do so, searching for direction in the instructions and in their recollections of what they learned at trial. But eventually another juror subsequently focuses them on "the main question" of who has caused the plaintiff's injury.

A second example is a car accident case between a female and a male driver. Liability was contested, and the jurors were given an instruction on comparative negligence, that is, the degree of responsibility of each party for the accident. Each juror had a copy of the instructions and referred to them as the discussion commenced.

> Juror 6: To answer his question too, it says here "If you find the defendant was not at fault, then your verdict must be . . ." wait a minute, that's not it.
>
> Juror 7: The part about if she's not fully [inaudible] don't worry about the damages percentage?
>
> Juror 6: Yeah, because you have to prove . . .
>
> Juror 1: It was his fault.
>
> Juror 6: . . . that it's his fault before you can say, like he was saying it was 10 percent his fault, but it has to proved that his story was less believable than hers before you can go to that.
>
> Juror 1: I don't . . .
>
> Juror 6: Percentage-wise it says that before you make your decision you have to say which story was most true. So if you say her story was most true then you have to go the next step, which was the percentage of it.
>
> Juror 1: To be honest what she says is irrelevant because she didn't see anything.
>
> Juror 6: Right, right . . .
>
> Juror 1: That answers the instructions on, you know if you're going to give her a percentage and say he's partly at fault, then you have to say her story was more believable than his story, that's what the instructions say.
>
> Juror 3: Unfortunately, we haven't found too many things believable about her story.
>
> Juror 1: She didn't even see it, so her story really is irrelevant too. It doesn't prove that it's his fault.
>
> Juror 3: The only thing I don't like about his, and he admitted it too, he said, "I never even considered that somebody could be approaching." He didn't see her, but he didn't even look.
>
> Juror 6: It says in the instructions, it states that before we get to that point of whether or not he's partly at fault . . .
>
> Juror 8: You have to decide which . . .
>
> Juror 7: You have to decide first . . .
>
> Juror 6: . . . you have to prove that he was . . .

Juror 1: At fault.

Juror 6: . . . more believable, or less believable than the defendant. Before you even get to whether he's 1 percent at fault or 100 percent at fault you have to go by the instructions . . .

[Additional discussion about credibility of testimony]

Juror 3: I believe he's 90 percent not guilty, but . . .

Juror 6: But that's what the instructions say, that you believe him more than you believe her.

Juror 3: Right.

Juror 6: Here, let me show you where it says that.

Juror 3: Let me see what page you're on.

Juror 1: They have to prove that . . .

Juror 7 [reading from instructions]: "if you find defendant liable to plaintiffs you must then decide the full amount of money that would reasonably and fairly compensate . . ."

Juror 1: Right. See, they have to prove that it was his fault.

Juror 6: See, I could agree with you and say that, you know, 5 percent was his fault.

Juror 2 [reading from instructions]: "If you find the party at fault . . ."

Juror 3: I was thinking 90, 10.

Juror 6: But that's only . . .

Juror 3: Let me read that page again.

Juror 7: Second to the last, at the top.

Juror 3: "If you find the defendant liable . . ."

Juror 6: It says here first, the page before that. [reading from the instructions] It says "If you find the defendant not at fault, then your verdict must be for the defendant. If you find that the defendant was at fault, then the defendant is liable to the plaintiff and your verdict must be for the plaintiff. You must then decide the full amount of the plaintiff's damages and enter the amount on the verdict form. You should then consider the defendant's claim that the plaintiff was at fault. On the defendant's claim that the plaintiffs were at fault, you must decide whether the defendant has proved that plaintiffs were at fault and under all the circumstances of the case whether any such fault should reduce the plaintiff's damages. These decisions are left to your sole discretion." So basically it's saying . . .

Juror 1: They did not prove that he was at fault.

Juror 6: Yeah. So what it's saying is that they have to prove that he was at fault first.

Juror 1: Before you can assign any percentages.

Here the jurors actively attempt to parse the meaning of the instructions, looking to them for advice on the sequencing of their decisions—first, deciding whether the defendant is at fault, and then considering the possibility of comparative fault. Once again we see the heavy use of the multiple copies of the instructions and the conferring among jurors about the meaning of particular phrases. Also we see them read from instructions, note relevant facts and credibility questions they learned at trial, and subsequently return to the instructions for guidance. Both of these examples underscore the fact that comprehending and applying legal instructions is definitely a group effort.

A CONCLUDING PERSPECTIVE ON JURY COMPETENCE

The studies showing sizeable agreement between jury verdicts and the decisions of judges yield support for the hypothesis that juries are competent, at least in the great majority of cases. As we have seen, some other studies that have taken a closer look at jury decision processes, such as case studies and mock jury projects, indicate that juries fall short on occasion. Some domains of evidence and law are more challenging than others. One particular challenge is the jury's ability to comprehend and follow particular legal instructions, especially when the instructions are at odds with their ideas about particular crimes or when the instructions ask them to engage in improbable mental gymnastics. Our brief peek at the deliberations of real juries provides some tantalizing perspectives on how jury members rely on one another to work through the legal instructions.

Richard Lempert, in his review of case studies of juries in complex trials that we mentioned earlier, made an important observation. Jury performance must be benchmarked against the likely performance of individual judges. Absent some dramatic changes in the American trial system, the judge is the alternative decision maker to the jury. In complex cases, he argues, there is no reason to think that judges will always perform optimally. Although judges have more formal education than the average person, judges, like jurors, are subject to many of the same cognitive illusions that characterize human decision making.

Although the jury's performance is generally good in the majority of cases, what about complex and highly technical disputes involving the evaluation of conflicting expert testimony? Let's turn to the topic of juries and experts.

Chapter 8

TRIALS IN A SCIENTIFIC AGE

Juries Judging Experts

CONTEMPORARY CONTROVERSY ABOUT JURIES AND EXPERTS

Despite the overall evidence that juries perform their jobs well, critics and some courts continue to argue that juries often become confused over expert testimony. Here's a sampling of opinion from a legal brief filed by one of the parties in *Kumho Tire v. Carmichael*, a 1999 US Supreme Court case about expert testimony:[1]

> [J]urors often "abdicate their fact-finding obligation" and simply "adopt" the expert's opinion.
>
> But "because experts often deal with esoteric matters of great complexity" jurors frequently are incapable of "critically evaluating the bases of an expert's testimony" and too often give "unquestioning deference to expert opinion."
>
> [Because of the "aura of infallibility"] even when jurors have a "basis for questioning the expert's reliability, [they] may be disinclined to do so."

Years ago a federal appeals court stated that expert testimony presented by scientists courted "a substantial danger of undue prejudice or of confusing the issues or of misleading the jury" because of its "aura of special reliability and trustworthiness."[2] In his 1991 book *Galileo's Revenge: Junk Science in the Courtroom*, legal commentator Peter Huber complained that plaintiff lawyers in civil cases were introducing highly questionable scientific evidence to win their cases. He asserted that they were often successful in large part because juries were "befuddled" by these experts and tended to be swayed by sympathies for badly injured plaintiffs.[3] Huber implied that judges could do a better job. In *Science on Trial*, Marcia Angell, the former editor of the *New England Journal of Medicine*, critiqued lawsuits over claims that leaking silicone gel from breast implants caused severe immune reactions.[4] She asserted that, while expert medical and scientific testimony is difficult for judges, "[f]or a jury it is especially difficult, because its members usually have no competence in the area. They are often left to make judgments largely on the basis of emotional appeals of the lawyers and their expert witnesses."

Concern about the possibility of jury reliance on unsound science underlay a series of rulings on expert evidence by the US Supreme Court in the 1990s. In these rulings, referred to as the *Daubert* trilogy after one of the cases, the Court held that trial judges should serve in a gatekeeper role, evaluating the scientific basis for expert testimony before permitting it to be introduced at a trial.[5]

Social scientists have pointed out that concerns about the jury's treatment of expert evidence are based on anecdote and appeals to common sense rather than systematic data.[6] Common sense would argue that complicated expert testimony with technical, scientific, economic, or statistical information should be challenging to the general public, and that the tendency would be to go along with a highly credentialed expert. But this reasonable-sounding notion that jurors are befuddled and dominated by scientific experts needs to be carefully examined.

We need to ask the following questions: Do juries understand expert scientific testimony and apply it reasonably and independently to the factual disputes before them, or do they abdicate their fact-finding function to the experts? Do jurors rely on superficial characteristics of the expert witness rather than analyzing the testimony's reliability? When experts for the opposing sides offer conflicting testimony, are jurors confused—or educated—by the battle of experts? Even if the jury cannot comprehend some scientific testimony presented in a trial, to what degree and how often does it make a difference in the ultimate verdict that the jury renders? How do juries fare in comparison to trial judges, the obvious alternative to the jury?

Before we answer these questions, however, it is useful to show, once again, that such controversy about juries is hardly new. Let us go back more than one hundred and fifty years.

THE TRIAL OF JOHN HENDRICKSON

In 1853 in Albany County, New York, John Hendrickson Jr. was accused of poisoning his wife, Maria, with aconitine, a derivative from the wolfsbane plant.[7] The circumstantial evidence was damning. Their marriage was rocky. Maria had left him once before because of domestic abuse, and the reconciliation was not working out. She had made arrangements to leave him again and live with her mother. Hendrickson had numerous liaisons with other women, including prostitutes, and had seriously assaulted one of them, which resulted in his fleeing the county for many months. Witnesses testified to his unsavory character. In hindsight the earlier death of their infant son also appeared suspicious. Albany druggists made tentative identification of Hendrickson as a purchaser of a medicine called aconitine and testified that he had inquired about prussic acid, another poison. Other evidence contradicted Hendrickson's claim that he awoke in the middle of the night to find Maria dead.

The circumstantial evidence, however, was probably insufficient to convict Hendrickson. To bolster their case, the prosecution called Dr. James H. Salisbury, turning the case into the major toxicology trial of the nineteenth century. Dr. Salisbury was only twenty-eight years old, but he held a medical degree and had a medical practice. He had previously testified in two trials. Most important of all, Salisbury had conducted research on the medicine aconitine. At the murder trial, he testified that Maria's intestines contained aconite poison.

Salisbury provided novel scientific evidence, since scientific laboratories in the United States and Europe had been unable to detect aconitine after it had entered body tissues. Salisbury, however, asserted that he had extracted aconitine from Maria's intestines and had literally put some on his finger and tasted it and then tested it in other ways. To double-check on his conclusion he fed the remainder to one of his laboratory cats. However, he failed to save a sample for later examination. Two other medical experts, including a Dr. Swineburn, also gave evidence consistent with Maria's being poisoned. The defense called two doctors to testify for Hendrikson, but their testimony was vague and did not directly confront Salisbury's testimony about the drug.

In closing arguments to the jury, a lead member of the prosecution team drew attention to the fact that many prominent members of the Albany medical profession had attended the trial as observers. They heard the testimony presented by Salisbury. None had come forward to refute Salisbury's testimony, which strongly implied that the findings were generally accepted by the medical community. In his lengthy summing up to the jury, Judge Richard P. Marvin, speaking for himself and the other two judges who presided over the trial (recall that major trials in the nineteenth century would typically have more than one judge), reviewed the testimony of Dr. Salisbury and emphasized that it was "very important" and that if Salisbury's opinion was "well founded . . . it places beyond all reasonable doubt the *cause of death*."[8]

Hendrickson was convicted and sentenced to hang. In the sentencing hearing, Judge Marvin commented again on Dr. Salisbury's testimony. He suggested that Hendrickson had chosen aconitine because someone had told him it could not be detected. But Judge Marvin said that this belief was now proven wrong through science: "Chemists are enabled now, through the wonderful developments of science . . . to detect almost all poisons . . . with almost unerring certainty," adding that the "[c]ommunity should understand that the crime of murder cannot be committed in this day of light . . . without leaving the evidence of guilt; and this evidence always points out, unerringly, to the guilty individual."[9]

Hendrickson's lawyer appealed, and the hoopla generated by the highly publicized trial and its verdict soon led the medical and scientific community to examine Salisbury's testimony in detail. They skewered Salisbury's scientific claims. A leader in this critical analysis was Charles A. Lee, a prominent and influential professor of pathology from Buffalo.[10] In an 1853 article in the *American Journal of the Medical Sciences*, Lee reviewed the evidence reported in the trial transcript. He concluded that aconitine could not be detected in the way that Salisbury claimed in his testimony. He also criticized the "confident and positive" demeanor that Salisbury and the other prosecution doctor displayed on the witness stand, which was in marked contrast to the more scientifically appropriate moderate and qualified testimony of the defense experts. Dr. Lee asserted that it was probable that Salisbury's and Swineburn's testimony had a greater influence on the jury than "the more careful and judicious testimony . . . of men of age, professional skill and enlarged experience" who had testified for the defense. (Indeed, we know that a witness's confidence can bolster the jury's judgment of the testimony's credibility.)

Through the efforts of Dr. Lee and others, the case became a cause célèbre among professionals in the United States and provoked responses from medical experts in England and Ireland. Some medical experts challenged Salisbury's testimony in the pages of the *New York Medical Journal* and the *New York Medical Times*. By early 1854, an overwhelming scientific majority emerged saying that Salisbury's failure to preserve the key evidence was unforgivable, that his methodology was flawed, that there were alternative explanations for his findings, and that his conclusions were inconsistent with or contradicted by research findings. The prosecution's evidence lacked what modern courts would call scientific reliability. In short, Salisbury was guilty of relying on junk science. David Wells, an expert in chemistry living in Cambridge, Massachusetts, was so agitated that he wrote four articles on the subject and, in his last piece, offered to come to Albany to testify about the chemical errors in the prosecution's evidence.

But it was too late. The court refused to reopen the case. Protests from prominent members of the medical community failed to persuade Governor Horatio Seymour to grant clemency, and public opinion was strongly against Hendrickson. A last-minute newspaper campaign to sway public opinion failed, and Hendrickson was hanged on May 5, 1854, in the courtyard of the Albany county jail.

Dr. Lee, citing the unwillingness of the courts and the governor to reconsider the case, concluded: "We pretend not to fathom the hearts or the motives of men, but we think we see in the present instance an example and illustration of the force of outward pressure—of popular excitement and prejudice—on witnesses, counsel, judges and jury, which makes us question at times, whether the boasted right and Privilege of trial by jury, be, indeed, a blessing or a curse."[11]

Should the jury have been blamed for the verdict, if indeed the verdict was wrong? Dr. Lee accused the jury of relying on superficial characteristics of the expert witnesses rather than on the substance of the evidence. But note that the scientific community's opinion that Salisbury's testimony was egregiously without scientific merit was developed only *after* the jury's verdict was rendered. The three judges who presided over the trial believed the prosecution's experts and disregarded testimony from the defendant's experts. Judge Marvin was almost in rapture about what he believed science could do. Then, too, the expert evidence was only one part of the trial. Substantial circumstantial evidence pointed to Hendrickson's guilt. The jury might have decided against Hendrickson without the expert testimony.

With these thoughts, let's return to the present day, where the testimony of experts is a frequent occurrence.

THE PREVALENCE OF EXPERT EVIDENCE IN MODERN TRIALS

Modern trials regularly include expert evidence about many subjects. Googling "expert witness" produces over a million hits, leading us to a host of directories and individual listings of people who are available to serve as experts in trials. For example, in criminal trials, experts provide testimony involving scientific or engineering-based technologies for such matters as police procedures, accident reconstruction, fire and arson analysis, handwriting, fingerprints, blood types, blood spatter patterns, DNA matches, and fiber composition. Pathologists and other medical experts are regularly called, as are mental health experts such as psychiatrists, psychologists, and social workers. Chemists, experimental psychologists, social and behavioral scientists, accountants, lawyers, and financial securities experts also provide expert testimony in criminal cases. The felony jury study in four state courts found that experts testified in over half of the criminal trials; prosecution experts were much more common than experts called by the defense.[12]

Civil trials appear even more likely to include expert testimony. Several surveys have tried to measure the typical number of experts who testify per trial. The surveys have found that the average number of experts in civil cases ranged between 3.7 and 4.1 experts per trial.[13] Combining results across these surveys, it appears that about 40 percent of the experts are in the field of medicine or mental health and another 25 percent of the experts have expertise in business, finance, or legal matters. Approximately 25 percent are specialists in engineering or safety matters, and the remainder have other scientific specialties. Medical malpractice trials require doctors to testify about standards and techniques of medical procedures. Product liability trials and patent infringement cases often require testimony from experts in biology, chemistry, physics, or engineering. In business disputes, accountants and economists testify about frequently arcane matters involving market shares or international corporate structures and accounting procedures.

This rise in the use of experts deeply concerns some observers. Attorneys can search for persuasive experts who favor the positions they are advocating. Observers worry about the ethics and reliability of expert witnesses and the adversarial pressures that could affect their testimony.

WHO IS AN EXPERT AND WHEN ARE EXPERTS ALLOWED TO TESTIFY?

To use a quaint legal phrase, experts are people who have knowledge that is ordinarily "beyond the ken" of the average person. The Federal Rules of Evidence locate expertise in training or experience and require that expert testimony "assist the trier of fact to understand the evidence or to determine a fact in issue."[14] Many states have followed the federal lead with similar rules that govern expert testimony. The expert's opinion is not intended to replace the jury's decision-making role. Rather, it is intended to help the jury comprehend the factual evidence and resolve the case.

The jury does not work autonomously; the trial judge makes procedural rulings about the expert evidence they are allowed to hear, relying on legal standards that help define when and under which conditions expert evidence is admissible. These guidelines include assessments of whether the testimony is from a competent expert in a field of knowledge, whether the testimony is relevant to the issues in the case, and whether it will assist the jury. It can be barred if it gets too close to the core legal questions for the jury. For example, in a rape trial, a judge would allow an expert to testify that a woman who was examined had had recent intercourse and that tears and bruises were consistent with forcible sex. The judge might allow another expert to testify that the woman's early refusal to admit she was raped was consistent with rape trauma syndrome. However, neither expert would be permitted to testify that the woman was raped. That judgment has elements that go beyond the witness's expertise and would be left for the jury.[15]

THE RELATIVE IMPORTANCE OF EXPERT EVIDENCE FOR THE JURY'S DECISION

We have already raised a question about how important Dr. Salisbury's testimony was in the Hendrickson case. Was the circumstantial evidence that Hendrickson had attempted to buy poison and that his story was contradicted by other witnesses sufficient evidence of guilt? Debate about juries and experts often employs examples of instances in which the expert evidence is central to a determination of guilt or negligence. For example, the defendant's DNA matches with the DNA from semen in the raped murder victim, or the surgeon severs the third sacral nerve rather than the fourth nerve in a rhizotomy operation. There may be other evidence in such cases, but the expert evidence makes or breaks the case. In many trials, however, the expert testimony may be only one piece of evidence among others that needs to be weighed by the jury. Consider some illustrative examples.

A woman ran over her adulterous husband. She claimed it was an accident, but others accused her of murder. Two eyewitnesses, who saw the incident from two different vantage points, testified that she ran her car over him three separate times. An accident reconstruction expert called by the defense testified that his examination of tire marks at the scene indicated that the husband was run over once. Which evidence was more credible?

In an environmental lawsuit, the expert for the plaintiff—the city—presented evidence that the defendant company was polluting the water in its lakes, the sources of the city's water supply. The defense, on the other hand, called civilian witnesses to testify about other sources of the pollution.

In short, an expert's testimony may be contradicted by the testimony of another expert, it may be contradicted by nonexpert evidence that is more persuasive, or it may be rendered irrelevant by a change in the nature of issues argued at the trial. In some trials it may never be intended to be the lynchpin of the case but is offered only because the lawyer is covering all of the bases and presenting evidence as thoroughly as possible. In other cases, such as toxic tort litigation, the expert evidence is so essential that if, prior to trial, the judge holds that the plaintiff's expert evidence is inadmissible, the case is dismissed. Thus, the expert evidence may be of major or minor importance in the jury's reaching a factually correct verdict.

JURY INSTRUCTIONS: WHAT IS EXPECTED OF JURORS

Recognition of what the law expects and instructs the jurors to do is central to the claims about juror responses to experts. This is particularly true with regard to the claims that jurors give undue attention to expert credentials and that they defer to experts while disregarding other evidence. A federal civil jury pattern instruction explains how jurors should treat expert testimony:

> You have heard testimony from [a] person[s] who, because of education or experience, [is] [are] permitted to state opinions and the reasons for those opinions. Opinion testimony should be judged just like any other testimony. You may accept it or reject it, and give it as much weight as you think it deserves, considering the witness' education and experience, the reasons given for the opinion, and all the other evidence in the case.[16]

Jurors are specifically admonished to treat expert testimony like any other testimony and to weigh that testimony against other evidence. Thus jury performance cannot be properly evaluated without considering the total context in which the jurors are asked to perform their task. It is essential for juries to be sensitive to the specific purpose of expert evidence as defined by the trial judge's ruling and jury instructions as well as its degree of relevance to the ultimate issue or issues of the case. Yet context and instructions are often ignored or misunderstood in debates about how well jurors evaluate expert testimony.

Under our adversary system of legal procedure, the experts who appear at trial are selected by each party for opinions that are consistent with its side. Nevertheless, the opposing side has an opportunity to cross-examine the expert and expose the expert evidence's weaknesses and irrelevancies. The opposing side may, and frequently does, call its own experts to offer an opposing opinion. While some critics say that the "battle of experts" only confuses jurors, an alternative view is that the whole process exposes jurors to and educates jurors about the nature of the evidence. In difficult cases, one or the other of these views may seem especially plausible.

THE INTELLECTUAL COMPETENCE OF JURIES REGARDING EXPERTS

Some critics assert that, by its very nature, many forms of expert evidence are not only "beyond the ken" of average laypersons but are also beyond their intellectual capacity. Some expert testimony, especially that containing scientific, medical, and economic material, involves issues such as determining causation, assessing statistical representativeness, and using conditional probabilities. In their daily lives, ordinary people are quite adept at applying complex causal reasoning and analyzing how representative certain events are. These abilities, called "domain-specific skills," are particular to one setting. They do not necessarily transfer to other settings like the courtroom that may require similar reasoning. Nevertheless, with even relatively brief training sessions, laypersons can be taught to transfer these skills to other domains. A key question regarding jurors' competence to evaluate and apply expert evidence is whether the trial process provides jurors with the domain-specific education needed to properly assess the quality of that testimony. If it does not, is that because of how that education is given or because the jury is incapable of being so educated?

Students of persuasion and decision making have in recent years paid particular attention to the cognitive processes by which information is received, weighed, and evaluated. Two basic types of information processing seem to exist: central and peripheral processing. As we've seen, sometimes people take mental shortcuts in processing information, especially when messages are complex or difficult. Instead of focusing on the central content of the message, they pay attention to peripheral cues like the length of the communication, the number of arguments, or the professed expertise of the speaker.

The argument that juries defer to the credentials of the expert and fail to scrutinize the logic of the expert's testimony is, in these terms, an assumption that jurors engage in peripheral processing. Confronted with a highly credentialed expert, jurors engaged in peripheral processing would decide the expert has impressive credentials and for this reason accept the expert's judgment. This need not be irrational or silly, particularly if issues are esoteric and complex or if one side's experts have stronger or more germane credentials than the other's.

Peripheral processing is less likely to occur when people are motivated to understand the message and have the intellectual ability to grapple with the arguments. Studies involving posttrial interviews with jurors and the tapes of actual deliberations show that jurors appear highly motivated to understand the facts of the case and that they pool their individual intellectual resources during deliberations. These factors encourage central as opposed to peripheral processing.

RESEARCH ON JUROR UNDERSTANDING OF EXPERT TESTIMONY

Earlier we described research revealing that judges have shown substantial agreement with jury verdicts in complex cases and that the agreement rate is about the same in both straightforward and complex cases. Both of these empirical facts lead to the reassuring conclusion that the jury's ability to understand complex expert testimony is sufficient to reach a sound verdict. A number of more specific studies and experiments have been undertaken in order to assess whether and under what conditions jurors understand expert testimony.[17]

Richard Lempert's insightful survey of twelve complex trials, discussed earlier, included careful analysis of the jurors' treatment of complex evidence, including expert testimony.[18] He drew attention to the fact that the juries in these longer than average trials contained few or no jurors with college degrees. Jurors with more formal education had a better chance at comprehending complex evidence and leading the jury, yet they were not fully represented on the juries who heard these demanding cases. Jurors reportedly struggled in several of these cases with complex evidence. Even so, Lempert concluded that the juries seemed to be able to differentiate between more and less reliable scientific evidence and that the inability to understand expert evidence rarely seemed to be a factor in erroneous verdicts. (Those Lempert attributed primarily to the mistakes of lawyers and judges.)

In the juror interview project Valerie Hans undertook on juries that decided business lawsuits, she and Sanja Kutnjak Ivković focused in-depth on the jurors' comments about trial experts in a set of fifty-five juror interviews.[19] These jurors served in trials concerning medical malpractice, workplace injuries, product liability, asbestos injuries, and motor vehicle accidents. On average each trial had slightly over four testifying experts. Ivković and Hans observed that rather than uncritically accepting expert opinion at face value, the jurors recognized that the experts were selected within an adversary process and from the outset regarded them with a critical eye. Jurors paid some attention to the experts' credentials, considering the witness's institutional affiliation, specialization, education, research, and professional activity. They also considered the role of an expert witness's motive for testifying. Often lawyers for the other side would ask about the amount of the expert fee. One juror observed: "I was very interested also in their fees, which were—it was funny . . . two or three were getting four hundred dollars an hour; one was getting two hundred and sixty-five dollars an hour; and we're saying, you know, "We're getting fifteen dollars a day."[20] Jurors looked down on some of the experts in asbestos cases because of their frequent appearances in court: "The defense attorney brought out that 95 percent of this guy's income is just testifying in asbestos cases all over the United States, and then you felt like he had a racket."[21] Jurors also perceived bias in the case of a friendship between the defendant doctor in a medical malpractice suit and the expert witness who testified on his behalf.

Jurors appeared to employ sensible techniques to evaluate expert testimony. The clarity and educational value of the presentation were important: "He was extremely knowledgeable. . . . The way he explained things to the jury and to the courtroom, we all understood perfectly. He would have been a great teacher."[22] They assessed the completeness and consistency of the testimony and evaluated it against their knowledge of related factors. Juries also relied on the members of the jury who possessed greater familiarity with the subject matter of the expert testimony.

In other research, Anthony Champagne, Daniel Shuman, and their collaborators have conducted juror surveys and other studies to examine juror reactions to experts. The majority of jurors agreed that expert testimony was important to their cases. They reportedly relied on the expert's ability to present complex information in a straightforward way, the expert's willingness to reach a definite conclusion, the expert's reputation, and the expert's credentials. The researchers concluded on the basis of their multiple studies that there was no "white coat syndrome." Instead, they discovered jurors who were demanding and skeptical in their evaluation of expert evidence: "Jurors made expert-specific decisions based on a sensible set of considerations—the expert's qualifications, reasoning, factual familiarity and impartiality. Our data do not lend support to the critics who paint jurors as gullible, naïve or thoughtless persons who resort to irrational decision-making strategies that rely on superficial considerations."[23]

Judith Fordham, an Australian barrister and professor of forensic science, attended criminal trials and then conducted detailed interviews with the jurors, specifically focusing on how the jurors understood the expert evidence.[24] The interviews revealed that the jurors were aware of conscious and even unconscious biases of experts. They appreciated experts who were willing to alter their opinions in the face of new information presented during the trial and they considered the congruence of the expert's opinion with other trial evidence. Fordham concluded that jurors are more sophisticated than they are given credit for. Detailed interviews with criminal trial jurors in New Zealand reached a conclusion consistent with the American and Australian jury studies.[25]

Not every set of juror interviews has yielded results that are a ringing endorsement of jury competence. Some of the case studies we've reviewed, and that were included in Lempert's case study analysis—the Rand asbestos study and Joseph Sanders's Bendectin juror interviews—uncovered problems in juror comprehension of expert evidence.[26] Researchers in both of these studies concluded that the jurors they interviewed misunderstood the epidemiological evidence presented by experts.[27] In the Bendectin case study, jurors had a difficult time distinguishing between experts and tended to view all of the experts as biased. They also overestimated the percentage of scientists who believed the drug Bendectin caused birth defects and confused the legal concept of general causation with causation in specific cases.

Still other research has been based on experiments, including mock jury studies in which jury-eligible people hear expert testimony presented in different formats and conditions. Although mock jury research lacks the contextual richness of a jury trial, it can provide some insights into factors that might influence juror treatment of expert witnesses. A number of studies have examined factors affecting the persuasiveness and comprehension of expert testimony. We present some illustrative examples of this work.

For instance, professors Shari Diamond and Jay Casper conducted a realistic mock jury experiment of an antitrust trial in which the expert testimony involved an estimate of damages suffered by the plaintiff.[28] Some jurors heard the expert provide a damage assessment using a complex statistical presentation, while others listened to an expert assess damages employing a more concrete "yardstick" model. The mock jurors saw the statistical expert as less clear but also as having greater expertise. The clarity of one side's expert canceled out the expertise advantage of the other. Although the statistical form of the evidence was harder to understand, jurors under both conditions showed generally good comprehension.

Joel Cooper and his colleagues conducted simulation studies in which they varied the complexity of expert testimony and the expert's credentials.[29] Recall that challenging material may encourage more peripheral than central processing. If mock jurors are more apt to use peripheral processing when the evidence is complex, then we should see that credentials are more important when the evidence is complicated, and that is what Cooper and his colleagues found in an initial experiment. In another effort to study when jurors might shift to peripheral processing, they varied the expert's pay along with the complexity of the evidence. When the testimony was simple, pay had no impact; but when it was complicated, the highest-paid expert was rated the least trustworthy. That suggests jurors shifted to peripheral processing. However, it's also possible that the mock jurors may have centrally processed the evidence but dismissed it when the expert's motives seemed suspect and the testimony was seen as purposefully confusing.[30]

An interesting experiment by University of Nebraska psychology and law professor Brian Bornstein contrasted how people responded to different types of expert scientific evidence in a civil lawsuit about lead contamination.[31] His study participants reviewed short descriptions of the case, including epidemiological evidence presented by a plaintiff's expert. The defense expert provided either anecdotal evidence (relevant case histories of three boys) or experimental evidence (a relevant animal study). The defendant's case was viewed more favorably when the anecdotal evidence was presented. Experts appeared to have more impact when they presented concrete examples than when they summarized research findings, a finding that is consistent with other work on psychological expert testimony.[32]

LIES, DAMN LIES, AND STATISTICS: FORENSIC EVIDENCE AND STATISTICAL MATCHES

A robber wearing a blue-hooded sweatshirt and gloves walks into a Connecticut bank and demands money from the bank teller. After receiving over $5,000, he flees on foot. A police manhunt ensues. The search for the robber is unsuccessful but does turn up wads of the marked money, together with a blue-hooded sweatshirt and a pair of gloves. Two strands of hair are discovered on the sweatshirt. The hairs are tested by using a novel form of DNA analysis—mitochondrial DNA (mtDNA) analysis—which is employed when there is minimal or degraded biological material for scientific testing. Police eventually receive a tip about the likely robber. The suspect's mtDNA is analyzed and found to match the mtDNA of the sweatshirt hairs. Prosecution and defense experts disagree about the exact likelihood of a match.

Two hairs may seem to be a slender basis for a criminal felony conviction, but they were a central part of the felony trial of Stephen Pappas, accused of being a Connecticut robber.[33] The hairs were not the only evidence—there was a web of circumstantial and testimonial evidence that also tied him to the robbery. But the mtDNA analysis was an integral tool for law enforcement and prosecutors as they assembled evidence for Pappas's criminal trial. One important question faced the judge and attorneys in the case: Would a lay jury be able to understand the importance and limits of mtDNA analysis, comprehend the claims of an expert about the likelihood of a match, and use the information appropriately in judging the guilt of Mr. Pappas?

The introduction and relevance of mitochondrial DNA, like many other forms of forensic evidence, relies on understanding the meaning of statistical probabilities. The interpretation of these probabilities can be important in deciding what weight to give specific trial evidence. Yet a growing body of research indicates that when posed with abstract statistical problems, most people who are not trained in making statistical inferences perform poorly, including both jurors and judges.[34]

Suppose that a forensic expert testifies about a match between biological or other evidence—blood type, DNA evidence, a hair sample, or a bite mark—at the crime scene and the defendant. The forensic expert will often make a statement about the likelihood that a random person in the population would match the crime scene evidence, a statistic called a random match probability. To understand and properly apply the evidence, the juror or judge has to understand some of the statistical reasoning behind probability estimates and random matches. Do jurors know, or can they learn, enough about the statistical reasoning to be able to weigh the evidence appropriately?

Researchers have identified two common mistakes that many of us make when reasoning about the probabilities involved in a match. One is called the "prosecutor's fallacy."[35] Suppose our forensic expert testifies that the random match probability of some DNA evidence—the probability that DNA from a randomly selected person in the population would match the crime scene DNA—is 1 percent. People tend to flip or transpose this number and conclude that because there is only a 1 percent chance that an innocent person's DNA would match, the likelihood of the defendant's guilt is 99 percent. That fails to take into account all of the other evidence in the case that may point to or be inconsistent with the defendant's guilt. Another misuse of statistics is labeled the "defense attorney's fallacy." Here, a defense attorney confronted with a 1 percent random match probability might argue that there are many other individuals whose DNA could match the crime scene DNA in a large population, and therefore the DNA evidence should be disregarded.[36] That, too, is a mistake—the DNA should still be an informative piece of evidence that can be combined with the rest of the evidence to assess the likelihood of the defendant's guilt.

William Thompson of the University of California at Irvine, along with his students and other collaborators, has spent decades studying how jurors handle statistical evidence.[37] Under some circumstances, mock jurors give statistical information too much weight, in others, too little. Thompson has also discovered that mock jurors have trouble discovering the flaws in arguments based on statistics. This means they could be especially prone to false arguments that might arise in an adversarial trial.

Other mock juror research studies confirm that people have trouble with concepts of statistical probability as they attempt to employ it in judging guilt.[38] DNA evidence might be less informative—or even worthless—if crime laboratory technicians make errors in the analysis or otherwise contaminate the DNA samples. This requires jurors to combine the random match probability with the likelihood that the crime lab made an error in its analysis. One simulation experiment found that mock jurors tended to give less than optimal weight to the possibility of a laboratory error in DNA analysis when it was accompanied by estimates of a low random match probability.[39] Another experiment also found that the mock jurors gave less weight to the evidence than was warranted. This was partly because the jurors did not understand how to combine probabilities of error in the match and errors in the laboratory and partly because of their prior beliefs about corruption of the original samples as they passed through the hands of the police and prosecutors.[40]

A study by Brian Smith, Steven Penrod, Amy Otto, and Roger Park had more encouraging findings.[41] These researchers varied the strength of forensic evidence presented to their study participants. Some learned that an enzyme test matched the defendant and that approximately 20 percent of the population shared that enzyme type. Others heard about the match but learned that 80 percent of the population shared the enzyme type. The former evidence is obviously more informative than the latter, and the participants' judgments about the likelihood of guilt appropriately reflected that difference. Furthermore, an instruction about how to combine probabilities helped participants avoid the defense attorney's fallacy described above.

A realistic mock jury study conducted by one of the authors (Hans) with several collaborators concerned jury comprehension of expert scientific evidence.[42] The key purpose of the experiment was to determine how different jury reforms might help jurors better understand scientific evidence. The study, conducted over a period of several months, included four hundred and eighty-eight people from the jury pool in Wilmington, Delaware, who were at the courthouse but not needed for trial. They watched a videotape of a mock trial based on the case of the Pappas robbery, mentioned earlier. The defendant, like Stephen Pappas, was charged with bank robbery, and, like Pappas, was linked to the crime through two human hairs found on a sweatshirt. (Pappas was convicted by his Connecticut jury.)

The FBI expert presented basic information about DNA, including mitochondrial DNA. Jurors then heard conflicting expert opinions by an FBI analyst for the prosecution and a geneticist for the defense regarding the significance of mitochondrial DNA analysis of the two human hairs. There was additional evidence in the trial, but the conflicting opinions provided estimates of the likelihood of a match. The FBI analyst estimated that only six men in the local geographical area of about forty thousand people could have the DNA profile, whereas the defense expert estimated as many as fifty-seven local men could have that DNA pattern.

The jury deliberations were videotaped and analyzed, and the jurors also filled out questionnaires about their understanding of the issues. The results showed that the jurors demonstrated a basic comprehension of the expert evidence. Many of the jurors understood and could explain some technical terms and their relevance to the contested issues. However, like the less realistic mock juror projects, some of the jurors showed susceptibility to the classic fallacies in reasoning about probabilities. The jurors did not appear to be overwhelmed by the prosecution evidence about an extremely low random match probability; instead, they seemed more inclined to agree with the defense attorney that the mitochondrial DNA evidence was irrelevant because of the number of other people who could be the source of the hairs.

Several factors were associated with improved comprehension of the scientific evidence. Not surprisingly, people who had more education and more background in science and mathematics were better able to understand the scientific evidence. Deliberations improved juror comprehension about the scientific issues. Furthermore, jurors who were able to use particular jury innovations—specifically, jury notebooks, which included the expert's slides and a glossary of terms, and a checklist to use with the scientific evidence—performed better in some instances. (Note taking and juror questions, shown to be useful in other contexts, did not improve comprehension of the scientific evidence in this study, perhaps because of the short time frame and the small number of questions asked.) Thus, modifications that judges and lawyers can use at trial can ameliorate some of the difficulties of juror comprehension.

One point to note is that as the science has improved, DNA random match probabilities—especially for nuclear DNA—are extremely close to zero. Therefore, in the absence of evidence of contamination or laboratory error, it may not matter much if jurors cannot handle probabilistic information well. That said, other types of forensic evidence that are not as diagnostic as DNA may continue to require jurors to engage in the meaningful assessment of probabilities. The insights derived from work with DNA should prove helpful with these other types of evidence. Another point is that many of the mock juror statistics studies involved relatively simple presentations of evidence, and we cannot be positive that such errors persist in a full-blown adversary jury trial, where attorneys have other avenues to try to convey the meaning of statistics to the jury. However, the consistent problems that statistical presentations appear to produce—even in the more realistic mock jury trial just described—indicate that, in cases that rely on statistical evidence, judges and attorneys should be open to employing jury innovations and even to exploring new approaches to evidence presentation to promote jury understanding.

THE JURY AT WORK: EXPERT EVIDENCE IN CIVIL TRIALS

The Arizona jury data provide examples of jurors responding to expert testimony. These examples illustrate that the jurors were actively engaged in collective efforts to understand expert testimony.

In one case the plaintiff said he had severe back and leg pain resulting from an accident. As is not infrequent in automobile claims that go to trial, this plaintiff had preexisting injuries and health problems. The treating physician and another physician testified for him regarding tests performed and the prescribed treatment. Recall that jurors in Arizona civil trials have the right to ask questions of witnesses. Here are questions jurors asked those experts:

> Why [are there] no medical records beyond the two years prior to the accident? What tests or determination besides subjective patient's say-so determined [your diagnosis of] a migraine? What exact symptoms did he have regarding a migraine? Why no other tests to rule out other neurological problems? Is there a measurement for the amount of serotonin in his brain? What causes serotonin not to work properly? Is surgery a last resort? What is indothomiacin? Can it cause problems if you have prostate problems?

In another automobile injury case, an overweight plaintiff alleged injury to her knee that required surgery. Her diagnostic radiologist testified and so did an accident reconstruction expert. The radiologist was asked these questions by jurors:

> Did you see the tears in the meniscus? Do you see degeneration in young people and what about people of the plaintiff's age? Is a tear in the meniscus a loosening, lack or gash in the cartilage? Can you tell the age of a tear due to an injury? Can you see healed tissue in an MRI? Do cartilage tears heal by themselves? Can healed tears appear younger [more recent] than they really are?

A defense medical expert in the same case was asked:

> Could the plaintiff have sustained a blunt meniscal tear during the accident? Could one tear cause another tear?

Questions to the plaintiff's accident reconstruction expert included the following:

Not knowing how she was sitting or her weight, how can you be sure she hit her knee? Would these factors change your estimate of 15ft/sec travel speed? If a body in motion stays in motion, and she was continuing motion from prior to the impact, how did this motion begin and what do you base this on? How tall is the person who sat in your exemplar car to reconstruct the accident and how heavy was he? What is the error in your 10 mph estimate? Is the time of 50–70 milliseconds based on an estimate of the size of the dent? Do you conclude that the Olds was slowed and pushed to the left by the Lincoln and [if so] how would the plaintiff move to the right and forward?

The above examples suggest that the jurors followed the evidence and perceived gaps in it. They are striking, not just for the information the jury sought, but also for what they tell us about the information that the parties' lawyers intentionally or unintentionally failed, it seems, to provide. Not only did the party calling the expert fail to ask about these issues on direct examination, but the opposing party failed to adequately inquire into them on cross-examination. One lawyer or the other had probably made a mistake, and together, absent the allowance of the juror questions, the jury would have been kept in the dark about facts that at least some jurors thought important.

In another trial involving an automobile accident, the defendant's vehicle hit the plaintiff's car, slipped under the bumper, and caused an alleged whiplash injury. The plaintiff and defendant presented conflicting evidence about how fast the defendant's vehicle was traveling. The plaintiff claimed it was traveling as much as forty-five miles per hour, and the defendant claimed it was going less than ten at the time of impact. An accident reconstruction expert corroborated the defendant's claim, yet a chiropractor testified that the plaintiff had sustained a serious injury. The jurors closely examined the accident scene photographs and compared their personal experience with the expert testimony:

Juror 6: Uh, it's [the bumper] pushed down. It's pushed down, but that's just the fact that if you hit down at the bottom it's going to push that down.

Juror 3: Well, uh, that guy [the expert] that uh, the defense brought down said it's just like running into one of those concrete curbs in the parking lot, you know, because I've rolled into those myself at 5 miles per hour.

Juror 6: Right, but you're hitting something underneath you're not hitting something that's got a shock on it, you're hitting frame and that's going to jar the snot out of you more than something hitting your bumper: But see, but there's, to me it doesn't look like there's that much physical damage to the thing and if it's going to be something that, I mean I've, you know, been bumped in a parking lot or been bumped on the street and no damage was done and nobody was hurt [Juror 9 nods in agreement]. And if he's laying a skid mark, he's doing, you know, 35 mile an hour, and he lays a 20 foot skid, and his, sort of, he's not going to look down to see how fast, he's not going "how fast am I going to hit her at?"

Juror 3: No.

Jurors 6 and 3 [in unison]: He's just guesstimating . . .

Juror 5: Well almost anything will cause the brakes to [inaudible phrase]

Juror 3 [interrupts]: Well, uh, I like the question you were asking [Juror 3 points to Juror 9] if someone's prepared and someone's not prepared. But 6 miles an hour, I mean . . .

Juror 3 [talking while staring at an exhibit and leaning back in his chair]: Um, I pretty much agree with the uh, with the uh, uh the gentleman the uh, defense brought down. Uh, in question of uh . . .

And uh, what I kind of find interesting is at the hospital all they found was uh, musculature, and uh, then he's [the chiropractor who testified for the plaintiff] finding stuff wrong with her spine which the hospital didn't find anything on their x-rays, so . . .

Juror 9: So the compelling evidence from you was [that of the accident reconstruction] expert?

Juror 3: Yeah.

In a business dispute, the plaintiff claimed that the defendant's fraudulent actions had caused the plaintiff's business to fail. Both plaintiff and defendant were experienced business people and both offered their own estimates of projected income if the business had succeeded. Both called financial experts to bolster their own positions:

Juror 4: I know they say to not speculate, but since the word there is desirous, we have to speculate on the purchase price.

Juror 8: When they say speculate I don't believe that's the instruction you refer to. I believe the whole case is about making a projection but I think speculation refers to things that are not in evidence, like, what did he do wrong. We have to make a projection—that's the only way to assess a value.

Juror 6: At that point we have to decide how valid [the plaintiff's] projections are, how credible was her projection . . .

Juror 5 interjects: Compared to?

Juror 6 continues: How credible was [expert] Olson's? I think he reinforced his report in the advertising area as opposed to [the defendant] and Seligman and Schultz [defense expert].

. . .

Juror 5: So how many of you guys think the [defendant]—I really don't think he did anything to hurt the plaintiff because all the information she gave was all factual.

Juror 1: I do too, although those projections . . . were not as optimistic as Olson's.

. . .

Juror 8: One of the things about Olson's testimony that I don't agree with [Juror 8 turns to Juror 1 and says he agrees that Olson was a bit too optimistic] is, I think he was too pessimistic because he almost discounted word of mouth . . .

Juror 6: He didn't consider product identification, either.

[Several jurors agree.]

Juror 5: As far as [the plaintiff] is concerned do we need to talk about him any more? Do we need to go on . . . ?

Juror 8: I put this up [pointing to a chart placed in front of jurors] because none of us disagreed with the methodology that [the defendant's expert] used—they only challenged his numbers. So we should go back and say do we believe these numbers or do they need to be adjusted. If we do that it will kind of focus us.

Juror 8: I had no problem with the cost reductions of [the defense expert]—they seemed reasonable. I'm not real convinced on the growth factors.

Juror 6: Were they based on a study?

Juror 8: They were based on Schulz's curve and they were less optimistic than Olson's.

Juror 1: So Schulz adjusted the advertising response curve less optimistically . . .

Juror 8: So these numbers [pointing to the chart] are less optimistic than Olson's.

Juror 6 asks: Do you think the defense was able to discredit Olson?

Several jurors: No.

Here we see jurors in a range of cases actively evaluating expert testimony, critically examining its implicit and explicit assumptions, and drawing, when possible, on their own knowledge and life experiences to place the expert claims in context. It seems to us that this is exactly what jurors should be doing. As to whether they get it right in each case, we could reasonably ask, could a judge alone, with a professional life ordinarily limited to judging and legal practice, do better?

JUDGES JUDGING SCIENCE

Recall that in *Hendrikson*, Judge Marvin was clearly enthralled with the scientific evidence bearing on the detection of poisons and that Dr. Lee castigated both the jury and the judges for their lack of acumen in detecting pseudoscience. In the modern era, some judges continued to allow Bendectin cases to come to trial even after the development of scientific consensus that Bendectin did not cause birth defects. Dr. Marcia Angell's assertion that a judge could do a better job in assessing breast implant illness claims ignored the fact that, on appeal, a *three-judge panel* also concluded that the defendant was responsible for exposing thousands of women to a devastating disease.

Case studies by a panel of statistical experts formed by the National Research Council concluded that judges frequently misinterpreted statistical information.[43] In 1999 a study of four hundred state trial court judges from all fifty states by Sophia Gatowski, James Richardson and their colleagues found that judges tended to view themselves as competent in assessing scientific evidence.[44] However, only about six percent of them could give adequate answers to questions about some of the scientific research terms that are essential for evaluating scientific procedures. As we discussed earlier, judges are subject to some of the same cognitive biases that cause jurors to misinterpret statistical evidence.[45]

These findings should not be taken to mean that judges are incompetent in deciding cases. They are highly educated and have expert training and experience in the law. Many judges do a heroic job attempting to master the intricacies of complex scientific issues in disputes before them. Depending on the jurisdiction's method of assigning cases to judges, judges with special expertise may also be selected to preside over cases involving very technical science or other matters. They can take advantage of judicial training programs and continuing legal education on the scientific issues that are likely to arise. Aids like the Science for Judges Program and the Federal Judicial Center's *Reference Manual on Scientific Evidence* can provide the background judges need to serve as a gatekeeper.[46] Judges also have the ability to study the evidence during the trial and formulate questions for the experts that jurors typically lack. All of these possibilities could give judges a fact-finding advantage over the jury, at least on the scientific issues.

Nevertheless, most judges are laypeople when it comes to understanding scientific procedures and interpreting statistical evidence. The difficulties that both judges and juries face in evaluating expert evidence challenge the easy assumption that, because of education or experience, a trial judge deciding alone will more often than not do better than the jury in judging scientific expert testimony. Moreover, there is no one to backstop the judge, but the judge can do this for the jury. In criminal trials where the jury convicts, and in all civil trials, the judge who is convinced the jury has erred in its verdict may enter a verdict for the other side or order a new trial. If judges frequently believed that jury verdicts in cases with complex scientific evidence were untenable, we should see more trial judges reversing jury verdicts than we do now.

JURIES AND EXPERT EVIDENCE IN PERSPECTIVE

Criticisms of the ways that juries deal with experts have been based on anecdotes and failures to adequately consider the legal instructions that jurors are given by the trial judges, the relative importance of expert evidence compared to other trial evidence, and the educative effects of competing expert testimony and cross-examination of experts. Contradicting the anecdotal evidence, we now have systematic findings from a series of research studies that show jurors to be diligent and skeptical in evaluating expert testimony.

At the same time, there can be little doubt that expert evidence, especially in cases with complex statistical evidence, poses difficulties for jurors. From what we can tell, jurors tend to give too little weight rather than too much weight to evidence they don't understand. They are susceptible to agreeing with fallacious reasoning about statistics. No doubt jurors sometimes get it wrong—just as trial judges have been shown to get it wrong.

The bright side is that we probably can do better. There are strong hints in the research findings that better evidence presentations by lawyers and their experts, supervised by alert trial judges, can eliminate some of the difficulties. Other trial reforms such as allowing jurors to take notes, ask questions, employ jury notebooks, and use evidence checklists may also help.

Chapter 9

JUDGING CRIMINAL RESPONSIBILITY

Erroneous Convictions, the CSI *Effect, and the Victim's Role*

Two competing yet equally troubling images of the criminal jury have emerged in recent years. Both feature the gullible and error-prone jury. The first image emerges from the work done by the Innocence Project and other investigators, who have assembled clear evidence of erroneous convictions by juries, some that have placed defendants on death row. The other is the so-called *CSI* effect, named after the television program and its spin-offs that highlight the world and work of crime scene investigators. Jurors who consume a steady diet of *CSI* television are reportedly reluctant to convict when the messy world of real criminal trials does not measure up to what they have come to expect from prosecutors trying to prove their cases. In one set of cases, the jury is seen as too keen to convict, in the other, too averse.

Our examination of the criminal jury highlights these and other key issues that have sparked controversy over the jury's role and performance. The role of both crime victim and criminal defendant are implicated. We've already described how jurors carefully evaluate trial evidence, arranging it in the form of a narrative story that is organized around the motives of key parties. Their evaluations are tested and refined in the jury deliberation. The results strongly overlap with those of legal experts, with the perceived strength of the evidence as the major determinant of jury verdicts. So, how do juries come to convict an innocent defendant or acquit a guilty one?

ERRONEOUS CONVICTIONS IN JURY TRIALS

On two occasions in the same evening in July 1984, a black male assailant broke into apartments in a North Carolina town, severed the phone wires, and sexually assaulted and robbed their female occupants.[1] The next month, Ronald Cotton, a young black man, was arrested for these crimes. In January 1985 Cotton was convicted by a jury of one count of rape and one count of burglary. His conviction, however, was overturned because one of the victims had identified another man in the police lineup. He was granted a second trial, and in 1987 he was found guilty of both rapes and two counts of burglary and sentenced to life plus fifty-four years.

The prosecution's evidence at the second trial included a photo identification by one of the victims, a flashlight from Cotton's home that resembled one used by the assailant, and rubber from Mr. Cotton's tennis shoe that was consistent with evidence at the crime scene. However, the most important evidence was the eyewitness identification of Cotton by one of the victims.

Twenty-two-year-old college student Jennifer Thompson was awakened at about three o'clock in the morning. A man held a knife to her throat and raped her. The quick-witted woman remained calm enough to talk to and scrutinize the face of her assailant and try to commit to memory any other distinguishing characteristics for later identification. She asked permission to go to the bathroom, and when he allowed her to do so, the light gave her further opportunity to look closely at the man. After the rape, she asked permission to get a drink of water and while in the kitchen she escaped to a neighbor's apartment from which the police were called.

After being taken to the hospital and submitting to a forensic exam to collect semen samples, Thompson was asked to go to the police department, where she developed a composite sketch of her assailant from a police identification kit. Using the sketch, the police identified several African American men, including Ronald Cotton, age twenty-two, who worked at a restaurant near her apartment and who had a minor criminal history. Ms. Thompson was shown a photo array that included Mr. Cotton and five other black males. She identified Cotton as similar to the man who had raped her, and he was arrested. Later, the police arranged a live lineup in which each person was asked to step forward and say a few sentences. After carefully scrutinizing the members of the lineup and asking to have the process repeated, Thompson again identified Cotton.

Before the second trial began, Ronald Cotton was optimistic about an acquittal. While in prison after the first trial, he learned that Bobby Poole, one of the other inmates—a tall black man convicted of rape who bore a strong resemblance to the composite sketch—had reportedly bragged to his fellow inmates that he had committed the rapes for which Cotton was charged. At the trial, out of the presence of the jury, Poole was brought into the courtroom with Cotton so that Jennifer Thompson could make the comparison. She identified Cotton again. As she told PBS's *Frontline* television program that produced a story on the Cotton case in 1997, when Bobby Poole was brought in to the courtroom: "I never remember looking at Bobby Poole, thinking, 'I've got the wrong person. . . . I've made a huge mistake. . . .' That never entered my head." Based on the two identifications made by Jennifer Thompson and the other victim, the jury, who never saw Bobby Poole, returned a guilty verdict.

In 1994 two new lawyers took over Ronald Cotton's defense. They filed a motion arguing that Mr. Cotton's original lawyers had provided ineffective assistance of counsel. The new lawyers asked for DNA testing of the semen samples taken at the time of the rapes. Their motion was granted in October 1994. The samples from one victim were too deteriorated to be conclusive, but the samples from the other victim's vaginal swab and underwear were subjected to PCR-based DNA testing and showed no match to Ronald Cotton. At the defense's request, the results were sent to the State Bureau of Investigation's DNA database, which contained the DNA patterns of convicted violent felons in North Carolina prisons. The state's database showed a match with Bobby Poole. In 1995, after serving ten and a half years in prison, Ronald Cotton was officially cleared of all charges and released. Subsequently, Ms. Thompson has spoken out courageously and publicly about her error and pointed to the dangers of relying solely on a very confident eyewitness.

How could the jury have gotten it wrong? The Innocence Project identifies a number of documented cases of erroneous convictions like that of Ronald Cotton.[2] The most important and most frequent cause is mistaken eyewitness identification, present in Cotton's case and in about three-quarters of the cases cleared by DNA evidence. Another factor is false confessions. It may seem difficult to believe that innocent defendants would confess to something they did not do. Nonetheless, research by Saul Kassin, Richard Leo, and others has convincingly shown that duress, coercive questioning, misunderstanding, and personal characteristics like a defendant's youth or mental problems can all lead a defendant to falsely admit to committing a crime.[3] A third factor in wrongful convictions is informants or so-called jailhouse snitches, who testify about a defendant's culpability in exchange for promised or anticipated personal benefits.[4] Another set of problematic issues arises with the presentation of forensic evidence—either its degree of unreliability is not presented fairly to the jury, or the state crime laboratory has mishandled the evidence or erred in the analysis. Finally, some of the key actors—the police, prosecutors, or the defense attorney, may have behaved badly or unethically, undermining the defendant's right to a fair trial and leading to an erroneous conviction. One caveat is that the relative frequency of these problems has, by necessity, been documented only in cases in which the defendants have been exonerated. It could be that in the broad range of cases, there are other significant sources of trial errors. Even taking that into account, we see that serious problems in the evidence presented to juries, and juries' reliance on that faulty evidence, can lead them to wrongfully convict.

EYEWITNESS IDENTIFICATION

In 1996 the US Department of Justice concluded that eyewitness misidentifications resulted in dozens of wrongful convictions.[5] Judges and legal scholars have recognized the problem for over a century and acknowledged that jurors frequently accord eyewitness identification too much weight. Many police departments have improved their lineups and other identification procedures in recent years, but these improvements still leave much to be desired. And, as the Ronald Cotton case clearly shows, even the most careful witness can be mistaken.

Elizabeth Loftus conducted a now classic study to demonstrate the compelling effects of eyewitness identification.[6] In her experiment, people acting as jurors heard circumstantial evidence in a robbery-murder case. Some of the mock jurors heard an additional piece of evidence, an eyewitness identification of the defendant. Others heard the circumstantial and eyewitness identification, but they also heard a cross-examination in which the eyewitness was totally discredited by showing that she could not have seen the person as she had claimed. The mock jurors who heard the discredited eyewitness should have discounted her testimony and yielded verdicts similar to the no-eyewitness condition, but that did not happen. Their verdicts were more similar to those of the jurors who had heard the eyewitness who was not discredited. Subsequent research has shown that a likely reason for this finding is that the testimony of an eyewitness increases the weight that jurors give to the various pieces of circumstantial evidence.[7] Even when the eyewitness is later discredited in cross-examination, the extra weight given to the circumstantial evidence still tilts the jurors toward a guilty verdict.

Many judges express high confidence that cross-examination of the witness will expose witness unreliability and that jurors will be able to detect inaccurate identifications. Psychologists Gary Wells and Rod Lindsay and their collaborators conducted a series of experiments in which eyewitnesses were put in a position to observe an ostensible theft.[8] Some of the witnesses later made accurate identifications of the thief, while others made false identifications. In the next part of the experiment, the mock jurors observed cross-examinations of these witnesses. These mock jurors then rated the witnesses' accuracy and confidence. Eyewitnesses were believed 80 percent of the time, regardless of whether they were accurate or had made a false identification. Perceived witness confidence was unrelated to accuracy, but it was highly correlated with the mock jurors' belief that the witness was accurate. A number of variations on this basic experiment yielded similar results. In short, people have trouble distinguishing between accurate and inaccurate witnesses.

Another problem is the legal status of witness confidence. In the 1973 case of *Neil v. Biggers*, the Supreme Court pronounced five criteria that judges need to consider in deciding whether to allow eyewitness testimony contested by the defense.[9] Most, like the opportunity to view the criminal, the degree of attention, and the length of time between the crime and the identification of the defendant, are sensible criteria supported by years of research on perception and memory. However, one criterion—the degree of certainty expressed by the eyewitness—has no scientific grounding. It may seem intuitively obvious that a person who is very confident in identifying another person is likely to be accurate. But, surprisingly, that intuition has been called into question by more than three decades of scientific research.[10] An eyewitness's certainty can mislead investigators so they do not explore other avenues. And when eyewitnesses testify in court, their strong confidence leads jurors and judges to rely on them too much.

Some state courts have attempted to avoid the problems that reliance on witness confidence might create by developing strong cautionary instructions to the jury about problems of potential eyewitness unreliability. Other courts have allowed psychologists to testify before the jury about factors that might affect witness reliability, testimony that can provide a social framework for jurors to interpret the evidence. The psychologists are not allowed to testify that the actual witness is wrong. Rather, the purpose of their testimony is to educate the jurors about what is known about factors that can cause people to have mistaken judgments. This way the jurors can better evaluate the testimony of the witness.

Some judges have objected to psychologist experts on the grounds that they might have too much influence on the jurors, causing them to undervalue, as opposed to overvalue, the eyewitness. However, a series of experiments conducted by different researchers have shown that this is not likely to happen.[11] The studies have found that testimony by an expert increased the amount of time that mock jurors spent discussing the reliability of the witness and made jurors more sensitive to the effects of different viewing conditions and other factors relevant to the ability to identify a defendant. There was no indication in the experiments that the jurors accepted the expert evidence uncritically or that they completely discounted the eyewitness testimony. The findings are consistent with research we've noted elsewhere regarding the ability of jurors to keep expert evidence in perspective and to evaluate it in conjunction with other evidence.

WRONGFUL ACQUITTALS?

DNA analysis of crime scene evidence, not available at the time of the original trial, provides us with definitive factual evidence that some juries have convicted innocent defendants. But what about the jury's acquittal of a defendant who, on the basis of the law and the evidence, should be convicted? The answer is complicated, in part because a factually based connection to a crime—the kind we might be able to establish through forensic evidence—may not be sufficient proof of legal guilt. In some cases juries apply societal norms and interpret legal rules to reach their verdicts. Furthermore, the criminal law insists on the high standard of proof of beyond a reasonable doubt. Thus, there will clearly be jury acquittals in which the defendant "did it" but the verdict of not guilty is justified because the prosecution failed to carry its burden of proof or the jury applied relevant community norms.

Research shows us that jury acquittals with which the trial judge disagrees are more likely to occur than jury convictions with which the trial judge disagrees. When the jury diverges from the legal expert, it is in the direction of acquitting rather than convicting. Strictly speaking, in many of these cases we cannot say that either the judge or the jury is right. The jury's tendency to acquit is consistent with the adage that it is better to let ten guilty persons go free than to convict one innocent person. The jury also incorporates community notions of justice in its decisions, and these may diverge at times from the strict application of legal rules, a point we will address shortly. Nonetheless, jury acquittals that seem to be unjustified can cause great distress to the public.

The jury verdict in the criminal trial of Orenthal James Simpson, the African American former football hero, on charges that he killed his wife, Nicole Brown Simpson, and her friend Ron Goldman, is often mentioned as an example of an erroneous acquittal. Dozens of books have been written about the high-profile trial, which lasted nine months, was televised in its entirety, and was eagerly watched by millions of Americans. Many years after the trial, the jury's acquittal remains controversial.[12]

The O. J. Simpson prosecution depended on circumstantial evidence. There were no eyewitnesses to the crime, and O. J. Simpson did not confess. The jury had to weigh motive, opportunity, and DNA evidence tying Simpson to the murders. At the trial, prosecution experts testified that the DNA found at the murder scene matched the DNA of O. J. Simpson. However, the defense team argued that the police may have tampered with the blood samples before they reached the testing laboratory. They called witnesses who testified about problems in the chain of custody. Furthermore, a key police detective was tripped up in a damaging cross-examination about statements he had made using the word *nigger*, raising serious concerns about racism and its impact on the investigation. Defense arguments about possible police misconduct and forensic evidence flaws carried the day, leading the racially mixed, largely African American jury to reasonable doubts and an acquittal.

One of the notable aspects of public opinion about the O. J. Simpson jury acquittal was the persistent racial divide in views of the case. From the start, African Americans were much more likely than whites to doubt Simpson's guilt. When the jury delivered its verdict, 80 percent of African Americans supported it, while 55 percent of whites disagreed with it.[13] Most cases do not generate such dramatic disagreement between racial and ethnic groups.

A civil jury subsequently found Simpson legally responsible for the wrongful deaths of Nicole Simpson and Ron Goldman and imposed a multimillion-dollar damage award. Recall that the civil jury uses a "preponderance of the evidence" standard to reach its decision. Over time, a number of observers of the trial came to the view that, although O. J. Simpson probably killed his wife and Ron Goldman, it seemed more understandable that the criminal jury, applying the "beyond a reasonable doubt" standard, might have arrived at the decision to acquit.

THE *CSI* EFFECT: DOES IT EXIST?

Erroneous jury acquittals might also be due to the alleged *CSI* effect. News media stories and prosecutors have raised the question of whether a steady diet of *CSI* television programming leads contemporary jurors to impose impossibly high standards for the prosecution in criminal cases. In one study, a substantial number of prosecutors from Maricopa County, Arizona—the location of Phoenix and surrounding cities and towns—voiced concerns that local jurors were unduly influenced by watching programs like *CSI*.[14] The prosecutors' complaints included the points that jurors now expect scientific evidence even when there is a full confession in the case, and that "the jury focused so much on presented scientific evidence that they paid too little attention to unscientific evidence" such as testimony by police and other witnesses.[15] In Arizona, jurors are permitted to ask questions, and their questions often included forensic science terms that had not been employed in the trial, such as "trace evidence" and "latent prints."[16]

There is no direct evidence—yet—of a *CSI* effect. It's not implausible that media depictions of the investigation and prosecution of criminal cases could affect jurors. After all, pretrial publicity has been shown to affect jurors' evaluation of evidence in trials. And, to the extent that jurors routinely draw on their world knowledge to inform their assessments of a case, television shows might well influence the stories jurors develop. But New York University psychology professor Tom Tyler observes that it's equally plausible to hypothesize that watching a lot of *CSI* shows will *lower* the standards of proof that jurors employ in their decision making, making convictions by juries more rather than less likely.[17] Tyler argues that the overall message of *CSI* is that scientific evidence is reliable, which may, in turn, lead jurors to overvalue forensic evidence in a trial and accept it uncritically. Tyler also observes that the need for closure, which is happily served by the tidy resolutions characteristic of the *CSI* programs, might interact with actual jurors' need to see justice done, increasing the pressure to convict the defendant. Thus, a careful consideration of the so-called *CSI* effect—if it exists at all—yields two diametrically opposed but plausible predictions. Whether a *CSI* effect exists at all and whether it has any impact remains to be demonstrated.

DEFENDANTS, VICTIMS, AND DEFENDANTS AS VICTIMS

Another set of topics relevant to our consideration of the criminal jury relates to the intersecting roles of the defendant and the victim. In some instances, observers say that hostility to the victim leads juries to a wrong decision to absolve the defendant. In other instances, the victim and defendant roles are intertwined, and the defendant's status as a victim is brought out in an effort to mitigate the punishment. The jury's willingness to consider the defendant's victimization is derogated as the naive acceptance of an "abuse excuse." Similar to testimony by eyewitness experts, healthcare professionals may testify about the phenomenon of abuse, providing jurors with a social framework to help them evaluate the contested issues.

SEXUAL ASSAULT CASES: FOCUS ON THE VICTIM

In 2003 basketball superstar Kobe Bryant was arraigned on rape charges. There was no dispute that Bryant and his accuser had had sexual intercourse, but he claimed the sex was consensual. The charges were eventually dropped after Bryant made a public apology to the woman, but many commentators suggested that one of the primary reasons that the prosecution stalled was that Bryant's legal team immediately and publicly shifted the blame to the accuser, insinuating that she was a promiscuous gold digger and that Bryant was the actual victim.[18] The Kobe Bryant case illustrates some of the continuing challenges in rape prosecutions, especially for sexual acts that occur between acquaintances. Some call it "date rape" and others label it "acquaintance rape." Date rape cases that go to trial pose the question for the jury of whether or not a crime occurred. Even if the jury decides that a forceful sexual act without the victim's consent did occur, how do juries consider the broader context and the behavior of the victim?

A victim's actions are critically important to juries. Years ago Kalven and Zeisel's *The American Jury* looked at rape cases.[19] Judge-jury disagreement was very high in this set of cases, with juries much more likely than judges to acquit defendants when the rape was not aggravated. Those authors noted that the primary legal issue in a rape trial involving an adult is whether there was consent at the moment of intercourse. Kalven and Zeisel observed that juries weighed the woman's conduct, ruthlessly examining her credibility. They tended to be lenient toward the defendant if the woman was seen as contributing in any way to the situation that led to the rape, such as hitchhiking or sharing a drink with the defendant. The juries that decided the above cases in the 1950s were almost all entirely composed of men, and it is likely that the jury verdicts reflected centuries-old attitudes that women had the responsibility to avoid rape victimization.

Even in the 1970s and 1980s, research showed that many people still tended to put blame on rape victims. Studies reviewed by Lynda Olsen-Fulero and Solomon Fulero found that between 50 and 78 percent of people surveyed endorsed a view that most reported rapes are false accusations intended for revenge or disguising promiscuous behavior on the part of women.[20] Males, compared to females, tended to be less sympathetic toward rape victims and saw them as less adversely affected by a rape experience and likely to have precipitated the rape by their clothing or behavior. One study found that over half of respondents endorsed views that "[a] woman who goes to the home or apartment of a man on a first date implies that she is willing to have sex," and "in the majority of rapes, the victim was promiscuous or had a bad reputation." It is important to point out, however, that these attitudes were not held exclusively by males. Women who were more traditional in their values were less inclined than other women to be supportive of rape victims.

But there was an additional factor in the cases included in Kalven and Zeisel's study, namely, the rules of evidence in the 1950s. Most typically, rapes are private crimes without observers, so juries often must weigh the accuser's word against the defendant's word. Commentators of that period expressed special fears of false rape claims, arguing that rape was a charge easy to make and difficult to disprove. Laws in some jurisdictions required that a woman's testimony that she was raped be corroborated by independent evidence. Judicial instructions at the time included special judicial cautions about the woman's credibility. The woman's prior sexual experiences were explored during cross-examination, which could be, and often was, a demoralizing and devastating exercise for the victim. These special rules in rape cases both reflected and reinforced existing stereotypes and prejudices. Research on rape trials showed that a woman's prior sexual behavior biased jurors against the woman, making it more difficult to prevail on a rape charge.[21]

Societal attitudes about women began to change in the 1970s, including increasing acceptance of the woman's right to say no. Another change was the recognition that men could be sexual assault victims, and that sexual assault could occur between men or between women. Today, in contrast to the 1950s, many states have gender-neutral laws for sexual assault. Laws recognize the right of a spouse, not to mention a former spouse, to refuse sexual relations. For example, in Ohio, marriage or cohabitation is not a defense to rape, nor can the defendant argue intoxication as a defense. The victim need not offer any physical resistance for there to be a viable rape charge. In California, the current law makes clear that even if a woman initially consents to sex, if she changes her mind at any point, a subsequent sexual act may be considered nonconsensual.

Rape shield provisions were introduced in all fifty states and into the Federal Rules of Evidence. In most cases, the defense is prohibited from bringing up a victim's prior sexual behavior with others. Evidence of consent to sex in the past is not to be considered probative of consent on a given occasion. (However, the defendant may introduce evidence of prior sexual relations with the complainant to demonstrate that he had a mistaken belief in her consent to sex from her verbal or nonverbal behavior.)

Modern research by healthcare professionals has demonstrated that women are often traumatized by date rape encounters. The trauma may lead them to behaviors that may seem inconsistent with jurors' preconceived notions of how rape victims should respond. The woman may delay reporting the rape for days, or even weeks. Or if she does report it immediately, her affect in relating what happened may be flat rather than highly emotional. And yet, at the same time, she may exhibit severe internal turmoil, self-blame, and other disturbances, a phenomenon known to these professionals as rape trauma syndrome, a form of post-traumatic stress disorder, or PTSD.[22]

In mid-August 1991, John Martens went to the home of his married coworker Phyllis G.[23] According to Martens, he and Phyllis had become close friends at work and had arranged for an intimate sexual rendezvous at her home. A sexual encounter did take place. Some six weeks later, in November, Phyllis G. informed her husband and the sheriff about the incident. According to Phyllis G., Martens had been making unwanted sexual advances to her at work. She said that he came to her home uninvited, forced her to the floor, and raped her. In December, Martens was indicted, and the trial took place in July 1992.

Since there were no witnesses to the event, the jurors were faced with determining who was telling the truth. An obvious problem for the prosecution and the jury was the six-week lag between the incident and when Phyllis G. reported it. The prosecutor called forensic psychologist Dr. Bergman to bolster the state's case. Dr. Bergman testified that Phyllis G. had been referred to her by the prosecutor. She had interviewed Phyllis G. on two occasions approximately eight months after the alleged incident. During the interviews Dr. Bergman inquired about Phyllis G.'s life before and after the alleged assault as well as the incident with Martens, and she administered a well-known psychological test, the Minnesota Multiphasic Personality Inventory, or MMPI. She also spoke with Phyllis G's husband and Phyllis G.'s work supervisor about any changes in her behavior. As a result, Dr. Bergman testified that she concluded that Phyllis G. suffered from post-traumatic stress disorder and that, in her opinion, the cause of the PTSD was the August 1991 incident. Dr. Bergman described the psychological checks that she had employed to support her conclusion and further offered the opinion that an extramarital affair or similarly stressful event would be insufficient to cause the PTSD.

Dr. Bergman was vigorously cross-examined about her opinion. She conceded that not all psychologists agree about the reliability of clinical judgments like the one that she had made and that she had no way of knowing with certainty that Phyllis G. had not lied to her, but she offered the opinion that Phyllis G.'s emotional demeanor was not feigned.

In pretrial hearings, Martens's defense lawyer had argued that Dr. Bergman's testimony should be excluded entirely because it spoke to a subject within the common understanding of layperson jurors and because it was more prejudicial than probative. The trial judge ruled that Dr. Bergman could testify about the impact of stess, but would not be allowed to mention rape trauma syndrome because that would imply that a rape had taken place and impinge on the fact-finding function of the jury.

After six hours of deliberation the jury foreman sent a note indicating that the jury was deadlocked. The judge called the jurors back to court and instructed them that "absolute certainty cannot be attained or expected" and "it is your duty to decide the case if you can conscientiously do so." The jury eventually returned a verdict of guilty. Martens appealed his conviction. An Ohio appellate court held that Dr. Bergman's testimony "was relevant and material to the issues to be decided by the jury. Because appellant asserted that [Phyllis G.] had consented to having sexual relations, [her] demeanor after the incident was relevant and important to corroborate that she was, in fact, raped." It further accepted Dr. Bergman's testimony in the pretrial hearing that the PTSD was only within jurors' knowledge "to a certain extent." The court commented that Dr. Bergman's testimony came perilously close to infringing on the decision of the jury when she testified that Phyllis G.'s emotional state was not feigned, but this had not crossed the line to improper testimony. Martens's conviction was upheld.

Expert evidence similar to that given by Dr. Bergman in the Martens case is now fairly common in acquaintance rape trials. While some early cases had allowed the expert to use the term *rape trauma syndrome*, most courts now restrict the testimony to PTSD. It remains controversial, particularly over the question of whether juries might be too influenced by psychological experts. However, studies by Nancy Brekke and Eugene Borgida suggested that some jurors do hold notions about rape and its aftermath that are inconsistent with what experts have discovered about the reactions of rape victims.[24] A series of simulation studies that they conducted indicated that such testimony caused laypeople to give attention to situational evidence and increased their attention to issues of the complainant's credibility. If the defense called an expert who offered a different opinion, this testimony reduced the influence of the prosecution's expert but did not eliminate it.

Juries will continue to be placed in the unenviable position of deciding whether the alleged victim's or the defendant's version of the sexual encounter is the "truth." Today, the scales between accusers and defendants are balanced a little more evenly due to changes in the public's understanding about the crime of rape, the substantive laws on sexual assault, and rape shield laws. However, even with these changes and a greater focus on psychological evidence, the examination of the accuser's prior sexual history remains an issue.[25]

DOMESTIC VIOLENCE: THE DEFENDANT AS A VICTIM

Perhaps the most visible instance in which the defendant is also a victim are cases in which a victim of domestic violence turns on and injures or kills the batterer. Violence between domestic partners is unquestionably as old as human history, but for most of this history it has been ignored or tolerated as a familial matter where the law does not belong. Only recently have attitudes changed. Some highly publicized cases began to draw the public's attention to the tragic lives of women (and sometimes, though much less frequently, of men) who endure years of physical and psychological abuse. In 1977 a Michigan housewife, Francine Hughes, had endured thirteen years of vicious beatings, death threats, and humiliation by her husband.[26] She had unsuccessfully tried to escape from the situation and sought help in vain from police, lawyers, and social workers. On a March day she told her children to put on their coats and wait in the car. While her drunken husband slept she poured gasoline in the bedroom and lit a match. As the house burst into flames, she and the children drove to the police station to confess. She stood trial for murder but was found not guilty by reason of temporary insanity. Her story was told in a best-selling book, *The Burning Bed*, and made into a widely viewed 1984 NBC television movie by the same title.

The 1991 movie *Sleeping with the Enemy*, starring Julia Roberts, drew attention to the fact that domestic violence is not confined to working class people. Numerous scientific studies have shown that the problem is extensive in American society. For instance one study found that one of every six wives reported that she was struck during the course of her marriage; the survey estimated that just under 11 percent were attacked during the year in which the survey was taken. Approximately 3 percent of these acts were characterized as involving "severe violence."[27]

Today, the term *battered woman* is commonly used in legal discussions and mass media and indeed is well understood by many in the general population. Courts and policy makers have sought solutions to prevent domestic violence, but it still occurs at an alarming rate.

A great deal of research since 1980 has shed light on the psychology of battered women.[28] Many who endure severely abusive relationships develop psychological states that can be classified as a post-traumatic stress disorder plus other symptoms that lead to the woman's perception of imminent harm and terror. These concomitant symptoms might include anxiety, depression, feelings of helplessness, fear for oneself and for one's children, passivity, psychological and social isolation, and feelings of unpredictability. Resorting to force, perhaps deadly force, may be perceived as the only way out of a desperate situation.

Pleading not guilty by reason of temporary insanity, as Francine Hughes did, is an "excuse defense." The perpetrator admits that a wrongful act occurred but claims that she or he lacked the mental capacity to appreciate the nature of the act.

A closely related defense is that of diminished capacity in which a defendant argues that his or her mental capacity was affected by intoxication, trauma, or mental disease so that the requisite mental state or intent to commit the crime was absent.

A third possibility is justification, or self-defense. The defendant claims that the abuser was engaging in an act of violence and the only resort was counterviolence, or self-defense. Under the law, the right to self-defense is taken so seriously that sometimes it is permissible to kill. The law of self-defense has been expanded over the centuries from the limited version in early English law that we discussed previously, but even today the threat of serious injury or death to the victim must usually still be imminent to justify killing in self-defense.

Unlike the situation in the Francine Hughes case, about 70 percent of battered women who kill their batterers do so during a confrontation. However, in many cases, imminent harm is disputed. In 1980 Gladys Kelly stabbed her husband, Ernest, with a pair of scissors.[29] He died shortly thereafter at a hospital. Gladys Kelly was then indicted for murder. At trial she did not deny the stabbing but claimed that she had done it in self-defense, fearing he would kill her. The couple had been married for seven years. The day after they were married, Ernest Kelly got drunk and knocked his wife down. During the next seven years, as often as once a week, he would beat his wife. In his drunken attacks he threatened to kill Gladys and cut off parts of her body if she tried to leave him. All but one of the attacks had occurred in private, but on the day of his death, Gladys, with her daughter in tow, found Ernest at a friend's house and asked for money to finish the family shopping. Ernest was intoxicated and told her to wait until they got home. Shortly thereafter the couple and their daughter left. After walking a short distance, he angrily asked, "What the hell did you come around here for?" and grabbed the collar of her dress, and the two fell to the ground. He began choking her, punched her in the face, and bit her leg. A crowd gathered, and two men separated them, just as Gladys felt she was passing out. She looked for her daughter in the crowd and retrieved her purse. Ernest began rushing toward her. She testified at the trial that, fearing for her life, she grabbed scissors from her purse and tried to scare him away, but he persisted, and only then did she stab him.

The prosecutor claimed a different version of the stabbing, asserting that Gladys had started the scuffle and that after the couple was disentangled, she was restrained by bystanders and threatened to kill Ernest. She then chased after him and stabbed him. Gladys's lawyer attempted to call a psychologist to testify about "battered woman syndrome" to support Gladys's claim that she felt that her life was threatened. The judge ruled that such testimony was inadmissible. The jury found Gladys guilty of second-degree murder, and she was sentenced to five years in prison.

Gladys Kelly appealed, and the Supreme Court of New Jersey overturned her conviction on the primary grounds that the trial judge should have allowed the testimony about battered woman syndrome because it was "relevant to the honesty and reasonableness of defendant's belief that deadly force was necessary to protect her against death or serious bodily harm."

Since the Kelly trial, testimony about battered woman syndrome has been admitted in many states, although some states allow only testimony about PTSD. When an expert is allowed to testify about battered woman syndrome, the testimony is typically restricted to descriptions of the states of mind of battered women as a general category and not of the state of mind of the defendant at the time of the incident. Otherwise, the courts believe, the testimony infringes on the ultimate facts that the jury should decide.

Battered woman syndrome testimony has been criticized. Some researchers find fault with the basic scientific research documenting characteristic reactions of battered women, pointing to problems in the studies as well as to the diversity of ways that battered women respond to violence. Another argument is that the dynamics of spousal abuse are, to use the old Scots phrase, "within the ken" of the jury: it is common knowledge. A third argument is that the testimony will cause jury members to rely too heavily on the opinion of the expert, thus leading them to ignore or downplay other evidence or testimony that is inconsistent with self-defense. Indeed, some might argue that although she was a victim of abuse, the evidence in Gladys Kelly's case was inconsistent with battered woman syndrome. For example, she fought back when being assaulted, actions that might be seen as inconsistent with a battered woman. If a woman's relational history is not completely consistent with a battered woman profile, the jury might reject her claim of self-defense.

Psychologist Regina Schuller has studied the battered woman syndrome, including the effects of expert testimony about battered women on jurors.[30] Some members of the general public hold conceptions about battered women that are inconsistent with what researchers have learned about the psychology of severely abused women. A number of experiments have examined the effects of expert testimony on the way that mock jurors evaluate evidence in homicide cases where abused women's claims of self-defense are invoked. The basic methodology of the experiments is to compare responses to trial evidence with or without various forms of expert testimony. Generally, the testimony is beneficial to the defendant, but, consistent with findings we've noted elsewhere, the jurors do not accept the evidence uncritically. They use it as a psychological framework to examine both the prosecution and defense evidence. The findings also do not show jurors rejecting a self-defense argument if the defendant does not perfectly fit a battered woman profile.

While we have focused on battered women, expert evidence similar to battered woman evidence has been permitted in trials of abuse in other rare cases. These may involve heterosexual men who claimed to be victims of abuse, homosexual relationships, and battered child syndrome, which has been offered by juveniles who kill their parents.

Brian Nemeth was verbally abused, beaten with coat hangers, and burned with cigarettes by his alcoholic mother.[31] In 1995 on her birthday, she threatened to kill him and then fell into a drunken stupor. The sixteen-year-old-boy took his bow and arrows and shot her five times in the head and neck. She died several days later. At trial he claimed that he believed he was in imminent danger, despite the undisputed fact that his mother was comatose. The judge refused to permit expert testimony on the effects of long-term child abuse, and Nemeth was convicted of murder. However, the Supreme Court of Ohio overturned the conviction on the primary grounds that expert testimony was relevant to his state of mind and that the average person and juror might have misperceptions about the context and consequences of abuse. It is reasonable to assume that jurors respond to battered child syndrome evidence as they do to battered woman evidence, namely, they consider it but do not accept it wholesale.

QUESTIONING VICTIMHOOD: THE "ABUSE EXCUSE"

Battered woman syndrome and battered child syndrome fit into the broad category of so-called abuse excuses. Other examples include the 1993 case of Lorena Bobbitt, who cut off her husband's penis with a kitchen knife, drove off with it, and flung it out her car window. Police found the severed appendage, and it was surgically reattached, but Bobbitt was charged with malicious wounding. At trial she claimed she had been subjected to years of physical and sexual abuse and as a response to marital rape, acted upon an irresistible impulse. A jury found her not guilty on grounds of temporary insanity, and she spent forty-five days in a psychiatric hospital. Alan Dershowitz's popular book *The Abuse Excuse* listed a plethora of other excuses to criminal responsibility that have included the "black rage" defense, "urban survival syndrome," the premenstrual syndrome defense, and a host of other nontraditional defenses.[32]

James Q. Wilson, however, has charged that claims about pervasive abuse excuses are a construction of "journalists and one or two law school professors."[33] The abuse stories are supposed to reflect moral decay and our society's unwillingness to hold people accountable for their criminal acts. Still, as Wilson points out, few killers are acquitted outright. In the majority of cases, he argues, the introduction of battered woman syndrome at trial rarely completely exonerates the woman. If it has any impact at all, it tends to produce less severe verdicts, such as manslaughter instead of murder. Wilson argues that jurors are drawn from the same public whose polls show very tough views on crime. Most important, the trial evidence may persuade the jurors to see the mental context of a crime in a way that is different from their preconceived notions and cause them to judge criminal responsibility in a more fair and just way.

DIFFERENT PROBLEMS FOR DIFFERENT JURIES

In our analysis of several key issues facing the jury in criminal cases, we have focused on types of cases that have highlighted the defendant's/victim's roles, including those that depend on eyewitness testimony or psychological evidence about the defendant's state of mind. The chapter has, of course, only scratched the surface of the variety of tasks that confront different juries. Some juries must attempt to determine if a crime has occurred, as in the acquaintance rape case. Was it consensual sex or was it sexual assault? The question of whether a crime occurred faced the jury in the highly publicized Durham, North Carolina, case of Mike Peterson, whose wife was found in a pool of blood at the bottom of the staircase in their home. The prosecution said it was murder: she was beaten by her husband and left to die. Mike Peterson's defense was that she had fallen, hit her head, and bled to death. There were no witnesses, the alleged murder weapon was never found, and the defendant exercised his constitutional right to not testify. The jury had to decide guilt or innocence based on their visit to the staircase, the testimony of forensic experts who produced contradictory testimony about blood spatter, coroner reports about the cause of death, and testimony about possible motives. They found Peterson guilty, thus concluding that a crime had occurred.[34]

In other instances, there is no question that a crime has occurred, but the issue before the jury is either the identity of the perpetrator or the culpability of the defendant. The cases of O. J. Simpson and Ronald Cotton illustrate the first issue; the battered woman cases the second.

In all these diverse types of cases, jurors perceive and interpret the evidence, incorporating their world knowledge and social norms to develop a coherent account of the case. Sometimes the evidence is faulty and juries don't fully appreciate its flaws. Other times their world knowledge—perhaps gained from television news programs—may provide a misleading framework for evaluating the evidence. But we see that although at times they may err, either in favor of the prosecution or in favor of the defense, for the most part the criminal jury's verdicts appear to be well grounded in the evidence.

Chapter 10

DECIDING INSANITY

Mad or Bad?

Juries sometimes have to decide cases involving acts that are so terrible that they defy explanation. Andrea Yates, the thirty-seven-year-old mother of five children ranging between six months and seven years, had appeared to many to be an ideal mother.[1] The family lived in a Houston, Texas, suburb, and Andrea homeschooled her children, took them to ball games, baked cookies for their friends, and with her husband, accompanied them to church. But on the morning of June 21, 2001, she systematically began drowning her children in their bathtub. When her oldest son, Noah, age seven, came into the bathroom and saw his six-month-old sister floating in the tub, he tried to run, but his mother chased him down, dragged him back to the bathtub, forced him into the water filled with the vomit and feces of his siblings, and held him under until he, too, was drowned. Andrea Yates then carefully laid Noah along with the other children side by side in her bed, strands of her hair still clutched in the little hand of Noah from his struggle to escape being held under the water. Andrea Yates then dialed 911 and told the police what she had done. Then she called her husband at work.

When Russell Yates arrived home and was told by police what his wife had done, he collapsed into a fetal position with grief and anger at the horror and loss. A few days later, however, he defended his wife because of the "illness." Andrea had suffered from postpartum depression and other mental illnesses for years and had been under the care of psychiatrists. Nonetheless, Andrea Yates was charged with capital murder and put on trial. Her lawyers entered a plea of not guilty by reason of insanity. Even though she had attempted suicide twice, had been hospitalized four times for psychiatric problems, and had experienced a delusional psychiatric episode just before the drownings, that was insufficient. In Texas, with one of the nation's most restrictive laws on the insanity defense, jurors would be instructed to find her guilty if the evidence showed that she could distinguish right from wrong despite her delusions and madness. Prosecutors would urge the jury to recommend death by lethal injection.

The Yates trial took place in Houston in March 2002. The evidence was complex and graphic. Jurors heard from police investigators and saw photographs of the dead children and the crime scene. They saw home videotapes of the laughing children and their parents during more pleasant times. They heard Andrea's taped confession taken by a detective. A jail psychiatrist testified that after her arrest, Andrea was put on medications that allowed her to talk about her visions and the voice of Satan in her head. That voice said she had to be executed to be rid of him and the way to get the death penalty was to kill her children. She told the psychiatrist: "It was the seventh deadly sin. My children weren't righteous. They stumbled because I was evil. The way I was raising them they could never be saved," and "they were doomed to perish in the fires of hell."

The most dramatic evidence came in the form of videotaped interviews undertaken by prosecution psychiatrist Park Dietz. He became famous for his testimony in the cases of John Hinckley, who had attempted to assassinate President Reagan, and serial killer Jeffrey Dahmer, who kept the heads of his victims in a freezer. The jailhouse videotapes showed Andrea Yates saying that she did not think drowning her children was wrong. In response to a follow-up question she explained, "If I didn't do it, they would be tormented by Satan. It was a bad choice. I shouldn't have done it. There was distress, but I still felt I had to do it." She said further that Satan left her when she killed the children.

Dietz testified that in his opinion Andrea Yates was not insane when she committed the crimes. Rather, her psychosis occurred only after the deaths. He offered the view that although he had initially been inclined to accept her statements that her actions were driven by her belief in Satan, her actions belied her claim: "I would expect her to try and comfort the children, telling them they are going with Jesus or with God, but she does not offer words of comfort to the children." Dietz further added that since thoughts of killing her children had been in her head for perhaps two years, he would have expected her to talk about her thoughts to her minister or a friend. He explained that she felt controlled by the onerous burden of homeschooling, but he dismissed her religious beliefs about demons. Instead, Dietz argued, she did not talk about her delusions because she believed that if she did, her husband or others would stop her from carrying out the killings. An especially crucial part of Dietz's testimony came from his assertion that Andrea Yates had gotten the idea of killing her children from a recent episode of the television show *Law & Order*, which, he had been told, she watched frequently. In that episode a woman drowned her child in a bathtub.

The defense produced its own psychiatrists who disputed Dietz's opinion. The jury was left to sort out whom to believe. After the testimony was completed, the lead prosecutor began her closing argument by explaining why the state of Texas was compelled to prosecute a mother with a history of mental illness. Attempting to draw on their emotions, she reminded them that the victims were helpless children, focusing particularly on the struggles of Noah as she held him under the fetid bathtub water. Asking the jurors to recall Andrea's confession—"I killed my kids"—when the police arrived at her home, she asked the jurors to take three minutes of silence when they began their deliberations, because that is how long it would have taken each child to lose consciousness.

After four weeks of testimony, the jury found Yates guilty of murder in the killing of her children. In Texas, as in other states, a capital murder trial proceeds in two phases. After the guilty verdict, the trial resumed for the penalty phase. One of the prosecutors stopped short of requesting a death sentence, but the lead prosecutor asked the jurors to take the photos into the deliberation room. She asserted that "[e]veryone is trying to make this woman's issue a political issue, but the issue to me is five dead children." The jurors also heard about the other side of Andrea. Defense lawyers called witnesses who described her life as a nurse before marriage and her desire to have as many children as God would give her. The testimony portrayed her as devoted mother who had always wanted the best for her children. They also heard about the dedicated care she gave to her father during an extended illness and Alzheimer's disease before his death. In their closing, the defense lawyers, choking back tears, described the tragedy of Andrea's life and her future suffering, knowing what she had done to her children, her husband, and herself.

As the jury of four men and eight women returned to the courtroom, none of them would look at the defendant as they took their seats. The judge took the verdict form and had the clerk read the verdict. The jurors had opted for life in prison. Andrea Yates was spared death by lethal injection. Later, some of the jurors explained the reasoning behind their verdicts. A central theme in their deliberations was the methodical way that she drowned the children, suggesting premeditation. One juror said, "She was able to describe what she did. I felt like she knew exactly what she was doing, and she knew it was wrong, or she would not have called the police." Another juror explained, "Andrea Yates, herself, in her interviews said she knew it was wrong in the eyes of society. She knew it was wrong in the eyes of God, and she knew it was illegal. And, you know, I don't know what wrong means if all those three things aren't factored in." Still another juror said, "A lot of people want you to have sympathy for her and feel sorry for her and that's okay, but you cannot forget those children." Originally, two jurors had favored the death penalty, but they acquiesced to the majority and the final verdict for life in prison without parole. Despite acknowledging that Andrea Yates was mentally ill, the jurors concluded that she had known right from wrong when she committed those horrifying acts. There is more to the Andrea Yates story. But first let us digress with a brief history of the insanity defense.

A SHORT HISTORY OF THE INSANITY DEFENSE

Insanity defenses implicate mens rea, that is, the "guilty mind," a cornerstone of criminal law. To be held responsible for a crime, typically one must not only commit the criminal act but also have the required mental state (usually, the intention to commit the act). The insanity defense is an important limit to culpability, whereby those who do not have the requisite mental state because of serious mental illness are not held accountable. Recognition of the central importance of the defendant's mental state has been a major element in Anglo American criminal law for centuries. In 1582, Englishman William Lambard advanced one criterion: "If a madman or a natural fool, or a lunatic in the time of his lunacy, or a child that apparently hath no knowledge of good or evil do kill a man, this is no felonious act, nor anything forfeited by it . . . for they cannot be said to have any understanding will. But if upon examination it fall out, that they knew what they did, and this it was ill, then seemeth it otherwise."[2]

Another standard developed in the 1724 trial of Edward Arnold. Known to his neighbors as "Crazy Ned," Arnold was accused of shooting and wounding Lord Onslow. The trial judge instructed the jury that to find the defendant not guilty by reason of insanity he must be "totally deprived of his understanding and memory, and doth not know what he is doing, no more than an infant, than a brute, or a wild beast."[3] This came to be known as the "wild beast" test. Perhaps because the test was so stringent, Crazy Ned was convicted and hanged. In subsequent cases the concept of insanity was refined, partially as a result of changes in medical theories about the brain and human psychology.[4] For instance, one popular theory in the 1700s was the notion of the compartmentalized mind, with different mental functions allocated to different physical areas of the brain. The famous English judge Sir Matthew Hale drew on this theory to differentiate between total insanity and partial insanity. Individuals afflicted with partial insanity were, he argued, insane in some ways but could function perfectly well in others. Some defendants relied on this theory to explain how they could have purchased a pistol, loaded it, and killed a person with it, despite suffering all the while from insane delusions.

In 1800, James Hadfield, a twenty-nine-year-old soldier, was released from the army for insanity because of brain damage sustained in battle. He fired a pistol at King George as the king was arriving to attend a play in Drury Lane. Although he missed, Hadfield was tried for regicide. During Hadfield's trial, the defense argued that he was laboring under the delusion of being the savior of the world, who could preserve humanity by sacrificing his own life. Because suicide was morally repugnant to him, and the punishment for attempted regicide was death, he fired his pistol at the king. The prosecution pointed out that Hadfield had enough sense to buy a pistol and ammunition and therefore could not be mad. The defense conceded that Hadfield knew right from wrong and was able to plan out his act, but the defense argued that the act was a direct consequence of his insane delusions. The jury agreed with the defense and found Hadfield not guilty by reason of insanity.

The most important of these early cases, however, arose in 1843. A young Scotsman named Daniel McNaughtan attempted to assassinate the Tory prime minister Sir Robert Peel, but mistakenly shot and killed Peel's private secretary instead.[5] At McNaughtan's trial on murder charges in London's Old Bailey, the only issue in dispute was his mental state. The Crown prosecutor maintained that McNaughtan must be held responsible for his actions, since he could distinguish right from wrong, but the defense argued that McNaughtan was suffering from partial insanity and should be relieved of criminal responsibility. Nine medical experts testified on behalf of the defense. According to these witnesses, McNaughtan's attempt on the life of the prime minister was a direct consequence of his delusions that he was persecuted by the Tories. The Crown prosecutor presented no medical testimony to rebut the defense claims, and the trial judge virtually directed the jury to acquit. Instead of retiring to their chambers, the jurors huddled in the jury box and in less than two minutes found McNaughtan not guilty by reason of insanity.[6] The verdict was wildly controversial and caused lengthy debates in the House of Lords because many feared that an expansion of the insanity defense would put the public in jeopardy. The House of Lords eventually pronounced the proper test for insanity was whether the defendant knew right from wrong. This legal test was inherited by the American colonies.

The McNaughtan right-wrong test was used in the trial of Charles Guiteau, who shot and fatally wounded President James Garfield in 1881.[7] The trial evidence revealed the defendant's history of repeated patterns of very bizarre behavior. Guiteau insisted on defending himself and carried out his defense in an erratic, theatrical manner during a trial lasting over ten weeks. He claimed that divine inspiration was the reason he killed Garfield. The jury deliberated for one hour and five minutes before returning a verdict of guilty, at which the spectators in the courtroom broke into applause. Guiteau was hanged, but an autopsy found syphilitic lesions in his brain. As a result, medical opinion shifted to thinking it likely that Guiteau's behavior was the result of organic causes.

In the early twentieth century, psychiatrists complained that what they considered to be insane behavior was not congruent with the legal definition of insanity, and some state legislatures were persuaded that the McNaughtan right-wrong test was too narrow.[8] Here we see what became a continuing pattern:

changing ideas in medicine and psychology led to shifts in the laws regarding insanity. In 1954 the Washington, DC, appellate court responded to criticisms of the McNaughtan test and articulated a new rule that became known as the Durham test after defendant Monte Durham.[9] Durham was a man with a troubled history of mental disease. He was charged with housebreaking. At the trial his lawyer called psychiatrists who testified that Durham was suffering from a psychopathic personality disorder with psychosis, but they could not determine if he knew right from wrong. Durham was convicted under the McNaughtan test, but the verdict was appealed. The appeals court overturned the conviction and articulated a new rule that received nationwide attention and was eventually adopted in some other jurisdictions: "An accused is not criminally responsible if his unlawful act was the product of mental disease or mental defect."

In 1962 the American Law Institute (ALI), which periodically promulgates its views about what the law is or should be, incorporated aspects of the Durham test into a suggested standard: a defendant is not responsible for his criminal conduct if, as a result of mental disease or defect, he "lacks substantial capacity either to appreciate the criminality of his conduct or to conform his conduct to the requirements of the law."[10] Thus, both the Durham test and the subsequent ALI test expanded the McNaughtan test to allow for a finding of not guilty by reason of insanity in the case of a defendant who might be able to understand an act was wrong but still be unable to control his or her actions. The ALI test was well known in the legal world, but it did not receive much public attention until 1982.

On a gray, drizzly morning in March 1981, John W. Hinckley Jr. waited for President Reagan to emerge from a speaking engagement at the Washington Hilton Hotel.[11] As President Reagan started to enter his limousine, Hinckley fired his pistol. One bullet seriously wounded the president, and other bullets gravely wounded press secretary James Brady and a police officer. The shooting was captured on videotape and broadcast to a stunned and worried nation.

At the 1982 trial, the prosecution produced evidence of a bizarre motive for the assassination attempt. Hinckley had been obsessed with movie star Jodie Foster since seeing her in the movie *Taxi Driver*. He believed that killing the president would draw Foster's attention to him and win her love. During the eight-week trial, jurors saw the videotape of the shooting and saw the dozens of love poems he had written that reflected his obsession. Several defense psychiatrists hired by Hinckley's wealthy parents testified that their son suffered from schizophrenia. The parents themselves testified that they had kicked him out of the house in an attempt to force him to get a job and do something with his life. The prosecution countered with their own psychiatrists (including Park Dietz) who offered opinions that while Hinckley suffered from personality disorders, he still had the capacity to recognize right from wrong. They characterized him as a manipulative, parasitic person who chose assassination as a way of becoming famous without working for it.

Although almost everyone assumed Hinckley would be found guilty, the predominantly blue-collar jury returned a verdict of not guilty by reason of insanity after twenty-five hours of deliberation. The trial judge, acting under the ALI formulation, had instructed them that the prosecution had to prove to them beyond a reasonable doubt that Hinckley was sane at the time of the shooting. Jurors were instructed to consider whether Hinckley did not know right from wrong *or* whether he could not conform his behavior to comport with the law (even if he knew right from wrong). If the defense raised a reasonable doubt in their minds about either of these conditions, they were required to acquit by reason of insanity.

The verdict produced a nationwide uproar about the insanity defense and gullible juries. A survey by Valerie Hans and Dan Slater found that most Americans did not believe Hinckley was insane.[12] They wanted him to be treated for his mental problems, but they also wanted him to be punished. In later interviews with the mass media and in their testimony at a US Senate hearing, five of the jurors indicated their own doubts about and anger toward Hinckley. Some said they believed that he knew what he was doing, but they insisted that they followed the judge's instructions. As a result, the jurors felt that they had no choice but to issue a not guilty by reason of insanity verdict. One juror explained, "I had all the opportunity to try to prove to the other jurors that he was sane. But the prosecution could not do it, how am I going to do it? I got ten other people to try to prove that he is sane. We went through all the evidence. Here the evidence shows he had a mental disorder. But he contradicted himself so much and made fools of a lot of the psychiatrists. How were we really to pinpoint what was his problem?"[13]

In the aftermath of the Hinckley case, the US Congress passed the Insanity Defense Reform Act of 1984.[14] It significantly modified the standard for insanity previously applied in the federal courts. The Act placed the burden of proof on the defendant to establish the defense by clear and convincing evidence; barred expert testimony on the ultimate issue of whether the defendant's mental condition met the legal requisites for insanity; eliminated the defense of diminished capacity; and created a special verdict of "not guilty only by reason of insanity," which required immediate commitment to a mental hospital. Thirteen states followed suit with similar legislation, moving away from the Durham/ALI standard and closer to the earlier McNaughtan right-wrong standard. However, some of the revised statutes also provided a new option, "guilty but mentally ill," or GBMI. The GBMI verdict is an attempt to allow juries to find criminal responsibility, thus allowing criminal punishment, but simultaneously allowing them to recognize that defendants are mentally ill, which might help the prisoner obtain treatment while in confinement.

Although the Andrea Yates jurors did not mention the Hinckley case in their posttrial interviews, could the Hinckley case been in the back of their minds? While Hinckley is still confined to a mental hospital, he has been granted supervised visits to his parents' home, which has angered many members of the public. Was it the Texas statute, which refers only to whether the defendant knew that the act was wrong? Was it partly from Texas citizens' attitudes that are reputed to be highly retributive and unsympathetic to defendants of all kinds? Was it the lack of enough defense evidence about the effects of severe postpartum psychosis from which Andrea Yates suffered? Was it the compelling testimony of psychiatrist Park Dietz? Or was it just that in the jurors' minds the facts supported a verdict of guilty of premeditated murder?

THE SECOND YATES TRIAL

Andrea Yates was given a second trial. A Texas appellate court overturned her conviction when it was belatedly discovered that Dietz had erred in telling the jurors that "as a matter of fact" the recent *Law & Order* episode involving a mother drowning her child in a bathtub had inspired Yates to kill her children. In their closing arguments, prosecutors had emphasized that episode as proof of premeditation. In reality, the episode was a figment of Dietz's memory. Dietz, a consultant for *Law & Order* and another program, had been confused about a pilot program that had had that theme but was never developed or aired. Dietz also later admitted that Andrea Yates had never told him about the episode or discussed *Law & Order* programs as implied in his testimony.[15]

The second Yates trial took place in 2006, again in Houston. In most respects the trial evidence was the same. Psychiatrist Dietz offered essentially the same testimony that in his opinion Yates knew her actions were wrong, but he omitted the *Law & Order* episode. Another prosecution expert testified that, in his opinion, Yates carried out efficient and well-planned murders. The defense called psychiatrist Philip Resnick, who testified that in his opinion Yates believed that killing the children was the right thing to do and that she believed that Satan had taken over her body. Despite the similarity in the trial evidence, this time Andrea Yates was found not guilty by reason of insanity. She may spend the rest of her life in a mental hospital. What explains the difference in the two outcomes?

We can only speculate about the reasons. Because the jury in the first trial had rejected the death penalty and prosecutors could find no new evidence to support capital murder, the prosecution did not ask for a death sentence in the second trial. This was likely of substantial benefit to Yates, because capital murder trials exclude people who oppose the death penalty. Thus, the pool of eligible jurors was more representative of the general population than in the first trial. Professor Phoebe Ellsworth and her colleagues found that people who support capital punishment tend to be more opposed to the insanity defense and are more favorable to prosecution arguments than people who are against the death penalty.[16] It is also possible that in the intervening time, publicity about Yates and general information about the effects of postpartum psychosis may have influenced the public. Many newspapers and other media had discussed postpartum psychosis.

During jury selection, substantial numbers of potential jurors said they had already decided that Andrea Yates was insane. Many others said they could not be impartial because of what they had already heard about the case. After the verdict, some of the jurors spoke about the case. During deliberations they asked to see the evidence relating to the opposing psychiatrists' evaluations, but the jury foreman said that they did not base their decision solely on the testimony of one expert. (That would be consistent with juries' general approach to cases with expert testimony, as discussed earlier.) The foreman added that he had a six-month-old child, and "[t]he first time I gave my son a bath after seeing those pictures, it was very hard." He commented that he and his fellow jurors endured the most "emotionally and intellectually challenging" event of their lives. Moreover, some of the jurors had had personal experiences with family members who suffer from mental illness.

The Yates trials may have been a turning point in the public understanding of the effects of postpartum psychosis by drawing attention to the frequency of postpartum illness and its sometimes severe effects on mothers' mental states. In the wake of the first Yates trial, three other Texas women were put on trial for the killing of their children.[17] Deanna Laney had used rocks to bash the heads of her three children because she believed God ordered her to kill them. Two of the children died. Lisa Ann Diaz drowned her three- and five-year-old daughters in a bathtub. Dena Schlosser cut off the arms of her ten-month-old daughter, then called 911 while a church hymn played in the background. All three women were found not guilty by reason of insanity. Yet, such verdicts remain a rarity. While the insanity defense holds a central place in the law, widespread animosity toward it exists.

JUROR ATTITUDES ABOUT INSANITY DEFENSES

Less than 1 percent of defendants facing felony charges plead not guilty by reason of insanity. Studies of court records confirm that only a tiny proportion of the small number of defendants who enter an insanity plea avoid criminal responsibility. Yet, studies of public opinion have found that, consistently, laypeople estimate that the insanity defense is raised far more frequently than it is, up to 40 percent of criminal trials in one study.[18] Many see it as an abused area of law, a "loophole" that defendants use to attempt to escape responsibility. Research has shown that even when members of the public are presented with correct information about the low frequency of insanity pleas and the still lower frequency of acquittals, about half maintain their belief in the misuse of insanity to escape criminal responsibility.[19] The public also has a mistaken notion about what happens to defendants found not guilty by reason of insanity, fueling fears that the insanity defense allows dangerous people to go free. Not surprisingly, people who think many defendants succeed at the insanity plea or who think that defendants acquitted by reason of insanity will be held only short periods of time have more negative attitudes toward the defense.

There is typically no set time that a person found not guilty by reason of insanity can be held. The decision is left to psychiatrists and other mental health professionals. Lisa Ann Diaz, one of the Dallas mothers who drowned her young daughters and was found not guilty by reason of insanity, was released from a state psychiatric hospital in November of 2006. The release prompted prosecutors to argue that Texas law should be changed to allow a "guilty but mentally ill" verdict. They argued that there should be a middle-ground option similar to the ones in thirteen other states.[20]

As we have seen, over the centuries legal authorities, first in England and then in the United States, have struggled with what it means to be insane in criminal cases and how to devise legal tests and jury instructions. In the 1950s, shortly after the District of Columbia pronounced the Durham insanity test, Rita James Simon conducted the first systematic research on juror reactions in insanity cases.[21] Through a series of jury simulation studies, she attempted to see if the Durham instructions would produce different results than McNaughtan instructions. She used two different cases. One was a housebreaking trial based on the actual case of Monte Durham. The other was modeled on another real case of a father without mental problems who was charged with incest. She discovered that whether or not the legal instructions for insanity mattered to jurors depended on the case. In the incest case, all of the juries found the defendant guilty under the McNaughtan instruction, but nineteen percent of juries instructed under the Durham rule found him not guilty. In the housebreaking case, over half of the juries found the defendant not guilty by reason of insanity, but the specific legal rule did not affect their verdicts.

Simon's studies also found that jurors were critical of psychiatric testimony. They accepted and understood the purpose of the testimony but were annoyed that the experts were not more conclusive. (It is not clear that Simon's jurors understood that the rules of evidence ordinarily constrict how far a psychiatrist or other mental health expert can go in making definitive statements about the defendant, because that ultimate question is the job of the jury.)

In later research, Norman Finkel's important work on "commonsense justice," examining how laypersons look at legal responsibility, has found that public perceptions of insanity are far more complex and nuanced than any of the forms of jury instructions that have been devised by judges and lawyers.[22] Simulation studies have repeatedly found that jurors apply their own norms and values in making decisions about guilt in such cases. Generally, the form of instruction has little effect on verdicts. Moreover, Jennifer Skeem and Stephen Golding have found that people have complex prototypes (formed mental images) of insanity that can't be easily reduced to legal or psychiatric definitions of insanity.[23] Different people hold different prototypes and these affect how the facts in a specific case are interpreted. This body of research helps to explain jurors' different reactions to insanity defenses.

The planning involved in the Yates murders appears to have been a central reason for the guilty verdict in her first trial and the cause of the troubled jurors in her second trial. The case of Wendell Williamson helps to further illustrate the problems that juries encounter with insanity defenses.

In January 1995, dressed in a camouflage jacket, carrying six hundred rounds of ammunition in a backpack, and armed with an M-1 rifle, Wendell Williamson—a twenty-six-year-old law student at the University of North Carolina—walked into downtown Chapel Hill, NC, and opened fire. An undergraduate student on a bicycle and one local resident sitting on his porch were killed; a police officer and ten other people were wounded. Williamson was finally shot in the legs by police and captured.

Williamson had shown many disturbing signs as a student, at times behaving normally, but sometimes disrupting classes. Referred to a student counselor, he told of hearing a voice talk to him and he expressed the belief that he was telepathic. Still, he refused treatment and medication. A hearing to determine potential involuntary commitment determined that he was not a danger, and so he was released.[24] In the spring of 1994, Williamson once again disrupted a class, claiming that he had telepathic powers. Eventually he was persuaded to meet with a psychiatrist who specialized in working with university students. The two met for six sessions over a ten-week period. During the sessions, Williamson told the psychiatrist of his belief that he was telepathic. The psychiatrist diagnosed Williamson with "delusional disorder grandiose" in order to give him a chance to eventually practice law, rather than entering a probably more appropriate diagnosis of paranoid schizophrenia in the medical record. Once on medication, Williamson improved vastly and finished the school year, returning for the fall semester and outwardly behaving normally. However, after the winter break, he started living in his car, stopped attending his classes, and began purchasing guns and ammunition. He cached the ammunition in several places on the campus, and his shooting rampage started shortly afterward.[25]

Following his capture, Williamson again expressed his belief that he was telepathic, was invincible to police bullets, and that he had to carry out a violent act in order to spread the word of his telepathy to President Clinton. He also said that he would receive the Congressional Medal of Honor for his telepathy.

In November 1995, Williamson was put on trial for noncapital murder and pleaded not guilty by reason of insanity. The prosecution argued that Williamson's purchase of six hundred rounds of ammunition, his targeting of males riding bicycles, his telling a woman to run away just before he leveled his rifle and shot another of his victims, and his admitted knowledge that shooting at people was illegal were all behaviors that indicated the presence of rationality and intention—and thus sanity. The jury found him not guilty by reason of insanity, and he was confined to North Carolina's Dorothea Dix mental hospital. Like the Hinckley case, the verdict was highly controversial, reflecting many people's perception that Williamson understood his actions and should have been found guilty. Further public outrage occurred after Williamson successfully sued his psychiatrist for medical malpractice for not monitoring and conducting follow-up treatment.

Caton Roberts, Stephen Golding, and their colleagues conducted simulation studies to investigate the effects of evidence about planning when a defendant pleads insanity.[26] Study participants construed planned acts as indicative of the defendant's ability to appreciate the nature of the crime. The greater the degree to which jurors perceived a defendant planning actions, the more inclined they were to reject an insanity verdict. Building on these findings, Mikaela Vidmar-Perrins found that, despite evidence indicating severe mental illness, when a defendant planned the purchase of a weapon, stalked his victim and the victim died from the assault, jury-eligible citizens were more likely to render a verdict of guilty than when the evidence indicated that using the weapon was a spontaneous act, the defendant did not stalk the victim, and the victim survived serious injury.[27] Evidence of planning, then, makes it difficult for a defendant to succeed in an insanity defense.

A series of experimental studies by Caton Roberts and his associates have also examined the effects of a new "guilty but mentally ill" (GBMI) verdict option that was introduced in many states after the Hinckley verdict ushered in widespread reform of insanity defense rules.[28] When a defendant pleads insanity in these states, the jury may be given the option to find the defendant guilty, not guilty by reason of insanity, or guilty but mentally ill. The option of a GBMI verdict shifts a significant number of people away from the NGRI verdict to the GBMI verdict. It seems that GBMI serves as a compromise verdict in which the illness is recognized but the defendant is still held culpable. It seems to capture people's desires to both treat and punish the mentally disturbed criminal defendant.

ADDITIONAL THOUGHTS

It seems likely that the insanity defense will remain controversial. The need to find responsibility and condemn for wrongful acts is as deeply embedded in our societal conceptions of justice as it is in the formal laws that judges and legislatures devise. Here again, as in other tasks that jurors are asked to undertake, their psychological schemas and social values affect the way that evidence is interpreted. Jurors' notions of insanity are complex and nuanced, taking into account the context of specific facts while reflecting the strong societal norm of accountability.

It's important to note another reason why the public reacts with both incredulity and hostility on the rare occasions when juries return insanity verdicts in publicized cases. The public does not have the evidence the jury has. Rather it hears only a few minutes on the evening news or reads only short accounts in the local paper on what transpired at trial. These stories are often devoted to descriptions of the horrors of the crime and the defendant's involvement in it. Expert testimony pertaining to the defendant's mental state may be summarized in a few sentences. The defendant's account of the actions leading up to the incident—either told directly or through police or psychiatrists—may sound like a ploy to avoid responsibility. It seems preposterous, for example, that an obsession with Jodie Foster could induce a person to shoot the president. How could a jury buy this story?

The fact is that jurors, if chosen in a way to represent the full community, are likely to hold the same doubts and hostilities toward the insanity defense that we see consistently in public opinion surveys. All of this indicates that cases of horrific acts by mentally disordered people—Andrea Yates, John Hinckley, and Wendell Williamson among them—will only rarely result in insanity verdicts.

Chapter 11

JURY NULLIFICATION

The War with the Law

March 17, 2003. Four members of the Catholic Worker Community in Ithaca, New York, made headlines in a St. Patrick's Day protest just days before the start of the Iraq war. War veteran Peter DeMott, Clare and Teresa Grady, and Daniel Burns traveled to the Army-Marine Recruiting Station located in a nearby shopping mall. They knelt down and prayed together. Evoking memories of Vietnam-era protests, the peace activists poured their own blood on the door, walls, and floors of the recruiting station and on an American flag, then read a statement:

> Our apologies, dear friends, for the fracture of good order. As our nation prepares to escalate a war on the people of Iraq by sending hundreds of thousands of US soldiers to invade, we pour our blood on the walls of this military recruiting center. We mark this recruiting office with our own blood to remind ourselves and others of the cost in human life of our government's war making.[1]

The activists sang, prayed, and spoke out against the war, emphasizing the significance of their blood as a symbol of the bloodshed in Iraq. Sheriff's deputies soon arrived, handcuffed the activists, and carted them off.[2] They were arraigned in the local court and jailed on charges of criminal mischief and trespass.[3] At their formal arraignment, when the defendants heard the specific charges against them and were asked whether they would like to enter a guilty or a not guilty plea, their responses were distinctive: "I plea for an end to war." "I plea for truth, so the truth can come out."[4] The district attorney, George Dentes, offered the four a plea bargain if they would plead guilty to a lesser charge in exchange for no jail time. But they refused.[5] One of the four, Teresa Grady, announced that they would represent themselves in the criminal trial: "I look forward to the trial and having all the jury understand and hear all the facts and what it means to have freedom of speech."[6]

A year later, with the war in Iraq bogged down by insurgents, mounting casualties on both sides, and American public opinion shifting against the war, the St. Patrick's Four stood trial in Ithaca. Experts on international law were prepared to testify that the Iraq invasion violated international law and therefore the St. Patrick's Four were protected under the Nuremberg Principles. However, Judge M. John Sherman, who presided over the trial, ruled that the experts could not testify because their testimony was not relevant to the case.[7] Thus, the four could not provide the jury with all of their legal justifications for the recruiting station incident. The judge did allow them to testify about their backgrounds, thoughts, and individual reasoning. On the witness stand, Clare Grady told the jury, "I believe my action was not criminal. I believe it was legal and required. When we discover that laws are responsible for hurting or killing, it's our responsibility to change them."[8] All four spoke at length from the witness box about their religious beliefs and their long involvement in charitable works and political actions against war. DA Dentes strongly protested the judge's decision to allow the four to explain themselves: "The moment I learned of that, I knew it was a hopeless case. . . . This case was about damaging government property. It was preposterous that the trial was not about whether they broke the law—they completely admitted they did—but a philosophical debate about the war."[9]

The jury spent twenty hours deliberating the case. Signs emerged that they were having trouble reaching consensus.[10] After telling the judge they were deadlocked and being sent back to the jury room for further deliberations, they asked two questions: how should they consider the defendants' knowledge at the time of their actions, and whether it was appropriate to take into account the effect this case might have on future cases. The judge instructed them to "consider the personal experiences described by the defendants in testimony and their stated legal, moral and religious beliefs to constitute what knowledge they had at that time," but to disregard the impact of their verdict on other cases.[11] In the end, though, the jury could not reach unanimity. Nine of the twelve insisted on acquittal, and the remaining three were adamant for conviction. As Judge Sherman announced a mistrial in the case, the courtroom erupted in applause, and supporters of the four clapped as the jury was dismissed.

Prosecutor Dentes was not pleased. Recognizing that a retrial in liberal Ithaca was unlikely to be successful, he referred the case to federal authorities, who chose to try the case in the more conservative city of Binghamton, New York.[12] It would be the first time that the federal government had asserted conspiracy charges against civilians who protested the Iraq war.[13]

So in the fall of 2005, the St. Patrick's Four, having evaded misdemeanor convictions by a local jury, faced more serious federal charges, including damaging $958 worth of government property and conspiracy to impede an officer of the United States by threat, intimidation, and force. The potential penalties were more serious as well; the defendants were now confronted with up to eight years in prison and $360,000 in fines if convicted on all of the charges.[14]

Right from the start, federal judge Thomas McAvoy exerted greater control over what the defendants were permitted to tell the jury about their motivations for the incident, ruling it "immaterial" whether defendants acted because of their antiwar views or because they thought they were protected by principles of international law.[15] The defendants complained directly to the jury:

> You, the jury, are now being asked by the prosecutor to render a verdict in this case based on half-truths and falsehoods. You also know that our explanations were often interrupted, and I am sorry that we have not been able to tell you the whole truth which prompted us to act as we did. I wish we could have explained more to you about our understanding regarding the Constitution and international law and how those beliefs informed, shaped and guided us in the actions that we took.[16]

Daniel Burns thanked the jury during his closing argument, saying: "We've come before you in the last few days and tried to share with you about ourselves and our reasons for going to the recruiting center and pouring our own blood. There's a lot we wanted to tell you and we are not allowed."[17] Nonetheless the defendants were able to talk about their states of mind at the time of the recruiting center action and to convey something of their motives. In any event, the jury was surely cognizant of the defendant's strong antiwar sentiments; the courthouse was surrounded by demonstrators during the trial.[18]

The federal prosecutor told the jury to ignore the defendants' motives and how they personally felt about the Iraq war: "You are here to decide, have criminal laws of our country been violated? And motive is irrelevant. If these laws were violated, the reasons for them are irrelevant . . ." He reminded the jurors of other people who justified lawbreaking:

> The KKK in the south. Those extremists thought they were right. That segregation is right. That murdering black people is right. That burning black people's homes is right. They really believe it. That doesn't make it right. It does not make it correct. It does not make it lawful. . . . Extremist groups that burn down and blow up buildings that house animals that are used in experiments in biological labs, the PETA people. . . . They believe they're righteous but the law says, we cannot condone your action because of your motives.[19]

Some might say that the prosecutor went over the top in his closing argument, referring to the Aryan brotherhood and Timothy McVeigh to exemplify people who had arrogant disregard for the law. He concluded by exhorting the jury to deny the defendants a license to break the law with an acquittal: "That's what this fight in this courtroom is all about. It's the license to be unlawful, go about and bring chaos. Go about and ignore the law or not. And you, all of you, hold that key."[20]

Judge McAvoy's final instructions to the jury again tried to focus the jury on the specific incident rather than the broader context:

> You've heard a great deal of philosophical, moral, religious and political comment about the war in Iraq, nuclear weapons and military wars in general, etcetera. Because you may think your job is to decide whether the United States foreign policy is morally proper, religiously sound or politically wise, let me be very clear that it is absolutely and unquestionably not your job. While you may consider the defendants' views, it would be a violation of your sworn duty for you to allow your consideration of this case to be influenced by your personal views on the moral, religious, or political aspects of the United States foreign policy. Your job is to apply the law stated in these instructions to the facts as you find them from the evidence. You will not be asked to determine and you should not concern yourself with the purpose or motive of any defendant in doing any act that you find the defendant committed.[21]

The federal jury deliberated seven and a half hours before delivering its verdict. The result was mixed, affording each side some satisfaction. The jury cleared the four defendants on the most serious charge of conspiracy, convicting them instead of two misdemeanor counts of trespassing and damaging federal property.[22] A legal adviser to the defense said the verdict was a sign that the government had overreached in charging the four with conspiracy, while the prosecutor emphasized that the defendants were finally held accountable. The four spent between four and eight months in federal prisons before their release.[23]

THE JURY'S POLITICAL ROLE

The St. Patrick's Four trials showcase what is arguably the most important function of the jury, its political role. The statements of the prosecution and the defense, the instructions of the judge—all centered around the scope of the jury's fact-finding in this politically charged case of an antiwar protest. The judge and prosecutor urged the jury to decide the case essentially out of context—"motive is irrelevant"—whereas the defendants asked that the jury consider their ultimate goal to bring attention to a greater harm through their protest action. Both juries had to balance the societal need for predictable sanctions for law violation against the particularized scrutiny of these defendants and the democratic tradition of nonviolent political protest.

At first blush, that calculus may have simply reflected the differences between the local communities of more liberal Ithaca and more conservative Binghamton. Yet the content of the two trials also differed; a federal conspiracy charge was added in the Binghamton trial, and the defendants were more limited in testifying about their motivations in Binghamton than they had been in Ithaca. Nonetheless, the two juries seemed to overlap more than diverge. The Ithaca jury appeared to be divided about how to consider the defendants' motives as well as the case's impact on the future, having submitted questions to the judge on these two issues. Ultimately the Ithaca jurors could not agree on the proper outcome. The Binghamton jury arrived at unanimity in splitting the difference, acquitting on the most serious charge and convicting on the misdemeanors. Both juries sent nuanced messages, rejecting extreme analogies to violent wrongdoers like Timothy McVeigh and the KKK but also resisting the protesters' desire for complete exoneration.

Many famous jury trials are well known precisely because the jury rejected the strict application of the law.[24] Earlier we talked about the significance of Bushell's case in seventeenth-century England in which the jury refused to convict Penn and Mead for unlawful assembly because they were preaching on the streets of London.[25] That case represents the principle that juries cannot be punished for their verdicts, even though their decision might be at odds with the judge's.[26] John Peter Zenger, whose case we also discussed earlier, was acquitted by a jury in 1735 despite strong evidence that he had published allegedly seditious material.[27] The verdicts of Northern juries who acquitted abolitionists on charges that they violated the Fugitive Slave Act around the time of the Civil War, the juries who found Prohibition-era producers of moonshine not guilty, and the juries who exonerated Vietnam War protesters are illustrations of the political role of the jury.[28] Jury nullification is not always in the service of what most people might regard as good. If Northern juries of the 1850s acquitted the courageous people who harbored slaves in defiance of the Fugitive Slave Act, Southern juries a hundred years later acquitted people who had beaten and killed the descendants of those slaves as they attempted to assert their legal rights.

The jury channels the community's political views within the rule of law. We've already seen that jurors' beliefs about justice influence their judgments. Usually these views of justice affect a verdict in cases where the law and the evidence are ambiguous enough to justify either verdict. However, in "jury nullification," juries acquit despite the law and despite evidence that would otherwise merit a conviction. In effect, a single jury has the potential to "nullify" a law passed by the legislature or interpreted by a judge, even though the impact is limited to just one case.

Those who oppose jury nullification in both principle and practice say that it is inconsistent with a society based on the rule of law. Allowing a jury to disregard the law and decide a case on the grounds of whatever it thinks is fair sets up a slippery slope. Opponents see it as an invitation to chaos. The federal prosecutor in the St. Patrick's Four case emphasized the theme of anarchy as he insisted that juries follow the law and convict the four defendants. An acquittal would constitute a "license to be unlawful, go about and bring chaos."

Although controversial, the possibility of jury nullification is integral to the jury's political role. In the US Supreme Court's decision in *Duncan v. Louisiana*, it stated that the prime purpose of the right to jury trial is "to prevent oppression by the government."[29] Similarly, in *Taylor v. Louisiana*, the Court stated that the jury's function is "to guard against the exercise of arbitrary power—to make available the commonsense judgment of the community as a hedge against the overzealous or mistaken prosecutor and in preference to the professional or perhaps overconditioned or biased response of a judge."[30] These decisions indicate that even the members of the Supreme Court can appreciate the jury's ability to deliver a verdict at odds with an unfair law or arbitrary prosecution.

The renowned legal scholar John Wigmore and venerated law school dean Roscoe Pound agreed on another benefit. Because laws cannot be written for every conceivable circumstance, applying a general law to a particular case may lead to injustice. It's the jury's job to consider the context and particulars of a case and make the necessary adjustments in applying the law so that justice is done. Dean Pound famously said that "[j]ury lawlessness is the great corrective of law in its actual administration."[31]

George Washington University law professor Paul Butler argues that targeted jury nullification can help to address societal causes of inequity. In a widely cited and controversial *Yale Law Journal* article on race-based jury nullification, Butler described the negative consequences of punitive sentencing policies in drug cases that left many African American communities depleted of its young men.[32] Citing statistics that over half of young black men were under criminal justice system supervision, and that more young black men were in prison than in college, Butler argued that on both practical and political grounds, the African American community was better off if nonviolent offenders stayed in the community. He asserted that African Americans should reserve the right to decide what type of crime should be punished, taking into account what would hurt or help the community, instead of having a criminal justice system dominated by whites do it for them. Jury nullification offered African American jurors the power to do just that.[33]

Butler identified a set of nonviolent crimes, especially drug cases, in which African American jurors could take a principled approach and consider the costs and benefits of jury nullification with African American defendants. These jurors should judge for themselves whether a conviction merited by the evidence would also do justice, and whether the defendant and the community would be best served by putting the defendant in prison or rehabilitating him or her in the community.

Nonetheless, since the late nineteenth century, American courts have consistently held that although juries have the *power* to disregard the law because they render general verdicts after secret deliberations without having to give reasons for their decision, they do not have the legal *right* to do so.

DEFINING JURY NULLIFICATION

It's important to say exactly what we mean by jury nullification. Commentators often throw the charge around if they strongly disagree with a jury verdict. Yet most scholars believe that the jury's intent to nullify is of paramount importance. For a verdict to qualify as jury nullification, jurors must vote to acquit the defendant even though they understand that the defendant is guilty under the law and the facts.[34] If jurors misunderstand the facts, don't comprehend the law, or misapply the law to the facts, they aren't engaged in jury nullification. They may be stupid, they may be wrong, and their verdict may have the same impact as one driven by jury nullification, but they are not nullifying.

Law professor Darryl Brown has outlined four distinct types of jury nullification, but he argues that only one constitutes actual lawlessness.[35] The other situations, he asserts, are within the scope of the law and the historic role of the jury. The first acceptable occasion is when a jury acquits the defendant of violating a law that the jury finds unjust. A Civil War–era Northern jury acquitting an abolitionist of violating the Fugitive Slave Act exemplifies this type of jury nullification. A second instance is when a just and fair law is applied in an unjust manner, such as when a conviction would result in a disproportionate punishment. Charging the St. Patrick's Four with conspiracy, a federal crime that carried the possibility of an eight-year sentence, even though they were tried in the local court for misdemeanor offenses, might, depending on how jurors view the law, be an example. Another would be an acquittal for a minor offense that, because of the three strikes rule in some jurisdictions, would put a defendant in prison for life. A third type of nullification results when a jury acquits because of its view that the state has engaged in serious misconduct and should be penalized by an acquittal even though the law is just and has been applied in a just manner. In Brown's view, all of these reasons for arriving at a not guilty verdict are principled and consistent with the rule of law.

The fourth type of nullification Brown regards differently. Here, a jury acquits because of bias or prejudice against the prosecution or for the defendant. That unprincipled form of nullification is inconsistent with the rule of law.

Most scholars limit jury nullification to criminal jury acquittals. Since a judge can overturn a jury conviction that is inconsistent with the law and the facts, the convicting jury does not have the same unreviewable opportunity to negate the law on the books as an acquitting jury does. Professor Norman Finkel, however, argues that some jury convictions, in which juries vengefully convict a defendant against the law and the evidence, should also be counted as nullification.[36]

One could make a similar argument about civil jury verdicts. Civil jury verdicts can be overturned and awards adjusted by a judge, so again, as a technical matter, a civil jury verdict cannot nullify the law in the way that a criminal acquittal does. Nonetheless, civil juries that decide cases apparently at odds with the law bear some resemblance to nullifying criminal juries.[37] University of Florida law professor Lars Noah argues that jury nullification should include civil verdicts. He points out that judges rarely have direct knowledge of the grounds for a jury's verdict, so they cannot tell whether jury nullification has occurred. Furthermore, he argues, judges are often reluctant to overturn a jury's judgment.[38]

DETECTING JURY NULLIFICATION

The idea that juries could "nullify" law would have sounded strange to our forebears. The early English jury verdict combined judgments on what we would today separately distinguish as the law and the facts.[39] Even as community customs developed into common law and judges began to give juries legal instructions, there was broad recognition and acceptance of the jury's prerogative to interpret both the law and the facts in light of community wisdom. As noted earlier, however, as the legal profession matured in the nineteenth-century United States, federal and state judges began to chip away at the jury's right to interpret the law, dealing it a death blow in the *Sparf* case in 1895.[40]

American juries now are routinely instructed that they must follow the law as handed down to them by the trial judge, except for in a few states like Indiana in which a jury's right to decide questions of law is still enshrined in the state constitution. Today, as in the St. Patrick's Four trials, prospective jurors are quizzed about their ability to follow the judicial instructions on the law; a citizen's unwillingness to comply is grounds for challenge. Unless jurors speak forthrightly during jury selection, however, or admit they are disregarding the law during jury deliberation, it's difficult to determine whether jury nullification is occurring and nearly impossible to police nullifying jurors.

Consider the case of Laura Kriho, a Colorado juror who was the lone holdout in a drug possession trial.[41]During deliberations, the jury on which she served had agreed to acquit on one charge and to convict on another, but the members were stuck on the third charge of drug possession. According to other jurors in the case, Kriho reportedly urged her fellow jurors to acquit, asserting that the evidence was weak and saying that in any event drug problems should be handled by the family and not by the courts. The judge eventually declared a mistrial. Outside the courthouse as the jury was departing, Kriho shared a pamphlet about jury nullification with another juror, who turned it in to the judge.

The prosecutor filed obstruction of justice charges against Laura Kriho. In addition to citing the pamphlet, the prosecutor also noted she had failed to volunteer during voir dire the information that she had previously been arrested for drug possession and was a member of the Boulder Hemp Initiative Project—a movement to legalize marijuana. Although the trial judge found Kriho in contempt on the ground that her withholding of relevant personal information prevented the selection of a fair and impartial jury, Colorado's Court of Appeals reversed the contempt charges and ordered a new trial. The appellate court said it was impermissible for the trial judge to rely on the testimony of other jurors concerning jury deliberations about Kriho's unwillingness to follow the law. The appeals court pointed to some testimony suggesting that Kriho's statements in the jury room were based on her perception of the weakness of the evidence, not simply her opposition to drug laws. Although a new trial was ordered, the case was eventually dismissed.[42]

The case of *United States v. Thomas*, like Laura Kriho's case, highlights the daunting challenge of preserving some modicum of jury independence while at the same time trying to determine whether a juror is engaging in nullification once a jury has started to deliberate. Members of the Thomas family stood trial on federal drug charges.[43] All the defendants were black. Juror No. 5, a black man, came to the court's attention during jury selection. The prosecutor attempted to exercise a peremptory challenge against Juror No. 5 but was overruled by the judge, who misapplied a legal rule (the *Batson* rule discussed earlier) and kept him on the otherwise all-white jury. A group of six other jurors complained about Juror No. 5 during the trial to the courtroom clerk and also the judge: "Juror No. 5 was distracting them in court by squeaking his shoe against the floor, rustling cough drop wrappers in his pocket, and showing agreement with points made by defense counsel by slapping his leg and, occasionally during the defense summations, saying '[y]eah, yes.'"[44]

Responding to the complaints, the trial judge met with each of the complaining jurors and Juror No. 5, inquiring about the matter. Juror No. 5 reassured the judge that he would try to be less distracting and that he would follow the judge's instructions. Once jury deliberations started, though, new problems erupted. Jurors complained to the judge that Juror No. 5 had voted to acquit and said he wouldn't change his mind. According to juror reports about the goings-on of the heated deliberation, Juror No. 5 had reportedly pretended to vomit and had almost struck another juror. Some jurors told the judge they thought Juror No. 5 favored an acquittal because of the evidence, while others thought it was due to his opposition to drug laws. After two rounds of individual juror interviews, the judge removed Juror No. 5 from the jury, which promptly convicted the defendants.

The appeals court overturned the verdict.[45] It said that a juror's unwillingness to follow the judge's legal instructions is proper grounds for dismissal. But, once deliberations begin, if the judge uncovers any evidence that the juror's stance could be due to his or her perceptions of the evidence, the judge must not remove the juror. Otherwise, there is too great a danger of judicial interference with jury deliberation. After all, if opinions are split in the jury room, the majority could well come to see the holdouts as being "unreasonable" and "irrational" and "failing to follow the judge's instructions."

Perhaps the only unassailable ground for removal is when the juror admits to being willing to disregard the law, including on occasion the requirement to deliberate. In a 2001 California trial of statutory rape, after the foreman had written a note to the judge alerting him to a problem, the trial judge interviewed a more forthcoming juror:[46]

> The Court: [I]t's been reported to me that you refuse to follow my instructions on the law in regard to rape and unlawful sexual intercourse, that you believe the law to be wrong and, therefore, you will not hear any discussion on that subject. Is that correct?
>
> Juror: Pretty much, yes . . .
>
> The Court: I would remind you too that you took an oath at the outset of the case in the following language: "Do you and each of you understand and agree that you will well and truly try the case now pending before this Court and a true verdict render according only to the evidence presented to you and to the instructions of the Court." You understand that if you would not follow the instructions that have been given to you by the court that you would be violating that oath? Do you understand that?
>
> Juror: I understand that . . .
>
> The Court: Well, you understand that statutory rape or unlawful sexual intercourse has been described to you as a misdemeanor? Did you follow that in the instructions?
>
> Juror: I've been told it is a misdemeanor. I still don't see—if it were a $10 fine, I just don't see convicting a man and staining his record for the rest of his life. I think that is wrong. I'm sorry, Judge . . . I'm trying as best I can, Judge. And I'm willing to follow all the rules and regulations on the entire rest of the charges, but on that particular charge, I just feel duty-bound to object.

Not surprisingly, this juror's candor got him bumped from the jury.

EVIDENCE OF JURY NULLIFICATION: KALVEN AND ZEISEL'S STUDY

For obvious reasons, we are not likely to get a clear reading on the extent of the jury's war with the law by examining trial or appellate court records. So, we need to turn to other forms of evidence to assess whether and how often jurors' views on the law lead them to nullify.

Kalven and Zeisel's classic study conducted in the 1950s, discussed earlier, examined the reasons that judges gave when they disagreed with the jury verdicts in their cases. They estimated that in 29 percent of the cases in which judge and jury disagreed, the disagreement appeared to be due at least in part to the jury's sentiments about the law.[47]

The clearest "war with the law," although evident in only a small number of cases, came in jury trials on morals violations. The so-called victimless crimes included gambling, liquor violations, noncompliance with game laws, and drunk driving. Jurors apparently objected to the government's intrusion in these domains, seeing no need to legislate morality. Judges wrote: "To the best of my recollection, there has never been a game law violation verdict of guilty in this county"[48] and "[a] very great number of persons maintain the belief that the law against selling such alcoholic drinks should not be enforced, and it is extremely difficult to get a conviction no matter how strong the evidence may be."[49] In a drunk driving case in which the defendant testified and the jury heard about his prior record of drunk driving yet acquitted, "[t]his is a mining community and the men in the community will not convict in gambling and drunk driving cases."[50]

Another set of cases involved self-defense, which jurors tended to interpret more liberally than the legal rule. The law permits a person to defend himself or herself with force if there is an immediate threat of violence, there is no chance to escape, and the force used in self-defense is no greater than what is necessary for self-protection. But even if these strict legal conditions had not been met, the jury tended to forgive defendants who acted to fend off personal injury or even property damage. Systematic studies of citizens' views versus the law confirm that people have an expansive notion of self-defense.[51]

A related group of trials that created judge-jury disagreement concerned the perceived responsibility of the victim for the crime. Contributory negligence is a tort doctrine that applies only to the civil justice system and inquires whether the person who is injured is partly at fault.[52] It is not a defense to criminal prosecution. Yet, Kalven and Zeisel identified cases where jury disagreement with judges appeared entirely or in part due to the fault attributed to crime victims. Earlier we noted how 1950s juries might acquit rape defendants even when the judge would have convicted because of juror perceptions of the victim's role. Today, as attitudes toward rape and sexual assault have changed and women are more likely to serve on juries, juries may show greater willingness to punish defendants in such trials.

Juries sometimes disagreed with judges when they saw the criminal offense or the damage caused as trivial. In these "de minimis" cases, juries focused not only on the law but also on the harm done. In cases with minor property damage, or where the victims were seen as undeserving, juries occasionally seemed inclined to let the matter go, either acquitting or convicting of a less serious crime than the one charged. Money stolen from a gambling game, theft of a few hot dogs, and stealing an auto that is recovered within a few hours all led to jury leniency. Other cases involved more serious harm, yet the jury did not convict, apparently because they derogated the victim. A wife who was acquitted after killing her husband during a drunken argument elicited this comment from the trial judge: "Community thought itself well rid of decedent."[53]

CONTEMPORARY EVIDENCE ABOUT JURY NULLIFICATION

What about contemporary juries? Are they, too, occasionally affected by these sentiments to nullify the law? In *Commonsense Justice*, Professor Norman Finkel differentiates between lawyers' black-letter law and citizens' commonsense ideas of what is fair and just.[54] Over a period of several decades, he has undertaken a series of experiments that have examined the extent to which commonsense justice and the law overlap or diverge. Finkel finds that lay sentiments are incorporated into and reflected in many legal rules, but sometimes imperfectly. When rules and sentiments diverge and citizens find that the just result is not always the outcome one would obtain from strictly following the law, they are understandably drawn toward the just result. Finkel identifies several areas in which commonsense justice and black-letter law are often at odds. Laypeople, as we've seen, have a more constricted view of legal insanity than the law allows, yet they have a more expansive approach to self-defense. Citizens value privacy rights very highly. Although euthanasia is not sanctioned by the law, many laypeople respect the right of terminally ill, suffering individuals to die with dignity and refuse to hold responsible those who hasten this process, especially when the deceased person has requested aid in departing.

Commonsense justice and concerns about fairness are reflected in contemporary juries. Paula Hannaford-Agor and one of the authors (Hans) analyzed the results of their national study of felony jury trials (described earlier) to look for evidence of jury nullification.[55] The study questionnaires filled out by jurors, judges, and attorneys included questions on the evidence and law as well as perceptions of legal fairness. The study overall showed that the weight of the evidence, whether measured by the perceptions of the jurors or the judge, was the most significant determinant of the jury's verdict. However, their perception of the fairness of the law was also important.

In general, jurors in the felony trials viewed the law that they were asked to apply as fair. But, those in juries that acquitted or were hung saw the law in the case as significantly less fair than the jurors who convicted on all or most charges. Jurors showed the same pattern when asked about the fairness of the legally correct outcome in the cases. This overall pattern was apparent across a wide variety of types of cases, including homicide, sexual assault, property crimes, and drug offenses. The findings raise the possibility that concerns about the fairness of the law or the legally correct outcome contribute to jurors acquitting or experiencing difficulty reaching a definitive verdict.

To examine whether these perceptions of fairness led to jury nullification, the study examined in closer detail those cases in which the evidence was evaluated by the judge or the jury as strong for the prosecution, the rated legal fairness was low, and the jury acquitted or were hung. These, it seemed, were the most likely cases to provide evidence that juries were nullifying against the weight of the evidence and the law. Jury (rather than judge) perceptions of the evidence are most relevant, since, following the definition we are using, a nullifying jury acquits despite perceiving the evidence and the law as favoring conviction. Of the fifty-three cases in which the jury saw the prosecution case as strong, most resulted in convictions. Of the acquittals, just two seemed to be potential nullification cases because the jury's collective rating of the fairness of the law and the legally correct outcome were both low.

One of the two cases involved drug sales. The defendant was convicted of one offense and acquitted of two others and received a five- to ten-year prison sentence. Through their ratings, jurors in this case reflected concern about the possible harshness of the likely prison sentence. However, they also found the police evidence to be not very believable. Therefore, the verdict in this case could have resulted because of combined distrust of the police testimony as well as worry about an excessive sentence for the defendant, and they did not let the defendant go completely free.

The second case of possible jury nullification involved sexual assault charges. Neither the defendant nor the victim was described as very sympathetic. The jury acquitted the defendant on five of the six charges, expressing concern about the consequences of a conviction on the defendant. The judge in this case rated the evidence as supporting the defense, in contrast to the jury's collective rating of the evidence as strong for the prosecution. So, the case presented a more mixed picture of possible evidentiary problems along with concerns about the impact of a conviction on the defendant. Similar to the jury in the drug sales case, the jury in the sexual assault case, although concerned about the fairness of a conviction and sentence, seemed to split the difference, convicting on one charge while acquitting the defendant on the other charges. It is reminiscent of the approach taken by the St. Patrick's Four jury in Binghamton.

Case outcomes in which the judge rated the evidence as strong for the prosecution yet the jury acquitted or were hung could be due to a whole range of factors, not just jury nullification. So, they are not as informative as the jury-rated strong evidence cases we've just discussed. Yet, because judges are legal experts, it's informative to examine those cases as well.

The first big difference is that judges saw many more cases as favoring the prosecution. (Recall that judges in this felony jury trial study were more likely to convict than juries.) Whereas juries rated only 53 cases as strong for the prosecution, judges perceived 126 cases as strong. Again, most of these 126 cases that the judge rated as strong resulted in convictions on all or most charges. But in 30 of the 126 cases, juries acquitted on most charges or were hung. Therefore, the jury fairness ratings and other characteristics of these thirty cases were closely examined to determine whether fairness concerns drove the verdicts. In seven of the thirty cases, fairness ratings were well below average; yet, in addition, in every one of the cases, juries rated the evidence as more ambiguous than did the judges. Problems with police evidence were also common in these seven cases. Although fairness concerns may have had some impact in leading juries to acquit or be hung in the cases judges rated as strong, evidentiary factors also seemed to have played an important role.

This detailed study of felony juries indicated that in a number of jury trials involving acquittals or hung juries, jurors expressed concerns about the fairness of the law, the legally correct outcome, or the impact on the defendant. There was, however, little evidence of outright nullification. Rather, fairness concerns were intertwined with evidentiary problems. This echoes the findings of Kalven and Zeisel's project half a century ago, which found that outright nullification was rare; that jurors' notions of justice affected judge-jury disagreement when the evidence was close.

NULLIFICATION IN CIVIL JURY TRIALS

What about civil trials? Despite the fact that civil jury verdicts for either party may be overturned by the judge, and are thus not technically a nullification, it's still of interest to examine whether the fairness of a civil law rule or its application affects civil jury decision making.

The story of jury decisions in contributory negligence cases is often used to illustrate the civil jury's role in changes in the law.[56] In the early nineteenth century, as we discussed earlier, the law in most jurisdictions was one of contributory negligence. The doctrine is a harsh one, for it holds that if a plaintiff's own carelessness contributed in any way to the harm that occurred, the plaintiff can recover nothing, no matter how much more responsible or careless the defendant was. Moreover, the "fellow servant" rule dictated that even when plaintiffs who were injured at work were blameless, they could not recover against their employers if the negligence that harmed them was that of a coworker. Finally, workers who undertook certain dangerous jobs were held to have "assumed the risk" of the dangerous activity. This doctrinal trilogy—contributory negligence, fellow servant rule, and assumption of risk—meant that workers who had been seriously injured, often through little or no fault of their own, could not recover if the law was strictly followed.

There were so many worker accidents as the Industrial Age swung into full gear that these limits created serious problems for law—and for society. Judges could direct verdicts against plaintiffs using the contributory negligence doctrine and other legal rules, and they did. But, if the plaintiff could suggest a way in which to avoid the doctrine, the judge might allow the case to go to the jury. We lack detailed quantitative studies, but it appears that juries often found for injured plaintiffs, even in the face of strong defense evidence. The result was an unpredictable legal regime: sometimes, injured workers got nothing; in other cases that varied little with regard to the facts, they received awards. This state of affairs eventually led to a compromise in which business, labor, and policy makers developed the system of workers' compensation that today provides smaller, predictable awards to people injured on the job. Most states today have replaced the contributory negligence doctrine with the approach of comparative negligence, in which juries apportion fault between the parties.

Experimental psychologists Kristin Sommer, Irwin Horowitz, and Martin Bourgeois, intrigued by these historical developments, designed a research study to examine whether the perceived fairness of contributory versus comparative negligence rules affects jury decisions today.[57] First, they surveyed a sample of respondents and determined that contributory negligence is seen as less fair than comparative negligence. Next, in an experiment, they presented to their mock jurors a product design defect case that included evidence that strongly suggested that the defendant was responsible but also that the plaintiff was partly at fault for the injury. One group of participants received contributory negligence instructions, while another had comparative negligence instructions.

If the contributory negligence mock jurors strictly followed the law given to them by the experimenters, then they should have found for the defendant. However, the mock jurors, though deciding under the rules of contributory negligence, adjusted their perceptions of fault to allow recovery. They were more likely to conclude that the plaintiff had not been even slightly negligent than the mock jurors who got the comparative negligence instructions. The law, not the evidence, had changed, but to achieve a fair result, the mock jurors appeared to adjust their assessment of the plaintiff's fault to avoid the harshness of the contributory negligence regime.[58] In a second, similar study, mock juries deliberated in groups, some under contributory and others under comparative negligence instructions. Mock juries who had to use the unfair contributory negligence rule were more likely to clear the plaintiff of fault.[59] In their jury deliberations, they tended to focus on evidence that was consistent with this view.

This type of deviation from the law benefits plaintiffs, but other examples show that plaintiffs can be disadvantaged when juries depart from the law. Even in the absence of fault, juries tend to attribute some measure of blame to a person who has suffered.[60] Psychologist Melvin Lerner first identified this psychological phenomenon, caused by people's need to believe in a just, predictable world in which people deserve what they get. Observers sometimes attempt to minimize their discomfort at seeing others suffer by minimizing the injury, criticizing the victim, or reinterpreting the injury as victim-caused. This tendency to blame the victim can affect juries.

For instance, Neal Feigenson and his colleagues conducted an experiment in which they varied whether or not the plaintiff was blameworthy.[61] In one version presented to participants, a worker had followed all of the rules and did not appear to be responsible at all for his injury. Yet study participants, on average, found him 22 percent responsible for his accident. Another featured a homeowner who was injured when the gas company's propane tank exploded; seemingly blameless, the homeowner was given 14 percent of the responsibility for his accident.[62] Why people have a strong tendency to hold victims responsible for their injuries is addressed elsewhere in the book; the examples above indicate instances where the jury's contextualized judgment of fairness and relative responsibility diverge from the law.

SHOULD JURIES BE INSTRUCTED ABOUT JURY NULLIFICATION?

The biggest academic debate over jury nullification, and one that has spilled over into the public realm, is whether juries should be instructed about their power to nullify in order to serve the interests of justice. If the jury is to serve as the conscience of the community and a corrective to imperfect laws, then, some argue, it should know that it has the ability to modify the strict application of the law in order to reach a just result. Instead, as we saw in the St. Patrick's Four case, most judges take the opposite approach, instructing the jury that it must follow the law and must disregard any personal views about whether the law or its application is just. B. Michael Dann, a retired Arizona judge, has written about the growing uneasiness he felt as a trial judge when he gave the typical legal instruction to jurors that if the law and the facts convinced them of the defendant's guilt beyond a reasonable doubt, they must convict.[63] He came to the view that he was intruding on the province of the jury.

In the Vietnam War–era case of *United States v. Dougherty*, antiwar activists stood trial for actions taken against the Dow Chemical Company, manufacturers of napalm. The defendants justified their actions on moral grounds and asked that the jury be instructed on its ability to nullify the law.[64] The trial judge refused, and the appellate court sustained the judge's refusal on appeal. Although the appellate opinion acknowledged that juries historically had rendered nullifying verdicts in important cases, it asserted that jurors knew about this ability and there was little need to specifically instruct them about it. An explicit instruction might make them all too willing to disregard the law.

They have the power, if not the right, to nullify. Do jurors know this? There are some signs they do not. Take the recent trial of medical marijuana provider Edward Rosenthal, charged in federal court with violating the federal Controlled Substances Act. In November 1996, California voters passed Proposition 215, the Compassionate Use Act, allowing patients to use marijuana for medical purposes that were approved by a physician.[65] A majority—56 percent—of California voters supported Proposition 215 and the idea of permitting the medical use of marijuana.[66]

The Compassionate Use Act is intended to shield patients and their caregivers from state prosecution on charges of possession and cultivation of marijuana. But even though California state law no longer forbids the use or cultivation of marijuana for medical purposes, those activities still run afoul of federal law. Federal authorities viewed California's permissiveness over medical marijuana as a challenge to its domain. Ed Rosenthal was under contract to cultivate and distribute marijuana for medical purposes on behalf of the Oakland City Council.[67] Federal agents raided Rosenthal's Oakland operation and seized 628 rooted marijuana plants. The federal prosecutor then charged Rosenthal with multiple counts of violating the federal Controlled Substances Act.

The jury trial commenced with a jury selection in which dozens of prospective jurors were eliminated from the pool because of their stated support for Proposition 215.[68] The trial judge instructed the jury to disregard anything said about medical marijuana during trial testimony. He did not permit Mr. Rosenthal to talk about his arrangement with the Oakland City Council group and he did not allow the defense to argue a medical justification for his marijuana growing. Finally, the judge strongly instructed the jury that it must follow federal law regardless of California's Proposition 215.

The evening before the jury arrived at a verdict, one of the jurors in the Rosenthal case called an attorney friend for help because she was confused and frustrated.[69] Even though the case appeared to be about medical marijuana, the judge had instructed them to pay attention only to the federal law. Did she have to follow the judge's instruction, or did she have "any leeway at all for independent thought"? The attorney responded that she had to follow the judicial instructions and if she did not, she could get into trouble. The jury subsequently convicted the defendant.

The appellate court overturned Rosenthal's convictions on the grounds that the communication was jury misconduct, and there was the possibility that the extraneous information from the attorney had affected the jury's decision. Appellate judge Betty Fletcher wrote: "Jurors cannot fairly determine the outcome of a case if they believe they will face 'trouble' for a conclusion they reach as jurors. The threat of punishment works a coercive influence on the jury's independence, and a juror who genuinely fears retribution might change his or her determination of the issue for fear of being punished."[70]

Lack of knowledge and confusion about the jury's capacity to nullify, evident in the Rosenthal case, was confirmed in a 1995 survey.[71] The researchers asked their respondents, mostly college students who might be expected to be more knowledgeable about history and politics, to answer a series of questions about jury nullification. Most thought, probably incorrectly, that a juror could be sanctioned by legal authorities for engaging in nullification.[72] Most also reported that juries had to follow the legal instructions of the judge. A strong majority, 69 percent, for example, said the jury could not disregard the written law and overwhelming evidence of guilt and find the defendant not guilty because the law was not fair in a case. Nor could a juror base the decision on community standards of right and wrong or nullify if the police had wrongfully assaulted the defendant.

The Fully Informed Jury Association would like to change that lack of knowledge. FIJA, dedicated to educating citizens and jurors about the jury's right to nullify the law, was formed in 1989 by a group of people who had previously been active in the American Libertarian Party.[73] Their lively Web site asserts the jury's power and right to nullify and argues that juries should routinely be instructed about their right to nullify the law. However, given the slim chance that judges will adopt this approach anytime soon, FIJA members have been engaged in grassroots activism to bring the knowledge of jury nullification power to the people. In addition to broad educational efforts through its Web site, FIJA activists have targeted potential jurors in certain high-profile cases, handing out leaflets and brochures describing and encouraging the practice of jury nullification.[74]

When trial judges learn about FIJA leafleting and brochure distribution, they often respond by excluding anyone from the jury who has read the leaflet or is familiar with nullification.[75] Vanderbilt Law School professor Nancy King catalogs a variety of cases in which trial judges clamped down after learning of efforts to inform the jury pool about the possibility of nullification: A California judge dismissed anyone who listened to a radio station that had publicized the issue of jury nullification; a judge in Dayton, Ohio, dismissed the entire jury pool after discovering that someone had distributed brochures describing nullification outside the courthouse; another pool of prospective jurors in Colorado was sent home after one of them passed around a FIJA brochure.[76]

What would happen if juries included people who were familiar with nullification doctrine? Or suppose they received instructions from the judge, or arguments from the attorneys, that nullification was a possible outcome in a jury trial? Psychologist Irwin Horowitz has studied the impact of nullification instructions for several decades, using the methodology of mock jury experiments.[77] His studies show that nullification instructions could have an impact, but the instructions must be quite detailed. Furthermore, they are likely to have an effect predominantly in cases that involve strong feelings of justice. In an initial study with Ohio jurors, some jurors heard an audiotape of a murder trial in which a grocery store owner was killed during a robbery. Others listened to the trial of a nurse who had allegedly engaged in a "mercy" killing of a terminal cancer patient. A final group heard the case of a college student defendant who had killed a pedestrian while driving drunk. Just before jurors were formed into mock juries to deliberate on one of these cases, they received judicial instructions. One set included no mention of nullification. Another was modeled on the instructions used in some states like Maryland in which jurors are told that they are the judges of both the law and the facts. A final type of instruction was labeled "radical nullification." It informed jurors of their power to nullify, said that it was appropriate to consider their own feelings of conscience and to express community sentiment, and provided historical information about famous cases of jury nullification.

The results were interesting. In the robbery murder case, the instructions had no impact at all. But in the other two types of cases, the radical nullification instructions created differences. In the euthanasia case, those who heard the radical nullification instruction were more likely to acquit the nurse than jurors given the other two instructions. In the drunk driving case, the radical nullification group was more likely to convict than the other instruction groups. This pattern makes sense; after all, the jurors were invited to consider their feelings of justice and they apparently did so, but in a targeted way.

Horowitz and his collaborators have continued to investigate the possible impact of nullification instructions. In most of these studies, nullification instructions have the expected specific, targeted effect. A recent experiment, done online with a predominantly undergraduate population, shows that nullification instructions might encourage the expression of a range of emotional reactions to trial participants.[78] The researchers created two versions of a trial in which a terminal cancer patient died of a drug overdose in the hospital. In the euthanasia version, the prosecution argued that the doctor who administered the drug was motivated by a desire to alleviate the victim's suffering. In an alternate "greed" version, the prosecution argued that the doctor was motivated by potential access to the victim's wealth. The evidence in each version was purposefully ambiguous. Half the participants who read each version learned that the victim was a generous philanthropist, while he was portrayed as a mobster and convicted child molester to the other half. The study also varied whether individuals received nullification instructions.

The information about the victim mattered only in the euthanasia case and only when participants were given nullification instructions that encouraged them to reflect their emotions in their decisions. When the victim of euthanasia was described in a sympathetic way, and people were given nullification instructions, they convicted the doctor of murder 59 percent of the time, compared to a 37 percent conviction rate for those who considered the doctor's alleged euthanasia of the mobster and heard nullification instructions. In the greed versions of the scenario, nullification instructions did not interact with the sympathetic versus unsympathetic information about the victim. So, as in the first Horowitz study in the grocery store robbery-murder, when a trial does not implicate nullification issues, instructions about the right to nullify appear to have minimal or no effects. But such instructions might liberate a jury to indulge in emotion-based decision making, at least under certain circumstances. As the authors note in reporting their findings: "It took a special set of circumstances to entice jurors to eat the forbidden fruit."[79]

It thus seems clear that juries do not frequently engage in acts of outright jury nullification. Recall Kalven and Zeisel's statement that "the jury's war with the law is a small one." Judges and juries mainly agree on verdicts, and when they disagree, although the perception of fairness is important, disagreements seldom reflect intentional nullification. Although some scholars and activists call for juries to be informed of their ability to nullify unfair laws or their unfair application, American judges appear to be vigilant in seeking out and removing potential sources of nullification advocacy and adamant in asserting the jury's duty to strictly follow judicial instructions. In most instances today, for jury nullification to succeed, it must remain subterranean, unacknowledged, and undetected.

We conclude that juries do not offer a freely roaming folk justice in which verdicts rest almost entirely on the composition of the jury. But in the exceptional case of state overreaching or technically defensible but morally indefensible prosecutions, the jury—even without knowing the full range of its powers—can stand between the accused and an out-of-touch state.

Chapter 12

DEATH IS DIFFERENT

Juries and Capital Punishment

In the landmark 1972 Supreme Court case of *Furman v. Georgia* that temporarily abolished the American death penalty, Justice Brennan, joined by four other justices of the US Supreme Court, somberly remarked that "[d]eath is a unique punishment."[1] In later cases, up through *Ring v. Arizona* in 2002,[2] members of the Court have repeated the theme that "death is different."[3] The sheer finality, severity, and irreversibility of execution distinguish it from all other punishments. A death sentence reflects the ethical judgment of the community, represented through the jury, that the criminal has morally lost the entitlement to live.[4]

Because death is different, the Court has asserted that death penalty cases require extraordinary procedural safeguards to attempt to ensure their accuracy and fairness. Only truly guilty persons should receive death sentences. Furthermore, capital punishment should be reserved for the most culpable, death-worthy defendants. Procedural safeguards promoting accuracy and fairness should apply at all stages of the criminal process, from prosecution through posttrial review of death sentences.

Juries, of course, play a central role in the process, determining not only the guilt of the defendant but also deciding whether the facts support a judgment that the ultimate punishment should be imposed. It is a highly controversial role and, as we shall see, a role that is filled with enormous problems, not all of which can be laid on the shoulders of the jury. Capital punishment law is too complex for full coverage here, but some background on the historical and legal context in which the jury operates is needed to understand the jury's role in this issue.[5]

A HISTORICAL SKETCH OF THE DEATH PENALTY IN THE UNITED STATES

The death penalty was an accepted punishment throughout the early history of the United States. The Fifth Amendment to the US Constitution, ratified in 1791, makes this clear in three places in a single compound sentence: "No person shall be held to answer for a *capital*, or other infamous crime . . . [nor] put in jeopardy of *life* . . . nor be deprived of *life*, liberty, or property, without due process of law." Part of the due process of law included the right to trial by jury guaranteed in the Sixth Amendment.

Nevertheless, by the nineteenth century, bills to abolish capital punishment were submitted to state legislatures in New York, Massachusetts, and Pennsylvania. In 1846 Michigan voted to abolish hanging for all crimes except treason. Rhode Island abolished the death penalty in 1852, and Wisconsin followed the next year. After the Civil War a number of other states abolished capital punishment but subsequently reinstated it. Late in the nineteenth century the electric chair and the gas chamber began to replace hanging because these devices were considered to result in more humane methods of execution. Concomitantly, executions began being carried out behind the walls of prisons rather than in the public square. During this same period, state legislatures began to limit the death penalty to more serious crimes, so that by the beginning of the twentieth century capital punishment was primarily reserved for murder, rape, and treason. One reason for this change was that juries increasingly refused to convict for lesser crimes, presumably on the grounds that the mandatory penalty of death was seen as too severe for these offenses. Judges had the primary duty to sentence criminal defendants, but some states began to allow the jury to make a recommendation to the judge about death sentences, while others required that the capital punishment decision be the sole responsibility of the jury.

Systematic statistics on American executions did not begin to be collected until around 1900. Large numbers of people were executed at the early part of the century, and the numbers declined over time. One estimate is that between 1900 and 1966 as many as 7,266 legal executions were carried out. This figure does not count the untold number of lynchings that took place during this time, especially in the southern states. The highest number of executions occurred around 1935 when 199 people were put to death, but then executions began to drop.[6] In the 1950s the number was half that of the 1940s. Between 1965 and 1967 only ten executions were carried out.

The rapid drop of executions in the 1960s must be understood against the backdrop of the legal and social climate and a strategy by lawyers involved with the NAACP's Legal Defense Fund. Beginning in the 1950s and extending into the 1960s, the US Supreme Court under the leadership of Chief Justice Earl Warren rendered a number of decisions that are characterized as a due process revolution that extended more procedural rights to defendants. These rights included the right to a court-appointed lawyer if the accused was too poor to afford one. Another factor was the school desegregation cases that exposed the invidious effects of racial prejudice in almost every area of American life. Not least among the various evils was the fact that records showed that blacks were disproportionately represented on death row and among those actually executed. Particularly striking were figures showing that in the deep South, many blacks were sentenced to death for rape (especially of white women). Lawyers for the NAACP's Legal Defense Fund developed legal strategies attacking the procedural fairness of capital punishment trials, even providing lawyers across the United States with a "Last Aid Kit" to assist them in preparing defenses and making appeals.

In 1972 the Supreme Court considered for the first time whether the death penalty violated the Eighth Amendment's proscription against cruel and unusual punishment.[7] Three cases, all involving black men sentenced to die, were consolidated under the lead case titled *Furman v. Georgia*. In a landmark five-to-four decision, the Court ruled that the death penalty violated that prohibition. All nine justices wrote separate opinions. Justice Marshall, adopting language from one of the few prior cases interpreting the Eighth Amendment, *Trop v. Dulles*, asserted that although capital punishment was accepted at the framing of the Bill of Rights, it was now inconsistent with "the evolving standards of decency that mark the progress of a maturing society." Justice Brennan also would have banned it outright, but the other three justices in the bare majority offered more limited opinions. Justice Douglas centered on the racial discrimination that resulted in members of minority groups being sentenced to die proportionately more often than whites. Justice Stewart emphasized capriciousness, arguing that the death penalty was "wantonly and freakishly applied" to only a random handful of persons. Justice White argued that "the death penalty is exacted with great infrequency even for the most atrocious crimes and . . . there is no meaningful basis for distinguishing the few cases in which it is imposed from the many cases in which it is not."

Justice White saw the jury as a central problem: "The short of it is that the policy of vesting sentencing authority primarily in juries—a decision largely motivated by the desire to mitigate the harshness of the law and to bring community judgment to bear upon the sentence as well as guilt or innocence—has so effectively achieved its aims that capital punishment within the confines of the statutes now before us has for all practical purposes run its course."[8]

A major problem was that in 1972, in most states the evidence about a defendant's guilt and the evidence about whether or not the defendant merited a death sentence were presented in a single trial phase. This put defense lawyers in a difficult position by forcing them to choose between trial strategies focusing on challenging the prosecution's evidence regarding guilt for the crime versus strategies that emphasized why a defendant did not deserve a death sentence.

Another central problem was that juries were pretty much left to their own devices when it came to deciding who deserved to die. Juries had no clear legal standards to guide their decision making about whether a defendant merited a death sentence. It's not surprising that different juries would come up with different verdicts in seemingly similar cases.

These problems of racial bias, unpredictability, lack of guidance, and unitary trials led the *Furman* court to conclude that all existing statutes had major due process flaws. *Furman* set aside all existing death sentences in the United States. Death rows across the nation were emptied.

Legislative reaction to *Furman* was swift. Thirty-five states revised their statutes to address *Furman*'s criticisms of unfettered jury discretion and lack of clear judicial oversight of those verdicts. Many statutes bifurcated capital trials, dividing them into a guilt phase and a sentencing phase. In the sentencing phase, the prosecution and defense were allowed to present evidence about aggravating and mitigating factors associated with the accused and the circumstances surrounding the crime.

Following the Supreme Court's concerns about lack of standards, the various states adopted guided discretion approaches to determining who should live and who should die. The new laws identified which elements and factors of a case should be considered in the death penalty decision. Aggravating factors, such as the existence of torture or multiple victims, made the crime or defendant more death-worthy. Mitigating factors, including such things as a defendant's age, abused childhood, or mental disturbance, made the defendant a less appropriate subject for capital punishment. Jurors were instructed to review the evidence in the case to determine whether these factors existed and to weigh them together to decide on life or death. In a number of states, the jury recommendation was made advisory and judges were given authority to overrule the jury's recommendation and substitute death or life in prison.

Most important, as a matter of law, appeals courts now were required to review each death sentence to ensure equity and proportionality in the application of the statutory guidelines.

In 1976 the Supreme Court upheld Georgia's new death penalty statute that provided for bifurcated trials, guided discretion, and appellate review in *Gregg v. Georgia*.[9] It concluded that the procedural problems had been solved by these new features. The Court acknowledged that "while some jury discretion still exists the discretion to be exercised is controlled by clear and objective standards so as to produce non-discriminatory application." Moreover, the Court asserted that review of sentences by state supreme courts would correct any remaining problems. The brief interlude in the banning of death sentences and executions came to an end.

In 1977 Gary Gilmore stopped appeals of his death sentence and was executed by a Utah firing squad, making him the first person to be executed in the post-*Furman* era. John Spinkellink, age twenty-four, a twice-convicted felon and drifter, was found guilty of the 1973 killing of a hitchhiker with whom he was sharing a hotel room.[10] In 1979 Spinkellink, the first post-*Gregg* person to be executed against his will, was strapped into Florida's three-legged chair, nicknamed "Old Sparky." A leather hood covered Spinkellink's shaved head; a heavy strap held his chin immobile. Thirty-two witnesses watched as the executioner threw the switch. Three separate 2,300-volt charges of electricity surged from Spinkellink's head to a wire strapped to his leg. His hands curled and blackened. His legs twitched. Smoke filled the execution chamber, and an official witness, a Democratic state representative, later said that "if you leaned forward and looked you could see that he sizzled and sizzled again." The death penalty had most definitely returned to America.

However, constitutional challenges to the death penalty continued. In 1977 in *Coker v Georgia*,[11] the Supreme Court ruled that the death penalty for rape was unconstitutional because, although rape was a heinous offense, the punishment was disproportionate to the crime. In 1983 the Court rejected a challenge to psychiatric evidence about a capital defendant's future dangerousness in *Barefoot v. Estelle*.[12] In that case, the American Psychiatric Association had tendered an amicus brief on behalf of the defendant, summarizing scientific research that showed that such predictions were highly unreliable. The Court, however, noted that the defendant could cross-examine the state's expert witnesses and call their own witnesses. Further, it asserted that juries were capable of assigning proper weight to the evidence. In the 1987 case of *McCleskey v. Kemp*, the Court did not dispute findings by Professor David Baldus and two colleagues that demonstrated continuing racial disparities in Georgia death penalty sentencing. However, the Court observed that McCleskey did not prove that his particular jury was biased or had impermissibly taken race into account. McCleskey had committed an armed robbery and then killed a police officer by firing a bullet into the officer's face. The McCleskey decision effectively closed the door on statistical challenges alleging racial bias.[13] (Warren McCleskey was electrocuted by the State of Georgia in 1991).

There were some victories for opponents of capital punishment. In 2002, in *Atkins v. Virginia*,[14] the Court ruled that the death sentence could not be given if the convicted person was mentally retarded. It cited legislative changes as evidence for a national consensus against executing the mentally retarded. In 2005, by a five-to-four vote in *Roper v. Simmons*,[15] the Court ruled that persons who were under the age of eighteen when they committed the capital crime could not be executed. Both of these limitations found broad support among the American public.[16] In limiting the death penalty in these two types of cases, the Supreme

Court alluded to the nation's evolving standards of decency and public consensus that juveniles and the mentally retarded were not as culpable for their crimes. For example, a Gallup poll taken before the *Roper* decision found that just 26 percent of Americans endorsed capital punishment for juveniles. A number of states had already barred the execution of juveniles, and statistics indicated that juries were highly reluctant to sentence juveniles to death. Capital Jury Project researchers, led by William Bowers, interviewed jurors in the rare juvenile death penalty cases and found that the jurors resisted juvenile death sentences because of young people's cognitive, social, and emotional immaturity and hence their reduced ability to act responsibly.[17]

Nine states—Arizona, Idaho, Montana, Nebraska, Colorado, Alabama, Delaware, Florida, and Indiana—had statutes that gave the judge rather than the jury the prime authority to decide on the punishment, although their approaches varied. In Delaware, for example, juries voted on whether or not aggravating factors existed in the case and whether the aggravating factors outweighed the mitigating factors. Judges considered these advisory jury judgments in making their own decisions about whether the defendant should live or die. In Nebraska, after a jury reached its decision on guilt, a three-judge panel decided on the sentence. But in 2002 in *Ring v. Arizona* the Supreme Court struck down these approaches, ruling that having a judge rather than a jury determine critical sentencing factors violated the defendant's right to a jury trial. At a minimum, the jury must determine whether aggravating factors that made the case eligible for the death penalty existed beyond a reasonable doubt.[18] Indiana, Colorado, and Arizona have since switched to a jury sentencing system, while other states have modified their statutes so that even though the judge still decides the final sentence, juries now determine whether a defendant is eligible for death by determining whether at least one aggravating factor exists beyond a reasonable doubt.[19]

From Spinkellink in 1977 through December of 2006, 1,057 people convicted of murder were put to death in 32 state execution chambers.[20] Of these, 152 were killed by electrocution, 11 died in gas chambers, 3 died by hanging, and 2 were executed by firing squad.[21] The remainder were killed by lethal injection, which has become the primary method of killing in most states. The Gilmore and Spinkellink executions were widely covered in the national media, but many subsequent executions have been carried out in near anonymity, warranting only a brief news item in local newspapers.

CONTINUING CAPRICE AND CONVICTION OF THE INNOCENT

Despite the Supreme Court's optimism in *Gregg v. Georgia* that the main procedural problems would be solved by jury guidelines and bifurcated sentencing procedures, three decades later problems of basic fairness continue to plague the imposition of death sentences. Two case examples help to illustrate the many problems associated with capital punishment in the United States.

Anthony Porter: Two teenagers were shot and killed near a swimming pool on the South Side of Chicago in 1982. A young man swimming in the pool implicated Anthony Porter in the killing after presenting the police with at least three different stories. Porter's lawyer did not meet with him until just before the proceedings and fell asleep during the short trial. Anthony Porter was sentenced to death. Appeals to both the Illinois Supreme Court and US Supreme Court were denied, but Porter continued to file appeals delaying his execution. In 1995, he was found to have an IQ of 51; a new appeal was launched claiming that he may not have understood his punishment. Another stay was granted fifty hours before his scheduled execution.

In 1998 a journalism class at Northwestern University decided to investigate the case. They discovered that the young man in the pool who had implicated Porter had recanted and said the police had intimidated him and forced him to implicate Porter. They also drew attention to evidence that the shots in the case had been made by a right-handed shooter, but Porter was left-handed. Finally, another witness came forward who identified Alstory Simon as the killer and said the killing resulted from a dispute over drugs. Simon later confessed to the crime on video. The journalism students reported the information they had gathered. Porter was eventually released from prison, and all charges against him were dropped. Alstory Simon was tried and convicted and received thirty-seven and a half years for the killings. After Anthony Porter was released, Governor George Ryan decided to issue a moratorium on executions in the State of Illinois and, shortly before his term ended, commuted all death penalty sentences in the state to life in prison.[22]

Henry Lee Hunt: In 1984, Dottie Ransom and her bigamous husband, Rogers Locklear, hired A. R. Barnes to kill her first husband, Jackie Ransom, to collect on an insurance policy. A. R. Barnes recruited his brother Elwell Barnes to assist in the murder, and, according to prosecutors, Elwell recruited Henry Hunt, a North Carolina Lumbee Indian, to join them. Jackie Ransom was shot in the head in the woods near a local bar on September 8, 1984. Following the murder, another man, Larry Jones, went to the police to talk about who was involved in the murder. Jones was later shot and buried in a shallow grave. At trial, state prosecutors led the jury to believe that Larry Jones had gone to the police to implicate Henry Hunt, giving Hunt a motive to kill Jones. In fact, Larry Jones had implicated Rogers Locklear as the person responsible for the murder. While the bullets that killed Jones matched Hunt's gun, there was little further physical evidence. State and local officials destroyed files on the investigation of the case before Henry Hunt's appellate lawyers were able to review them.

A. R. Barnes originally confessed to the murders but later recanted and pointed the blame at his brother Elwell and Henry Lee Hunt. A. R. Barnes failed a lie detector test. Hunt passed two lie detector tests administered by a respected polygraph expert. Many of the people who testified for the prosecution were either involved in the murders or had reason to deflect blame away from themselves. Elwell Barnes and Henry Hunt were both charged with capital murder and both received a death sentence. In 1989 Elwell Barnes signed an affidavit that he, his brother A. R. Barnes, and others—but not Henry Hunt—committed both murders and that Henry Hunt had nothing to do with either murder. Elwell Barnes died in prison in 2001. On September 12, 2003, Henry Hunt became the twenty-fifth person and first Native American executed in North Carolina in the post-*Furman* era. Everyone else involved in the case served less than ten years in prison.[23]

THE CONTINUING PROBLEM OF RACE

At the end of October 2006, a tally of those under sentence of death in the United States produced the following findings: fully 3,344 people were on death row; of these, 1,572 were white, 1,396 were black, 358 were Hispanic, 78 were of unknown race. Fifty-seven were women.[24] While blacks constitute only about 13 percent of the US population, they accounted for almost 42 percent of death row inmates. In the modern era of American capital punishment, fifteen white people have been executed for killing a black; 213 black people have been executed for killing a white.

In *Furman*, the Supreme Court justices cited the evident racism in the death penalty system in which blacks were disproportionately likely to be sentenced to death. Modern-era death penalty procedural reforms were designed to eradicate such racial factors. The Baldus study of Georgia's new death penalty system showed some apparent success insofar that the race of the defendant was, by itself, not a statistically significant factor. However, Baldus and his colleagues discovered a striking statistical pattern that involved the *victim's* race. Prosecutors sought the death penalty for 70 percent of black defendants with white victims but only 15 percent of black defendants with black victims. A case with a white victim was *over four times* more likely to result in a death sentence than was a comparable black victim case.[25]

Maryland governor Parris Glendening commissioned a thorough study of the death penalty after a preliminary report indicated that black defendants who killed white victims were more likely to receive a death sentence. University of Maryland criminologist Ray Paternoster and his collaborators collected extensive information on homicides that occurred during the period 1978–1999, including background data about the offender and potentially aggravating and mitigating factors in those cases. The Maryland study found, as Baldus's Georgia study found, that controlling for relevant case factors, those who killed whites were more apt to receive a death sentence. The effect appeared to be due to the prosecutor's initial decision to seek the death penalty and to stick with the pursuit of a death sentence as the case progressed, rather than any differential treatment by the jury during the sentencing phase.[26]

Research undertaken by Bowers and Pierce as part of the Capital Punishment Project showed that patterns of racial disparity were not confined to southern states.[27] In Ohio, for example, 22 percent of blacks convicted of killing a white received a death sentence compared to 5 percent of whites who killed whites and 0.6 percent of blacks who killed blacks. No whites who killed blacks were sentenced to death. In almost all of the states where there have been reviews of race and the death penalty, data show a pattern of race effects.[28] A 2003 study by Amnesty International covering all US jurisdictions concluded that even though blacks and whites are murder victims in nearly equal numbers, 80 percent of the people executed since the death penalty was reinstated in 1976 have been for murders of white victims. Furthermore, more than 20 percent of executed blacks were convicted by all-white juries.[29] A 2001 report by the New Jersey Supreme Court concluded: "There is unsettling statistical evidence indicating that cases involving killers of White victims are more likely to progress to a penalty phase than cases involving killers of African-American victims."[30] The effects of the race of the victim and the race of the defendant are not always found, but their discovery in multiple jurisdictions gives cause for concern.[31]

THE CENTRAL ROLE OF JURIES

The jury is the lynchpin in the process of capital punishment. Yet, problems begin with the process that selects a "death-qualified" jury and do not end with the final verdict. Some of the best data we have come from the Capital Jury Project, a consortium of researchers in fourteen states that attempted to interview four randomly selected jurors from numerous death penalty trials. The trials were chosen to provide equal numbers of cases in which the verdict was death and cases in which the jury decided against a death sentence.[32]

THE JURORS WHO SERVE AND THOSE WHO CAN'T

Before 1968, any juror who expressed opposition or reservations for any reason about capital punishment was automatically excluded from serving on a capital jury. The legal reasoning was simple. Democratically elected legislatures had passed laws saying that capital punishment was appropriate for certain crimes. Jurors who were opposed to capital punishment were saying that they would not uphold the law even if the evidence supported a death sentence. Therefore, at the beginning of the trial the judge would question and dismiss any jurors who had scruples against death sentences. (In Texas this questioning was actually called "scrupling.")

William Witherspoon was convicted of murder in Cook County, Illinois, and sentenced to die. At his trial the judge began jury selection by saying, "Okay, let's first eliminate the conscientious objectors" and proceeded to dismiss jurors with scruples against capital punishment. Witherspoon's lawyer appealed the conviction and death sentence, arguing that this winnowing process produced a jury that was prone to convict and more apt to give the death sentence. His argument was that under the Illinois statute, large numbers of people were eliminated, even people who expressed mild reservations about the punishment, leaving a jury composed of people who staunchly supported capital punishment. Thus, the lawyer argued, the jury was composed of people more likely than the general public to be prone to choosing the death penalty. Moreover, he claimed that the jury was even biased on the question of guilt. Those who favored the death penalty held views that were tough on law and order, causing them to be conviction-prone, that is, biased in favor of the prosecution.

In 1968, in *Witherspoon v. Illinois* the US Supreme Court rejected Witherspoon's argument that his jury was conviction-prone, saying that currently there was insufficient evidence of a relation between death penalty attitudes and the tendency to convict.[33] But the Court did conclude that it was "obvious" that the members of the jury had been selected for their harsh attitudes favoring punishment and were "uncommonly willing to condemn a man to die." In short, death qualification procedures produced a jury that was biased on the issue of death. Witherspoon's sentence was reduced to life imprisonment.

The *Witherspoon* decision effectively changed the way that capital juries are selected. Potential jurors who have reservations about capital punishment but who say that they can nevertheless follow the law and consider the death penalty are not automatically disqualified from serving on the jury. In 1985 the Supreme Court revisited the issue in *Wainwright v. Witt* and clarified the standard to be used.[34] A juror may be dismissed for cause if he or she feels so strongly that those personal views will "prevent or substantially impair the performance of his duties as a juror in accordance with his instructions and his oath." This standard also applies to any juror who would automatically vote for the death penalty upon a finding of guilt. Under *Witt*, the trial judge has considerable discretion in deciding if a juror is qualified to serve.

A number of studies bearing on the *Witherspoon* claims of conviction-proneness and death-proneness were carried out by University of Michigan psychology and law professor Phoebe Ellsworth and her collaborators. Their data produced compelling support for those claims of bias. Yet, in *Lockhart v. McCree*, the Supreme Court rejected the studies.[35] The Supreme Court has the final word, but, regardless, many subsequent studies of jurors who served in capital trials indicate that capital juries are tilted toward both finding guilt and recommending death.

The voir dire questioning following the *Witherspoon* and *Witt* decisions is supposed to be a net that eliminates those people who too strongly favor death as well as those opposed to death. The Capital Jury Project's many interviews of jurors have shown the screening process to be badly flawed. One study in South Carolina found that 14 percent of jurors who actually served as jurors in capital cases believed that the death penalty was the only acceptable punishment for murder, 57 percent believed that it was the only acceptable punishment for premeditated murder, and 48 percent believed it was required for killing a policeman or prison guard.[36] These basic findings have been replicated in many other studies.[37] One study estimated that as many as 30 percent of jurors who serve may not be qualified under the *Witherspoon* criteria because they would automatically vote for death.[38]

Juror interviews by William Bowers and his colleagues led them to conclude: "There appears to be a presumption that clear unequivocal proof of guilt justifies the death penalty."[39] Here are some examples they provided:

> A Florida juror: "When I knew in my heart he was guilty . . . as I knew he was guilty, I knew he should get death."
>
> A Kentucky juror: "We found him guilty, and I again believed in the death sentence, believe in it, so in my mind I knew what my vote would be."
>
> A California juror: "After the jury voted guilty. The weight of the fact that all twelve individuals all believed the defendant to be guilty, made me lean toward death."

These jurors seemed to foreclose the possibility of a life sentence even before hearing any evidence in the sentencing phase of the trial in contradiction of the legal standard that clearly requires that jurors be open to both alternatives as they hear and review the evidence.

We know from the research on the story model of juror decision making that a juror's prior attitudes can shape the way that trial evidence is interpreted and assimilated into a decision about guilt. It would appear to also be true about punishment. Research from the Capital Jury Project has found that the more strongly a juror believes in death as the appropriate punishment for murder, the more likely that juror is to vote for death on the first ballot during the penalty phase of the trial.[40]

THE IMPACT OF THE DEATH QUALIFICATION PROCESS

Jury selection in capital cases is complex. At the very beginning of the proceedings, before hearing any of the evidence, jurors have to be questioned about their ability to consider the death penalty in the sentencing phase of the trial if the defendant is found guilty. Professor Craig Haney was among the first to recognize that the very process of questioning prospective jurors about their willingness to give a death sentence could tilt the jurors toward a guilty verdict in the first stage of the trial.[41] He pointed out that all of the fuss about a second stage will make jurors inclined to believe that a death sentencing stage is expected. Moreover, some jurors may come to believe that not only the prosecutor but also the judge hold a view that death is the appropriate verdict. Haney provided an example from a New Jersey judge's instruction manual from the early 1980s:

> When I instruct the jury at the close of this trial, I will outline in detail the factors to be weighed in deciding whether to impose a death penalty. Let me give you a general idea of what I will say so that you can understand what we need to know now of your views.[42]

Note that the instructions telegraph a message that the jury is likely to find the defendant guilty and that a second phase will follow. Moreover, Haney hypothesized, the instructions and the dismissal of jurors because of their opposition to capital punishment may create the impression in juror's minds that the judge considers some persons fit for service while others are unfit.

Haney tested these propositions in a clever experiment.[43] A group of jury-eligible adults were asked to observe a two-hour videotape of jury selection for a murder trial and asked to imagine that they were jurors in the case. Half of the group was assigned to a standard voir dire condition, but the other half was assigned to a death qualification condition that contained not only the standard voir dire questions but also death qualification questions. After they had viewed the tape, all participants were asked a series of questions about the videotape. Participants in the "death qualification" condition were more likely to indicate that they believed the defendant was guilty of first-degree murder and that he would be convicted of that charge. They were also more likely to believe that the judge thought the defendant was guilty and favored the death penalty. Furthermore, they were also more likely to indicate that the law disapproved of people who opposed capital punishment. In short, Haney's experiment supported the prediction that the voir dire biased jurors toward guilt and death.

In subsequent years, many states have modified their jury instructions to attempt to overcome some of this biasing effect. For example, in the state of Washington, the trial judge reads a list of instructions before voir dire begins.[44] Instructions include information that capital trials involve a "two phase procedure for determining whether or not the death penalty should be imposed." The jurors are told that the first phase is for determining guilt and are then instructed:

> However, if you find the defendant guilty of the crime of premeditated first-degree murder with aggravating circumstances then you will be reconvened for

> a second phase called a sentencing phase. During the sentencing phase proceeding you may hear additional evidence and argument concerning the penalty to be imposed.

The potential jurors are given additional instructions about aggravating and mitigating circumstances and the need for unanimity, and then are told:

> Since you may become a juror in this case and possibly be required to participate in the sentencing phase determination involving the question of the death penalty, you can be expected to be questioned about your views, if any, about the death penalty and to the extent that these views might influence your decisions in this case.

Thus, Washington's instruction is crafted to emphasize that the sentencing stage is more hypothetical than already a sure bet.

But continuing problems lie in the questioning. Here is one among several real trial examples that Haney provided wherein the prosecutor asked jurors:

> In an appropriate case, based upon the information that will be given to you, and the law as his Honor, Judge Matia, will give you, if you come to the conclusion that the imposition of capital punishment is the appropriate verdict at the second trial, do you feel that you could join with your fellow jurors and sign a verdict form indicating that?[45]

Or, consider an example from a case in North Carolina:[46]

> The Judge: Do you have any personal convictions about the death penalty which would prevent you or substantially hinder the performance of your duty in accordance with the Court's instructions and your oath as a juror?
>
> Juror: No sir.
>
> The Judge: If you sit as a juror at the sentencing phase of the trial, will you follow the instructions of the Court?
>
> Juror: Yes, sir.
>
> . . . .
>
> District Attorney: If you're satisfied of all the things . . . it would be your duty under the law to come back to this courtroom and announce as your verdict that this Defendant should be sentenced to death. Do you understand that?
>
> Juror: Yes, sir.
>
> District Attorney: A part of this process and a part of the system that you have to go through is that you alone are required to stand there where you're seated now and face this Defendant and say, "I agree with the verdict. It is my verdict that he be put to death, and I still assent to that verdict." Are you strong enough to do that?
>
> Juror: Yes, sir . . .
>
> District Attorney: If there is some small doubt in the back of your mind that

> you can't come back in this courtroom after the State has met its burden and done all that it's required to do, if you don't think you can come back in here and stand up there alone and answer those questions out loud that you sentence this man right down here . . . this isn't just some person that we're talking about that's not in the courtroom. That man seated right down there. Do you understand that?
>
> Juror: Yes, sir.

Several aspects of this last example require comment. Under the law the juror would *not* have to "stand alone," look the defendant in the eye, and sentence the man to death. Despite stating several times that he could follow the law, under relentless questioning, the prospective juror began to hesitate when the district attorney asked essentially the same question again. The trial judge refused defense counsel an opportunity to further examine the juror and granted the district attorney's motion to excuse the juror for cause. Other prospective jurors saw this process unfold. Several other jurors who said they could vote for the death penalty but hesitated over the "stand alone" question were also excused by the judge.

Scott Sundby, who has studied death penalty jurors as part of the Capital Jury Project, notes that jurors are often exposed to back-and-forth questioning from the prosecutor and the defense lawyer after the judge is finished with his questioning.[47] As he explains, the prosecutor may ask: "Mrs. Jones, it sounds to me that after much soul-searching [pause], as much as you'd like to follow the law, you really could not sentence another human being to the gas chamber, wouldn't you agree?" The defense lawyer, on the other hand, may say, "Now, Mrs. Jones, you would be able to impose the death penalty on Adolf Hitler, for instance, wouldn't you?" Jurors may waver back and forth in the face of such examination to the point that they may be confused about where they stand. As Professor Haney has observed, the death qualification process in several ways helps jurors to become more comfortable with the idea of delivering a death sentence.[48]

In *Adams v. Texas*, the Supreme Court acknowledged that far more anti–death penalty jurors than pro–death penalty jurors are likely to be disqualified from serving in capital cases: "Despite the hypothetical existence of the juror who believes literally in the Biblical admonition 'an eye for an eye,' . . . it is undeniable . . . that such jurors will be few indeed as compared with those excluded because of scruples against capital punishment."[49]

A process in which jurors are systematically eliminated from the jury pool by the judge because they are opposed to capital punishment can send a message that the legal system supports the imposition of the death penalty in this case. Jurors are asked repeatedly in voir dire if they are willing to "follow the law" and impose the death penalty to the point that the questions become a sort of obedience drill. Professor Haney pointed out that these factors are likely to persist when the jury deliberates, especially because some jurors may consider that they have made a promise to the judge that they will vote for it. They may use this reasoning to persuade wavering jurors, even arguing that a holdout juror has a duty to follow through with the implied promise.

In an ideal world we might be able to cope with the conviction proneness of the death-qualified jury by having one jury selected to decide guilt without death qualification questions. Then, if guilt is found, a second jury would be death qualified to decide on the punishment. For administrative and financial reasons, a two-jury plan is not usually feasible, but even if it were, the problems of the death-proneness of the sentencing jury would persist. Moreover, we have not yet discussed the pernicious effects of peremptory challenges on jury composition in capital cases.

RACE AND PEREMPTORY CHALLENGES

The *New York Times* documented a 1984 Georgia case in which the only black jury member in the trial of a convicted black man, Henry Hance, had reservations about sentencing Hance to death.[50] In fact she never voted for death but was bullied by the other eleven jurors into acquiescing in a death sentence. She was afraid that she might be charged with perjury for not going along because she had said in voir dire that she could vote for death. Her account was verified by one of the white jurors, who also reported that another white juror described Hance as "just one more sorry nigger that no one would miss."

Even if we assume that such blatant racism is absent in many capital juries, there is evidence that racial bias may appear in more subtle forms. A recent analysis of photos of Philadelphia capital defendants by Jennifer Eberhardt and her colleagues revealed that defendants who had "stereotypically black features"—broad noses, thick lips, dark hair, and dark skin—were more likely to be sentenced to death than black defendants with less stereotypical features.[51] In cases with white victims, a total of 58 percent of the stereotypically black defendants were sentenced to death. In contrast, only 24 percent of the defendants who had less stereotypically black features were given a death sentence. There was no difference in the black defendant-black victim cases, however.

Research has shown that the racial and gender composition of death penalty juries is related to whether or not a defendant gets the death sentence.[52] As already noted, a black defendant convicted of killing a white victim is substantially more likely to receive a death sentence verdict than any of the other three racial combinations. When we look at the composition of the juries that render death sentences in these cases, gender and racial composition makes a difference. Data from fourteen states indicate that the death penalty is three times as likely for the defendant in a black-kills-white case if the jury is composed of five or more white males. A life sentence is twice as likely if there is at least one black male juror. Professor Bowers and his coauthors have found that the thinking of black and white jurors regarding appropriate punishment changes as the trial proceeds.[53] By the time of the jury's first vote on punishment, two out of three whites favor death and two out of three blacks favor life. Posttrial interviews indicate that whites are less receptive to mitigating circumstances and are more likely to see the defendant as a continuing danger to society. Whites are less likely to consider the defendant's upbringing as part of the context of the crime.

The racial and gender problems would be problematic enough if the process by which death-qualified jurors were eliminated was neutral with regard to race and gender—but it is not. As we discussed earlier, Professor Baldus and his collaborators found a racial pattern in peremptory challenge strikes in the Philadelphia courts that they concluded made a difference in the likelihood of a death sentence. The biases of prosecutors to prefer whites and defense attorneys to prefer blacks did not in the end cancel each other out. Philadelphia prosecutors were more successful in eliminating their target groups because there were fewer of them.

In short, despite the line of Supreme Court decisions prohibiting attorney consideration of race in the exercise of peremptory challenges, the data indicate that the problems of racial discrimination persist in capital cases. Thus, in addition to pro-prosecution biases arising out of the death qualification process, the use of peremptory challenges further disadvantages black defendants in capital cases.

EVIDENCE DURING TRIAL

During the trial, prosecutors routinely introduce photographs of the body, the death scene, and other compelling evidence, such as bloody clothes or recordings of a victim's 911 call. This is relevant evidence bearing on the facts of the case with respect to guilt and punishment. Nevertheless, interviews with jurors indicate that such evidence plays a major role in their decision for death, particularly for jurors who are initially most inclined toward a death sentence.[54]

Another important factor in deciding life or death is the jurors' perception of the defendant's remorse. Professor Sundby has examined the role of remorse in death penalty cases.[55] Jurors want to see remorse. They seldom ever see it. The reasons are complex. Most defendants sit quietly during the trial and show little expression. Perhaps some actually have no remorse. Others may have come from childhood and adult environments filled with violence where showing any emotion is a sign of weakness. Some may feel that to express remorse is a sign of shame or that by expressing remorse they will be seen as insincere. And there is also the advice of their lawyers who inform them that the trial will be filled with emotional testimony and perhaps even testimony that the defendant believes is in error or even a lie. Concerned about a harmful emotional outburst in court, the lawyer might instruct the client that it is in his best interest to not display emotion.

Jurors frequently reacted strongly to a perceived lack of defendant remorse. Professor Sundby reported examples of posttrial responses of jurors who voted for a death sentence:

> "It was just like, 'I'll get off.' I mean really it was stone face. There was no emotion."
>
> "I felt sick thinking how anyone could do such a thing and sit there and act like nothing is going on."
>
> "Just sat there. He didn't do much expression at all. He didn't show any emotion at all."
>
> "He appeared relaxed, just like another day, and of course, no remorse, because he didn't do it, so why should he be sorry?"
>
> "He was very casual about everything that was happening. He was trying to be cool, you know, he was just trying to be a tough guy."

Interestingly, other research has shown that when juveniles failed to show remorse, jurors chalked it up to their immaturity and lack of awareness of the seriousness of the proceedings.[56]

Finally, the issue of race is again implicated in death penalty decisions. Professor Thomas Brewer analyzed data from 865 jurors interviewed for the Capital Jury Project.[57] He concluded that blacks and whites tended to give the same amount of consideration to mitigating evidence except in cases in which a black defendant was convicted of killing a white person. In this latter case, he argued, the data show that black jurors were more receptive to mitigation than their white co-jurors. Under these circumstances, blacks were more likely than whites to have lingering doubts about the defendant's guilt, to view the defendant as remorseful, and to believe that remorse was grounds for mercy. Blacks were also more likely to believe the jury rushed to a verdict and that the deliberations were dominated by a few outspoken white jurors who were intolerant of differing opinions. No one can say if these perceptions were accurate, but the findings again point to the inseparable problems of race in death sentences.

Research findings also indicate that during the guilt phase of the trial, well before any evidence about the appropriateness of the death penalty is presented in the penalty phase, jurors attempt to evaluate whether the defendant is a continuing threat to society.[58] Remorse is one component of this evaluation, but so is evidence of past violent crimes. Almost always jurors who return a death sentence strongly believe that the defendant is a continuing menace to the lives of others.

Testimony from expert and layperson witnesses bearing on the defendant's character is especially significant in the sentencing phase of a trial. The prosecution can produce testimony about aggravating circumstances that warrant a death penalty. Prosecutors often call the families of the victims to testify about the impact of the murder on their lives. The prosecution usually also calls a psychiatrist or psychologist to testify that the defendant shows proclivities toward being a continuing menace to society. The most infamous prosecution expert was Dr. James Grigson, a psychiatrist who earned the moniker "Dr. Death" and was expelled from the American Psychiatric Association because of his frequent testimony (in more than one hundred and fifty trials) that the chances of the defendant being dangerous in the future were 1,000 percent.[59] Such testimony by prosecution experts is compatible with the beliefs of jurors who lean toward a death sentence, but it is also misleading.[60] Psychological assessment tools are often inaccurate in predicting risk, particularly when they are predicting dangerousness in a prison population.[61]

The defense is also entitled to call witnesses to provide evidence of mitigating circumstances. In *Lockett v. Ohio*, the Supreme Court ruled that a defendant constitutionally must be allowed to present "any aspect of a defendant's character or record and any of the circumstances of the offense that the defendant proffers as a basis for a sentence less than death."[62] In many trials the financially hard-pressed or incompetent defense counsel present little or no such evidence; but in other cases, the defendants' family members or experts may be called to testify about the horrendous childhood of the defendant, prior drug use, potential brain damage, or low IQ. Sometimes lay testimony by prison guards is called in an attempt to show the good behavior of the defendant while awaiting trial. Posttrial juror interviews, however, reveal a great deal of skepticism toward such testimony.

Professor Sundby analyzed interviews with 152 jurors in thirty-six California capital trials.[63] The study revealed three consistent themes regarding these experts: experts were viewed as "hired guns," jurors were skeptical of the experts' ability to explain human behavior, and the experts often failed to draw a link between their testimony and the defendant's specific situation. When they were questioned about their reactions to the expert evidence, the jurors often referred to these professional witnesses in a derogatory manner. Some focused on their high fees. In one case a juror said: "The final witness was [Dr. X], a practicing clinical psychologist and teacher, who was hired by the defense to put together a psychological profile. . . . It was rather exasperating that at $200 per hour for over 240 hours of his time—which equates to $48,000 of taxpayer dollars—he really didn't tell us anything we hadn't learned already from witnesses and family members."[64] Jurors frequently relayed with pleasure their view that during cross-examination the prosecutor had "picked apart," "ripped . . . to threads," "chopped up," and "blow[n] . . . out of the box" the defense expert.[65]

Similar to our earlier discussions of jurors' commonsense reasoning, the capital jurors often applied their own common sense or personal experience in evaluating the expert testimony as well as their values regarding personal responsibility. Here is an exchange between the interviewer and a juror regarding why a claim of a mitigating factor was not valid:

Juror: [The expert] talked about methamphetamines and that they can make you not aware of your doings and such. . . . I thought it was a crock, because when I was in college . . . I did this stuff . . .

Interviewer: Have you used methamphetamines?

Juror: Yeah, yeah so when I was sitting there listening to this drug expert I was thinking, "Have you ever done this stuff? Do you actually know what was, I mean, is this all just textbook knowledge?" Because he knew nothing. . . . I had done this stuff, I know, and everything he was saying was just so far-fetched. I wondered where he got all this from.

Interviewer: Did you share that with the jury?

Juror: Oh yeah. Because there was another girl in there too, she was a former addict and . . . a recovering alcoholic, and she told the jury too, "I've done this stuff . . ." We both told the jury, "I've used it, I've done it, and I would no more go out and say, 'Let's go kill somebody today and let's get cash and get more drugs.'" I never was up for four or five or six days as he apparently was. Even so, when you do the drugs you know it's illegal, you know it's wrong, so I just believe you're responsible for your actions.[66]

Professor Sundby reported that a number of jurors or their close relatives had been involved with or had been a victim of the same types of mitigating and hardship circumstances described by the expert as an excuse. Many responded with some variation of, "Yeah, well, I went through that and I didn't end up a killer."[67] As one juror stated, "I was asking myself, you are crazy to blame his past. . . . As a justification for his lifestyle, just forget it."[68]

In other instances the jurors thought the expert provided useful information but failed to tie it directly to the defendant:

Juror: I think they were trying to paint a picture of getting our sympathy for this defendant because he had this traumatic experience in his life. But it was sort of like, okay, well, what do we do with that? It was very hard . . . hard for us to hear that. All the other jurors had great empathy for this thirteen-year-old boy who lost his brother, and we had a lot of feeling for it, but we didn't know what to do with it! . . .

Interviewer: So you would say the other jurors did feel empathy for the brother's death, but they didn't know where to go with it?

Juror: Very much. It wasn't enough to make sense. Like if we could somehow tie it in, and say it was so damaging psychologically, you know, in some way make us realize that that could permanently affect a person.[69]

As a consequence, the jury essentially ignored the testimony.

Jurors might have been quite sensible in their rejection of the expert testimony.

However, the examples show the reasoning of death-qualified jurors and raise the question of whether the many jurors who are excluded from serving on capital trials might hold different views about the relevance of the expert testimony bearing on mitigating circumstances.

JURY INSTRUCTIONS

Consider (slightly edited) instructions given to jurors in Oklahoma in the sentencing phase of the trial:[70]

> You are instructed that, in arriving at your determination of punishment, you must first determine whether any one or more of the following aggravating circumstances exists beyond a reasonable doubt.

The judge then lists all relevant factors as they pertain to the case, which may include prior felony convictions; knowingly putting more than one person at risk of death; whether the act was especially heinous, atrocious, or cruel or committed to avoid arrest; whether the act was committed against a peace officer; or if the individual was likely to commit further criminal acts of violence. The judge then goes on to introduce the issue of what the jurors may consider as mitigating circumstances:

> Mitigating circumstances are those which, in fairness, sympathy, and mercy, may extenuate or reduce the degree of moral culpability or blame. The determination of what circumstances are mitigating is for you to resolve under the facts and circumstances of this case.

The judge goes on to explain that aggravating circumstances need to be unanimously agreed upon by all the jurors; the State has to have established beyond a reasonable doubt the existence of at least one aggravating circumstance before the death penalty can be considered. He also points out to the jurors that they do not need to unanimously agree on mitigating circumstances, though, nor do such circumstances need to be proven beyond a reasonable doubt to be considered. The judge will then go on to enumerate the individual mitigating circumstances that could be applicable in the case, which may include such things as lack of prior criminal history; impairment of ability to conform one's activities to the law (for example, acting under duress); the presence of mental or emotional disturbance; defendant's age, character, or emotional and family history; if the victim was a willing participant; the defendant could be rehabilitated; or other mitigating circumstances that the jury might find. The judge then explains the weighing of aggravating and mitigating circumstances as such:

> If you unanimously find that one or more of the aggravating circumstances existed beyond a reasonable doubt, the death penalty shall not be imposed unless you also unanimously find that any such aggravating circumstance or circumstances outweigh the finding of one or more mitigating circumstances. Even if you find that the aggravating circumstance(s) outweigh(s) the mitigating circumstance(s), you may impose a sentence of imprisonment for life with the possibility of parole or imprisonment for life without the possibility of parole.

In Oklahoma, as in other states, the prosecution must prove aggravating factors beyond a reasonable doubt, but the defense is required to prove mitigating factors only to the juror's satisfaction. There must be unanimity on one or more aggravating factors, but unanimity is not required for mitigating circumstances. Thus, the defense is held to a less stringent standard of proof for establishing the existence of mitigating factors than the prosecution is for establishing aggravating factors.

A number of studies in different states have shown that many jurors are confused by these obviously complex instructions. James Luginbuhl and Julie Howe interviewed eighty-three jurors from North Carolina capital trials on their understanding of North Carolina jury instructions, which are comparable to the Oklahoma instructions.[71] Some elements are better understood than others. Two-thirds of the jurors correctly understood that an aggravating factor had to be proven beyond a reasonable doubt, and three-fourths understood that unanimity was required to find the existence of an aggravating factor. However, misunderstandings are common. Forty-eight percent of the jurors incorrectly believed that they could have considered non-enumerated aggravating circumstances, and one-fourth incorrectly believed that aggravating factors needed only to be proven by a preponderance of the evidence or to the satisfaction of the juror. Only 36 percent correctly understood that they were restricted to the specific list of aggravating factors mentioned by the judge. Fifty-nine percent were aware that they could consider any evidence they desired as a mitigating factor, but only 47 percent correctly understood that mitigating factors did not require proof beyond a reasonable doubt. Forty-one percent incorrectly thought that the standard of proof for mitigating factors was proof beyond a reasonable doubt. Similarly, only 47 percent were aware that unanimity was not required to find the existence of mitigating factors, while 42 percent incorrectly believed that unanimity was required.

Research by Professor Edie Greene found that when capital jurors were asked, "What do you remember most about the judge's instructions?" several jurors complained that they were lengthy and hard to remember and that when they asked for clarification, the judge "simply reread the instructions."[72]

Cornell professors Theodore Eisenberg and Martin Wells found similar confusion in interviews with South Carolina capital jurors.[73] Almost one-half of the jurors believed that mitigating circumstances must be proved beyond a reasonable doubt rather than only to the satisfaction of the juror. And the misunderstandings have an impact: Professor Richard Weiner found in one study that the less jurors understood mitigation instructions, the more likely they were to recommend the death penalty.[74]

The instructions provided to capital jurors about aggravating and mitigating factors, burdens of proof, and the unanimity requirements typically use complex language and unfamiliar words without an explanation of their legal meanings; sentence structures contain multiple negatives. Shari Diamond and Judith Levi analyzed the sources of juror misunderstandings.[75] Those authors also attempted to improve juror understanding of the instructions by rewriting the Illinois instructions in accordance with psycholinguistic principles and then testing the comprehensibility of the revisions against the original instructions on samples of jury-eligible people. Jurors who received the revised instructions were better able to understand them and—like the Weiner study above—were less likely to lean toward a death sentence. Nevertheless, many people still had an inadequate grasp of the intended meaning.

PERCEIVED NONRESPONSIBILITY FOR THE ACTUAL DEATH SENTENCE

The jury verdict in the punishment phase is a critical stage in the death penalty process, but many jurors seem to underappreciate its significance. A number of related studies conducted as part of the Capital Jury Project reveal that many capital jurors believed that their verdict would be reviewed by the judge or by an appellate court and reversed if the judges thought that the verdict was incorrect. Some did not think the defendant would actually be executed. One juror said, "[W]e all pretty much knew that when you vote for death you don't necessarily or even usually get death. Ninety-nine percent of the time they don't put you to death. You sit on death row and get old."[76] Eisenberg, Garvey, and Wells found that a majority of jurors endorsed the view that "very few" defendants sentenced to death would ever be executed.[77] Roughly 70 percent believed that less than half would actually be executed. Jurors also came to feel that they were not personally responsible for the death sentence. The effect was even more pronounced in states like Indiana in which judges before *Ring* shared the sentencing authority with the jury. The whole process of the trial from opening instructions through death qualification, final arguments and instructions, encourages jurors, in Professor Craig Haney's memorable phrase, to a form of "moral disengagement."[78] In short, many jurors do not fully appreciate, nor do they accept, the actual responsibility for their verdict.

PROCEDURAL FAIRNESS PROBLEMS EXTEND BEYOND THE JURY'S ROLE

Between 1973 and February 2006 a total of 123 people in twenty-five different states were released from death row. Some of those released were proven innocent through DNA or other evidence; some were not exonerated, but enough doubt about trial fairness resulted in concerns about executing them.[79] DNA evidence has played a significant role in some of these cases, showing observers that even with evidence that satisfies prosecutors and juries, the capital jury trial is not infallible. Recognizing the problem of wrongful conviction and sentencing, the American Bar Association passed a resolution in 1997 calling for a moratorium on the death penalty.[80] Among its supporters were lawyers who favored capital punishment in principle but who recognized the problems of unfairness in its administration.

The jury is a significant factor in the unfairness and caprice, but it is essential to point to other difficulties in capital litigation. Studies show that problems arise from the very inception of a capital case, which in turn affect the quality of the evidence that juries will hear.[81] One key factor is the adequacy of legal representation. Blacks and poor people are more likely to have a court-assigned lawyer for the simple reason that they cannot afford a private attorney.[82] Ineffective assistance of counsel claims are common. Some states do not even require prior death penalty experience for these difficult cases. Research has shown that among lawyers assigned to defend capital defendants there is a high incidence of alcoholism, previously suspended legal licenses, other disciplinary matters, or total lack of previous experience in capital litigation. Sometimes it appears that judges assign these lawyers to give them a chance to redeem themselves, but in many instances it is probably because other lawyers will not take the case. In 2004 the state of Mississippi paid lead counsel $25 per hour up to a grand total of $1,000! Maryland paid $30 per hour up to a total of $12,500. Colorado paid $65 per hour up to a total of $10,000. Florida paid $40 per hour, and Georgia paid $45 per hour. The amounts available for experts is often either paltry or nothing at all. It would be difficult for a lawyer to pay for an office, copy machine, and secretary at $45 per hour. One conscientious Alabama lawyer who was granted only $500 for expert and investigative resources said: "Without more than $500, there was only one choice, and that is to go to the bank and to finance this litigation, myself, and I was just financially unable to do that. It would cost probably in excess of thirty to forty thousand dollars, and I just could not justify taking those funds from my practice, or my family at that time."[83] The lawyer could not find resources to do routine nonlegal investigation bearing on the factual matters in the case. He pointed out, however, that the district attorney's office and law enforcement agencies had all of the resources they needed to prosecute the case.

In 2006 the American Bar Association's Death Penalty Moratorium Project published an in-depth study of the death penalty system in Georgia.[84] The members of the study commission contained judges as well as prosecutors and defense lawyers. The study identified numerous problems. Funding for defense counsel was often inadequate. The state provided no lawyers for appeals of death sentences for indigent defendants. Racial disparities still existed. The burden of proof for mentally retarded defendants was inadequate. The pattern jury instructions on mitigating circumstances were inadequate. The mandatory proportionality review of death sentences by the Georgia Supreme Court proved to be nearly meaningless.

CONCLUSION

Throughout this book much of the empirical evidence shows that the jury is a competent and responsible decision-making institution that injects societal values into the criminal and civil litigation process. The data on capital juries are anomalous to those conclusions. Death is indeed different.

Clearly, central problems lie in the way that juries are selected and instructed. Other problems lie in whether jurors truly understand the consequences of their actions. But juries are also at the mercy of the complicated litigation process that produces underfunded or incompetent defense attorneys or zealous prosecutors who rely on questionable evidence.[85] Under the best circumstances the legal system as a human institution is subject to error, but in the case of death sentences that are carried out, it is irreversible. And since cases are tried on an individual basis, there is the practical challenge of treating like cases alike.

The Supreme Court's decisions in both *Furman* and *Gregg*, more than three decades ago, recognized that "the evolving standards of decency that mark the progress of a maturing society" required procedural fairness. The optimism of the *Gregg* court that new standards and procedures would solve the problems of the capital jury has not been borne out by empirical evidence. In 1994 in *Callins v. Collins*, Supreme Court justice Harry Blackmun wrote:

> From this day forward, I no longer shall tinker with the machinery of death. For more than 20 years I have endeavored . . . to develop . . . rules that would lend more than the mere appearance of fairness to the death penalty endeavor. . . . Rather than continue to coddle the Court's delusion that the desired level of fairness has been achieved . . . I feel . . . obligated simply to concede that the death penalty experiment has failed.[86]

Legislators, the Supreme Court, and the American citizenry may eventually arrive at the same conclusion.

A POSTSCRIPT: THE END OF THE DEATH PENALTY?

Death sentences have been in a steady decline over the past decade, despite the fact that the murder rate has remained relatively constant and that public opinion polls also show some diminution of support for the death penalty.[87] Yet Professor Scott Sundby, whose work we have cited here, cautions that the death penalty may not be completely on its way out in the near term because of what he calls "the McVeigh factor."

Some of the decline, he suggests, is probably due to the Supreme Court decisions forbidding the killing of mentally incompetent defendants and juveniles, which by itself lessens the numbers of those potentially eligible for death. Some of the decline may be the result of improved lawyering skills among those who represent defendants; juries that are more representative of the population, including minorities; and controls on prosecutorial discretion in seeking the death penalty. Some states have put moratoriums on the death penalty until its fairness can be established. Another factor may be the widespread publicity about racial unfairness and innocent people being sent to death row, which, in turn, may make even death-qualified jurors more cautious in voting for death. So far, there has been no definitive proof that an innocent person has been put to death, but if such a case is proven—most experts say it is not a question of "if" but "when"—it may further turn the public against capital punishment. Sundby's article was written before the widely publicized "botched execution" of Angel Diaz in Florida in December 2006.[88] Diaz's apparently painful thirty-four-minute death due to improper injection of the needle carrying the toxic fluids to his body caused a public outcry. The execution problems are compounded by medical societies increasingly ruling that medical ethics forbid doctors from taking any part in executions.[89]

Professors Carol Steiker and Jordan Steiker have suggested that if the trend toward decreasing execution rates continues, the Supreme Court may eventually be forced to rule that it is so infrequent that it has become "cruel and unusual" in practice and thus violates the Eighth Amendment to the Constitution.[90]

Yet, Sundby notes, there is still the "McVeigh factor" at work in public opinion. Horrific crimes like those perpetrated by Timothy McVeigh, Ted Bundy (rapist and serial killer of scores of women),[91] and Scott Peterson (who killed his pregnant wife) bring forth cries for continued use of the death penalty. Desire for retribution runs deep in such cases.

Chapter 13

CIVIL LIABILITY

Plaintiff vs. Defendant in the Eyes of the Jury

Jury verdicts in civil cases have led to the sharpest attacks on the institution of trial by jury in recent decades. Although the civil jury system has many supporters, civil jurors are routinely pilloried for their supposed hostility to businesses and insurance companies.[1] Members of the American Tort Reform Association (ATRA), an organization underwritten by business interests, have argued that unjustified jury verdicts encourage excessive litigation and harm the American economy. ATRA has identified what it calls "judicial hellholes," jurisdictions in which plaintiff lawyers enjoy great and, in ATRA's opinion, unwarranted success.[2]

To evaluate these arguments, we take a close look at how civil jurors approach their multiple tasks—first, deciding liability, and second, arriving at damage awards. We begin by examining how the civil jury determines whether the defendant should be held legally responsible for the plaintiff's injuries. After that we will address the process by which juries arrive at damage awards to compensate the plaintiff or to punish the defendant.

THE BOY IN THE PAINT STORE

Consider the jury decision-making process in the case of a young boy who injured himself in a paint store. It illustrates how civil juries evaluate and combine evidence to arrive at a liability decision.[3] A five-year-old went to the paint store with his mother, who began to look through wallpaper samples. While his mother was distracted, he proceeded to get into mischief and then into serious trouble. He first ran around the store and, according to the store clerk who complained to the mother, messed up some of the store displays. In his wanderings he discovered a small spring-loaded knife, which was bright orange and looked very much like a toy. He tried to open the knife, but in the process he cut his finger badly, severing the tendon. The store clerk offered to call an ambulance, but the mother declined, saying that she would take the boy to his pediatrician, who could look at the finger and determine what needed to be done. The pediatrician saw the boy and sewed up the skin, apparently not realizing that the tendon beneath had been cut. Because of the botched operation, the boy lost the full use of his finger.

The family sued the paint store, charging that the store was negligent for having dangerous objects accessible to children. Unlike most civil actions, this one was neither dismissed nor settled. Because the case was brought in a comparative negligence jurisdiction, jurors also had to determine whether the boy's mother was negligent in her care for the boy. Interestingly, the doctor who had made a medical error in the boy's care was not involved in the trial. We can only guess, but it's reasonable to assume that the doctor and his insurance company settled with the boy's family prior to trial.

Posttrial interviews with the jurors revealed how they assessed the relative responsibilities of the store and the mother. They drew upon their own backgrounds and experiences as well as on widely shared ideas about responsibility to reach a verdict. Earlier we described the story model of jury decision making. Consistent with the story model's assumptions, the jurors organized the evidence to form a narrative about responsibility. The predominant theme was the mother's essential responsibility. Yet other narratives emerged during the group deliberations and were recounted in the interviews.

Women jurors, whom one might stereotype as particularly sympathetic to injured children, vigorously proclaimed the mother completely responsible for her son. A mother should be aware of dangerous elements in any environment that could harm her child and do whatever she can to limit the child's exposure to them. For example: "Knowing the accessories that come with wallpaper, she should have been a little more careful than to let her son run around. . . . She was at fault for just letting him run around."[4] Another juror agreed: "The mother should have known that she had an active five-year-old and either left him in the car . . . or if she had him in the store she had him tied to her belt or took him to his grandmother's house and then went back to the store. But the mother was the one responsible for the safety of that child in the store, and she did not exercise the right or reasonable care."[5] Jurors drew on their own experiences, as did this mother of nine: "I would not take one of my kids out to a store with me, because I felt if I can't make it mind, it's not going with me. And they didn't go with me either."[6] In a word, these jurors reasoned that a responsible mother would be vigilant in watching her child in a paint store.

Although most jurors agreed that the mother had been negligent, some jurors also blamed the store. Because the paint store was a site with potentially dangerous materials, "the clerk and the store share a greater responsibility in this regard for watching the child because the mother doesn't know that in a paint store and wallpaper store there are any hazardous materials . . . I'm sure that it would never dawn on her that the kid could really get into . . . trouble."[7] A business should anticipate that parents will be looking at the merchandise and children will run around: "The company should definitely not have anything out where a kid might get hurt on it."[8] A grandfather of two drew on his own personal experience making his home safe for his young granddaughters: "When my daughter used to come my wife would check right away to make sure she doesn't have anything out for the kids to hurt themselves on, any pills or anything like that."[9]

Jurors voiced some suspicions about the mother's motives in bringing this lawsuit: "My impression of the mother was that she was a person who saw an opportunity to recover a lot of money, a significant amount of money, and was taking every opportunity she had to do that."[10] The absence of testimony from the doctor bothered some of the jurors. She should be suing the doctor rather than the store, one juror pointed out. The doctor's mistake in sewing up the boy's finger made him a clear culprit; so where was he? One of the jurors shared her view that the doctor probably settled a lawsuit with the parents.

Ultimately the jury found both the mother and the store negligent, allocating some responsibility to each of them. Because they concluded that the mother was more than 50 percent at fault, under the comparative negligence laws of the jurisdiction, she could not recover. Thus, the defense had to pay nothing.

THE CIVIL JURY AND THE REASONABLE PERSON

One reason its supporters think the American jury is a particularly appropriate decision maker for lawsuits of this kind is that legal doctrines often invoke the concept of a "reasonable person," a mythical human who is not ultracareful but who never acts unreasonably in taking risks or puts others at risk and who otherwise follows a community's accepted norms of behavior. A defendant's conduct in a negligence action is judged against this standard. What would a reasonable person in the defendant's position have anticipated or done? Were consequences like the plaintiff's injury reasonably foreseeable as a result of the defendant's action? The plaintiff's behavior, too, is assessed using a reasonable-person standard. Jurors from the community are familiar with how ordinary people behave in the situations that are under dispute. Knowing communal norms of behavior, jurors are especially well suited to evaluate the plaintiff's and defendant's conduct against these standards. In this they typically differ from the judge, who is likely to be a member of a socioeconomic elite and whose views might become jaded from hearing case after case. More importantly, since what is reasonable is often unclear, jurors can discuss it and sort out competing concerns and values. Judges don't have the benefit of a community sounding board. As a stand-in for the community, the representative jury reflects current local expectations about duty and responsibility. Civil jury verdicts also are able to reflect changes in community standards over time. Jurors' assessments of reasonable conduct consider the behavior of both parties—plaintiff and defendant—comparatively and holistically in the context of responsibility.

ASSESSING THE PLAINTIFF'S DEGREE OF RESPONSIBILITY AND THE EXISTENCE OF AN INJURY: JUROR SKEPTICISM TOWARD PLAINTIFFS

Asked to identify a character from fiction that best symbolizes the typical civil juror, many people might choose Robin Hood, the valiant defender of the oppressed, eager to transfer wealth from the rich (defendants) to give to the poor (plaintiffs). Indeed, assertions about the overly sympathetic civil jury are regularly included in business and industry demands for tort reform. Such claims also find their way into judicial opinions, which limit the types of evidence that can be presented to a jury.

Based on our research with civil juries, if we had to identify a fictional character to typify the jury, Scrooge rather than Robin Hood might be more apt. Interviews with civil jurors and public opinion polls show that many jurors start off with great skepticism about claims brought by plaintiffs. Plaintiffs have the burden of proof, according to the law, so it is appropriate for jurors to examine their claims carefully. But civil jurors seem to go beyond that. They draw on nineteenth-century notions of assumption of risk and contributory negligence, in which people were held strictly accountable for their actions and sometimes even their injuries. Jurors regularly express worries about greedy plaintiffs and believe they should be alert for frauds who try to blame others for injuries they have faked or problems they have caused themselves. Surveys of jurors—and the public from which juries are drawn—reveal that many citizens believe emphatically in a litigation explosion (90 percent or more in most surveys), propelled by unjustified claims. In juror interviews conducted for *Business on Trial*, Hans discovered that many jurors held negative views of people who brought lawsuits. Approximately four out of five jurors agreed that "people are too quick to sue" and that "there are far too many frivolous lawsuits today." These attitudes were shared by people at all levels of education and income.[11]

Deliberations from the Arizona Civil Jury Project reveal how these skeptical attitudes play out in discussions of civil cases. Consider this exchange, typical of many juries:

> Juror 5: Every time somebody gets hurt they want to sue somebody.
> Juror 7: I agree.
> Juror 5: Nobody wants to take responsibility for their own actions anymore.
> Juror 7: Everything is someone else's fault.

Other studies have uncovered similar beliefs among the public about runaway juries and a litigation crisis.[12] As we will see, these attitudes affect how evidence is evaluated, which in turn affects civil jury verdicts.

Influenced by these background assumptions, civil jurors begin with a strong presumption of personal responsibility and focus intensively on the conduct of the plaintiff. Was the plaintiff acting in a reasonable manner when she was injured? Did the plaintiff's behavior contribute in any way to her injury? Are her claims of injury false or exaggerated? Is she trying to get money for a trumped-up injury?

Although suspicions of plaintiff deceit occur even when a plaintiff is seriously injured, they are even more prevalent when jurors confront more common and more moderate injuries, such as the whiplash that many drivers suffer after being in an auto accident. Whiplash injuries, caused by damage to muscles and connective tissue, can be very painful and debilitating. Yet, within the context of a lawsuit, whiplash is often perceived as fraudulent. Valerie Hans undertook several studies of reactions to whiplash that included focus groups, surveys, and mock juries. In the focus group study, participants in Colorado and Kentucky engaged in group discussions about whiplash injuries.[13] Many expressed doubts about plaintiffs claiming whiplash. One person stated:

> A lot of people complain of it when they have an accident and a lot of lawsuits are won because you can't see it. I just figure when they go with a whiplash, a lot of times they don't have whiplash, but the first thing they think of is, "Oh, my neck . . . like how much can I get for this one."[14]

Another voiced a similar preconception about plaintiff claims:

> Nowadays if you have an accident, everyone is hurt whether they are injured or not. . . . They fake injury for the lawsuit. . . . It happens all the time.[15]

Even when jurors are not openly suspicious of plaintiff fraud or malingering, they take seriously the fact that the burden of proof is on the plaintiff and search for reasons to disbelieve the plaintiff's story. The Arizona Civil Jury Project yielded many examples. Consider a trial in which doctors testified for the plaintiff about ongoing pain from an accident. The jurors applied their own observations that contradicted the expert testimony:

> Juror 4: There's only one thing I want you all to think about and notice during the entire trial, every single doctor that he had testify said that he could not sit still longer than fifteen or twenty minutes, every doctor said that, I want you to note (Juror 6, [consulting her notes]: Before the accident), No, after it.
>
> Juror 6 [interrupting]: Yeah, but let's differentiate doctors' testimony before the accident from doctors after . . .
>
> Juror 4: No, after the accident, he cannot sit, he's got a 'whoopy' cushion and he can not sit for more than 15–20 minutes without getting up out of his chair at work and walking around. (Juror 2: The trial, he sat through the entire thing) The entire trial, from 2 to 3 pm in court, he did not move from [his] chair, I took notes as to every single day when he was sitting (Juror 2: My Lord!) starting on Tuesday, I can tell you how long that man sat in his chair (Juror 1: You know something) he never got out of his chair (Juror 1: You're good), (Juror 2: You're good), and that he never got out of that chair the entire trial.
>
> Juror 1: You know something, I was moving more than he was.
>
> Juror 4: And my butt hurt.
>
> Juror 1: He sat like a rock, didn't he?
>
> [Laughter from group]
>
> Juror 4: He did.
>
> Juror 1: He looked more comfortable than us.
>
> Juror 4: Every one of you guys moved, you either crossed your legs, moved this way, sat up or sat back . . .
>
> Juror 3: . . . but I definitely felt, there was a couple times, I thought, I didn't know whether he [the plaintiff] moved his pillow just a hair, I didn't think he moved he didn't get up and walk.

In another of the Arizona trials, a woman claimed that as a result of an automobile accident she continued to have severe back pain. During discussions, one of the jurors observed that she was wearing high heels, and that when she stepped off the raised witness stand after her testimony, she didn't even wince, an observation seconded by other female jurors. These examples show jurors being attentive to all aspects of behavior, what plaintiffs did as well as what was said by them and their experts during testimony.

In a pertinent deliberation from still another of the Arizona civil juries, the following exchange took place in a case in which a female driver was hit from behind and claimed a continuing injury resulting from the impact. Her young child and a passenger were also in the car. The plaintiff estimated the speed at impact at thirty to forty miles per hour. The defendant admitted negligence but contested the injury as at best minor, and called a biomechanical engineer who estimated the speed of impact at approximately eight miles per hour. Let us listen in as the jurors work through the evidence, searching for confirmation of the plaintiff's testimony from other evidence in the case. The jurors offer their own interpretations about evidence and raise questions about missing testimony, causing them to draw a negative inference from its absence. The conversation has a rapid flow, with jurors interjecting comments signifying agreement with one another:

> Juror 3: And the weight of the SUV (Juror 8: Sure.) you know (Juror 4: Yeah.) even going very slowly.
>
> Juror 8: And her car didn't move 25 feet, it moved a couple inches. A [car like that] is just gonna 'puck' [uses her hands to illustrate a car collapsing due to collision], I mean they're not made of much, (Juror 3 and Juror 7: Yeah.) and I think it was really . . .
>
> Juror 5 [interrupting]: It would at least crack the, uh, bumper, crack the tail light, something like that, if she hit her hard enough.

A few minutes later the jurors returned to the speed of impact, with Juror 5 giving the dialogue and other jurors acting like a Greek chorus as they interjected agreement.

> Juror 5: If the child was standing in there, and if she hit her at 40 miles an hour, 20 miles an hour . . . that child would've flown into the dashboard. (Juror 3: Yes.) (Juror 2: Into her brain.) (Jurors 4 and 8: Yeah.) Regardless how much they tried to restrain that child, that child would've fell into it. (Juror 3: Yeah.) (Juror 2: Out of control.) She claimed that, uh, a, a cup of soda (Juror 4: On the floor.), between her feet ended up in the back. (Juror 2: Right.) (Juror 3: Well, apparently this . . .) Now if that was true, that child would've hit that dash.
>
> Juror 3: No, that could be true.
>
> Juror 4: That child would've been injured by it.
>
> Juror 3: Actually, just uh, I think that, uh, sliding under the seat, if there's a smooth surface under the seat, it could've . . .
>
> Juror 1 [very softly]: Uh. [clears throat] What happened to Nancy [the passenger] and the kid? Uh, (Juror 5: Yeah.) Did they get hurt?
>
> Juror 5: That, that's the one that I wondered. Why Nancy wasn't brought in as a witness as to how hard the impact was and all this . . .
>
> Juror 3: Especially that little baby. Restrained or not restrained, that little baby would've been hurt either way.

These examples suggest careful, highly observant jurors trying to make sense of the evidence. They place the burden of proof on the plaintiff, which is where it should be. We also see them scrutinizing the evidence to evaluate the plaintiff's credibility and story of the events of the accident. These examples give some of the flavor of how jurors use their own preexisting ideas about personal responsibility to assess evidence for the plaintiff's case.

Jurors often begin with strong assumptions about unjustified lawsuits and concern for a litigation explosion. As the trial proceeds, they pay particular attention to evidence that can help them assess the credibility and merits of the plaintiff's claim against this broader backdrop. But their background assumptions appear to have an impact. Systematic research with actual and mock juries reveals that anti-plaintiff attitudes that jurors bring with them to the jury box translate into anti-plaintiff tendencies in the courtroom. Jurors who think there are many unjustified lawsuits and who believe in a litigation explosion, for example, are much more likely to find for the defendant in civil cases.[16]

On the other hand, while many jurors may begin with a presumption about unjustified lawsuits, they can be persuaded by evidence. Indeed, juries in the Arizona project ruled in favor of plaintiffs almost 60 percent of the time, although they also occasionally found the plaintiff was partly responsible for the injury and gave awards that were often considerably lower than the amount the plaintiff was asking for.

But what about the severely injured plaintiff? There is a presumption that plaintiffs who are very severely injured pluck at the heartstrings of civil jurors, leading them to find liability when the facts are questionable. This may happen on occasion. Many experiments and mock jury studies have attempted to test this widely presumed tendency of the civil jury. In these studies, the facts surrounding a defendant's conduct are described identically, but some study participants are told that the plaintiff is badly injured, while others hear that the plaintiff is only moderately injured. The results of these studies are mixed. In some, there is no difference, while in others there is a greater tendency to find liable a defendant who badly injured a plaintiff. University of Illinois law professor Jennifer Robbennolt reviewed seventy-five studies of the phenomenon and concluded that on balance people tend to attribute greater responsibility for the outcome of a negative event when the outcome is more rather than less severe.[17]

THE COMPLICATION OF A PLAINTIFF'S PRIOR INJURIES AND ILLNESSES

Although jurors may become convinced that a plaintiff is really injured, they must also assess the extent of the injury and determine whether and to what extent the defendant's misconduct caused it. Particularly difficult problems arise when an injured plaintiff has previously suffered a similar or related injury. A common example is a history of back problems when a plaintiff claims they were caused or made worse by an accident. The same kind of critical stance that jurors reveal in determining whether there is an injury at all is also apparent when jurors try to determine the extent to which the defendant is responsible for a plaintiff's injury.

Many plaintiffs in the Arizona civil jury trials had experienced related injuries or illnesses prior to the accident. This was especially true of automobile injury cases. Of twenty-three automobile trials in the study sample, eighteen defendants admitted that they were at fault in the accident. Some defendants contested only the damage amounts but others argued that their actions had not produced the claimed injuries. In almost every one of these latter cases, the plaintiff had suffered from prior injuries or illnesses that might have caused some of the problems the plaintiff attributed to the accident. It seems safe to assume that the plaintiff's prior condition led the defendant's liability insurer to contest rather than settle the case. The law is relatively clear. A plaintiff cannot recover for disability or pain due to a prior injury or accident but can recover to the degree that the accident augmented the disability or pain.

Prior injuries played a significant role in the way that the jurors viewed the plaintiff's claim. In the example below, two jurors steer comments sympathetic to the plaintiff back to the issue of preexisting conditions.

> Juror 2: He was hospitalized three times and it wasn't within a long period of time.
>
> Juror 3: It was a good idea to bring John's [plaintiff's] wife in because she seems very credible.
>
> Juror 2: John and his wife have been through some hardships, but it's a matter of whether the hardships were caused by the accident.
>
> Juror 3: John has been a heck of a guy.
>
> Juror 6: They spend a lot of time showing damages, but I don't think that has anything to do with the car accident. John had preexisting conditions that were exacerbated.

Prior injuries or illnesses also played a role in the trial evidence for some non-automobile cases as well. An employee had long suffered from depression. She alleged that sexual harassment from her boss had occurred over a long period and the employer company had done nothing to stop it. She alleged that as a result of the hostile environment she suffered a form of post-traumatic stress disorder and could not work. Her claim was bolstered by testimony from a psychologist and her doctor. Part of the disputed issue involved the phenomenon of the "eggshell" plaintiff, one who is unusually vulnerable to suffer substantial harm if injured. In tort law, the fact that a person who is negligently injured and is more vulnerable than the average person provides no excuse for the injurer. In the famous case of *Vosburg v. Putney*, which many new law students encounter in their first exposure to the law of torts, a Wisconsin schoolboy's kick to the leg of one of his young comrades led to catastrophic consequences for the victim, in part because the victim was previously injured. The Wisconsin Supreme Court confirmed the rule that wrongdoers are liable for all of the injuries resulting from their actions, even extraordinary injuries they did not foresee, so long as any harm was foreseeable.[18] Generations of law students, and contemporary jurors, have problems with the apparent imbalance between the defendant's action and the plaintiff's injury. Their commonsense justice is at odds with the legal rule.

During closing arguments in the sexual harassment trial, the plaintiff's lawyer drew an analogy to attempt to persuade the jury that the defendant should pay for the full consequences of a negligent action. The lawyer asked jurors to consider a cracked antique bowl sitting in a display case with the crack hidden from view. As long as it is sitting undisturbed, it is still a valuable antique, even though it is vulnerable. Now, someone carelessly and negligently knocks into the case and the antique bowl falls and breaks. Without the negligent action, the bowl will keep its value. With the negligent action, the antique bowl's value is lost. Therefore, the lawyer argued to the jury, the negligent person should be held fully responsible.

Still, after having heard this, the jurors found the law on this point unfair and struggled over how to treat the plaintiff's prior illness. Juror 5 read the judge's instructions bearing on the susceptibility of a person who has a prior disorder to be more readily injured than a normally healthy person would be. This produced the following exchange:

> Juror 3: I have some contention with that, um, I think this is like kind of what we were saying about, yesterday, or what I was saying earlier about fault, or whatever, um, if someone, and I hate to kind of get away from the case, if someone tripped, yesterday you had your leg sticking out, if someone is walking alone and trips over your leg, And they break their hip, but you were asleep, sitting there, you were in clear view and everything, it's not really your fault, but, on the other hand, if you come up and trip them, that's where you start getting into outrageous behavior or inappropriate behavior and fault, I see it as legal fault, you can't . . .
>
> Juror 2: You're talking two different things (Juror 4: Exactly), if I tripped over his leg and a normal healthy person would not have broken their leg.
>
> Juror 3: But, I broke my leg, you cannot come back and say, hey, a hundred people have tripped over my leg, no one ever broke their leg so I don't see how you can break your leg, they are saying here [pointing to instructions], that a normally healthy person don't regard that as the standard of what you think was the sustained injury . . .
>
> Juror 7: But if he had tripped on my leg and had previously broken his leg, that's what this is saying. In Mildred's situation, she had problems previously and that was the crack in the vase and he [the defendant] was at fault for this because he triggered it, I don't agree with it, but . . .
>
> Juror 3: That's the law.
>
> . . .
>
> Juror 3: She, her doctor, listen to me, her doctor testified that she will not return back to work.
>
> Juror 2: Exactly, that was caused by what, her PTSD, not because she was sexually harassed?
>
> Juror 7: That was caused by a preexisting condition.

The jurors in the above case found the defendant liable and awarded modest damages on other grounds, but the important point is that when the law is in tension with community ideas about justice and fairness, the inconsistencies find their way into the jury room.

OTHER INJURIES

In addition to the problems identified above, plaintiffs also face an uphill battle when they make claims for injuries that do not have clear physical and economic evidence. Harassment, harms to dignity and to reputation, emotional distress, fear and worry, and loss of significant personal relationships are all psychological and emotional injuries that people acknowledge are extremely important in their everyday lives. However, claims for compensation for such injuries meet with resistance in the law and in the jury box. Some of the reluctance is due to the difficulty of proving these injuries to the satisfaction of the jury, especially a jury that is predisposed to question plaintiff claims. Many of the claims rest almost exclusively on plaintiffs' reports of their internal states of pain or emotional trauma. Law professor Lucinda Finley and other legal scholars have suggested that women more than men are disadvantaged by this tendency to recognize as real only those injuries that have obvious physical manifestations or economic correlates.[19] For example, a man who has lost a week's wages due to an injury will find it easy to prove his loss; a stay-at-home mother who is incapacitated for a week following an accident will have a harder time proving her loss. We will have more to say about how jurors value diverse injuries in the next chapter on compensatory damages.

EVALUATING THE DEFENDANT'S RESPONSIBILITY AND LEGAL LIABILITY

The legal rules that govern the defendant's liability vary, depending on the type of case.[20] Certain rules apply when a defendant intentionally acts to injure another person. Other rules govern injuries from products made by businesses. Disputes over property and contracts have given rise to other distinctive legal rules.[21] But most commonly today, civil jurors are asked to determine whether the defendant's conduct directly or indirectly caused the plaintiff's injury and whether the conduct was negligent. Once the jury concludes that a plaintiff's injury was actually caused by the defendant's conduct, most often the negligence decision rests on whether what the defendant did was reasonable considering all of the circumstances. Would a reasonable person have behaved in the same way? Should a reasonable person have anticipated that someone would be harmed by the action?

Here again jurors draw on their knowledge and personal experiences of community norms and expectations.

Determining whether the defendant is a "reasonable person" is complicated by the fact that in at least half of American civil jury trials, a corporation rather than a physical person is on trial.[22] How does the civil jury decide what is reasonable conduct for a corporate entity? That question led Valerie Hans to conduct a series of studies on the civil jury and corporate responsibility.[23]

To assess whether people take a distinctive approach in a lawsuit when a corporation is the defendant, she began with a simple experiment. Along with her collaborator, M. David Ermann, a sociologist who studies corporate deviance, Hans devised a brief case scenario. In the scenario, workers were injured by clearing toxic waste from a site. Half the participants received a scenario in which the workers were hired by one Mr. Jones, who asked them to clear a lot he owned, while the other half were hired by the Jones Corporation. All of the other facts surrounding Jones's conduct and the workers' injuries were identical. Nonetheless, participants responded very differently to the two scenarios. Given the same facts, the corporation was seen as more likely to have known beforehand about the toxic waste, more likely to be viewed as reckless, and more likely to be found negligent.[24]

But why? Was it, as businesses often claim, that corporations have "deep pockets" so juries have no qualms about rendering verdicts against them? In subsequent research summarized in *Business on Trial*, Hans interviewed jurors who decided cases with corporate parties (including the boy in the paint store case) and conducted additional experiments along the same lines. She discovered that jurors seem to use the same basic template to assess individual and corporate responsibility, often relying on their ideas about what would be appropriate for a person in the same situation. One of the jurors interviewed in the paint store case used the following analogy to describe the approach taken to deciding the liability of the store: "I thought of it in the same way I would treat my premises. I would not want somebody to be injured on my premises, and I see a store owner as having a similar obligation, just from a safety standpoint."[25] A juror from an asbestos trial likened it to "me trying to give you a bottle of poison . . . and I don't tell you what it's gonna do to you."[26]

However, although the actions of a person and a corporation are evaluated using much the same criteria, more is expected of a reasonable corporation than a reasonable person. This is because corporations are typically seen as having greater knowledge and expertise than individuals, as well as a special professional responsibility to take care. Corporations have specialized knowledge about their environments and products, and the perception of this greater expertise leads jurors to expect that they will be knowledgeable about potential risks. A defendant's intentions, foresight, and knowledge about potential harms are all factors that the law instructs jurors to weigh in determining a defendant's legal responsibility, and they are factors that jurors consider as they assign responsibility.[27] One juror pointed out the knowledge benefits that come with the corporate structure: "[T]hey do have more resources available to them. . . . It's a lot easier for a corporation to get the information that they need to make an intelligent decision than it is for an individual. They also have the resources of capital to make an informed decision. I think they should be held to a set of higher standards."[28] Jurors assume there was—and should be—more deliberate decision making when a corporation is deciding on a course of action: "An individual is just one person, one bad moment and it's bad. Corporations, you got a whole board you act through and move through, so there should be some reasonable answer there. You could do a lot more damage as a corporation."[29]

The last comment adds a further dimension; the negligent actions of business corporations are seen as more likely to cause substantial harm to many people. "Of course they've got to exercise a great deal more safety awareness, they've got many more people in there to worry about."[30] The potential for substantial impact raises the stakes and the expectations for how a careful corporation will act.

These elevated expectations translate into greater liability for corporations. In a hypothetical slip and fall experiment modeled on the Jones experiment described above, half the participants read a scenario about a person who slipped and fell in defendant Mr. Wilson's home, where he had been holding a tag sale. The other half read a nearly identical scenario, except that the fall occurred in a store of the Wilson Furniture Corporation. Even though the facts pertaining to the fall were the same, Hans found that mock jurors were much more likely to ascribe responsibility to the store than to the individual. The plaintiff was attributed 53 percent of the fault when she fell in a private home, compared to just 23 percent of the fault when she fell in the store. The corporate context altered the meaning and significance of her fall; it changed from an action that was largely her responsibility to one that was primarily the store's fault.[31]

Just as concerns about frivolous lawsuits lead jurors to take a critical view of the plaintiff's injuries in specific lawsuits, so, too, do high standards for corporate conduct create a greater likelihood of liability for the business corporation. Jurors who believe that corporations should be held to higher levels of responsibility carry through on that promise and are more apt to hold businesses legally responsible for a plaintiff's injuries.[32]

In sum, the idea that jurors approach trials with a proclivity to rule in favor of plaintiffs is belied by careful survey research and by studies of mock juries and real juries. Instead, we observe jurors subjecting plaintiffs to careful, and sometimes harsh, scrutiny, looking to the evidence in the case to bolster or undermine the plaintiff's story, and filling in gaps with social knowledge about lawsuits that they have gleaned from others in the community and from the media. As with criminal cases, jurors compare and contrast the roles and expectations of the two parties. Thus when corporations are defendants in the case, higher expectations about the defendant translate into greater likelihood of the plaintiff prevailing.

Chapter 14

DECIDING COMPENSATORY DAMAGES

Million-Dollar Questions

Civil juries are undoubtedly most controversial because of their role in arriving at damage awards. The arguments against juries are often sprinkled with fictitious or distorted views of awards that appear in the mass media. Some stories are advanced by interest groups and politicians urging legal reform because of "lawsuit abuse."

One of the classic stories intended to show that American courts are filled with frivolous lawsuits and irresponsible juries was based on a real medical malpractice case, *Haimes v. Temple University Hospital and Hart*, in 1986.[1] The widely reported story had a jury awarding Ms. Haimes almost $1 million for the loss of her psychic powers from a bungled CAT scan. The case was covered in the *New York Times*, the *Los Angeles Times*, and, in subsequent years, was repeated in *Forbes* magazine and many other sources, including books aimed at influencing the public about the need for tort reform. It is true that Ms. Haimes had worked as a psychic, a position that included consulting for national and local law enforcement organizations. However, the complete facts of *Haimes v. Hart* reveal a far different story than the one that has been bandied about.

Ms. Haimes underwent surgery to discover the nature and causes of tumors on her ear. Before surgery Ms. Haimes warned the radiologist that she had previously experienced a strong allergic reaction to a contrast dye used for the scan. The radiologist dismissed her concerns as "ridiculous" and persuaded her to allow him to inject a small dose of the dye. She immediately went into anaphylactic shock and experienced severe pain. Another doctor intervened and probably saved her life. At trial she testified that she had continued to suffer for days from severe nausea, vomiting, extreme headaches, and hives. She further claimed that afterward she suffered severe headaches whenever she attempted deep mental concentration. The judges instructed the jury to ignore her claim about loss of psychic powers, because she failed to produce expert testimony linking her continuing headaches to the alleged loss of income. The jury awarded her $600,000 in compensatory damages for her immediate reactions to the contrast dye, and with accrued interest from the time the lawsuit was filed, permitted under Pennsylvania law, the total came to $986,000. The trial judge denied the award as "grossly excessive" and ordered a new trial. A second trial was dismissed when the new judge ruled that Haimes's expert witness lacked proper medical qualifications. A divided Pennsylvania Supreme Court agreed with the judge, and Ms. Haimes never recovered a penny for her contrast dye injury.

Haimes offers a cautionary lesson about the use of anecdotes by interest groups to influence the opinion of the public and legislators in regard to civil jury behavior. The facts also help to illustrate, once again, that trial by jury is more properly conceived as "trial by judge and jury." A trial judge controlled the evidence that the jury was allowed to hear and instructed it on what was relevant. The judge also policed the jury verdict, in this instance overturning the jury's decision and ordering a new trial.

Regardless, damages arising out of jury trials remain controversial. The so-called pain and suffering portion of damage verdicts receives special attention. Critics of juries view "excessive" pain and suffering awards as particularly pernicious and call for limits, or "caps," on jury awards for these damages. A number of lobbying campaigns to install caps on some types of compensatory damages have been successful, especially with state legislatures.

The criticisms of pain and suffering are not confined to members of the American Tort Reform Association. Richard Abel, a respected legal scholar and noted liberal, has written that pain and suffering verdicts are "incoherent, incalculable, incommensurable, and inegalitarian."[2] Still other independent researchers have expressed concern about the unreliability of jury awards because there is a great deal of variation in the awards given to people with similar injuries.[3]

Where does the truth lie? We will concentrate here on compensatory damages, that is, monetary awards that, in common lawyer parlance, are intended to make an injured plaintiff "whole" again. Punitive damages will be discussed as a separate topic in the following chapter.

A PROFILE OF COMPENSATORY DAMAGE AWARDS

News reports of civil litigation are written not only to inform but also to entertain, so it's not surprising that such news coverage tends to feature cases in which juries make eye-popping damage awards. A systematic examination of the awards that civil juries reach in the broad range of cases provides a very different picture. In 2001 the Bureau of Justice Statistics/National Center for State Courts study surveyed 11,681 trials in state courts that represented the seventy-five largest counties in the United States.[4] Plaintiffs won in 55 percent of tort trials (e.g., personal injuries, libel, false arrest) and 65 percent of contract cases (e.g., fraud, buyer-seller disputes, partnership disputes). For all tort trials the median award from juries was $27,000, with about 8 percent of awards exceeding one million dollars. In contract disputes, the median award was $45,000, while slightly over 5 percent resulted in million-dollar awards.

Business corporations and governments were the plaintiffs in only about 8 percent of all civil trials, but often the amounts in dispute were very large. For example, a Texas company attempted to establish franchises in Mexico, but the Mexican business partners broke off negotiations and used information obtained from the plaintiff to buy the franchises. In 2001, after seventeen days of trial, a Texas jury found in favor of the plaintiff and awarded $90 million in actual damages and $364.5 million in punitive damages. Trials in federal courts tend to involve larger claims because of rules about the types of cases that can be tried in these courts. In 2002 to 2003 the median award in all federal tort trials was $244,000.[5] In some trials there are multiple plaintiffs. Following an airplane crash or a mass chemical spill, the various claims by plaintiffs or their survivors may be consolidated into a single trial, increasing the amounts that juries award if the plaintiffs prevail on liability. Newspapers sometimes report only the final verdict without mentioning that it will be divided among tens, hundreds, or thousands of plaintiffs.

Are these amounts unreasonable? What criteria can we use to judge them? A necessary first step in addressing these questions is understanding the elements of compensable damages.

THE LEGAL CONTEXT IN WHICH DAMAGES ARE DECIDED

Elements of Damages

American law recognizes three basic types of damages.[6]

Special damages involve the economic losses that can be itemized as out-of-pocket expenses. In personal injury cases, special damages include such things as past and future medical expenses, lost income, and property losses. In breached contract, antitrust, or trademark infringement disputes, special damages are the monetary losses due to the defendant's wrongful behavior. Many special damages are problematic, and expert testimony is needed to prove them. In a personal injury case, healthcare experts may testify about the degree of disability and the life care needs of the plaintiff. An expert testifying on behalf of lifetime lost income for a permanently injured child may build into the economic equation the assumption that she would have gone to college or graduate school. In a breach of contract dispute, experts may be called to testify about what the past and future sales of the plaintiff company would have been but for the actions of the defendant. The defendant's lawyer may attempt to point out questionable assumptions or errors in the plaintiff's estimates during cross-examination, or the lawyer may call opposing experts who offer much lower estimates. Economic losses are often not hard facts. The trials involve contested claims about the degree of losses, if any. The jury may choose either side or, as we will show shortly, make its own decision about the appropriate amount.

General damages are the losses for which the only metric is fairness. The most well-known subcategory of general damages is "pain and suffering." Compensation for pain and suffering has a long history in Anglo-American law.[7] Jurors are asked to determine a dollar amount to compensate the plaintiff for past and future pain, but in doing so they are faced with the problem of how that is to be translated into a dollar amount. General damages are frequently called noneconomic damages. This label may be appropriate for pain and suffering or "loss of consortium" (i.e., loss of marital relations, including sexual intercourse). However, there are other legally compensable losses that are lumped under noneconomic damages that have similar unclear metrics about dollars but that have economic consequences. For example, a severe disfigurement may cause psychological and emotional anguish, but in addition there may be economic consequences such as reduced employment or marriage opportunities. The Illinois Supreme Court, to take one example, has ruled that disability, loss of a normal life, increased risk of harm, loss of society, and wrongful death involve economic damages.[8] The New York pattern instructions for wrongful death include components that instruct jurors that while they should not award money for sorrow or mental anguish, plaintiffs are entitled to pecuniary losses for the "intellectual, moral and physical training and education that the parent would have given."[9] Similar to pain and suffering, these additional elements of general damages require social judgments about the appropriate level of compensation because the losses vary, depending on the facts of the case. There is no way to place an exact figure on what such injuries are worth. The jury has to consider the individual circumstances and local community norms. At trial, plaintiffs or spouses testify about what the injury has done to their lives, providing the jury with insight about the consequences of the injury. In short, although damage statutes in many states refer to noneconomic damages, and lawyers use the term as shorthand for general damages, it is a misleading characterization.

Punitive damages are given to punish and deter behaviors that are regarded as wanton, reckless, or reprehensible. Punitive damages will be considered separately because they have a different purpose than the other elements of damages.

COMPARATIVE AND CONTRIBUTORY NEGLIGENCE

Earlier we showed how civil juries evaluate the relative culpability of both plaintiff and defendant to determine whether the defendant is legally responsible for the plaintiff's injuries. Most states now have a comparative negligence rule.[10] The jury is instructed to first apportion responsibility between the two parties and then decide the total amount of the plaintiff's losses independent of responsibility. In many jurisdictions, the judge adjusts the damages in proportion to the plaintiff's fault before entering the formal trial judgment. In some states if the plaintiff is judged to be more than 50 percent at fault, she cannot recover anything, as we saw in the case of the boy in the paint store described earlier.

A minority of states such as Alabama, Maryland, North Carolina, and Virginia still rely on a contributory negligence rule, which, in its harshest form, states that no matter how slight the plaintiff's responsibility, even if only 1 percent, she cannot recover anything. However, the instructions in contributory fault states have been modified in various ways to overcome the harshness of the rule.

While comparative and contributory negligence speak to issues of liability, questions have arisen about whether juries sometimes discount their awards to consider the degree of the plaintiff negligence even though their instructions direct them to put degree of plaintiff negligence aside and assess the actual losses suffered.[11] A mock juror study by Neal Feigenson and his colleagues showed that participants discounted the plaintiff's awards in line with their judgments of the plaintiff's fault.[12] Those authors observed that if actual jurors take this same approach, the results are double-discounting: once when the jurors reduce the value of an injury due to the plaintiff's perceived fault, and a second time when the judge reduces it following a comparative negligence rule.

JUROR CHARACTERISTICS AFFECTING DAMAGE AWARDS: IRISHMEN VERSUS NORWEGIANS?

Lawyers are always interested in the issue of whether jurors with certain demographic characteristics or personalities are prone to give higher or lower damage awards. Law practice manuals make for amusing—and sometimes infuriating—reading on this score.[13] One manual, for example, suggests that nurses are not good for civil plaintiffs because they are too intolerant of pain. Another manual suggests that plaintiffs should try to select owners of small businesses, salespeople, students, and people on welfare because they are generous to plaintiffs. Suburban housewives have been said to be conservative on damages. Jurors between the ages of thirty-five and fifty were said to be more favorable toward civil plaintiffs than younger or older plaintiffs. One manual stated that Jews, blacks, Irish, Italians, and people of Mediterranean background favored plaintiffs whereas people of "German, Norwegian, Swedish, English and Oriental" ethnic backgrounds favored defendants.

In their comprehensive book surveying the topic of jury damage awards, *Determining Damages*, Edie Greene and Brian Bornstein reviewed research on stereotypes of generous and stingy jurors and found little support for such generalizations.[14] Comparisons of such variables as gender, education, income level, or personality tended to show either no relationship or inconsistent relationships across studies. Vidmar and Jeffrey Rice found a weak correlation between a juror's income and the amount awarded to a medical malpractice plaintiff.[15] Less wealthy jurors awarded less money for pain and suffering and disfigurement. They tended to view a $10,000 award as a lot of money, whereas an upper-middle-class worker tended to view $10,000 as insufficient. However, these correlations were only modest. Moreover, juries are usually composed of people with different income levels, so it can be expected that extreme differences in preferences for an award would cancel one another out.

Some sources have referred to a "Bronx effect" in which it is alleged that juries in some locales around the country are more prone to give larger awards than others. The "Bronx effect" can possibly be traced to Tom Wolfe's 1987 novel *Bonfire of the Vanities*, in which a lawyer used a creative legal rationale to move his case from Westchester County, New York, to Bronx County because he believed that Bronx juries were more generous in their awards. The "Bronx effect" story was repeated in the *New York Times* and the *Wall Street Journal*, with anecdotal examples. The basic claims have been perpetuated in some litigation manuals used by trial lawyers. Although it is usually stated without explicit reference to race, underlying claims about a Bronx effect are implicit assumptions that counties with large racial minorities and poor people, often one and the same, are friendly to plaintiffs and produce staggering losses for defendants.

Theodore Eisenberg and Martin Wells tested the assumption of demographic effects with nationwide statistics of federal jury verdicts.[16] They found "no robust evidence" that award levels correlated with population demographics. In fact, awards in jurisdictions with large black populations tended to have lower awards than other jurisdictions. The data did indicate, however, that plaintiffs were more likely to prevail at trial in jurisdictions with large black populations when the case involved job discrimination, product liability, or torts. Data from state courts produced roughly the same results, although counties with high poverty rates did have slightly larger awards in tort cases. Overall, however, Eisenberg and Wells found few consistent demographic influences on trial outcomes.[17] In a complement to the Eisenberg and Wells research, Mary Rose and Neil Vidmar specifically compared Bronx jury trial outcomes in medical malpractice and product liability trials with adjacent New York counties.[18] The win rates were somewhat higher in the Bronx for both types of cases, but, strikingly, average malpractice and product liability awards in Manhattan, Brooklyn, and Westchester counties were higher than those in the Bronx. In short, the "Bronx effect" wasn't even found in the Bronx.

ATTITUDES ABOUT INSURANCE

The litigation crisis attitudes discussed earlier should not be ascribed exclusively to the propaganda of tort reform advocates or to selective newspaper accounts. The conservatism may be ascribed to more general American values about getting only what you deserve. Years before the propaganda about a litigation crisis, an important study by David Engel indicated that many people from the American heartland endorsed the view that people should not sue for minor injuries and that it is wrong to attempt to get unwarranted benefits.[19] These conservative attitudes are reflected in jurors' attitudes about the role of insurance in personal injury cases.

American law has a rule called the "collateral source rule." The rule states that if a person or corporation injured through negligence receives compensation for injuries, say, from health insurance, and later sues the negligent party to recover for injuries, the insurance payments should not be deducted from any award that is received.[20] As a consequence of this legal reasoning, jurors are kept in the dark about insurance so they are not influenced by irrelevant legal considerations.[21] If the jurors ask for information on insurance during their deliberations, the judge will typically instruct them that they should not consider it and that they should focus exclusively on the evidence presented at trial.

Most legal commentators have assumed that jurors discuss insurance anyway, particularly whether the defendant has insurance. This belief has been tied to claims that juries act like Robin Hood because they assume the defendant will not bear the burden of the award. Diamond and Vidmar's analyses of the taped deliberations of Arizona civil juries have confirmed that insurance is frequently a subject of discussion in the jury room.[22] Conversations about insurance occurred in thirty-four out of forty trials. On average, insurance came up about four times during any jury deliberation. Contrary to conventional legal lore, however, more often than not the focus was on the plaintiff's insurance, not the defendant's insurance. In some instances the comments reflected skepticism of the plaintiff's damage claim. For instance:

Juror 6: This is another thing that was not brought up: How much of the medical has been paid?

Juror 5: They never tell that . . .

Juror 3: Insurance usually covers chiropractic care. Why should we give her above and beyond what she is probably going to get [for future medical expenses] on her insurance?

In some cases the jurors followed the judge's instructions even when a juror mentioned insurance:

Juror 6: They didn't say anything about insurance.
Juror 8: No . . .
Juror 5: We were told not to.
Juror 8: Told not to. So we can't . . .
Juror 5: Not consider car insurance anything.
[Silence. Juror 8 looks back at her notes.]

About half of the time discussion of insurance was casual or perfunctory, but in the remaining cases the potential influence of insurance on damage awards could not be ruled in or out.

Consistent with these excerpts from actual deliberations, posttrial interviews with actual jurors and simulation experiments with jury-eligible citizens by one of the present authors (Hans) yielded a similar conclusion.[23] A minority of the jurors said that the likely presence of the defendant's insurance made reaching the award easier for them because it would not be coming from the defendant's pocket. However, this view was strongly contested by other jurors who insisted that their verdict should be decided solely on the merits. Hans also found much jury interest in the plaintiff's insurance coverage. Both the Diamond and Vidmar and the Hans studies indicate that if insurance does play a role in awards, it is probably a complex and subtle one.

THE "DEEP POCKETS" HYPOTHESIS

Closely related to the insurance debate are claims about a "deep pockets effect," that is, regardless of the merits of the evidence on damages, juries award more money when the defendant is perceived to be rich. Researchers at the Rand Corporation analyzed jury verdicts awarded in Cook County, Illinois (Chicago), from 1959 through 1979.[24] They found that the average award to individuals who sued other individuals was $18,500, but for individuals who sued corporations, the average award was $120,800. Of course, some of this difference could have been due to the fact that individual and corporate defendants were involved in different types of cases, but even when some of these differences, such as severity of the plaintiff's injury, were taken into consideration, corporations still paid more. These and other findings led legal commentator Peter Huber, in a widely read 1988 book *Liability: The Legal Revolution and Its Consequences*, to assert that juries (along with some like-minded judges) were "committed to running a generous sort of charity. If the tort system cannot find a careless defendant after an accident, it will often settle for a merely wealthy one."[25] The Mobil Corporation in a public service missive claimed, in part: "Defendants with seemingly deep pockets (big companies, professionals, etc,) are paralyzed by the threat of huge jury awards and/or the likelihood of paying damages grossly out of proportion to their share of the blame."[26]

Several experiments have attempted to assess the deep pockets hypothesis. Hans conducted an experiment, related to the ones described earlier, in which a plaintiff was injured and then sued an individual, a nonprofit organization, or a corporation.[27] In one scenario the mock jurors learned nothing about the defendant's finances, in another they were told that the defendant had low financial resources, and in a third they learned that the defendant had large financial resources. The average compensatory awards to the plaintiff did not differ as a function of the defendant's wealth. Robert MacCoun[28] and Vidmar[29] conducted similar experiments and also found little support for the deep pockets hypothesis.

These findings were generally supported in Hans's interviews with actual jurors.[30] Many jurors said that they considered the process of arriving at a damage award one of the most difficult and challenging aspects of their jury task. However, 77 percent of the jurors indicated that their juries neither discussed nor considered whether the defendant could afford to pay a large damage award. Eighteen percent said they had considered the issue, and the remaining 5 percent said that while some discussion had occurred, it had not figured in their ultimate verdict. The majority of jurors stated that their deliberations centered on whether or not negligence was proven, on the plaintiff's needs, and on fairness.

One factor that came out in Hans's juror interviews was a general concern about excessive awards. Jurors frequently mentioned their apprehension about the potentially negative impact of jury awards on business costs and insurance rates. Some jurors said they had discussed the defendant's ability to pay because they wanted to assure themselves that their award would not seriously harm or even destroy the defendant. A juror in a trial involving asbestos said: "Yeah, [the plaintiff lawyers] kept coming up and saying they were bigger companies and, and we thought that they could handle it more so than a smaller company. A smaller company, a big award would wipe them out . . . I didn't want to wipe them out, and I know a lot of other [jurors] didn't want to wipe them out. . . . We figured what we had decided [for the verdict] wasn't gonna wipe these corporations out."[31] Some jurors did express the view that a large award would not really affect the defendant because it would probably be covered by insurance.

Hans concluded that there was only a modest degree of support for the deep pockets hypothesis. She also observed that while much attention has been directed to claims about inflated awards against wealthy defendants, some of her findings hint that "empty pockets" are also a significant factor in some trials. Some jurors expressed concern that their award might financially harm an individual or corporate defendant. These research findings will not end the controversy about deep pockets, but they do suggest that the deep pockets claim may be exaggerated.

THE EFFECTS OF PSYCHOLOGICAL ANCHORS

In states that permit it, during closing arguments, the plaintiff's lawyer will typically suggest an amount of the damages, called the *ad damnum*. Typically the lawyer reviews the evidence and recommends an amount for each component of the claim, such as medical costs, lost wages, and pain and suffering. The defense may offer alternative figures. These suggestions by the lawyers are intended to provide what cognitive psychologists call "psychological anchors"—numbers that influence final judgments by setting a base from which adjustment occurs.

Research based on jury simulations has attempted to assess the effects of anchors on verdicts. As Edie Greene and Brian Bornstein have concluded in their review of that research, the figure suggested by the plaintiff's lawyer generally provides an upper boundary on the amount the jury awards. [32] When the defense offers a counter-figure, that number usually serves as a lower boundary. However, one experiment suggests that if the *ad damnum* requested by the plaintiff is too high it may produce a boomerang effect.[33] In that study a plaintiff's request for $25 million resulted in a significantly lower award than a request for $15 million.

The figures offered by the plaintiff and the defendant set the boundaries within which the damage award is made. However, as will be seen shortly, examples from the deliberations of Arizona jurors suggest that between these boundaries juries pay careful attention to the actual evidence bearing on damages and conduct their own calculations.

EXPERT TESTIMONY ON FINANCIAL LOSS

Experts are frequently called to testify about financial losses in personal injury cases. A twenty-one-year-old college student from North Carolina was killed when a tow truck driver swerved in front of her.[34] At trial, an economist detailed the young woman's potential earnings as a teacher, her intended vocation, and the financial contributions she would have made to her parents in their old age. The economist's testimony included a variety of factors to arrive at a projection, including current teacher salaries, inflation, reduction to present value, tax rates, fringe benefits, self-maintenance, and morbidity rates. He calculated her economic worth to her parents at $188,663. Posttrial interviews with the jurors revealed that in deliberations, they challenged the economist's assumptions, particularly his failure to consider the deceased's plan to marry and have children, which likely would have lessened the amount of financial support she could have given to aging parents. The jurors recalculated the economic loss to be $64,866.

Central to an Arizona case was a breach of an agreement that caused a printing business to fail. At the trial, the plaintiff testified about a projected substantial increase of sales and profit with the business plan and the goodwill that was in place at the time that the defendant breached the agreement. Several valuation and marketing experts were called to bolster that projection and estimated a total loss of $2.3 million. The defendant produced experts who testified that the only worth of the company was its hard assets, approximately $550,000.

After discussing the issues in some detail, the jurors took a secret ballot and were split. Then they reanalyzed the projections of the experts, including each component of the claims of fair market value. A process of negotiation began around a chart the jurors developed near the beginning of deliberations. Here is a sample of discussion about a plaintiff's expert:

> Juror 3: I don't think it is realistic to assume the highest number.
>
> Juror 4: The highest is $1.9 mil.
>
> Juror 3: But not on his chart . . . let's say [stands and goes to chart] you're already going with the lowest return, discount rate, and you're getting the highest possible number for the last year on the projections and I think that is far too high. If you took even this number, at 30 percent, that's a huge difference and that's still going up to 2007. I know you feel this is all very conservative, but you are taking the very highest figure and . . . I'm not sure that is realistic . . .
>
> Juror 7: Was there a reason he [plaintiff expert] came up with this last figure?
>
> Juror 8: He talked about changes, he was doing an analysis that's only as good as the data that goes into it, and he talked about how the numbers changed over time, and not just the discount numbers but the owner's salary and such, so all those things were as he learned more about the business, as he got the management consultants and as he got a figure to put on the brand equity, that all plays into the rate of return. I don't have a problem with those numbers changing—they're going to evolve as you keep . . . and hopefully, you're getting closer to the truth. The only way to find the truth is to sell it and we can't do that.
>
> Juror 3: Don't you think he changed those numbers to get to a higher number for the market value, like using the $78,000 for the owner's salary—I know where he came up with the number but it wasn't reflective of what he was getting before.
>
> Juror 8: Someone with his background, it wouldn't take 200 hours to figure out how to play with the discount rate. . . . He would of said, "Gee, let's go to a lower discount rate," . . . I don't think that was all he was trying to do.

The jury eventually made a $1.7 million award.

These brief examples suggest that claims about jurors uncritically deferring to experts and the respective lawyers' final arguments on the appropriate award are overblown. The Arizona juries had a collective mind of their own, and there is no reason to believe they are different from juries in other states. Moreover, the issues that arise in many trials further complicate the picture. Let's examine the process of deliberating about damages a little further.

INJURY ASSESSMENTS AND DAMAGES CALCULATIONS

The facts and issues at trial provide a rich context in which the jurors are encouraged to use their own experience and reasoning. Even when the jury has decided that the defendant is the only person at fault, the task of determining compensatory damages is often complicated. Judicial instructions direct the jury to consider the nature, the extent, and the duration of the injury. The following example shows one jury doing just that following a claim for an industrial accident:

> Juror 1: My opinion is if we say he has, uh, an injury related to this thing, it's a minor injury and you've got to understand that he did work continuously for seven or eight weeks. I don't think this injury could . . .
>
> Juror 4: 6 weeks.
>
> Juror 1: Is it 6 weeks?
>
> Juror 4: Uh huh.
>
> Juror 1: Well then I don't think the injury he had here would have lasted 5 weeks. And so I don't think he has any wage claim whatsoever that's valid. We can look at all his medical expenses up say for 3 to 4 weeks . . . from this kind of a thing and say we'll pay those medical expenses.
>
> Juror 8: I agree with him [pointing to Juror 1] on a lot of parts, but he [plaintiff] had the accident, he went back to work, and I haven't heard anybody say that he didn't want to work except the defendant. . . . But he worked for 5 weeks and now his back got worse and then he goes back to the doctor again and they put him off work and then later they said he could go back to light duty so he goes back to light duty . . . and when was that date?
>
> Juror 6: January.
>
> Juror 5: No, February.
>
> Juror 8: Ok so in February he gets hurt again.
>
> Juror 7: Yeah, middle of February.
>
> Juror 8: Which adds to the problem. So my estimation is he deserves things up to mid-February because this was related to all his problems.

FAILURE TO MITIGATE

In the preceding chapter we explored how jurors assess the seriousness of the plaintiff's claim of injury and also how previous injuries can complicate that assessment. In assessing damages, the jurors may also take into account a plaintiff's failure to mitigate the effects of an injury. Thus, in a breach of contract case where the defendant is solely at fault, the plaintiff's injuries may be greater than they otherwise might have been because he failed to act after the injury. For instance, the jury may be told that the plaintiff had a legal responsibility to take action to stop further losses. This could also occur in a personal injury case as well. The theme of "failure to mitigate" was raised repeatedly by the jurors themselves.

In a first example a man injured in an automobile accident failed to follow the instructions of his treating doctor and instead eventually went to a chiropractor. Juror 5 expressed the views of most of the other jurors as they discounted the worth of the injury.

> Juror 5: Number one, he didn't get any of the medication filled for the 10 days after, and I see it hard that somebody that hurt as bad as he didn't do anything for 10 days. He didn't see a doctor for 15 days afterwards and that was when his wife finally made him go.

In a second example a carpenter was injured at work. His doctor told him to stay off work for several weeks. He went back anyway. Discounting the possibility that the man may have needed the money, the jurors were not very sympathetic. They acknowledged he had been injured as a result of his employer's negligence but also blamed him:

> Juror 4: So to me it's, there's still fault there. But I also think he's at fault.
>
> Juror 8: Right.
>
> Juror 4: For trying to work when the doctor (Juror 8: Right.) even told him he shouldn't be working, and he said I don't care, I want to work anyway.
>
> (Juror 5: Um hum.) And I do think that under that responsibility thing. It's your responsibility to take care of your body, and if your doctor said you shouldn't have been working you shouldn't be working.
>
> Juror 8: Cause he had a bad back and went to work for almost a month and a half at the least . . .
>
> Juror 1: Seven weeks.
>
> Juror 8: He could have hurt his back just doing that.

Here we see again, but in the context of assessing damages, the jurors' shared tendency to scrutinize the plaintiff's possible contributions to his own injury.

JURORS AS ACCOUNTANTS

Some lawyers and academics have speculated that jurors do not concern themselves with the details of the damages but instead search for a single amount that "seems right" and then work backward from that figure.[35] Consistently, Arizona juries did not fit this pattern during their deliberations, instead considering invoices in detail. Here is an example:

> Juror 4: We have to find the doctor bills, so we can make a determination of the money. Let me take a look at that one [Juror 5 hands her an exhibit] . . .
>
> Juror 4: I found it guys, the medical bills.
>
> Juror 7: I knew we had you as foreman for a reason.
>
> Juror 5 [to Juror 4]: Do they have them broken down by dates?
>
> Juror 4: Yes they do, okay, um [Everyone is talking] . . .
>
> Juror 6: The plaintiff said $175,000 and the defendant said $15,000, so I think it would help me to know the total of medical bills and then take a look at what the plaintiff is asking . . .
>
> Juror 4 [interrupting]: Okay, a question, I want to ask everybody the first question. There is no doubt that he missed one week of work after the accident, okay? (Juror 3: I thought he missed two.), (Juror 5: 1½ weeks) Well both attorneys agree on that figure, the figure is $1,753, can this jury agree to $1,753 in the figure?

The jurors agreed and moved on to another part of the claim.

> Juror 4: Okay, now the other thing . . . okay, we have to figure out what the rest of it is. Can people here agree on the emergency room visit?
>
> Juror 7: Absolutely.
>
> Juror 2: Yes. [Others nod their heads in agreement.]
>
> Juror 4: Now, let's figure out what that is. Okay, um, [looking at the exhibit of hospital visits and medical bills] the accident was on 10/15, so that would have to be what happened on 10/16. Okay, on 10/16, Dr. Phelps, well, now that says, [reading the medical records] 10/16 to 4/22, 10/16 to 10/28. (Juror 6: It should say 10/16.) Oh, here it is, emergency room 10/15/96 is $557.26.
>
> Jurors 6 and 7 [simultaneously]: $600 . . .
>
> Juror 4 [writes it down]: $600 for the ER visit.
>
> Juror 4 [continues]: Lenscrafters, that was for his broken glasses, $52.10 and we'll round it to (Juror 5: that's right)
>
> Juror 1: $50.
>
> Juror 4: Okay, Eckerd Drugs, that was $171.91.
>
> Juror 7: What was that for?
>
> Juror 4: That was for pain medication, that was for and the emergency room visit, whatever they gave him. Okay, now here's what we have to figure out, um, who did he see for, because we have two doctors here, at the emergency clinic for 10/16. But they didn't break it down for just the 10/16, they extended it through 4/22 and it amounts to $286.
>
> Juror 6: That's fine. Do you want to agree to that?

Everyone seemed to agree. They moved on to other documents related to the plaintiff's expenses and calculated in the same manner until they agreed on the individual items and then summed the individual items to arrive at a total.

The pattern of close scrutiny of medical bills, wage slips, tax forms, and other expenses was repeated many times among the other Arizona juries. The best characterization would be jurors acting as tightfisted accountants, not wanting to give plaintiffs a dollar more than they deserved.

GENERAL DAMAGES

The calculation of general damages in personal injury trials involves a more amorphous task for the jury. There are no bills and receipts. There is only the testimony of the plaintiff on how she suffered and perhaps medical experts to describe the nature and causes of pain. The jury is in a position to decide, as well as anyone, the special circumstances of pain suffered by the plaintiff. Consider people who have lost a leg due to negligence. Sometimes amputees experience excruciating "phantom pain" that is unabating, and doctors can do little but prescribe heavy doses of pain medicine. In contrast, a second person with an identical amputation injury will experience no pain; a third person will have intermittent pain. Similar differences occur with whiplash injuries. Some people have stronger tolerance for pain or mental anguish, but others have weaker tolerance. The jury is asked to consider the special circumstances of the plaintiff.

Sometimes lawyers suggest a general figure in closing. Other lawyers suggest an hourly or daily amount that should be awarded for the pain or disfigurement or loss of society and ask the jurors to apply that figure to calculate the amount of time that the plaintiff suffered. If it is a lifelong injury, they suggest calculating the figure over the plaintiff's expected remaining life span.

Instructions on pain and suffering implicitly acknowledge the vagueness of the jury's task. For instance, a North Carolina instruction says:

> Damages should include such amount as you find, by the greater weight of the evidence, is fair compensation for the actual physical pain and mental suffering which were the immediate and necessary consequences of the injury. There is no fixed formula for evaluating pain and suffering. You will determine what is fair compensation by applying logic and common sense to the evidence.

In one case from the Arizona Jury Project, a previously healthy woman in her thirties was badly and permanently injured in an industrial accident. The jury heard medical testimony indicating that she faced additional surgeries, permanent pain, brain damage, and depression. In his closing argument, her lawyer suggested an amount per day and calculated it over the plaintiff's expected lifetime, arriving at a figure just short of five million dollars. The defense lawyer suggested $5 million was inappropriate for pain and suffering and argued that the figure should be no more than $1 million.

The jury deliberations on general damages were lengthy and intertwined with contested estimates of future medical expenses and income losses. After initial discussion, the jurors agreed on a tentative upper limit of $5 million for the total award. The deliberations involved vacillations and backtracking over previous discussions. The jurors tried to put themselves in the plaintiff's place and considered how such an injury would affect their relationships with their own children and grandchildren. The following edited excerpts give the flavor of the deliberations. These excerpts are a bit longer than other examples, but since general damages are the subject of so much criticism of juries, it is important to look closely at the process.

> Juror 4: So what would you say, this guy [plaintiff lawyer] is asking for $5 million the other one said to give her $1 million?
>
> Juror 6: I say $2 or $3 million.
>
> Juror 7: Well, like you say, $5 million (Juror 3: Well, he wanted . . .) is too high and $1 million is too low.
>
> Juror 6: That's everything, pain and suffering and everything.
>
> . . . .
>
> Juror 8: I think that's the problem, I think that as the physical gets worse (Juror 4: The pressure goes up) it's probably likely to say that the mental gets worse I don't know how it will work, I don't know if the mental gets better if the physical doesn't get better.
>
> Juror 6: Yeah, she's in pain all the time.
>
> Juror 8: So, if that's how you are for the rest of your life what amount of money makes your life okay? (Juror 6: Yeah.)
>
> Juror 8: I would say no amount of money . . .
>
> Juror 4: You can't put a dollar amount on it.
>
> Juror 8: Exactly.
>
> Juror 3: I know I've been trying to think of a number.
>
> Juror 4: You can't put a dollar amount, but do you guys have a number?
>
> Juror 6: We have to.
>
> Juror 3: I mean, right now, everybody, can everybody come up with a number they have thought of?
>
> . . . .
>
> Juror 6: It's hard it really is, I keep thinking of the permanent damage I keep thinking of the permanent damage she's going to have for the rest of her life, you can't think of just now.
>
> Juror 4: When she testified, there's so much to relate to, I have a granddaughter and play with her.
>
> Juror 6: She's [plaintiff] never going to be the same.
>
> Juror 4: I have asthma and can't run after her that much and it irks me and now this lady now can't but it's not something she did (Juror 6: That's right) there's a lot of things . . .

Juror 8: And I think of even in terms of if she can get another job not only will it pay very low it probably won't be very satisfying but if it takes her seven more years to be medically at a place where she can work and then, given by then she will be in her mid forties she's not going to have a lot of time to build anything up that she can retire on.

Juror 7: Here's some numbers I came up with, there was the $1,249,000 for the salary . . . (Juror 4: So, what did you come up with?) I came up with $2,490,000.

. . . .

Juror 8: I think she'll have more than a couple of hundred for future medical; I think you have to double that almost (Juror 3: yeah) if not a little more, because it's only been a year and a half and she's already accrued more than $163,000 [in medical bills].

. . . .

Juror 3: So, that means you'd only be giving her (Juror 8: She gets less than a million for pain and suffering?) yeah, that's what you're saying is she is getting less than a million for pain and suffering.

Juror 8: Yeah, that her pain and suffering is less than a million.

Juror 4: No, it's not, it's $1.2 million.

Juror 3: No, cause you're not equating the future medical expenses.

Juror 8: Exactly, you have to subtract out the future medical expenses. What if she spends $500,000 on medical expenses and then getting $650,000 for pain and suffering?

Juror 4: Yeah.

Juror 3: That number right there, that $2.8.

Juror 4: Add another $300,000 to it, and give her $3.1.

. . . .

Juror 7: I like $3.1. It gives her a cushion, say okay we don't know what's happening to the dollar, we don't know what's happening . . .

. . . .

Juror 8: I think she's got to have over one million for pain and suffering.

Juror 6: I wouldn't want to go through what she did.

Juror 3: Yeah, I wouldn't want to know that I could never play with my children or grandchildren again, that I couldn't walk without a cane anymore.

Juror 3: There's a lot of things that have been taken away from her (Juror 4: I agree) and I think a lot of those things are things in life that she needs and that she's not going to have anymore.

Juror 4: There's all this compensation and things you can do.

Juror 3: That's what we're trying to do, compensate her . . .

Juror 3: What number did you [pointing to Juror 5] come up with?

Juror 5: $3.5 million.

Juror 3: So, we have five $3's and three $3.5's.

Juror 7: Let's average it out.

In this example, jurors all seem to agree that the injury is devastating and that a substantial award for pain and suffering is merited, yet all have difficulty in identifying an appropriate amount. They look to one another for a number that will somehow represent a fair award. The jurors settled on $3.2 million for a total verdict.

For injuries that were relatively minor in comparison to the very serious injury suffered by the plaintiff in the above example, many jurors strongly felt no award should be given for pain and suffering. In one case concerning a nonpermanent injury following an automobile accident, the plaintiff's lawyer had suggested a figure of $250 per day for six weeks. Some jurors wanted to give nothing, while others wanted to give some award. They eventually compromised:

> Juror 1: Let's say she had 2 bad days. [Her lawyer] even said, even at the first time, for three nights, I didn't believe that. Let's go with this, and say maybe for that 15 weeks she has two bad nights. You got to think, it also tapered. It probably got better over that time. . . . So maybe we give her three days a week pain and suffering for the first three weeks. Maybe two days a week for three weeks.
>
> Juror 2: At what pretense?
>
> Juror 1: That's what we have to decide. I don't think, I can't see giving someone, I mean, $250 a day for pain and suffering?
>
> Juror 6: No.
>
> Juror 1: That's a bunch of crap.
>
> Juror 2: I think she should get her babysitting fee and maybe a mileage and that's it.
>
> . . . .
>
> Juror 2 [to Juror 7]: You want the pain and suffering. It seems like you are the proponent of pain and suffering. How much do you want . . . ?
>
> Juror 5 [interrupting]: Why don't you take the amount of the compensation for the doctor's bills and just divide it by half, and that's it? So give her the doctor's bills, $1,725.
>
> Juror 1: Plus half that?
>
> Juror 5: Plus half of that for pain and suffering.
>
> Juror 1: So we end up giving her what, $2,500 dollars?
>
> Juror 5: Yeah.
>
> Juror 1: I can live with that if you all can.

INSIGHTS FROM THE JURY DELIBERATION EXAMPLES

The context out of which jury awards arise is complex and nuanced. Jurors have many things to consider as they struggle with the award: the testimony of the plaintiff, accountants, life care specialists, documents—and the alternative perspective of the defendant that might range from an argument that no award should be given to one that is drastically lower than the plaintiff's request. What becomes very clear is that hypotheses about the impact of juror gender or race or economic status, the effects of psychological anchors provided by the lawyers, or any other single variable are far too simplistic. The examples given above are typical of thirty cases in which the Arizona civil juries rendered awards to plaintiffs. They took their task very seriously, often to the extent of calculating and arguing down to the last dollar.

JUDGING DAMAGE AWARDS

Even if, as we have seen, juries take their job conscientiously, how well do they perform in this role? There can be no clear, unequivocal answer, since the amount of damages is in dispute. Nevertheless, there are several different ways to obtain rough measures of jury performance.

One way is to compare the award with the seriousness of the injury. A number of studies have done just that. In one California study, the claim files of medical malpractice insurance companies were checked to determine the plaintiff's economic losses, severity of injury, and age.[36] These variables were then compared to the award. In general, the magnitudes of the awards were positively related to the size of the losses. Several subsequent studies compared the amounts awarded by juries and the seriousness of the injury sustained by the plaintiff, and found that the more serious the injury the larger the award, except for injuries resulting in death, which produced lesser amounts than other very serious injuries.[37] The drop in awards for death can be explained by the fact that there are no future medical expenses, as there are with seriously injured plaintiffs who may require around-the-clock nursing care over many years. Nor is there ongoing pain and suffering. These statistical findings, like those from the Arizona juries, lead to the conclusion that jury awards are reasonably related to injury seriousness.

However, the statistical studies do show considerable variability within each level of injury severity. That is, people with the same level of injury received different dollar awards. This could be evidence of jury unreliability, but there is a very plausible alternative interpretation. Damages may differ greatly even with the same level of injury. For instance, a child who suffers a debilitating injury faces many years of medical bills and lost wages, whereas an elderly person, with a shorter life span, would have lower bills and fewer lost wages. A person who earns $200,000 per year will suffer greater wage loss than someone who makes $20,000 per year. A single parent with four dependent children who was incapacitated or died would justify a much larger award than a childless person with the same injury. Pain and suffering may differ from case to case as we pointed out with the leg amputation example: one patient who loses a leg may experience excruciating phantom pain whereas another with the same injury has no pain at all. Author Vidmar and colleagues Kara MacKillop and Paul Lee studied medical malpractice settlements exceeding $1 million.[38] Their findings documented the variability of damages. Even when the patient died, losses varied: one patient left a minor child; another was survived by three minor children; still another left four minor children needing financial support.[39]

That is not to say that two juries hearing the same case would arrive at exactly the same damage award. Human variability is inherent in the jury's task. Experts called by the opposing sides often have widely differing estimates of the worth of the case. Which expert is right? One jury might see it one way and another jury in a different way. Legal specialists often differ on these amounts. In one study, experienced trial lawyers were randomly assigned to represent either a plaintiff or a defendant and each was provided extensive but identical materials about the case.[40] Regardless of the side they represented, lawyers showed great variability in how they evaluated the worth of the plaintiff's losses. Furthermore, as Michael Saks has noted, even insurance claims adjusters whose full-time job is to make valuations of injuries show great variability in their estimates of damages.[41]

To examine some of these issues, Roselle Wissler and her colleagues conducted an experiment involving 558 jury-eligible citizens, 224 judges, and 248 defense and plaintiff personal injury lawyers from the states of New York and Illinois.[42] Each participant was presented with two case summaries adapted from actual personal injury cases. The cases differed across a wide range of physical symptoms and seriousness of injury (e.g., from quadriplegia and a vegetative state to temporary paralysis of two fingers or burns on legs). Each participant was asked to rate the seriousness of the injury and then indicate the appropriate amount of general damages, plus make some additional judgments.

Wissler and her colleagues found that jurors, judges, and lawyers thought about the relative severity of injuries in remarkably similar ways. Disability and mental suffering were the strongest predictors of estimated overall severity, although disfigurement and pain made smaller contributions to the judgments. Interestingly, the sociodemographic characteristics (age, education, gender) of the various people in the study were unrelated to assessments of severity. Judgments of the appropriate amount of dollar damages produced slightly less clear results, but, nevertheless, the different groups of decision makers showed important similarities in their assessments. Greater perceived disability and mental suffering were strongly associated with larger awards, disfigurement had a smaller effect, and pain itself was related to awards only indirectly through its association with other attributes of the injury.

Edie Greene and Brian Bornstein review additional research on how juries decide the pain and suffering component of damages.[43] They point out that while all American jurisdictions allow recovery for pain and suffering for physical injury and most jurisdictions allow recovery for the infliction of emotional distress, the jurisdictions differ in their specific instructions about how to decide pain and suffering. Research with mock jurors suggests that different instructions can influence the amounts of awards. However, Greene and Bornstein point out that in real trials these effects may be offset by expert evidence and by the arguments of the opposing lawyers.

The pain and suffering component of awards, as we have noted, gets the greatest attention of critics. Many have claimed that legal training and experience make judges better qualified to apply more reasoned—and better—judgment to this component of damages. The pain and suffering component was only one element in the Wissler research, but two additional studies by Vidmar specifically looked at damages for pain and suffering and disfigurement. In the first study, two groups of jurors awaiting jury duty and a group of twenty-one senior lawyers—six of whom were former judges—were provided a detailed description of a female who suffered a severe burn on her knee.[44] The injury left a large, disfiguring scar, but there were no effects on her mobility. Liability was admitted, and the only issue was how much she should receive for her pain and suffering and disfigurement. The mean and median damage awards of the jurors and the senior lawyers were the same, approximately $50,000. Both the lawyer-judges and the jurors showed quite a bit of variability in their estimates of the appropriate award, but juror verdicts had a greater range of high and low awards. However, unlike a decision of a single-trial judge, jury verdicts are a result of collaboration of between six and twelve people. When the individual juror awards were averaged together, in an effort to model actual jury awards, the statistical jury awards were less variable and extreme than the individual judge awards. Thus, when jury awards were modeled by averaging the individual awards of its members, jury awards were more stable.

A second experiment, similar to the one described above, was based on a substantially greater injury to a teenage girl and involved different groups of lawyers and jurors. Once again the estimated average jury award was about the same as that of judges, but as in the first experiment, statistical juries were estimated to be less likely to produce awards that were as variable as those that would be expected from any randomly chosen judge. The findings from these two studies need to be accompanied by an important qualification. The jurors did not deliberate, and thus we cannot be sure of the degree to which discussion would have changed individual jurors' awards. Nevertheless, the findings show variability among legal professionals and hint that juries may produce more stable estimates of the community's evaluation of the injury than a single judge acting alone.

As we noted earlier, in *The American Jury*, Kalven and Zeisel made the point that there is no reason to assume that when juries and judges differ in their verdicts that the jury's verdict is wrong and the judge's is right. After all, if the reason for the jury's divergence from the judge is that the jury is applying community norms and values in order to achieve a just and fair result, why shouldn't its decision be the correct standard? Furthermore, the other data show that juries tend to give damages in proportion to the seriousness of the harm and they appear to apply approximately the same reasoning as judges do. (We will have a few more things to say about pain and suffering awards when we consider medical malpractice in chapter 16.)

CONCLUDING PERSPECTIVE

Clearly, juries treat damage awards as serious business, dispelling the myths about juries being irresponsible or the legally sanctioned equivalent of contemporary Robin Hoods. Evidentiary rules that keep some evidence like insurance away from the jury, and judicial instructions on the law, attempt to provide for consistency across cases and constrain juries to their fact-finding role. Juries allow equity and community values to slip between the legal rules. As we have seen, these values are often conservative rather than irresponsibly generous, as we would have assumed if we only read news reports of civil jury awards, reports that tend to overrepresent the cases with the highest awards. There are undoubtedly occasions in which juries go astray, but trial judges and appeals courts can and do reduce awards or reject them entirely.

The key question in evaluating jury damage determinations is not simply whether damage awards vary in cases with similar injuries. We observe such variability, but other aspects of the case may differ in ways that reasonably relate to the jury award. What is important is the degree of variation, whether that variation can be explained by other factors, and whether, as always, we would do better if a judge rather than a jury made the decision.

Professor James Oldham has documented the fact that long before the Seventh Amendment was adopted in the United States, both English common law and American practice had made it clear that juries were far better suited than judges to determine compensatory damages, although judges had the right to review the awards if they believed the jury had made an error. As recently as 1999, a US Supreme Court decision affirmed that historically derived wisdom.[45] We have left the door open to consider these same issues with respect to punitive damages.

Chapter 15

PUNITIVE DAMAGES

Coffee Spills and Marlboro Cigarettes

> Reform is urgently needed to restore balance, fairness, and predictability to punitive damages law. The civil justice system should not be a "litigation lottery" characterized by excessiveness and arbitrariness.
>
> American Tort Reform Association (2006)

Jury verdicts that involve large punitive damage awards grab the attention of the mass media, legislators, and the public. Punitive damages drive the proponents of tort reform and the American business community to apoplexy. Declarations are made that punitive damages inhibits invention of products and harms America's global business competitiveness.[1]

The McDonald's coffee spill case involving an elderly woman who spilled hot coffee on her lap and received compensatory damages of $200,000 and punitive damages of $2.7 million—and which we will discuss shortly—has become a poster child for the ills of punitive damages.[2] In 1994 an Alaska jury awarded $287 million in compensatory damages and $5 billion in punitive damages following the *Exxon Valdez* oil spill. In 2000 a Florida jury awarded $145 billion in punitive damages on behalf of all Florida smokers against the R. J. Reynolds Tobacco Company.[3] In 2006 a New Jersey jury awarded $4.5 million in compensatory damages and $9 million in punitive damages against drug manufacturer Merck & Co. after a man had a heart attack after taking Merck's arthritis painkiller drug, Vioxx. The award followed a Texas verdict against Merck of $7 million in compensatory damages and $25 million in punitive damages.[4]

Beginning in the 1990s, the Supreme Court has addressed the issue of punitive damages numerous times. There is a general perception that punitive damage awards have increased in both size and frequency over the past couple of decades. Professor George Priest of Yale Law School has argued that juries are capricious and unreliable when rendering punitive awards.[5] Although acknowledging the relative infrequency of punitive damages generally, Priest asserted that a principal problem is that the standards provided to juries in punitive damages cases "are extremely vague and employ terms that are largely undefined," thereby causing different juries to use different metrics in calculating punitive awards. Additionally, Professor Priest and others have claimed that the threat of highly unpredictable and outrageously high jury punitive damages affects the settlement process, causing defendants to settle without a trial for much more than the case is actually worth.[6] Lawyers refer to this as the *in terrorem* (literally, the "fear") effect.

Following the *Exxon Valdez* award, the Exxon Corporation began to underwrite a series of simulation studies about juries and punitive damages.[7] These experiments were compiled in Cass Sunstein and others, *Punitive Damages: How Jurors Decide* (2002).[8] In the book the authors asserted that their findings supported the conclusion that "the legally required decision tasks often seemed to exceed [jurors'] individual and social capacities. . . . Jurors' good intentions and high levels of motivation were thwarted by the inherent complexity of the legal decision task and by lack of clear instructions or other effective guidance. The result is a decision process that is unreliable, erratic and unpredictable."[9]

Are these claims valid? As we will show below, the vast bulk of the hard evidence refutes these claims. First, however, let us briefly review the history of punitive damages and two recent US Supreme Court cases that set forth guidelines for their application.

THE HISTORY AND PURPOSES OF PUNITIVE DAMAGES

As Thomas Koenig and Michael Rustad have pointed out, American law on punitive damages has its origin in English common law, which developed the concept of exemplary damages to punish abuses of power by the Crown.[10] In 1763 agents for King George III conducted an unlawful search and seizure of a newspaper. Exemplary damages were awarded to the plaintiff on the grounds that actual damages would be insufficient to punish and deter future conduct by the Crown's agents. The doctrine was later expanded to punish private individuals who deliberately committed torts with malicious intentions, such as destruction of property or an assault. Exemplary damages were frequently used in cases involving aristocrats who abused their power, abuses including the mistreatment of servants or the intentional violation of property rights. By the beginning of the nineteenth century, exemplary damages were awarded in a wide range of instances involving abuses of power.

American tort law followed the English example. In 1784, the South Carolina Supreme Court awarded "vindictive damages" against a doctor who used his medical knowledge to deliberately cause pain in a man, with whom he had had a quarrel, by spiking his wine with a large dose of Spanish fly. Later American law tended to refer to exemplary damages as punitive damages, and by the middle of the nineteenth century punitive damages were levied in a wide variety of cases of abuses of power, including instances in which women were assaulted or raped, or in cases in which a physically stronger man attacked a weaker man. Punitive damages were also levied for intentional or malicious acts regarding property, interference in domestic relations, reputation, and liberty interests. In 1872, a Massachusetts court explained in a case involving trespass that the jury award was consistent with a societal norm: "the right of the poor against the aggressions of power and violence."

In the latter half of the nineteenth century, American courts began to gradually allow punitive damages in commercial transactions in which a defendant had engaged in egregious acts of malice, fraud, insult, misrepresentation, or wanton disregard of the rights of others. After the Civil War, a Colorado Supreme Court decision stated that punitive damages could be imposed for classes of acts "extremely injurious to individuals, of which the criminal law takes no cognizance, and yet . . . which [affects] the public interest." In the twentieth century, the doctrine of punitive damages was expanded to include, among other things, product liability. Some statutes, such as those dealing with antitrust or discrimination, provide for automatic doubling or tripling of compensatory awards if a violation is found, thus adding a punishing component designed to have a deterrent effect.

Punitive damages thus have two goals. One is to punish behaviors that, while perhaps not criminal, offend important moral values—abuses of power or the blatant disregard of the rights of others. The second goal is to deter such behaviors by making it more likely that the costs of wrongful actions will exceed the benefits. The deterrence goal is directed not only to the defendant to deter future bad actions but also to other persons or corporations who might contemplate similar unacceptable behavior. A representative jury is trusted to reflect the community's judgment and commonsense justice about such abuses.

Punitive damages blend civil law—which deals with private wrongs—in the direction of criminal law to punish behaviors that are not typically covered by criminal statutes. Moreover, while the government itself may in some instances do the prosecuting, American law encourages private enforcement of public policy. At the risk of oversimplification, the theory of private enforcement is that individuals with a grievance are allowed to file lawsuits seeking punitive damages for themselves, but the effect will be to the greater good of society if the wrongdoer is punished for behaviors that harm more than just the person who brought the lawsuit.[11] While in the past, the plaintiff recovered all of the punitive award, today many state statutes, such as those in Utah and Oregon, provide that as much as 75 percent of a punitive award will go into the public coffers; the plaintiff (and the plaintiff's lawyers) will receive the remainder.

PROPORTIONALITY: *BMW* AND *STATE FARM*

BMW v. Gore

An Alabama doctor purchased a $40,000 new BMW automobile.[12] He learned that parts of it had been repainted after it had been exposed to acid rain, so he sued on the grounds that it was not a new car as represented. During the trial, BMW revealed that their policy was to sell damaged cars as new if the damage could be fixed for less than 3 percent of the cost of the car. However, the doctor's lawyers argued that BMW's policy of repainting cars and selling them as new was fraudulent. Moreover, BMW had committed the fraud at least a thousand times in Alabama or other states. Although the repair was minor, the lawyers argued that a large punitive award should be given to punish BMW for its overall behavior and send a message that would deter other companies from engaging in similar behavior. The jury awarded $4,000 in compensatory damages and $4,000,000 in punitive damages.

When the case was appealed to the US Supreme Court, the justices expressed a number of interrelated concerns. One was that it was inappropriate for the jury to award punitive damages for actions that occurred outside of Alabama because BMW's actions might be legal in other states. A second concern of the Court was that the harm was economic in nature, as opposed to personal harm. It held that BMW's actions were not really so reprehensible, since there was no evidence of reckless disregard for the health or safety of its customers. Most important, however, the Court was disturbed by the relationship between the size of punitive damage award and the amount of the compensatory award. The punitive award was one thousand times larger than the compensatory award. The ratio of actual and potential harm, said the Court, should not ordinarily exceed a single digit.

The *BMW* Court set forth three guidelines for judges to follow in determining if the award was inappropriate. The most important of these is the degree of reprehensibility of the defendant's conduct. A second criterion is the ratio of compensatory damages awarded for actual or potential harm. The third criterion is a comparison with civil or criminal penalties that might be imposed for comparable misconduct.

The Court concluded that the amount of the punitive award in *BMW* violated substantive due process under the Constitution. It was sent back to the Alabama court for review under the guidelines. Eventually the case settled for under several hundred thousand dollars. But *BMW v. Gore* serves as the leading case on how judges should determine whether a jury award is out of line with constitutional standards.

State Farm v. Campbell

Curtis Campbell, a man of modest means, caused an automobile accident in which two people were killed.[13] Despite the willingness of the estates of the deceased to settle for Mr. Campbell's policy limit of $25,000 and Mr. Campbell's plea to settle, State Farm refused to settle. Mr. Campbell was sued, and a jury awarded one deceased's estate $135,000 and the other $50,849. Mr. Campbell did not have the money to pay the awards, and State Farm still would not pay. A State Farm agent even wisecracked to poor Mr. Campbell that he should sell his home to pay the award. In an interesting legal move the plaintiffs' estates then entered into agreement with Mr. Campbell to have him sue State Farm for bad faith failure to settle and seek damages for fraud and intentional infliction of emotional distress.

At the trial State Farm argued that failure to settle was an "honest mistake." However, Mr. Campbell's lawyer showed through documents and expert testimony that for twenty years State Farm had a policy of not settling claims—especially when the policyholder was poor, a member of a racial minority, a woman, or elderly. It deliberately concealed and destroyed documents bearing on its profit scheme. State Farm lawyers instructed their insurance adjusters to ask personal questions of their policyholders who made claims in order to intimidate them. Furthermore, the company had an internal policy that the outcomes of lawsuits should not be forwarded to corporate headquarters so that their executives could plead ignorance about the actions of its agents.

The jury awarded Mr. and Mrs. Campbell $3.6 million in compensatory damages for emotional distress plus punitive damages of $145 million. The trial judge reduced the compensatory damages to $1 million and the punitive damages to $25 million. The case was appealed to the Utah Supreme Court, which condemned State Farm's behavior and reinstated the original jury award, observing that the $145 million should be compared to State Farm's overall worth of $547 billion. By that measure the award was only 0.26 percent of State Farm's overall worth. Under the statute then in existence, after subtracting $20,000 and allowances for reasonable attorney fees, the State of Utah would receive 50 percent of the punitive award.

The case was then appealed to the US Supreme Court, which held that an award of $145 million in punitive damages compared to $1 million of compensatory damages violated due process. The decision noted that as in *BMW v. Gore*, the defendant was being punished for actions outside as well as inside Utah and that the harm to the Campbells was economic rather than physical. It also noted that a criminal fine for grand fraud was only $10,000. The Court reiterated that the primary standard for punitive damages was the degree of reprehensibility of the defendant's conduct:

> We have instructed courts to determine the reprehensibility of a defendant by considering whether: the harm caused was physical as opposed to economic; the tortious conduct evinced an indifference to a reckless disregard of the health or safety of others; the target of the conduct had financial vulnerability; the conduct involved repeated actions or was an isolated incident; and the harm was the result of intentional malice, trickery or deceit, or mere accident.

The case was sent back to the Utah Supreme Court for reconsideration. In a detailed decision continuing to note the reprehensible behavior, the Utah Supreme Court reduced the punitive award to $9,018,780.75—nine times the compensatory damages.

State Farm helps to show that courts can agree or disagree with a jury verdict on punitive damages. It also shows the role of both trial judges and appellate judges in scrutinizing and adjusting exceptional jury verdicts.

EMPIRICAL FACTS ABOUT PUNITIVE AWARDS

Because punitive damages have become so controversial, a substantial body of research has been devoted to documenting their frequency, the types of cases in which they are given, and the ratios between compensatory and punitive awards.[14] The findings largely contradict many of the assertions made about juries in punitive damages cases.

JURIES RARELY AWARD PUNITIVE DAMAGES

Based on systematic surveys of state courts in 1992, 1996, and 2001 by the US Bureau of Justice Statistics (BJS) and the National Center for State Courts (NCSC), it can be estimated that punitive damages are awarded in less than 1 percent of all civil cases in state courts.[15] A review of several different databases by Thomas Eaton and his colleagues concluded that "for every 1000 tort claims filed, typically only 50 or more are resolved by trial, only 25 produce trial outcomes favorable to the plaintiff, and only 1.25 [of 1,000] have a punitive damage award."[16]

THE INCIDENCE OF PUNITIVE DAMAGES HAS NOT INCREASED

The BJS/NCSC survey showed that the actual number of punitive awards was half a percent lower in 2001 compared to 1992, and the number of awards exceeding a million dollars did not differ between the two time periods. This same conclusion was reached by other researchers who reviewed additional studies of the incidence of awards.

PUNITIVE DAMAGES MOSTLY OCCUR IN CASES INVOLVING INTENTIONAL TORTS AND FRAUD

Empirical studies of punitive damages have concluded that punitive damages against businesses tended to involve allegations of acts that show either a knowing and active disregard for the law, such as illegal toxic dumping, providing minors with alcohol that resulted in a death, or falsely reporting inspections of equipment. They rarely, if ever, involved commonly accepted business practices or instances where the business followed normal precautions for safety.[17] These findings from studies of court statistics are consistent with a number of simulation studies that indicate that jurors render awards roughly commensurate with the reprehensibility of alleged conduct.[18]

While most of the tort reform rhetoric focuses on individuals or groups of individuals suing businesses, particularly in product liability cases, in fact Professor Rustad concluded that the growth in most large punitive damage awards involved businesses suing other businesses alleging economic harm from opportunistic business practices.[19] Data from the Bureau of Justice Statistics revealed that in the 2001 sample of state courts, there were only three punitive damage awards out of seventy product liability cases won by plaintiffs. A wide-ranging study of punitive damages concluded that the growth area for punitive damages was not personal injury cases but in business and contract litigation involving economic harms resulting from "opportunistic business practices." For example, a jury awarded IGEN International $105.4 million in compensatory damages and $400 million in punitive damages against Roche Diagnostics.[20] Pioneer Commercial Corporation won $13.5 million in compensatory damages and $337.5 million in punitive damages.[21] The State of Alabama sued Exxon Mobil Corporation over breach of contract and fraudulent accounting practices concerning natural gas leases in the Gulf of Mexico. The jury awarded Alabama $102.8 million in compensatory damages for breach of contract and fraud and $11.8 billion in punitive damages. However, the punitive damages were reduced to $3.5 billion by the trial judge. (The case was still being appealed by Exxon in 2007. Strikingly, however, Exxon did not contest the jury's finding that it had engaged in fraudulent practices.)

PUNITIVE DAMAGES TEND TO BE MODEST AND IN PROPORTION TO COMPENSATORY DAMAGES

The BJS/NCSC study found that in 2001 the median punitive award was only $50,000. In comparison, after adjustments for inflation, the median award in 1992 was $63,000. One study of Florida verdicts found that the median punitive award was only 70 percent of the compensatory award. A study of twenty-five years of punitive damage awards in product liability trials showed a higher overall ratio of 1.67 to 1, but even then punitive damages were lower than compensatory damages in 36 percent of the verdicts.[22]

Some academic critics have conceded that the proportionality ratios are modest in ordinary cases, but they argue that in "blockbuster" cases involving very large awards, such as the hundreds of millions of dollars awarded in asbestos, cigarette, and business-to-business cases, there is no proportionality. One study by Joni Hersch and Kip Viscusi claimed there was no relationship between compensatory and punitive damages in these cases.[23] However, Ted Eisenberg and Martin Wells challenged their statistical analysis and recalculated the data. Their new statistical analysis found a reliable relationship between compensatory and punitive damages even in the blockbuster cases. More recently, Eisenberg and Wells teamed up with Hans to analyze a combined data set that included compensatory and punitive damage awards from the BJS/NCSC research, the Hersh-Viscusi study of blockbuster awards, and another set of mega-awards compiled by the *National Law Journal*. This integrated dataset provided the most comprehensive picture of American punitive damages to date. The results showed once again a strong, statistically reliable relationship exists between compensatory and punitive damages.[24]

JURIES VERSUS JUDGES

Although many critics would prefer to eliminate punitive damages altogether, others argue that, at minimum, punitive assessment should be made by judges. The ostensible reasons are similar to the arguments discussed earlier in reference to compensatory damages: judges have more training and experience that allow them to make more reasoned judgments. It turns out that between 18 and 20 percent of disputes are tried before judges rather than juries. Of course, the problem is that these cases are often, for various reasons, different than the one tried before juries. Bearing this difference in mind, Eisenberg and his colleagues compared a sample of 101 judge awards with 438 jury awards. Sophisticated statistical analyses attempted to control for differences in the types of cases.[25] The findings revealed that juries and judges awarded about the same amount of punitive damages per dollar of compensatory damages. Eisenberg and associates concluded that there was "no substantial evidence that judges and juries behave differently in any meaningful and systematic manner." Similarly, Thomas Eaton and his coauthors studied over twenty-five thousand civil cases filed in Georgia state courts and, after controlling for differences, concluded that juries were not more likely than judges to give punitive damages.[26] While we can't be sure that these studies controlled for all of the differences in the cases tried before judges versus juries—they probably have not—the overall picture is one of similarity rather than difference.

Jennifer Robbennolt used a different approach to study the issue.[27] She persuaded eighty-seven federal and state trial judges to render decisions in several variations of a lawsuit and compared the results to the decisions of 140 jury-eligible citizens who responded to the identical lawsuits. She found that the decision making of judges and citizens was quite similar. Both actual and potential injury influenced both groups. When the defendant's actions were perceived to be more offensive to expected standards of behavior, both judges and juries awarded more damages.

SUMMARY PERSPECTIVE ON THE EVIDENCE

In a separate article, Robbennolt reviewed the body of empirical research on juries and punitive damages. Her conclusion provides a clear summary to the empirical research:

> [T]he research examining the processes by which jurors determine punitive damages suggests that jurors take into account important characteristics of the cases in making their punitive damages awards . . . [J]urors do not appear to make decisions that clearly differ from the decisions that judges would make, certainly not to the dramatic extent that most critics of the jury would suggest.[28]

UNDERSTANDING WHY: THE TRIAL PROCESS

Because the empirical facts about punitive damages so strongly contradict the claims about incompetent juries, it is important to explore the trial process that leads—or doesn't lead—to these awards. The first part of a trial involving punitive damages is similar to any other civil trial except that in the voir dire process and opening statements, the jurors ordinarily learn that punitive damages will be requested. During the trial, the jurors will hear evidence about the case and reach a decision about liability and compensatory damages. Only if the plaintiff prevails on liability and compensation does the jury consider punitive damages. States differ in the way the trial proceeds on the punitive damages issue. Some states conduct the trial in a single phase. In these states, in addition to liability and compensatory damages, the verdict form asks whether punitive damages are appropriate and, if so, how much should be awarded. Other states use a bifurcated procedure. The verdict form asks only whether punitive damages should be awarded. If the jury says yes, a second stage of the trial begins and it is devoted entirely to punitive damages.

The jury instructions on punitive damages define the legal conditions necessary to award punitive damages. In personal injury cases, the instructions usually specify the punitive damages must be awarded only if the jury finds "wanton and willful conduct." The conduct must be under "circumstances which show that [he/she/corporate officials] was/were aware from . . . knowledge of existing conditions that it is probable that the injury would result from [the] acts and omissions, and nevertheless proceeded with reckless indifference as to the consequences and without care for the rights of others."[29] A standard instruction for "fraud" says it is "an intentional misrepresentation, deceit or concealment of a material fact known to the defendant with the intention on the part of the defendant of thereby depriving a person of property or legal rights or otherwise causing injury."[30]

Most courts set a higher level of proof for punitive damages than the "preponderance of evidence" standard used to determine liability for compensatory damages. Instead, the jury is instructed that it needs to find "clear and convincing evidence" that the legal conditions are met.[31] In deciding the amount of the award, the jury is typically instructed that while there is no fixed standard, it should assess the "reprehensibility of the conduct" and "the amount of damages that will have a deterrent effect on the defendant in the light of the defendant's financial condition." The jury is further instructed that the punitive award "must bear a reasonable relation to the injury, harm or damage [actually] suffered by the plaintiff."[32]

In making their decisions, the jurors have the benefit of having seen or heard, over a period of days or weeks of trial, documents and testimonial evidence bearing on the conduct of the defendant. The evidence the plaintiff may present includes incriminating documents, calculated behaviors, clear warnings about the dangers of conduct—and possibly the economic worth of the defendant. To counter the plaintiff's evidence, the defendant may cross-examine or otherwise dispute the evidence and produce counter-evidence, including expert testimony. In closing statements both sides can present arguments about the appropriateness and amount of awards.

THE FACTS AND OUTCOME OF THE McDONALD'S COFFEE SPILL CASE

On the surface it seems absurd that a woman who spilled coffee on her lap should end up with a $2.7 million punitive award.[33] Surely this must be a case of an irresponsible jury. However, most people only know about the jury verdict of this famous case, not the facts involved in the litigation. William Haltom and Michael McCann have thoroughly documented all of the facts.[34]

In 1992, seventy-nine-year-old Stella Liebeck ordered a cup of coffee at a McDonald's drive-through in Albuquerque, New Mexico. The car was not moving, but the coffee spilled into her lap. Mrs. Liebeck suffered third-degree burns to her thighs, buttocks, genitals, and groin area (about 6 percent of her body) and lesser burns on 16 percent of her body that left permanent scars. She was in the hospital for over a week; her injuries required a vascular surgeon; eventually she was forced to undergo a series of very painful skin grafts. The surgeon reported that Liebeck's injuries resulted in one of the worst burn cases from hot liquids that he had ever seen. Mrs. Liebeck, a conservative Republican, had never been involved in a lawsuit and did not immediately consult a lawyer. Rather, she sent a letter of grievance to McDonald's corporate office acknowledging that she had spilled the coffee but claiming there was no warning about the danger of the product. She asked McDonald's to reevaluate its coffee temperature and to check the coffee machine to determine if it was faulty, reevaluate its standards for coffee temperature, and to pay her approximately $20,000 in medical expenses that were not entirely covered by Medicare. In reply, McDonald's offered Mrs. Liebeck $800.

Only then did Liebeck consult a lawyer, one who had settled a prior coffee burn case against McDonald's for $27,000. The lawyer asked McDonald's for $90,000 for Liebeck's medical bills plus pain and suffering. McDonald's refused and made no counteroffer. Mrs. Liebeck then filed a lawsuit, but she still offered to settle, albeit the nominal ante was upped to $300,000. The case went before a mediator who recommended a settlement of $225,000. Again McDonald's refused to negotiate a settlement.

When the case went to trial, Mrs. Liebeck did not dispute that she had spilled the coffee on herself. Two medical experts testified about the effects of burns, including the facts that 190-degree coffee can cause third-degree burns that can penetrate through the skin into the underlying fat, muscle, and bone. Only seven seconds of exposure, not enough time to wipe the liquid off or remove clothing, can produce the burns. Liebeck's lawyer charged that McDonald's failed to comply with industry standards. Trial evidence showed that McDonald's coffee manual instructions said to make the coffee at 195–205 degrees and serve it at 180–190 degrees. Most coffee in restaurants and home coffeemakers is served at 160 degrees. McDonald's claimed its coffee tasted better at this high temperature. Other evidence showed that most customers were unaware of the hazards of such hot coffee. Moreover, McDonald's had received over seven hundred complaints about its hot coffee, had paid out over $750,000 in previous claims, and had never once consulted a burn specialist. Finally, a witness for McDonald's dismissed the dangers, said the claims were statistically irrelevant, but admitted that he had seen photos of previous coffee burns from claimants. He further testified that McDonald's had no current plan to change its coffee standards.

The trial was held in two stages. In the first stage, the jury found for Mrs. Liebeck and awarded her $200,000 for compensatory damages. However, it also found Mrs. Liebeck was 20 percent responsible for the accident, thus reducing these damages to $160,000. The second stage involved punitive damages. Mrs. Liebeck's lawyer noted that McDonald's sold over a billion cups of coffee each year and generated daily revenues of $1.35 million. He argued that two days worth of coffee revenues was a sufficient and reasonable punitive award. The jury agreed and rendered its verdict of $2.7 million.

But here is the additional point that is ignored in the scorn associated with Mrs. Liebeck's award. Following the verdict, the trial judge reviewed the evidence and in his judgment reduced the punitive award to $480,000. Eventually the case settled for an undisclosed sum, reportedly for a fraction of the $480,000 judgment. And McDonald's coffee is now sold at temperatures similar to those used by other restaurants. Very arguably, rather than a symbol of jury injustice, the McDonald's case might be seen as the symbol of the desirable deterrent value of punitive damages in tort law.

JUDICIAL OVERSIGHT AND POSTVERDICT SETTLEMENTS

The judge's reduction of the McDonald's award draws attention to a largely overlooked factor in the debate about punitive damages. In both *BMW* and *State Farm* the US Supreme Court made it clear that judges had a duty to review the punitive damages in accordance with the criteria enunciated in those cases. Critics of punitive damages conveniently tend to ignore that fact. Recall that the trial judge in *State Farm* reduced the original punitive award to $25 million. To be sure, after a thorough review of the facts of the case, the Utah Supreme Court decided the original award was correct and reinstated it. As we know, the US Supreme Court disagreed with that decision as it reiterated the *BMW* guidelines. One lesson is that judges, even groups of judges, can disagree, but the other lesson is that jury awards do receive judicial scrutiny. Each state provides its own standards for judicial review, and many existed before *BMW* was decided. Judges may reduce awards that show "passion or prejudice" or that "shock the conscience." A number of research studies have shown that punitive damages are in fact often reduced.[35]

Finally, even if punitive awards are not reduced by the trial judge, studies have shown that some punitive damages cases are settled for compensatory damages only, and in others, the settlement results in a greatly reduced payment.[36]

THE EXXON STUDIES

The findings reported above contradict the claims made in the book *Punitive Damages: How Jurors Decide*, mentioned at the beginning of the chapter, that concluded that juries are not competent to decide punitive damages. The authors of the Exxon Corporation's research are respected scholars who undertook a series of simulation studies involving various issues related to juries' punitive damage decisions. Some of the studies yield interesting insights about some of the decision processes that jurors may engage in, but they have a number of deficiencies in both experimental design and legal relevance. One of this book's authors (Vidmar) and other scholars have drawn attention to major problems with those experiments and their authors' conclusions about real jury behavior.[37]

Some of the experiments involved short summaries—most ranged between eight and twenty sentences—of cases involving people who had been injured. The mock jurors in the experiments were told that compensatory damages had already been awarded to the plaintiff. Their task was only to award punitive damages. The summaries described the allegations from the perspective of the plaintiff, without rebuttal evidence from the defendant. Then, the simulating jurors were asked to make decisions based on these summaries. With minimal instruction on the relevant law, the mock jurors were asked to specify the amount of punitive damages that they believed was appropriate. No other information was given about the rich factual context out of which the disputes arose, nor did the subjects have an opportunity to compare their individual views with those of other subjects.

Another experiment involved over three thousand jury-eligible people formed into five hundred six-person deliberating juries. The authors further reported that the individual jurors viewed a videotaped narration of one of a number of personal injury trials read by a professional actor. Then approximately half of the people were asked to make a personal judgment on an eight-point scale of the degree to which the defendant should be punished, while the remainder were asked instead to assess an amount of damages that the defendant should be required to pay. Next, they were assigned to six-person groups and asked to reach a unanimous decision on the judgment they had just made individually, either responding on the eight-point scale or awarding dollars. During deliberations, subjects were required to reach their decision in thirty minutes.

Based on these and similar experiments, the authors concluded that their data showed that jurors were reasonably consistent in rating the reprehensibility of the defendant's behavior but very erratic in awarding dollar amounts for that behavior.

It should be obvious that the experiments did not take into consideration the complex trial settings out of which real juries reach their decisions. Juries in real punitive damages cases hear all of the evidence, first decide on liability, and next decide on compensatory damages. Then they see documents and are given detailed instructions on the burden of proof necessary to award punitive damages.

The lawyers for the defendant are allowed to present evidence and arguments favoring a lower award or no award at all. Thus, the context of the task in the simulating juries was very different in significant ways from that of real juries. Moreover, in drawing conclusions that juries were erratic and unreliable, the authors of the research ignored many studies of real juries, some of which we have reported here, that contradicted their findings.

MARLBOROS AND THE MIND OF A JURY

A case recently before the US Supreme Court forms the third leg of a trilogy of cases on legal review of punitive damages that include *BMW* and *State Farm*. The case, *Philip Morris v. Williams*, highlights many of the points of controversy about punitive damages and provides insight into the mind of the jury that rendered the verdict.[38]

Jesse Williams, an African American retired school custodian from Portland, Oregon, was a devoted husband and father of six children. He smoked Marlboro cigarettes, as many as three packs a day, for forty-seven years. His wife and children had continually urged him to quit the habit with entreaties about the dangers of smoking. He regularly resisted these efforts by arguing that the cigarette companies said they were safe. Jesse Williams developed inoperable lung cancer. After his diagnosis, his wife later testified, he said, "Those darned cigarette companies lied to me." He died six months later at age sixty-seven.

The Trial

Mayola Williams sued Philip Morris on behalf of her husband's estate and asked for compensatory and punitive damages. The case went to trial in 1999. The lawsuit admitted an unspecified degree of comparative negligence on Mr. Williams's part and left it to the jury to decide his degree of fault. The punitive damages portion of the lawsuit focused on Philip Morris's forty-year practice of denying that cigarette smoking was dangerous to health. Evidence at trial attempted to show the effects of the company's advertising and denial of health dangers on all Oregon smokers. Plaintiff lawyers were careful in their evidence and final arguments to the jury to limit the claim to Oregon in order to comply with the US Supreme Court's rulings in *BMW* and *State Farm*.

Mrs.Williams's evidence at trial included many internal company documents that did not put Philip Morris in a very good light. Her lawyers argued that the company knew of the potential health risks for fifty years but knowingly hid the information from the public. In 1952 a *Reader's Digest* article reported new research linking smoking with cancer, causing cigarette sales to fall. Trial evidence indicated that Philip Morris and other tobacco companies began an advertising campaign with a publication titled "A Frank Statement to Smokers" sent to 448 newspapers throughout the United States. It asserted that "the products we make are not injurious to health" and ridiculed "experiments with mice." Philip Morris, along with other tobacco companies, later set up the Council for Tobacco Research that they trumpeted would conduct research into "all phases of tobacco and health." Evidence indicated, however, that the council's real purpose was to offer alternative explanations for the epidemic of lung cancer among smokers.

Yet at a 1953 meeting of company executives one official admitted, "It's fortunate for us that cigarettes are a habit they can't break." In 1958 only one of thirty-two scientists from the tobacco industry was not convinced that "smoking causes lung cancer." Also in 1958, Philip Morris's research chief wrote a memo acknowledging that evidence "is building up that heavy cigarette smoking contributes to lung cancer." Despite this knowledge, a company vice president produced another public document saying that Philip Morris would "stop business tomorrow," if the company thought its product was harming smokers, and another spokesperson said that "there was no connection" between smoking and disease, but if there was, Philip Morris "wouldn't be in the business." After the 1964 surgeon general's report on the dangers of smoking, a Philip Morris executive wrote that "we must in the near future . . . give smokers a psychological and self-rationale to continue smoking." In the 1970s Philip Morris publicly denied that nicotine was addictive and falsely denied reports that it manipulated the nicotine content in cigarettes. At the same time internal memos said that "no other rationale is adequate to sustain the habit [of smoking] in the absence of nicotine." Moreover, even as the company switched to lower tar and nicotine cigarettes, a memo gloated that the consequence would be increased cigarette sales because smokers would have to purchase more to feed their need for nicotine.

In its trial defense, Philip Morris downplayed the efficacy of the hundreds of millions of dollars it spent in advertising, despite other internal company memos that claimed a "brilliantly conceived and executed" public relations campaign to defend the company. Their lawyers argued to the twelve-person jury that the case was about the choices that Jesse Williams made and his personal responsibility.

The Verdict and Judgment

Mrs. Williams asked for $100,000 million in punitive damages. Oregon requires agreement of only nine of the twelve jurors for a valid verdict. Three of the jurors were smokers and four were former smokers. After four weeks of trial, the jurors retired to deliberate with piles of notebooks of expert testimony from physicians, addiction specialists, historians, and an expert on growing tobacco, as well as copies of Philip Morris's internal documents. On March 31, 1999, after two and a half days of deliberations, nine of the twelve jurors found that Jesse Williams and Philip Morris were equally negligent in Williams's death and awarded the family

$21,485 for medical expenses and $800,000 for pain and suffering. For the claim that Phillip Morris lied about the link between smoking and disease, the jury awarded $79.5 million in punitive damages. The trial judge found that, based on the trial record, the punitive award was a rational one, but, believing that the award was "excessive under federal standards," reduced it to $32 million.

The Jurors Explain

Several of the jurors explained their verdict to Portland's *Oregonian*.[39] Juror April Dewees, a high school science teacher, was quoted as saying that she and other jurors "were upset by documents that showed Philip Morris apparently knew about the addictive properties and cancer-causing potential of cigarette smoke but avoided telling its customers." Additionally, Dewees said that she thought that the company over the years discovered the disease-causing potential of cigarettes, but, rather than warning customers, the company executives decided to "keep going until they couldn't go any further." Juror Debra Barton agreed with Dewees, "I'd have to say it was the documents." Dewees was quoted as elaborating further, saying that the jurors "felt that Philip Morris misrepresents the facts and makes it easy for people to have conflicts in their mind about what's really true. I'm not so much bothered by the fact that they put the product out, but the fact that they muddy the water I find unacceptable." In her view the company hid behind semantics and refused to admit that cigarettes are addictive, saying only that some smokers have a difficult time quitting. Dewees reported that jurors were angered by their perception that the company refused to admit that cigarettes cause disease. Dewees was not impressed by Philip Morris's defense. "They want it to be everyone's responsibility, but theirs. That would work if they told the people, 'Yes, this is addictive, and you may be one of those who can't quit.' Are people really making an informed decision when they don't have the information?" Finally, she said, "Of course, Jesse was at fault, but Philip Morris does business with the public and has a responsibility to be forthright about the product."

On the other hand, three jurors opposed awarding punitive damages. Alisa Duffy, a customer service representative, was quoted as saying that "tobacco-makers shouldn't be blamed for an individual's decision to use their product" and found the internal Philip Morris documents unconvincing. She elaborated to the reporters, "This is basically what it boils down to for me: personal responsibility. I don't want to offend any of my fellow jurors—I respect their decision. I just think Philip Morris and the tobacco industry have become an easy target."

The Appeals

Of no surprise, Phillip Morris appealed the verdict. The Oregon Supreme Court thoroughly reviewed the evidence and reinstated the jury's original $79.5 million award. It concluded that Philip Morris "inflicted potential harm on the members of the public in Oregon through its fraudulent promotional scheme." Noting that the jury could have reasonably concluded that Philip Morris's actions were so reprehensible over forty years, the court concluded that it was appropriate to exceed the single-digit ratio set forth in *State Farm*. Additionally, the court ruled that the large award was also appropriate when the defendant's wealth was weighed against the profitability of its conduct over the many decades.

Philip Morris appealed the decision to the US Supreme Court. In February 2007 the Court, in a narrow five-to-four decision, "vacated" the Oregon Supreme Court's decision.[40] It ruled that the jury was improperly instructed on the punitive damages issue. Specifically, it said that a jury may not punish a defendant for harm to other persons (in this case, the other Oregon smokers) who are not part of the lawsuit. To do so violates the Due Process clause of the Constitution. However, at the same time, the decision said that reprehensibility is the main consideration in assessing punitive damages and that the jury may consider "the harm that Phillip Morris was prepared to inflict on the smoking public at large." If this seems puzzling or trivial, Justice Ginsburg and the three other justices who dissented from the opinion thought so as well. They would have upheld the Oregon Supreme Court's decision. In any event, the case was referred back to the Oregon Supreme Court for reconsideration in the light of the new standard. The reconsideration, said the US Supreme Court, could result in a new trial or a change in the amount of the punitive damages. If Mrs. Williams eventually prevails and receives the original punitive award or some lesser amount, 60 percent of the money will go to the state's Victim Compensation Fund. Mrs. Williams and her lawyers will receive the balance.

The lesson from the *Philip Morris* case is that the Supreme Court recognizes that juries have a crucial role in deciding punitive damages, but that judges disagree about the instructions they should be given and the constraints that should be placed on their verdicts.

CONCLUDING PERSPECTIVE

Jury punitive damage awards will probably remain controversial, but they are likely to remain part of our legal landscape, even if the US Supreme Court imposes further restrictions on the punitive to compensatory damages ratios or if it further modifies how juries can decide. Interestingly, in the 1980s a survey of business executives found many in favor of punitive damages for business disputes involving egregious behavior.[41] Elected legislators in various states have approved punitive damages, and in Oregon and elsewhere, appellate courts have affirmed jury verdicts. The empirical evidence indicates that juries perform reasonably well and that judges have been shown to exercise their supervisory powers over errant verdicts.

Chapter 16

JURIES AND MEDICAL MALPRACTICE

Antidoctor, Incompetent, and Irresponsible?

> The jury system seems to show a desire for punitive [action] and retribution above and beyond the degree of injury—"let's get the rich doctor."
>
> North Carolina Plastic Surgery Society (1986)

> Problems with medical malpractice juries include decisions that are not based on a thorough understanding of the medical facts and awards that increase at an alarming rate and in a fashion that seems uniquely to disadvantage physicians as compared with other individuals who have acted negligently.
>
> American Medical Association Task Force (1988)

> The primary cause of the growing liability crisis is the unrestrained escalation in jury awards that are a part of a legal system that in many states is simply out of control.
>
> American Medical Association (2003)[1]

For more than three decades, the jury has been at the center of a major controversy about medical malpractice lawsuits and their subsequent impact on the medical profession. Beginning in 1975 and at eight- to ten-year intervals, the professional liability insurance premiums for medical malpractice have spiked sharply upward, causing considerable distress to doctors, hospitals, and other healthcare providers. While scholars, such as Tom Baker,[2] and other commentators have argued that the jump in medical malpractice insurance rates are due to fluctuations in the insurance business cycle and other causes, doctors and business groups assert that the problem is due to rapacious plaintiff lawyers who file frivolous lawsuits—and to the juries that decide medical malpractice cases. Juries, as the above quotations from medical sources indicate, are alleged to be antidoctor, incompetent, gullible, confused by plaintiff experts, swayed by sympathies for sick or injured patients, and irresponsible in awarding extravagant damage awards.

An examination of these claims requires a brief survey of the context out of which malpractice claims arise and the percentage of all malpractice lawsuits decided by juries.

THE MALPRACTICE CONTEXT

Incidence of Malpractice

In 1990 a groundbreaking Harvard study of medical negligence examined hospital records of thirty-one thousand patients and concluded that one out of every one hundred patients admitted to a hospital had an actionable legal claim based on medical negligence.[3] Some of these patients' injuries were minor or transient, but 14 percent of the time the adverse event had resulted in death, and 10 percent of the time the incident resulted in hospitalization for more than six months. Generally, the Harvard Study concluded, the more serious the injury, the more likely it was caused by negligence.[4] In 2000 the Institute of Medicine produced a report that relied on these studies and other data.[5] The report concluded that each year, ninety-eight thousand people die and that many other patients sustain serious injuries due to medical negligence. In 2004, HealthGrades, Inc., a company that rates hospitals on healthcare for insurance companies and health plans, studied Medicare records in all fifty states for the years 2000 to 2002 and stated that a better estimate was 195,000 annual deaths.[6] In 2005 HealthGrades upped the figure to over two hundred and fifty thousand people.[7] In short, medical negligence is a serious problem.

THE COSTS OF MEDICAL INJURIES DUE TO NEGLIGENCE

In 1989 economists Frank Sloan and Stephen van Wert conducted systematic assessments of economic losses (medical costs, income losses, and other expenses) in a sample of claims of medical negligence occurring as a result of birth-related and emergency room incidents.[8] Adjusted to 2007 dollars, the average loss in these cases was approximately $2.4 million. Economic losses for people who survived an emergency room incident were estimated at $2.2 million, and for people who died in an emergency room incident the loss to their survivors was estimated at $0.9 million. There was substantial variability in these estimated averages: some patients had much higher economic losses, and, conversely, others had lesser losses.

THE FREQUENCY OF LAWSUITS, JURY TRIALS, AND OUTCOMES

There is a widespread public belief that injured patients sue at the drop of a hat. In fact, the opposite seems to be true. One of the most striking findings from the Harvard medical negligence study is that only one out of eight people experiencing a serious injury due to medical negligence filed a claim.[9] To be sure, claims were also filed in cases in which the research team of healthcare providers concluded that there was no negligence. However, the bottom line is that for every doctor or hospital charged with a claim where no negligence was found, there were many more valid claims that were not filed.[10] Why not? There are a number of reasons.[11] One reason is that some patients never discover that negligence led to their bad outcome; they ascribe it to the illness or injury that caused them to seek medical help in the first place. Another is that, because of their personal relationship with the doctor, they forgive the negligence. A third reason is that they cannot find a lawyer willing to take the case; lawyers find many cases too difficult and expensive to litigate. Most plaintiff lawyers work on a contingency fee basis in which they get a percentage of the plaintiff's recovery. Malpractice litigation is complex, and paying for testifying medical experts is very costly—experts and other litigation costs can range from $100,000 or even triple that amount. Almost always, the lawyer advances the money to pay these costs. If the plaintiff recovers nothing in the lawsuit, the lawyer will not only lose that money but the many days of her own time devoted to the case. As a result, lawyers carefully screen cases before agreeing to take them. If a patient has a valid claim but the potential damage recovery is too small, lawyers cannot afford to take the case.

Only about 7 percent of medical malpractice lawsuits are eventually tried by juries. Most cases are settled without a jury trial. Most payments made to plaintiffs following medical negligence are a result of private negotiations resulting in settlements with the plaintiff. This statistic applies even to cases in which plaintiffs receive awards of a million dollars or more. Nevertheless, in absolute numbers, juries decide a large number of cases. In 2001, the latest year for which there were figures, the US Bureau of Justice Statistics estimated that in the nation's seventy-five largest counties, there were over 1,100 malpractice cases tried before juries.[12] In these trials, plaintiffs won only 26 percent of the time, that is, about one case out of four. (In some jurisdictions, the plaintiff win rate is closer to only one case out of five.) However, when plaintiffs did win, the median award was $422,000, and in 16 percent of the cases the award equaled or exceeded $1 million. This is well above the median awards in most other types of cases.

Most states forbid punitive damages in medical malpractice cases except in instances of gross malfeasance, such as sexual assaults on patients, or the fraudulent altering of the medical records.[13] The Bureau of Justice Statistics indicates that punitive damages were awarded in 4 percent of medical malpractice cases.

JURY VERDICTS, "SHADOW EFFECTS," AND "PAIN AND SUFFERING"

Why are juries so controversial in the medical malpractice debate if they decide only a small percentage of cases and if, even in those cases, they side with the doctors 75 to 80 percent of the time? The answer offered by jury critics is that the jury verdicts and awards set the standard around which settlements are negotiated. This is referred to as the "shadow effect." Doctors' fear of an unjustified mega-award, it is said, drives them to settle some cases in which there is no liability and settle other cases for more than the cases are worth. Moreover, critics argue that "pain and suffering" rather than medical care and lost income constitute the major portion of the mega-awards. Some critics have asserted that pain and suffering constitutes as much as 90 percent of the verdict. These critics also say that juries have continuously inflated awards over the years, and they claim that jury verdicts are capricious, resulting in some patients not getting what they are due while others get undeserved and excessive awards.

We need to examine these claims carefully, and the best way to start is to consider some selected examples of cases with serious injuries that went to trial.

JURY TRIAL ISSUES: SOME CASE EXAMPLES

There is no prototypical medical malpractice trial. Some recent examples from Illinois and Pennsylvania, however, illustrate the kinds of issues that juries consider.[14] Keep in mind, as we have already discussed, that plaintiffs win only between 20 and 25 percent of trials. Four examples in which the plaintiff prevailed are included because these are the types of cases that evoke the criticism of juries. A final example resulted in a defense win, but the plaintiff received some money anyway. We have retained some of the medical terminology in these examples because jurors are faced with such terminology at trial. To be sure, if the lawyers and their experts do their job properly, the jurors will learn what these terms mean and what role they play in the dispute about negligence.

Cerebral Palsy

On Thanksgiving a woman entered a hospital to deliver her first baby. She was placed on an external fetal monitor. After a short time, the monitor showed variable decelerations in the heart rate of the fetus for over two hours. At trial the mother claimed that despite these signs of distress, the obstetrical nurses allowed the obstetrician to use the only available operating room for another patient's nonemergency tubal ligation. The fetal monitor readings showed further deterioration until the nurses noted a prolapsed umbilical cord that was depriving the baby of oxygen and blood flow to the brain. There was a twenty-minute delay to ready an operating room and assemble personnel for an emergency cesarean delivery, but by then the baby had suffered permanent brain damage. Twelve years old at the time of trial, the child had cerebral palsy, spastic quadriparesis, no bowel or bladder control, and the inability to walk or talk. The defense contended that the child had a preexisting condition of "inflammatory response syndrome" (an infection of the whole body without a proven source of infection) that was responsible for his condition. Three medical experts and one economist testified for the plaintiff. Three experts testified for the defense. The jury awarded $12,500,000: $5 million for past and future loss of a normal life, $3,750,000 for future medical expenses, $1,120,000 for loss of earnings, $1 million for past and future pain and suffering, $1 million for disfigurement, $450,000 for the father's services in caring for the child at home, and $180,000 for past medical expenses.

A Leg Amputation

In 1997 a Polish immigrant, age sixty, living in Illinois, was treated for recurrent thrombosis (blood clot) by means of a Gortex bypass graft in her femoral artery. In 1999 the graft clotted, requiring a thromboidectomy (surgical removal of the clot). Following this operation, the patient was instructed to stop smoking, lower her cholesterol, take medication to reduce her high blood pressure, and take an anticoagulant to prevent further bypass clotting. The patient did not comply with these instructions, and another blood clot occurred. The defendant surgeon conducted two more thromboidectomies, but they failed, and the woman's leg was amputated above the knee. At trial the plaintiff's expert contended that the standard of care required that the surgeon should have harvested the plaintiff's saphenous vein and performed a new bypass from her femoral artery to her tibial artery. The defense contended that the standard of care did not require a new bypass: the Gortex graft was appropriate, the success rates of the Gortex graft were no different from those of saphenous vein bypasses, and the patient's noncompliance with medical instructions was the causal factor in her amputation. The jury awarded the plaintiff a total of $590,000 for loss of a normal life and disfigurement.

A Fatal Heart Attack

In May 1998, a fifty-four-year-old Pennsylvania draftsman was brought by ambulance to a hospital and admitted with tightening of the chest, angina symptoms, shortness of breath, cold sweating, and a history of coronary disease. The attending cardiologist ordered a stress test, concluded that the patient's condition was stable, and deduced that many of the symptoms were due to the patient's asthma. The patient was discharged two days later with instructions to follow up with his personal cardiologist. The cardiologist performed an angiogram, which showed significant occlusion and blockage of arteries, but he did not recommend surgery and instead treated the patient with medication. The patient, a married father of seven children, suffered a heart attack in August that led to his death in September. The plaintiff's estate sued the hospital cardiologist, contending that he should have told the patient that he was at increased risk for death, that the stress test was markedly abnormal, and that he needed an angiogram. The defendant testified that he did not recall what he told the man, claimed it was his practice to review stress test findings with patients, and admitted he did not tell the man he was at risk and needed a heart catheterization to further determine the extent of the coronary disease. The defendant also maintained that the patient indicated he wanted all future care to be done at a different hospital with his personal cardiologist, but this was not documented in the hospital records. One expert testified for the plaintiff and one testified for the defendant. The jury awarded the plaintiff's estate $500,000. His personal cardiologist and the hospital were dismissed from the lawsuit before trial after the former offered a settlement of $975,000 and the latter offered $175,000.

Quadriplegia

A Pennsylvania man in his mid-forties suffered severe back pain and was advised that he should undergo surgery to relieve spinal compression. During the operation, the surgeon was advised by a specialist, who was monitoring motor-evoked potentials, that the motor signals to the spinal cord had been lost. Nevertheless, the surgeon continued with the operation, decompressing the spinal cord, and fusing a section of the cervical spine with metal hardware and a bone grafted from the patient's hip. The patient arrived in the recovery room paralyzed and quadriplegic. Postoperative imaging taken on the day of surgery suggested persistent compression of the man's spinal cord in the region of the surgery, consisting of the presence of bone fragments or spicules within the spinal canal, which were compressed and had flattened the spinal cord. The surgeon again operated on the man, this time to decompress the spinal cord in the area of the prior surgery, but the man remained paralyzed. He suffers permanent pain and depression and is totally restricted in the activities of daily life. He is subject to infections and deterioration of tissues and is unemployable.

The patient sued the surgeon, the assisting surgeon, and the hospital. Before trial the parties reached an agreement that in the event of a plaintiff's verdict, the damages would be capped at $3 million. Furthermore, the parties agreed that if there was a defense verdict $1 million would be paid to the plaintiff. The jury verdict was $2 million.

Permanent Blindness

A woman entered the emergency room of a hospital with complaints of severe headache and blurry vision. She was diagnosed with sinusitis. Her personal physician was contacted, and he prescribed an antibiotic and Tylenol #3 by phone. She continued to get worse. The doctor advised her to discontinue the Tylenol and make an office visit the next day. Instead, two days later the woman went to the emergency room at a different hospital and was diagnosed with a blood clot that resulted in strangulation of the optic nerves. The plaintiff is now totally blind and needs a seeing eye dog. She sued the emergency room doctors at the first hospital. The physicians who treated her at the second hospital and other medical experts testified at trial that had she been correctly diagnosed earlier, her vision would have been saved. The jury found both defendants not liable. We cannot be sure, of course, but we can speculate that the woman's failure to make the recommended office visit contributed to the defense verdict. Our earlier discussion about liability and compensation pointed out that juries sometimes look skeptically at plaintiffs who do not take actions that could have mitigated an injury. (Despite the verdict, the defendant's insurer eventually paid the woman $200,000.)

INSIGHTS FROM THE EXAMPLES

Medical malpractice plaintiffs seek medical treatment for an illness or injury. When they, or their estates (if the patient died), sue a healthcare provider, the jury has to decide whether the treatment they received—or did not receive—was consistent with prevailing standards of medical care. However, in addition, the jury must also determine whether the injury was the "proximate cause" of the injury or whether the injury was the result of the patient's underlying condition or an unavoidable risk of proper treatment. Juries are aided in these determinations by the medical experts who testify at trial. The "standard of medical care" differs from the "reasonable person" test by which most other negligence is judged. Since juries are composed of laypeople, medical experts are needed to instruct them on the standard of care. The standard of care varies by medical specialty. A general practitioner may be held to a lesser standard than a specialist treating the same condition. Often the medical experts who testify disagree about whether the standard of care was violated. The jury is usually aided by the patient's medical records, which are supposed to document all actions taken by health providers, including what the patient was told. It is, however, not unusual for information to be missing from the records, perhaps only because a busy doctor failed to make complete notations.

The Illinois and Pennsylvania research yields some other insights. Because medical care today often involves a team approach to treatment, it is not unusual, indeed, it is common, for lawsuits to have multiple defendants, including a hospital. (Many malpractice cases revolve around issues of different healthcare providers failing to communicate with one another over the course of a treatment.) The juries in these studies sometimes found one or more parties liable but decided other doctors were not liable. This shows that juries do not make wholesale judgments against all defendants but rather make distinctions between them based on the trial evidence.

Sometimes the jury receives only part of the full story during trial. If some defendants "settle out," as in the example of the patient who died of a heart attack, they may not testify, and jurors are rarely told why they did not testify. Consequently, the jurors have to infer what role, if any, the other healthcare providers played in the injury. Jurors are also not told about prior agreements to settle cases for a certain amount, as in the case of the Pennsylvania man who became quadriplegic.

The jury may be aided in the determination of damage awards through the expert testimony of economists or life care specialists who testify about the expected future healthcare needs of the plaintiff and the costs associated with this care. Defendants may provide their own experts who offer testimony that favors their version of the case. Previous research on medical malpractice trials indicated that defendants often choose to not call experts to testify about damages but, instead, restrict their trial strategy to vigorous cross-examination of the plaintiff's experts. There are two main and interrelated reasons for this choice. Doctors and hospitals contest the case on the issue of liability. Defense lawyers believe that if they present experts to counter the plaintiff's experts on damages, the jury will perceive the defense as admitting liability. In these frequent instances, the jury does not have the advantage of comparative opinions on the amount of damages. In one striking example, jurors who decided for the plaintiff in the case of serious birth injury expressed concern that the estimates of the plaintiff's experts regarding future medical care were too high, but they followed the judge's instructions to decide the case only on the trial evidence and used the plaintiff's estimate in awarding damages. In these instances the jury should not be blamed if the award seems excessive, since they are following the law. Besides, as we will explain shortly, the final payments paid by the doctors and hospitals are often much less than the jury's verdict.

Deciding which side should prevail in a medical malpractice trial is a difficult task. There is often no absolutely correct answer to a medical malpractice claim. Both sides can muster medical experts to testify that the treatment did or did not deviate from the standard of care and was or was not a proximate cause of harm. Even if the case was decided by a judge or a panel of experts, there would often be serious grounds for disagreement or even minority reports.

A number of studies have examined rates of agreement among medical professionals as to whether malpractice occurred. In one study, medical experts disagreed about negligent medical error in 30 percent of ratings.[15] Another study involving anesthesiologists found that disagreement rates among medical professionals increased with the seriousness of the injury.[16] A recent study published in the *New England Journal of Medicine*, and discussed in more detail below, found that medical professionals expressed high confidence in their judgments of medical error in 44 percent of over 1,400 cases and moderate levels of confidence in 30 percent of the cases, but in 23 percent of the cases the professionals rated them as "close calls; that is, the experts could not agree on whether negligence had occurred."[17] In short, doctors often disagree about whether medical negligence occurred. The jury has to decide which doctor is most likely correct.

The central questions about jury performance, therefore, are relative ones. But, as the quotes that began this chapter indicate, juries have been charged with a number of serious faults. Among them are the following: damage awards are increasing at an alarming rate and in amounts that cannot be justified; juries are biased against doctors and hospitals and in recent decades have increasingly favored injured plaintiffs; juries often give awards to plaintiffs out of sympathy for their plight, even if there is no evidence of negligence; there is a "deep pockets" effect where jurors give larger awards against doctors because they assume that doctors can more easily afford to pay the costs of the injury; juries are not competent to decide the complex technical issues in medical negligence cases and are often confused by the testimony of experts, particularly "hired gun" experts; and juries evaluate the expert evidence on legally irrelevant dimensions.[18]

So, how well do juries perform in deciding these difficult cases?

AGREEMENT BETWEEN HEALTH PROFESSIONALS AND JURIES IN MEDICAL MALPRACTICE CASES

In 1989 authors associated with the American Medical Association proposed the use of administrative tribunals composed of doctors to settle medical malpractice cases.[19] They described the challenges, which often require fact finders to make judgments about the cause of an injury in the face of substantial uncertainty, and which force laypeople to judge a question upon which experts disagree: "Lay juries are ill-equipped to resolve the arcane issues involved. . . . Even under the best of circumstances, juries can never be as effective as specialized triers of fact at deciding malpractice cases because jurors are exposed to the medical issues only once; consequently, they cannot develop an institutional memory to aid them in deciding a specific dispute."[20] The claim appears to be a plausible one, but it rests on a testable empirical assumption, namely that juries decide cases differently than doctors would decide them.

Mark Taragin and his associates conducted a study of 8,231 insurance claims from a major New Jersey doctors' liability insurance company that put these assumptions to a test.[21] Each time a malpractice claim was made against a doctor, the insurance company had its own independent experts review the medical records to assess whether the doctor had been negligent. The purpose of the review was to aid the insurer in deciding whether to contest the claim or try to settle it before trial. The reviewing doctors did not always agree with one another, and in other instances they concluded that the evidence was ambiguous as to whether the doctor had breached the expected standard of medical care. Based on these ratings, the cases were classified as "defensible," "indefensible," and "unclear." In addition to having access to these ratings, the researchers also classified the case according to three levels of injury suffered by the patient: minor, moderate, and severe.

While most cases were settled without a trial, 12 percent, or 988 cases, went to trial and were decided by juries. Taragin and his colleagues compared the jury verdicts against the doctors' ratings of negligence and the research team's ratings of injury severity. The jury verdicts outcomes were positively related to the doctors' ratings. That is, jury verdicts favoring the doctor tended to be ones that had been classified as "defensible," and verdicts favoring the plaintiff tended to be ones classified as "indefensible" or "unclear." In addition, the researchers found that the jury outcome was *not* related to severity of the patient's injury, which strongly suggests that sympathy for the plaintiff did not play a role in the juries' decisions. The correlations between the doctor ratings and jury verdicts were not perfect, but the study generally supported a conclusion that medical malpractice juries are neither incompetent nor generally swayed by sympathies when the plaintiff is severely injured.

In 2006 the *New England Journal of Medicine* published a study by a group of researchers associated with the Harvard School of Public Health that produced results similar to those found in Taragin's study.[22] The team of medically trained personnel systematically examined the medical records and other data from over fourteen hundred randomly chosen closed insurance claims in four different regions of the United States. Ratings were made as to whether the case involved a negligent error or no negligent medical error. Fifteen percent of the claims, or 208 cases, were decided at trial, and in the trials, plaintiffs prevailed only 21 percent of the time, that is, in only about one case in five. Their verdicts were largely consistent with the medical experts' judgments on negligence.

Overall, these two studies indicate that jury verdicts compare very favorably to decisions made by medical professionals. Indeed, it is in line with the substantial judge-jury agreement rate in criminal and civil trials that we documented earlier. Such high agreement also bears on the issue of whether jurors are confused and overwhelmed by the medical evidence. In an earlier chapter we discussed research bearing on how jurors approach expert evidence and concluded that they are not overwhelmed by experts. That appears to be the case in medical malpractice cases as well. We must remember that both sides call experts and each side is permitted to thoroughly cross-examine the other side's experts. The deliberation process, moreover, allows the jury to apply its collective wisdom. If jury confusion over medical evidence was in fact a frequent cause of bad decisions on liability, we would expect greater disagreement between juries and the ratings of medical experts. The studies indicate this does not happen.

THE JURY SYMPATHY ARGUMENT

One of the most persistent claims against juries is that they are swayed in favor of the plaintiff by sympathies. We have already drawn attention to the fact that at trial doctors win about four cases out of five. This statistic by itself seems inconsistent with the assertions that juries tend to tilt toward plaintiffs, since many losing plaintiffs have experienced debilitating injuries or death. Data from the Taragin study, just discussed, are also inconsistent with the sympathy argument: whether the jury decided for or against the plaintiff was not related to the severity of the alleged injury.

Interviews with North Carolina jurors who decided medical malpractice cases led the first author of this book (Vidmar) to the conclusion that many jurors initially viewed the plaintiffs' claims with great skepticism.[23] Their attitudes were expressed in two main themes. First, they said that too many people want to get something for nothing, a skeptical attitude about claiming that we discussed earlier in other contexts. Second, they expressed the belief that most doctors try to do a good job and should not be blamed for a simple human misjudgment. Indeed, these attitudes were even expressed in some of the cases in which jurors decided for the plaintiff. One jury that gave a multimillion-dollar award for a baby with severe brain injuries was very concerned about the possible adverse effect on the doctor's medical practice. This does not mean that in every such case jurors held these views. Sometimes, evidence of the doctor's seemingly careless behavior caused jurors to be angry about what happened. However, even in these latter cases, the interviews indicated that the jurors had initially approached the case with open minds.

NO EVIDENCE SUPPORTING CLAIMS OF A "DEEP POCKETS" EFFECT

Closely related to the claim of jury sympathy is the charge that juries are more likely to render verdicts against doctors and hospitals, not because they are seen as negligent, but because the jurors perceive them as having the ability to pay large awards.[24] In an earlier chapter we described how researchers have not been able to document systematic evidence of a deep pockets mentality in cases with businesses and corporations, and the same appears to be true in the medical context. Vidmar conducted experiments that specifically tested for a deep pockets effect in medical malpractice cases.[25] In a first experiment, 147 people called for jury duty were asked to award damages for pain and suffering in the case of a young woman who suffered a broken leg and resulting complications. For one set of jurors, the cause was ascribed to medical negligence. For other jurors, the cause of the broken leg was described as a motor vehicle accident. There was no statistically significant difference in awards. A second experiment was similar, except that the case involved more severe and permanent injuries. Results again showed no statistically significant difference between awards in the medical malpractice and automobile cases.

VERTICAL AND HORIZONTAL EQUITIES

Professor Michael Saks has used the terms *vertical* and *horizontal* equity to categorize issues related to jury variability.[26] Vertical equity refers to the degree to which jury awards are positively related to the seriousness of the injury. Horizontal equity is the similarity of awards within levels of injury severity.

Randall Bovbjerg and his colleagues found evidence of vertical equity in a sample of medical malpractice cases. The magnitude of jury awards was positively correlated with the severity of the plaintiffs' injuries, except that injuries resulting in death tended to result in awards substantially lower than injuries resulting in severe permanent injury, such as quadriplegia.[27] Another study of malpractice verdicts in New York, Florida, and California also found that jury awards to prevailing plaintiffs in malpractice cases were correlated with the severity of the injury.[28]

Bovbjerg and his colleagues concluded, however, that there was horizontal inequity: damage awards varied considerably within categories of injury severity. This finding raises a question about the reliability of jury verdicts, but, as we discussed in regard to compensatory damages, there is a plausible alternative explanation—that both economic losses and pain and suffering of individuals can differ dramatically even for similar injuries. Research by Frank Sloan and Stephen van Wert supports this reasoning.[29] They closely examined economic losses in samples of Florida malpractice cases involving birth and emergency room injuries. The costs for medical care and anticipated lost income showed great variability with the same level of injury. An earlier study by Patricia Danzon in California also compared the plaintiffs' age, economic loss, and the severity of the injury with jury verdicts.[30] The amounts of the verdicts were consistent with the patients' injuries.

JURY DAMAGE AWARDS HAVE INCREASED, BUT THERE ARE MANY POSSIBLE EXPLANATIONS

The Bureau of Justice Statistics/National Center for State Courts study found that in 2001 the median verdict when plaintiffs prevailed in medical malpractice trials was $431,000, compared to $253,000 in 1992.[31] There are at least five possible reasons for this increase, and they are not mutually exclusive of one another. Juries may have become more generous. Patients may have sustained more serious injuries. Plaintiff lawyers may have become more adept at proving damages by using experts who document economic losses better than in the past. The cost of negligent medical injuries and lost income has increased: during the 1990s medical costs for illnesses and injuries increased by almost 52 percent and in the future there will be more inflation, which must be taken into account in assessing the effects of long-term disability and illness. Claims tried before juries in 2001 may have involved more serious injuries than in 1992; as a consequence, juries may be deciding different cases rather than deciding cases differently.

Since these alternative explanations are quite plausible and consistent with other findings—including findings that jury awards are positively related to injuries and economic losses—the burden of proof seems to lie with those who claim the increases in awards are inappropriate.

POSTVERDICT ADJUSTMENTS

The fact that the jury verdict is not the end of litigation is often overlooked in discussions of the role of the jury. This is especially true of medical malpractice trials. Consider these examples from Illinois.[32]

Waliczek v. Ghandhigutta and Alexian Brothers Medical Center involved the death of a forty-seven-year-old construction worker who was hospitalized following a construction accident. The man had multiple fractures in his arms, wrists, and legs, bleeding in the stomach, and a small amount of bleeding in the brain. The plaintiff's estate contended that the man was administered the blood-thinning agent, heparin, that was intended for another patient. The defendants disputed both negligence and causation. On June 28, 2001, the jury rendered a verdict of $6,500,000. However, the case settled for $800,000.

Skonieczny v. Gardner, Northwest Professional Obstetrics and Gynecology, Levy and Northwest Community Hospital concerned a claim that a brachial plexus injury during delivery resulted in permanent loss of the use of a child's left arm and shoulder plus the likelihood of future arthritis and pain. The plaintiff claimed that the obstetrician applied excessive traction to the baby's head and that hospital nurses inappropriately pushed down on the mother's stomach during delivery. The jury awarded $13,298,052, but defendant Levy was found not liable. Defendants Gardner and Northwest Professional each had a $1 million liability policy, and the plaintiff settled for those amounts. Thus, the Skonieczny child and parents ended up with $2 million, not $13 million.

Large awards get the attention of the public, causing concern about such outlier awards. Many times, the economic damages are enormous. A brain-damaged child may have a normal life expectancy with enormous expenses being incurred for lifelong care.

The Illinois examples suggest another explanation that has already been discussed. In some instances doctors contest the case solely on liability and do not call experts on damages or contest damages at all. The plaintiff, on the other hand, presents the losses through experts who give a "Cadillac" version of the plaintiff's losses. The jury is then instructed by the judge to decide damages solely on the evidence, and the jurors have only the plaintiff's figures to work with. Despite reservations, the jurors follow the judge's instructions and accept the plaintiff's suggested award because that is the only evidence they have. In other instances, the defense may call an economist who offers an alternative to the plaintiff's evidence of damages. The estimate may still be quite high due to the seriousness of the injury, and the jury uses this as a floor from which damages are estimated.

Of course, huge outlier awards may occasionally be due to jury anger. Because of evidence brought out at trial, jurors may become so outraged at the negligence of the defendant or an attempt to alter medical records after the fact (an act that occurs more often than people might expect) that they essentially violate the judge's instructions and appear to add a punitive component into their compensatory award. These outlier awards are not frequent, but they unquestionably do occur, as Vidmar documented in *Medical Malpractice and the American Jury*.[33]

Nevertheless, the two Illinois examples of postverdict reductions of awards are far from exceptions. Research consistently indicates that outlier verdicts seldom withstand postverdict proceedings. The judge may reduce the award by *remittitur* (the legal term for a reduction), or the case may be appealed to a higher court at which time the award may be reduced. Perhaps most common of all, the plaintiff and the defendant negotiate a posttrial settlement that is less than the jury verdict. Plaintiffs are willing to negotiate lesser amounts because they need the money immediately and cannot wait for the years it will take to get the money if the case is appealed. Also, there is always a risk that an appeals court will reduce the award or even overturn the verdict. Most of these large awards greatly exceed the medical provider's insurance coverage, and while plaintiffs and their lawyers could attempt to foreclose on the defendant's assets, they are reluctant to do so for a number of reasons. The assets may be legally protected. More often, however, as Tom Baker's research revealed, plaintiff lawyers are reluctant to destroy a doctor and her reputation.[34] Therefore, the plaintiff negotiates a settlement around the defendant's insurance coverage.

Some of the largest malpractice awards in New York that made national headlines ultimately resulted in settlements between 5 and 10 percent of the original jury verdict actually being paid.[35] Vidmar's Illinois study found that settlements in his sample of large jury awards averaged only 43 percent of the original verdicts.[36] A study of Texas malpractice cases by David Hyman and his colleagues yielded similar results.[37] Like the New York research, the Texas study found that the larger the award, the more it was reduced in postverdict negotiations.

COMPARING JURY VERDICT SETTLEMENTS TO PRELAWSUIT SETTLEMENTS

Florida requires malpractice insurance companies to file detailed reports on each malpractice case, whether it is settled or goes to trial. A study of these data by author Vidmar and his colleagues found that among 801 cases occurring between 1990 and 2003, only 60 (about 7.5 percent) resulted in a payment following a jury trial; the rest were settled without a trial.[38] Twenty-three of the cases in the sample had payments equal to or exceeding $5 million. However, only two of the twenty-three followed jury verdicts; the rest were a result of pretrial settlements.

In a follow-up study, Vidmar, MacKillop and Lee examined cases in which insurers paid patients a million dollars or more without a lawsuit even being filed.[39] There were approximately twice as many of these no-lawsuit cases as there were jury verdict cases. The no-lawsuit settlements involved instances in which the healthcare provider's negligence was so clear that it made economic sense for the providers and their insurance companies to negotiate immediately and avoid the expenses of a lawsuit they would almost certainly lose if they went to trial. The no-lawsuit cases were compared to postverdict settlements from jury cases, roughly controlling for the patients' levels of injury and economic losses. Essentially, the payments in both pre-lawsuit and jury verdict cases did not differ from one another. These findings strongly suggest that the large payments made to patients were made on the basis of the patients' true losses regardless of whether they resulted from a settlement or a jury verdict. Incidentally, other data in the Florida files showed that the long-term economic consequences for many injured patients were tremendous, sometimes involving many millions of dollars.

These findings strongly suggest that the emphasis on jury verdicts is misplaced. The bulk of malpractice payouts occur around the negotiation table rather than in the jury room.

"NONECONOMIC" OR PAIN AND SUFFERING AWARDS

The largest complaint about jury awards in medical malpractice cases involves the argument that jury largess is primarily related to "pain and suffering" awards, not economic damages.[40] Proponents of tort reform have advocated for a "cap" on pain and suffering and other general damages, arguing that they result in unreasonable windfalls for plaintiffs and their lawyers who are paid a percentage of the award. California imposed a cap of $250,000 in 1975 and it has served as a model that other states have followed.

We discussed pain and suffering in Chapter 14, but there are additional issues in medical malpractice that further our understanding of this component of jury awards. Most important is the finding that posttrial settlements are often dramatically lower than verdicts. Economics professor Frank Sloan and his coauthors studied the final amounts received by plaintiffs after lawsuits from their sample of birth and emergency room injuries. They concluded that plaintiffs who went to trial before a jury eventually received, on average, only about 20 percent more in compensation than their actual economic losses.[41] Most people would not consider 20 percent a "windfall" for a badly injured plaintiff.

But there is another matter to be considered. What are the effects of caps on general damages? First, caps seem inequitable when comparing medical negligence to other negligent injuries. A person injured in an automobile accident, in an industrial accident, or by a dangerous product can collect whatever pain and suffering component the jury decides is reasonable and fair. Yet a patient who is just as badly injured through medical negligence is limited by the cap. Second, as the Wisconsin Supreme Court reasoned when it overturned that state's $350,000 cap on pain and suffering in medical malpractice cases, caps have inequitable effects among patients injured by medical malpractice.[42]

The Wisconsin Court reasoned that the most severely injured plaintiffs were most likely to be inadequately compensated. For example, a patient suffering a severe infection for a period of, say, four months but who eventually recovered could receive $350,000 for pain and suffering in a jury award. In contrast, a patient who was so badly injured that she would suffer excruciating pain for the rest of her life would be limited to the same amount. In the Wisconsin Supreme Court's words, "[t]he cap's greatest impact falls on the most severely injured persons." The plaintiff in the Wisconsin case was a boy who was severely deformed at birth due to medical negligence. He can be expected to live for another sixty-nine years. He was awarded $10,000 per year for pain and suffering. Under the cap, the Wisconsin Court concluded, that amount would be almost halved. The Wisconsin decision additionally concluded that many cases that would be affected by caps involve children similar to the injured boy.

The inequitable effects of caps have also been studied empirically. David Studdert and his colleagues examined California's $250,000 cap on noneconomic damages.[43] Their findings indicated that reductions under the cap affected the patients with the most severe injuries, causing them to conclude: "Plaintiffs with the most severe injuries appear to be at the highest risk for inadequate compensation. Hence, the worst-off may suffer a kind of 'double jeopardy' under caps."

In another study, Professor Lucinda Finley systematically examined jury verdicts in California, Florida, and Maryland to determine if caps had a disparate effect on the monetary recoveries of women and elderly people.[44] She found that indeed to be the case. Finley's research pointed out that cap laws tend to "place an effective ceiling on recovery for certain types of injuries disproportionately experienced by women, including sexual assault and gynecological injuries that impair child bearing or sexual functioning." In wrongful death cases, women, as compared to men, were shown to be disadvantaged in the awards they received.

Thus, the Wisconsin Supreme Court and two studies by respected researchers arrived at the same conclusion. Caps on pain and suffering have a disproportionate negative impact on the fairness of compensation for people injured through medical negligence. As we discussed earlier in this book, constant pain may cause depression or prevent a patient from working. Severe disfigurement may affect employment opportunities. Children who are orphaned by the death of their mother or father can receive money for what is often called "loss of society," but it in fact can provide for their future education.

Juries do, of course, sometimes award very substantial sums for pain and suffering and other noneconomic costs. However, the posttrial adjustment findings described above often render this portion of the award moot. A jury could award a hundred million dollars for pain and suffering, but if the case settles for an amount that covers only medical and income losses, and sometimes barely covers them, the settlement amount is the one the defendant pays.

TRIAL BY JUDGE ALONE CAN PRODUCE SOME VERY LARGE AWARDS

Most medical malpractice trials are by jury. Sometimes, however, the only option is by judge alone. *Coleman v. United States of America and Touchette Regional Hospital* (2003) involved a claim against a physician who was a federal employee of the United States.[45] The Federal Tort Claims Act specifies that trials involving federal employees can take place only before a judge, not a jury. The plaintiff's mother alleged that during the birthing process the physician attempted to apply a vacuum extractor to the baby's head about fifteen times rather than the manufacturer's recommendation of no more than three times. The result was severe brain injury to the child. The lawsuit further alleged that although a cesarean section was eventually performed, it should have been performed much earlier. The physician denied that fifteen attempts were made with the vacuum extractor and claimed the injury was due to an arrest of labor and aggravated by an infection contracted by the mother. Defendant Touchette Regional Hospital was dismissed from the suit before trial. After hearing the evidence, the federal judge rendered a verdict for the plaintiff for $19,253,549. (The plaintiff reportedly had offered to settle for $8 million before trial, and the defendant's last offer was reported as $3.1 million.)

This case suggests the enormous costs of lifetime medical care required for a child who is so badly injured. One suspects that had a jury rather than a federal judge made the award, it would have been excoriated in the media and its decision cited by critics as another example of jury malfeasance.

CONCLUSION

There is no question that medical malpractice cases are often difficult and complex. Yet research does not support the claims that juries are incompetent or biased or both. Jury verdicts on liability compare favorably to judgments of medical experts. There is no evidence to support claims of jury sympathy or antidoctor verdicts. Payments following jury verdicts are not different from payments in similar cases that result from cases settled without a jury trial. Ultimately, in most cases, the money that negligently injured patients receive goes almost entirely to cover their medical care and income losses. Claims that juries have created a malpractice crisis are unwarranted.

Chapter 17

CONCLUDING

The Verdict on Juries

This book has presented the charges and countercharges concerning trial by jury. We have surveyed the historical landscape, tracing the beginnings of the jury system in England and early colonial America, and described the evolutionary steps that created our contemporary institution. We have identified the distinctive political and legal contexts of the criminal and civil jury systems. Detailed case examples have allowed us to illustrate the wide range of social, moral, and cognitive judgments that today's juries are called upon to make. Finally, we have summarized the empirical evidence—gathered over more than fifty years—bearing on how the American jury functions and the values that it serves. Now it is time for us to integrate all of this evidence and deliver our verdict.

SIGNS OF STRENGTH

As we evaluate the case for the jury, we observe many signs that the American jury is a sound decision maker in the majority of both civil and criminal trials. Very significant to us are the research findings that identify the strength of the evidence presented at the trial as the major determinant of jury verdicts. Civil jury damage awards are strongly correlated with the negligence and degree of injury.

These reasonable patterns in jury decisions go a long way to reassuring us that juries, by and large, listen to the judge and decide cases on the merits of the evidence rather than on biases and prejudice.

Furthermore, in systematic studies spanning five decades, we find that judges agree with jury verdicts in most cases. Disagreement between judges and juries in criminal trials is related most to judges' greater willingness to convict. In both civil and criminal trials, the disagreement is not related to the complexity of the trial evidence, as would be expected if juries misunderstood law and evidence that in contrast legal experts correctly comprehended. Nor is it related to whether a business or a corporation is the defendant, as would be expected if juries were more biased than judges against these corporate actors. Most judges say that jurors make a serious attempt to apply the law, and they do not see jurors relying on their feelings rather than the law in deciding on a verdict.

The jury's distinctive approach of commonsense justice best explains the divergence between judge and jury. These juror values affect the verdicts primarily in trials in which the evidence is relatively evenly balanced and a verdict for either side could be justified. Other studies, showing that the judgments of medical experts and arbitrators converge with jury decisions, reinforce this basic conclusion.

Mock jury studies that allow a fine-grained examination of the decision process also put the jury in a good light. Jurors' individual and collective recall and comprehension of evidence are substantial. Jurors critically evaluate the content and consistency of testimony provided by both lay and expert witnesses and do not appear to rubber-stamp expert conclusions. Our inclusion of excerpts from actual Arizona civil jury deliberations illustrates jurors' detailed assessment of the accuracy and reliability of testimony and their scrutiny of the reasonableness of litigants' behavior.

A key element contributing to jury competence is the deliberation process. A representative, diverse jury promotes vigorous debate. One of the most dramatic and important changes over the last half century is the increasing diversity of the American jury. Diverse juries have an edge in fact-finding, especially when the matters at issue incorporate social norms and judgments, as jury trials often do. Deliberation improves comprehension. Jurors with expertise on a topic often take a lead role when the jury discusses that topic, and errors made by one juror are frequently corrected by another juror. Deliberations encourage the sharing of knowledge and also the testing of narrative accounts. The representative jury and its verdicts are also seen as more legitimate by the public, an important strength of the jury as an institution.

We have explored the claims of doctors and business and corporate executives about unfair treatment by biased juries. However, the empirical evidence provides little support for these charges. The notion of the pro-plaintiff jury is contradicted by many studies that show that both actual and mock jurors subject plaintiffs' evidence to strict scrutiny. Most members of the public adhere to an ethic of individual responsibility and question why plaintiffs bring their claims to court. That is reflected in jurors' initial stances as they begin to evaluate the testimony and form narrative accounts. Although the research finds that juries treat corporate actors differently, the differential treatment appears to be linked primarily to jurors setting higher standards for corporate and professional behavior and not to antibusiness sentiments or the "deep pockets" effect. Members of the public, and juries in turn, believe that it is appropriate to hold corporations to higher standards because of their greater knowledge, resources, and potential for impact. The distinctive treatment that businesses receive at the hands of juries is a reflection of the jury's translation of community values about the role of business in society.

SIGNS OF VULNERABILITY

The overall picture of general competence is marred by some areas of particular vulnerability. First, the jury system is strong to the extent that its members reflect a broad range of the community. Therefore, the low participation rates observed in some jurisdictions, and problems with seating representative juries in others, constitute a serious threat to the jury's integrity and strength as a community fact finder. So does the evidence that peremptory challenges are exercised on the basis of a prospective juror's race or gender.

Prejudice is the dark side of commonsense justice. We saw in cases with extensive pretrial publicity that jurors exposed to incriminating news stories and community gossip are sometimes affected in their judgments of the parties, in their estimations of the strength of the evidence, and in their deliberations. In capital trials we find that death-qualified juries often tilt toward the prosecution in their evidence assessments, taking a dim view of capital defendants and their lawyers. Other especially troubling cases involving mental illness and acquaintance rape engender stereotypes that may be hard to overcome. In the civil arena, plaintiffs' attorneys might reasonably argue that they, too, face an uphill fight against juries that are predisposed against their claims. In both criminal and civil justice contexts, the community's inclinations and limitations translate into the inclinations and limitations of the jury.

Those who want better justice for the disadvantaged can attempt it in the courtroom, where the adversarial context allows advocates to bring their cases before the public. A more representative jury helps here, too, as biases in some segments of the community can perhaps be counteracted when different jurors bring divergent perspectives into the deliberations. A case in point is that the typically low conviction rate in rape trials in New York changed over time as more women began to serve on juries.[1] However, when it comes to widely shared stereotypes that disadvantage particular litigants, the surest way to improve juries is to expand the public's understanding.

Bias in decision making has been documented in many cognitive psychology studies. It is an inescapable part of the human condition, and we have to deal with it as best we can if we want to continue to include a human element to our judicial system. We have not found compelling evidence that bias is markedly worse in juries than in judges.[2] Repeated exposure to similar cases, as judges experience, might lead them to be better able to manage certain kinds of bias but may introduce other ones. For example regular exposure to particular types of cases, defenses, and even specific litigants may create expectations in judges that are hard to overcome. Because a jury is composed of persons without repetitive exposure the jury system gives every litigant the benefit of a fresh look.

Another factor to consider about the judge as the alternative to the jury is that although judges are markedly more diverse than twenty-five years ago when they were nearly all white men, judges, as a group, do not reflect the broad range of community perspectives and values as well as juries do. But even more important, the fact that juries typically make a single decision and then disperse may disrupt to some degree the substantial advantages that repeat players have in the legal system.[3] The potential for being beholden to special interests is greater when identifiable judges, as opposed to ad hoc juries, make the justice system's central decisions. On the civil justice side, both plaintiff and defense lawyers who make up the trial bar and repeat-player litigants are apt to lobby for the selection of congenial judges. In states where judges are elected, these groups contribute money to the judicial campaign funds of judges they believe are more likely to render favorable rulings.[4] But even without political considerations, judges, whether appointed or elected, who sit on the bench over many years may become jaded or develop a tendency to favor one side or the other.

A final but serious problem is the jury's documented difficulty in understanding legal instructions. This issue has plagued the courts since judges first took over the law-finding role from juries. In our experience, judges are surprised to learn just how badly their instructions can sometimes be mangled by the jurors who are expected to understand them. The remedy has been known since at least the 1970s, when Charrow and Charrow wrote a leading article on how to improve jury instructions, followed by Elwork, Sales, and Alfini's book *Making Jury Instructions Understandable*. These researchers showed that straightforward revisions to complicated legal instructions produce better understanding and better application of the law. Professor Peter Tiersma has recently pulled all of these findings into a single source, *Communicating with Juries*.[5] Simple testing procedures can be used to determine whether current legal instructions are clearly understood by the range of citizens who sit on juries. We strongly advise the systematic testing of proposed legal instructions. Several states have introduced plain-English legal instructions, a move we applaud.

REFORMS AND REMEDIES

Our historical survey showed that the jury has always been in a process of evolution and it will undoubtedly continue to change, responding to social conditions and emerging societal needs. In recent decades the changes have become more proactive. B. Michael Dann, then an Arizona state trial judge, wrote an influential law review article in 1993 that jump-started active jury reforms.[6] In the article he summarized research from the diverse fields of education, communication, psychology, and jury studies and identified the ways in which jury trials departed from ideal educational practices. Judge Dann argued that it made sense to reform jury trial procedures so that they promoted the jury's ability to become educated about the evidence. He chaired an important committee, the Arizona Supreme Court Committee on More Effective Use of Juries, which assessed Arizona's jury system, studied the available research, and made a host of recommendations to improve trial by jury. The committee's report, *Jurors, The Power of Twelve*, is a persuasive document that has spurred changes in other courts.[7]

Many states in addition to Arizona have formed jury reform commissions to examine the operation of the jury system, to review current knowledge about juries, and to propose improvements in jury selection and jury trial procedures. Building on these state efforts, in 2005 the American Bar Association, under the direction of its President, Robert Grey, Jr., adopted a revised set of "Principles for Juries and Jury Trials that incorporates these new ideas for jury trials."[8]

We've already reviewed many of these jury reforms as we traveled through this book. One set has involved modifications to the jury selection process to further democratize the jury. A broader range of people are now called for jury duty. There are fewer exclusions and exemptions. Many courts have moved to a "one day–one trial" system and concomitantly have become less open to accepting excuses from people who think they are just too busy to serve on a jury. As a result, a record number of Americans have served on juries.

Another set of reforms involves changes in trial procedures that allow jurors to take a more active role during the trial. Although the changes still remain controversial to many judges and lawyers, "active jury reforms" are based on cognitive and educational research that shows the well-documented benefits of active and interactive learning.[9] The adversary system's emphasis on ensuring a neutral decision maker has led to a largely passive formal role for juries. Evidence scholar Mirjan Damaška trenchantly noted that "[w]hile evidence is being adduced, [jurors] sit silent, cast—one might say—into the role of potted courtroom plants."[10] Jurors absorb the evidence presented by both sides, waiting until the end of the trial to make their judgment. Yet how passive are they in practice? We know that long before they embark on their deliberations, jurors are attempting to organize the evidence into a narrative account and to test the coherence and consistency of each side's story. And several studies have confirmed what many lawyers and judges suspect: on occasion jurors, disregarding instructions, discuss the trial with friends and family while it is going on.[11]

Although some of the active jury reforms, such as note taking, enjoy broad support, others are more controversial. Attorneys in particular worry about allowing jurors to ask questions of witnesses, discuss the case with one another during the trial, and seek additional arguments and assistance from the two sides if they are stuck. Their caution is understandable. Allowing jurors to ask questions takes over a slice of the adversary attorney's role in the trial. Discussing the evidence when only one side has had a chance to present its case raises fears of prejudgment, especially for the side that goes second. The side that has the burden of proof might be seen as getting an advantage if jurors cannot arrive at a verdict and the two sides are allowed additional time for arguments focused on the issues that most trouble the jury. Yet if confusion and biases develop during the process of evidence presentation, and these shape how later testimony is viewed, then timely questions or discussions with other jurors could promote better fact-finding.

In collaboration with judges and other researchers, both of us have been involved in assessing the impact of active jury reforms.[12] On the whole, the findings of our studies and those of other researchers show that there are some benefits in particular cases; the feared harms such as prejudgment, distraction, and asymmetrical benefits do not materialize.[13] At the same time, the most passionate advocates of jury reform may oversell the benefits. Although in the past, attorneys and judges could only speculate about the likely impact of specific innovations, there is now substantial empirical evidence about the merits of particular reforms that attorneys and judges can review to decide whether they will employ them as a general rule or utilize them only for particular trials.

SIGNS OF VITALITY

The promulgation of jury reform commissions in many states and the work on jury trials by organizations like the American Bar Association, the National Center for State Courts, and the American Judicature Society show that a broad range of policy makers in and outside the legal system are committed to modernizing state jury systems. We see these efforts as a positive way to reconfigure the jury in order to keep it relevant to contemporary society. There are also other signs of vitality.

In the second chapter we brought attention to the historical pattern of a decline in the number of American jury trials. While once the American jury decided a good proportion of all disputes, today it resolves only a fraction of them. Whether or not the jury's report card is good, the declines in both criminal and civil jury trials raise the question of whether it is nonetheless on a slow road to extinction, doomed by trial expenses and delay, made irrelevant by the rise of expertise, and killed off by segments of society who believe their interests are better served bypassing the citizenry.

The story of the decline of jury trials is a complex one. In the state courts, where most jury trials take place, the overall number of jury trials declined from 1976 to 2002, and the fraction of court cases that were resolved by jury trials also decreased over the period. The pattern of decline was especially pronounced in serious criminal cases. But in some states there was a slight increase in the jury trial rate for civil cases.[14] In the federal court system, although again there has been an overall decline in trials, jury trials are not decreasing as rapidly as judge trials. Professor Marc Galanter's analysis of federal civil trials over the last several decades, for example, found that in 1962, judge trials were slightly more numerous than jury trials. Civil trials climbed, and the pattern in which judge trials were more frequent than jury trials held until the early 1980s. However, starting in the 1990s, although trials in general decreased, jury trials then became more common than bench trials, and that has persisted at least through the latest data from 2002.[15] Whether or not jury trials have declined, the judiciary and the American public continue to hold the jury in high regard, even if people disagree with particular verdicts from time to time. The jury system is strongly supported by the public. In one recent poll, three-quarters of respondents say that if they were on trial, they would prefer a jury to a judge. Other polls demonstrated similar findings.[16]

There are other signs that lay decision makers add value to a legal system.[17] Over fifty countries around the world have jury systems modeled in varying degrees after the original English common law jury. Many European nations use "mixed tribunals" of judges and laypersons to decide serious criminal offenses.[18] In recent years, a number of countries have introduced or reintroduced the jury or other forms of lay decision making into their legal systems. Juries seem to constitute part of a move away from a totalitarian regime to one of greater democracy. Russia resurrected its jury system in the early 1990s as the Soviet Union collapsed.[19] The right to jury trial is included in a number of post-Soviet constitutions, including those of Armenia, Kazakhstan, Ukraine, and Azerbaijan.[20] Similarly, as Spanish dictator Franco's regime ended, Spain introduced trial by jury.[21] Japan is scheduled to debut Saiban-in Seido, a form of mixed tribunal, beginning in 2009.[22] Three professional judges will decide serious felony cases jointly with six lay judges chosen from the general population. In the wake of political controversy over the fairness and integrity of the legal system in Argentina, serious debates about the benefits of a jury system have been sparked in that country. The Argentine constitution provides for trial by jury but enabling legislation has not yet been passed.[23] In South Korea, after political and democratic reforms there, the legislature recently passed a bill providing for jury trials in serious criminal cases. For now, juries will participate only in cases in which the defendant agrees. Furthermore, to comport with the constitutional guarantee of judicial decision making, the jury's decision currently will be only advisory to the judge. Nonetheless it is a significant expansion of the public's role in the Korean legal system.[24]

The juries or mixed tribunals in these countries will not, of course, necessarily be identical to the American jury. The form and procedure will develop from within these nations' different legal systems as well as their social and political worlds. However, the international interest and emergence of jury systems suggest that there are some enduring benefits to the direct involvement of citizens as legal decision makers. Most significantly, the jury system appears to shore up democratic impulses. Recent research by a multidisciplinary team of US researchers has found that meaningful participation on a jury increases the juror's likelihood of voting in subsequent elections.[25] Deliberating with other jurors to resolve a criminal case appears to reinforce the bonds that link citizens to their democratic society.

ON BALANCE

In 1986, we wrote our first book together, *Judging the Jury*.[26] The field of jury studies was at an early stage, trial consultants were just beginning to emerge as occasional players in high-profile trials, and concerted attacks on the civil jury were about to commence. Over two decades have passed. We have the benefit of many new empirical studies of the jury system, particularly of the civil jury that has undergone so much scrutiny and criticism. Thus, we know a great deal more now about how the jury functions and the values that it serves in contemporary society than we did then. The conclusion we reached in 1986 about the basic soundness of the American jury has been reinforced by this new scholarship. After evaluating all of the evidence, our verdict is strongly in favor of the American jury.

NOTES

INTRODUCTION

1. Thomas Jefferson to Thomas Paine, 1789, in 7 THE WRITINGS OF THOMAS JEFFERSON 408 (Albert Ellery Bergh ed., definitive edition, 1905). Text available at University of Virginia's online materials on Thomas Jefferson: http://etext.virginia.edu/jefferson/quotations/jeff1520.htm#Trial.

2. *The View from the Bench: A National Law Journal Poll*, NATIONAL LAW JOURNAL, August 10, 1987 at 1; John Setar, *Comments on Judges' Opinions on Procedural Issues*, 69 BOSTON UNIVERSITY LAW REVIEW 765 (1989).

3. See, e.g., MICHAEL PELLOWSKI, THE O.J. SIMPSON MURDER TRIAL: A HEADLINE COURT CASE (2001).

4. ALAN M. DERSHOWITZ, THE ABUSE EXCUSE: AND OTHER COP-OUTS, SOB STORIES, AND EVASIONS OF RESPONSIBILITY (1994).

5. JIM DWYER ET AL., ACTUAL INNOCENCE (2000).

6. Stuart Taylor & Evan Thomas, *Civil Wars*, NEWSWEEK, December 15, 2003, at 43.

7. Neil Vidmar et al., *Should We Rush to Reform the Criminal Jury? Consider Conviction Rate Data*, 80 JUDICATURE 286 (1997).

8. See Jonathan Turley, *Legal Myths: Hardly the Whole Truth*, USA TODAY, January 30, 2005, available at http://www.usatoday.com/news/opinion/2005-01-30-tort-reform_x.htm. For example, in June 2003, publisher Morton Zuckerman wrote a column in *U.S. News & World Report* that bemoaned the state of litigious America. He wrote, "A

woman throws a soft drink at her boyfriend at a restaurant, then slips on the floor she wet and breaks her tailbone. She sues. Bingo—a jury says the restaurant owes her $100,000. A woman tries to sneak through a restroom window at a nightclub to avoid paying the $3.50 cover charge. She falls, knocks out two front teeth, and sues. A jury awards her $12,000 for dental expenses." The publisher subsequently had to issue a correction because both were fabrications. Stephanie Mencimer, *The Fake Crisis over Lawsuits: Who's Paying to Keep the Myths Alive*, http://www.aliciapatterson.org/APF2102/Mencimer/Mencimer.html.

9. Milton Rokeach & Neil Vidmar, *Testimony Concerning Possible Jury Bias in a Black Panther Murder Trial*, 3 JOURNAL OF APPLIED SOCIAL PSYCHOLOGY 19 (1973).

10. See, e.g., Shari Diamond, Neil Vidmar, Mary Rose, Leslie Ellis & Beth Murphy, *Juror Discussions during Trials: Studying an Arizona Innovation*, 45 ARIZONA LAW REVIEW 1 (2003). Financial support was provided by the following sources: Neil Vidmar & Shari S. Diamond, National Science Foundation Grant SBR 9818806; State Justice Institute Grant SJI-97-N-247; American Bar Foundation; Duke University School of Law and Northwestern University School of Law. The research included a condition that names, facts, and other evidence were to be altered to protect confidentiality of the trial process and the anonymity of the jurors. The authors have always complied with this important condition.

11. Anthony N. Doob & Hershi M. Kirshenbaum, *Some Empirical Evidence on the Effect of s.12 of the Canada Evidence Act upon the Accused*, 15 CRIMINAL LAW QUARTERLY 88 (1972).

12. Her first project was a master's thesis attempting to replicate her adviser's study on criminal record: Valerie P. Hans, "The Effect of Criminal Record on Individual and Group Judgments of Guilt in a Jury Simulation Paradigm" (1974) (MA thesis, University of Toronto); later published as Valerie P. Hans & Anthony N. Doob, *Section 12 of the Canada Evidence Act and the Deliberations of Simulated Juries*, 18 CRIMINAL LAW QUARTERLY 235 (1976).

13. Valerie P. Hans, "Effects of the Unanimity Requirement on Group Decision Processes in Simulated Juries" (1978) (PhD dissertation, University of Toronto). The law reform process is described in Valerie P. Hans, *Evaluating the Jury: The Uses of Research in Policy Formation*, in EVALUATION AND CRIMINAL JUSTICE POLICY 143 (Ronald Roesch & Ray Corrado eds., 1981).

14. VALERIE P. HANS, BUSINESS ON TRIAL: THE CIVIL JURY AND CORPORATE RESPONSIBILITY (2000).

15. Valerie P. Hans, Paula L. Hannaford-Agor, G. Thomas Munsterman, Nicole L. Mott & G. Thomas Munsterman, *The Hung Jury: The American Jury's Insights and Contemporary Understanding*, 39 CRIMINAL LAW BULLETIN 33 (2003).

CHAPTER 1: THE ENGLISH ORIGINS OF THE MODERN JURY

1. WILLIAM BLACKSTONE, COMMENTARIES ON THE LAWS OF ENGLAND (Clarendon edition, 1966) (1769).

2. PATRICK DEVLIN, TRIAL BY JURY 164–65 (1956).

3. Although we researched and cite additional material, this chapter draws heavily from the following sources: JOHN BEATTIE CRIME AND THE COURTS IN ENGLAND, 1600–1800

(1986); DAVID BENTLEY, ENGLISH CRIMINAL JUSTICE IN THE NINETEENTH CENTURY (1998); TWELVE GOOD MEN AND TRUE: THE CRIMINAL TRIAL JURY IN ENGLAND, 1200–1800 (J. S. Cockburn & Thomas A. Green eds., 1988); THOMAS A. GREEN, VERDICT ACCORDING TO CONSCIENCE: PERSPECTIVES ON THE ENGLISH CRIMINAL TRIAL JURY, 1200–1800 (1985).

4. Donald J. Evans, *Forgotten Trial Techniques: The Wager of Battle*, ABA JOURNAL, May 1985, at 66; ROSCOE POUND, READINGS ON THE HISTORY AND SYSTEM OF THE COMMON LAW 88–110 (Jacob North & Co., 1904).

5. POUND, READINGS ON THE HISTORY AND SYSTEM OF THE COMMON LAW, note 4, at 93.

6. GREEN, VERDICT ACCORDING TO CONSCIENCE, note 3, at 3–27.

7. FREDERICK POLLOCK & FREDERICK MAITLAND, THE HISTORY OF ENGLISH LAW BEFORE THE TIME OF EDWARD I 138 (Lawbook Exchange Ltd., 2nd ed., 1996) (1898); JOHN DAWSON, A HISTORY OF LAY JUDGES 119 (1960).

8. DAWSON, HISTORY OF LAY JUDGES, note 7, at 119, 122.

9. *Id.* at 120.

10. *Id.* at 123, note 16.

11. GREEN, VERDICT ACCORDING TO CONSCIENCE, note 3, at 15; Charles Wells, *The Origin of the Petty Jury*, 347 LAW QUARTERLY REVIEW (1911).

12. BEATTIE, CRIME AND THE COURTS IN ENGLAND, note 3, at 337–38, note 54.

13. T. F. T. PLUNCKNETT, A CONCISE HISTORY OF THE COMMON LAW 125–26 (5th ed. 1956).

14. PLUNCKNETT, CONCISE HISTORY OF THE COMMON LAW, note 13, at 129, quoting Bracton.

15. GREEN, VERDICT ACCORDING TO CONSCIENCE, note 3, at 19, 200.

16. *Id.* at 16.

17. *Id.* at 32.

18. *Id.* at 35.

19. *Id.* at 42.

20. *Id.* at 43.

21. *Id.* at 42.

22. *Id.* at 42–43.

23. See generally GREEN, VERDICT ACCORDING TO CONSCIENCE, note 3; Stephen Landsman, *The Rise of the Contentious Spirit: Adversary Procedure in Eighteenth-Century England*, 75 CORNELL LAW REVIEW 497–609 (1990).

24. GREEN, VERDICT ACCORDING TO CONSCIENCE, note 3, at 233–34.

25. WILLIAM FORSYTHE, HISTORY OF TRIAL BY JURY (Burt Franklin, 2nd ed., 1971) (1878).

26. *Id.* at 25; GREEN, VERDICT ACCORDING TO CONSCIENCE, note 3, at chapter 6, 200–64.

27. See H. W. BRANDS, THE FIRST AMERICAN: THE LIFE AND TIMES OF BENJAMIN FRANKLIN, 35–37 (2002) (providing a brief recounting of Penn's troubles).

28. BEATTIE, CRIME AND THE COURTS IN ENGLAND, note 3, at 398–99.

29. GREEN, VERDICT ACCORDING TO CONSCIENCE, note 3, at 200–201.

30. BRANDS, FIRST AMERICAN, note 27.

31. Edith Henderson, *The Background of the Seventh Amendment*, 80 HARVARD LAW REVIEW 289, 330 (1966); W.K. Stewart, *The Trial of the Seven Bishops*, 55 CALIFORNIA STATE BAR JOURNAL 70 (1980).

32. See generally GREEN, VERDICT ACCORDING TO CONSCIENCE, note 3, at chapter 8, 318–55.

33. GREEN, VERDICT ACCORDING TO CONSCIENCE, note 3, at 328–53; Henderson, *Background of the Seventh Amendment*, note 31, at 328–35.

34. BEATTIE, CRIME AND THE COURTS IN ENGLAND, note 3, at 316–18.

35. *Id.* at 316.

36. *Id.* at 340–52.

37. *Id.* at 341.

38. *Id.* at 349.

39. *Id.* at 340–62; Landsman, *Rise of the Contentious Spirit*, note 23.

40. BEATTIE, CRIME AND THE COURTS IN ENGLAND, note 3, at 352–62.

41. *Id.* at 375.

42. *Id.* at 106.

43. *Id.* at 364–76.

44. *Id.* at 378–89.

45. BLACKSTONE, COMMENTARIES ON THE LAWS OF ENGLAND, note 1. See also JAMES KENNEDY, LAW AND PRACTICE OF JURIES 90 (1826).

46. Nancy King, *Silencing Nullification Advocacy Inside the Jury Room and Outside the Courtroom*, 65 UNIVERSITY OF CHICAGO LAW REVIEW 433 (1998).

47. Neil Vidmar, *The Canadian Criminal Jury: Searching for a Middle Ground*, in WORLD JURY SYSTEMS 211 (Neil Vidmar ed., 2000).

48. BLACKSTONE, COMMENTARIES ON THE LAWS OF ENGLAND, note 1. KENNEDY, LAW AND PRACTICE OF JURIES, note 45, confirmed their use a century later.

49. See generally VIDMAR, WORLD JURY SYSTEMS, note 47.

50. BEATTIE, CRIME AND THE COURTS IN ENGLAND, note 3, at 376.

51. *Id.* at 377.

52. See generally BENTLEY, ENGLISH CRIMINAL JUSTICE IN THE NINETEENTH CENTURY, note 3.

53. *Id.* at 341.

54. *Id.* at 91.

55. *Id.* at 205.

56. *Id.* at 315.

57. *Id.* at 19.

58. See WORLD JURY SYSTEMS, note 47.

59. LORD JUSTICE AULD, REVIEW OF THE CRIMINAL COURTS OF ENGLAND AND WALES: REPORT 135–139 (September 2001) available at http://www.criminal-courts-review.org.uk/auldconts.htm.

60. Sally Lloyd-Bostock & Cheryl Thomas, *The Continuing Decline of the English Jury*, in WORLD JURY SYSTEMS, note 47, at 53.

61. JAMES GOBERT, JUSTICE, DEMOCRACY AND THE JURY 24, note 1 (1997).

62. AULD, REVIEW OF THE CRIMINAL COURTS OF ENGLAND AND WALES, note 59, at 135 and appendix IV.

63. See BENTLEY, ENGLISH CRIMINAL JUSTICE IN THE NINETEENTH CENTURY, note 3, at 135–38; Lloyd-Bostock & Thomas, *Continuing Decline of the English Jury*, note 60, at 61–66.

64. AULD, REVIEW OF THE CRIMINAL COURTS OF ENGLAND AND WALES, note 59, at chapter 4, 94–134; Penny Darbyshire, *An Essay on the Importance and Neglect of the Mag-*

istry, CRIMINAL LAW REVIEW 627 (1997) (exploring the role of lay magistrates in the United Kingdom and discussing the dearth of scholarly research on this legal institution).

65. Lloyd-Bostock & Thomas, *Continuing Decline of the English Jury*, note 60, at 68–72; AULD, REVIEW OF THE CRIMINAL COURTS OF ENGLAND AND WALES, note 59, at 140–45.

66. AULD, REVIEW OF THE CRIMINAL COURTS OF ENGLAND AND WALES, note 59, at 164; Lloyd-Bostock & Thomas, *Continuing Decline of the English Jury*, note 60, at 86–87.

67. Lloyd-Bostock & Thomas, *Continuing Decline of the English Jury*, note 60, at 86.

68. *Id.* at 72–76.

69. *Id.* at 76–77.

70. *Id.* at 82–83.

71. AULD, REVIEW OF THE CRIMINAL COURTS OF ENGLAND AND WALES, note 59, at 200–14; see also Lloyd-Bostock & Thomas, *Continuing Decline of the English Jury*, note 60, at 66–67.

72. See David Barrett, *Goldsmith Defends Jury-Free Fraud Trials Move*, INDEPENDENT, online edition, June 21, 2005, http://news.independent.co.uk/uk/legal/article293994.ece; *Head to Head: Fraud Trial Juries*, BBC NEWS, June 21, 2005, http://news.bbc.co.uk/1/hi/uk/4114934.stm.

CHAPTER 2: FROM COLONIAL TIMES TO THE PRESENT DAY

1. This discussion of the trial of Peter Zenger is derived from the following sources: JAMES ALEXANDER, A BRIEF NARRATIVE OF THE CASE AND TRIAL OF JOHN PETER ZENGER (Stanley Katz ed., 1963); THE TRIAL OF PETER ZENGER (Vincent Buranelli ed., 1957); Ellen James, *Decoding the Zenger Trial: Andrew Hamilton's "Fraudful Dexterity" with Language*, in THE LAW IN AMERICA: 1607–1861 (William Pencak & Wythe Holt Jr. eds., 1989); FRANK LATHAM, THE TRIAL OF JOHN PETER ZENGER (1970); WILLIAM PUTNAM, JOHN PETER ZENGER AND THE FUNDAMENTAL FREEDOM (1997); LIVINGSTON RUTHERFORD, JOHN PETER ZENGER: HIS PRESS AND HIS TRIAL (Johnson Reprint Corporation, 1968) (1904).

2. Quoted in PUTNAM, JOHN PETER ZENGER, note 1, at 4.

3. ALEXANDER, A BRIEF NARRATIVE, note 1, at 109–38.

4. RUTHERFORD, JOHN PETER ZENGER, note 1, at 31.

5. *Id.*

6. PUTNAM, JOHN PETER ZENGER, note 1, at 80.

7. *Id.* at 83.

8. *Id* at 86, taken from the account of the trial published by Zenger himself.

9. BURANELLI, THE TRIAL, note 1, at 49.

10. *Id.* at 102–105.

11. *Id.* at 108.

12. *Id.* at 112.

13. *Id.* at 131.

14. *Id.* at 132.

15. However, Zenger eventually lost both positions on the official grounds that he was an indifferent printer and had an inadequate grasp of the English language; see PUTNAM, JOHN PETER ZENGER, note 1, at 119.

16. *Id.* at 118–32.

17. See Morris Forkosch, *Zenger versus Crosswell and the Rule of Law*, in THE LAW IN AMERICA, note 1; Catherine Menand, *Juries, Judges and the Politics of Justice in Pre-Revolutionary Boston*, note 1.

18. PUTNAM, JOHN PETER ZENGER, note 1, at 105–106.

19. This section is developed primarily from the following sources: BRADLEY CHAPIN, CRIMINAL JUSTICE IN COLONIAL AMERICA, 1606–1600 (1983); LAWRENCE FRIEDMAN, A HISTORY OF AMERICAN LAW (2nd ed., 1985); GEORGE HASKINS, LAW AND AUTHORITY IN EARLY MASSACHUSETTS: A STUDY IN TRADITION AND DESIGN (1960); Stephen Landsman, *The Civil Jury in America: Scenes from an Unappreciated History*, 44 HASTINGS LAW JOURNAL 579 (1993); EDGAR MCMANUS, LAW AND LIBERTY IN EARLY NEW ENGLAND: CRIMINAL JUSTICE AND DUE PROCESS, 1620–1692 (1993); WILLIAM NELSON, AMERICANIZATION OF THE COMMON LAW: THE IMPACT OF LEGAL CHANGE ON MASSACHUSETTS SOCIETY, 1760–1830 (1975).

20. MCMANUS, LAW AND LIBERTY, note 19, at 99.

21. Landsman, *The Civil Jury*, note 19, at 592.

22. MCMANUS, LAW AND LIBERTY, note 19, at 99. The colony of New Haven, which had a strong preference for applying the laws of God through its religious leaders, was an exception, but eventually as it was incorporated into the colony of Connecticut, it gave way and introduced trial by jury. It is noteworthy, however, that in Connecticut juries were used in civil cases before criminal defendants had the statutory right to jury trial; see NELSON, AMERICANIZATION, note 19, at 100.

23. DAVID BODENHAMER, FAIR TRIAL: RIGHTS OF ACCUSED IN AMERICAN HISTORY (1992).

24. *Id.* at 10–11.

25. HASKINS, LAW AND AUTHORITY, note 19, at 144–45. This was not unique to American colonies as the instructions were contained in an English manual, *id.* at 144.

26. *Id.* at 5.

27. *See* MCMANUS, LAW AND LIBERTY, note 19, at 90–114.

28. FRIEDMAN, A HISTORY, note 19, at 94–100.

29. It is very important in this brief sketch of colonial juries to keep in mind not only that they varied from colony to colony but also that they also were evolving over time. A prime example of this process is attitudes toward legal counsel. From the beginning, Connecticut and Rhode Island permitted legal counsel for civil cases. Rhode Island also permitted felony defendants to have paid counsel to argue technical legal questions. Rhode Island made use of public prosecutors in some instances, whereas Massachusetts and Connecticut seldom did so. See MCMANUS, LAW AND LIBERTY, note 19, at 95–98.

30. NELSON, AMERICANIZATION, note 19, at 13–23.

31. *Id.* at 21.

32. HASKINS, LAW AND AUTHORITY, note 19, at 212.

33. ARTHUR SCOTT, CRIMINAL LAW IN COLONIAL VIRGINIA 84–91 (1930).

34. 24 CYCLOPEDIA OF LAW & PROCEDURE (William Mack ed., 1908); Albert Alschuler & Andrew Deiss, *A Brief History of the Criminal Jury in the United States*, 61 CHICAGO LAW REVIEW 867, 911 (1994).

35. Alschuler & Deiss, *A Brief History*, note 34, at 881.

36. WILLIAM BLACKSTONE, COMMENTARIES ON THE LAWS OF ENGLAND 359–65 (Clarendon edition, 1966) (3rd ed. 1769).

37. For criminal cases, Massachusetts allowed unlimited challenges for cause based on bias or incompetence of the juror, but there was no provision for peremptory challenges. Massachusetts allowed no challenges at all in civil cases. JOHN P. REID, IN A DEFIANT STANCE: THE CONDITIONS OF LAW IN MASSACHUSETTS BAY, THE IRISH COMPARISON, AND THE COMING OF THE AMERICAN REVOLUTION 29 (1977). Rhode Island allowed unlimited challenges for cause and twenty peremptory challenges in capital cases. New Plymouth allowed unlimited challenges for cause and eight peremptory challenges. Connecticut had no laws on jury selection, and there were no provisions for challenges of any kind, although it is likely that a defendant or civil litigant could appeal to the judges about bias in potential jurors. MCMANUS, LAW AND LIBERTY, note 19, at 100–101. In Virginia a criminal defendant was allowed any number of challenges for cause and twenty peremptory challenges, but in some cases a defendant who exercised more than twenty peremptories could be considered convicted. SCOTT, CRIMINAL LAW, note 33, at 90.

38. 1 THE LEGAL PAPERS OF JOHN ADAMS 230 (L. Kinivin Wroth & Hiller B. Zobel eds., 1965).

39. MCMANUS, LAW AND LIBERTY, note 19, at 93.

40. NELSON, AMERICANIZATION, note 19, at 24.

41. *Id.*

42. John Murrin, *Trial by Jury in Seventeenth-Century New England*, in SAINTS & REVOLUTIONARIES: ESSAYS ON EARLY AMERICAN HISTORY (David T. Hall et al. eds., 1984).

43. HASKINS, LAW AND AUTHORITY, note 19, at 212–14. There appeared to be some abuse of the system with trivial and vexatious lawsuits; see *id.* at 213.

44. *Id.* at 213.

45. *Id.*

46. *Id.* at 214.

47. Daniel Blinka, *Trial by Jury on the Eve of Revolution: The Virginia Experience*, 71 UNIVERSITY OF MISSOURI-KANSAS CITY LAW REVIEW 529 (2003).

48. *Id.* at 579.

49. NELSON, AMERICANIZATION, note 19, at 20–30.

50. *Id.* at 21.

51. REID, DEFIANT STANCE, note 37, at 30–35.

52. *Id.* at 31.

53. Matthew P. Harrington, *The Economic Origins of the Seventh Amendment*, 87 IOWA LAW REVIEW 145, 166 (2001).

54. REID, DEFIANT STANCE, note 37, at 27–40.

55. *Id.* at 32.

56. *Id.* at 31.

57. *Id.* at 41–54.

58. *Id.* at 55–64.

59. Harrington, *Economic Origins*, note 53, at 167.

60. *Id.*, whole article. See NELSON, AMERICANIZATION, note 19, at 89–97; Daniel Blinka, *"This Germ of Rottedness": Federal Trials in the New Republic, 1789–1807*, 36 CREIGHTON LAW REVIEW 135 (2003).

61. Harrington, *Economic Origins*, note 53, at 185.

62. *Id.* at 187.

63. *Id.* at 189.

64. *Id.* at 209.

65. NELSON, AMERICANIZATION, note 19, at 165–74.

66. F. THORNTON MILLER, JURIES AND JUDGES VERSUS THE LAW: VIRGINIA'S PROVINCIAL LEGAL PERSPECTIVE 1783–1828, 98–101 (1994).

67. David Bodenhamer, *The Democratic Impulse and Legal Change in the Age of Jackson: The Example of Criminal Juries in Antebellum Indiana*, 45 HISTORY 206, 209 (1982); *Sparf et al. v. United States*, 156 U.S. 51, 83–91 (1895).

68. Mark DeWolf Howe, *Juries as Judges of the Criminal Law*, 52 HARVARD LAW REVIEW 582, 582 (1939).

69. Bodenhamer, *Democratic Impulse*, note 67, at 211.

70. Article 1, § 19 of the Indiana Bill of Rights of the State Constitution reads: "In all criminal cases whatever, the jury shall have the right to determine the law and the facts." This article of the Indiana Constitution is available at http://www.in.gov/legislative /ic/code/const/art1.html.

71. Bodenhamer, *Democratic Impulse*, note 67, at 212.

72. Reported in DAVID MCCULLOUGH, JOHN ADAMS 536–37 (2001).

73. Calendar's Case, reported in FRANCIS WHARTON, STATE TRIALS OF THE UNITED STATES DURING THE ADMINISTRATIONS OF WASHINGTON AND ADAMS (1849); See also *Sparf et al. v. United States*, 156 U.S. 51 (1895), at 69.

74. *Sparf et al. v. United States*, 156 U.S. 51 (1895), at 69.

75. Howe, *Juries as Judges of the Criminal Law*, note 68, at 612.

76. Alschuler & Deiss, *A Brief History*, note 34.

77. Jenia Iontcheva, *Jury Sentencing as Democratic Practice*, 89 VIRGINIA LAW REVIEW 311 (2003); Nancy King, *The Origins of Felony Jury Sentencing in the United States*, 74 CHICAGO-KENT LAW REVIEW 101 (2003).

78. This account is taken from ANONYMOUS, THE WEBSTER AND DURANT MURDER CASES (Collector Publishing Co., 1897) and HELEN THOMPSON, MURDER AT HARVARD (1971). For an interesting variation on the story of George Parkman's murder, see SIMON SCHAMA, DEAD CERTAINTIES: UNWARRANTED SPECULATIONS (1991).

79. Apparently the prosecution had no peremptory challenges. The record is not clear, but in any event, none were exercised by the prosecution.

80. LAWRENCE FRIEDMAN, CRIME AND PUNISHMENT IN AMERICAN HISTORY 61–260 (1993); LAWRENCE FRIEDMAN & ROBERT PERCIVAL, THE ROOTS OF JUSTICE: CRIME AND PUNISHMENT IN ALAMEDA COUNTY, CALIFORNIA 1870–1910 (1981).

81. FRIEDMAN, CRIME AND PUNISHMENT, note 80, at 245.

82. FRIEDMAN & PERCIVAL, ROOTS OF JUSTICE, note 80, at 189.

83. *Id.* at 194.

84. *Id.*

85. *Gideon v. Wainright*, 372 U.S. 335 (1963).

86. FRIEDMAN, CRIME AND PUNISHMENT, note 80, at 251–52.

87. FRIEDMAN & PERCIVAL, ROOTS OF JUSTICE, note 80, at 173.

88. For historical perspectives on the development of plea bargaining and the decline of jury trials, see Bruce P. Smith, *Plea Bargaining and the Eclipse of Trial by Jury*, 1 ANNUAL REVIEW OF LAW & SOCIAL SCIENCE 131–49 (2005). See also MILTON HEUMANN, PLEA BARGAINING: THE EXPERIENCES OF PROSECUTORS, JUDGES, AND DEFENSE ATTORNEYS (1978).

89. Smith, *Plea Bargaining,* note 88, at 182.

90. Albert Alschuler, *Foreword: The Vanishing Civil Jury*, 1990 UNIVERSITY OF CHICAGO LEGAL FORUM 1 (1990); George Priest, *The Role of the Civil Jury in a System of Private Litigation*, 1990 UNIVERSITY OF CHICAGO LEGAL FORUM 161 (1990).

91. See KENNETH DEVILLE, MEDICAL MALPRACTICE IN NINETEENTH-CENTURY AMERICA: ORIGINS AND LEGACY (1990).

92. The material in this section is drawn from the following sources: STEPHEN DANIELS & JOANNE MARTIN, CIVIL JURIES AND THE POLITICS OF REFORM (1995); Theodore Eisenberg et al., *Juries, Judges and Punitive Damages: An Empirical Study*, 87 CORNELL LAW REVIEW 743 (2002); FRIEDMAN, A HISTORY OF AMERICAN LAW, note 19; MORTON HORWITZ, THE TRANSFORMATION OF AMERICAN LAW: 1780–1860 (1977); THOMAS KOENIG & MICHAEL RUSTAD, IN DEFENSE OF TORT LAW (2001); George Priest, *The Invention of Enterprise Liability: A Critical History of the Intellectual Foundations of Modern Tort Law*, 14 JOURNAL OF LEGAL STUDIES 461 (1985); Gary Schwartz, *The Beginning and Possible End of Modern American Tort Law*, 20 GEORGIA LAW REVIEW 601 (1992); Anthony Sebok, *The Rise and Fall of Blame in American Tort Law*, 68 BROOKLYN LAW REVIEW 1031 (2003); Anthony Sebok, *What Did Punitive Damages Do? Why Misunderstanding of Punitive Damages Matters Today*, 78 CHICAGO-KENT LAW REVIEW 163 (2003).

93. Priest, *Invention of Enterprise Liability*, note 92; Steven Croley & Jon Hanson, *Rescuing the Revolution: The Revived Case for Enterprise Liability*, 91 MICHIGAN LAW REVIEW 683 (1993); Anthony Sebok, *What Did Punitive Damages Do?* note 92.

94. Marc Galanter, *The Life and Times of the Big Six; Or, The Federal Courts Since the Good Old Days*, 1988 WISCONSIN LAW REVIEW 921 (1988).

95. See THOMAS PETZINGER JR., OIL AND HONOR: THE TEXACO PENNZOIL WARS (1987).

96. See Marc Galanter, *The Vanishing Trial: An Examination of Trials and Related Matters in Federal and State Courts*, 3 JOURNAL OF EMPIRICAL LEGAL STUDIES 459 (2004).

97. *Id.*

98. *Id.* at 462–63.

99. *Id.* at 493 and 554.

100. *Id.* at 506.

101. *Id.* at 507 (civil) and p. 512 (criminal). The study examined filings in the general jurisdiction courts of twenty-one states, the District of Columbia, and Puerto Rico, with slightly different numbers of states for civil and criminal comparisons. For additional analysis of state court data, see Brian J. Ostrom, Shauna M. Strickland & Paula L. Hannaford-Agor, *Examining Trial Trends in State Courts: 1976–2002*, 3 JOURNAL OF EMPIRICAL LEGAL STUDIES 755 (2004).

102. ELLEN E. SWARD, THE DECLINE OF THE CIVIL JURY (2001).

CHAPTER 3: A JURY OF PEERS

1. Transcription of the deliberation of a civil jury deliberation, from the Arizona Jury Project. See Shari Diamond, Neil Vidmar, Mary Rose, Leslie Ellis & Beth Murphy, *Juror Discussions during Trials: Studying an Arizona Innovation*, 45 ARIZONA LAW REVIEW 1 (2003).

2. *Glasser v. United States*, 315 U.S. 60 (1942). The source of information about the composition of the jury pool was said to come from the article *Women and the Law*, 26 AMERICAN BAR ASSOCIATION JOURNAL 354, 354–56 (1940).

3. *Glasser v. United States*, 315 U.S., at 86. Although the Court did not set aside Mr. Glasser's conviction on jury selection grounds (*id.* at 87), it was overturned on an assistance of counsel claim. *Id.* at 76.

4. For an excellent discussion of the historical development and current status of the special jury, see JAMES C. OLDHAM, TRIAL BY JURY: THE SEVENTH AMENDMENT AND ANGLO-AMERICAN SPECIAL JURIES (2006). *See also* James C. Oldham, *The Origins of the Special Jury*, 50 UNIVERSITY OF CHICAGO LAW REVIEW 137 (1983); and modern essays on the desirability of resurrecting the special jury: William V. Luneberg & Mark A. Nordenberg, *Specially Qualified Juries and Expert Nonjury Tribunals: Alternatives for Coping with the Complexities of Modern Civil Litigation*, 67 VIRGINIA LAW REVIEW 904 (1981); Michael A. Fisher, *Going for the Blue Ribbon: The Legality of Expert Juries in Patent Litigation*, 2 COLUMBIA SCIENCE AND TECHNOLOGY LAW REVIEW 1 (2000–2001).

5. Alan Feigenbaum, *Special Juries: Deterring Spurious Medical Malpractice Litigation in State Courts*, 24 CARDOZO LAW REVIEW 1361 (2003).

6. Oldham, *The Origins of the Special Jury*, note 4, at 171–72; Susan A. Lentz, *Without Peers: A History of Women and Trial by Jury Part One—From the Women's Sphere to Suffrage*, 11 WOMEN & CRIMINAL JUSTICE 83, 91–92 (2000); Gretchen Ritter, *Jury Service and Women's Citizenship Before and After the Nineteenth Amendment*, 20 LAW & HISTORY REVIEW 479, 493–94 (2002). The jury of matrons was also used in a few other contexts, such as in disputes over inheritance.

7. Oldham, *The Origins of the Special Jury*, note 4.

8. Jeannette E. Thatcher, *Why Not Use the Special Jury?* 31 MINNESOTA LAW REVIEW 232, 233 (1947).

9. *New Windsor Turnpike Co. v. Ellison*, 1 Johns. 141 (NY Supp. 1806).

10. *Industrial & Gen. Trust. v. Tod*, 95 N. Y. S. 44, 45 (1905).

11. *Fay v. New York*, 332 U.S. 261 (1947).

12. FOURTH ANNUAL REPORT OF THE JUDICIAL COUNCIL OF THE STATE OF NEW YORK (1938), cited in *Fay v. New York*, 332 U.S. 261 (1947).

13. *Id.*

14. E.g., *Moore v. New York*, 333 U.S. 565 (1948).

15. OLDHAM, TRIAL BY JURY, note 4.

16. Fisher, *Going for the Blue Ribbon*, note 4. See also the detailed discussion of Delaware's use of the special jury in OLDHAM, TRIAL BY JURY, note 4, at 207–209.

17. See generally MARIANNE CONSTABLE, THE LAW OF THE OTHER (1994); Deborah A. Ramirez, *The Mixed Jury and the Ancient Custom of Trial by Jury de Medietate Linguae: A History and a Proposal for Change*, 74 BOSTON UNIVERSITY LAW REVIEW 777 (1994).

18. Ramirez, *Mixed Jury*, note 17.

19. *Id.* at 786.

20. *Id.* at 787.

21. *Id.* at 790–91.

22. HIROSHI FUKURAI, EDGAR W. BUTLER, & RICHARD KROOTH, RACE AND THE JURY: RACIAL DISENFRANCHISEMENT AND THE SEARCH FOR JUSTICE 86–89 (1993) (describing the early history of Supreme Court cases involving race, citizenship, and jury service).

23. *Strauder v. West Virginia*, 100 U.S. 306 (1880).

24. *Id.* at 308.

25. Sources for the Scottsboro case and trials: DAN T. CARTER, SCOTTSBORO: A TRAGEDY OF THE AMERICAN SOUTH (1979); Douglas Linder, *Famous American Trials: The Scottsboro Boys Trials: 1931–1937*, FAMOUS TRIALS WEB SITE, http://law.umkc.edu/faculty/projects/ftrials/Scottsboro/scottsb.htm; Faust Rossi, *The First Scottsboro Trials: A Legal Lynching*, Vol. 29 #2 CORNELL LAW FORUM 1 (2002); Faust Rossi, *The Scottsboro Trials: A Legal Lynching (Part II)*, Vol. 29 #3 CORNELL LAW FORUM 3 (2003). See also Cornell Law School's library Web site on the Scottsboro trial: http://lawschool.cornell.edu/library/Scottsboro (accessed February 17, 2007).

26. *Norris v. Alabama*, 294 U.S. 587 (1935). See the discussion of the Norris case in FUKURAI ET AL., RACE AND THE JURY, note 22, at 89–91.

27. *Avery v. Georgia*, 345 U.S. 559 (1953).

28. As the Court recounted: "[T]here were 534 names on the grand jury list and of this number only six were Negroes. Of the six Negroes, one did not reside in the county and the other five testified in this proceeding. Two were over 80 years of age; one was partially deaf and the other in poor health. The remaining three were 62 years of age. Each of the witnesses had lived in the county for at least 30 years. None had ever served on a grand jury nor heard of any other Negroes serving on a grand jury in the county." *Reece v. Georgia*, 350 U.S. 85, 88 (1955). The sizable black population in the county and the dominance of all-white juries constituted, in the Court's view, a strong showing of systematic exclusion.

29. *Swain v. Alabama*, 380 U.S. 207 (1965).

30. FUKURAI ET AL., RACE AND THE JURY, note 22, at 100–102; and WALLACE D. LOH, SOCIAL RESEARCH IN THE JUDICIAL PROCESS: CASES, READINGS, AND TEXT (1984) at 362, for discussions of statistical errors in *Swain*.

31. Citations to excellent articles on women's jury service include the following: Carol Weisbrod, *Images of the Woman Juror*, 9 HARVARD WOMEN'S LAW JOURNAL 59 (1986); Cristina M. Rodriguez, *Clearing the Smoke-Filled Room: Women Jurors and the Disruption of an Old Boys' Network in Nineteenth-Century America*, 108 YALE LAW JOURNAL 1805 (1998–1999); Barbara Allen Babcock, *A Place in the Palladium: Women's Rights and Jury Service*, 61 UNIVERSITY OF CINCINNATI LAW REVIEW 1139 (1993); Joanna L. Grossman, *Women's Jury Service: Right of Citizenship or Privilege of Difference?* 46 STANFORD LAW REVIEW 1115 (1994); Susan A. Lentz, *Without Peers: A History of Women and Trial by Jury Part Two—The Law of Jury Service in the Twentieth Century*, 11 WOMEN & CRIMINAL JUSTICE 81 (2000); Lentz, *Without Peers*, note 6; Ritter, *Jury Service*, note 6.

32. Albert Alschuler & Andrew Deiss, *A Brief History of the Criminal Jury in the United States*, 61 CHICAGO LAW REVIEW 867, 898–99 (1994).

33. *Id.* at 900, text and note 171.

34. *Id.*

35. *Hoyt v. Florida*, 368 U.S. 57 (1961). See also Alschuler & Deiss, *Brief History*, note 32, at 900.

36. *Hoyt v. Florida*, 368 U.S. at 62.

37. *Taylor v. Louisiana*, 419 U.S. 522 (1975).

38. *Duren v. Missouri*, 439 U.S. 357 (1979).

39. See generally Andrew Leipold, *Constitutionalizing Jury Selection in Criminal Cases: A Critical Evaluation*, 86 GEORGETOWN LAW JOURNAL 945 (1998).

40. *Thiel v. Southern Pacific Company*, 328 U.S. 217, 220, 223–24 (1946).

41. *Georgia v. McCollum*, 505 U.S. 42 (1992).

42. See, e.g., Phoebe Ellsworth, *Are Twelve Heads Better than One?* 52 LAW & CONTEMPORARY PROBLEMS 205 (1989); Samuel R. Sommers, *On Racial Diversity and Group Decision Making: Identifying Multiple Effects of Racial Composition on Jury Deliberations*, 90 JOURNAL OF PERSONALITY & SOCIAL PSYCHOLOGY 597 (2006). In a compelling essay on jury size, Richard O. Lempert identified multiple ways that diversity could enhance fact-finding; see *Uncovering "Nondiscernible" Differences: Jury Research and the Jury Size Cases*, 73 MICHIGAN LAW REVIEW 644, 670–71 (1974–1975).

43. Sommers, *On Racial Diversity*, note 42.

44. *Georgia v. McCollum*, 505 U.S. 42, 68 (1992) (O'Connor, dissenting).

45. Quoted in Steve McGonigle, Holly Becka, Jennifer LaFleur, & Tim Wyatt, *A Process of Juror Elimination*, DALLAS MORNING NEWS, August 21, 2005, available at http://www.dallasnews.com/sharedcontent/dws/news/longterm/stories/082105dnproprosecutors.378d9eb.html (accessed February 17, 2007); see also Sommers, *On Racial Diversity*, note 42.

46. During a five-year period, the phrase "all-white jury" appeared over two hundred times in three major newspapers. *Georgia v. McCollum*, 505 U.S. 42, 52–53 n.1 (1992) (Thomas, concurring).

47. Doug Linder, *The Trials of Los Angeles Police Officers' in Connection with the Beating of Rodney King*, FAMOUS TRIALS WEB SITE (2001), http://www.law.umkc.edu/faculty/projects/ftrials/lapd/lapdaccount.html (accessed February 17, 2007).

48. *Id.*

49. JEFFREY ABRAMSON, WE THE JURY: THE JURY SYSTEM AND THE IDEAL OF DEMOCRACY 139–41 (1994).

50. Robert G. BOATRIGHT, IMPROVING CITIZEN RESPONSE TO JURY SUMMONSES: A REPORT WITH RECOMMENDATIONS (American Judicature Society, 1998). See also a number of informative articles summarizing different aspects of the report by Boatright and colleagues: Robert G. Boatright, *Why Citizens Don't Respond to Jury Summonses, and What Courts Can Do about It*, 82 JUDICATURE 156 (1999); Robert G. Boatright, *Generational and Age-Based Differences in Attitudes towards Jury Service*, 19 BEHAVIORAL SCIENCES AND THE LAW 285 (2001); Susan Carol Losh & Robert G. Boatright, *Life-Cycle Factors, Status, and Civil Engagement: Issues of Age and Attitudes toward Jury Service*, 23 JUSTICE SYSTEM JOURNAL 221 (2002).

51. Curriden (1996), cited in BOATRIGHT, IMPROVING CITIZEN RESPONSE, note 50, at 15.

52. BOATRIGHT, IMPROVING CITIZEN RESPONSE, note 50.

53. See HIROSHI FUKURAI ET AL., RACE AND THE JURY, note 22. For analysis of Texas, see Mary R. Rose, Shari Seidman Diamond & Marc A. Musick, *Who Gets to Be a Juror? An Analysis of Prevalence in the Multi-stage Process of Jury Selection*, paper presented at the CLS-JELS Junior Empirical Scholars Meeting, Cornell Law School, Ithaca, NY (October 2005). Texas jury selection problems are also described in McGonigle et al., *Process of Juror Elimination*, note 45.

54. BOATRIGHT, IMPROVING CITIZEN RESPONSE, note 50.

55. John Paul Ryan, *What Do Americans Believe about Jury Service?* 5.2 INSIGHTS ON LAW & SOCIETY 19 (Winter 2005).

56. David Letterman, *Top 10 Ways to Get Out of Jury Duty* (CBS television broadcast

November 14, 1990; reprinted in JUR-E BULLETIN, September 23, 2005, http://www.ncsconline.org/WC/Publications/KIS_JurInnJurE09-23-05.pdf)(accessed August 8, 2007).

57. *Tom Munsterman's Exceptional Excuses*. JUR-E BULLETIN, September 23, 2005, http://www.ncsconline.org/WC/Publications/KIS_JurInnJurE09-23-05.pdf (accessed August 8, 2007).

58. KING JAMES I, A PROCLAMATION FOR JURORS (1607).

59. ROBERT S. SUTCLIFFE, IMPRESSIONS OF AN AVERAGE JURYMAN 65–66 (1922).

60. *The Dog Ate My Summons*, JUR-E BULLETIN, January 9, 2004, http://www.ncsconline.org/WC/Publications/KIS_JuryInnJurE01-09-04.pdf (accessed February 17, 2007).

61. *Puritanical Crackdown*, JUR-E BULLETIN, October 1, 2004, http://www.ncsconline.org/WC/Publications/KIS_JurInnJurE10-1-04.pdf (accessed February 17, 2007).

62. BOATRIGHT, IMPROVING CITIZEN RESPONSE, note 50.

63. *Id.*

64. Brian C. Kalt, *The Exclusion of Felons from Jury Service*, 53 AMERICAN UNIVERSITY LAW REVIEW 65 (2003); Amanda L. Kutz, *A Jury of One's Peers: Virginia's Restoration of Rights Process and Its Disproportionate Impact on the African American Community*, 46 WILLIAM & MARY LAW REVIEW 2109, 2110 (2005).

65. Kutz, *Jury of One's Peers*, note 64, at 2122–23.

66. Kalt, *Exclusion of Felons from Jury Service*, note 64, at 65.

67. Kutz, *Jury of One's Peers*, note 64, at 2135–39.

68. See *id.*, and Kalt, *Exclusion of Felons from Jury Service*, note 64, for their cogent analyses.

69. Kalt, *Exclusion of Felons from Jury Service*, note 64, at 65.

70. See, e.g., Deborah Ann A'Hearn, *Blind Injustice: Seeing beyond the DC Superior Court Exclusion of Blind Citizens from Jury Duty*, 2 DISTRICT OF COLUMBIA LAW REVIEW 431 (1993–1994); Nancy Lawler Dickhute, *Jury Duty for the Blind in the Time of Reasonable Accommodations: The ADA's Interface with a Litigant's Right to a Fair Trial*, 32 CREIGHTON LAW REVIEW 849 (1999); Andrew Philip McGuire, *Blind Justice: Should the Courts Ban Blind and Deaf Citizens from Serving as Jurors?* 10 WASHINGTON LAW REVIEW 30 (1996).

71. New York's history of jury exclusions and exemptions provides an illustrative example. See Phylis Skloot Bamberger, *Democratizing the Supreme Court: 300 Years of the Jury*, in LOOKING BACK ON A GLORIOUS PAST 1691–1991 (Historical Society of the Courts of the State of New York e-book), http://www.nycourts.gov/history/pdf/Library/Events/Glorious_Past.pdf (accessed February 17, 2007). See also Judith S. Kaye, *My Life as Chief Judge: The Chapter on Juries*, 78 NEW YORK STATE BAR ASSOCIATION JOURNAL 10 (October 2006); she describes the sweeping changes that led to an expansion of the jury pool.

72. Jonna Spillbor, *The Ultimate Jury-Duty Excuse: "I'm President."* LOS ANGELES DAILY JOURNAL, December 23, 2005, at 6.

73. Shirley S. Abramson, *Justice and Juror*, 20 GEORGIA LAW REVIEW 257, 297 (1986). For a law professor's intriguing essay on her experience on a criminal jury, see Stacy Caplow, *The Impossible Dream Comes True: A Criminal Law Professor Becomes Juror # 7*, 67 BROOKLYN LAW REVIEW 785 (2002).

74. SANJA KUTNJAK IVKOVIĆ, LAY PARTICIPATION IN CRIMINAL TRIALS: THE CASE OF CROATIA 165–202 (1999).

CHAPTER 4: JURY SELECTION

1. Information about the case was obtained from news articles, case files, and separate interviews with the trial judge and one of the jurors. News articles included Sean O'Sullivan, *Family Sues Doctor Who Performed Abortion*, NEWS JOURNAL (Wilmington, DE), January 8, 2002; Sean O'Sullivan, *Doctor's Malpractice Case Goes to Jury Today*, NEWS JOURNAL (Wilmington, DE), January 15, 2002; Sean O'Sullivan, *$2.2 Million Awarded in Abortion Death*, NEWS JOURNAL (Wilmington, DE), January 16, 2002. Antiabortion Web sites also carried news stories on the Harris case; see, e.g., http://www.priestsforlife.org/news/infonet/infonet02-01-11.htm (accessed January 19, 2004). Case files: *Harris v. National Women's Health Organization of Delaware, Inc. et al.*, Jury selection, Superior Court of the State of Delaware, New Castle County, January 2, 2002; *Harris v. National Women's Health Organization of Delaware, Inc. et al.*, Jury selection and conference in chambers at 4–8, Superior Court of the State of Delaware, New Castle County, January 3, 2002; *Mohammad Imran M.D. v. George A. Harris Jr. et al.*, C. A. No. 99C-09-138, Superior Court of the State of Delaware, New Castle County; affirmed by Del. Supreme Ct., June 26, 2003. Interviews include one by Valerie Hans with Judge Jan Jurden, in Wilmington, Delaware (June 30, 2003), also by Valerie Hans with a Harris case juror (name withheld to protect confidentiality), in Wilmington, Delaware (October 13, 2004). Case transcripts are on file with the authors.

2. O'Sullivan, *Family Sues Doctor Who Performed Abortion*, note 1.

3. *Harris v. National Women's Health Organization*, Jury selection, note 1, at 194–95.

4. *Id.* at 192.

5. *Id.* at 99.

6. *Id.* at 22.

7. *Id.* at 25–26.

8. *Id.* at 221.

9. *Id.* at 167–68.

10. *Id.* at 119–20.

11. *Id.* at 148–50.

12. *Id.* at 108–10.

13. *Id.* at 97–98.

14. *Id.* at. 276.

15. *Harris v. National Women's Health Organization*, Jury selection and conference in chambers, note 1, at 4–8.

16. *Harris v. National Women's Health Organization*, Jury selection, note 1, at 271–72.

17. *Harris v. National Women's Health Organization*, Jury selection and conference in chambers, note 1, at 5.

18. Specific details of the expert testimony were covered in the story on the Harris case at http://www.priestsforlife.org/news/infonet/infonet02-01-11.htm, note 1.

19. *Id.*; see also O'Sullivan, *Doctor's Malpractice Case Goes to Jury Today*, note 1.

20. Interview by Valerie Hans with Harris juror, note 1.

21. O'Sullivan, *$2.2 Million Awarded in Abortion Death*, note 1.

22. *Miles v. United States*, 103 U.S. 304 (1880). Prospective juror Dunn's statement is taken verbatim from p. 306.

23. Nancy King, *Silencing Nullification Advocacy Inside the Jury Room and Outside the Courtroom*, 65 UNIVERSITY OF CHICAGO LAW REVIEW 433, 469 (1998).

24. For Massachusetts, see PETER OXENBRIDGE THATCHER, OBSERVATION OF SOME METHODS KNOWN IN THE LAW OF MASSACHUSETTS, TO SECURE THE SELECTION AND APPOINTMENT OF AN IMPARTIAL JURY IN CASES CIVIL AND CRIMINAL (1834); for other states, see 24 CYCLOPEDIA OF LAW & PROCEDURE, 348–51 (William Mack ed., 1908).

25. CYCLOPEDIA OF LAW & PROCEDURE, note 24, at 348.

26. *Id.* at 351.

27. King, *Silencing Nullification Advocacy*, note 23, at 472.

28. See CYCLOPEDIA OF LAW & PROCEDURE, note 24, at 311–12.

29. *Id.*; see also *Commonwealth v. Brown*, 23 Pa. Super. 470 (1903).

30. *United States v. Butler*, 25 F. Cas. 213 (1877).

31. As quoted in S. Mac Guttman, *The Attorney-Conducted Voir Dire of Jurors: A Constitutional Right*, 39 BROOKLYN LAW REVIEW 290, 296–97 (1972).

32. *Id.*; see also CYCLOPEDIA OF LAW & PROCEDURE, note 24, at 338–39, 345 (1908).

33. Barbara Babcock, *Voir Dire: Preserving "Its Wonderful Power,"* 27 STANFORD LAW REVIEW 545 (1975).

34. Federal Rule of Criminal Procedure 24(a).

35. David Suggs & Bruce Sales, *Juror Self-Disclosure in the Voir Dire: A Social Psychological Analysis*, 56 INDIANA LAW JOURNAL 245, 251 (1981).

36. *Id.*

37. DAVID B. ROTTMAN ET AL., STATE COURT ORGANIZATION 1998, 279 tbl. 41 (2000), available at http://www.ojp.usdoj.gov/bjs/pub/pdf/sco98.pdf (accessed February 17, 2007).

38. John Shapard & Molly Johnson, *Memorandum to Advisory Committee on Civil Rules and Advisory Committee on Criminal Rules, re: Survey Concerning Voir Dire*, October 4, 1994. Researchers mailed a questionnaire to a randomly selected sample of one hundred and fifty active federal district court judges, and 83 percent (124 judges) responded to the survey.

39. *Id.* at 1.

40. GREGORY E. MIZE, PAULA HANNAFORD-AGOR & NICOLE L. WATERS, THE STATE-OF-THE-STATES SURVEY OF JURY IMPROVEMENT EFFORTS: A COMPENDIUM REPORT (2007), available at http://www.ncsconline.org/D_Research/cjs/pdf/SOSCompendiumFinal.pdf.

41. PAULA L. HANNAFORD-AGOR & NICOLE L. WATERS, EXAMINING VOIR DIRE IN CALIFORNIA (2004), available at http://www.ncsconline.org/juries/CAVOIRREP.pdf (accessed February 13, 2007).

42. Peggy Lowe & Charlie Brennan, *Jury Pool Is Queried*, ROCKY MOUNTAIN NEWS, August 28, 2004; Peggy Lowe, *Bryant Jury Pool Grows*, ROCKY MOUNTAIN NEWS, August 30, 2004.

43. See generally Neal Bush, *The Case for Expansive Voir Dire*, 2 LAW & PSYCHOLOGY REVIEW 9 (1976); Douglas B. Catts, *Jury Bias*, ADVOCATE, Winter 2001, at 20; Valerie P. Hans, *The Conduct of Voir Dire: A Psychological Analysis*, 11 JUSTICE SYSTEM JOURNAL 40 (1986); Frederick W. Iobst, *The Goal of Expanded Voir Dire*, ADVOCATE,

Winter 2001, at 24; JURYWORK: SYSTEMATIC TECHNIQUES, 2nd ed., release 21 (Elissa Krauss & Beth Bonora eds., 2000).

44. Gregory E. Mize, *On Better Jury Selection: Spotting UFO Jurors before They Enter the Jury Room*, COURT REVIEW, Spring 1999, at 10.

45. *Id.* at 12.

46. *Id.* at 12–13.

47. *Id.* at 12.

48. Valerie P. Hans & Alayna Jehle, *Avoid Bald Men and People with Green Socks? Other Ways to Improve the Voir Dire Process in Jury Selection*, 78 CHICAGO-KENT LAW REVIEW 1179 (2003); Dale Broeder, *Voir Dire Examinations: An Empirical Study*, 38 SOUTHERN CALIFORNIA LAW REVIEW 503, 505 (1965).

49. Richard Seltzer, Mark A. Venuti & Grace M. Lopes, *Juror Honesty during the Voir Dire*, 19 JOURNAL OF CRIMINAL JUSTICE 451 (1991).

50. *Id.* at 456. Eight percent came forward; 30 percent did not.

51. *Id.* at 455.

52. *Id.* at 457–58.

53. Cathy Johnson & Craig Haney, *Felony Voir Dire: An Exploratory Study of Its Content and Effect*, 18 LAW & HUMAN BEHAVIOR 487 (1994).

54. *Id.* at 498–99.

55. *Id.* at 499.

56. Michael T. Nietzel & Ronald C. Dillehay, *The Effects of Variations in Voir Dire Procedures in Capital Murder Trials*, 6 LAW & HUMAN BEHAVIOR 1 (1982).

57. Michael T. Nietzel, Ronald C. Dillehay & Melissa J. Himelein, *Effects of Voir Dire Variations in Capital Trials: A Replication and Extension*, 5 BEHAVIORAL SCIENCES AND THE LAW 467 (1987). One puzzle is why defense challenges were affected by voir dire variations but prosecution challenges were not. Their studies predated the use of the *Witt* standard first enunciated in *Wainwright v. Witt*, 469 U.S. 412 (1985). The authors predict that more heterogeneous dismissals (by both prosecution and defense) will result from the more ambiguous *Witt* standard.

58. Nietzel et al., *Voir Dire Variations*, note 57, at 476.

59. VALERIE P. HANS, BUSINESS ON TRIAL: THE CIVIL JURY AND CORPORATE RESPONSIBILITY (2000).

60. Hazel Markus & R. B. Zajonc, *The Cognitive Perspective in Social Psychology*, in THE HANDBOOK OF SOCIAL PSYCHOLOGY 137, 184 (Gardner Lindzey & Elliot Aronson eds., 3rd ed. 1985).

61. Kathi Middendorf & James Luginbuhl, *The Value of a Nondirective Voir Dire Style in Jury Selection*, 22 CRIMINAL JUSTICE AND BEHAVIOR 129 (1995).

62. Richard E. Nisbett & Timothy Wilson, *Telling More Than We Can Know: Verbal Reports on Mental Processes*, 84 PSYCHOLOGICAL REVIEW 231 (1977); Robert W. Pearson, Michael Ross & Robyn M. Dawes, *Personal Recall and the Limits of Retrospective Questions in Surveys*, in QUESTIONS ABOUT QUESTIONS: INQUIRIES IN THE COGNITIVE BASES OF SURVEYS 64 (Judith M. Tanur ed., 1992).

63. David Suggs & Bruce Sales, *Juror Self-Disclosure in the Voir Dire: A Social Science Analysis*, 56 INDIANA LAW JOURNAL 245 (1981); Susan E. Jones, *Judge- Versus Attorney-Conducted Voir Dire*, 11 LAW & HUMAN BEHAVIOR 131 (1987).

64. Some advantages of juror questionnaires are described in Diane Wiley, *Pre–Voir*

Dire, Case-Specific Supplemental Juror Questionnaires, in HANDBOOK OF JURY RESEARCH (Walter F. Abbott & John Batt eds., 1999).

65. *Harris v. National Women's Health Organization*, jury selection, note 1, at 135–43.

66. Mary R. Rose & Shari Seidman Diamond, *Evaluating Bias in Challenges for Cause*, paper presented at the annual meeting of the Law & Society Association, Pittsburgh, PA (2003) (on file with authors).

67. Mary R. Rose & Shari S. Diamond, *Assessing Juror Bias from Multiple Angles: Judges, Attorneys and Jurors*, paper presented at the annual meeting of the American Psychology-Law Society, Phoenix, AZ (2004). This line of work is summarized in Mary R. Rose & Shari S. Diamond, *Judging Bias: Role-Based Decision Strategies and Perceptions of the Impartial Juror* (2007) (unpublished manuscript on file with the authors).

68. HANNAFORD-AGOR & WATERS, EXAMINING VOIR DIRE IN CALIFORNIA, note 41, at 26.

69. *Id.*

70. JURY SELECTION WITH JACK MCMAHON, DATV Productions videotape, no date. See discussion in David Baldus et al., *The Use of Peremptory Challenges in Capital Murder Trials: A Legal and Empirical Analysis*, 3 UNIVERSITY OF PENNSYLVANIA JOURNAL OF CONSTITUTIONAL LAW 3, 41–43 (2001). Baldus et al. quote from a transcript of the McMahon tape; our quotes are taken from the transcript as reported by Baldus et al.

71. Baldus et al., *Use of Peremptory Challenges*, note 70, at 43 note 153.

72. *J. E. B. v. Alabama ex rel. T. B.*, 511 U.S. 127 (1994).

73. *Swain v. Alabama*, 380 U.S. 202 (1965).

74. *Swain v. State*, 290 Ala. 123 (1973).

75. *Batson v. Kentucky*, 476 U.S. 79 (1986).

76. In 1991, the US Supreme Court forbade attorneys in civil cases to base their peremptory challenges on race in *Edmondson v. Leesville Concrete Co.*, 500 U.S. 614 (1991). Criminal defense attorneys were prohibited from considering race in exercising their peremptories in *Georgia v. McCollum*, 505 U.S. 42 (1992).

77. *J. E. B. v. Alabama ex rel. T. B.*, at 129. The prohibited categories may expand beyond race and gender; see John H. Mansfield & John H. Watson Jr., *Peremptory Challenges to Jurors Based Upon or Affecting Religion*, 34 SETON HALL LAW REVIEW 435 (2004).

78. Baldus et al., *Use of Peremptory Challenges*, note 70, at 31; Barbara Underwood, *Ending Race Discrimination in Jury Selection: Whose Right Is It Anyway?* 92 COLUMBIA LAW REVIEW 725 (1992).

79. Nancy S. Marder, *Justice Stevens, the Peremptory Challenge, and the Jury*, 74 FORDHAM LAW REVIEW 1683 (2006).

80. K. J. Mellili, *Batson in Practice: What We Have Learned about Batson and Peremptory Challenges*, 71 NOTRE DAME LAW REVIEW 447 (1996).

81. See discussion in Baldus et al., *Use of Peremptory Challenges*, note 70, at 43.

82. *Miller-El v. Dretke*, 545 U.S. 231 (2005).

83. Baldus et al., *Use of Peremptory Challenges*, note 70, at 52–53 (see also tbl. 2 at 53).

84. Mary Rose, *The Peremptory Challenge Accused of Race or Gender Discrimination? Some Data from One County*, 23 LAW & HUMAN BEHAVIOR 695–702 (1999).

85. Samuel R. Sommers & Michael I. Norton, *Race-Based Judgments, Race-Neutral*

Justifications: Experimental Examination of Peremptory Use and the Batson Challenge Procedure, 31 LAW & HUMAN BEHAVIOR 261 (2007).

86. Steve McGonigle et al., *Jurors' Race a Focal Point for Defense*, DALLAS MORNING NEWS, January 24, 2005, available at http://www.dallasnews.com/s/dws /spe/2005 /jury/index_jury.html.

87. Marder, *Justice Stevens*, note 79, at 1706–1707.

88. Solomon Fulero & Steven Penrod, *The Myths and Realities of Attorney Jury Selection Folklore and Scientific Jury Selection*, 27 OHIO NORTHERN UNIVERSITY LAW REVIEW 229 (1990).

89. Hans Zeisel & Shari Seidman Diamond, *The Effect of Peremptory Challenges on Jury and Verdict: An Experiment in a Federal District Court*, 30 STANFORD LAW REVIEW 491, 507 (1978). Two caveats: the sample is small, and the analysis rests on assumptions about the relationship between initial and final verdicts.

90. Baldus et al., *Use of Peremptory Challenges*, note 70, at 125–27.

91. *Id.* at 126.

92. Cathy Johnson & Craig Haney, *Felony Voir Dire: An Exploratory Study of Its Content and Effect*, 18 LAW & HUMAN BEHAVIOR 487 (1994).

93. *Batson v. Kentucky*, 476 U.S. 79, 102–103, 107 (1986).

94. Criminal Justice Act 1988, § 118. See discussion in Sally Lloyd-Bostock & Cheryl Thomas, *The Continuing Decline of the English Jury*, in WORLD JURY SYSTEMS 53–91 (Neil Vidmar ed., 2000).

95. COUNCIL FOR COURT EXCELLENCE, JURIES FOR THE YEAR 2000 AND BEYOND: PROPOSALS TO IMPROVE THE JURY SYSTEMS IN WASHINGTON, DC (1998), available at http:// www.courtexcellence.org/juryreform/juries2000_final_report.pdf (accessed February 17, 2007). See Recommendation 19d, eliminating or drastically reducing the number of peremptory strikes, at 24–37.

96. Mary R. Rose, *A Voir Dire of Voir Dire: Listening to Juror's Views regarding the Peremptory Challenge*, 78 CHICAGO-KENT LAW REVIEW 1061 (2003). See also Mary R. Rose, *A Dutiful Voice: Justice in the Distribution of Jury Service*, 39 LAW & SOCIETY REVIEW 601 (2005).

97. HANNAFORD-AGOR & WATERS, EXAMINING VOIR DIRE IN CALIFORNIA, note 41, at 21–23.

98. See discussion of the history of systematic approaches to jury selection in VALERIE P. HANS & NEIL VIDMAR, JUDGING THE JURY 80–82 (1986).

99. Brenda Sandburg, *Flight Plan*, AMERICAN LAWYER, September 2006, available at http://www.americanlawyer.com/contents0906.shtml. (accessed February 17, 2007).

100. *Id.*

101. *Id.*

102. In addition to the discussion of the effectiveness of jury consulting techniques in HANS & VIDMAR, JUDGING THE JURY, note 98, at 89–92, other excellent treatments of the topic can be found in NEIL J. KRESSEL & DORIT F. KRESSEL, STACK AND SWAY: THE NEW SCIENCE OF JURY CONSULTING (2002); JOEL D. LIEBERMAN & BRUCE D. SALES, SCIENTIFIC JURY SELECTION (2007); and AMY J. POSEY & LAWRENCE S. WRIGHTSMAN, TRIAL CONSULTING (2005).

103. See generally KRESSEL & KRESSEL, STACK AND SWAY, note 102; POSEY & WRIGHTSMAN, note 102. See also the thoughtful discussion of issues in the overall effec-

tiveness of systematic jury selection in LIEBERMAN & SALES, SCIENTIFIC JURY SELECTION, note 102, at 143–65.

CHAPTER 5: PROBLEM CASES

1. See Petition for Review with Request for Stay, *Peterson v. Superior Ct. of San Mateo County*, No. S129466 (CA, November 24, 2004), denied November 29, 2004. The defense petitioned for a new penalty phase jury, making the argument that refusing to sequester the Peterson jury between the guilt and penalty phases biased the Peterson jury. The court, however, denied the request. For the perspective of several Peterson jurors who wrote a book about the case, see GREG BERATLIS ET AL., WE, THE JURY: DECIDING THE SCOTT PETERSON CASE (2006).

2. See, generally, MICHAEL J. PELLOWSKI, THE O. J. SIMPSON MURDER TRIAL: A HEADLINE COURT CASE (2001); JANICE E. SCHUETZ & LIN S. LILLEY, THE O. J. SIMPSON TRIALS: RHETORIC, MEDIA, AND THE LAW (1999).

3. Globe Wire Services, *Merck Fails in Bid to Postpone Vioxx Trial: Texas Judge Rejects Firm's Request for Two-Month Delay*. BOSTON GLOBE, July 6, 2005, available at www.boston.com; Kristen Hays, *Judge Refuses to Delay Vioxx Jury Selection*, BUSINESS WEEK, July 5, 2005, available at www.businessweek.com (accessed February 21, 2007).

4. Globe Wire Services, *Merck Fails in Bid to Postpone Vioxx Trial*, note 3; Hays, *Judge Refuses to Delay Vioxx Jury Selection*, note 3.

5. David P. Brown, *Growth of Lawsuits Creates Litigation Communications*, BUSINESS REVIEW (Albany), February 16, 1998. See a related discussion of the impact of litigation publicity on company reputations in VALERIE P. HANS, BUSINESS ON TRIAL: THE CIVIL JURY AND CORPORATE RESPONSIBILITY 4–5 (2000).

6. Geoffrey P. Kramer, Norbert L. Kerr & John S. Carroll, *Pretrial Publicity, Judicial Remedies, and Jury Bias*, 14 LAW & HUMAN BEHAVIOR 409 (1990); see also *Special Issue: Law and the Media* (Valerie P. Hans ed.), 14 LAW & HUMAN BEHAVIOR 399 (1990); Valerie P. Hans, *Juror Bias Is a Special Problem in High-Profile Trials*, 5.2 AMERICAN BAR ASSOCIATION INSIGHTS ON LAW & SOCIETY 14 (2005); JON BRUSCHKE & WILLIAM E. LOGES, FREE PRESS VS. FAIR TRIALS: EXAMINING PUBLICITY'S ROLE IN TRIAL OUTCOMES (2004).

7. See, e.g., TIMOTHY MURPHY ET AL., MANAGING NOTORIOUS TRIALS (1998).

8. Sally Lloyd-Bostock & Cheryl Thomas, *The Continuing Decline of the English Jury*, in WORLD JURY SYSTEMS 53 (Neil Vidmar ed., 2000). See also David Corker & Michael Levi, *Pre-trial Publicity and Its Treatment in the English Courts*, 1996 CRIMINAL LAW REVIEW 622 (1996); and more generally, Neil Vidmar, *A Historical and Comparative Perspective on the Common Law Jury*, in WORLD JURY SYSTEMS, supra, at 1.

9. See Nancy Jean King, *The American Criminal Jury*, in WORLD JURY SYSTEMS, note 8, at 93.

10. For extended discussion of problems involving juror conduct, see JURY ETHICS: JUROR CONDUCT AND JURY DYNAMICS (John Kleinig & James Levine eds., 2006).

11. *Irvin v. Dowd*, 366 U.S. 717 (1961). Quotations cited in the text appear on pages 727 and 728 of the Court's opinion.

12. *Rideau v. Louisiana*, 373 U.S. 723 (1963).

13. *Sheppard v. Maxwell*, 384 U.S. 333 (1966).

14. *Id.* at 362.

15. Information on the Sam Sheppard case is widely available. See, e.g., Douglas O. Linder, *Dr. Sam Sheppard Trials (1954 and 1966)*, FAMOUS TRIALS WEB SITE, http://www.law.umkc.edu/faculty/projects/FTrials/sheppard/Sheppard.htm; Sam Sheppard Wikipedia entry, http://en.wikipedia.org/wiki/Sam_Sheppard (accessed February 21, 2007).

16. *Mu'Min v. Virginia*, 500 U.S. 415 (1991).

17. See Timothy McVeigh trial information at Douglas O. Linder, *Oklahoma City Bombing Trial (Timothy McVeigh Trial) 1997*, FAMOUS TRIALS WEB SITE, http://www.law.umkc.edu/faculty/projects/ftrials/mcveigh/mcveightrial.html; Oklahoma City Nat'l Memorial, http://www.oklahomacitynationalmemorial.org/hist.htm (accessed February 21, 2007).

18. Christina Studebaker & Steven D. Penrod, *Pretrial Publicity: The Media, the Law and Common Sense*, 3 PSYCHOLOGY, PUBLIC POLICY & LAW 428 (1997); Christina Studebaker et al., *Assessing Pretrial Publicity Effects: Integrating Content Analytic Results*, 24 LAW & HUMAN BEHAVIOR 317 (2000). The trial was moved to Denver; during the same nine-month period, the major Denver newspaper published 174 articles, including 9 photographs and 24 front-page stories. Just 18 percent of the Denver survey respondents said they were absolutely confident in McVeigh's guilt before the trial.

19. Studebaker & Penrod, *Pretrial Publicity*, note 18; Studebaker et al., *Assessing Pretrial Publicity Effects*, note 18.

20. *U.S. v. McVeigh*, 955 F. Supp. 1281 (D. Colo. 1997); see also *U.S. v. McVeigh*, F. Supp. 1467, 1473 (W.D. Okla. 1996). See also Stephen Jones & Holly Hillerman, *McVeigh, McJustice, McMedia*, 1998 UNIVERSITY OF CHICAGO LEGAL FORUM 53 (1998).

21. *City of Tulsa v. Tyson Foods et al.*, No. 01-CV-0900-EA (N.D. Okla. 2003).

22. *City of Durham v. Lodhal* (1995), as described in Neil Vidmar, *Case Studies of Pre- and Midtrial Prejudice in Criminal and Civil Litigation*, 26 LAW & HUMAN BEHAVIOR 73, 77 (2002).

23. Amy L. Otto, Steven D. Penrod & H. R. Dexter, *The Biasing Impact of Pretrial Publicity on Juror Judgments*, 18 LAW & HUMAN BEHAVIOR 453 (1994); Christina A. Studebaker & Steven D. Penrod, *Pretrial Publicity and Its Influence on Juror Decision Making*, in PSYCHOLOGY AND LAW: AN EMPIRICAL PERSPECTIVE 254, 254–55 (Neil Brewer & Kipling D. Williams eds., 2005). See Neil Vidmar, *When All of Us Are Victims*, 78 CHICAGO-KENT LAW REVIEW 1143, 1151 (2003) for a list of the different points in the trial process that the effects of pretrial publicity might be found. BRUSCHKE & LOGES, FREE PRESS VS. FAIR TRIALS, note 6, point out that studies designed to examine the impact of pretrial publicity show that the impact can vary, sometimes biasing juror judgments and sometimes not. They argue that legal remedies may be able to address negative effects of pretrial publicity. Most other scholars working in the area are not so optimistic.

24. KAI ERIKSON, WAYWARD PURITANS 4 (1966).

25. Neil Vidmar & Julius Melnitzer, *Juror Prejudice: An Empirical Study of a Challenge for Cause*, 22 OSGOODE HALL LAW JOURNAL 487 (1984).

26. Gerald Wetherington et al., *Preparing for the High Profile Case: An Omnibus Treatment for Judges and Lawyers*, 51 FLORIDA LAW REVIEW 425 (1999).

27. See, e.g., Neal Feigenson, *Sympathy and Legal Judgment: A Psychological Analysis*, 65 TENNESSEE LAW REVIEW 1 (1997); Vicki L. Fishfader et al., *Evidential and Extralegal Factors in Juror Decisions: Presentation Mode, Retention, and Level of Emo-*

tionality, 20 LAW & HUMAN BEHAVIOR 565 (1996); Norbert L. Kerr et al., *On the Effectiveness of Voir Dire in Criminal Cases with Prejudicial Pretrial Publicity: An Empirical Study*, 40 AMERICAN UNIVERSITY LAW REVIEW 665 (1991); Geoffrey P. Kramer et al., *Pretrial Publicity, Judicial Remedies, and Jury Bias*, 14 LAW & HUMAN BEHAVIOR 409 (1990); James Ogloff & Neil Vidmar, *The Impact of Pretrial Publicity on Jurors: A Study to Compare the Effects of Television and Print Media in a Child Sex Abuse Case*, 18 LAW & HUMAN BEHAVIOR 507 (1994); Nancy Steblay et al., *The Effects of Pretrial Publicity on Juror Verdicts: A Meta-analytic Review*, 23 LAW & HUMAN BEHAVIOR 219 (1999).

28. For reviews of this research, see Steblay et al., *Effects of Pretrial Publicity on Juror Verdicts*, note 27; Studebaker & Penrod, *Pretrial Publicity and Its Influence on Juror Decision Making*, note 18; Vidmar, *When All of Us Are Victims*, note 23.

29. Terry Honess, E. Charman & Michael Levi, *Factual and Affective/Evaluative Recall of Pretrial Publicity: Their Relative Influence on Juror Reasoning and Verdict in a Simulated Fraud Trial*, 33 JOURNAL OF APPLIED SOCIAL PSYCHOLOGY 1404 (2003).

30. See, generally, Vidmar, *When All of Us Are Victims*, note 23.

31. See J. Doppelt, *Generic Prejudice: How Drug Fervor Threatens Right to a Fair Trial*, 40 AMERICAN UNIVERSITY LAW REVIEW 821–36 (1991).

32. Neil Vidmar, *Generic Prejudice and the Presumption of Guilt in Sex Abuse Trials*, 21 LAW & HUMAN BEHAVIOR 5–25 (1997).

33. Lucy Arnot et al., *Generic Prejudice and the Law: Sexual Assault and Homicide*, 28 BASIC & APPLIED SOCIAL PSYCHOLOGY 145–55 (2006).

34. See, e.g., TRACY KENNEDY ET AL., MISTRIAL OF THE CENTURY: A PRIVATE DIARY OF THE JURY SYSTEM ON TRIAL 176–203 (1995); James Levine, *The Impact of Sequestration on Juries*, 79 JUDICATURE 266 (1996). Marcia Clark's remark quoted in the text may be found on p. 444 of MARCIA CLARK WITH TERESA CARPENTER, WITHOUT A DOUBT (1997).

35. Edward Bronson, *The Effectiveness of Voir Dire in Discovering Prejudice in High-publicity Cases: As Archival Study of the Minimization Effect*, unpublished manuscript, College of Behavioral and Social Sciences, California State University, Chico, CA (1989) (on file with authors). The quotes in the text are taken from Bronson's manuscript at pages 20–21 and 33–39.

36. Michael Nietzel & Ronald Dillehay, *Effects of Voir Dire Variations in Capital Trials: A Replication and Extension*, 5 BEHAVIORAL SCIENCE & LAW 467–77 (1987).

37. Archives of the September 11, 2001, Terrorist Attack on America at the World Trade Center Towers in New York City and the Pentagon in Washington, http://www.september11news.com/ (accessed February 21, 2007).

38. Indictment, *United States v. Lindh*, No. 02-37-A (E.D. Va. 2002). Case available at 227 F. Supp. 2d 565 (2002).

39. See Vidmar, *When All of Us are Victims*, note 23. Quotes from the survey respondents that appear in the text are taken from this source, and/or from the original questionnaires. See Vidmar, *When All of Us are Victims*, at 1164–66.

40. The case of Sami Al-Arian was covered extensively in the Tampa Bay newspapers; for a summary of the events and trial see Al-Arian Special Report, Tampa Bay Online, http://reports.tbo.com/reports/alarian/ (accessed February 21, 2007).

41. *Id.*

42. See Michael Fechter & Buddy Jaudon, *From the Beginning: A Timeline of the Sami Al-Arian Trial*, TAMPA TRIBUNE (December 7, 2005). The *Tampa Tribune* is available in its online format at http://www.TBO.com.

43. Declaration of Neil Vidmar, *United States v. Sami Amin Al-Arian et al.*, No. 8:03-CR-77-T-30TBM (M.D. Fla., Tampa Div., Apr. 28, 2005); Declaration of Edward J. Bronson, *United States v. Sami Amin Al-Arian et al.*, No. 8:03-CR-77-T-30TBM (M.D. Fla., Tampa Div., Apr. 28, 2005).

44. Declaration of Bronson, *United States v. Sami Amin Al-Arian et al.*, note 43, at 23.

45. *Id.* at 25.

46. *Id.* at 25–26.

47. *Id.* at 35.

48. *Id.* at 39–43.

49. Declaration of Vidmar, *United States v. Sami Amin Al-Arian et al.*, note 43.

50. *Id.* at 12.

51. *Id.* at 11.

52. *Id.* at 12.

53. *Id.*

54. *Id.* at 16.

55. Elaine Silvestrini, *Judge Says Al-Arian Trial Stays in Tampa*, TAMPA TRIBUNE, May 24, 2005, available at http://www.tbo.com (accessed February 21, 2007).

56. Michael Fechter, Elaine Silvestrini & Lenny Savino, *No Guilty Verdicts in the Al-Arian Trial*, TAMPA TRIBUNE, December 6, 2005.

57. Steblay et al., *Effects of Pretrial Publicity on Juror Verdicts*, note 27.

CHAPTER 6: THE TASKS OF THE JURY

1. E.g., PETER M. TIERSMA, LEGAL LANGUAGE (1999).

2. TOM R. TYLER, WHY PEOPLE OBEY THE LAW (2006).

3. This is not the place to explore the many differences in legal procedure between countries, but drawing attention to the uniqueness of adversary procedure sensitizes us to the unique way that facts are presented to the jury and the conditions under which they have to reconstruct what happened in order to reach a verdict. For background, see STEPHAN LANDSMAN, THE ADVERSARY SYSTEM: A DESCRIPTION AND DEFENSE (1984); MIRJAN R. DAMAŠKA, THE FACES OF JUSTICE AND STATE AUTHORITY: A COMPARATIVE APPROACH TO THE LEGAL PROCESS (1991).

4. PRINCIPLES FOR JURIES AND JURY TRIALS (American Bar Association, 2005). Principle 13C advocates juror questions in civil trials and suggests they be considered in criminal trials along with other factors: "In civil cases, jurors should, ordinarily, be permitted to submit written questions for witnesses. In deciding whether to permit jurors to submit written questions in criminal cases, the court should take into consideration the historic reasons why courts in a number of jurisdictions have discouraged juror questions and the experience in those jurisdictions that have allowed it." *Id.* at 91. For a discussion of research on juror questions and the issues that arise in their use in the adversary system, see Valerie P. Hans, *U.S. Jury Reform: The Active Jury and the Adversarial Ideal*, 21 SAINT LOUIS UNIVERSITY PUBLIC LAW REVIEW 85 (2002).

5. See, e.g., John Jackson & Nikolay Kovalev, *Lay Adjudication and Human Rights in Europe*, 13 COLUMBIA JOURNAL OF EUROPEAN LAW 20 (2006).

6. PRINCIPLES FOR JURIES AND JURY TRIALS, note 4. Principle 13A advocates that jurors be permitted to take notes.

7. Valerie P. Hans & Anthony N. Doob, *Section 12 of the Canada Evidence Act and the Deliberations of Simulated Juries*, 18 CRIMINAL LAW QUARTERLY 235 (1976); Roselle L. Wissler & Michael J. Saks, *On the Inefficacy of Limiting Instructions: When Jurors Use Prior Conviction Evidence to Decide on Guilt*, 9 LAW & HUMAN BEHAVIOR 37 (1985); Theodore Eisenberg & Valerie P. Hans, *Taking a Stand on Taking the Stand: The Effect of a Prior Criminal Record on the Decision to Testify and on Trial Outcomes*, paper presented at the meeting of the Law & Society Association, Berlin, Germany (2007), available at http://ssrn.com/id=998529.

8. John H. Blume, Sheri Lynn Johnson & Emily Paavola, *Every Juror Wants a Story, Story: Narrative Relevance, Third Party Guilt, and the Right to Present a Defense*, Cornell Law School Legal Studies Research Paper Series (2006), available at http://.ssrn .com/id=942653 (accessed February 18, 2007).

9. An excellent summary of the literature on hindsight bias, and how it affects judges as well as ordinary people, may be found in Chris Guthrie, Jeffrey J. Rachlinski & Andrew J. Wistrich, *Inside the Judicial Mind*, 86 CORNELL LAW REVIEW 777 (2001). See also Kim A. Kamin & Jeffrey J. Rachlinski, *Ex Post ≠ Ex Ante: Determining Liability in Hindsight*, 19 LAW & HUMAN BEHAVIOR 89 (1995).

10. W. LANCE BENNETT & MARTHA FELDMAN, RECONSTRUCTING REALITY IN THE COURTROOM: JUSTICE AND JUDGMENT IN AMERICAN CULTURE (1981).

11. *Id.* at 57–59.

12. See NEAL FEIGENSON, LEGAL BLAME: HOW JURORS THINK AND TALK ABOUT ACCIDENTS (Washington, DC: APA Books, 2000). Chapters 2 and 3 provide a highly useful review of the literature with particular reference to juror decisions.

13. Nancy Pennington & Reid Hastie, *A Cognitive Theory of Juror Decision Making: The Story Model*, 13 CARDOZO LAW REVIEW 519 (1991).

14. *Id.* at 524–25.

15. *Id.* at 521.

16. Vicki Smith, *How Jurors Make Decisions: The Value of Trial Innovations*, in JURY TRIAL INNOVATIONS 7 (G. Thomas Munsterman et al. eds., 2006).

17. REID HASTIE & ROBYN M. DAWES, RATIONAL CHOICE IN AN UNCERTAIN WORLD: THE PSYCHOLOGY OF JUDGMENT AND DECISION MAKING (2001).

18. Vicki Smith, *Prototypes in the Courtroom: Lay Representation of Legal Concepts*, 61 JOURNAL OF PERSONALITY & SOCIAL PSYCHOLOGY 857 (1991); NORMAN J. FINKEL, COMMONSENSE JUSTICE: JURORS' NOTIONS OF THE LAW (1995).

19. James A. Holstein, *Jurors' Interpretations and Jury Decision Making*, 9 LAW & HUMAN BEHAVIOR 83 (1985). Quotes from the mock jurors included in our text appear on p. 89 of Holstein's article.

20. FEIGENSON, LEGAL BLAME, note 12, at 171–210.

21. *Id.* at 183. Reprinted with permission of Neal Feigenson and APA Books.

22. Shari S. Diamond, Neil Vidmar, Mary Rose, Leslie Ellis & Beth Murphy, *Inside the Jury Room: Evaluating Juror Discussions during Trial*, JUDICATURE, September–October 2003, at 54.

23. John Manzo, *"You Wouldn't Take a Seven-Year-Old and Ask Him All These Questions": Jurors' Use of Practical Reasoning in Supporting Their Arguments*, 19 LAW &

SOCIAL INQUIRY 639 (1994). In the excerpts here, taken from pages 246–48 of the article, the article's original transcripts have been edited slightly to make them more understandable.

24. For a summary of the project, see Valerie P. Hans & Neil Vidmar, *The American Jury at Twenty-five Years*, 16 LAW & SOCIAL INQUIRY 323 (1991); Charles Hawkins, "Interaction and Coalition Realignments in Consensus-Seeking Groups: A Study of Experimental Jury Deliberations" (1960) (unpublished PhD dissertation, University of Chicago); Charles H. Hawkins, *Interaction Rates of Jurors Aligned in Factions*, 27 AMERICAN SOCIOLOGICAL REVIEW 689 (1962); Fred L. Strodtbeck, Rita M. James & Charles Hawkins, *Social Status in Jury Deliberations*, 22 AMERICAN SOCIOLOGICAL REVIEW 713 (1957).

25. Dennis J. Devine et al., *Jury Decision Making: 45 Years of Empirical Research on Deliberating Groups*, 7 PSYCHOLOGY, PUBLIC POLICY & LAW 622 (2001).

26. Hawkins, *Interaction Rates of Jurors Aligned in Factions*, note 24. PSYCHOLOGICAL REVIEW.

27. Two classic articles are James H. Davis, *Group Decision and Social Interaction: A Theory of Social Decision Schemes,* 80 PHYCHOLOGICAL REVIEW 97 (1973); and Norbert L. Kerr, *Social Transition Schemes: Charting the Group's Road to Agreement*, 41 JOURNAL OF PERSONALITY & SOCIAL PSYCHOLOGY 684 (1981). See also the excellent review by Devine et al., note 25.

CHAPTER 7: JUDGING THE JURY

1. HARRY KALVEN & HANS ZEISEL, THE AMERICAN JURY (1966).

2. The hung juries presented a problem, since there was no jury verdict with which to agree or disagree. They resolved it by counting each hung jury as half of a conviction and half of an acquittal.

3. A number of research articles report the findings of this study, which used the judge-jury agreement method to examine the frequency and causes of hung juries. See the original report: PAULA L. HANNAFORD-AGOR, VALERIE P. HANS, NICOLE L. MOTT & G. THOMAS MUNSTERMAN, ARE HUNG JURIES A PROBLEM? (National Center for State Courts, 2002), available at http://www.ncsconline.org/WC/Publications/Res_Juries_HungJuriesPub.pdf. See also Stephen P. Garvey, Paula Hannaford-Agor, Valerie P. Hans, Nicole L. Mott, G. Thomas Munsterman & Martin T. Wells, *Juror First Votes in Criminal Trials*, 1 JOURNAL OF EMPIRICAL LEGAL STUDIES 371 (2004); Valerie P. Hans, Paula L. Hannaford-Agor, Nicole L. Mott & G. Thomas Munsterman, *The Hung Jury: The American Jury's Insights and Contemporary Understanding*, 39 CRIMINAL LAW BULLETIN 33 (2003); Michael Heise, *Criminal Case Complexity: An Empirical Perspective*, JOURNAL OF EMPIRICAL LEGAL STUDIES 331 (2004); Theodore Eisenberg, Paula L. Hannaford-Agor, Valerie P. Hans, Nicole L. Mott, G. Thomas Munsterman, Stewart J. Schwab & Martin T. Wells, *Judge-Jury Agreement in Criminal Cases: A Partial Replication of Kalven & Zeisel's* THE AMERICAN JURY, 2 JOURNAL OF EMPIRICAL LEGAL STUDIES 171 (2005).

4. Eisenberg et al., *Judge-Jury Agreement in Criminal Cases*, note 3, at 185–89.

5. *Id.*, note 3, at 196–97.

6. Paula L. Hannaford, Valerie P. Hans & G. Thomas Munsterman, *Permitting Jury Discussions during Trial: Impact of the Arizona Jury Reform*, 24 LAW & HUMAN BEHAVIOR 359 (2000).

7. G. Thomas Munsterman et al., A Comparison of the Performance of Eight- and Twelve-Person Juries (National Center for State Courts, 1990).

8. Larry Heuer & Steven D. Penrod, *Trial Complexity: A Field Investigation of Its Meaning and Effects*, 18 Law & Human Behavior 29 (1994).

9. The literature on judge surveys is reviewed in Valerie P. Hans, *Attitudes toward the Civil Jury: A Crisis of Confidence?* in Verdict: Assessing the Civil Jury System 248, 261–65 (Robert E. Litan ed., 2003). Specific studies mentioned here include R. Perry Sentell, *The Georgia Jury and Negligence: The View from the Bench*, 26 Georgia Law Review 85 (1991); R. Perry Sentell, *The Georgia Jury and Negligence: The View from the (Federal) Bench*, 27 Georgia Law Review 59 (1992); Louis Harris & Associates, *Judges' Opinions on Procedural Issues: A Survey of State and Federal Judges Who Spend at Least Half Their Time on General Civil Cases* (1987); Ellen L. Rosen, *The View from the Bench: A National Law Journal Poll*, National Law Journal, August 10, 1987, at S1–S19; Gordon Bermant et al., Protracted Civil Trials: A View from the Bench (Federal Judicial Center, 1982).

10. Richard H. Field, Benjamin Kaplan & Kevin M. Clermont, Civil Procedure: Materials for a Basic Course (9th ed., 2007). Pages 1459–1508 discuss the legal issues in the right to a civil jury trial. In the federal system, not all matters may be tried to a jury; furthermore, the jury trial right is waived unless there is a timely demand for it.

11. Neil Vidmar, *Pap and Circumstance: What Jury Verdict Statistics Can Tell Us about Jury Behavior and the Tort System*, 28 Suffolk University Law Review 1205 (1994).

12. Kimberly A. Moore, *Judges, Juries, and Patent Cases—An Empirical Peek Inside the Black Box*, 99 Michigan Law Review 365 (2000).

13. *Id.* at 368.

14. Kimberly A. Moore, *Xenophobia in American Courts*, 97 Northwestern University Law Review 1497 (2003).

15. Kevin M. Clermont & Theodore Eisenberg, *Xenophilia in American Court*, 109 Harvard Law Review 1120 (1996). See also Kevin M. Clermont & Theodore Eisenberg, *Xenophilia or Xenophobia in American Courts? Before and After 9/11*, 4 Journal of Empirical Legal Studies 441 (2007).

16. Richard Lempert, *Civil Juries and Complex Cases: Taking Stock after Twelve Years*, in Verdict: Assessing the Civil Jury System 181 (Robert Litan ed., 1993).

17. Vidmar, Medical Malpractice and the American Jury 121–44 (1995).

18. Joseph Sanders, *The Jury Decision in a Complex Case: Havener v. Merrel Dow Pharmaceuticals*, 16 Justice System Journal 46 (1993). Sanders's conclusion, which we quote in the text, appears on p. 65 of this article. For a more extensive discussion of juries in the Bendectin litigation, see chapter 5 in Joseph Sanders, Bendectin on Trial: A Study of Mass Tort Litigation (1998).

19. Molly Selvin & Larry Picus, The Debate Over Jury Performance: Observations from a Recent Asbestos Case (1987).

20. See Tom Bower, Maxwell: The Outsider (1992).

21. Lord Justice Auld, Review of the Criminal Courts of England and Wales 135–39 (September 2001), available at http://www.criminal-courts-review.org.uk/auldconts.htm. The Fraud (Trials Without Jury) Bill 2006, which passed the House of Commons but is not certain to pass in the House of Lords in 2007, will require the prosecution in each case to obtain the approval of the Lord Chief Justice and to apply to a High Court

judge for an order agreeing to proceed without a jury. See http://www.publications.parliament.uk/pa/pabills/200607/fraud_trials_without_a_jury.htm.

22. Terry Honess, Michael Levi, & Elizabeth Charman, *Juror Competence in Processing Complex Trial Information: Implications from a Simulation of the Maxwell Trial*, 1998 CRIMINAL LAW REVIEW 763–73 (1998).

23. Sarah Tanford, Steven D. Penrod & Rebecca Collins, *Decision Making in Joined Criminal Trials: The Influence of Charge Similarity, Evidence Similarity, and Limiting Instructions*, 9 LAW & HUMAN BEHAVIOR 319 (1985).

24. See *id.*; see also Kenneth Bordens & Irwin Horowitz, *Joinder of Criminal Offenses: A Review of the Legal and Psychological Literature*, 9 LAW & HUMAN BEHAVIOR 339 (1985).

25. See *Cimino v. Raymark Industries, Inc.*, 751 F. Supp. 649 (1990).

26. Kenneth Bordens & Irwin Horowitz, *Mass Tort Civil Litigation: The Impact of Procedural Changes on Jury Decisions*, 73 JUDICATURE 22 (2003).

27. Lynne Foster Lee & Irwin Horowitz, *The Effects of Jury-aid Innovations on Juror Performance in Complex Civil Trials*, 86 JUDICATURE 184 (2003).

28. For excellent reviews of the legal and policy issues and relevant empirical evidence, see Joel Lieberman & Bruce Sales, *What Social Science Teaches Us about the Jury Instruction Process*, 3 PSYCHOLOGY, PUBLIC POLICY & LAW 589 (1997) and Peter English & Bruce Sales, *A Ceiling or Consistency Effect for the Comprehension of Jury Instructions*, 3 PSYCHOLOGY, PUBLIC POLICY & LAW 381 (1997).

29. NEWSWEEK, October 20, 1975, as described in AMIRAM ELWORK, BRUCE SALES & JAMES ALFINI, MAKING JURY INSTRUCTIONS UNDERSTANDABLE (1982).

30. *Id.*

31. Cal. Superior Court (LA County), Committee on Standard Jury Instructions, *California Jury Instructions: Criminal* 8.11 (6th ed., 1966).

32. Peter Tiersma, *The Rocky Road to Legal Reform: Improving the Language of Jury Instructions*, 66 BROOKLYN LAW REVIEW 1081, 1104 (2001).

33. ELWORK ET AL., MAKING JURY INSTRUCTIONS UNDERSTANDABLE, note 29, at 33.

34. Tiersma, *Rocky Road to Legal Reform*, note 32.

35. Vicki L. Smith, *When Prior Knowledge and Law Collide: Helping Jurors Use the Law*, 17 LAW & HUMAN BEHAVIOR 507 (1993).

36. *Id.*; See also Vicki L. Smith & Christina Studebaker, *What Do You Expect? The Influence of People's Prior Knowledge of Crime Categories on Fact Finding*, 20 LAW & HUMAN BEHAVIOR 517 (1996).

37. English & Sales, *Ceiling or Consistency Effect*, note 28.

38. Geoffrey Kramer & Dorean Koening, *Do Jurors Understand Criminal Jury Instructions? Analyzing the Results of the Michigan Juror Comprehension Project*, 23 UNIVERSITY OF MICHIGAN JOURNAL OF LAW REFORM 401, 414–15 (1990).

39. Norbert Kerr et al., *Guilt Beyond a Reasonable Doubt: Effects of Concept Definition and Assigned Decision Rule on the Judgments of Mock Jurors*, 34 JOURNAL OF PERSONALITY & SOCIAL PSYCHOLOGY 282 (1976).

40. Lieberman & Sales, *What Social Science Teaches Us*, note 28, at 559–600.

41. *Id.* at 600–601.

42. Valerie P. Hans & Anthony N. Doob, *Section 12 of the Canada Evidence Act and the Deliberations of Simulated Juries*, 18 CRIMINAL LAW QUARTERLY 235 (1976).

43. Roselle L. Wissler & Michael J. Saks, *On the Inefficacy of Limiting Instructions: When Jurors Use Prior Conviction Evidence to Decide on Guilt*, 9 LAW & HUMAN BEHAVIOR 37 (1985); Kerri L. Pickel, *Inducing Jurors to Disregard Inadmissible Evidence: A Legal Explanation Does Not Help*, 19 LAW & HUMAN BEHAVIOR 407 (1995).

44. Sally Lloyd-Bostock, *The Effects on Juries of Hearing about the Defendant's Previous Criminal Record: A Simulation Study*, 2000 CRIMINAL LAW REVIEW 734 (2000).

45. Stephan Landsman & Richard Rakos, *A Preliminary Inquiry into the Effect of Potentially Biasing Information on Judges and Jurors in Civil Litigation*, 12 BEHAVIORAL SCIENCES & THE LAW 113 (1994).

46. Chris Guthrie, Jeffrey J. Rachlinski & Andrew J. Wistrich, *Inside the Judicial Mind*, 86 CORNELL LAW REVIEW 777 (2001). A brief overview of this research may be found in Chris Guthrie, Jeffrey J. Rachlinski & Andrew J. Wistrich, *Judging by Heuristic: Cognitive Illusions in Judicial Decision Making*, 86 JUDICATURE 44 (July–August 2002).

CHAPTER 8: TRIALS IN A SCIENTIFIC AGE

1. Brief for Petitioners, *Kumho Tire Co. v. Carmichael*, 1997 U.S. Briefs 1709; *Kumho Tire Co., Ltd. v. Carmichael*, 526 U.S. 137 (1999). Quotes may be found on pp. 23–24 of Petitioners' brief.

2. *United States v. Amaral*, 488 F.2d 1148, 1152 (9th Cir. 1973).

3. PETER HUBER, GALILEO'S REVENGE: JUNK SCIENCE IN THE COURTROOM (1991).

4. MARCIA ANGELL, SCIENCE ON TRIAL: THE CLASH OF MEDICAL EVIDENCE AND THE LAW IN THE BREAST IMPLANT CASE (1996) at 204.

5. *Daubert v. Merrell Dow Pharmaceuticals*, 509 U.S. 579 (1993); *General Electric v. Joiner*, 522 U.S. 136 (1997); *Kumho Tire v. Carmichael*, note 1.

6. Anthony Champagne et al., *Expert Witnesses in the Courts: An Empirical Examination*, 76 JUDICATURE 5 (1992); Neil Vidmar & Shari S. Diamond, *Juries and Expert Evidence*, 66 BROOKLYN LAW REVIEW 1121 (2001); Sanja Kutnjak Ivković & Valerie P. Hans, *Jurors' Evaluations of Expert Testimony: Judging the Messenger and the Message*, 28 LAW & SOCIAL INQUIRY 441 (2003).

7. Hendrickson's case is described and analyzed in detail in JAMES C. MOHR, DOCTORS AND THE LAW (1993) at 122. This synopsis of the case and quotations are taken from Mohr's entertaining and lengthy account and from the original sources: DAVID BARNES & W. S. HEVENOR, TRIAL OF JOHN HENDRICKSON, JR., FOR THE MURDER OF HIS WIFE MARIA (1853); REVIEW, OPINIONS &C., OF DR. CHARLES A. LEE, AND OTHERS OF THE TESTIMONY OF DRS. SALISBURY AND SWINEBURNE, ON THE TRIAL OF JOHN HENDRICKSON, JR. FOR THE MURDER OF HIS WIFE, BY POISONING (1855).

8. BARNES & HEVENOR, TRIAL OF JOHN HENDRICKSON, note 7, at 167–68.

9. *Id.* at 172–73.

10. REVIEW, OPINIONS &C., note 7.

11. *Id.* at 40–41.

12. The felony jury study results on experts in criminal trials are described in Valerie P. Hans, *The Twenty-first Century Jury: Worst of Times or Best of Times?* 1 CRIMINAL LAW BULLETIN 3 (Spring 2006). For surveys of the use of experts, see Jennifer L. Grosscup, Steven D. Penrod, Christina A. Studebaker, Matthew T. Huss & Kevin M. O'Neil, *The Effects of Daubert on the Admissibility of Expert Testimony in State and Federal Criminal*

Cases, 8 PSYCHOLOGY, PUBLIC POLICY & LAW 339 (2002); Samuel R. Gross, *Expert Evidence*, 1991 WISCONSIN LAW REVIEW 1113 (1991); Carol Krafka, Meghan A. Dunn, Molly Treadway Johnson, Joe S. Cecil & Dean Miletich, *Judge and Attorney Experiences, Practices, and Concerns Regarding Expert Testimony in Federal Civil Trials*, 8 PSYCHOLOGY, PUBLIC POLICY & LAW 309 (2002).

13. Gross, *Expert Evidence*, note 12; Krafka et al., *Judge and Attorney Experiences*, note 12.

14. Federal Rule of Evidence 702.

15. Laura Boeschen et al., *Rape Trauma Experts in the Courtroom*, 4 PSYCHOLOGY, PUBLIC POLICY & LAW 414 (1998).

16. MANUAL OF MODEL CIVIL JURY INSTRUCTIONS FOR THE NINTH FEDERAL CIRCUIT, Rule 3.7.

17. For reviews of this literature, see Champagne et al., *Expert Witnesses in the Courts*, note 6; Vidmar & Diamond, *Juries and Expert Evidence*, note 6; Ivković & Hans, *Jurors' Evaluations of Expert Testimony*, note 6.

18. Richard O. Lempert, *Civil Juries and Complex Cases: Taking Stock after Twelve Years*, in VERDICT: ASSESSING THE CIVIL JURY SYSTEM 181 (Robert E. Litan ed., 1993).

19. Ivković & Hans, *Jurors' Evaluations of Expert Testimony*, note 6.

20. *Id.* at 464.

21. *Id.* at 466.

22. *Id.* at 470.

23. Daniel Schuman and Anthony Champagne, *Removing the People from the Legal Process: The Rhetoric and Research on Judicial Selection and Juries*, 3 PSYCHOLOGY, PUBLIC POLICY & LAW 242, 255 (1997). The researchers have conducted extensive research on the jury system; see Champagne et al., *Expert Witnesses in the Courts*, note 6; Daniel W. Shuman et al., *An Empirical Examination of the Use of Expert Witnesses in the Courts—Part Two: A Three City Study*, 34 JURIMETRICS JOURNAL 193 (1994); Daniel W. Shuman et al., *Juror Assessments of the Believability of Expert Witnesses: A Literature Review*, 36 JURIMETRICS JOURNAL 371 (1996); Daniel W. Shuman et al., *Assessing the Believability of Expert Witnesses: Science in the Jurybox*, 37 JURIMETRICS JOURNAL 23 (1996).

24. Judith Fordham, *Illuminating or Blurring the Truth: Jurors, Juries and Expert Evidence*, in LAW AND PSYCHOLOGY: CURRENT LEGAL ISSUES (Belinda Brooks-Gordon & Michael Freeman eds., 2007).

25. WARREN YOUNG ET AL., JURIES SURVEY—REPORT OF FINDINGS, NEW ZEALAND LAW COMMISSION (1999).

26. See Vidmar & Diamond, *Juries and Expert Evidence*, note 6, at 1146–47.

27. See Joseph Sanders, *The Jury Deliberation in a "Complex Case:" Havener v. Merrill Dow Pharmaceuticals*, 16 JUSTICE SYSTEM JOURNAL 45 (1993); JOSEPH SANDERS, BENDECTIN ON TRIAL: A STUDY OF MASS TORT LITIGATION (1998).

28. Shari Diamond & Jonathan Casper, *Blindfolding the Jury to Verdict Consequences: Damages, Experts and the Civil Jury*, 26 LAW & SOCIETY REVIEW 513 (1992).

29. Joel Cooper & Isaac M. Neuhaus, *The "Hired Gun" Effect: Assessing the Effect of Pay, Frequency of Testifying, and Credentials on the Perception of Expert Testimony*, 24 LAW & HUMAN BEHAVIOR 149 (2000); Joel Cooper, Elizabeth A. Bennett & Holly L. Sukel, *Complex Scientific Testimony: How Do Jurors Make Decisions?* 20 LAW & HUMAN BEHAVIOR 379 (1996).

30. Vidmar & Diamond, *Juries and Expert Evidence*, note 6, offer this alternative explanation.

31. Brian H. Bornstein, *The Impact of Different Types of Expert Scientific Testimony on Mock Jurors' Liability Verdicts*, 10 PSYCHOLOGY, CRIME & LAW 429 (2004).

32. See, for example, Regina Schuller, *The Impact of Battered Woman Syndrome Evidence on Jury Decisions*, 16 LAW & HUMAN BEHAVIOR 597 (1992).

33. 256 Conn. 854, 776 A.2d 1091 (2001). The case is discussed in Marlan D. Walker, *Mitochondrial DNA Evidence in State v. Pappas*, 43 JURIMETRICS JOURNAL 427 (2003).

34. See Vidmar and Diamond, *Juries and Expert Evidence*, note 6, at 1135–37.

35. In statistical parlance, it is labeled the "fallacy of the transposed conditional." David H. Kaye & George F. Sensabaugh Jr., *Reference Guide on DNA Evidenc*e, in REFERENCE MANUAL ON SCIENTIFIC EVIDENCE 485, 539 (2nd ed., Federal Judicial Center 2002).

36. *Id.* at 539; see also Kaye and Sensabaugh's general discussion of DNA match probabilities at 537–43.

37. William C. Thompson & Edward L. Schumann, *Interpretation of Statistical Evidence in Criminal Trials: The Prosecutor's Fallacy and the Defense Attorney's Fallacy*, 11 LAW & HUMAN BEHAVIOR 167 (1987); William C. Thompson, *Are Juries Competent to Evaluate Statistical Evidence?* 52 LAW & CONTEMPORARY PROBLEMS 9 (1989).

38. See discussion of prior research in David H. Kaye, Valerie P. Hans, B. Michael Dann, Erin Farley & Stephanie Albertson, *Statistics in the Jury Box: How Jurors Respond to Mitochondrial DNA Match Probabilities*, JOURNAL OF EMPIRICAL LEGAL STUDIES (forthcoming 2007). For a description of the research project, see B. Michael Dann, Valerie P. Hans & David H. Kaye, *Can Jury Trial Innovations Improve Juror Understanding of DNA Evidence?* 90 JUDICATURE 152 (2007).

39. Jonathan Koehler et al., *The Random Match Probability in DNA Evidence: Irrelevant and Prejudicial?* 37 JURIMETRICS JOURNAL 425 (1995).

40. Jason Schklar & Shari S. Diamond, *Juror Reactions to DNA Evidence: Errors and Expectancies*, 23 LAW & HUMAN BEHAVIOR 159 (1999).

41. Brian C. Smith, Steven D. Penrod, Amy L. Otto & Roger C. Park, *Jurors' Use of Probabilistic Evidence*, 20 LAW & HUMAN BEHAVIOR 49 (1996).

42. Dann et al., note 38.

43. THE EVOLVING ROLE OF STATISTICAL ASSESSMENTS AS EVIDENCE IN THE COURTS (Stephen Feinberg ed., 1989).

44. Sophia Gatowski et al., *Asking the Gatekeepers: Results of a National Survey of Judges on Judging Expert Evidence in a Post-Daubert World*, 25 LAW & HUMAN BEHAVIOR 433 (2001). Indeed, the need for expertise in scientific and other domains has led one law professor to suggest that lay justices with expertise in particular scientific fields might make important contributions as members of the US Supreme Court. Adrian Verneule, *Should We Have Lay Justices?* 59 STANFORD LAW REVIEW 1569 (2007).

45. Chris Guthrie, Jeffrey J. Rachlinski & Andrew Wistrich, *Inside the Judicial Mind: Heuristics and Biases*, 86 CORNELL LAW REVIEW 777 (2001).

46. REFERENCE MANUAL ON SCIENTIFIC EVIDENCE (2nd ed., Federal Judicial Center, 2002). Professor Margaret Berger of Brooklyn Law School heads the Science for Judges Program initiative; see http://www.brooklaw.edu/centers/scienceforjudges/.

CHAPTER 9: JUDGING CRIMINAL RESPONSIBILITY

1. This description of the Cotton case was the subject of a PBS *Frontline* documentary, "What Jennifer Saw," that originally aired on February 25, 1997, accessed at www.pbs.org/wgbh/pages/frontline/shows/dna; the show's transcript may be found at http://www.pbs.org/wgbh/pages/frontline/shows/dna/etc/script.html (accessed February 25, 2007). Jennifer's statements in our text come from the program transcript. For more information see http://www.ojp.usdoj.gov/ovc/publications/bulletins/dna_4_2001/dna11_4_01.html; http://cds.aas.duke.edu/exhibits/innocentspast.html; *The Innocents: Headshots*, Photographs and Video by Taryn Simon, Case Profiles by Peter Neufeld, Barry Scheck, and Huy Dao, http://cds.aas.duke.edu/exhibits/innocentspast.html; Innocence Project at http://www.innocenceproject.org/case/display_profile.php?id=06.

2. See the Innocence Project Web site at http://www.innocenceproject.org/understand/ (accessed February 25, 2007) for information about the most frequent causes of erroneous convictions. See also Samuel R. Gross et al., *Exonerations in the United States 1989 through 2003*, 95 JOURNAL OF CRIMINAL LAW & CRIMINOLOGY 523 (2005).

3. See, generally, Saul Kassin, *Internalized False Confessions*, in THE HANDBOOK OF EYEWITNESS PSYCHOLOGY Vol. 1 (Michael Toglia, J. Don Reid, David Ross & R. C. L. Lindsay eds., 2007) at 175; Richard Leo, Steven Drizin, Peter Neufeld, Brad Hall & Amy Vatner, *Bringing Reliability Back In: False Confessions and Legal Safeguards in the Twenty-first Century*, 2006 WISCONSIN LAW REVIEW 479 (2006).

4. The Center on Wrongful Convictions at Northwestern University School of Law has done an insightful analysis of the problematic use of snitches, http://www.innocenceproject.org/docs/SnitchSystemBooklet.pdf.

5. US DEPARTMENT OF JUSTICE, NATIONAL INSTITUTE OF JUSTICE, CONVICTED BY JURIES, EXONERATED BY SCIENCE: CASE STUDIES IN THE USE OF DNA EVIDENCE TO ESTABLISH INNOCENCE AFTER TRIAL (1996).

6. Elizabeth Loftus, *The Incredible Eyewitness*, 8 PSYCHOLOGY TODAY 116 (1974).

7. David Saunders et al., *Eyewitness Testimony and the Discrediting Effect*, in EVALUATING WITNESS EVIDENCE: RECENT PSYCHOLOGICAL RESEARCH AND NEW PERSPECTIVES (Sally M. A. Lloyd-Bostock & Brian R. Clifford eds., 1983) at 57.

8. Gary Wells & R. C. Lindsay, *How Do People Infer the Accuracy of Eyewitness Memory? Studies of Performance and a Metamemory Analysis*, in EVALUATING WITNESS EVIDENCE, note 7, at 41.

9. *Neil v. Biggers*, 409 U.S. 188, 198 (1972). See, generally, Brief of Neil Vidmar et al., Amicus Brief on Writ of Certiorari in *Le Quan Ledbetter v. State of Connecticut*, No. 05–9500 (2006).

10. Brief of Neil Vidmar et al., Amicus Brief, note 9, provides a review of the recent research. See also BRIAN L. CUTLER & STEVEN D. PENROD, MISTAKEN IDENTIFICATION: THE EYEWITNESS, PSYCHOLOGY, AND LAW (1995); Steven D. Penrod & Brian L. Cutler, *Witness Confidence and Witness Accuracy: Assessing Their Forensic Relation*, 1 PSYCHOLOGY, PUBLIC POLICY & LAW 817 (1995); Gary L. Wells & Elizabeth A. Olson, *Eyewitness Testimony*, 54 ANNUAL REVIEW OF PSYCHOLOGY 277 (2003).

11. Neil Vidmar & Regina A. Schuller, *Juries and Expert Evidence: Social Framework Testimony*, 52 LAW & CONTEMPORARY PROBLEMS 133 (1989).

12. Many excellent articles and books have been written about the O. J. Simpson trial,

including POSTMORTEM: THE O. J. SIMPSON CASE: JUSTICE CONFRONTS RACE, DOMESTIC VIOLENCE, LAWYERS, MONEY, AND THE MEDIA (Jeffrey Abramson ed., 1996) and JEFFREY TOOBIN, THE RUN OF HIS LIFE: THE PEOPLE V. O. J. SIMPSON (1996). Several jurors shared their perspectives on the trial in ARMANDA COOLEY, CARRIE BESS & MARSHA RUBIN-JACKSON, MADAM FOREMAN: A RUSH TO JUDGMENT? (1995). There is also a comprehensive Web site devoted to a presentation and analysis of the trial: Doug Linder, The Trial of Orenthal James Simpson, http://www.law.umkc.edu/faculty/projects/ftrials/Simpson/Simpsonaccount.htm.

13. Jeffrey Abramson, Editor's Introduction, 1, 10–11 in POSTMORTEM, note 12.

14. *CSI: Maricopa County: The CSI Effect and Its Real-Life Impact on Justice. A Study by the Maricopa County Attorney's Office* (June 30, 2005), http://www.maricopacountyattorney.org/Press/PDF/CSIReport.pdf.

15. *CSI: Maricopa County*, note 14, at 6.

16. *Id.*

17. Tom Tyler, *Viewing CSI and the Threshold of Guilt: Managing Truth and Justice in Reality and Fiction*, 115 YALE LAW JOURNAL 1050 (2006). For a recent study that finds no differences between frequent and nonfrequent viewers of *CSI* programs, see Kimberlianne Podlas, *"The CSI Effect": Exposing the Media Myth*, 16 FORDHAM INTELLECTUAL PROPERTY, MEDIA & ENTERTAINMENT LAW JOURNAL 429 (2006).

18. In our account, we draw on Court TV's coverage of the background and legal proceedings in the failed prosecution of Kobe Bryant on sexual assault charges, at http://www.courttv.com/trials/bryant/index.html (accessed February 26, 2007).

19. HARRY KALVEN JR. & HANS ZEISEL, THE AMERICAN JURY 249 (Little Brown & Company, 1966).

20. For a review, see Lynda Olsen-Fulero & Solomon M. Fulero, *Commonsense Rape Judgments: An Empathy-Complexity Theory of Rape Juror Story Making*, 3 PSYCHOLOGY, PUBLIC POLICY & LAW 402 (1997); Martha Burt, *Cultural Myths and Support for Rape*, 38 JOURNAL OF PERSONALITY & SOCIAL PSYCHOLOGY 217 (1980).

21. See discussion of the relevant research in VALERIE P. HANS & NEIL VIDMAR, JUDGING THE JURY 210–14 (1986). There is a substantial amount of mock jury research on the factors that influence decision making in rape cases; for recent reviews, see D. D. Koski, *Jury Decisionmaking in Rape Trials: A Review and Empirical Assessment*, 38 CRIMINAL LAW BULLETIN 21 (2002); J. W. Schutte & Harmon M. Hosch, *Gender Differences in Sexual Assault Verdicts*, 12 JOURNAL OF SOCIAL BEHAVIOR & PERSONALITY 759 (1997); Ashley A. Wenger & Brian B. Bornstein, *The Effects of Victim's Substance Use and Relationship Closeness on Mock Jurors' Judgments in an Acquaintance Rape Case*, 54 SEX ROLES 547 (2006).

22. SCIENCE IN THE LAW: SOCIAL AND BEHAVIOR SCIENCE ISSUES 269–307 (David L. Faigman, David H. Kaye, Michael J. Saks & Joseph Sanders eds., 2002).

23. *State v. Martens*, 629 N.E.2d 462 (Ohio Ct. App. 1993).

24. Vidmar & Schuller, *Juries and Expert Evidence*, note 11.

25. Regina A. Schuller & Marc A. Klippenstine, *The Impact of Complainant Sexual History Evidence on Jurors' Decisions*, 10 PSYCHOLOGY, PUBLIC POLICY & LAW 321 (2004).

26. FAITH MCNULTY, THE BURNING BED (Harcourt, 1980).

27. RICHARD GELLES AND MURRAY STRAUSS, INTIMATE VIOLENCE: THE CAUSES AND CONSEQUENCES OF ABUSE IN THE AMERICAN FAMILY (1988).

28. Regina A. Schuller & Sara Rzepa, *Battered Woman Syndrome and Other Psycho-*

logical Effects of Domestic Violence against Women, in 2 MODERN SCIENTIFIC EVIDENCE: THE LAW AND SCIENCE OF EXPERT TESTIMONY 37, 47–48 (David L. Faigman et al. eds., 2nd ed., 2002).

29. *State v. Kelly*, 478 A.2d 364, 368 (NJ 1984).

30. Regina A. Schuller, *Expert Evidence and Its Impact on Jurors' Decisions in Homicide Trials Involving Battered Women*, 10 DUKE JOURNAL OF GENDER, LAW & POLICY 225 (2003); Schuller & Rzepa, *Battered Woman Syndrome*, note 28.

31. *State v. Nemeth*, 694 NE 2d 1332, 1333 (Ohio 1998).

32. ALAN M. DERSHOWITZ, THE ABUSE EXCUSE (1994).

33. JAMES Q. WILSON, MORAL JUDGMENT: DOES THE ABUSE EXCUSE THREATEN OUR LEGAL SYSTEM? (1997).

34. The Michael Peterson case description is derived from multiple sources, including Neil Vidmar's notes as the trial occurred; live broadcasts on a local television channel, WRAL; articles from the *Raleigh News and Observer* and *Durham Herald Sun*, and *NBC Dateline*'s documentary "Mystery on Cedar Street," broadcast on February 13, 2004.

CHAPTER 10: DECIDING INSANITY

1. The primary sources for information about Andrea Yates's first trial are Deborah Denno, *Who Is Andrea Yates? A Short Story about Insanity*, 10 DUKE JOURNAL OF LAW & POLICY 1 (2003) and Sherry Colb, *The Conviction of Andrea Yates: A Narrative of Denial*, 10 DUKE JOURNAL OF LAW & POLICY 141 (2003), plus many sources in the mass media. Information about the second trial was obtained from mass media accounts available on the Internet; see, e.g., the thorough coverage by Court TV, http://www.courttv.com/trials/yates/. Quotes from jurors in the first Yates trial are taken from *Jurors: Yates' Drowning of Her Children Seemed Premeditated*, CourtTV, March 18, 2002, http://www.courttv.com/trials/yates/031802-b_ap.html. Quotes from the jury foreman in the second Yates trial are taken from Lisa Sweetingham, *Andrea Yates Found Not Guilty by Reason of Insanity for Children's Deaths*, CourtTV, July 26, 2006, http://www.courttv.com/trials/yates/072606_verdict2_ctv.html.

2. Cited in J. M. Quen, *A History of the Anglo-American Legal Psychiatry of Violence and Responsibility*, in VIOLENCE AND RESPONSIBILITY: THE INDIVIDUAL, THE FAMILY, AND SOCIETY (Robert L. Sadoff ed., 1978).

3. Quen, *History of the Anglo-American Legal Psychiatry of Violence and Responsibility*, note 2, at 21.

4. VALERIE P. HANS & NEIL VIDMAR, 179 JUDGING THE JURY (1986); Valerie P. Hans, *An Analysis of Public Attitudes toward the Insanity Defense*, 24 CRIMINOLOGY 383 (1986).

5. RICHARD MORAN, KNOWING RIGHT FROM WRONG: THE INSANITY DEFENSE OF DANIEL MCNAUGHTAN (1981); NORVAL MORRIS, MADNESS AND THE CRIMINAL LAW (1982).

6. MORAN, KNOWING RIGHT FROM WRONG, note 5.

7. CHARLES ROSENBERG, THE TRIAL OF THE ASSASSIN GUITEAU (1968).

8. CURT BARTOL, PSYCHOLOGY AND AMERICAN LAW (1983).

9. Nancy Beran & Beverley Tooney, *The Mentally Disordered Offender*, in MENTALLY ILL OFFENDERS AND THE CRIMINAL JUSTICE SYSTEM (Nancy Beram & Beverley Tooney eds., 1979).

10. Discussion of the American Law Institute, 1962 statement can be found at http://www.diminishedcapacity.com/sec3.htm or http://www.mentalhealthamerica.net/go/position-statements/57.

11. See LINCOLN CAPLAN, THE INSANITY DEFENSE AND THE TRIAL OF JOHN W. HINCKLEY, JR. (1987).

12. Valerie P. Hans and Dan Slater, *John Hinckley, Jr., and the Insanity Defense: The Public's Verdict*, 47 PUBLIC OPINION QUARTERLY 202 (1983).

13. United States Congress, *Limiting the Insanity Defense*. Hearing before the Subcommittee on Criminal Law of the Committee of the Judiciary, United States Senate, 97th Congress, 2nd Session, June 24, 1982, at 155–201.

14. See http://www.co.uscourts.gov/forms/cja_app_h.pdf.

15. *Psychiatrist Whose Testimony Led to Andrea Yates' Overturned Conviction Takes Stand in Retrial*, CourtTV News, http://www.courttv.com/trials/yates/071406_ap.html. The psychiatrist Park Dietz has also posted relevant documents relating to his testimony in the Yates trial on his professional Web site, at http://www.parkdietzassociates.com/index7.htm.

16. Phoebe Ellsworth et al., *The Death Qualified Jury and the Defense of Insanity*, 8 LAW & HUMAN BEHAVIOR 81 (1984).

17. Angela Brown, *Yates' Retrial Keeps Focus on Mental Health*, DURHAM HERALD SUN, June 26, 2006.

18. The literature is reviewed in Jennifer Skeem & Stephen Golding, *Describing Jurors' Personal Conceptions of Insanity and Their Relationship to Case Judgments*, 7 PSYCHOLOGY, PUBLIC POLICY & LAW 561 (2001).

19. *Id.* at 563.

20. Jeff Carlton, *Woman Who Killed Children Released*, RALEIGH NEWS AND OBSERVER, November 11, 2006, at 18A.

21. RITA JAMES SIMON, JURIES AND THE DEFENSE OF INSANITY (1967).

22. NORMAN FINKEL, COMMONSENSE JUSTICE: JURORS' NOTIONS OF THE LAW 261–97 (1995).

23. Skeem & Golding, *Describing Jurors' Personal Conceptions of Insanity*, note 18.

24. *Williamson v. Lipztsin*, 539 S.E.2d 313 (N.C. Ct. App. 2000).

25. *Id.*

26. Caton Roberts & Stephen Golding, *The Social Construction of Criminal Responsibility and Insanity*, 15 LAW & HUMAN BEHAVIOR 349 (1991); Caton Roberts et al., *Implicit Theories of Criminal Responsibility: Decision Making and the Insanity Defense*, 11 LAW & HUMAN BEHAVIOR 207 (1987).

27. Mikaela Vidmar-Perrins, "The Construction of Insanity: The Impact of Informational Cues on Perceptions of Criminal Responsibility" (1999) (unpublished MS thesis, Acadia University).

28. Roberts et al., *Implicit Theories of Criminal Responsibility*, note 26; Roberts & Golding, *Social Construction of Criminal Responsibility and Insanity*, note 26; Caton Roberts et al., *Verdict Selection Processes in Insanity Cases: Juror Construals and the Effects of Guilty But Mentally Ill Instructions*, 17 LAW & HUMAN BEHAVIOR 261 (1993).

CHAPTER 11: JURY NULLIFICATION

1. Details about the protest action and trials were obtained from a variety of sources, including the St. Patrick's Four Web site, http://stpatricksfour.org/ (accessed February 28, 2007), archived articles in the ITHACA JOURNAL, and other news sources listed in footnotes 2–23.

2. Diana LaMattina, *Protesters Splash Blood on American Flag*, ITHACA JOURNAL, March 18, 2003, at 1A.

3. Diana LaMattina, *Protesters Stand by Actions*, ITHACA JOURNAL, March 19, 2003, at 2A. Later, a grand jury handed down an indictment. Diana LaMattina, *War Protesters Indicted by Tompkins Grand Jury*, ITHACA JOURNAL, July 10, 2003, at 1B.

4. Dan Higgins, *Not Guilty Pleas for Blood-Throwing Protesters*, ITHACA JOURNAL, July 15, 2003; Diana LaMattina, *Defendants Charged with Criminal Mischief*, ITHACA JOURNAL, July 15, 2003.

5. Michelle York, *After Hung Jury, 4 Who Poured Blood at Upstate Army Center Face US Trial*, NEW YORK TIMES, September 18, 2005, at 39.

6. LaMattina, *War Protesters Indicted by Tompkins Grand Jury*, note 3.

7. Adam Wilson, *Testifies Blood Spilling Was Legal*, ITHACA JOURNAL, April 10, 2004, at 1B.

8. *Id.*

9. York, *After Hung Jury*, note 5, at 39.

10. Diana LaMattina, *Sherman Declares Mistrial*, ITHACA JOURNAL, April 14, 2004, at 1A.

11. *Id.*

12. York, *After Hung Jury*, note 5.

13. *First Federal Conspiracy Trial of Anti-war Protesters Since Vietnam Begins Sept. 19*, US Newswire, September 15, 2005.

14. News articles differed in their claims about the maximum penalties for the federal trial, but all claims far exceeded the maximum potential sentence the defendants faced in the state trial.

15. Rebecca James, *Anti-war Protesters Face Years in Prison; County Jury Didn't Convict Ithaca Demonstrators; Now Federal Trial Begins*, POST-STANDARD (Syracuse, NY), September 18, 2005, at A1.

16. Transcript of Proceedings at 716, *U.S. v. DeMott, et al.*, No. 05-CR-73, 2005 U.S. Dist. LEXIS 37599 (N.D.N.Y. September 26, 2005), http://stpatricksfour.org/documents/T92305StPats4edited.txt.

17. Transcript of Proceedings at 718, *U.S. v. DeMott, et al.*, No. 05-CR-73, 2005 U.S. Dist. LEXIS 37599 (N.D.N.Y. September 26, 2005), http://stpatricksfour.org/documents/T92305StPats4edited.txt.

18. Mary Pat Hyland, *Impressions of a Demonstration*, PRESS & SUN-BULLETIN (Binghamton, NY), September 25, 2006, at 14A. The defendants and their supporters organized a "Citizens' Tribunal on Iraq" that was held in Binghamton during the trial, September 18–23, 2005. See DVD: *The Saint Patrick's Four: Citizens' Tribunal on Iraq* (2006).

19. Transcript of Proceedings at 701–03, *U.S. v. DeMott, et al.*, No. 05-CR-73, 2005 U.S. Dist. LEXIS 37599 (N.D.N.Y. September 26, 2005), http://stpatricksfour.org/documents/T92305StPats4edited.txt.

20. Transcript of Proceedings at 758, *U.S. v. DeMott, et al.*, No. 05-CR-73, 2005 U.S. Dist. LEXIS 37599 (N.D.N.Y. September 26, 2005), http://stpatricksfour.org/documents /T92305StPats4edited.txt.

21. Transcript of Proceedings at 800, *U.S. v. DeMott, et al.*, No. 05-CR-73, 2005 U.S. Dist. LEXIS 37599 (N.D.N.Y. September 26, 2005), http://stpatricksfour.org/documents /T92305StPats4edited.txt.

22. Nancy Dooling, *The St. Patrick's Four Verdict—Protestors Go Free with a Warning*, PRESS & SUN-BULLETIN (Binghamton, NY), September 27, 2005, at 1A.

23. *Id.* Teresa Grady and Peter DeMott each spent four months in federal detention centers; DeMott spent an additional four months in a halfway house to complete his sentence. Dan Burns and Clare Grade each spent six months in federal detention centers. See http://www.stpatricksfour.org (accessed February 28, 2007).

24. We draw in this section on Paula L. Hannaford-Agor & Valerie P. Hans, *Nullification at Work: A Glimpse from the National Center for State Courts Study of Hung Juries*, 78 CHICAGO-KENT LAW REVIEW 1249 (2003).

25. *T. Jones*, 13, s.c. 6 Howell's State Trials 999, 124 English Reports 1006, 1009 (C.P. 1670).

26. THOMAS ANDREW GREEN, VERDICT ACCORDING TO CONSCIENCE: PERSPECTIVES ON THE ENGLISH CRIMINAL TRIAL JURY, 1200–1800 (1985).

27. JAMES ALEXANDER, A BRIEF NARRATIVE OF THE CASE AND TRIAL OF JOHN PETER ZENGER (Stanley Nider Katz ed., 2nd ed. 1972).

28. CLAY S. CONRAD, JURY NULLIFICATION: THE EVOLUTION OF A DOCTRINE (1998). See also Arie M. Rubenstein, *Note: Verdicts of Conscience: Nullification and the Modern Jury Trial*, 106 COLUMBIA LAW REVIEW 959 (2006); W. William Hodes, *Lord Broughham, the Dream Team, and Jury Nullification of the Third Kind*, 67 UNIVERSITY OF COLORADO LAW REVIEW 1075, 1088–89 (1996).

29. *Duncan v. Louisiana*, 391 U.S. 145, 155 (1968).

30. *Taylor v. Louisiana*, 419 U.S. 522, 530 (1975).

31. Roscoe Pound, *Law in Books and Law in Action*, 44 AMERICAN LAW REVIEW 12, 18 (1910).

32. Paul Butler, *Racially Based Jury Nullification: Black Power in the Criminal Justice System*, 105 YALE LAW JOURNAL 677 (1995).

33. *Id.* at 679.

34. See discussion in Hannaford-Agor & Hans, *Nullification at Work*, note 24, at 1254–55; Also, Nancy Marder, *The Myth of the Nullifying Jury*, 93 NORTHWESTERN UNIVERSITY LAW REVIEW 877 (1999).

35. Darryl Brown, *Jury Nullification within the Rule of Law*, 81 MINNESOTA LAW REVIEW 1149 (1997).

36. NORMAN FINKEL, COMMONSENSE JUSTICE: JURORS' NOTIONS OF THE LAW (1995).

37. Lars Noah, *Civil Jury Nullification*, 86 IOWA LAW REVIEW 1601 (2001); see also Steven M. Fernandes, Comment, *Jury Nullification and Tort Reform in California: Eviscerating the Power of the Civil Jury by Keeping Citizens Ignorant of the Law*, 27 SOUTHWESTERN UNIVERSITY LAW REVIEW 99 (1997); Noel Fidel, *Preeminently a Political Institution: The Right of Arizona Juries to Nullify the Law of Contributory Negligence*, 23 ARIZONA STATE LAW REVIEW 1 (1991).

38. Noah, *Civil Jury Nullification*, note 37, at 1603.

39. Marianne Constable, The Law of the Other: The Mixed Jury and Changing Conceptions of Citizenship, Law, and Knowledge 15 (1994).

40. Hannaford-Agor & Hans, *Nullification at Work*, note 24, at 1258; *Sparf et al. v. United States*, 156 U.S. 51 (1895).

41. *People v. Kriho*, 996 P.2d 158 (Colo. Ct. App. 1999).

42. See the decision to dismiss charges, described at http://www.levellers.org/jrp/ (accessed July 25, 2006).

43. *United States v. Thomas*, 116 F.3d 606 (2d Cir. 1997).

44. *Id.* at 610.

45. *U.S. v. Thomas*, note 43.

46. *People v. Williams*, 21 P.3d 1209, 1212–13 (Cal. 2001).

47. Harry Kalven Jr. & Hans Zeisel, The American Jury 115 (1966).

48. *Id.* at 288.

49. *Id.* at 292.

50. *Id.* at 295.

51. Paul H. Robinson & John M. Darley, Justice, Liability, and Blame: Community Views and the Criminal Law (1995); Finkel, Commonsense Justice, note 36.

52. James A. Henderson Jr., Richard N. Pearson & John A. Siliciano, 353–54 The Torts Process, 6th ed. (2003); *Butterfield v. Forrester*, 11 East 60, 103 English Reports 926 (K.B. 1809); *Smith v. Smith*, 19 Mass. (2 Pick.) 621 (1824); Restatement (Third) of Torts, Apportionment of Liability §3 (definition of plaintiff negligence).

53. Kalven & Zeisel, The American Jury, note 47, at 283.

54. Finkel, Commonsense Justice, note 36.

55. Hannaford-Agor & Hans, *Nullification at Work*, note 24.

56. Lawrence Friedman & Jack Ladinsky, *Social Change and the Law of Industrial Accidents*, 67 Columbia Law Review 50 (1967).

57. Kristin L. Sommer, Irwin A. Horowitz & Martin J. Bourgeois, *When Juries Fail to Comply with the Law: Biased Evidence Processing in Individual and Group Decision Making*, 27 Personality & Social Psychology Bulletin 309 (2001). For a general discussion of this program of research, see Irwin A. Horowitz, Norbert L. Kerr & Keith E. Niedermeier, *Jury Nullification: Legal and Psychological Perspectives*, 66 Brooklyn Law Review 1207 (2001).

58. Sommer et al., *When Juries Fail*, note 57, at 313.

59. *Id.* at 315.

60. Melvin Lerner, Belief in a Just World: A Fundamental Delusion (1990).

61. Neal Feigenson et al., *Effect of Blameworthiness and Outcome Severity on Attributions of Responsibility and Damage Awards in Comparative Negligence Cases*, 21 Law & Human Behavior 597 (1997). Other examples of plaintiff blame may be found in Douglas J. Zickafoose & Brian H. Bornstein, *Double Discounting: The Effects of Comparative Negligence on Mock Juror Decision Making*, 23 Law & Human Behavior 577 (1999); Sommer et al., *When Juries Fail*, note 57.

62. Feigenson et al., *Effect of Blameworthiness*, note 61.

63. B. Michael Dann, *The Constitutional and Ethical Implications of "Must-Find-the-Defendant-Guilty" Jury Instructions*, in Jury Ethics: Juror Conduct and Jury Dynamics 93 (John Kleinig & James P. Levine eds., 2006).

64. *U.S. v. Dougherty*, 473 F. 2d 1113 (D.C. Cir. 1972).

65. California Health & Safety Code §11362.5(d).

66. Election results may be found at http://www.marijuana.org/Election%20results1.htm (accessed July 25, 2006).

67. The Oakland City Council designated a group, the Oakland Cannabis Buyers' Cooperative, to cultivate and distribute marijuana to authorized users, and Ed Rosenthal was designated by the OCBC to undertake this work.

68. Claire Cooper, *Reluctant Jury Convicts Medical Pot Grower*, SACRAMENTO BEE, February 1, 2003, available at http://www.sacbee.com. See also Sherry F. Colb, *The Conviction of Ed Rosenthal for Growing Medicinal Marijuana: Why It Was Wrong to Prosecute* (Findlaw column), February 12, 2003, http://writ.news.findlaw.com/colb/20030212.html.

69. *United States v. Rosenthal*, 454 F.3d 943 (2006). Rosenthal awaits another trial, *United States v. Watts*, 2006 U.S. Dist. LEXIS 9345 (2006).

70. *U.S. v Rosenthal*, note 69, at 950.

71. David C. Brody & Craig Rivera, *Examining the Dougherty "All-Knowing Assumption": Do Jurors Know about Their Jury Nullification Power?* 1995 CRIMINAL LAW BULLETIN 151 (1995).

72. Some types of activities could arguably give rise to judicial sanctions. A prospective juror lying to the court during jury selection, for example, could lead to a contempt of court citation.

73. The History of FIJA, http://www.fija.org/index.php?page=staticpage&id=3 (accessed July 25, 2006).

74. Nancy J. King, *Silencing Nullification Advocacy Inside the Jury Room and Outside the Courtroom*, 65 UNIVERSITY OF CHICAGO LAW REVIEW 433, 438–43 (1998).

75. King, *Silencing Nullification Advocacy*, note 74, provides a sampling of cases in which trial judges clamped down after discovering FIJA activity that might have affected the jury or jury pool.

76. *Id.* at 439.

77. Irwin Horowitz, *The Effect of Jury Nullification Instruction on Verdicts and Jury Functioning in Criminal Trials*, 9 LAW & HUMAN BEHAVIOR 25 (1985); see also VALERIE P. HANS & NEIL VIDMAR, 159–60 JUDGING THE JURY (1986).

78. Irwin A. Horowitz, Norbert L. Kerr, Ernest S. Park & Christine Gockel, *Chaos in the Courtroom Reconsidered: Emotional Bias and Juror Nullification*, 30 LAW & HUMAN BEHAVIOR 163 (2006).

79. *Id.* at 177. Further, the authors note the artificial nature of their scenarios, the Internet data collection, and the limited sample in calling for replication of their results.

CHAPTER 12: DEATH IS DIFFERENT

1. *Furman v. Georgia*, 408 U.S. 238, 286 (1972).

2. *Ring v. Arizona*, 536 U.S. 584, 606 (2002).

3. See Jeffrey Abramson, *Death-Is-Different Jurisprudence and the Role of the Capital Jury*, 2 OHIO STATE JOURNAL OF CRIMINAL LAW 117 (2004).

4. *Id.* at 119.

5. For an excellent review of all the issues, see BEYOND REPAIR? AMERICA'S DEATH PENALTY (Stephen Garvey ed., 2003).

6. THE DEATH PENALTY IN AMERICA 25 (Hugo Bedau ed., 3rd ed., 1982).

7. MICHAEL MELTSNER, CRUEL AND UNUSUAL: THE SUPREME COURT AND CAPITAL PUNISHMENT (1974).

8. *Furman v. Georgia*, 408 U.S. 238, 313 (1972).

9. *Gregg v. Georgia*, 428 U.S. 153 (1976).

10. Ramsey Clark, *Spinkellink's Last Appeal*, NATION, October 27, 1979, at 385. The "sizzled" quotation comes from a May 23, 1999, Associated Press story about the Spinkellink execution, http://venus.soci .niu.edu/~archives/ABOLISH/rick-halperin/mar 99/0700.html.

11. *Coker v. Georgia*, 433 U.S. 584 (1977).

12. *Barefoot v. Estelle*, 463 U.S. 880 (1983).

13. *McCleskey v. Kemp*, 481 U.S. 279 (1987); see also Abramson, *Death-Is-Different Jurisprudence*, note 3.

14. *Atkins v. Virginia*, 536 U.S. 304 (2002).

15. *Roper v. Simmons*, 534 U.S. 551 (2005).

16. William J. Bowers, Benjamin Fleury-Steiner, Valerie P. Hans & Michael E. Antonio, *Too Young for the Death Penalty: An Empirical Examination of Community Conscience and the Juvenile Death Penalty from the Perspective of Capital Jurors*, 84 BOSTON UNIVERSITY LAW REVIEW 609, 626 (2004).

17. *Id.* at 689–91.

18. *Ring v. Arizona*, 536 U.S. 584 (2002).

19. 11 Del. C. § 4209 (2006) shows the Delaware approach: "(3) a. Upon the conclusion of the evidence and arguments the judge shall give the jury appropriate instructions and the jury shall retire to deliberate and report to the Court an answer to the following questions: 1. Whether the evidence shows beyond a reasonable doubt the existence of at least 1 aggravating circumstance as enumerated in subsection (e) of this section; and 2. Whether, by a preponderance of the evidence, after weighing all relevant evidence in aggravation or mitigation which bear upon the particular circumstances or details of the commission of the offense and the character and propensities of the offender, the aggravating circumstances found to exist outweigh the mitigating circumstances found to exist." It goes on to state specifically: "In order to find the existence of a statutory aggravating circumstance as enumerated in subsection (e) of this section beyond a reasonable doubt, the jury must be unanimous as to the existence of that statutory aggravating circumstance."

20. Death Penalty Information Center, *Facts about the Death Penalty, Feb. 16, 2007*, http://www.deathpenaltyinfo.org/FactSheet.pdf (accessed February 16, 2007).

21. *Id.*

22. See http://en.wikipedia.org/wiki/Anthony_Porter (accessed July 12, 2006).

23. Compiled from numerous news sources; information on Henry Lee Hunt's trial and execution can be found on the Clark County Prosecutor's Web site, http://www.clarkprosecutor.org/html/death/US/hunt875.htm (accessed February 16, 2007).

24. Death Penalty Information Center, *Facts*, note 20.

25. David C. Baldus, George Woodworth & Charles A. Pulaski Jr., *Law and Statistics in Conflict: Reflections on McCleskey v. Kemp*, in HANDBOOK OF PSYCHOLOGY AND LAW 251 (D. K. Kagehiro & W. S. Laufer eds., 1992).

26. For a general review, see SAMUEL GROSS & ROBERT MAURO, DEATH AND DISCRIMINATION: RACIAL DISPARITIES IN CAPITAL SENTENCING (1989). Some of the key studies are David C. Baldus, George Woodworth, Catherine M. Grosso & Aaron M. Christ, *Arbitrari-*

ness and Discrimination in the Administration of the Death Penalty: A Legal and Empirical Analysis of the Nebraska Experience (1973–1999), 81 NEBRASKA LAW REVIEW 486 (2002); RAY PATERNOSTER ET AL., AN EMPIRICAL ANALYSIS OF MARYLAND'S DEATH SENTENCING SYSTEM WITH RESPECT TO THE INFLUENCE OF RACE AND LEGAL JURISDICTION, FINAL REPORT (2003).

27. William J. Bowers & Glenn Pierce, *Deterrence or Brutalization*, 26 CRIME & DELINQUENCY 453 (1980).

28. See David Baldus et al., *In the Post-Furman Era: An Empirical and Legal Overview, with Recent Findings from Philadelphia*, 83 CORNELL LAW REVIEW 1638 (1998).

29. AMNESTY INTERNATIONAL, DEATH BY DISCRIMINATION—THE CONTINUING ROLE OF RACE IN CAPITAL CASES, Document AMR 51/046/2003.

30. DAVID S. BAIME, REPORT TO THE SUPREME COURT SYSTEMIC PROPORTIONALITY REVIEW PROJECT, 2000–2001 Term, Asbury Park Press, August 13, 2001, at 5; http://www.judiciary.state.nj.us/pressrel/baimereport.pdf (accessed June 23, 2007).

31. An excellent summary may be found in Baldus et al., *Arbitrariness and Discrimination*, note 26, at 500–502. A new study of the federal death penalty examined the role of race in the all-important decision to seek the federal death penalty. United States attorneys were more likely to seek the death penalty in cases with black defendants and cases with white victims. However, once controls were introduced for case characteristics and the district of the country, the race effects were not statistically significant. One problem is that jurisdictions vary in their racial composition, and jurisdictional and racial factors in crime may be related. PATERNOSTER ET AL., AN EMPIRICAL ANALYSIS OF MARYLAND'S DEATH SENTENCING SYSTEM, for example, note 26, at 38, found that in Maryland the jurisdiction and race were confounded. As more sophisticated analyses are done of the death penalty systems in various regions, we should be able to get a better sense of the true impact of race. See STEPHEN P. KLEIN, RICHARD A. BERK & LAURA J. HICKMAN, RACE AND THE DECISION TO SEEK THE DEATH PENALTY IN FEDERAL CASES, RAND REPORT (2006).

32. See William J. Bowers, *The Capital Jury: Is It Tilted toward Death*? 79 JUDICATURE 220 (1996).

33. *Witherspoon v. Illinois*, 391 U.S. 510 (1968).

34. *Wainwright v. Witt*, 469 U.S. 412 (1985). For a comparison of the standards, see William Thompson, *Death Qualification after Wainwright v. Witt and Lockhart v. McCree*, 13 LAW & HUMAN BEHAVIOR 185 (1989).

35. *Lockhart v. McCree*, 476 U.S. 162 (1986).

36. John Blume, Theodore Eisenberg & Stephen Garvey, *Lessons from the Capital Jury Project*, in BEYOND REPAIR? AMERICA'S DEATH PENALTY, note 5.

37. William J. Bowers, Marla Sandys & Benjamin D. Steiner, *Foreclosed Impartiality in Capital Sentencing: Jurors' Predispositions, Attitudes and Premature Decision-Making* 83 CORNELL LAW REVIEW 1476 (1998); Theodore Eisenberg, Stephen Garvey & Martin Wells, *Forecasting Life and Death: Juror Race, Religion, and Attitudes toward the Death Penalty*, 30 JOURNAL OF LEGAL STUDIES 277 (2001).

38. Ronald Dillehay & Marla Sandys, *Life under Wainwright v. Witt: Juror Dispositions and Death Qualification*, 20 LAW & HUMAN BEHAVIOR 147 (1996).

39. Bowers et al., *Foreclosed Impartiality*, note 37. The juror comments quoted in our text appear on p. 1497.

40. *Id.* at 1531–33.

41. Craig Haney, *On the Selection of Capital Juries: The Biasing Effects of the Death-Qualification Process*, 8 LAW & HUMAN BEHAVIOR 121 (1984). Additional discussion of the death qualification process is in chapter 5 of CRAIG HANEY, DEATH BY DESIGN (2005).

42. Craig Haney, *Examining Death Qualification: Further Analysis of the Process Effect*, 8 LAW & HUMAN BEHAVIOR 133, 138 (1984).

43. Haney, *On the Selection of Capital Juries*, note 41.

44. 11 Washington Practice Pattern Jury Instructions, Criminal WPIC 31.01 (2nd ed.).

45. Haney, *Examining Death Qualification,* note 42, at 143.

46. See *State v. Prevatte*, 570 S.E.2d 440 (2002).

47. SCOTT SUNDBY, A LIFE AND DEATH DECISION: A JURY WEIGHS THE DEATH PENALTY (2005). The hypothetical questions posed by the prosecutor and the defense attorney, quoted in our text, appear on pp. 24–25.

48. Craig Haney, *Violence and the Capital Jury: Mechanisms of Moral Disengagement and the Impulse to Condemn to Death*, 49 STANFORD LAW REVIEW 1147, 1482 (1997).

49. *Adams v. Texas*, 448 U.S. 38, 49 (1980).

50. Bob Hebert, *In America: Mr. Hance's "Perfect Punishment*," NEW YORK TIMES, March 27, 1994 (The Week in Review), at 17.

51. Jennifer Eberhardt et al., *Looking Deathworthy: Perceived Stereotypicality of Black Defendants Predicts Capital Sentencing Outcomes*, 17 PSYCHOLOGICAL SCIENCE 383 (2006).

52. William J. Bowers, Benjamin D. Steiner & Marla Sandys, *Death Sentencing in Black and White: An Empirical Analysis of the Role of Jurors' Race and Jury Racial Composition*, 3 PENNSYLVANIA JOURNAL OF CONSTITUTIONAL LAW 173 (2001).

53. *Id.*

54. See Bowers et al., *Foreclosed Impartiality*, note 37; William Geimer & Jonathan Amsterdam, *Why Jurors Vote Life or Death: Operative Factors in Ten Florida Death Penalty Trials*, 15 AMERICAN JOURNAL OF CRIMINAL LAW 1 (1988).

55. Scott Sundby, *The Capital Jury and Absolution: The Intersection of Trial Strategy, Remorse and the Death Penalty*, 83 CORNELL LAW REVIEW 1557 (1998). Juror comments about the defendant's lack of remorse, quoted in our text, appear on p. 1566 of Sundby's article.

56. Bowers et al., *Too Young for the Death Penalty*, note 16.

57. Thomas Brewer, *Race and Jurors' Receptivity to Mitigation in Capital Cases: The Effect of Jurors', Defendants', and Victims' Race in Combination*, 28 LAW & HUMAN BEHAVIOR 529 (2004).

58. John Blume, Stephen Garvey & Sheri Johnson, *Future Dangerousness in Capital Cases: Always "At Issue,"* 86 CORNELL LAW REVIEW 397 (2001).

59. Laura Bell, *Groups Expel Texas Psychiatrist Known for Murder Cases*, DALLAS MORNING NEWS, July 26, 1995, available at http://www.ccadp.org/DrDeath.htm (accessed July 23, 2006).

60. See William J. Bowers, Benjamin D. Steiner & Michael E. Antonio, *The Capital Sentencing Decision: Guided Discretion, Reasoned Moral Judgment, or Legal Fiction*, in AMERICA'S EXPERIMENT WITH CAPITAL PUNISHMENT: REFLECTIONS ON THE PAST, PRESENT, AND FUTURE OF THE ULTIMATE PENAL SANCTION 413 (James R. Acker, Robert M. Bohm & Charles S. Lanier eds., 2nd ed., 2003).

61. See, generally, Daniel Krauss & Bruce Sales, *The Effects of Clinical and Scientific Expert Testimony on Juror Decisionmaking in Capital Sentencing*, 7 PSYCHOLOGY, PUBLIC POLICY & LAW 267 (2001).

62. *Lockett v. Ohio*, 438 U.S. 586 (1978).

63. Scott Sundby, *The Jury as Critic: An Empirical Look at How Capital Juries Perceive Expert and Lay Testimony*, 83 VIRGINIA LAW REVIEW 1109 (1997).

64. *Id.* at 1127.

65. *Id.* at 1130.

66. *Id.* at 1137.

67. *Id.*

68. *Id.* at 1141.

69. *Id.*

70. Oklahoma Jury Instructions—Criminal, Chapter c Homicide, available at http://www.oscn.net/applications/OCISWeb/index.asp?level=1&ftdb=STOKJUCR#1.MURDERINTHEFIRSTDEGREE.

71. James Luginbuhl & Julie Howe, *Discretion in Capital Sentencing Instructions: Guided or Misguided*? 70 INDIANA LAW JOURNAL 1161 (1995).

72. Edith Greene, Heather Koehring & Melinda Quait, *Victim Impact Evidence in Capital Cases: Does the Victim's Character Matter?* 28 JOURNAL OF APPLIED SOCIAL PSYCHOLOGY 145 (1998); see also Edith Greene, *The Many Guises of Victim Impact Evidence and Effects on Jurors' Judgments*, 5 PSYCHOLOGY, CRIME & LAW 331 (1999).

73. Theodore Eisenberg & Martin Wells, *Deadly Confusion: Juror Instructions in Capital Cases*, 79 CORNELL LAW REVIEW 1 (1993).

74. Richard Wiener, *The Role of Declarative Knowledge in Capital Murder Sentencing*, 28 JOURNAL OF APPLIED PSYCHOLOGY 124 (1998); see also Mark Costanzo & Sally Costanzo, *Jury Decision Making in the Capital Penalty Phase*, 16 LAW & HUMAN BEHAVIOR 185 (1992).

75. Shari Diamond & Judith Levi, *Improving Decisions on Death by Revising and Testing Jury Instructions*, 79 JUDICATURE 224 (1996).

76. Austin Sarat, *Representation and Responsibility in Capital Trials: The View from the Jury*, 70 INDIANA LAW JOURNAL 1103, 1133 (1995).

77. Theodore Eisenberg, Stephen Garvey & Martin Wells, *Jury Responsibility in Capital Sentencing: An Empirical Study*, 44 BUFFALO LAW REVIEW 339 (1996).

78. Craig Haney, *Violence and the Capital Jury: Mechanisms of Moral Disengagement and the Impulse to Condemn to Death*, 49 STANFORD LAW REVIEW 1147 (1997).

79. Death Penalty Information Center, http://www.deathpenaltyinfo.org.

80. Information on the ABA's moratorium on the death penalty is available at http://www.abanet.org/moratorium/home.html.

81. Hugo Bedau & Michael Radelet, *Miscarriages of Justice in Potentially Capital Cases*, 40 STANFORD LAW REVIEW 21 (1987); Samuel Gross, *Lost Lives: Miscarriages of Justice in Capital Cases*, 61 LAW & CONTEMPORARY PROBLEMS 125 (1998).

82. Stephen Bright, *Counsel for the Poor: The Death Sentence Not for the Worst Crime but for the Worst Lawyer*, 103 YALE LAW JOURNAL 1835 (1994).

83. *Id.* at 1847.

84. American Bar Association Death Penalty Moratorium Implementation project, Georgia Assessment, http://www.abanet.org/moratorium/assessmentproject/georgia.html.

85. Bright, *Counsel for the Poor*, note 82.

86. *Callins v. Collins*, 510 U.S. 1141, 1145 (1994).

87. Scott Sundby, *The Death Penalty's Future: Charting the Crosscurrents of Declining Death Sentences and the McVeigh Factor*, 84 TEXAS LAW REVIEW 1929 (2006).

88. See Chris Tisch and Curtis Kreuger, *Second Dose Needed to Kill Inmate*, ST. PETERSBURG TIMES, December 14, 2006, available at http://www.sptimes.com/2006/12/14/State/Second_dose_needed_to.shtml.

89. See, for example, Andrea Weigl, *New Ethics Policy Bars Doctor's Aid in Executions*, RALEIGH NEWS AND OBSERVER, January 19, 2007, available at http://www.newsobserver.com/644/story/533836.html.

90. Carol Steiker & Jordan Steiker, *Abolition in Our Time*, 1 OHIO STATE JOURNAL OF CRIMINAL LAW 323 (2003).

91. See Wikipedia's entry for Ted Bundy, http://en.wikipedia.org/wiki/Ted Bundy.

CHAPTER 13: CIVIL LIABILITY

1. See VALERIE P. HANS, BUSINESS ON TRIAL: THE CIVIL JURY AND CORPORATE RESPONSIBILITY (2000); EDIE GREENE & BRIAN BORNSTEIN, DETERMINING DAMAGES: THE PSYCHOLOGY OF DAMAGE AWARDS (2003).

2. See American Tort Reform Association, http://www.atra.org.

3. The boy in the paint store case is described in detail in HANS, BUSINESS ON TRIAL, note 1, at 24–28.

4. *Id.* at 25–26.

5. *Id.* at 27.

6. *Id.* at 26.

7. *Id.* at 24.

8. *Id.* at 25.

9. *Id.*

10. *Id.* at 27.

11. *Id.* at 50–78.

12. GREENE & BORNSTEIN, DETERMINING DAMAGES, note 1, at 91–92.

13. Valerie P. Hans & Nicole Vadino, *Whipped by Whiplash? The Challenges of Jury Communication in Lawsuits Involving Connective Tissue Damage*, 67 TENNESSEE LAW REVIEW 569 (2000). See also Valerie P. Hans & Juliet Dee, *Whiplash: Who's to Blame?* 68 BROOKLYN LAW REVIEW 1093 (2003).

14. Hans & Vadino, *Whipped by Whiplash?* note 13, at 575.

15. *Id.* at 573.

16. HANS, BUSINESS ON TRIAL, note 1, at 74–76.

17. Jennifer K. Robbennolt, *Outcome Severity and Judgments of "Responsibility:" A Meta-analytic Review*, 30 JOURNAL OF APPLIED SOCIAL PSYCHOLOGY 2575 (2000).

18. *Vosburg v. Putney*, 80 Wis. 523, 50 N.W. 403 (1891). In 1992, the *Wisconsin Law Review* published a special issue devoted to this classic torts case. As it turns out, the injured boy probably received little if any compensation. For more details about the litigation, see Zigurds L. Zile, *Vosburg v. Putney: A Centennial Story*, 1992 WISCONSIN LAW REVIEW 877 (1992).

19. Lucinda Finley, *The Hidden Victims of Tort Reform: Women, Children, and the Elderly*, 53 EMORY LAW JOURNAL 1263 (2004); Leslie Bender, *A Lawyer's Primer on Feminist Theory and Tort*, 38 JOURNAL OF LEGAL EDUCATION 3 (1988).

20. See, for example, JAMES A. HENDERSON JR., RICHARD N. PEARSON, DOUGLAS A. KYSAR & JOHN A. SILICIANO, THE TORTS PROCESS, 7th ed. (2007).

21. ROBERT S. SUMMERS & ROBERT A. HILLMAN, CONTRACT AND RELATED OBLIGATION: THEORY, DOCTRINE & PRACTICE (5th ed., 2006).

22. See, for example, Brian J. Ostrom, David B. Rottman & John A. Goerdt, *A Step above Anecdote: A Profile of the Civil Jury in the 1990s*, 79 JUDICATURE 233 (1996).

23. HANS, BUSINESS ON TRIAL, note 1.

24. Valerie P. Hans & M. David Ermann, *Responses to Corporate versus Individual Wrongdoing*, 15 LAW & HUMAN BEHAVIOR 151 (1989).

25. HANS, BUSINESS ON TRIAL, note 1, at 90.

26. *Id.*

27. KELLY G. SHAVER, THE ATTRIBUTION OF BLAME: CAUSALITY, RESPONSIBILITY, AND BLAMEWORTHINESS (1985); Mark D. Alicke, *Culpable Control and the Psychology of Blame*, 126 PSYCHOLOGICAL BULLETIN 556 (2000); M. Karlovac & John M. Darley, *Attribution of Responsibility for Accidents: A Negligence Law Analogy*, 6 SOCIAL COGNITION 287 (1988); PAUL H. ROBINSON & JOHN M. DARLEY, JUSTICE, LIABILITY AND BLAME: COMMUNITY VIEWS AND THE CRIMINAL LAW (1995).

28. HANS, BUSINESS ON TRIAL, note 1, at 123.

29. *Id.*

30. *Id.* at 130.

31. *Id.* at 43.

32. *Id.* at 133–34.

CHAPTER 14: DECIDING COMPENSATORY DAMAGES

1. See WILLIAM HALTOM & MICHAEL MCCANN, DISTORTING THE LAW: POLITICS, MEDIA AND THE LITIGATION CRISIS 1–5 (2004). Our description draws on Haltom and McCann's trenchant analysis of the case.

2. See, e.g., Richard Abel, *General Damages Are Incoherent, Incalculable, Incommensurable, and Inegalitarian (But Otherwise a Great Idea)*, 55 DEPAUL LAW REVIEW 253 (2006); Mark Geistfeld, *Due Process and the Determination of Pain and Suffering Tort Damages*, 55 DEPAUL LAW REVIEW 331 (2006).

3. Randall Bovbjerg et al., *Valuing Life and Limb in Tort: Scheduling "Pain and Suffering,"* 83 NORTHWESTERN UNIVERSITY LAW REVIEW 908 (1989).

4. THOMAS COHEN & STEVEN SMITH, CIVIL TRIAL CASES AND VERDICTS IN LARGE COUNTIES, 2001 (US Department of Justice, Bureau of Justice Statistics, April 2001, NCJ 202803).

5. THOMAS COHEN, FEDERAL TORT TRIALS AND VERDICTS, 2002–2003 (US Department of Justice, Bureau of Justice Statistics, August 2005, NCJ 208713).

6. See, generally, DAN B. DOBBS, HANDBOOK ON THE LAW OF REMEDIES (1973).

7. J. O'Connell and T. Bailey, *The History of Payment for Pain and Suffering*, 1972 UNIVERSITY OF ILLINOIS LEGAL FORUM 83 (1972).

8. West's Smith-Hurd Illinois Compiled Statutes Annotated (2006).

9. New York Pattern Jury Instructions, Civil 2–320 (West Supplement, 1996).

10. See, generally, George Christie et al., Cases and Materials on the Law of Torts (2004).

11. Edie Greene & Brian H. Bornstein, Determining Damages: The Psychology of Jury Awards 127–46 (2002).

12. Neal Feigenson et al., *Effects of Blameworthiness and Outcome Severity on Attributions of Responsibility and Damage Awards in Comparative Negligence Cases*, 21 Law & Human Behavior 597 (1997); Neal Feigenson et al., *The Role of Emotions in Comparative Negligence Cases*, 31 Journal of Applied Social Psychology 576 (2001).

13. For a summary of the folklore surrounding the tendencies of civil jurors and damage awards, including the claims we note here, see Solomon Fulero & Steven Penrod, *Attorney Selection Folklore: What Do They Think and How Can Psychologists Help?* 3 Forensic Reports 233 (1990); and Greene & Bornstein, Determining Damages, note 11, at 81.

14. See Greene & Bornstein, Determining Damages, note 11, at 80–89.

15. Neil Vidmar & Jeffrey Rice, *Assessments of Non-economic Damage Awards in Medical Malpractice Negligence: A Comparison of Jurors with Legal Professionals*, 78 Iowa Law Review 883 (1993); Roselle Wissler et al., *Decision-Making about General Damages: A Comparison of Jurors, Judges and Lawyers*, 98 Michigan Law Review 751 (1999).

16. See Theodore Eisenberg & Martin Wells, *Trial Outcomes and Demographics: Is There a Bronx Effect?* 80 Texas Law Review 1839 (2002).

17. *Id.* at 1840.

18. Mary Rose & Neil Vidmar, *The Bronx "Bronx Jury": A Profile of Civil Jury Awards in New York Counties*, 80 Texas Law Review 1889 (2002).

19. David Engel, *The Ovenbird's Song: Insiders, Outsiders and Personal Injuries in an American Community*, 18 Law and Society Review 551 (1984).

20. The reasoning behind this rule is that the wrongdoer should bear full responsibility for the costs of the whole accident and should not benefit from paying less just because the injured party had the foresight or good luck to have insurance. Similarly, the fact that a defendant carries insurance should not be grounds for holding him or her responsible just because he or she has the ability to pay. See, e.g., *Kirtland & Packard v. Superior Court for County of Los Angeles*, 59 Cal. App.3d 140, 131 Ca. Reporter 418 (1976).

21. Federal Rule of Evidence 411; Unified Rule of Evidence 54.

22. Shari S. Diamond & Neil Vidmar, *Jury Room Ruminations on Forbidden Topics*, 87 Virginia Law Review 1857 (2001).

23. Valerie P. Hans, Business on Trial 195–214 (2000).

24. Audrey Chin & Mark Peterson, Deep Pockets, Empty Pockets: Who Wins in Cook County Jury Trials (1985).

25. Peter Huber, Liability: The Legal Revolution and Its Consequences 11 (1988).

26. *Sensible Solutions #3*, New York Times, February 16, 1995, at A15.

27. Hans, Business on Trial, note 23, at 184–85.

28. Robert MacCoun, *Differential Treatment of Corporate Defendants by Juries: An Examination of the "Deep Pockets" Hypothesis*, 30 Law & Society Review 121 (1996).

29. NEIL VIDMAR, MEDICAL MALPRACTICE AND THE AMERICAN JURY 203–20 (1995).

30. HANS, BUSINESS ON TRIAL, note 23, at 187–92.

31. *Id.* at 195.

32. GREENE & BORNSTEIN, DETERMINING DAMAGES, note 11.

33. Mollie Marti and Roselle Wissler, *Be Careful What You Ask For: The Effect of Anchors on Personal Injury Damage Awards*, 6 JOURNAL OF EXPERIMENTAL PSYCHOLOGY: APPLIED 91–103 (2000).

34. VIDMAR, MEDICAL MALPRACTICE AND THE AMERICAN JURY, note 29, at 243–46.

35. For a discussion of these claims, see Edie Greene, *On Juries and Damage Awards: The Process of Decision Making*, 52 LAW & CONTEMPORARY PROBLEMS 225 (1989).

36. PATRICIA DANZON, MEDICAL MALPRACTICE: THEORY, EVIDENCE, AND PUBLIC POLICY 40–42 (1985).

37. Bovbjerg, et al., *Valuing Life and Limb in Tort*, note 3; STEPHEN DANIELS & JOANNE MARTIN, CIVIL JURIES AND THE POLITICS OF REFORM (1995); W. KIP VISCUSI, REFORMING PRODUCTS LIABILITY (1991).

38. Neil Vidmar, Kara MacKillop & Paul Lee, *Million Dollar Medical Malpractice Cases in Florida: Post-verdict and Pre-suit Settlements*, 59 VANDERBILT LAW REVIEW 1343 (2006).

39. *Id.* at 1375–78.

40. GERALD R. WILLIAMS, LEGAL NEGOTIATION AND SETTLEMENT 7 (1983).

41. Michael J. Saks, *Do We Really Know Anything about the Behavior of the Tort System—and Why Not?* 140 UNIVERSITY OF PENNSYLVANIA LAW REVIEW 1147, 1214–15, 1222 (1992).

42. Wissler et al., *Decision-Making about General Damages*, note 15.

43. GREENE & BORNSTEIN, DETERMINING DAMAGES, note 11, at 109.

44. VIDMAR, MEDICAL MALPRACTICE AND THE AMERICAN JURY, note 29, at 221–36.

45. JAMES OLDHAM, TRIAL BY JURY: THE SEVENTH AMENDMENT AND ANGLO-AMERICAN SPECIAL JURIES (2006) at 5–16 and 45–79.

CHAPTER 15: PUNITIVE DAMAGES

1. For a review of this claim, see Michael Rustad, *Unraveling Punitive Damages: Current Data and Further Inquiry*, 1998 WISCONSIN LAW REVIEW 15 (1998).

2. For a detailed account of this case, see WILLIAM HALTOM & MICHAEL MCCANN, DISTORTING THE LAW: POLITICS, MEDIA AND THE LITIGATION CRISIS 183–226 (2004).

3. See *R. J. Reynolds v. Engle*, 806 So. 2d 503 (1999).

4. *Garza, et al. v. Merck & Co. Inc.*, DC-03-84 (Tex. Dist. Ct. 2006); *McDarby v. Merck*, ATL-L-3553-05 (Atlantic Cty. Ct., NJ, 2006).

5. George Priest, *Introduction* to CASS SUNSTEIN ET AL., PUNITIVE DAMAGES: HOW JURIES DECIDE (2002); George Priest, *Punitive Damages Reform: The Case of Alabama*, 56 LOUISIANA LAW REVIEW 825 (1996).

6. For a critique of these views see Marc Galanter, *Shadow Play: The Fabled Menace of Punitive Damages*, 1998 WISCONSIN LAW REVIEW 1–14 (1998).

7. See Elizabeth Amon, *Exxon Bankrolls Critics of Punitives, Then Cites the Research in Appeal of $5.3 Billion Valdez Award*, NATIONAL LAW JOURNAL, May 17, 1999;

Alan Zarembo, *Funding Studies to Suit Need: In the 1990s Exxon Began Paying for Research into Juries and the Damages They Award; The Findings Have Served the Firm Well in Court*, LOS ANGELES TIMES, December 3, 2003.

8. CASS SUNSTEIN ET AL., PUNITIVE DAMAGES, note 5.

9. *Id.* at 241.

10. Most of the section is based on discussion in THOMAS KOENIG & MICHAEL RUSTAD, IN DEFENSE OF TORT LAW (2001).

11. An excellent summary of the theory of private enforcement is contained in Paul Carrington, *The American Tradition of Private Law Enforcement*, BITBURGER GESPRACHE JAHRBUCH (2003).

12. *BMW of N. Am., Inc. v. Gore*, 517 U.S. 559 (1996).

13. *State Farm Mut. Auto Ins. Co. v. Campbell*, 538 U.S. 408 (2003).

14. More studies than are covered in this summary of empirical facts are reported in Neil Vidmar et al., *Brief in Support of Respondent, Phillip Morris USA v. Mayola Williams*, 2005 U.S. Briefs 1256 (U.S. S. Ct. Briefs 2006).

15. Theodore Eisenberg et al., *Juries, Judges and Punitive Damages: Empirical Analyses Using the Civil Justice Survey of State Courts 1992, 1996 and 2001 Data*, 3 JOURNAL OF EMPIRICAL LEGAL STUDIES 263 (2006).

16. Thomas Eaton et al., *The Effects of Seeking Punitive Damages on the Processing of Tort Claims*, 34 JOURNAL OF LEGAL STUDIES 344 (2005).

17. Vidmar et al., *Brief*, note 14, at 9–10.

18. See Jennifer Robbennolt, *Determining Punitive Damages: Empirical Insights and Implications for Reform*, 50 BUFFALO LAW REVIEW 103 (2002); EDIE GREENE & BRIAN BORNSTEIN, DETERMINING DAMAGES: THE PSYCHOLOGY OF JURY AWARDS (2003).

19. Rustad, *Unraveling Punitive Damages*, note 1.

20. *IGEN Intern., Inc. v. Roche Diagnostics GmbH*, 335 F.3d 303 (4th Cir. 2003).

21. *Pioneer Commercial Funding Corp. v. American Financial Mortg. Corp.*, 855 A. 2d 818 (Pa. 2004).

22. Vidmar et al., *Brief*, note 14, at 10–13.

23. Joni Hersch & W. Kip Viscusi, *Punitive Damages: How Judges and Juries Perform*, 33 JOURNAL OF LEGAL STUDIES 1 (2004).

24. Theodore Eisenberg & Martin T. Wells, *The Significant Association between Punitive and Compensatory Damages in Blockbuster Cases: A Methodological Primer*, 3 JOURNAL OF EMPIRICAL LEGAL STUDIES 175 (2006); Theodore Eisenberg, Valerie P. Hans & Martin T. Wells, *The Relation between Punitive and Compensatory Awards: Combining Extreme Data with the Mass of Awards*, in CIVIL JURIES AND CIVIL JUSTICE: PSYCHOLOGICAL AND LEGAL EXPLANATIONS (Brian Bornstein et al. eds., forthcoming), available at http://ssrn.com/id=929565.

25. Eisenberg et al., *Juries, Judges and Punitive Damages*, note 15.

26. Thomas Eaton et al., *Another Brick in the Wall: An Empirical Look at Georgia Tort Litigation in the 1990's*, 34 GEORGIA LAW REVIEW 1049 (2000).

27. Jennifer Robbennolt, *Punitive Damage Decision Making: The Decisions of Citizens and Trial Court Judges*, 26 LAW & HUMAN BEHAVIOR 315 (2002).

28. Robbennolt, *Determining Punitive Damages*, note 18, at 158.

29. RONALD EADES, JURY INSTRUCTIONS ON DAMAGES IN TORT ACTIONS §§ 2–8 (4th ed., 1998).

30. CALIFORNIA JURY INSTRUCTIONS—CIV.14.71 (BAJI 14.71) (2005 Revision).

31. E.g., see Judicial Council of California, CIVIL JURY INSTRUCTIONS FOR EVIDENCE CODE SECTION 502 (2005).

32. CALIFORNIA JURY INSTRUCTIONS—Civ.14.71 (BAJI 14.71) (2005 Revision).

33. *Liebeck v. McDonald's Restaurants*, P.T.S., Inc., No. CV-93-02419, 1995 WL 36039 (NM Dist. Ct. August 18, 1994).

34. Additional details about the case can be found in HALTOM & MCCANN, DISTORTING THE LAW, note 2.

35. For a review of this research see Vidmar et al., *Brief*, note 14.

36. *Id.*

37. See Vidmar, *Experimental Simulations and Tort Reform: Avoidance, Error and Overreaching in Sunstein et al.'s Punitive Damages*, 53 EMORY LAW JOURNAL 1359–1404 (2004) for documentation of the research sponsorship and a detailed critique of the research. Also, see Richard Lempert, *Juries, Hindsight, and Punitive Damage Awards: Failures of a Social Science Case for Change*, 48 DEPAUL LAW REVIEW 867 (1999).

38. See *Williams v. Philip Morris Inc.* 340 Ore. 35, 127 P.3d 1165 (2006); *Philip Morris USA v. Williams*, 127 S. Ct. 1057 (2007).

39. Patrick O'Neill & Joe Rojas-Burke, *Company Documents Prove Key to Verdict*, OREGONIAN, March 31, 1999, at A1.

40. *Philip Morris USA v. Williams*, 127 S. Ct. 1057 (2007).

41. GALLUP ORGANIZATION, ATTITUDES TOWARD THE LIABILITY AND LITIGATION SYSTEM: A SURVEY OF THE GENERAL PUBLIC AND BUSINESS EXECUTIVES (1982).

CHAPTER 16: JURIES AND MEDICAL MALPRACTICE

1. *Statement for the Record of the American Medical Association to the Senate Health, Education, Labor, and Pensions Committee and the Senate Judiciary Committee. RE: Patient Access Crisis: The Role of Medical Litigation*, February 11, 2003.

2. TOM BAKER, THE MEDICAL MALPRACTICE MYTH (2005).

3. Harvard Medical Practice Study, *Patients, Doctors, and Lawyers: Medical Injury, Malpractice Litigation and Patient Compensation in New York* (1990). See also PAUL C. WEILER ET AL., A MEASURE OF MALPRACTICE: MEDICAL INJURY, MALPRACTICE LITIGATION, AND PATIENT COMPENSATION (1993).

4. Harvard Medical Malpractice Study, note 3, at 44, tbl. 3.2.

5. INSTITUTE OF MEDICINE, TO ERR IS HUMAN: BUILDING A SAFER HEALTH CARE SYSTEM (Linda Kohn et al. eds., 2000), available at http://books.nap.edu/catalog/9728.html?onpi_newsdoc112999 (accessed February 27, 2007); Lucian L. Leape, *Institute of Medicine Medical Error Figures Are Not Exaggerated*, 284 JOURNAL OF THE AMERICAN MEDICAL ASSOCIATION 95 (2000).

6. Reuters News, *Report Says 195,000 Deaths Due to Hospital Error* (July 27, 2004), WL 7/27/04 Reuters Eng. News Serv. 22:23:11.

7. HEALTHGRADES, THIRD ANNUAL PATIENT SAFETY IN AMERICAN HOSPITALS STUDY (April 2006).

8. Frank A. Sloan & Stephen S. van Wert, *Cost of Injuries*, in FRANK A. SLOAN ET AL., SUING FOR MEDICAL MALPRACTICE 123, 139–40 (1993).

9. Harvard Medical Practice Study, note 3.

10. Michael Saks, *Medical Malpractice: Facing Real Problems and Finding Real Solutions*, 35 WILLIAM & MARY LAW REVIEW 693, 702–703 (1994), presents one of the clearest expositions of these findings.

11. For an extended discussion of these matters, see Neil Vidmar, *Medical Malpractice Lawsuits: An Essay on Patient Interests, the Contingency Fee System, Juries and Social Policy*, 38 LOYOLA OF LOS ANGELES LAW REVIEW 1217 (2005).

12. Thomas Cohen, *Tort Trials and Verdicts in Large Counties, 2001*, BUREAU OF JUSTICE STATISTICS BULLETIN NOVEMBER 2004, NCJ 206240.

13. See THOMAS KOENIG & MICHAEL RUSTAD, IN DEFENSE OF TORT LAW 127–28, 140–45 (2001).

14. See Vidmar, *Medical Malpractice and the Tort System in Illinois: A Report to the Illinois State Bar Association* (May 2003); Vidmar, *Medical Malpractice Litigation in Pennsylvania: A Report for the Pennsylvania Bar Association* (May 2006).

15. Henry Farber & Michelle White, *A Comparison of Formal and Informal Dispute Resolution in Medical Malpractice*, 23 JOURNAL OF LEGAL STUDIES 277 (1994).

16. Robert Caplan et al., *Effect of Outcome on Physician Judgments of Appropriateness of Care*, 265 JOURNAL OF THE AMERICAN MEDICAL ASSOCIATION 1957 (1991).

17. David M. Studdert et al., *Claims, Errors and Compensation Payments in Medical Malpractice Litigation*, 354 NEW ENGLAND JOURNAL OF MEDICINE 2024 (2006).

18. For additional discussion of these claims see Vidmar, *Medical Malpractice Lawsuits*, note 11.

19. Kirk Johnson, Carter Phillips & David Orentlichter, *A Fault-Based Administrative System for Resolving Medical Malpractice Claims*, 42 VANDERBILT LAW REVIEW 1365 (1989).

20. *Id.* at 1370–71.

21. Mark Taragin et al., *The Influence of Standard of Care and Severity of Injury on the Resolution of Medical Malpractice Claims*, 117 ANNALS OF INTERNAL MEDICINE 780 (1992).

22. Studdert et al., *Claims, Errors and Compensation Payments*, note 17.

23. VIDMAR, MEDICAL MALPRACTICE AND THE AMERICAN JURY 169–71 (1995).

24. For a review of this research, see VALERIE P. HANS, BUSINESS ON TRIAL (2000).

25. Vidmar, *Empirical Evidence on the Deep Pockets Hypothesis: Jury Awards for Pain and Suffering in Medical Malpractice Cases*, 43 DUKE LAW JOURNAL 885 (1994).

26. Michael Saks et al., *Reducing Variability in Civil Jury Awards*, 21 LAW & HUMAN BEHAVIOR 243 (1997).

27. Randall Bovbjerg et al., *Valuing Life and Limb in Tort: Scheduling Pain and Suffering*, 83 NORTHWESTERN LAW REVIEW 908 (1989).

28. Neil Vidmar, Felicia Gross & Mary Rose, *Jury Awards for Medical Malpractice and Post-verdict Adjustments of Those Awards*, 48 DEPAUL LAW REVIEW 265, 287 (1998).

29. Sloan & Van Wert, *Cost of Injuries*, note 8.

30. PATRICIA DANZON, MEDICAL MALPRACTICE: THEORY, EVIDENCE, AND PUBLIC POLICY 40–42 (1985).

31. Thomas Cohen, *Tort Trials*, note 12, at 7, tbl. 7.

32. See Vidmar, *Medical Malpractice and the Tort System in Illinois*, note 14.

33. VIDMAR, MEDICAL MALPRACTICE AND THE AMERICAN JURY, note 23, chaps. 9 and 10.

34. Tom Baker, *Blood Money, New Money and the Moral Code of the Personal Injury Bar*, 35 LAW & SOCIETY REVIEW 257 (2002).

35. Vidmar et al., *Jury Awards for Medical Malpractice*, note 28.

36. See Vidmar *Medical Malpractice and the Tort System in Illinois*, note 14; also Neil Vidmar, *Juries and Jury Verdicts in Medical Malpractice Cases: Implications for Tort Reform in Pennsylvania* (January 28, 2002) (unpublished report, on file with the author).

37. David A. Hyman, Bernard Black, Kathryn Zeiler, Charles Silver & William M. Sage, *Do Defendants Pay What Juries Award? Post-verdict Haircuts in Texas Medical Malpractice Cases:1988–2003*, 4 JOURNAL OF EMPIRICAL LEGAL STUDIES 3 (2007).

38. Neil Vidmar, Paul Lee, Kara MacKillop & Kieran McCarthy, *Uncovering the "Invisible" Profile of Medical Malpractice Litigation*, 54 DEPAUL LAW REVIEW 315 (2005).

39. Neil Vidmar, Kara MacKillop & Paul Lee, *Million Dollar Medical Malpractice Cases in Florida: Post-verdict and Pre-suit Settlements*, 59 VANDERBILT LAW REVIEW 1309 (2006).

40. BAKER, THE MEDICAL MALPRACTICE MYTH, note 2.

41. Frank A. Sloan, Penny B. Githens, Gerald Hickson & Stephen S. van Wert, *Compensation*, in SUING FOR MEDICAL MALPRACTICE 187, 195 (Frank A. Sloan et al. eds., 1993).

42. *Ferdon v. Wis. Patients' Comp. Fund*, 701 N.W.2d 440 (Wis. 2005).

43. David Studdert, Tony Yang & Michelle Mello, *Are Damage Caps Regressive? A Study of Malpractice Jury Verdicts in California*, 21 HEALTH AFFAIRS 54 (2004).

44. Lucinda Finley, *The Hidden Victims of Tort Reform: Women, Children and the Elderly*, 53 EMORY LAW JOURNAL 1263 (2004). The quote taken from the article appears on p. 1313.

45. See Vidmar, *Medical Malpractice and the Tort System in Illinois*, note 14.

CHAPTER 17: CONCLUSION

1. James P. Levine, *Using Jury Verdict Forecasts in Criminal Defense Strategy*, 66 JUDICATURE 448 (1983); James P. Levine, *Jury Toughness: The Impact of Conservatism on Criminal Court Verdicts*, 29 CRIME & DELINQUENCY 71 (1983).

2. Chris Guthrie, Jeffrey J. Rachlinski & Andrew Wistrich, *Inside the Judicial Mind: Heuristics and Biases*, 86 CORNELL LAW REVIEW 777 (2001).

3. On the advantages of repeat players in the legal system, see Marc Galanter, *Why the "Haves" Come Out Ahead: Speculations on the Limits of Legal Change*, 9 LAW & SOCIETY REVIEW 95 (1974); IN LITIGATION: DO THE "HAVES" STILL COME OUT AHEAD? (Herbert M. Kritzer & Susan Silbey eds., 2003).

4. Richard Lempert, *Juries, Hindsight and Punitive Damage Awards: Failures of a Social Science Case for Change*, 48 DEPAUL LAW REVIEW 867–94 (1999); Daniel W. Shuman & Anthony Champagne, *Removing the People from the Legal Process: The Rhetoric and Research on Judicial Selection and Juries*, 3 PSYCHOLOGY, PUBLIC POLICY & LAW 242 (1997).

5. Peter Tiersma, *Communication with Juries: How to Draft More Understandable Jury Instructions*, National Center for State Courts (2006), available at http://ncsconline.org/Communicating.pdf (accessed March 1, 2007).

6. B. Michael Dann, *"Learning Lessons" and "Speaking Rights:" Creating Edu-*

cated and Democratic Juries, 68 INDIANA LAW JOURNAL 1229 (1993). Judge Dann is now retired.

7. ARIZONA SUPREME COURT COMMITTEE ON MORE EFFECTIVE USE OF JURIES, JURORS, THE POWER OF TWELVE (1993).

8. AMERICAN BAR ASSOCIATION, PRINCIPLES FOR JURIES AND JURY TRIALS (2005), http://www.abanet.org/juryprojectstandards/principles.pdf (accessed March 1, 2007).

9. Dann, *"Learning Lessons,"* note 6.

10. MIRJAN R. DAMAŠKA, EVIDENCE LAW ADRIFT 90 (1997).

11. Elizabeth F. Loftus & Douglas Leber, *Do Jurors Talk?* 22 TRIAL 59 (1986) (estimating that about 10 percent of jurors engage in forbidden discussions); Paula L. Hannaford, Valerie P. Hans & G. Thomas Munsterman, *Permitting Juror Discussions during Trial: Impact of the Arizona Reform*, 24 LAW & HUMAN BEHAVIOR 359, 371 (2000) (11 percent of jurors in cases in which they could talk to other jurors and 14 percent of jurors who were forbidden to talk to other jurors during the trial reported that they spoke to friends and family about the case during the trial).

12. See, for example: Shari S. Diamond, Neil Vidmar, Mary Rose, Leslie Ellis & Beth Murphy, *Jury Discussions during Civil Trials: Studying an Arizona Innovation*, 45 ARIZONA LAW REVIEW 1 (2003); Hannaford et al., *Permitting Juror Discussions during Trial*, note 11; Valerie P. Hans, Paula L. Hannaford & G. Thomas Munsterman, *The Arizona Jury Reform Permitting Civil Jury Trial Discussions: The Views of Trial Participants, Judges, and Jurors*, 32 UNIVERSITY OF MICHIGAN JOURNAL OF LAW REFORM 349 (1999); B. MICHAEL DANN, VALERIE P. HANS & DAVID H. KAYE, TESTING THE EFFECTS OF SELECTED JURY TRIAL INNOVATIONS ON JUROR COMPREHENSION OF CONTESTED MTDNA EVIDENCE (Final Technical Report to National Institute of Justice, Washington, DC, 2004).

13. The research literature on jury reforms is substantial and is summarized in a number of places. JURY TRIAL INNOVATIONS (G. Thomas Munsterman, Paula L. Hannaford-Agor & G. Marc Whitehead, eds., 2nd ed., 2006) is a comprehensive compendium of jury reforms that lists for each reform the relevant issues, procedures, advantages, disadvantages, and representative studies. The American Bar Association's PRINCIPLES FOR JURIES AND JURY TRIALS, note 8, is another excellent resource. See also B. Michael Dann & Valerie P. Hans, *Recent Evaluative Research on Jury Trial Innovations*, COURT REVIEW, Spring 2004, at 12.

14. Brian J. Ostrom, Shauna M. Strickland & Paula L. Hannaford-Agor, *Examining Trial Trends in State Courts: 1976–2002*, 1 JOURNAL OF EMPIRICAL LEGAL STUDIES 755, 764 (2004).

15. Marc Galanter, *The Vanishing Trial: An Examination of Trials and Related Matters in Federal and State Courts*, 1 JOURNAL OF EMPIRICAL LEGAL STUDIES 459, 465–66 (2004).

16. *Jury Service: Is Fulfilling Your Civic Duty a Trial?* Harris Interactive Poll prepared for American Bar Association (2004), http://www.abanews.org/releases/juryreport.pdf. For a summary of other surveys, see Valerie P. Hans, *Attitudes toward the Civil Jury*, in VERDICT: ASSESSING THE CIVIL JURY SYSTEM 248, 253–61 (Robert E. Litan ed., 1993).

17. Theodore Eisenberg and Jeffrey P. Miller report a recent analysis in which they find that when corporations write complex contracts with each other, they are apt to retain the jury trial right rather than allow an arbitrator to resolve the case. One interpretation of this pattern is that even some of the harshest critics of the jury believe that it adds value in

litigation. Theodore Eisenberg & Jeffrey P. Miller, *Do Juries Add Value?: Evidence from an Empirical Study of Jury Trial Waiver Clauses in Large Corporate Contracts*, 3 JOURNAL OF EMPIRICAL LEGAL STUDIES 539 (forthcoming 2007), available at http://ssrn.com abstract =946465.

18. See WORLD JURY SYSTEMS (Neil Vidmar ed., 2000); John D. Jackson & Nikolay P. Kovalev, *Lay Adjudication and Human Rights in Europe*, 13 COLUMBIA JOURNAL OF EUROPEAN LAW 83 (2006–2007).

19. Stephen C. Thaman, *The Resurrection of Trial by Jury in Russia*, 31 STANFORD JOURNAL OF INTERNATIONAL LAW 61 (1995).

20. Stephen C. Thaman, *The Nullification of the Russian Jury: Lessons for Jury Inspired Reform in Eurasia and Beyond*, CORNELL JOURNAL OF INTERNATIONAL LAW (forthcoming 2007).

21. Stephen C. Thaman, *Spain Returns to Trial by Jury*, 21 HASTINGS INTERNATIONAL & COMPARATIVE LAW REVIEW 241 (1998).

22. See discussion in Hiroshi Fukurai, *The Rebirth of Japan's Petit Quasi-Jury and Grand Jury Systems: Cross-National Analysis of Legal Consciousness and Lay Participatory Experience in Japan and the US*, CORNELL JOURNAL OF INTERNATIONAL LAW (forthcoming 2007); TAKASHI MARUTA, SAIBAN-IN SEIDO [The Quasi-Jury System] (2004).

23. In 2004 one of us was privileged to travel to Argentina for a speaking tour about the jury trial as Argentines were considering various bills that would introduce trial by jury. Valerie P. Hans, *Trip Report: Citizen Participation in the Judicial System: Trial by Jury, US Speaker and Specialist Program*, US Department of State, Buenos Aires, Argentina, August 29–September 4, 2004 (available from the author). The right to jury trial in Argentina has been extensively discussed in Edmundo S. Hendler, *Lay Participation in the Judicial Process: The Situation in Argentina*, 2001 SAINT LOUIS–WARSAW TRANSATLANTIC LAW JOURNAL 81 (2001–2002). See also RICARDO J. CAVALLERO & EDMUNDO S. HENDLER, JUSTICIA Y PARTICIPACION: EL JUCIO POR JURADOS EN MATERIA PENAL (1988).

24. *Jury Bill Gets Parliamentary Go-Ahead*, Digital Chosunilbo (English edition), May 1, 2007, http://english.chosun.com/w21data/html/news/200705/200705010023.html; *What the New Jury System Will Mean for Korea*, Digital Chosunilbo (English edition), May 3, 2007, http://english.chosun.com/w21data/html/news/200705/200705030023.html. See also Sanghoon Han, Sangjoon Kim & Kwang Bai Park, *Preparing the Ground: The Case of Lay Participation in Korea*, paper presented at the annual meeting of the Law & Society Association, Baltimore, MD (July 2006)(describing the background work they and other members of the Presidential Reform Commission in Korea conducted to evaluate a jury system for Korea).

25. John Gastil, E. Pierre Deess & Phil Weiser, *Civic Awakening in the Jury Room: A Test of the Connection between Jury Deliberation and Political Participation*, 64 JOURNAL OF POLITICS 585 (2002); John Gastil, E. Pierre Deess, Phil Weiser & Jordan Larner, *Jury Service and Electoral Participation: A Strong Test of the Participation Hypothesis*, JOURNAL OF POLITICS (forthcoming), available at http://depts.washington.edu/jurydem/JuryService AndElectoralParticipation.pdf (accessed June 24, 2007).

26. VALERIE P. HANS & NEIL VIDMAR, JUDGING THE JURY (1986).

INDEX

Abbott, Walter F., 363
Abel, Richard, 282, 389
abortion views as bias in Harris case, 83–87
Abramson, Jeffrey, 76, 358, 377, 383
Abramson, Shirley, 81, 359
Abuse Excuse, The (Dershowitz), 205
acceptable business practices, 126
accident cases
 determining responsibility, 127, 137–38, 140, 166–67, 184–86, 236, 274–75, 314, 390
 injuries from, 271–73, 292–93, 295–98, 336
  impact of previous injuries, 127, 139, 184, 274–77, 388
accountants, jurors acting as in determining damages, 294–98
Acker, James R., 386
aconitine (poison), 171, 172
acquaintance rape, 198, 201, 206, 341
acquittals, wrongful, 195–97
Adams, John, 49, 55
Adams v. Texas, 254
ad damnum, 290
ADR. *See* alternative dispute resolution
adversary procedure, 129–35
African Americans. *See* race
age discrimination and use of peremptory challenges, 97, 100
aggravating circumstances, 59, 126, 198, 244, 246, 248, 252, 253, 257, 260–61, 384
agreement between juries and judges, 148–51, 370
A'Hearn, Deborah Ann, 359
Alabama
 capital punishment cases in, 246
 contributory negligence rules, 285
 expert witnesses budget for defendant, 263
 state's suit against Exxon Mobil Corporation, 309
Alameda County, California, 59–60

Al-Arian case, 119–22, 123
Albertson, Stephanie, 375
Alexander, James, 42, 43, 44, 351, 381
Alfini, James J., 342, 372
Alfred P. Murrah Federal Building, 110
ALI. See American Law Institute
Alicke, Mark D., 389
Alien and Sedition laws, 55
ALI test, 212, 213
all-white jury, 72, 75, 96, 229, 249, 357, 358
al Qaeda, 117
Alschuler, Albert, 352, 354, 355, 357
alternative dispute resolution, 63
American Bar Association, 10, 77, 263, 343, 344, 368, 369, 387, 396
Americanization of the Common Law (Nelson), 48
American Journal of the Medical Sciences, 172
American Judicature Society, 79, 344
American Jury, The (Kalven and Zeisel), 148–51, 198–99, 230–31, 234, 240, 301
American Law Institute, 212
American Lawyer (magazine), 103
American Libertarian Party, 238
American Medical Association, 15, 329
  Task Force, 321
American Psychiatric Association, 245, 258
American Taliban case, 117–19
American Tort Reform Association, 15, 267, 282, 303
Amnesty International, 249, 385
Amon, Elizabeth, 391
amputation, unnecessary (malpractice suit), 325
Amsterdam, Jonathan, 386
anchor numbers, 164, 290, 298
Andrea Yates case, 19, 108, 207–10, 213–14
Angell, Marcia, 170, 187, 373
angiogram (malpractice suit), 326
Anti-Federalists, 53, 54
Antonio, Michael E., 384, 386
Argentina, jury trials in, 345, 397
Arian, Sami Al-, 119–22
Arizona
  capital punishment cases in, 246
  Supreme Court of, 18, 137
    Committee on More Effective Use of Juries, 343
Arizona Civil Jury Project (National Center for State Courts), 150, 271, 272, 274
Arizona Jury Project (Arizona Supreme Court), 18, 137–40, 164, 184–87, 287, 295–96, 355
Arkansas, 111
  sentencing authority, 56
Armenia and jury system, 345
Arnold, Edward, 210
Arnot, Lucy, 367
Aryan Brotherhood, 224
asbestos trials, 128, 156, 178, 278, 289, 310
  Rand asbestos study, 154, 179
Ashcroft, John, 118
assizes, 32, 35
  Assize of Clarendon (1166), 23
  Assize of Northampton (1176), 23
assumption of risk, 61–62, 234, 270
Atkins v. Virginia, 245
ATRA. *See* American Tort Reform Association
attaint, 25, 27
Auld, Robin, 38, 350, 351, 371
Austin, Arthur D., 154
Australia
  jury system, 36, 179
  limiting mass media coverage of criminal trials, 108
awards
  anchor numbers, 164
  fictitious, 15, 17, 347–48
  impact of on corporations, 62, 306, 307
  judges' review of, 147, 228, 302, 310, 311, 314, 334–35, 337–38
  juries arriving at damage awards, 127, 267, 274, 277
    acting as accountants, 294–98
    caps on, 282, 336–37

compensatory damages, 281–302
malpractice cases, 321–38
outlier awards, 156–57, 334
pain and suffering, 16, 284, 295, 298, 299, 300–302, 324, 332, 336–37
postverdict reductions, 314, 333–35
punitive damages, 303–20
reliability of jury awards, 282
juror characteristics affecting damage awards, 285–87
median compensatory damage awards, 283
median punitive damage awards, 310
overgenerous, 16, 281, 282, 289–90, 302, 318, 324, 390
See also damages
Azerbaijan and jury system, 345

Babcock, Barbara Allen, 357, 361
Bailey, T., 389
Baime, David S., 385
Baker, Tom, 321–22, 335, 393, 395
Baldus, David, 97, 100, 245, 248, 256, 363, 364, 384, 385
Bamberger, Phylis Skloot, 359
Barefoot v. Estelle, 245
Barnes, A. R., 247–48
Barnes, David, 373
Barnes, Elwell, 247–48
Barrett, David, 351
Bartol, Curt, 378
Barton, Debra, 318
Batson challenge, 97, 229
Batson v. Kentucky, 96–97, 100
Batt, John, 363
battered child syndrome, 204–205
battered woman syndrome, 202–205
Beattie, John, 32, 33, 35, 349, 350
Beccaria, Cesare, 55
Becka, Holly, 358
Bedau, Hugo, 383, 387
Bell, Laura, 386
Bendectin (drug), 153, 179, 187
Bender, Leslie, 389
Bennett, Elizabeth A., 374
Bennett, Lance, 132–33, 141, 369
Bentley, David, 349, 350
Beran, Nancy, 378
Berger, Margaret, 375
Berk, Richard A., 385
Bermant, Gordon, 371
Bernard, Francis, 51–52
Bess, Carrie, 377
beyond a reasonable doubt, 129, 150, 159, 160, 161, 196, 197, 213, 236, 246, 260–61
bias
affecting judges, 83–93, 342
affecting jurors, 340, 366
counteracting of, 341–42
removing jurors for cause, 93–95
hindsight bias, 131
Bible, Teresa, 95–96
Bill of Rights
Eighth Amendment, 243, 265
First Amendment, 114
Sixth Amendment, 115, 242
See also Constitution
Black, Bernard, 395
Blackmun, Harry, 264
Blackstone, William, 21, 34, 37, 348, 350, 352
blindness (malpractice suit), 327
Blinka, Daniel, 353
blue ribbon jury, 67–69. *See also* special juries
Blume, John H., 369, 385, 386
BMW v. Gore, 306–307, 314, 316
Boatright, Robert G., 358, 359
Bobbitt, Lorena, 205
Bodenhamer, David, 48, 352, 354
Boeschen, Laura, 374
Bohm, Robert M., 386
Bonfire of the Vanities (Wolfe), 286
Bordens, Kenneth, 372
Borgida, Eugene, 201
Bornstein, Brian, 180, 286, 290, 300–301, 375, 377, 382, 388, 390, 391, 392
Boston Massacre, 52
Boulder Hemp Initiative Project, 229

Bourgeois, Martin, 235, 382
Bousserman, Robert, 27
Bovbjerg, Randall, 332, 389, 391, 394
Bower, Tom, 371
Bowers, William, 246, 249, 251, 255–56, 384, 385, 386
Bowman, James E., 95–96
brachial plexus injury (malpractice case), 334
Bracton, Henry de, 25
Bradford, William, 47
Brady, James, 212
brain injury (malpractice case), 337–38
Brands, H. W., 349
Brekke, Nancy, 201
Brennan, Charlie, 361
Brennan, William J., 241, 243
Brewer, Neil, 366
Brewer, Thomas, 257, 386
Bright, Stephen, 387, 388
Brody, David C., 383
Broeder, Dale, 362
Bronson, Edward, 116, 117, 120, 367, 368
Bronx effect, 286, 287
Brown, Angela, 379
Brown, Darryl, 227, 381
Brown, David P., 365
Bruschke, Jon, 365, 366
Bryant, Kobe, 89, 198, 377
BJS. *See* US Bureau of Justice Statistics
Bundy, Ted, 265
Buranelli, Vincent, 351
Bureau of Justice Statistics. *See* US Bureau of Justice Statistics
Burger, Warren, 73, 88
burglary, legal vs. familiar meaning of, 159–60
Burning Bed, The (TV movie), 202
Burns, Daniel, 221–24, 381
Bush, Neal, 361
Bushel's case, 27–30, 225
business disputes, 61–62, 68. *See also* corporations
Business on Trial (Hans), 270, 278
Butler, Edgar W., 356
Butler, Paul, 226, 381
Caldwell/Johnson simulated case, 133–34, 141
Calendar, James, 55
California
  caps on malpractice awards, 337
  Compassionate Use Act, 237
  removing jurors for cause, 94–95
  and voir dire, 89, 91
California Jury study (National Center for State Courts), 150
Callins v. Collins, 264
Cambridge University, 30
Campbell, Curtis, 307
Canada, 36
  abolition of stand bys, 35
  and generic prejudice of jurors, 113–14
  Law Reform Commission, 18
  limiting mass media coverage of criminal trials, 108, 112
Capital Jury Project, 246, 251, 254, 257, 262
capital murder trials, 17, 89, 209, 238, 252
  Hendrickson case, 171–73
  Webster case, 56–59
  Yates case, 19, 108, 207–10, 213–14
  See also capital punishment; criminal trials; death penalty
capital punishment, 56, 57, 214, 241–65. *See also* death penalty
Capital Punishment Project, 249
Caplan, Lincoln, 379
Caplan, Robert, 394
Caplow, Stacy, 359
caps on awards, 282, 336–37
Carlton, Jeff, 379
Carolina colonies, 48
  use of jury trials, 50
  See also North Carolina; South Carolina
Carpenter, Teresa, 367
Carrington, Paul, 392
Carroll, John, 365
Carter, Dan T., 357
Casper, Jay, 179
Casper, Jonathan, 374
Castor, Betty, 119
Catholic Worker Community, 221

Catts, Douglas B., 361
causation and liability, 156–57
cause
challenge for cause, 87, 91, 362
removing jurors for, 91, 93–95, 362
Cavallero, Ricardo J., 397
Cecil, Joe S., 374
cerebral palsy, unnecessary (malpractice suit), 325
challenge for cause, 87, 91, 362
Chambers, John, 43–46
Champagne, Anthony, 178, 373, 374, 395
change of venue, 114–15, 116, 366
Arian trial, 121
Copeland trial, 116
Durham garbage truck case, 111
Lindh trial, 118–19
Oklahoma City bombing case, 110
Chapin, Bradley, 352
Charles II (king), 30
Charman, Elizabeth, 155, 367, 372
Charrow, Robert, 342
Charrow, Veda, 342
Chase, Samuel, 55
Chicago Jury Project, 143
Chicago jury selection study, 99
child abuse
battered child syndrome, 204–205
and generic prejudice of jurors, 113–14
Chin, Audrey, 390
Christ, Aaron M., 384
Christie, George, 390
Church of England, 28
Citizens' Tribunal on Iraq, 380
civil liability, 267–79
plaintiff's degree of responsibility in, 61, 128, 129, 166–67, 234–36, 267, 270–74, 279, 285
prior injuries and illnesses in, 127, 139, 184, 274–77, 388
reasonable person standard, 127–28, 154, 166, 269–70
civil traverse juries, 51–52
civil trials
civil liability, 267–79
plaintiff's degree of responsibility in, 61, 128, 129, 166–67, 234–36, 267, 270–74, 279, 285
prior injuries and illnesses in, 127, 139, 184, 274–77, 388
reasonable person standard, 127–28, 154, 166, 269–70
deciding compensatory damages, 281–302
decline in number of trials by jury, 62–63, 344–45
expert evidence and, 184–87
and historical facts, 127–28
impact of complex cases on competency of jury, 156–57
judges and juries agreeing on verdicts, 339–40
and jury nullification, 228, 231, 234–36
in nineteenth-century America, 54
origins of contemporary controversy, 61–64
personal injury cases, 37, 61, 92, 231, 300
and compensatory damages, 283–84, 290–92, 295
failure to mitigate, 65, 293
and punitive damages, 309, 312
role of insurance in, 287–88, 320
questioning witnesses, 130, 368
severed and joined civil trials, 156–57
trial process, 311–12
Clarendon, Assize of (1166), 23
Clark, Marcia, 115, 367
Clark, Ramsey, 384
class action suits, 62, 156
clear and convincing evidence, 129, 213, 312
Clermont, Kevin M., 152, 371
Clifford, Brian R., 376
Clinton, Bill, 217
closing arguments, 59, 104, 131, 160, 161, 171, 209, 214, 223–24, 276, 290, 295–96
CNN, 117
Cockburn, J. S., 349
coffee spill case, 15, 16, 19, 303, 312–14
cognitive illusions, 164
and expert witnesses, 177

Cohen, Thomas, 389, 394
Coker v. Georgia, 245
Colb, Sherry, 378, 383
Colden, Cadwaller, 42
cold water, trial by, 22
Coleman v. United States of America and Touchette Regional Hospital, 337–38
Coles, John, Jr., 26
Coles, John, Sr., 26
collateral source rule, 287
Collins, Rebecca, 372
colonial America, juries in, 41–52
Colorado
  capital punishment cases in, 246
  pay rate for defendant's counsel, 263
  Supreme Court of, 305
Columbia Law School, 18
Commentaries on the Laws of England (Blackstone), 21
Committee on More Effective Use of Juries (Arizona Supreme Court), 343
Common Council of New York, 46
Commonsense Justice (Finkel), 232
Communicating with Juries (Tiersma), 342
comparative negligence, 166, 235, 268, 269, 285, 316
Compassionate Use Act (California), 237
compensatory damages, 281–302
  deep pockets hypothesis, 288–90, 332, 341
  financial losses and, 290–92
  impact of insurance on, 287–88
  injury assessment and, 292, 298
    competence of juries in awarding of damages, 299–302
    plaintiff's failure to mitigate effects of injuries, 65, 293
  median awards for plaintiffs, 283
  personal injury cases and, 283–84, 290–92, 295
  psychological anchors, 290
competence of juries, 153–54, 339–46
  agreement between juries and judges, 148–54, 370
  in awarding damages, 299–302, 315
  on expert witnesses, 176–77
  impact of complex cases on, 156–57
  in malpractice cases, 330–31
  overall competence of, 340
  studied through mock trials, 154–57
complex trials, 154–57
compurgation, 21, 23
confidence of jurors, 94
conflicting narratives, 132–35, 138
Connecticut as a colony
  allowing legal counsel, 352
  exclusion of lawyers from trials, 48
  New Haven Colony, 50, 352
  use of jury trials, 50, 352, 353
Conrad, Clay S., 381
Constable, Marianne, 356, 382
Constitution, 9, 101, 319
  Bill of Rights, 73, 114, 115, 242, 243, 265
  juries in the constitutional debates, 52–54
consultants. *See* trial consultants
contempt
  of court, 29, 78, 108, 229, 383
  of the king, 28
contingency fees for lawyers, 61–62, 323
contract cases, 68, 283, 293
contributory fault doctrine, 62
contributory negligence, 62, 231, 234–35, 270, 285
Controlled Substance Act (US), 237
convictions, wrongful, 191, 192–95, 262–63, 376. *See also* Innocence Project
Cook County, Illinois, 288–89
Cooley, Armanda, 377
Cooper, Claire, 383
Cooper, Joel, 180, 374
Copeland, Johnny, 116–17, 118, 120
Corker, David, 365
corporations, 61–62, 68
  held to higher standards, 278–79, 341
  individuals vs. corporations as defendants in civil trials, 278–79
  as plaintiffs, 283
  suffering economic harm in damage awards, 62, 306, 307
  use of jury trials, 396–97

corsnaed, 22–23
Cosby, William, 41–43, 44, 52
Cotton, Ronald, 192–93, 194
Council for Tobacco Research, 317
CourtTV, 109, 377
Cradock, George, 51–52
"Crazy Ned." *See* Arnold, Edward
credibility of evidence, juries judging, 162–63
Criminal Justice Act of 1976 (England), 38
Criminal Justice and Public Order Act of 1974 (England), 38
criminal liability, 52
criminal responsibility, 191–206
criminal trials
  in America
    early America, 31
    nineteenth century, 55, 59–61
  decline in number of trials by jury, 17, 60, 62–63, 344–45
  judge-jury disagreements, 227, 339–40
  judging criminal responsibility, 191–206
  and jury nullification, 226, 227, 228–34
  severed and joined criminal trials, 155–56
  and use of expert witnesses, 173
Croley, Steven, 355
cross-examination of witnesses, 32, 33, 57, 58–59, 104, 130–31, 176, 194, 196, 199, 200, 245, 258, 284, 312, 328, 331
Croswell, Harry, 46–47
CSI effect, 16, 17, 191, 197, 377
Cutler, Brian L., 376

Dahmer, Jeffrey, 208
Dallas Morning News, 99
damages
  ad damnum, 290
  compensatory damages, 281–302
    deep pockets hypothesis, 288–90
    financial losses and, 290–92
    impact of insurance on, 287–88
    injury assessment and, 292
    median awards for plaintiffs, 283
    psychological anchors, 290
  competence of juries in awarding of, 299–302
  deep pockets hypothesis, 332, 341
  exemplary damages, 304–305
  financial status of juror affecting damage award, 286
  general damages, 284–85, 295–99. *See also* pain and suffering
  juries versus judges, 301
  juror characteristics affecting damage awards, 285–87
  punitive damages, 16, 128, 129, 157, 282, 285, 303–20
    as deterrence, 305
    frequency of, 308–309
    judicial oversight of, 314
    median awards, 310
    postverdict settlements, 314
  special damages, 283–84
  vindictive damages, 305
  variability, 299–300
  See also awards
Damaška, Mirjan, 343, 368, 396
Danelaw, 24
Daniels, Stephen, 355, 391
Dann, B. Michael, 236, 343, 375, 382, 395, 396
Danzon, Patricia, 333, 391, 394
Darbyshire, Penny, 350
Darley, John M., 382, 389
date rape, 198
Daubert trilogy of cases, 170
Davis, James H., 370
Dawes, Robyn M., 362, 369
Dawson, John, 349
death penalty, 18, 56, 57, 107, 116, 126, 208, 214, 241–65
  botched executions, 265
  death qualified juries, 251–55, 341
  judges rather than juries deciding on, 246, 384
  juries as determiner of, 243–44, 246, 249–65
    not feeling responsibility for, 262
  jury selection in death penalty cases, 57, 59, 68–69, 91, 97, 214, 249–56

life sentence vs. death penalty, 251
methods of execution, 110, 208, 209, 242, 245, 246, 254, 265
moratorium on, 247, 263, 387
numbers of executions in US, 242–43, 246, 248
racial bias in death penalty cases, 243, 244, 245, 248–49, 255, 385
voir dire in death penalty cases, 91, 251, 252–53, 255, 362
wrongful convictions, 262–63
Death Penalty Moratorium Project, 263
decision making and juries, 141–42, 144–45, 149
Declaration of Indulgence, 30
decline in number of trials by jury, 17, 60, 62–63, 345
deep pockets hypothesis, 278, 288–90, 341
and malpractice cases, 332
and compensatory damages, 288–90
Deess, E. Pierre, 397
defendants
defendant responsibility in civil trials, 277–79
intersecting roles of defendant and victim, 198–205
defendants as victims, 198, 202–205, 259
plaintiff vs. defendant in civil trials, 267–79
presenting no case, 131
receiving poor legal assistance, 263
testimony from, 58, 59
verdicts in favor of, 149, 150, 283, 308, 324, 330, 331
defense attorney's fallacy, 181
Deiss, Andrew, 352, 354, 357
DeLancey, James, 43, 44, 45, 47
Delaware
capital punishment cases in, 246, 384
and voir dire, 89
Delaware Right to Life organization, 83
Delaware Women's Health Organization, 83
Delinquent Juror Prosecution Program, 78
de minimis cases, 231–32
Democrat (newspaper), 117
demographic of jurors affecting awards, 285–87
DeMott, Peter, 221–24, 381
Denno, Deborah, 378
Dentes, George, 221
Dershowitz, Alan, 205, 347, 378
Determining Damages (Greene and Bornstein), 286
DeVille, Kenneth, 355
Devine, Dennis J., 370
Devlin, Patrick, 21, 348
Dewees, April, 318
Dexter, H. R., 366
Diamond, Shari, 18, 94, 99, 137, 179, 261–62, 287, 288, 348, 355, 358, 363, 364, 369, 373, 374, 375, 387, 390, 396
Diaz, Angel, 265
Diaz, Lisa Ann, 215, 216
Dickhute, Nancy Lawler, 359
Dietz, Park, 208–209, 212, 214, 379
Dillehay, Ronald, 91, 362, 367, 385
diminished capacity. *See* mental capacity, diminished or impaired
Dimitrius, Jo-Ellan, 103
disagreements between judges and juries, 340
in punitive awards, 310–11
in rape cases, 198–99, 231
reasons for, 230–32
disqualifications for jury duty, 79–81
District of Columbia jury reform commission, 101–102
DNA evidence, 15, 16, 95, 175, 193, 262–63
mtDNA analysis, 180–83
Dobbs, Dan B., 389
"Dr. Death." *See* Grigson, James
Domesday Book, 23–24
domestic violence, 202–205
Doob, Anthony, 18, 131, 162, 348, 369, 373
Dooling, Nancy, 381
Doppelt, J., 367
Dougherty, John, 27

Douglas, William O., 243
Dow Chemical Company, 236
drivers' license lists, 76–77
Drizin, Steven, 376
due process clause, 319
Duffy, Alisa, 318
Duncan v. Louisiana, 226
Dunn, Meghan A., 374
Dunn, Oscar, 87
Duren v. Missouri, 74
Durham, Monte, 212
Durham test, 212, 213, 216
Dwyer, Jim, 347

Eades, Ronald, 392
Eaton, Thomas, 308, 311, 392
Eberhardt, Jennifer, 255, 386
economic losses and compensatory damages, 290–92
Edmondson v. Leesville Concrete Co., 363
Eighth Amendment of the Bill of Rights, 243, 265
Eisenberg, Theodore, 152, 261, 262, 286, 287, 310–11, 355, 369, 370, 371, 385, 387, 390, 392, 396, 397
elderly as jurors and use of peremptory challenges against, 97, 100
electric chair, 242, 245, 246
Ellis, Leslie, 18, 348, 355, 369, 396
Ellsworth, Phoebe, 75, 214, 250, 358, 379
Elwork, Amiram, 342, 372
emotional distress, 307
empty pockets hypothesis, 290
Engel, David, 287, 390
England
  limiting mass media coverage of criminal trials, 108
  study of pretrial prejudice, 112–13
English, Peter, 372
English origins of the modern jury, 21–39
Enron trial, 103–104, 108
enterprise liability, 62
Erikson, Kai, 111–12, 366
Ermann, M. David, 278, 389
erroneous convictions, 191, 192–95
error, writ of, 59
Erving, John, 51–52
Erving v. Cradock, 51–52
euthanasia, 239
evading jury duty, 77–78
Evans, Donald J., 349
evidence, rules of, 50
  evolution of, 33, 36
  exclusion of some evidence, 131
  and expert witnesses, 174, 216
  Federal Rules of Evidence, 174, 199
  limiting instructions, 163–64
  rape cases, 131, 199
evidence driven deliberation approach, 143
evidence evaluation and juries, 125–45
  credibility, juries judging, 162–63
  in death penalty cases, 256–59
  evaluating their comprehension of evidence and law, 147–68
  impact of complex cases on competency of jury, 154–57
  impact of inadmissible evidence on, 162–64
  judging testimony of expert witnesses, 169–89
  legal instructions and factual determinations, 164–68
  in punitive awards, 312
  statistical evidence and juries, 180–84
examples
  of complex trials, 154–57
  determining financial losses in civil cases, 291–92
  determining general damages, 296–97, 298
  determining injuries in civil cases, 292
  insurance considerations in civil cases, 288
  of jurors analyzing evidence, 137–40, 141–42
  of jurors as accountants in determining damages, 294–95
  of jurors evaluating plaintiffs in civil cases, 271–73
  of jurors' use of instructions, 164–68
  of jury response to expert evidence in civil trials, 184–87

of negligence cases, 276
plaintiff's failure to mitigate effects of injuries, 293
See also mock juries
excuses to get out of jury duty, 77, 79–81
execution. *See* death penalty
exemplary damages, 304–305. *See also* punitive damages
exemptions from jury duty, 79–81
expert witnesses, 127, 131, 138, 149
ability of the jury to understand, 177–80
Andrea Yates case, 208–209, 214–15
defining expertise, 174
vs. eyewitnesses, 175
on financial losses, 290–92, 300
Hendrickson murder case and, 171–73
juries judging testimony of, 169–89
lacking proper credentials, 282
as lay justices, 375
in malpractice cases, 328
in penalty phase of trial, 258
St. Patrick's Four, 222
Exxon Corporation, 304
Exxon Mobil Corporation, 309
Exxon studies, 304, 315–16
Exxon Valdez (tanker), 303, 304
eyewitnesses, 134, 198, 206
vs. expert witnesses, 175
misidentification by, 192, 193, 194–95

Faigman, David L., 377, 378
failure to mitigate, 65, 293
fallacy of the transposed conditional, 181, 375
false admission of a crime, 193
false identification by eyewitnesses, 192, 193, 194–95
false verdict, 25
Farber, Henry, 394
Farley, Erin, 375
Fay v. New York, 68–69
Fechter, Michael, 367, 368
Federalists, 53, 54
Federal Judicial Center, 151
Reference Manual on Scientific Evidence, 188
Federal Rules of Criminal Procedure, 88
Federal Rules of Evidence, 174, 199
Federal Tort Claims Act (US), 337
Feigenbaum, Alan, 356
Feigenson, Neal, 136–37, 236, 285, 366, 369, 382, 390
Feldman, Martha, 132–33, 141, 369
fellow servant rule, 61, 234
felons and jury duty, 79–80
Fernandes, Steven M., 381
fictitious lawsuits, 347–48
lawn mower as hedge clipper, 17
slippery floor, 15, 17
Fidel, Noel, 381
Field, Richard H., 371
FIJA. *See* Fully Informed Jury Association
financial losses and compensatory damages, 290–92
financial status of juror affecting damage award, 286
Finkel, Norman, 216, 227–28, 232, 369, 379, 381, 382
Finley, Lucinda, 277, 337, 389, 395
First Amendment of the Bill of Rights, 114
Fisher, Michael A., 356
Fishfader, Vicki L., 367
Fletcher, Betty, 237
Fleury-Steiner, Benjamin, 384
Florida
capital punishment cases in, 246
pay rate for defendant's counsel, 263
and stand bys, 88
Fonda, Henry, 129
Forbes, 281
Ford Foundation, 143
Fordham, Judith, 179, 374
foreperson, 143, 144, 161
Forkosch, Morris, 352
Forsythe, William, 349
Foster, Jodie, 212, 219
Fourth Lateran Council (1215), 23
Fox Network, 119
Fox's Libel Act, 32, 47
Franco, Francisco, 345
"Frank Statement to Smokers, A" (Philip Morris), 317

Fraud (Trials Without Jury) Bill (England), 371–72
fraud cases, 37, 38–39, 67, 127, 128, 283, 312
  BMW, 306–307
  Enron, 19, 103
  Maxwell case, 112, 154–55
  Medicare fraud, 108
  punitive damages occurring in cases of, 309
  State Farm, 307–308
fraudulent accounting practices, 126
freedom of the jury, 27–30
freedom of the press, 41–47, 50
freemen, 66
Friedman, Lawrence, 59–60, 352, 354, 355, 382
frivolous lawsuits, 271, 279, 281, 322
Frontline (TV show), 193, 376
Fugitive Slave Act (US), 225, 227
Fukurai, Hiroshi, 77, 356, 357, 358, 397
Fulero, Solomon, 99, 199, 364, 377, 390
Fully Informed Jury Association, 238, 383
Furman v. Georgia, 18, 241, 243, 244, 248, 264

Galanter, Marc, 345, 355, 391, 395, 396
Galileo's Revenge: Junk Science in the Courtroom (Huber), 170
Garfield, James, 211
Garvey, Stephen, 262, 370, 383, 385, 386, 387
gas chamber, 242, 246, 254
Gastil, John, 397
Gatowski, Sophia, 187–88, 375
Geimer, William, 386
Geistfeld, Mark, 389
Gelles, Richard, 377
gender of jurors
  and death penalty cases, 255–56
  use of peremptory challenges based on, 96–98
  women
    eligibility to serve on juries, 37, 59, 66, 67, 70, 73–74
    in mixed juries, 70
    negative impact of negligence cases on, 277
    women jurors and rape trials, 341
general damages, 284–85, 295–99. *See also* pain and suffering
generic prejudice, 113–14
George III (king), 52, 210, 304
George Washington University, 226
Georgia
  death penalty system in, 263–64
  Georgia Constitution, 55
  pay rate for defendant's counsel, 263
  sentencing authority, 56
  and stand bys, 88
  Supreme Court of, 263–64
Georgia survey of death penalty system, 245, 248
Georgia survey of judges, 151
Georgia v. McCollum, 363
Gilmore, Gary, 245
Ginsburg, Ruth Bader, 319
Githens, Penny B., 395
Glasser v. United States, 67, 356
Glendening, Parris, 248
Glorious Revolution, 31
GMBI. *See* guilty but mentally ill verdict
Gobert, James, 350
Gockel, Christine, 383
God, hand of, 22
Goerdt, John A., 389
Golding, Stephen, 216–17, 218, 379
Goldman, Ron, 196, 197
Gortex bypass graft (malpractice suit), 325
Gracealynn Harris case, 83–87, 93–94, 95
Grady, Clare, 221–24, 381
Grady, Teresa, 221–24, 381
Granger, Thomas, 47–48
Green, Thomas, 26, 27, 349, 350, 381
Greene, Edith "Edie," 261, 286, 290, 300–301, 387, 388, 390, 391
Gregg v. Georgia, 244, 246, 264
Grey, Robert J., Jr., 9–10, 343
Grigson, James, 258
Gross, Felecia, 394
Gross, Samuel R., 374, 376, 384
Grosscup, Jennifer L., 373

Grossman, Joanna L., 357
Grosso, Catherine M., 384
group deliberation, 142–44
group questioning of jurors, 89, 90, 92. *See also* voir dire
guest statutes, 61
guilty but mentally ill verdict, 213, 216, 218
guilty mind. *See* mens rea
guilty people acquitted, 195–97
guilty until proven innocent, 32–33
Guiteau, Charles, 211
Guthrie, Chris, 164, 369, 373, 375, 395
Guttman, S. Mac, 361

Hadfield, James, 210–11
Haimes v. Temple University and Hart, 281–82
Hale, Matthew, 210
half-tongue jury. *See jury de medietate linguae*
Hall, Brad, 376
Hall, David T., 353
Haltom, William, 313, 389, 391, 393
Hamilton, Andrew, 44–47
Han, Sanghoon, 397
Hance, Henry, 255
Haney, Craig, 100, 252, 253, 254, 262, 362, 364, 386, 387
hangings, 242, 246
Hannaford-Agor, Paula, 232, 355, 361, 363, 364, 370, 381, 382, 396
Hans, Valerie, 18–19, 92, 101, 131, 149–50, 162, 178, 182, 213, 232, 270–71, 278, 288, 289–90, 348, 360, 361, 362, 364, 365, 369, 370, 371, 373, 374, 375, 377, 378, 379, 381, 382, 384, 388, 389, 390, 391, 392, 396, 397
Hanson, Hans, 55
Hanson, Jon, 355
Harald (king), 23
Harlan, John Marshall, 55
Harrington, Matthew P., 353
Harris, Gracealynn, 83–87, 93–94, 95
Harris, Louis, 371
Harvard Medical Practice Study, 393, 394
Harvard Study of medical negligence, 322, 323
Haskins, George, 352, 353
Hastie, Reid, 133–35, 141, 369
Hasuike, Reiko, 103, 104
Hawkins, Charles, 370
Hays, Kristen, 365
HealthGrades, Inc., 322, 393
health professionals and juries in malpractice cases, 329–31
Hearst, Patricia, 132–33, 142–43
heart attack (malpractice suit), 326
Heise, Michael, 370
Helpers of God's Precious Infants, 85–86
Henderson, Edith, 349, 350
Henderson, James A., Jr., 382, 389
Hendler, Edmundo S., 397
Hendrickson, John, Jr., 171–73, 175, 187
Hendrickson, Maria, 171–73
Henry, Patrick, 88
Henry II (king), 23
heparin, 333
Herbert, Bob, 386
Hersch, Joni, 310, 392
Heuer, Larry, 150, 371
Heumann, Milton, 354
Hevenor, W. S., 373
Hickman, Laura J., 385
Hickson, Gerald, 395
Higgins, Dan, 380
Hillerman, Holly, 366
Hillman, Robert A., 389
Himelein, Melissa J., 362
Hinckley, John, Jr., 15, 208, 212–14
hindsight bias, 131, 164
Hirschhorn, Robert, 103
historical facts, 125–28
Hodes, W. William, 381
Holstein, James, 135, 369
Holt, Wythe, Jr., 351
Honess, Terry, 155, 367, 372
horizontal equity, 332
Horowitz, Irwin, 156, 157, 235, 238–39, 372, 382, 383
Horwitz, Morton, 355

Hosch, Harmon M., 377
hot iron, trial by, 22
hot water, trial by, 22
housewives as jurors, 286
Howe, Julie, 261, 387
Howe, Mark DeWolf, 354
Hoyt v. Florida, 73
Huber, Peter, 170, 289, 373, 390
Hughes, Francine, 202, 203
hung juries, 17, 60, 122, 234, 370
Hunt, Henry Lee, 247–48
Huss, Matthew T., 374
Hyland, Mary Pat, 380
Hyman, David, 335, 395

Idaho, capital punishment cases in, 246
IGEN International, 309
Illinois
  moratorium on death penalty, 247
  sentencing authority, 56
  Supreme Court of, 247, 284
  women serving on juries, 73
impaired mental capacity. *See* mental capacity, diminished or impaired
Impressions of an Average Juryman (Sutcliffe), 77–78
Imran, Mohammad, 83, 86
inadmissible evidence, impact on juries, 162–64
Indiana
  capital punishment cases in, 246
  Indiana Constitution, 55
  Bill of Rights, 354
  sentencing authority, 56
  Supreme Court of, 55
individuals vs. corporations as defendants in civil trials, 278–79
inflammatory response syndrome (malpractice suit), 325
injury assessment and compensatory damages, 292, 298
  competence of juries in awarding of damages, 299–302
  plaintiff's failure to mitigate effects of injuries, 65, 293
Innocence Project, 191, 193, 376
innocent people convicted of crimes, 191, 192–95, 262–63
innocent until proven guilty, 32–33, 36, 91
inquisitorial procedures, 130
insanity defense, 15, 108, 126, 152, 159, 207–19, 232
  ALI test, 212, 213
  Durham test, 212, 213
  guilty but mentally ill verdict, 213, 216, 218
  juror attitudes about, 215–19
  partial insanity, 210, 211
  planning a crime as proof of sanity, 217–18
  right-wrong test for insanity, 126, 208, 210, 211, 212, 213, 216
  temporary insanity, 202, 205
Insanity Defense Reform Act of 1984 (US), 213
Institute of Medicine, 393
instructions to jury
  about expert witnesses, 175–76
  biasing jury to guilty verdict, 252
  in death penalty cases, 252–53, 260–62
  jurors not abiding by, 343–44, 396
  legal instructions and factual determinations, 164–68
  limiting instructions, 161–64
  and nullification, 236–40
  on pain and suffering, 295
  in Philip Morris case, 319
  presumption instructions, 161
  procedural instructions, 161
  in punitive awards, 312
  understanding and following, 158–64, 342
insurance
  juror attitudes toward, 287–88, 390
  medical malpractice insurance, 322, 330, 335
integrating juror narratives into deliberations, 135–37, 141, 142–43
Internet, impact of on pretrial publicity, 122
Iobst, Frederick W., 362
Iontcheva, Jenia, 354

Iraq War, protests against, 221–24
Irvin v. Dowd, 109
Ivković, Sanja Kutnjak, 178, 360, 373, 374

Jackson, John, 130, 368, 397
Jackson, Michael, 108
Jackson County, Alabama, 95–96
jailhouse snitches, 193, 376
James, Ellen, 351
James, Rebecca, 380
James, Rita M., 370
James I (king), 77
James II (king), 30–31
Jaudon, Buddy, 367
J. E. B. v. Alabama, 96, 363
Jefferson, Thomas, 16, 46, 347
Jehle, Alayna, 362
Johnny Copeland trial, 116–17, 118, 120
Johnson, Cathy, 100, 362, 364
Johnson, Kirk, 394
Johnson, Molly, 361, 374
Johnson, Sheri Lynn, 369, 386
Johnson/Caldwell simulated case, 133–34, 141
joined trials
  civil cases, 156–57
  criminal cases, 155–56
Jones, Larry, 247
Jones, Stephen, 366
Jones, Susan E., 362
judges
  as determiner of capital punishment, 246
    sharing responsibility with jury, 262
  disagreeing with an acquittal, 196
  experts as lay justices, 375
  and expert witnesses
    defining expertise of witnesses, 174
    evaluating expert testimony, 187–88
    as gatekeepers for expert testimony, 170
    refusing to allow expert testimony, 203–204, 205, 222
  and eyewitnesses misidentification of defendant, 194–95
  and instructions to juries, 163–64, 236–40
  judge-jury agreements, 148–51, 370
  judge-jury disagreements, 340
    in punitive awards, 310–11
    in rape cases, 198–99, 231
    reasons for, 230–32
  judge trials vs. jury trials, 151–52
    as alternate to juries, 342
    decline in number of trials by jury, 62–63, 345
    judge as sole determiner in malpractice, 337–38
  judicial oversight
    of malpractice damages, 334–35
    of punitive damages, 314, 318
  magistrates, trial by
    rise of in nineteenth century, 36
    in twentieth-century England, 37–39
  questioning witnesses, 32, 130
Judging the Jury (Hans and Vidmar), 346
judicial hellholes, 15, 267
Judicium Dei, 21–23
Jurden, Jan, 84, 90, 93, 360
Jurors: The Power of Twelve (Arizona Supreme Court Committee on More Effective Use of Juries), 343
jury awards, unreliability of, 282
jury de medietate linguae, 69–70
jury trials vs. judge trials, 151–52
  decline in number of trials by jury, 62–63, 345
  judge trials vs. jury trials
    as alternate to juries, 342
    judge as sole determiner in malpractice, 337–38
juveniles and capital punishment, 245–46, 265

Kalt, Brian C., 359
Kalven, Harry, 148–49, 150–51, 198, 199, 230–32, 234, 240, 301
Kamin, Kim A., 369

Kansas, women serving on juries in, 73
Kaplan, Benjamin, 371
Karlovac, M., 389
Kassin, Saul, 193, 376
Katz, Stanley, 351
Kaye, David H., 375, 377, 396
Kaye, Judith S., 359
Kazakhstan and jury system, 345
Kelly, Ernest, 203
Kelly, Gladys, 203–204
Kennedy, James, 350
Kennedy, Tracy, 367
Kentucky
  sentencing authority, 56
  and voir dire, 91
Kerr, Norbert L., 365, 367, 370, 372, 382, 383
Kim, Sangjoon, 397
King, James I., 359
King, Nancy, 238, 350, 354, 361, 365, 383
King, Rodney, 17, 75
Kirshenbaum, Hershi M., 348
KKK, 225
Klein, Stephen P., 385
Kleinig, John, 365
Klippenstine, Marc A., 377
Koehler, Jonathan, 375
Koehring, Heather, 387
Koenig, Thomas, 304, 355, 392, 394
Koening, Dorean, 161, 372
Kohn, Linda, 393
Koski, D. D., 377
Kovalev, Nikolay, 130, 368, 397
Krafka, Carol, 374
Kramer, Geoffrey, 161, 365, 367, 372
Krauss, Daniel, 387
Kressel, Dorit F., 364
Kressel, Neil J., 364
Kreuger, Curtis, 388
Kriho, Laura, 228–29
Kritzer, Herbert M., 395
Krooth, Richard, 356
Kumho Tire v. Carmichael, 169
Kutz, Amanda L., 359
Kysar, Douglas A., 389
Ladinsky, Jack, 382
Lady Ghislaine (yacht), 154
LaFleur, Jennifer, 358
LaMattina, Diana, 380
Lambard, William, 210
Landsman, Stephen, 163, 349, 352, 368, 373
Laney, Deanna, 215
Lanier, Charles S., 386
Larner, Jordan, 397
"Last Aid Kit" (NAACP), 243
Lateran Council, Fourth (1215), 23
Latham, Frank, 351
law, evaluating jurors' comprehension of evidence and law, 147–68
Law & Order (TV show), 208, 214
Law Reform Commission (Canada), 18
lawsuits, unjustified, 267, 274
lawyers, advent of, 33
Lay, Kenneth, 103–104, 108
Leber, Douglas, 396
Lee, Charles A., 172, 173, 187
Lee, Lynne Foster, 372
Lee, Paul, 299, 335, 391, 395
Legal Blame (Feigenson), 136–37
Legal Defense Fund (NAACP), 243
legal facts and the adversary procedure, 129–32
leg amputation, unnecessary (malpractice suit), 325
Leibowitz, Sam, 71–72
Leipold, Andrew, 357
Lempert, Richard, 153, 168, 177–78, 358, 371, 374, 393, 395
length of trials, 59–61
Lentz, Susan A., 356, 357
Leo, Richard, 193, 376
Leon County, Florida, 60
Lerner, Melvin, 235–36, 382
lethal injections, 110, 208, 209, 246, 265
Letterman, David, 77, 359
Levi, Judith, 261–62, 387
Levi, Michael, 155, 365, 367, 372
Levine, James, 365, 367, 395
liability, 127–28, 161, 283, 285, 289, 301, 311–12, 315

causation and liability, 156–57
civil liability, 267–79
deciding compensatory damages, 281–302
plaintiff's degree of responsibility in, 61, 128, 129, 166–67, 234–36, 267, 270–74, 279, 285
prior injuries and illnesses in, 274–77, 388
reasonable person standard, 127–28, 154, 166, 269–70
criminal liability, 52
enterprise liability, 62
in malpractice cases, 321, 324, 327, 328, 331, 334, 338
product liability cases, 163, 174, 178, 286–87, 305, 309, 310
and punitive damages, 311–12
Liability: The Legal Revolution and Its Consequences (Huber), 289
libel trials
Croswell trial, 46
Seven Bishops Trial, 30–32
Zenger trial, 41–47, 50
Liebeck, Stella, 313
Lieberman, Joel D., 364, 365, 372
life experiences shaping jurors' perceptions, 65–66
life sentence vs. death penalty, 251
Lilley, Lin S., 365
limiting instructions, 161–64
Linder, Douglas, 357, 358, 366, 377
Lindh, John Walker, 117–19
Lindsay, Rod, 194, 376
Litan, Robert E., 371, 374
litigation communications, 108
little parliament, 21
decline of, 37–39
Lloyd-Bostock, Sally, 162, 350, 351, 364, 365, 373, 376
locality rule, 62
Lockett v. Ohio, 258
Locklear, Rogers, 247
Loftus, Elizabeth, 194, 376, 396
Loges, William E., 365, 366
Loh, Wallace D., 357
Lopes, Grace M., 362
Los Angeles Times, 281
Losh, Susan Carol, 358
Lowe, Peggy, 361
Lozano v. State, 112
Lucas County, Ohio, 17–18
Luginbuhl, James, 261, 362, 387
Lumbee Indians, 247
Luneberg, William V., 356

MacCoun, Robert, 289, 390
MacKillop, Kara, 299, 335, 391, 395
Madison, James, 54
mad or bad. *See* insanity defense
magistrates, trial by
rise of in nineteenth century, 36
in twentieth-century England, 37–39
See also judges
Magna Carta, 66
Maitland, William Frederick, 23, 24, 349
Making Jury Instructions Understandable (Elwork, Sales, and Alfini), 342
malpractice, 62, 127–28, 321–38
agreements between juries and health professionals, 329
caps on malpractice awards, 336–37
case examples, 324–29
competence of juries in malpractice cases, 330–31
costs of medical injuries due to negligence, 322–23
disagreement of health professionals on occurrence of, 329
doctors' fears of high awards, 324
frequency of malpractice cases, 323–24
median awards for plaintiffs, 324
rise in, 333
prelawsuit settlements, 335–36
settlements, 299–300
standard of medical care, 157, 164, 327–28, 333
sympathy of jury for plaintiff in malpractice cases, 331
and use of expert witnesses, 174
vertical and horizontal equity of awards, 332

manifest prejudice, 34
Mansfield, John H., 363
Manzo, John, 141, 369
Marder, Nancy, 97, 363, 364, 381
marijuana for medical use, 237, 383
Markus, Hazel, 362
Marlboros, 316
Marshall, Thurgood, 100, 243
Martens, John, 200–201
Marti, Mollie, 391
Martin, Joanne, 355, 391
Maruta, Takashi, 397
Marvin, Richard P., 171–72, 173, 187
Mary (queen), 27
Maryland
  contributory negligence rules, 285
  Maryland Constitution, 55
  pay rate for defendant's counsel, 263
  sentencing authority, 56
Maryland study of death penalty system, 248–49
Massachusetts
  abolition of capital punishment, 242
  civil juries in, 54
  as a colony
    allowing legal counsel, 352
    exclusion of lawyers from trials, 48
    jury selection in, 49
    Massachusetts Bay Colony, 47
    New Plymouth Colony, 47, 353
    use of jury trials, 50
    use of peremptory challenges, 353
  jury selection in, 57
mass tort, 62, 156
Matsch, Richard, 110, 112, 119
Mauro, Robert, 384
Maxwell, Ian, 154
Maxwell, Kevin, 112–13, 154
Maxwell, Robert, 154–55
Maxwell fraud trial, 112, 154–55
McAvoy, Thomas, 223, 224
McCann, Michael, 313, 389, 391, 393
McCarthy, Kieran, 395
McCleskey, Warren, 245
McCleskey v. Kemp, 245
McCullough, David, 354
McDonald's coffee spill case, 15, 16, 19, 303, 312–14
McGonigle, Steve, 358, 364
McGuire, Andrew Philip, 359
McMahon, Jack, 95, 97
McManus, Edgar, 352, 353
McNaughtan, Daniel, 211
McNaughtan test. *See* right-wrong test for insanity
McNulty, Faith, 377
McVeigh, Timothy, 108, 110, 112, 114–15, 120, 224, 225, 265, 366
McVeigh factor, 264, 265
Mead, William, 28, 225
media and pretrial publicity, 108, 111–14, 122–23
medical malpractice. *See* malpractice
Medical Malpractice and the American Jury (Vidmar), 334
Medicare, 322
  Medicare fraud, 108
medicinal marijuana, 237, 383
mega verdicts, 62
Mellili, K. J., 363
Mello, Michelle, 395
Melnitzer, Julius, 366
Meltsner, Michael, 384
men, peremptory challenges against, 96
Menand, Catherine, 352
Menendez Brothers, 17
Menicimer, Stephanie, 347–48
mens rea, 210
mental capacity, diminished or impaired, 123, 126, 203, 213
  and death penalty, 245, 247, 265
mental disease or mental defect, 203, 212
mental illness, 209, 210, 341. *See also* insanity defense
mental shortcuts and juries, 164, 177
mental suffering, 300
Merck & Co., 108, 114, 303–304
Merrick, Pliny, 57
Michigan, abolition of hanging, 242
Middendorf, Kathi, 362
Mikva, Abner, 113
Miles, John, 87

Miletich, Dean, 374
Miller, F. Thornton, 354
Miller, Jeffrey P., 396, 397
Miller, John, 24
minimization effect, 117
minorities
as defendants
and generic prejudice of jurors, 116
lack of suitable defense, 263
as jurors, 71–76, 357
eligibility to serve on juries, 66–67, 71–73
use of peremptory challenges against, 96–99, 100, 255–56, 363
See also race
Mirror Group, 154–55
misidentification by eyewitnesses, 192, 193, 194–95
Mississippi, pay rate for defendant's counsel, 263
Missouri
use of juries, 56
women on juries, 74
mistaken identity, 125
mistrials, 222, 228
mitigating circumstances, 59, 126, 244, 246, 248, 253, 260–61, 263–64, 384
plaintiff's failure to mitigate effects of injuries, 65, 293
mitochondrial DNA analysis, 180–83
mixed jury. *See jury de medietate linguae*
mixed tribunals, 345
Mize, Gregory, 90, 361, 362
Mobil Corporation, 289
mock juries, 340–41
complex trials, 154–57
contributory and comparative negligence, 235
and deep pockets hypothesis, 289
determining damages, 300, 315
determining damages (comparing juries, judges, and lawyers), 301
discredited eyewitnesses, 194
impact of expert witnesses, 179–80, 182–83
individuals vs. corporations as defendants in civil trials, 279
jury nullification, 238–39
not guilty by reason of insanity, 216
plaintiff's degree of responsibility in civil trials, 285
studies of instructions to juries, 161
studies of jury understanding of legal terms, 160–61
See also examples
Moffitt, William, 122
Mohr, James C., 373
Montana, capital punishment cases in, 246
Moody, James S., Jr., 121
Moore, Kimberly, 152, 371
Moran, Richard, 378
moratorium on death penalty, 247, 263, 387
Moreno, Linda, 122
Morris, Gouverneur, 41
Morris, Lewis, 42
Morris, Norval, 378
Mott, Nicole L., 370
Mu'Min, Dawaud, 109–10
Mu'Min v. Virginia, 109–10
Munsterman, G. Thomas "Tom," 77, 370, 371, 396
murder trials, 17, 89, 209, 238, 252
Hendrickson case, 171–73
O. J. Simpson trial, 15, 17, 19, 103, 107–108, 109, 115, 196–97
Webster case, 56–59
Yates case, 19, 108, 207–10, 213–14
See also criminal trials; death penalty
"Murder with Malice Aforethought," 158–59
Murphy, Beth, 18, 348, 355, 369, 396
Murphy, Frank, 69
Murphy, Timothy, 365
Murrin, John, 353
Musick, Marc A., 358

NAACP, 243
narratives, integrating of by jury, 135–37, 141, 142–43
National Association for the Advancement of Colored People. *See* NAACP

National Center for State Courts, 19, 77, 101, 149–50, 283, 308, 309, 310, 333, 344
National Institute of Justice (US Dept. of Justice), 376
nationality of juror affecting damage awards, 285–87
National Law Journal, 310
National Research Council, 187
Native Americans, 70, 248. *See also* race
Naturalization Act of 1870 (England), 70
NBC, 202
NCSC. *See* National Center for State Courts
Nebraska, capital punishment cases in, 246
negligence, 15, 127, 277
  boy in the paint store, 268–69
  comparative negligence, 166, 235, 268, 269, 285, 316
  contributory negligence, 62, 231, 234–35, 270, 285
  and corporations, 279
  relative responsibility, 268–69
    plaintiff's degree of responsibility in, 268–69
  See also civil trials
Neil v. Biggers, 195
Nelson, William, 48, 51, 352, 353, 354
Nemeth, Brian, 205
Neufeld, Peter, 376
Neuhaus, Isaac M., 374
neutrality of jurors, 129
New Amsterdam and Zenger trial, 41–47
New England Journal of Medicine, 170, 329, 330
New Haven Colony, 50, 352
New Jersey
  Supreme Court of, 203–204, 249
  West New Jersey Colony
    exclusion of lawyers from trials, 48
    recognition of jury trials, 47
    use of jury trials, 50
  women serving on juries, 73
New Plymouth Colony
  recognition of jury trials, 47
  use of peremptory challenges, 353
New Windsor Turnpike Company, 68
New York
  abolition of capital punishment, 242
  instructions to jury on wrongful death, 284
  New York State Judicial Council, 69
  sentencing authority, 56
New York Daily News, 154–55
New York Medical Journal, 172
New York Medical Times, 172
New York Times, 255, 281, 286
New York Weekly Journal, 42, 43, 46
New Zealand, limiting mass media coverage of criminal trials, 108
NGRI. *See* not guilty by reason of insanity
nicotine addiction, 317, 318
Niedermeier, Keith E., 382
Nietzel, Michael, 91, 362, 367
Nineteenth Amendment of the Constitution, 73
Nisbett, Richard E., 362
Noah, Lars, 228, 381
no-lawsuit settlements, 335–36
noneconomic damages. *See* general damages
nonresponders to jury duty, 78–79
nonunanimous verdicts, 18, 38
Nordenberg, Mark A., 356
norms and values in decision making, 141–42, 144–45, 149
Norris v. Alabama, 72
Northampton, Assize of (1176), 23
North Carolina
  as a colony, 50
    Carolina colonies, 48, 50
  contributory negligence rules, 285
  Durham garbage truck case, 111
  sentencing authority, 56
  and stand bys, 88
North Carolina Plastic Surgery Society, 321
North Carolina study on jury instructions, 261
Northern District of Virginia, 118
Northwestern University, 247
Northwest Professional Obstetrics and Gynecology, 334

Norton, Michael, 98, 364
note taking by jurors, 130, 369
not guilty by reason of insanity, 15, 108, 126, 208, 210, 211, 212–13, 214–16, 217–18. *See also* insanity defense
nullification, jury, 221–40
  Bushel's case, 27–30
  race-based jury nullification, 226
  radical nullification, 239
  Seven Bishops Trial, 31
  war with the law, 232–33
Nuremberg Principles, 222
nurses as jurors, 285–86

Oakland Cannabis Buyers' Cooperative, 383
Oakland City Council, 237, 383
OCBC. *See* Oakland Cannabis Buyers' Cooperative
O'Connell, J., 389
O'Connor, Sandra Day, 75
Ogloff, James, 367
Ohio
  capital punishment cases in, 249
  nonrepresentative juries, 17–18
  rape cases, 199
  Supreme Court of, 205
oil spill, 303
O. J. Simpson trial. *See* Simpson, Orenthal James "O. J."
Oklahoma
  instructions to jury, 261
  sentencing authority, 56
Oklahoma City bombing, 108, 110, 112, 114–15, 120, 366
Old Bailey, 28, 33, 36, 211
older jurors and use of peremptory challenges against, 97, 100
Oldham, James, 302, 356, 391
Old Sparky, 245
Olsen-Fulero, Lynda, 199, 377
Olson, Elizabeth A., 376
O'Neil, Kevin M., 374
O'Neill, Patrick, 393
Onslow, Lord, 210
On the Laws and Customs of England (Bracton), 25
opening statements, 58, 59, 104, 130, 311
optical nerve damage (malpractice suit), 327
ordeal, trial by, 21–23, 24
ordeal of the morsel, 22–23
Oregon
  punitive awards, 306, 320
  Supreme Court of, 319
  valid verdicts in, 317
  women on juries, 73
Oregonian (newspaper), 318
O'Reilly, Bill, 119
Orentlichter, David, 394
Ostrom, Brian J., 355, 389, 396
O'Sullivan, Sean, 360, 361
Otto, Amy, 182, 366, 375
outliers, 156–57, 334

Paavola, Emily, 369
pain and suffering, 16, 284, 295, 298, 299, 300–302, 324, 332, 336–37
paint store case, 268–69, 278
Palestinian Islamic Jihad, 119, 122
Pappas, Stephen, 180–82
Park, Ernest S., 383
Park, Kwang Bai, 397
Park, Roger, 182, 375
Parker, Robert, 156
Parkman, George, 56–57
partial insanity, 210, 211. *See also* insanity defense
Paternoster, Ray, 385
Patricia Hearst case, 132–33, 142–43
Pearson, Richard N., 382, 389
Pearson, Robert W., 362
Peel, Robert, 211
peers, jury of, 34–35, 65–81
peine forte et dure, 24–25
Pellowski, Michael, 347, 365
penalty phase, 59, 107, 209, 249, 251, 257–58, 365
Pencak, William, 351
Penn, William, 19, 28–30, 33, 225
Pennington, Nancy, 133–35, 141, 369
Pennsylvania
  abolition of capital punishment, 242

as a colony
exclusion of lawyers from trials, 48
recognition of jury trials, 47
compensatory damages, 282
sentencing authority, 56
and stand bys, 88
Supreme Court of, 282
Pennzoil, 62
Penrod, Steven, 99, 150, 182, 364, 366, 367, 371, 372, 374, 375, 376, 390
Percival, Robert, 59–60, 354
peremptory challenges, 34, 87, 95–102, 354, 362, 363
abolition of, 100–102
effectiveness of, 99–100
race and, 255–56
peripheral processing of information, 177, 180
personal injury cases, 37, 61, 92, 231, 300
and compensatory damages, 283–84, 290–92, 295
failure to mitigate, 65, 293
and punitive damages, 309, 312
role of insurance in, 287–88, 320
Peterson, Laci, 107
Peterson, Mark, 390
Peterson, Mike, 206
Peterson, Scott, 107, 108, 265, 365
Peterson v. Superior Ct. of San Mateo County, 365
petit jury, 25–27, 50, 72–73
Petzinger, Thomas, Jr., 355
Philadelphia jury selection study, 97, 100
Philip Morris v. Williams, 316–19
Philipse, Frederick, 43
Phillips, Carter, 394
Phyllis G., 200–201
Pickel, Kerri L., 373
Picus, Larry, 371
Pierce, Glenn, 249, 385
Pioneer Commercial Corporation, 309
plaintiffs, 52, 131, 141, 267–79, 340–41, 342
assessing damages suffered by, 179, 186–87
compensatory damages, 283–85, 288–89, 290–92, 294–98, 299–302
and malpractice cases, 325, 326, 327, 328, 332–33, 336–37
postverdict settlements, 333–35
prelawsuit settlements, 335–36
punitive damages, 304, 306, 307, 309, 312, 315
choosing jurors who favor plaintiffs, 285–87
expert witnesses and, 170, 175, 180, 184–86
failure to mitigate, 65, 293
Gracealynn Harris case, 83–87
jurors having similar backgrounds, 65, 115
median awards for plaintiffs, 283
multiple plaintiffs, 156–57, 283
plaintiff's degree of responsibility in civil trials, 61, 128, 129, 166–67, 234–36, 267, 270–74, 279, 285
plaintiff vs. defendant in civil trials, 267–79
preexisting conditions of, 127, 139, 184, 274–77, 388
and reasonable person standard, 269–70, 278, 327
sympathy of jury for, 331, 340–41
verdicts in favor of, 149, 150, 283, 308, 324, 330, 331
planning a crime as proof of sanity, 217–18
plea bargaining, 35, 60, 63, 222
Plucknett, T. F. T., 349
Plymouth Plantation
mixed jury in, 70
recognition of jury trials, 47
political role of juries, 66, 224–27
Pollock, Frederick, 23, 349
Poole, Bobby, 192–93
Porter, Anthony, 247
Port of Boston, 51
Posey, Amy J., 364
post-traumatic stress disorder, 200, 201, 275
postverdict settlements, 314
postverdict adjustments, 333–35

potential jurors, 34, 89, 90, 95, 97, 123, 238, 250, 253
determining bias of, 17, 84, 86, 87, 91, 117, 118, 120–21, 215, 353
sources for, 67, 76
surveys of, 118, 120–21
Pound, Roscoe, 226, 349, 381
Power of God, The (book), 85
prejudice, pretrial, 111–14, 122–23, 339–46
prelawsuit settlements, 335–36
preponderance of evidence, 129, 312
presenting jury, 25, 27
presumption
of guilt, 33, 116, 120
of innocence, 32–33, 36, 91
judicial instructions, 161
pretrial prejudice, 111–14, 122–23
pretrial publicity, 107–23, 366
remedies for, 114–17
Priest, George, 304, 355, 391
"Principles for Juries and Jury Trials" (American Bar Association), 343, 368, 369, 396
prior injuries and illnesses in civil cases, 127, 139, 184, 274–77, 388
procedural instructions, 161
"Proclamation for Jurors, A" (King James I), 77
product liability cases, 163, 174, 178, 286–87, 305, 309, 310
property tax lists, 67
pro-plaintiff juries, 340–41
Proposition 215 (California), 237
prosecutors, 130
prosecutor's fallacy, 181, 375
psychic powers, 281
psychological anchors, 290
PTSD. *See* post-traumatic stress disorder
publicity before the trial, 107–23
remedies for effect of pretrial publicity, 114–17
Pulaski, Charles A., Jr., 384
punishment
attaint, 25, 27
death penalty, 18, 56, 57, 107, 116, 126, 208, 214, 241–65
botched executions, 265
death qualified juries, 251–55, 341
judges rather than juries deciding on, 246, 384
juries as determiner of, 243–44, 246, 249–65, 262
jury selection in death penalty cases, 57, 59, 68–69, 91, 97, 214, 249–56
methods of execution, 110, 208, 209, 242, 245, 246, 254, 265
moratorium on, 247, 263, 387
numbers of executions in US, 242–43, 246, 248
racial bias in death penalty cases, 243, 244, 245, 248–49, 255, 385
wrongful convictions, 262–63
for felonies in thirteenth to fifteenth centuries, 26–27
for not submitting to jury trial, 24–25
See also death penalty
punitive damages, 16, 128, 129, 157, 282, 285
frequency the awarding of, 308–309
goals of, 305
in terrorem effect, 304
judicial oversight of, 314
juries and, 303–20
McDonald's coffee spill case, 312–14
median awards, 310
personal injury cases and, 309, 312
postverdict settlements, 314
Punitive Damages: How Jurors Decide (Sunstein), 304, 315
Putnam, William, 351, 352

quadriplegia (malpractice suit), 326–27
Quait, Melinda, 387
Quakers, 27–30
qualifications for juries, 34–35, 79–81
Quen, J. M., 378
questioning witnesses by judges, 32, 130
questioning witnesses by juries, 32, 130, 184, 344, 368

race
  all-white jury, 72, 75, 96, 229, 249, 357, 358
  impact of O. J. Simpson trial, 196
  impact on damage awards, 286
  mixed juries, 69–70
  race-based jury nullification, 226
  racial bias in death penalty cases, 243, 244, 245, 248–49, 255, 257, 263, 265, 385
  racial minorities as defendants
    and generic prejudice of jurors, 116
    lack of suitable defense, 263
  racial minorities as jurors
    eligibility to serve on juries, 66–67, 71–73, 357
    use of peremptory challenges against, 96–99, 100, 255–56, 363
Rachlinski, Jeffrey, 164, 369, 373, 375, 395
Radelet, Michael, 387
radical nullification instructions, 239
Rakos, Richard, 163, 373
Ramirez, Deborah, 70, 356
Rand Corporation, 154, 179
  analysis of jury verdicts in Cook County, 288–89
Ransom, Dottie, 247
Ransom, Jackie, 247
rape
  acquaintance rape, 198, 201, 206, 341
  rape shield laws, 199–200
Reader's Digest, 316
Reagan, Ronald, 15, 208, 212
reasonable corporation standard, 278–79
reasonable person standard, 269–70, 278, 327
reexamination of witnesses, 131
Reference Manual on Scientific Evidence (Federal Judicial Center), 188
reform of jury system, 343–44
  and use of peremptory challenges, 101–102
Rehnquist, William, 110
Reid, J. Don, 376
Reid, John P., 353
relative responsibility in negligence cases, 268–69
    plaintiff's degree of responsibility, 270–74
remittitur, 334
remorse, 126
  in death penalty cases, 256–57
removing jurors
  challenge for cause, 87, 91, 362
  in death penalty cases, 250, 254
  determining when appropriate, 229–30
  removing jurors for cause, 91, 93–95, 362
representativeness in juries, 65–81, 96–97, 115, 144, 265, 270, 305, 340, 341
Resnick, Philip, 214
Review of the Criminal Courts of England and Wales (Auld), 38
Rhode Island
  abolition of capital punishment, 242
  as a colony
    allowing legal counsel, 352
    recognition of jury trials, 47
    use of jury trials, 50
    use of peremptory challenges, 353
Rice, Jeffrey, 286, 390
Richardson, James, 187–88
Rideau v. Louisiana, 109
right-wrong test for insanity, 126, 208, 210, 211, 212, 213, 216. *See also* insanity defense
Ring v. Arizona, 241, 246, 262
Ritter, Gretchen, 356
Rivera, Craig, 383
R. J. Reynolds Tobacco Company, 303
Robbennolt, Jennifer, 311, 388, 392
Roberts, Caton, 218, 379
Roberts, Julia, 202
Robin Hood, 16, 270, 287, 302
Robinson, Paul H., 382, 389
Roche Diagnostics, 309
Rodney King case, 17, 75
Rodriguez, Cristina M., 357
Roe v. Wade, 85

Rojas-Burke, Joe, 393
Rokeach, Milton, 18, 348
Roper v. Simmons, 245–46
Rose, Mary, 18, 94, 98, 101, 287, 348, 355, 358, 363, 364, 369, 390, 394, 396
Rosen, Ellen L., 371
Rosenberg, Charles, 378
Rosenthal, Edward, 237–38, 383, 383
Ross, David, 376
Ross, Michael, 362
Rossi, Faust, 357
Rottman, David B., 361, 389
Rubenstein, Arie M., 381
Rubin-Jackson, Marsha, 377
rules of evidence, 50
  evolution of, 33, 36
  exclusion of some evidence, 131
  and expert witnesses, 174, 216
  Federal Rules of Evidence, 174, 199
  limiting instructions, 163
  rape cases, 131, 199
  regarding research studies, 153
Russia and jury system, 345
Rustad, Michael, 304, 309, 355, 391, 392, 394
Rutherford, Livingston, 351
Ryan, George, 247
Ryan, John Paul, 358
Rzepa, Sara, 377

Sadoff, Robert L., 378
Sage, William M., 395
Saiban-in Seido, 345
St. Patrick's Four, 221–24, 225, 226, 227, 228, 233, 236, 380, 381
Saks, Michael, 300, 332, 369, 373, 377, 391, 394
Sales, Bruce D., 342, 361, 362, 364, 365, 372, 387
Salisbury, James H., 171, 172, 173, 175
sanctioning of jurors, 25, 27–28, 238, 383
Sandburg, Brenda, 364
Sanders, Joseph, 153, 179, 371, 374, 377
Sandys, Marla, 385, 386
Sarat, Austin, 387
Satan, voice of, 208, 214
Saunders, David, 376
Savino, Lenny, 368
Schama, Simon, 354
schemas, 133, 134, 218
Schklar, Jason, 375
Schlosser, Dena, 215
Schuetz, Janice E., 365
Schuller, Regina, 204, 375, 376, 377, 378
Schuman, Daniel, 374
Schumann, Edward L., 375
Schutte, J. W., 377
Schwab, Stewart J., 370
Schwartz, Gary, 355
Science for Judges Program, 188
Science on Trial (Angell), 170
Scofflaw Court, 78
Scott, Arthur, 352, 353
Scottsboro case, 71–72
scripts, 133, 134, 135
scrupling, 250. *See also* death penalty, jury selection
Sebok, Anthony, 355
seditious libel trials
  Croswell trial, 46
  Seven Bishops Trial, 30–32
  Zenger trial, 41–47, 50
selection of juries, 57, 83–105
  in colonial America, 49
  in death penalty cases, 57, 59, 68–69, 91, 97, 214, 249–56
  selective approach to, 66–67
self-defense, 26, 126, 134, 135, 158, 203, 204, 231, 232
Sellars, Andre, 158
Seltzer, Richard, 90–91, 362
Selvin, Molly, 371
Sensabaugh, George F., Jr., 375
Sentell, R. Perry, 371
September 11, 2001, attacks, 119
sequestering the jury, 108, 115, 365
sessions court. *See* assizes
Setar, John, 347
Seven Bishops Trial, 30–32
severed trials
  civil cases, 156–57
  criminal cases, 155

sexual assault and focusing on victim, 198–201
Seymour, Horatio, 172
shadow effects, 324
Shapard, John, 361
Shaver, Kelly G., 389
Shaw, Lemuel, 57, 58, 59
Shepherde, William, 26
Sheppard, Sam, 109
Sherman, M. John, 222
Shuman, Daniel, 178, 395
Silbey, Susan, 395
Siliciano, John A., 382, 389
Silver, Charles, 395
Silvestrini, Elaine, 368
Simon, Alstory, 247
Simon, Rita James, 216, 379
Simpson, Nicole Brown, 196, 197
Simpson, Orenthal James "O. J.," 19
  civil trial, 197
  criminal trial, 15, 17, 103, 107–108, 109, 115, 196–97
Sixth Amendment of the Bill of Rights, 115, 242
Skeem, Jennifer, 216–17, 379
Skilling, Jeffrey, 103–104, 108
Skonieczny v. Gardner, Northwest Professional Obstetrics and Gynecology, Levy and Northwest Community Hospital, 334
Slater, Dan, 213, 379
Sleeping with the Enemy (movie), 202
Sloan, Frank, 322, 332–33, 336, 393, 394, 395
Smith, Brian, 182, 375
Smith, Bruce P., 354, 355
Smith, Steven, 389
Smith, Susan, 108
Smith, Vicki, 161, 369, 372
Smith, William, 42, 43, 44
snitches, 139, 376
social desirability effect, 92
Sohier, Edward, 57
Sommer, Kristin, 235, 382
Sommers, Samuel, 74, 98, 358, 364
source lists for jurors, 76–77
South Carolina
  Carolina colonies, 48, 50
  sentencing authority, 56
  and stand bys, 88
  Supreme Court of, 305
  and voir dire, 91
South Carolina study on jury instructions, 261
South Korea and jury system, 345–46
Spain and jury system, 345
Spann, Johnny "Mike," 117, 118
Sparf, Herman, 55
Sparf et. al. v. United States, 55, 228
special damages, 283–84
special juries, 68–69, 73. *See also* blue ribbon jury
special verdicts, 31, 45, 50, 213
Spillbor, Jonna, 359
Spinkellink, John, 245, 246
spread of jury system, 36–37, 345–46
standard of medical care, 157, 164, 327–28, 330
stand bys, 34–35, 38, 88
Star Chamber, 27, 46
State Farm v. Campbell, 307–308, 314, 316, 319
statistical evidence and juries, 180–84
Statute of Westminister (1275), 24
Steblay, Nancy, 367, 368
Steiker, Carol, 265, 388
Steiker, Jordan, 265, 388
Steiner, Benjamin D., 385, 386
Stewart, Potter, 243
Stewart, W. K., 349
story model of juror decision making, 135–37, 139, 141–42, 144–45, 251, 268
Strauder v. West Virginia, 71–76
Strauss, Murray, 377
Strickland, Shauna M., 355, 396
Strodtbeck, Fred L., 370
struck jury, 34, 43
Stuart, Mildred, 165
Studdert, David M., 394, 395
Studebaker, Christina, 366, 367, 372, 374
Suggs, David, 361, 362

Sukel, Holly L., 374
Summers, Robert S., 389
summons for jury duty, 77–79, 81
Sundby, Scott, 254, 256, 257, 258, 259, 264–65, 386, 387, 388
Sunstein, Cass, 304, 392
Supreme Court. *See* individual states; US Supreme Court
Supreme Court Act of 1981 (England), 37
surgery, damage during (malpractice suit), 326–27
surveys of potential jurors, 118, 120–21
Sutcliffe, Robert, 77–78, 359
Swain, Robert, 72–73
Swain v. Alabama, 72–73, 96
Sward, Ellen E., 355
Sweetingham, Lisa, 378
Swineburn, John, 171, 172
Symbionese Liberation Army, 132
sympathy of jury for plaintiff, 331

Taliban, 117, 118
Tanford, Sarah, 372
Tanur, Judith M., 362
Taragin, Mark, 329, 394
tasks of juries, 125–45
Taxi Driver (movie), 212
Taylor, Stuart, 347
Taylor v. Louisiana, 73–74, 226
temporary insanity, 202, 205. *See also* insanity defense
Tennessee, sentencing authority in, 56
Texaco, 62
Texas
  capital punishment cases in, 250
  laws on the insanity defense, 208, 209, 214, 216
  peremptory challenges in, 99
  sentencing authority, 56
Thaman, Stephen C., 397
Thatcher, Jeannette E., 356
Thatcher, Peter Oxenbridge, 361
Thiel v. Southern Pacific Co., 74
Thomas, Cheryl, 350, 351, 364, 365
Thomas, Clarence, 75
Thomas, Evan, 347
Thomas family, 229
Thompson, Helen, 354
Thompson, William, 181–82, 375, 385
Thompson, Jennifer, 192–93
three strikes rule, 227
Throckmorton, Nicholas, 27
thrombosis (malpractice suit), 325
Tiersma, Peter, 158, 342, 368, 372, 395
Tisch, Chris, 388
Toglia, Michael, 376
Toledo, Ohio, 17–18
Toobin, Jeffrey, 377
Tooney, Beverley, 378
"Top Ten Ways to Get Out of Jury Duty" (Letterman), 77
tort law, 52, 156, 175, 283, 289, 305, 314
  contributory negligence as tort doctrine, 231
  expansion of, 61–64
  intentional tort, 309
  median awards in tort trials, 283
  success of tort claims, 308
  tort reform, 85, 270, 281, 287, 303, 309, 336
  Vosburg v. Putney, 275–76
  See also civil trials
to see them say. *See* voir dire
Touchete Regional Hospital, 337–38
Townsend v. State, 55
trial atmosphere in Old Bailey (London), 28
trial by jury
  decline in number of, 17, 60, 62–63, 345
  right of, 9, 16, 37, 74, 88, 115, 147, 242
trial consultants, 102–105
trial length, 59–61
Trial of the Seven Bishops, 30–32
trials, types of
  judge trials vs. jury trials, 151–52
    as alternate to juries, 342
    decline in number of trials by jury, 62–63, 345
    judge as sole determiner in malpractice, 337–38
  trial by jury, right of in US, 9, 16, 37, 74, 88, 115, 147, 242

trial by magistrates in England, 36, 37–39
trial by ordeal, 21–23, 24
trial by wager of battle, 21–22
trial by witnesses, 21, 23
trial without juries in England, 155, 371–72
wager of law, 23
trior procedure, 34, 49, 57, 87–88
Trop v. Dulles, 243
Tucson, Arizona, 18
Tulsa v. Tyson, 111
Turley, Jonathan, 347
Twelve Angry Men (movie), 129
Tyler, Tom, 129, 197, 368, 377
Tyson Foods, 111

Ukraine and jury system, 345
Underwood, Barbara, 363
unfair jury selection, 96
United States and mass media coverage of criminal trials, 108–109
United States v. Dougherty, 236
United States v. Thomas, 229
unjustified lawsuits, 267, 274
unlawful assembly, 28–29
unreliability of jury awards, 282
US Bureau of Justice Statistics, 283, 308, 309, 310, 323, 333
US Chamber of Commerce, 15
US Department of Justice, 194, 376
US Federal Bureau of Investigation, 122
U.S. News & World Report (magazine), 15, 347–48
US Supreme Court, 69, 245, 247, 256, 265, 302, 375
Adams v. Texas, 254
Barefoot v. Estelle, 245
Batson v. Kentucky, 96–97
BMW v. Gore, 306, 314, 316–19
Callins v. Collins, 264
Coker v. Georgia, 245
Daubert trilogy of cases, 170
Duncan v. Louisiana, 226
Duren v. Missouri, 74
Edmondson v. Leesville Concrete Co., 363
Furman v. Georgia, 241, 243, 244, 248, 264
Georgia v. McCollum, 363
Gregg v. Georgia, 244–45, 246, 264
Hoyt v. Florida, 73
Irvin v. Dowd, 109
J. E. B. v. Alabama, 96, 363
Kumho Tire v. Carmichael, 169
Lockett v. Ohio, 258
McCleskey v. Kemp, 245
Mu'Min v. Virginia, 109–10
Neil v. Bigger, 195
Norris v. Alabama, 72
opinions on capital punishment, 243–46
Philip Morris v. Williams, 316, 319
on punitive damages, 304, 319–20
Rideau v. Louisiana, 109
Ring v. Arizona, 241, 246
Roper v. Simmons, 245–46
Sam Sheppard case, 109
Scottsboro case, 72
State Farm v. Campbell, 307–308, 314, 316
Swain v. Alabama, 72–73
Taylor v. Louisiana, 73–74, 226
Thiel v. Southern Pacific Co., 74
Trop v. Dulles, 243
Wainwright v. Witt, 250
Witherspoon v. Illinois, 250
Utah
receiving a portion of punitive award, 307
Supreme Court of, 307, 308
women serving on juries, 73

Vadino, Nicole, 388
values and norms in decision making, 141–42, 144–45, 149
Van Dam, Rip, 41–42
Vanderbilt Law School, 238
van Wert, Stephen, 322, 332–33, 393, 394, 395
Vatner, Amy, 376
Vaughn, Chief Justice, 28–29
venue, change of, 114–15, 116, 366
Arian trial, 121

Copeland trial, 116
Durham garbage truck case, 111
Lindh trial, 118–19
Oklahoma City bombing case, 110
Venuti, Mark A., 362
verdict on juries, 339–46
verdicts
false verdict, 25
judges and juries agreeing on, 148–51, 339–40, 370
jury instructions biasing jury to guilty verdict, 252
jury prejudice affecting, 111–14, 122–23, 341–42
mega verdicts, 62
nonunanimous verdicts, 18, 38
postverdict reductions, 333–35
postverdict settlements, 314
Rand analysis of jury verdicts in Cook County, 288–89
special verdicts, 31, 45, 50, 213. *See also* guilty but mentally ill verdict
statistics on verdicts in favor of defendants and plaintiffs, 149, 150, 283, 308, 324, 330, 331
verdict driven deliberation approach, 143–44
wrongful convictions, 191, 192–95, 262–63
See also death penalty; nullification, jury
Verneule, Adrian, 375
vertical equity, 332
victims
battered child syndrome, 204–205
battered woman syndrome, 202–205
defendants as victims, 198, 202–205, 259
intersecting roles of defendant and victim, 198–205
seen as responsible for the crime, 231
sexual assault and focusing on victim, 198–201
white victims and black defendants, 249, 385
Vidmar, Neil, 17–18, 101, 111, 120, 137, 153, 286, 287, 288, 289, 299, 301, 315, 331, 332, 334, 335, 347, 348, 350, 355, 364, 365, 366, 367, 368, 369, 370, 371, 373, 374, 375, 376, 377, 378, 390, 391, 392, 393, 394, 395, 396, 397
Vidmar-Perrins, Mikaela, 218, 379
Vietnam War protesters, 225
vindictive damages, 305
Vioxx (drug), 108, 114, 304
Virginia
civil juries in, 54
as a colony
exclusion of lawyers from trials, 48
judges authority in, 51
jury selection in, 49
use of peremptory challenges, 353
Virginia Company and juries, 47, 50
contributory negligence rules, 285
sentencing authority, 56
Viscusi, Kip, 310, 392
voir dire, 87–93, 109, 229
in death penalty cases, 91, 251, 252–53, 255, 362
and punitive damages, 311–12
as remedy for pretrial publicity, 116–17
Vosburg v. Putney, 275–76, 388
voter registration lists, 67, 76–77

wager of battle, 21–22
wager of law, 23
Wainwright v. Witt, 250, 362
Waliczek v. Ghandhigutta and Alexian Brothers Medical Center, 333
Walker, Marlan D., 375
Wall Street Journal, 286
Warren, Earl, 73, 243
war with the law, 232–33. *See also* nullification, jury
Washington
instructions to jury, 252–53
women serving on juries, 73
water, trial by, 22
Waters, Nicole L., 361, 363, 364
Watson, John H., Jr., 363

Webster, George, 56–59
Weigl, Andrea, 388
Weiner, Richard, 261
Weisbrod, Carol, 357
Weiser, Phil, 397
Wells, Charles, 349
Wells, David, 172
Wells, Gary, 194, 376
Wells, Martin, 261, 262, 286, 287, 310, 370, 385, 387, 390, 392
Wenger, Ashley A., 377
West New Jersey Colony
  exclusion of lawyers from trials, 48
  recognition of jury trials, 47
  use of jury trials, 50
Wetherington, Gerald, 366
Wharton, Francis, 354
Whigs, 51–52
whiplash, 185, 271–72, 295
White, Byron, 72–73, 243
White, Michelle, 394
white coat syndrome, 178
Whitehead, G. Marc, 396
Wiener, Richard, 387
Wigmore, John, 226
Wiley, Diane, 363
William III (king), 34
William of Orange (king), 31
Williams, Gerald R., 391
Williams, Jesse, 316, 317
Williams, Kipling D., 366
Williams, Mayola, 316–19
Williamson, Wendell, 217–18
William the Conqueror (king), 23
Wilson, Adam, 380
Wilson, James Q., 205, 378
Wilson, Timothy, 362
Wilson Furniture Corporation, 279
Wisconsin
  abolition of capital punishment, 242
  caps on malpractice awards, 336–37
  Supreme Court of, 275–76, 336–37
Wissler, Roselle, 300, 301, 369, 373, 375, 390, 391
Wistrich, Andrew, 164, 369, 373, 395
Witherspoon, William, 250
Witherspoon v. Illinois, 250, 251
witnesses, 194–95
  eyewitnesses, 134, 198, 206
    vs. expert witnesses, 175
    misidentification by, 192, 193, 194–95
  questioning of. *See also* cross-examination of witnesses
    by judges, 32, 130
    by juries, 32, 130, 184, 344
    reexamination of witnesses, 131
  trial by witnesses, 21, 23
  See also evidence evaluation and juries; expert witnesses
Witt standard, 362
Wolfe, Tom, 286
women
  battered woman syndrome, 202–205
  eligibility to serve on juries, 37, 59, 66, 67, 70, 73–74
  in mixed juries, 70
  negative impact of negligence cases on, 277
  peremptory challenges against, 95–98
  women jurors and rape trials, 341
Woodworth, George, 384
Wrightsman, Lawrence S., 364, 365
writ of attaint, 25
writ of error, 59
wrongful acquittals, 195–97
wrongful convictions, 191, 192–95, 262–63, 376. *See also* Innocence Project
wrongful death, 108, 153, 197, 284, 337
Wroth, L. Kinivin, 353
Wyatt, Tim, 358
Wyoming Territory, 73

Yang, Tony, 395
Yates, Andrea, 19, 108, 207–10, 213–14
  second trial of, 214–15
Yates, Russell, 207
York, Michelle, 380
Young, Warren, 374
younger jurors and use of peremptory challenges against, 97

Zajonc, R. B., 362
Zeiler, Kathryn, 395
Zeisel, Hans, 99, 148–49, 150–51, 198, 199, 230–32, 234, 240, 301, 364
Zembro, Alan, 392
Zenger, Anna Catherina, 43
Zenger, John Peter, 41–47, 50, 52, 225, 351
Zickafoose, Douglas J., 382
Zile, Sigurds L., 388
Zobel, Hiller B., 353
Zuckerman, Morton, 347